T0190427

Lecture Notes in Computer Science 13942

Founding Editors

Gerhard Goos
Juris Hartmanis

Editorial Board Members

Elisa Bertino, *Purdue University, West Lafayette, IN, USA*
Wen Gao, *Peking University, Beijing, China*
Bernhard Steffen , *TU Dortmund University, Dortmund, Germany*
Moti Yung , *Columbia University, New York, NY, USA*

The series Lecture Notes in Computer Science (LNCS), including its subseries Lecture Notes in Artificial Intelligence (LNAI) and Lecture Notes in Bioinformatics (LNBI), has established itself as a medium for the publication of new developments in computer science and information technology research, teaching, and education.

LNCS enjoys close cooperation with the computer science R & D community, the series counts many renowned academics among its volume editors and paper authors, and collaborates with prestigious societies. Its mission is to serve this international community by providing an invaluable service, mainly focused on the publication of conference and workshop proceedings and postproceedings. LNCS commenced publication in 1973.

Vijayalakshmi Atluri · Anna Lisa Ferrara
Editors

Data and Applications Security and Privacy XXXVII

37th Annual IFIP WG 11.3 Conference, DBSec 2023
Sophia-Antipolis, France, July 19–21, 2023
Proceedings

 Springer

Editors
Vijayalakshmi Atluri 🆔
Rutgers University
Newark, NJ, USA

Anna Lisa Ferrara 🆔
University of Molise
Campobasso, Italy

ISSN 0302-9743   ISSN 1611-3349 (electronic)
Lecture Notes in Computer Science
ISBN 978-3-031-37585-9   ISBN 978-3-031-37586-6 (eBook)
https://doi.org/10.1007/978-3-031-37586-6

© IFIP International Federation for Information Processing 2023

This work is subject to copyright. All rights are reserved by the Publisher, whether the whole or part of the material is concerned, specifically the rights of translation, reprinting, reuse of illustrations, recitation, broadcasting, reproduction on microfilms or in any other physical way, and transmission or information storage and retrieval, electronic adaptation, computer software, or by similar or dissimilar methodology now known or hereafter developed.
The use of general descriptive names, registered names, trademarks, service marks, etc. in this publication does not imply, even in the absence of a specific statement, that such names are exempt from the relevant protective laws and regulations and therefore free for general use.
The publisher, the authors, and the editors are safe to assume that the advice and information in this book are believed to be true and accurate at the date of publication. Neither the publisher nor the authors or the editors give a warranty, expressed or implied, with respect to the material contained herein or for any errors or omissions that may have been made. The publisher remains neutral with regard to jurisdictional claims in published maps and institutional affiliations.

This Springer imprint is published by the registered company Springer Nature Switzerland AG
The registered company address is: Gewerbestrasse 11, 6330 Cham, Switzerland

Preface

This volume contains the papers presented at DBSec 2023: the 37th Annual IFIP WG 11.3 Conference on Data and Applications Security and Privacy (DBSec 2023), Sophia Antipolis, France – July 19–21, 2023.

In response to the call for papers of this edition, 56 submissions were received. Each submission went through a thorough single-blind peer review evaluation process, assessing its significance, novelty, and technical quality. The Program Committee, consisting of 49 members, did an outstanding job in reviewing all the submitted works, with additional reviewers providing assistance. Each submission received between three and five reviews. The Program Committee's work was carried out electronically, resulting in extensive discussions. Of the submitted papers, 19 full papers and 5 short papers were selected for presentation at the conference.

The success of DBSec 2023 was made possible thanks to the dedicated efforts of many individuals, and we would like to extend our sincere appreciation to all those who deserve special recognition. We express our gratitude to all the members of the Program Committee and the external reviewers for their hard work in evaluating the papers and actively participating in the discussion and selection process. We are thankful to all those who readily provided assistance and ensured a smooth organization process, particularly Michele Bezzi for his effort as DBSec 2023 general chair. We would also like to acknowledge Sara Foresti (IFIP WG11.3 chair) for her guidance and support, Valentina Piantadosi (publicity chair) for her assistance with publicity, and Marco Rosa for his contributions to other conference arrangements.

The use of EasyChair greatly facilitated the conference review and publication process, ensuring its smooth execution.

Last but certainly not least, we extend our gratitude to all the authors who submitted their contributions and to all the conference attendees. We hope that the proceedings of DBSec 2023 prove to be interesting, stimulating, and inspiring for your future research endeavors.

July 2023

Vijayalakshmi Atluri
Anna Lisa Ferrara

Organization

General Chair

Michele Bezzi   SAP Security Research, France

Program Committee Chairs

Vijay Atluri   Rutgers University, USA
Anna Lisa Ferrara   University of Molise, Italy

IFIP WG11.3 Chair

Sara Foresti   Università degli Studi di Milano, Italy

Publicity and Web Chair

Valentina Piantadosi   University of Molise, Italy

Local Arrangement Chair

Marco Rosa   SAP Security Research, France

Program Committee

Ayesha Afzal   Air University, Pakistan
Hafiz Asif   Rutgers University, USA
Vijay Atluri   Rutgers University, USA
Gunjan Batra   Kennesaw State University, USA
Francesco Buccafurri   UNIRC, Italy

Sergiu Bursuc	University of Luxembourg, Luxembourg
Frédéric Cuppens	Polytechnique Montréal, Canada
Nora Cuppens-Boulahia	Polytechnique Montréal, Canada
Sabrina De Capitani di Vimercati	Università degli Studi di Milano, Italy
Csilla Farkas	University of South Carolina, USA
Fausto Fasano	University of Molise, Italy
Anna Lisa Ferrara	University of Molise, Italy
Barbara Fila	INSA Rennes, IRISA, France
Sara Foresti Di	Università degli Studi di Milano, Italy
Steven Furnell	University of Nottingham, UK
Essam Ghadafi	University College London, UK
Ehud Gudes	Ben-Gurion University, Israel
Javier Herranz	Universitat Politècnica de Catalunya, Spain
Sokratis Katsikas	Norwegian University of Science and Technology, Norway
Ram Krishnan	University of Texas at San Antonio, USA
Costas Lambrinoudakis	University of Piraeus, Greece
Adam J. Lee	University of Pittsburgh, USA
Xiang Li	Santa Clara University, USA
Giovanni Livraga	University of Milan, Italy
Javier Lopez	University of Malaga, Spain
Haibing Lu	Santa Clara University, USA
Maryam Majedi	University of Southern California, USA
Brad Malin	Vanderbilt University, USA
Amir Masoumzadeh	University at Albany – SUNY, USA
Barbara Masucci	University of Salerno, Italy
Charles Morisset	Newcastle University, UK
Martin Olivier	University of Pretoria, South Africa
Federica Paci	University of Verona, Italy
Stefano Paraboschi	Università di Bergamo, Italy
Günther Pernul	Universität Regensburg, Germany
Silvio Ranise	University of Trento and Fondazione Bruno Kessler, Italy
Indrajit Ray	Colorado State University, USA
Indrakshi Ray	Colorado State University, USA
Pierangela Samarati	Università degli Studi di Milano, Italy
Andreas Schaad	HS Offenburg, Germany
Basit Shafiq	Lahore University of Management Sciences, Pakistan
Anoop Singhal	NIST, USA
Scott D. Stoller	Stony Brook University, USA
Shamik Sural	Indian Institute of Technology Kharagpur, India

Helen Treharne   University of Surrey, UK
Jaideep Vaidya   Rutgers University, USA
Lingyu Wang   Concordia University, Canada
Edgar Weippl   University of Vienna, Austria
Nicola Zannone   Eindhoven University of Technology,
                                  The Netherlands

Additional Reviewers

Al-Amin, Md.
Alcaraz, Cristina
Amer, Safwa
Bashir, Shadaab Kawnain
Baumer, Thomas
Berlato, Stefano
Binder, Dominik
Carpent, Xavier
Cerulli, Andrea
Cimato, Stelvio
Dankner, Alon
Datta, Pratish
Friedl, Sabrina
Ghavamnia, Seyedhamed
Grill, Johannes
Guerra, Michele
Karakoç, Ferhat

Khan, Latifur
Liu, Peng
Majedi, Maryam
Mayer, Rudolf
McCarthy, Andrew
Merzdovnik, Georg
Muller, Tim
Musale, Pratik
Muñoz, Antonio
Pasquini, Cecilia
Rios, Ruben
Rizzi, Matteo
Rodriguez, David
Schlette, Daniel
Shepherd, Carlton
Sáez, Germán
Xu, Andrew

Contents

Mobile Applications

Defense Mechanisms

Differential Privacy

(Local) Differential Privacy has NO Disparate Impact on Fairness

Héber H. Arcolezi$^{(\boxtimes)}$ ⓘ, Karima Makhlouf ⓘ, and Catuscia Palamidessi ⓘ

Inria and École Polytechnique (IPP), Palaiseau, France
{heber.hwang-arcolezi,karima.makhlouf,catuscia}@lix.polytechnique.fr

Abstract. In recent years, Local Differential Privacy (LDP), a robust privacy-preserving methodology, has gained widespread adoption in real-world applications. With LDP, users can perturb their data on their devices before sending it out for analysis. However, as the collection of multiple sensitive information becomes more prevalent across various industries, collecting a single sensitive attribute under LDP may not be sufficient. Correlated attributes in the data may still lead to inferences about the sensitive attribute. This paper empirically studies the impact of collecting multiple sensitive attributes under LDP on fairness. We propose a novel privacy budget allocation scheme that considers the varying domain size of sensitive attributes. This generally led to a better privacy-utility-fairness trade-off in our experiments than the state-of-art solution. Our results show that LDP leads to slightly improved fairness in learning problems without significantly affecting the performance of the models. We conduct extensive experiments evaluating three benchmark datasets using several group fairness metrics and seven state-of-the-art LDP protocols. Overall, this study challenges the common belief that differential privacy necessarily leads to worsened fairness in machine learning.

Keywords: Fairness · Local Differential Privacy · Machine Learning

1 Introduction

The advent of the Big Data era has brought many benefits but has also raised significant concerns about privacy and algorithm bias in Machine Learning (ML). On the one hand, with massive amounts of data generated and collected by various entities, protecting individuals' personal information has become increasingly challenging. In this context, research communities have proposed different methods to preserve privacy, with ϵ-differential privacy (ϵ-DP) [17] standing out as a formal definition that allows quantifying the privacy-utility trade-off with the parameter ϵ (the smaller, the more private). At the same time, there have been many efforts to develop methods and metrics to evaluate and promote fairness in ML due to unequal treatments of individuals or groups based on factors such as race, gender, or socio-economic status [5,30–32].

This means that privacy and fairness are essential for ML to apply in practice successfully. In real-life scenarios, it is not common anymore for entities to have

© IFIP International Federation for Information Processing 2023
Published by Springer Nature Switzerland AG 2023
V. Atluri and A. L. Ferrara (Eds.): DBSec 2023, LNCS 13942, pp. 3–21, 2023.
https://doi.org/10.1007/978-3-031-37586-6_1

access to *sensitive* (or *protected*[1]) attributes like race due to legal restrictions and regulations[2] governing their collection. Therefore, it can be difficult for these entities to quantify/assess the fairness of the models they deploy since they cannot access the protected attributes used for the fairness assessment. One way to address this problem [33], ignoring legal feasibility, is to enable users to share their sensitive attributes using protocols satisfying Local Differential Privacy (LDP) [26], and learn a non-discriminatory predictor.

However, while collecting the sensitive attribute in a privacy-preserving manner may seem sufficient, it is worth noting that proxy variables can exist [25] and can still lead to inferences about the sensitive attribute (*e.g.*, by exploiting correlations). It is also important to acknowledge that proxy variables may be considered as personal information under the GDPR, requiring the same level of privacy protection. Thus, as collecting multiple sensitive information (*i.e.*, *multidimensional data*) becomes increasingly prevalent in various industries, protecting this information is a legal obligation and an ethical responsibility.

Therefore, this paper contributes to an in-depth empirical analysis of how pre-processing multidimensional data with ϵ-LDP affects the fairness and utility in ML binary classification tasks. We evaluated several group fairness metrics [5,31], including disparate impact [10], equal opportunity [22], and overall accuracy [13], on benchmark datasets, namely, Adult [15], ACSCoverage [15], and LSAC [41]. To broaden the scope of our study, we have experimentally assessed seven state-of-the-art LDP protocols, namely, Generalized Randomized Response (GRR) [24], Binary Local Hashing (BLH) [11], Optimal Local Hashing (OLH) [40], RAPPOR [19], Optimal Unary Encoding (OUE) [40], Subset Selection (SS) [39,42], and Thresholding with Histogram Encoding (THE) [40].

Moreover, since proxy variables can still introduce unintended biases and thus lead to unfair decisions [25], we consider the setting in which each proxy (sensitive attribute) is collected independently under LDP guarantees. In other words, applying this independent setting automatically removes the correlation between the proxy attributes. To this end, the privacy budget ϵ should be divided among all sensitive attributes to ensure ϵ-LDP under sequential composition [18]. Let d_s be the total number of sensitive attributes, the LDP literature for multidimensional data [6,38] considers a **uniform** solution that collects each sensitive attribute under $\frac{\epsilon}{d_s}$-LDP. In this paper, we propose a new **k-based** solution that considers the varying domain size k of different sensitive attributes. More precisely, for the j-th sensitive attribute, we allocate $\epsilon_j = \frac{\epsilon \cdot k_j}{\sum_{i=1}^{d_s} k_i}$.

Overall, our study challenges the common belief that using DP necessarily leads to worsened fairness in ML [9,21]. Our findings show that training a classifier on LDP-based multidimensional data slightly improved fairness results without significantly affecting classifier performance. We hope this work can aid practitioners in collecting multidimensional user data in a privacy-preserving

---

[1] Throughout this paper, we use the term *sensitive* attribute from a privacy perspective and the term *protected* attribute from a fairness perspective. Note that we always consider *protected* attributes as *sensitive* attributes.

[2] For example, the General Data Protection Regulation (GDPR) [3].

manner by providing insights into which LDP protocol and privacy budget-splitting solutions are best suited to their needs.

In summary, the three main contributions of this paper are:

- We empirically analyze the impact of pre-processing multidimensional data with ϵ-LDP on fairness and utility;
- We compare the impact of seven state-of-the-art LDP protocols under a homogeneous encoding when training ML binary classifiers (see Fig. 1) on fairness and utility;
- We propose a new privacy budget splitting solution named k-based, which generally led to a better privacy-utility-fairness trade-off in our experiments.

All our codes are available in a **GitHub repository** [2].

Outline. The rest of this paper is organized as follows. Section 2 discusses related work. In Sect. 3, we present the notation, fairness, and LDP protocols used. Next, Sect. 4 states the problem addressed in this paper and the proposed k-based solution. Section 5 details the experimental setting and main results. Finally, we conclude this work indicating future perspectives in Sect. 6.

2 Related Work

The recent survey work by Fioretto *et al.* [20] discusses two views about the relationship between central DP and fairness in learning and decision tasks. The first view considers DP and fairness in an aligned space (*e.g.*, [16]), which mainly corresponds to individual fairness metrics. The other view regards DP and fairness as "enemies" (*e.g.*, [9,21,35]), which mainly corresponds to group fairness notions. For instance, Pujol *et al.* [35] investigated disparities in decision tasks using ϵ-DP data. Regarding learning tasks, Bagdasaryan, Poursaeed, & Shmatikov [9] studied the impact of training ϵ-DP deep learning (*a.k.a. gradient perturbation*) models on unprivileged groups. By keeping the same hyperparameters as the non-private baseline model, the authors noticed that the accuracy for the unprivileged group dropped more than for the privileged one. Similarly, Ganev et al. [21] have also noticed disparities for the unprivileged group when generating ϵ-DP synthetic data for training ML models by also keeping default hyperparameters of the differentially private generative models. In this paper, we aim to explore to what extent training an ML classifier on ϵ-LDP multidimensional data (*a.k.a. input perturbation*) while fixing the same set of hyperparameters negatively impacts the unprivileged group is valid.

Regarding the local DP setting, the work of Mozannar, Ohannessian, & Srebro [33] was the first one to propose a fair classifier when sanitizing only the protected attribute with ϵ-LDP in both training and testing sets. More recently, the work of Chen *et al.* [14] considers a "semi-private" setting in which a small portion of users share their protected attribute with no sanitization and all other users apply an ϵ-LDP protocol. While the two aforementioned research works [14,33] answer interesting questions by collecting a single sensitive attribute using only the GRR [24] protocol, we consider in this work multiple sensitive attributes, which reflects real-world data collections, seven ϵ-LDP protocols, and several fairness and utility metrics. In addition, we also propose a new privacy budget splitting solution named k-based, which generally leads to better fairness and performance in ML binary classification tasks.

3   Preliminaries and Background

This section briefly reviews the group fairness metrics, LDP, and LDP protocols. The notation used throughout this paper is summarized in Table 1.

Table 1. Notations

Symbol	Description
n	Number of users
$[n]$	Set of integers, $\{1, 2, \ldots, n\}$
$\mathbf{x}_i$	i-th coordinate of vector $\mathbf{x}$
$z = \mathcal{M}(v)$	Protocol $\mathcal{M}$ perturbs v into z under ϵ-LDP
X	Set of "non-sensitive" attributes
A_s	Set of sensitive attributes (**privacy viewpoint**)
A_p	Protected attribute (**fairness viewpoint**), $A_p \in A_s$
Z_s	Set of locally differentially private sensitive attributes, $Z_s = \mathcal{M}(A_s)$
k_j	Domain size of the j-th attribute
d_s	Number of sensitive attributes, $d_s = |A_s|$
Y	Set of target values, $Y = \{0, 1\}$
D	Original dataset, $D = (X, A_s, Y)$
D_z	Dataset with sanitized sensitive attributes, $D_z = (X, Z_s, Y)$

Note that in this work, we always consider a single protected attribute and assess fairness w.r.t. that attribute. For LDP, we consider a set of sensitive attributes instead. Moreover, the protected attribute is always considered sensitive, but the opposite is untrue.

3.1   Group Fairness Metrics

In this paper, we focus on group fairness metrics, which assess the fairness of ML models for different demographic groups that differ by the protected attribute (*e.g.*, race, gender, age, ...). Let A_p be the protected attribute, $\hat{Y}$ be a predictor of a binary target $Y \in \{0, 1\}$. The metrics we use to evaluate fairness are:

– **Disparate Impact (DI)** [10]. DI is defined as the ratio of the proportion of positive predictions ($\hat{Y} = 1$) for the *unprivileged* group ($A_p = 0$) over the ratio of the proportion of positive predictions for the *privileged* group ($A_p = 1$). The formula for DI is:

$$DI = \frac{\Pr[\hat{Y} = 1 | A_p = 0]}{\Pr[\hat{Y} = 1 | A_p = 1]}. \tag{1}$$

Note that a perfect DI value is equal to 1.

– **Statistical Parity Difference (SPD)** [4]. Instead of the ratio, SDP computes the difference in the proportion of positive predictions for *unprivileged* and *privileged* groups and is defined as:

$$SPD = \Pr[\hat{Y} = 1 | A_p = 1] - \Pr[\hat{Y} = 1 | A_p = 0]. \tag{2}$$

A perfect SPD value is equal to 0.

– **Equal Opportunity Difference (EOD)** [22]. EOD measures the difference between the true positive rates (*i.e.*, recall) of the *unprivileged* group and the *privileged* groups. Formally, EOD is defined as:

$$EOD = \Pr[\hat{Y} = 1 | Y = 1, A_p = 1] - \Pr[\hat{Y} = 1 | Y = 1, A_p = 0]. \tag{3}$$

A perfect EOD value is equal to 0.

– **Overall Accuracy Difference (OAD)** [13]. OAD measures the difference between the overall accuracy rates between the *privileged* group and the *unprivileged* group. Formally, OAD is represented as:

$$OAD = \Pr[\hat{Y} = Y | A_p = 1] - \Pr[\hat{Y} = Y | A_p = 0]. \tag{4}$$

A perfect OAD value is equal to 0.

3.2   Local Differential Privacy

In this article, we use LDP [26] as the privacy model, which is formalized as:

Definition 1 (ϵ-Local Differential Privacy). *A randomized algorithm $\mathcal{M}$ satisfies ϵ-local-differential-privacy (ϵ-LDP), where $\epsilon > 0$, if for any pair of input values $v_1, v_2 \in Domain(\mathcal{M})$ and any possible output z of $\mathcal{M}$:*

$$\Pr[\mathcal{M}(v_1) = z] \le e^\epsilon \cdot \Pr[\mathcal{M}(v_2) = z].$$

Proposition 1 (Post-Processing [18]). *If $\mathcal{M}$ is ϵ-LDP, then for any function f, the composition of $\mathcal{M}$ and f, i.e., $f(\mathcal{M})$ satisfies ϵ-LDP.*

Proposition 2 (Sequential Composition [18]). *Let $\mathcal{M}_1$ be an ϵ_1-LDP protocol and $\mathcal{M}_2$ be an ϵ_2-LDP protocol. Then, the protocol $\mathcal{M}_{1,2}(v) = (\mathcal{M}_1(v), \mathcal{M}_2(v))$ is $(\epsilon_1 + \epsilon_2)$-LDP.*

3.3   LDP Protocols

Let $A_s = \{v_1, \dots, v_k\}$ be a sensitive attribute with a discrete domain of size $k = |A_s|$, in this subsection, we briefly review seven state-of-the-art LDP protocols.

Generalized Randomized Response (GRR). GRR [24] uses no particular encoding. Given a value $v \in A_s$, $GRR(v)$ outputs the true value v with probability p, and any other value $v' \in A_s \setminus \{v\}$, otherwise. More formally:

$$\forall z \in A_s : \quad \Pr[z = a] = \begin{cases} p = \frac{e^\epsilon}{e^\epsilon + k - 1} & \text{if } z = a \\ q = \frac{1}{e^\epsilon + k - 1} & \text{otherwise,} \end{cases}$$

in which z is the perturbed value sent to the server.

Binary Local Hashing (BLH). Local Hashing (LH) protocols [11,40] can handle a large domain size k by first using hash functions to map an input value to a smaller domain of size g (typically $2 \leq g \ll k$), and then applying GRR to the hashed value. Let $\mathcal{H}$ be a universal hash function family such that each hash function $H \in \mathcal{H}$ hashes a value in A_s into $[g]$, i.e., $H : A_s \rightarrow [g]$. With BLH, $[g] = \{0, 1\}$, each user selects at random one hash function H, calculates $b = H(v)$, and perturbs b to z as:

$$\Pr[z = 1] = \begin{cases} p = \frac{e^\epsilon}{e^\epsilon + 1} & \text{if } b = 1 \\ q = \frac{1}{e^\epsilon + 1} & \text{if } b = 0. \end{cases}$$

The user sends the tuple $\langle H, z \rangle$, i.e., the hash function and the perturbed value. Thus, for each user, the server can calculate $S\left(\langle H, z \rangle\right) = \{v | H(v) = z\}$.

Optimal LH (OLH). To improve the utility of LH protocols, Wang *et al.* [40] proposed OLH in which the output space of the hash functions in family $\mathcal{H}$ is no longer binary as in BLH. Thus, with OLH, $g = \lfloor e^\epsilon + 1 \rfloor$, each user selects at random one hash function H, calculates $b = H(v)$, and perturbs b to z as:

$$\forall i \in [g] : \quad \Pr[z = i] = \begin{cases} p = \frac{e^\epsilon}{e^\epsilon + g - 1} & \text{if } b = i \\ q = \frac{1}{e^\epsilon + g - 1} & \text{if } b \neq i. \end{cases}$$

Similar to BLH, the user sends the tuple $\langle H, z \rangle$ and, for each user, the server can calculate $S\left(\langle H, z \rangle\right) = \{v | H(v) = z\}$.

RAPPOR. The RAPPOR [19] protocol uses One-Hot Encoding (OHE) to interpret the user's input $v \in A_s$ as a one-hot k-dimensional vector. More precisely, $\mathbf{v} = OHE(v)$ is a binary vector with only the bit at position v set to 1 and the other bits set to 0. Then, RAPPOR randomizes the bits from $\mathbf{v}$ independently to generate $\mathbf{z}$ as follows:

$$\forall i \in [k] : \quad \Pr[\mathbf{z}_i = 1] = \begin{cases} p = \frac{e^{\epsilon/2}}{e^{\epsilon/2} + 1} & \text{if } \mathbf{v}_i = 1, \\ q = \frac{1}{e^{\epsilon/2} + 1} & \text{if } \mathbf{v}_i = 0, \end{cases}$$

where $p + q = 1$ (i.e., symmetric). Afterwards, the user sends $\mathbf{z}$ to the server.

Optimal Unary Encoding (OUE). To minimize the variance of RAPPOR, Wang *et al.* [40] proposed OUE, which perturbs the 0 and 1 bits asymmetrically, *i.e.*, $p + q \neq 1$. Thus, OUE generates $\mathbf{z}$ by perturbing $\mathbf{v}$ as follows:

$$\forall i \in [k]: \quad \Pr[\mathbf{z}_i = 1] = \begin{cases} p = \frac{1}{2} & \text{if } \mathbf{v}_i = 1, \\ q = \frac{1}{e^\epsilon + 1} & \text{if } \mathbf{v}_i = 0. \end{cases}$$

Afterwards, the user sends $\mathbf{z}$ to the server.

Subset Selection (SS). The SS [39,42] protocol randomly selects $1 \leq \omega \leq k$ items within the input domain to report a subset of values $\Omega \subseteq A_s$. The user's true value v has higher probability of being included in the subset Ω, compared to the other values in $A_s \setminus \{v\}$. The optimal subset size that minimizes the variance is $\omega = \lfloor \frac{k}{e^\epsilon + 1} \rfloor$. Given a value $v \in A_s$, $SS(v)$ starts by initializing an empty subset Ω. Afterwards, the true value v is added to Ω with probability $p = \frac{\omega e^\epsilon}{\omega e^\epsilon + k - \omega}$. Finally, it adds values to Ω as follows:

- If $v \in \Omega$, then $\omega - 1$ values are sampled from $A_s \setminus \{v\}$ uniformly at random (without replacement) and are added to Ω;
- If $v \notin \Omega$, then ω values are sampled from $A_s \setminus \{v\}$ uniformly at random (without replacement) and are added to Ω.

Afterwards, the user sends the subset Ω to the server.

Thresholding with Histogram Encoding (THE). Histogram Encoding (HE) [40] encodes the user value as a one-hot k-dimensional histogram, *i.e.*, $\mathbf{v} = [0.0, 0.0, \ldots, 1.0, 0.0, \ldots, 0.0]$ in which only the v-th component is 1.0. $HE(\mathbf{v})$ perturbs each bit of $\mathbf{v}$ independently using the Laplace mechanism [17]. Two different input values $v_1, v_2 \in A_s$ will result in two vectors with L1 distance of $\Delta = 2$. Thus, HE will output $\mathbf{z}$ such that $\mathbf{z}_i = \mathbf{v}_i + \mathrm{Lap}\left(\frac{2}{\epsilon}\right)$. To improve the utility of HE, Wang *et al.* [40] proposed THE such that the user reports (or the server computes): $S(\mathbf{z}) = \{v \mid \mathbf{z}_v > \theta\}$, in which θ is the threshold with optimal value in $(0.5, 1)$. In this work, we use `scipy.minimize_scalar` to optimize θ for a fixed ϵ as: $\min\limits_{\theta \in (0.5, 1)} \frac{2e^{\epsilon\theta/2} - 1}{(1 + e^{\epsilon(\theta - 1/2)} - 2e^{\epsilon\theta/2})^2}$.

4 Problem Setting and Methodology

We consider the scenario in which the server collects a set of multiple sensitive attributes A_s under ϵ-LDP guarantees from n distributed users $U = \{u_1, \ldots, u_n\}$. Furthermore, in addition to the LDP-based multidimensional data, we assume that the users will also provide non-sanitized data X, which we consider as "non-sensitive" attributes. The server aims to use both sanitized $Z_s = \mathcal{M}(A_s)$ and non-sanitized data X to train an ML classifier with a binary target variable $Y = \{0, 1\}$. Notice, however, that we will be training an ML classifier on $D_z = (X, Z_s, Y)$ but testing on $D = (X, A_s, Y)$ as the main goal is to *protect the privacy of the data used to train the ML model* (e.g., to avoid membership inference attacks [23], reconstruction attacks [36], and other privacy threats [29]). In other words, instead of considering a system for on-the-fly LDP sanitization of test data, as in [33], we only sanitize the training set.

With these elements in mind, our primary goal is to study the impact of training an ML classifier on $D_z = (X, Z_s, Y)$ compared to $D = (X, A_s, Y)$ on fairness and utility, using different LDP protocols and privacy budget splitting solutions. More precisely, we consider the setting where each sensitive attribute in A_s is collected independently under LDP guarantees. In this case, to satisfy ϵ-LDP following Proposition 2, the privacy budget ϵ must be split among the total number of sensitive attributes $d_s = |A_s|$. To this end, the state-of-the-art [6,38] solution, named **uniform**, propose to split the privacy budget ϵ uniformly among all attributes, *i.e.*, allocating $\frac{\epsilon}{d_s}$ for each attribute. However, as different sensitive attributes have different domain sizes k_j, for $j \in [d_s]$, we propose a new solution named **k-based** that splits the privacy budget ϵ proportionally to the domain size of the attribute. That is, for the j-th attribute, we will allocate $\epsilon_j = \frac{\epsilon \cdot k_j}{\sum_{i=1}^{d_s} k_i}$.

In addition, each LDP protocol has a different way of encoding and perturbing user's data. We thus propose to compare all LDP protocols under the same encoding when training the ML classifier. More specifically, we will use OHE and Indicator Vector Encoding (IVE) [1] as all LDP protocols from Sect. 3.3 are designed for categorical data or discrete data with known domain. For example, let Ω be the reported subset of a user after using SS as LDP protocol. Following IVE, we create a binary vector $\mathbf{z} = [b_1, \ldots, b_k] \in \{0, 1\}^k$ of length k, where the v-th entry is set to 1 if $v \in \Omega$, and 0, otherwise. In other words, $\mathbf{z}$ represents the subset Ω in a binary format. Figure 1 illustrates the LDP encoding and perturbation at the user side and how to achieve a "homogeneous encoding" for all the seven LDP protocols at the server side. Last, all "non-sensitive" attributes X are encoded using OHE.

5   Experimental Evaluation

In this section, we present our experiments' setting and main results. Supplementary results can be found in [8]. Our main Research Questions (RQ) are:

- **RQ1.** Overall, how does preprocessing multidimensional data with ϵ-LDP affect the fairness and utility of ML binary classifiers with the same hyperparameters used before and after sanitization?
- **RQ2.** Which privacy budget-splitting solution leads to less harm to the fairness and utility of an ML binary classifier?
- **RQ3.** How do different LDP protocols affect the fairness and utility of an ML binary classifier, and which one is more suitable for the different real-world scenarios applied?

5.1   Setup of Experiments

General Setting. For all experiments, we consider the following setting:

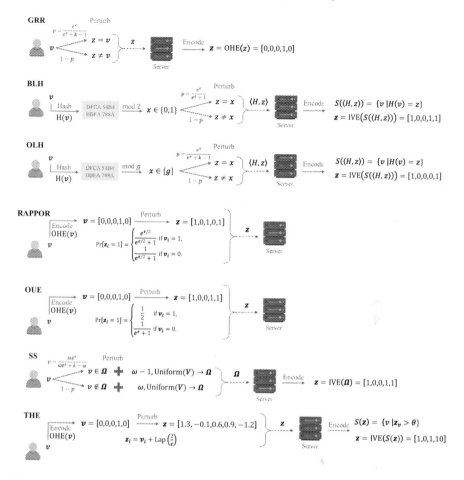

Fig. 1. Overview of client-side encoding and perturbation steps for the seven different LDP protocols applied. On the server side, there is also a post-processing step with one-hot encoding (OHE) or indicator vector encoding (IVE), if needed.

- **Environment.** All algorithms are implemented in Python 3 with Numpy [37], Numba [28], and Multi-Freq-LDPy [7] libraries, and run on a local machine with 2.50 GHz Intel Core i9 and 64 GB RAM. The codes we develop for all experiments are available in a **GitHub repository** [2].
- **ML classifier.** We used the state-of-the-art[3] LGBM [27] as predictor $\hat{Y}$.
- **Encoding.** We only use discrete and categorical attributes, which are encoded using OHE or IVE (see Fig. 1) and the target is binary, *i.e.*, $Y \in \{0, 1\}$.
- **Training and testing sets.** We randomly select 80% as training set and the remaining 20% as testing set. We apply LDP on the training set only. That is, the samples in the testing set are the original samples (*i.e.*, no LDP).

---

[3] https://www.kaggle.com/kaggle-survey-2022.

– **Stability.** Since LDP protocols, train/test splitting, and ML algorithms are randomized, we report average results over 20 runs.

Datasets. Table 2 summarizes all datasets used in our experiments. For ease of reproducibility, we use real-world and open datasets.

Table 2. Description of the datasets used in the experiments.

Dataset	n	A_p	A_s, domain size k	Y
Adult	45849	gender	- gender, $k = 2$ - race, $k = 5$ - native country, $k = 41$ - age, $k = 74$	income
ACSCoverage	98739	DIS	- DIS, $k = 2$ - AGEP, $k = 50$ - SEX, $k = 2$ - SCHL, $k = 24$	PUBCOV
LSAC	20427	race	- race, $k = 2$ - gender, $k = 2$ - family income, $k = 5$ - full time, $k = 2$	pass bar

– **Adult.** We use 26000 as threshold to binarize the target variable "income" of the *reconstructed Adult* dataset [15]. After cleaning, $n = 45849$ samples are kept. We excluded "capital-gain" and "capital-loss" and used the remaining 10 discrete and categorical attributes. We considered $A_s = \{$gender, race, native-country, age$\}$ as sensitive attributes for LDP sanitization and $A_p =$ gender as the protected attribute for fairness assessment.

– **ACSCoverage.** This dataset[4] is retrieved with the `folktables` [15] Python package and the binary target "PUBCOV" designates whether an individual is covered by public health insurance or not. We select the year 2018 and the "Texas" state, with $n = 98739$ samples. We removed "DEAR", "DEYE", "DREM", and "PINCP" and used the remaining 15 discrete and categorical attributes. We considered $A_s = \{$DIS, AGEP, SEX, SCHL$\}$ as sensitive attributes for LDP sanitization and $A_p =$ DIS as the protected attribute (*i.e.*, disability) for fairness assessment.

– **LSAC.** This dataset is from the Law School Admissions Council (LSAC) National Bar Passage Study [41] and the binary target "pass_bar" indicates whether or not a candidate has passed the bar exam. After cleaning, $n = 20427$ samples are kept. We only consider as attributes:

---

[4] The full documentation for the description of all attributes is in https://www.census. gov/programs-surveys/acs/microdata/documentation.html.

'gender', 'race', 'family income', 'full time', 'undergrad GPA score' (discretized to $\{1.5, 2.0, ..., 4.5\}$), and 'LSAT score' (rounded to the closest integer). The 'race' attribute was binarized to $\{black, other\}$. We set $A_s = \{race, gender, family income, full time\}$ as sensitive attributes for LDP sanitization and $A_p = race$ as the protected attribute for fairness assessment.

Evaluated Methods. The methods we use and compare are:

- **(Baseline) NonDP.** This is our baseline with LGBM trained over original data (*i.e.*, $D = (X, A_s, Y)$). We searched for the best hyperparameters using Bayesian optimization [12] through 100 iterations varying: $max\_depth \in [3, 50]$, $n\_estimators \in [50, 2000]$, and $learning\_rate \in (0.01, 0.25)$;
- **LDP protocols.** We pre-processed $Z_s = \mathcal{M}(A_s)$ of the training sets using all seven LDP protocols from Sect. 3.3 (*i.e.*, GRR, RAPPOR, OUE, SS, BLH, OLH, and THE) as $\mathcal{M}$. We used the best hyperparameters found for the NonDP model and trained LGBM over $D_z = (X, Z_s, Y)$. For all datasets, we set d_s to 4. That is, $d_s = |A_s| = 4$. To satisfy ϵ-LDP (*cf.* Definition 2), we split the privacy budget ϵ following the two solutions described in Sect. 4 (*i.e.*, the state-of-the-art uniform and our k-based solution).

Metrics. We evaluate the performance of LGBM trained over the original data (*i.e.*, NonDP baseline) and LDP-based data on privacy, utility, and fairness:

- **Privacy.** We vary the privacy parameter in the range of $\epsilon = \{0.25, 0.5, 1, 2, 4, 8, 10, 20, 50\}$. At $\epsilon = 0.25$ the ratio of probabilities is bounded by $e^{0.25} \approx 1.3$ giving nearly indistinguishable distributions, whereas at $\epsilon = 50$ almost no privacy is guaranteed.
- **Utility.** We use accuracy (acc), f1-score (f1), area under the receiver operating characteristic curve (auc), and recall as utility metrics;
- **Fairness.** We use the metrics of Sect. 3.1 (*i.e.*, DI, SPD, EOD, and OAD).

5.2   Main Results

LDP Impact on Fairness. Figure 2 (Adult), Fig. 3 (ACSCoverage), and Fig. 4 (LSAC) illustrate the privacy-fairness trade-off for the NonDP baseline and all the seven LDP protocols, considering both uniform and our k-based privacy budget splitting solutions. From these figures, one can notice that fairness is, in general, slightly improved for all seven LDP protocols under both the uniform and the k-based solution. For instance, for the DI metric in Fig. 2, the NonDP data indicates a value of 0.44 showing discrimination against women and, by applying LDP protocols, DI tended to increase to ~0.48 (with $\epsilon = 0.25$) resulting in a slight improvement in fairness. Similarly, SPD decreased from 0.37 to ~0.34 after applying LDP protocols. The same behavior is obtained for EOD. The exception was in Fig. 3 for the OAD metric in which the gap between privileged and unprivileged groups was accentuated (favoring the unprivileged group). More specifically, the NonDP baseline has OAD equal to -0.17, and after satisfying LDP for both uniform and k-based solutions and using all LDP protocols, the gap between the privileged and unprivileged groups increased to -0.3. In other words, we start with favoritism towards the unprivileged group (negative value) and this favoritism increased after LDP.

Note also that when applying the uniform privacy budget splitting solution (see left-side plots), all fairness metrics were less robust to LDP than our k-based solution and, thus, returned to the NonDP baseline value in low privacy regimes. With our k-based solution (see right-side plots), all fairness metrics continued to be slightly better for all privacy regimes for the Adult dataset in Fig. 2. For the ACSCoverage dataset, not all fairness metrics returned to the NonDP baseline value and for the LSAC dataset, a similar behavior was noticed for both uniform and k-based solutions. These differences are mainly influenced by the domain size k of the sensitive attributes. For instance, while Adult has sensitive attributes with higher values of k, LSAC has many binary sensitive attributes.

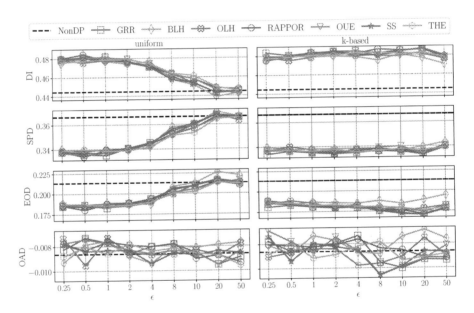

Fig. 2. Fairness metrics (y-axis) by varying the privacy guarantees (x-axis), the ϵ-LDP protocol, and the privacy budget splitting solution (*i.e.*, uniform on the left-side and our k-based on the right-side), on the Adult [15] dataset.

LDP Impact on Utility. Figure 5 (Adult), Fig. 6 (ACSCoverage), and Fig. 7 (LSAC) illustrate the privacy-utility trade-off for the NonDP baseline and all the seven LDP protocols, considering both uniform and our k-based privacy budget splitting solutions. From these figures, one can note that, in general, the impact of ϵ-LDP on utility metrics is minor. For instance, for the Adult dataset (Fig. 5), only $\sim 1\%$ of utility loss for all metrics is observed. Regarding privacy budget splitting, for the Adult dataset, our k-based solution is more robust to

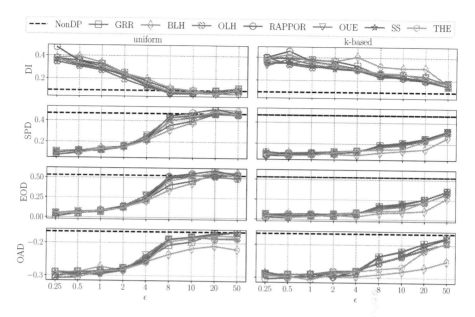

Fig. 3. Fairness metrics (y-axis) by varying the privacy guarantees (x-axis), the ϵ-LDP protocol, and the privacy budget splitting solution (*i.e.*, uniform on the left-side and our k-based on the right-side), on the ACSCoverage [15] dataset.

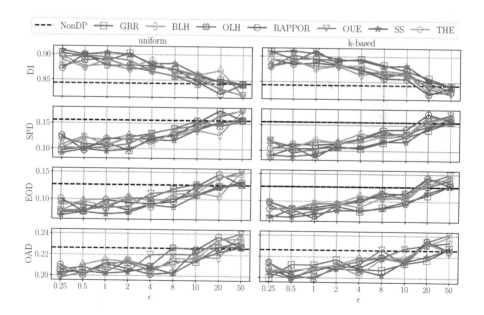

Fig. 4. Fairness metrics (y-axis) by varying the privacy guarantees (x-axis), the ϵ-LDP protocol, and the privacy budget splitting solution (*i.e.*, uniform on the left-side and our k-based on the right-side), on the LSAC [41] dataset.

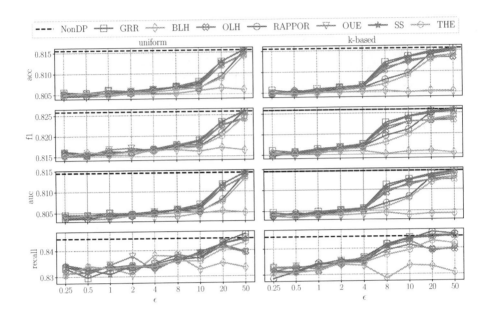

Fig. 5. Utility metrics (y-axis) by varying the privacy guarantees (x-axis), the ϵ-LDP protocol, and the privacy budget splitting solution (*i.e.*, uniform on the left-side and our k-based on the right-side), on the Adult [15] dataset.

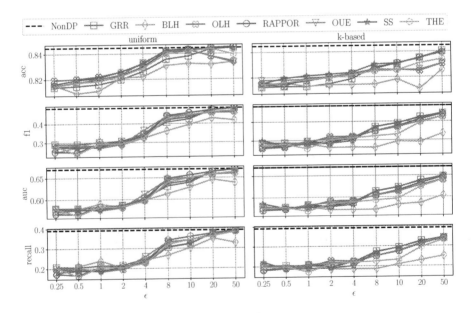

Fig. 6. Utility metrics (y-axis) by varying the privacy guarantees (x-axis), the ϵ-LDP protocol, and the privacy budget splitting solution (*i.e.*, uniform on the left-side and our k-based on the right-side), on the ACSCoverage [15] dataset.

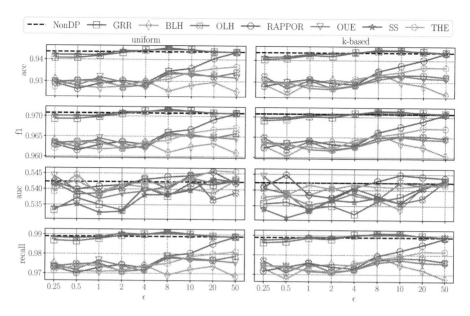

Fig. 7. Utility metrics (y-axis) by varying the privacy guarantees (x-axis), the ϵ-LDP protocol, and the privacy budget splitting solution (*i.e.*, uniform on the left-side and our k-based on the right-side), on the LSAC [41] dataset.

LDP as it only drops in higher privacy regimes (*i.e.*, smaller ϵ values) than the uniform solution. One main explanation for this behavior is because there is more discrepancy in the domain size k's of the sensitive attributes A_s and, consequently, more privacy budget ϵ are allocated to those attributes with high k. For this reason, the uniform solution preserved more utility for the ACSCoverage dataset in Fig. 6, and both solutions had similar results for the LSAC dataset in Fig. 7 due to sensitive attributes with small domain size k.

Summary. We summarize our main findings for the three research questions formulated at the beginning of Sect. 5. We highlight these findings are generic and were also confirmed in additional experiments presented in the full version of this paper [8]. **(RQ1)** Using the same hyperparameters configuration, ϵ-LDP positively affects fairness in ML (see Figs. 2, 2 and 4) while having a negligible impact on model's utility (see Figs. 5, 2 and 7). This contrasts the findings of [9,21] that state that under the same hyperparameters configuration, ϵ-DP negatively impacts fairness. Although the aforementioned research works concern *gradient perturbation* in central DP, the recent work of de Oliveira *et al.* [34] has shown that when searching for the best hyperparameters for both non-private and DP models, the ϵ-DP impact on fairness is negligible. In our case, we focused on *input perturbation, i.e.*, randomizing multiple sensitive attributes before training any ML algorithm, and discovered a positive impact of ϵ-(L)DP on fairness. **(RQ2)** Our k-based solution consistently led to better fairness than the state-of-the-art uniform solution when there exist sensitive attributes with high domain size k (*e.g.*, for both Adult and ACSCoverage datasets). Naturally, when all sensitive attributes have a binary domain, our k-based solution is equivalent to the uniform solution. For this reason, both state-of-the-art uniform and our k-based solution led to similar privacy-utility-fairness trade-off for the LSAC dataset (see Figs. 4 and 7). Therefore, regarding utility, k-based is better when sensitive attributes have higher domain sizes k, which coincides with real-world data collections. **(RQ3)** In general, GRR and SS presented the best privacy-utility-fairness trade-off for all three datasets. This is because GRR has only one perturbed output value and because SS is equivalent to GRR when $\omega = 1$, thus, not introducing inconsistencies for a user's profile. The term *inconsistency* refers to an user being multiple categories in a given attribute, *i.e.*, being both woman and man at the same time. In fact, this is precisely what happens with UE protocols that perturb each bit independently or with LH protocols in which many values can hash to the same perturbed value. For this reason, since BLH hashes the input set $V \to \{0, 1\}$, it consistently presented the worst utility results for all three datasets, and only for ACSCoverage (see Fig. 3), it presented slightly better fairness results than all other LDP protocols.

6   Conclusion and Perspectives

This paper presented an in-depth empirical study of the impact of pre-processing multidimensional data with seven state-of-the-art ϵ-LDP protocols on fairness and utility in binary classification tasks. In our experiments, GRR [24] and SS [39,42] presented the best privacy-utility-fairness trade-off than RAPPOR [19], OUE [40], THE [40], BLH [11], and OLH [40]. In addition, we proposed a new privacy budget splitting solution named k-based, which generally led to better fairness and performance results than the state-of-the-art solution that splits ϵ uniformly [6,38]. Globally, while previous research [9,21] has highlighted that DP worsens fairness in ML under the same hyperparameter configuration, our study finds that LDP slightly improves fairness and does not significantly impair utility. Indeed, there is still much to explore in the area of privacy-fairness-aware ML, and this study's empirical results can serve as a basis for future research directions. For instance, we intend to formally investigate the privacy-utility-fairness trade-off on binary classification tasks when varying the distribution of the protected attribute, the target, and their joint, and propose new methods accordingly. Last, we plan to investigate the impact of LDP pre-processing on different ML algorithms, such as deep neural networks.

Acknowledgements. This work was supported by the European Research Council (ERC) project HYPATIA under the European Union's Horizon 2020 research and innovation programme. Grant agreement n. 835294.

References

1. Indicator vector. https://en.wikipedia.org/wiki/Indicator_vector. Accessed on 04 April 2023
2. LDP impact on fairness repository. https://github.com/hharcolezi/ldp-fairness-impact
3. General data protection regulation (GDPR) (2018). https://gdpr-info.eu/. Accessed on 26 March 2023
4. Agarwal, A., Agarwal, H., Agarwal, N.: Fairness score and process standardization: framework for fairness certification in artificial intelligence systems. AI and Ethics, pp. 1–13 (2022)
5. Alves, G., Bernier, F., Couceiro, M., Makhlouf, K., Palamidessi, C., Zhioua, S.: Survey on fairness notions and related tensions. arXiv preprint arXiv:2209.13012 (2022)
6. Arcolezi, H.H., Couchot, J.F., Al Bouna, B., Xiao, X.: Random sampling plus fake data: Multidimensional frequency estimates with local differential privacy. In: Proceedings of the 30th ACM International Conference on Information & Knowledge Management, CIKM 2021, pp. 47–57. Association for Computing Machinery, New York (2021). https://doi.org/10.1145/3459637.3482467
7. Arcolezi, H.H., Couchot, J.F., Gambs, S., Palamidessi, C., Zolfaghari, M.: Multi-freq-ldpy: multiple frequency estimation under local differential privacy in python. In: Atluri, V., Di Pietro, R., Jensen, C.D., Meng, W. (eds.) Computer Security - ESORICS 2022, pp. 770–775. Springer, Cham (2022). https://doi.org/10.1007/978-3-031-17143-7_40
8. Arcolezi, H.H., Makhlouf, K., Palamidessi, C.: (local) differential privacy has no disparate impact on fairness. arXiv preprint arXiv:2304.12845 (2023)
9. Bagdasaryan, E., Poursaeed, O., Shmatikov, V.: Differential privacy has disparate impact on model accuracy. In: Wallach, H., Larochelle, H., Beygelzimer, A., d'Alché-Buc, F., Fox, E., Garnett, R. (eds.) Advances in Neural Information Processing Systems, vol. 32. Curran Associates, Inc. (2019)
10. Barocas, S., Selbst, A.D.: Big data's disparate impact. Calif. L. Rev. **104**, 671 (2016)
11. Bassily, R., Smith, A.: Local, private, efficient protocols for succinct histograms. In: Proceedings of the Forty-Seventh Annual ACM Symposium on Theory of Computing, STOC 2015, pp. 127–135. Association for Computing Machinery, New York (2015). https://doi.org/10.1145/2746539.2746632
12. Bergstra, J., Yamins, D., Cox, D.D.: Making a science of model search: hyper-parameter optimization in hundreds of dimensions for vision architectures. In: Proceedings of the 30th International Conference on International Conference on Machine Learning, ICML 2013, pp. I-115-I-123. JMLR (2013)
13. Berk, R., Heidari, H., Jabbari, S., Kearns, M., Roth, A.: Fairness in criminal justice risk assessments: The state of the art. Sociological Methods & Research (2018)
14. Chen, C., Liang, Y., Xu, X., Xie, S., Hong, Y., Shu, K.: On fair classification with mostly private sensitive attributes. arXiv preprint arXiv:2207.08336 (2022)
15. Ding, F., Hardt, M., Miller, J., Schmidt, L.: Retiring adult: new datasets for fair machine learning. Advances in Neural Information Processing Systems 34 (2021)
16. Dwork, C., Hardt, M., Pitassi, T., Reingold, O., Zemel, R.: Fairness through awareness. In: Proceedings of the 3rd Innovations in Theoretical Computer Science Conference. ACM, January 2012. https://doi.org/10.1145/2090236.2090255

17. Dwork, C., McSherry, F., Nissim, K., Smith, A.: Calibrating noise to sensitivity in private data analysis. In: Theory of Cryptography, pp. 265–284. Springer, Heidelberg (2006). https://doi.org/10.1007/11681878_14

18. Dwork, C., Roth, A., et al.: The algorithmic foundations of differential privacy. Found. Trends Theoretical Comput. Sci. 9(3–4), 211–407 (2014)

19. Erlingsson, U., Pihur, V., Korolova, A.: RAPPOR: Randomized aggregatable privacy-preserving ordinal response. In: Proceedings of the 2014 ACM SIGSAC Conference on Computer and Communications Security. pp. 1054–1067. ACM, New York (2014). https://doi.org/10.1145/2660267.2660348

20. Fioretto, F., Tran, C., Hentenryck, P.V., Zhu, K.: Differential privacy and fairness in decisions and learning tasks: A survey. In: Proceedings of the Thirty-First International Joint Conference on Artificial Intelligence (Jul 2022). https://doi.org/10.24963/ijcai.2022/766

21. Ganev, G., Oprisanu, B., De Cristofaro, E.: Robin hood and matthew effects: Differential privacy has disparate impact on synthetic data. In: Chaudhuri, K., Jegelka, S., Song, L., Szepesvari, C., Niu, G., Sabato, S. (eds.) Proceedings of the 39th International Conference on Machine Learning. Proceedings of Machine Learning Research, vol. 162, pp. 6944–6959. PMLR (17–23 Jul 2022)

22. Hardt, M., Price, E., Srebro, N.: Equality of opportunity in supervised learning. Advances in neural information processing systems 29 (2016)

23. Hu, H., Salcic, Z., Sun, L., Dobbie, G., Yu, P.S., Zhang, X.: Membership inference attacks on machine learning: a survey. ACM Comput. Surv. 54(11s), 1–37 (2022). https://doi.org/10.1145/3523273

24. Kairouz, P., Bonawitz, K., Ramage, D.: Discrete distribution estimation under local privacy. In: International Conference on Machine Learning, pp. 2436–2444. PMLR (2016)

25. Kallus, N., Mao, X., Zhou, A.: Assessing algorithmic fairness with unobserved protected class using data combination. Manage. Sci. 68(3), 1959–1981 (2022). https://doi.org/10.1287/mnsc.2020.3850

26. Kasiviswanathan, S.P., Lee, H.K., Nissim, K., Raskhodnikova, S., Smith, A.: What can we learn privately? In: 2008 49th Annual IEEE Symposium on Foundations of Computer Science, pp. 531–540 (2008). https://doi.org/10.1109/FOCS.2008.27

27. Ke, G., et al.: Lightgbm: a highly efficient gradient boosting decision tree. In: Guyon, I., Luxburg, U.V., Bengio, S., Wallach, H., Fergus, R., Vishwanathan, S., Garnett, R. (eds.) Advances in Neural Information Processing Systems, vol. 30. Curran Associates, Inc. (2017)

28. Lam, S.K., Pitrou, A., Seibert, S.: Numba: a llvm-based python jit compiler. In: Proceedings of the Second Workshop on the LLVM Compiler Infrastructure in HPC. LLVM 2015. Association for Computing Machinery, New York (2015). https://doi.org/10.1145/2833157.2833162

29. Liu, B., Ding, M., Shaham, S., Rahayu, W., Farokhi, F., Lin, Z.: When machine learning meets privacy. ACM Comput. Surv. 54(2), 1–36 (2021). https://doi.org/10.1145/3436755

30. Makhlouf, K., Zhioua, S., Palamidessi, C.: Machine learning fairness notions: bridging the gap with real-world applications. Inf. Process. Manage. 58(5), 102642 (2021). https://doi.org/10.1016/j.ipm.2021.102642

31. Makhlouf, K., Zhioua, S., Palamidessi, C.: On the applicability of machine learning fairness notions. ACM SIGKDD Explorations Newsl. 23(1), 14–23 (2021). https://doi.org/10.1145/3468507.3468511

32. Mehrabi, N., Morstatter, F., Saxena, N., Lerman, K., Galstyan, A.: A survey on bias and fairness in machine learning. ACM Comput. Surv. **54**(6), 1–35 (2021). https://doi.org/10.1145/3457607

33. Mozannar, H., Ohannessian, M., Srebro, N.: Fair learning with private demographic data. In: III, H.D., Singh, A. (eds.) Proceedings of the 37th International Conference on Machine Learning. Proceedings of Machine Learning Research, vol. 119, pp. 7066–7075. PMLR (13–18 Jul 2020)

34. de Oliveira, A.S., Kaplan, C., Mallat, K., Chakraborty, T.: An empirical analysis of fairness notions under differential privacy. In: PPAI 2023, 4th AAAI Workshop on Privacy-Preserving Artificial Intelligence, 13 February 2023, Washington DC, USA (2023)

35. Pujol, D., McKenna, R., Kuppam, S., Hay, M., Machanavajjhala, A., Miklau, G.: Fair decision making using privacy-protected data. In: Proceedings of the 2020 Conference on Fairness, Accountability, and Transparency. ACM, January 2020. https://doi.org/10.1145/3351095.3372872

36. Salem, A.M.G., Bhattacharyya, A., Backes, M., Fritz, M., Zhang, Y.: Updates-leak: Data set inference and reconstruction attacks in online learning. In: 29th USENIX Security Symposium, pp. 1291–1308. USENIX (2020)

37. van der Walt, S., Colbert, S.C., Varoquaux, G.: The numpy array: a structure for efficient numerical computation. Comput. Sci. Eng. **13**(2), 22–30 (2011). https://doi.org/10.1109/MCSE.2011.37

38. Wang, N., et al.: Collecting and analyzing multidimensional data with local differential privacy. In: 2019 IEEE 35th International Conference on Data Engineering (ICDE). IEEE, April 2019. https://doi.org/10.1109/icde.2019.00063

39. Wang, S., et al.: Mutual information optimally local private discrete distribution estimation. arXiv preprint arXiv:1607.08025 (2016)

40. Wang, T., Blocki, J., Li, N., Jha, S.: Locally differentially private protocols for frequency estimation. In: 26th USENIX Security Symposium (USENIX Security 17), pp. 729–745. USENIX Association, Vancouver, BC, August 2017

41. Wightman, L.F.: Lsac national longitudinal bar passage study. lsac research report series (1998)

42. Ye, M., Barg, A.: Optimal schemes for discrete distribution estimation under locally differential privacy. IEEE Trans. Inf. Theory **64**(8), 5662–5676 (2018). https://doi.org/10.1109/TIT.2018.2809790

Building Quadtrees for Spatial Data Under Local Differential Privacy

Ece Alptekin and M. Emre Gursoy[✉]

Department of Computer Engineering, Koç University, Istanbul, Turkey
{ealptekin21,emregursoy}@ku.edu.tr

Abstract. Spatial decompositions are commonly used in the privacy literature for various purposes such as range query answering, spatial indexing, count-of-counts histograms, data summarization, and visualization. Among spatial decomposition techniques, quadtrees are a popular and well-known method. In this paper, we study the problem of building quadtrees for spatial data under the emerging notion of Local Differential Privacy (LDP). We first propose a baseline solution inspired from a state-of-the-art method from the centralized DP literature and adapt it to LDP. Motivated by the observation that the baseline solution causes large noise accumulation due to its iterative strategy, we then propose a novel solution which utilizes a single data collection step from users, propagates density estimates to all nodes, and finally performs structural corrections to the quadtree. We experimentally evaluate the baseline solution and the proposed solution using four real-world location datasets and three utility metrics. Results show that our proposed solution consistently outperforms the baseline solution, and furthermore, the resulting quadtrees provide high accuracy in practical tasks such as spatial query answering under conventional privacy levels.

Keywords: Privacy · local differential privacy · location-based services · spatial data · spatial decompositions

1 Introduction

Location-based services (LBSs) have become ubiquitous, thanks to the popularity of smartphones, GPS-equipped mobile devices, online social networks, and connected car applications. This results in growing volumes of spatial data which are available for collection, storage and analysis; however, the privacy of the data must be protected. A common method to deal with big spatial data in the privacy literature has been to adopt *spatial decompositions* which partition (decompose) the geometric space into smaller subspaces through the likes of tree-based and grid-based data structures. Spatial decompositions have been commonly used in the differential privacy literature for various purposes such as range query answering [8,29,34], spatial indexing and modeling [26,39], count-of-counts histograms [22], data summarization and visualization [2,27], as well as synthetic data generation [15,16,19].

Among spatial decomposition techniques, quadtrees are a popular and well-known method [8,23,28]. Indeed, the problem of building quadtrees under centralized differential privacy (DP) has been actively studied [8,24,26,34,39]. However, a major drawback

© IFIP International Federation for Information Processing 2023
Published by Springer Nature Switzerland AG 2023
V. Atluri and A. L. Ferrara (Eds.): DBSec 2023, LNCS 13942, pp. 22–39, 2023.
https://doi.org/10.1007/978-3-031-37586-6_2

of centralized DP is that it assumes all data is collected and stored in a centralized location before the algorithm is executed (i.e., before a quadtree is built). On the other hand, the recently emerging notion of *Local Differential Privacy (LDP)* enables each user to locally perturb their data on their own device and send the perturbed output to the data collector [7, 13]. This way, the data collector cannot observe the true data (in our context, the true location) of any user; yet, the data collector can still build a quadtree by estimating aggregate statistics pertaining to the general population. Due to its desirable privacy guarantee, LDP has recently received significant attention from the academia and industry [7, 14, 37]. It has also been deployed in consumer-facing products of tech companies such as Apple, Google and Microsoft [1, 10, 13].

Motivated by the above, in this paper, we study the problem of building quadtrees for spatial data under LDP. We first propose a *baseline solution* inspired from a state-of-the-art method from the centralized DP literature [39] and adapt it to LDP by making modifications. However, we observe that this baseline solution yields low utility in practice. This is because the baseline solution divides the total ε privacy budget into several pieces, each used for LDP estimation in one depth of the quadtree. Since the privacy budget used per estimation is smaller, higher noise is added to satisfy LDP, which causes noisy node densities and erroneous structure in the resulting quadtrees since estimation results also affect whether an internal tree node should split (have children). To address these weaknesses, we then develop a new, *proposed solution* which performs a single LDP estimation. This single-step estimation is performed at the hypothetical leaves of the quadtree and results in low noise, thereby enabling high-quality estimates to be obtained at the leaves. Then, leaves' densities are propagated upwards (in bottom-up fashion) to populate the densities of remaining nodes. Finally, structural corrections and consistency is achieved for the quadtree in top-down manner.

We experimentally evaluate the baseline solution and the proposed solution using four real-world location datasets and three utility metrics: Average Query Error (AQE) which measures the correctness of query results issued on the quadtrees, Tree Edit Distance (TED) which measures the structural difference between the LDP quadtree and a noise-free, gold-standard quadtree, and Node Density Difference (NDD) which measures the error in the densities of quadtree nodes. Typical privacy values such as $\varepsilon = 0.1, 0.5, 1, 2$ are used throughout the experiments. Results show that our proposed solution consistently outperforms the baseline solution in a variety of settings and quadtree parameters. Furthermore, in many cases, quadtrees built using our proposed solution enable query answering with less than 5% error, demonstrating the practicality and usefulness of our solution.

In short, the contributions of this paper can be summarized as follows:

- We formulate the problem of building quadtrees for spatial data under LDP and propose two solutions: a *baseline solution* inspired from the centralized DP literature, and a *proposed solution* which relies on a single step of LDP data collection to address the iterative noise accumulation in the baseline solution.
- We develop three utility metrics to measure the accuracy of quadtrees built under LDP: Average Query Error (AQE), Tree Edit Distance (TED) and Node Density Difference (NDD).
- We experimentally evaluate the baseline and proposed solutions using four-real world location datasets and the three aforementioned metrics, under varying ε

privacy budgets as well as varying quadtree parameters (max height h^* and split threshold θ). Results show that the proposed solution is superior to the baseline solution, and furthermore, quadtrees built using the proposed solution can be used in practice with low utility loss.

2   Preliminaries

2.1   Data Model and Notation

Consider a two-dimensional geolocation space Ω and let $\mathcal{U} = \{u_1, u_2, u_3, ...\}$ be the collection of users, where $n = |\mathcal{U}|$ denotes the number of users. For each user $u_i \in \mathcal{U}$, the user's true location l_i is a tuple consisting of latitude and longitude coordinates. Each location l_i falls within the boundaries of Ω. For example, if users are from the city of London, then Ω corresponds to the geographic boundaries of London and each location l_i corresponds to some GPS coordinates within London. We assume that Ω by itself is not sensitive, as it can be learned from public resources.

2.2   Local Differential Privacy

Local Differential Privacy (LDP) has recently emerged as a popular privacy standard and it has been deployed in consumer-facing products of companies such as Apple, Google and Microsoft [1,7,10,13,37]. In LDP, each user locally perturbs their true data on their own device using a randomized algorithm Ψ and sends the perturbed output to the server (i.e., the data collector). After the server collects perturbed data from many users, it performs estimation to recover aggregate statistics pertaining to the general user population. The main reasons why LDP is a good fit for the problem considered in this paper are twofold. First, since perturbation is performed on the user's side, the server does not observe the true location of any user, which protects the privacy of the user's location from a potentially untrusted server. Second, while the server cannot infer any particular user's true location, it can recover aggregate statistics pertaining the general user population, which enables the server to estimate location densities and build spatial decomposition structures pertaining to the overall population.

In our context, the sensitive data that needs to be protected using LDP is each user's location. Accordingly, we formalize LDP as follows.

Definition 1 (ε-LDP). *A randomized algorithm Ψ satisfies ε-local differential privacy (ε-LDP), where $\varepsilon > 0$, if and only if for any two inputs l_i, l_i^*, it holds that:*

$$\forall y \in Range(\Psi) : \quad \frac{Pr[\Psi(l_i) = y]}{Pr[\Psi(l_i^*) = y]} \le e^\varepsilon \tag{1}$$

where $Range(\Psi)$ stands for the set of all possible outputs of the algorithm Ψ.

Given the perturbed output y, ε-LDP ensures that the server (or any third party who observes y) will not be able to distinguish between user's actual location l_i and fake location l_i^* beyond the probability odds ratio controlled by e^ε. The strength of privacy is controlled by the parameter ε, commonly known as the *privacy budget*. Lower ε yields stronger privacy.

Similar to centralized DP, LDP enjoys the *sequential composition* property [11, 33, 38] which can be formalized as follows.

Definition 2 (Sequential Composition). *Consider algorithms* $\Psi_1, \Psi_2, ..., \Psi_m$ *such that each* Ψ_j *satisfies* ε_j-*LDP. Then, the sequential execution of* $\Psi_1(l_i), \Psi_2(l_i), ..., \Psi_m(l_i)$ *satisfies* $(\sum_{j=1}^{m} \varepsilon_j)$-*LDP.*

The popularity of LDP has led to the development of several LDP protocols [3, 13, 31, 32]. New systems and applications often use these LDP protocols as building blocks. In particular, we will use the *Optimized Unary Encoding (OUE)* protocol as a building block in this paper, since it was shown to provide higher accuracy than many other protocols [32]. As in other protocols, OUE consists of two main components: (i) user-side encoding and perturbation to satisfy LDP on users' devices, and (ii) server-side estimation after collecting perturbed data from the user population.

User-Side Perturbation in OUE: OUE assumes that the user's data is encoded as a unary bitvector (vector of bits), i.e., only one position in the user's vector contains a 1 bit and all remaining positions contain 0 bits. Let B_i denote user u_i's unary bitvector. The perturbation algorithm Ψ of OUE takes B_i as input and outputs perturbed bitvector B'_i as:

$$\Pr\left[B'_i[j] = \Psi(B_i[j]) = 1\right] = \begin{cases} \frac{1}{2} & \text{if } B_i[j] = 1 \\ \frac{1}{e^\varepsilon + 1} & \text{if } B_i[j] = 0 \end{cases} \tag{2}$$

In other words, each position $j \in [1, |B_i|]$ is considered independently from others, and the bit that exists in $B_i[j]$ is either kept or flipped according to the above probabilities. After this perturbation is complete, u_i sends the perturbed bitvector B'_i to the server.

Server-Side Estimation in OUE: The server receives perturbed bitvectors from many users, collectively denoted by $\{B'_1, B'_2, ..., B'_n\}$. Then, the server computes the reported counts of each position $j \in [1, |B_i|]$, which we denote by $\widehat{C}(j)$:

$$\widehat{C}(j) = \sum_{i=1}^{n} B'_i[j] \tag{3}$$

Finally, the server computes the estimate for position j, i.e., how many users have 1 bit in the j'th position of their original bitvectors. This estimate, denoted by $\bar{C}(j)$, is computed as:

$$\bar{C}(j) = \frac{2 \cdot \left((e^\varepsilon + 1) \cdot \widehat{C}(j) - |\mathcal{U}|\right)}{e^\varepsilon - 1} \tag{4}$$

2.3   Spatial Decompositions and Quadtrees

A spatial decomposition decomposes a geometric space into smaller subspaces. Tree-based (hierarchical) decompositions are quite common, in which data points are divided among the leaf nodes [8, 19, 22, 23, 39]. Tree-based decompositions are usually computed down to a level in which either the leaves contain a small number of points or each leaf covers a small enough area.

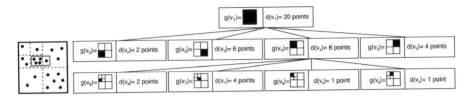

Fig. 1. Sample users with their locations represented as points (on the left) and the corresponding quadtree (on the right).

Among tree-based spatial decomposition techniques, quadtrees are a popular and well-known method [8,23,28]. A quadtree recursively divides the geographical space into four equi-sized quadrants (top left, top right, bottom left, bottom right) at each step. A sample quadtree is illustrated in Fig. 1. The root corresponds to Ω as a whole. In the next level of the tree, Ω is divided into four quadrants, each of which corresponds to a child of the root node. The division of a node into four quadrants will keep occurring recursively, until: (i) the maximum height limit h^* is reached, or (ii) the current node contains fewer number of points than a pre-defined threshold θ.

We establish some notation and terminology with the help of Fig. 1. Let Q denote a quadtree and let $\mathcal{V} = \{v_1, v_2, v_3, ...\}$ denote the set of nodes (vertices) in Q. The depth of a node v is denoted by $h(v)$, e.g., in Fig. 1, $h(v_1) = 1$, $h(v_2) = h(v_3) = 2$, $h(v_7) = 3$. Nodes with the same $h(v)$ are found at the same depth of Q. Each node corresponds to a region of the geographical space as shown in Fig. 1, e.g., v_1 corresponds to Ω, v_2 corresponds to bottom left quadrant of Ω, and so forth. We denote the geographical space corresponding to vertex v by $g(v)$. Furthermore, the number of data points located in the corresponding region of v is called the *density* of v and it is denoted by $d(v)$. In Fig. 1, $d(v_1) = 20$, $d(v_2) = 2$, $d(v_3) = 6$, etc. By definition, the root node v_1 has density $d(v_1) = n$ since all users are assumed to be located within Ω.

We denote the children of a node v by $c(v)$, e.g., according to Fig. 1, $c(v_4) = \{v_6, v_7, v_8, v_9\}$. If a node has children, it will always have exactly 4 children. If a node does not have children, then it is called a *leaf* node. The parent of a node v is denoted by $p(v)$, e.g., $p(v_6) = p(v_8) = v_4$.

In general, let v_i denote a node with set of children $c(v_i) = \{v_{i1}, v_{i2}, v_{i3}, v_{i4}\}$. By definition of Q and from the example in Fig. 1, it can be verified that:

$$g(v_i) = g(v_{i1}) \cup g(v_{i2}) \cup g(v_{i3}) \cup g(v_{i4}) \tag{5}$$

and the pairwise intersection $g(v_{ij}) \cap g(v_{ik})$ is empty for all $j \neq k$. Furthermore, the sum of densities of all children equals the density of the parent:

$$d(v_i) = d(v_{i1}) + d(v_{i2}) + d(v_{i3}) + d(v_{i4}) \tag{6}$$

One of the key applications of quadtrees is in answering spatial count (density) queries [8,23,39]. Consider a query q. Initially, the answer of q is set to 0, i.e., $ans_q = 0$. Then, starting from the root, the quadtree is traversed in-top down fashion. For each node v that is visited:

1. If $g(v)$ is disjoint from q, then v is ignored.
2. If $g(v)$ is fully contained in q, then ans_q is increased by $d(v)$.
3. If $g(v)$ partially intersects q and v is not a leaf node, then every child of v with a region not disjoint from q must be visited.
4. If $g(v)$ partially intersects q and v is a leaf node, then ans_q is incremented by:

$$ans_q = ans_q + d(v) \times \frac{||g(v) \cap q||}{||g(v)||}$$

Here, $|| \cdot ||$ denotes the size of a geographical region.

We exemplify this process with the help of Fig. 1. Let q be a query denoted using the red rectangle. Starting from v_1, we first find that $g(v)$ intersects with v_1, therefore v_1's children must be visited. Since v_2 and v_3 have no intersection with q, they are ignored. v_5 has intersection with q and it is a leaf node, therefore ans_q is incremented by $d(v_5) \times \frac{||g(v_5) \cap q||}{||g(v_5)||}$. v_4 has intersection with q but it is not a leaf node, therefore v_4's children must be visited next. Among v_4's children, v_6, v_8 and v_9 are ignored. Since v_7 intersects with q, ans_q is incremented by $d(v_7) \times \frac{||g(v_7) \cap q||}{||g(v_7)||}$.

2.4 Problem Formulation

Let $\mathcal{U}$ be the collection of users where l_i denotes the location of user u_i. Let Ω, θ and h^* parameters be known by the server. The server would like to construct a quadtree according to these parameters. If the server was able to access the real location l_i of each user, then a noise-free quadtree Q can be built. However, each user's location must be protected by ε-LDP, which causes users' responses to the server to be perturbed (noisy) to achieve privacy protection. Given the noisy responses, the server can build a *noisy* quadtree, denoted by Q'. For Q' to be useful in practice, it is desired that Q' has high similarity to Q. In other words, it is desired to build a quadtree Q' while satisfying ε-LDP, such that Q' has high similarity to the hypothetical, noise-free Q that would have been built if privacy protection did not exist.

In short, the problem that we study in this paper is to design and develop a solution in which: (i) the privacy of each user's location l_i is protected via ε-LDP, and (ii) the server is able to build a quadtree Q' such that Q' has high similarity to quadtree Q which would have been built if privacy protection had not been applied.

3 Building Quadtrees Under LDP

In this section, we describe two solutions for the problem formulated in Sect. 2.4. Our first solution is inspired by a differentially private quadtree building algorithm from the centralized DP literature, which we modify in order to adapt to LDP. We explain the centralized algorithm and the key modifications we need to perform to adapt it to LDP in Sect. 3.1. Then, our baseline solution is given in Sect. 3.2. However, we observe that although the iterative noise addition approach used in the baseline solution satisfies LDP, it is not a desirable solution in practice since it causes large noise accumulation and therefore low utility. This motivates the proposal of our new approach in Sect. 3.3, which yields higher utility than the baseline solution.

3.1   Quadtrees Under Centralized DP

Consider the quadtree building algorithm presented in [39], which satisfies centralized DP. The algorithm starts by initializing quadtree Q with a root node v_1 such that $g(v_1) = \Omega$ and marks v_1 as unvisited. Then, the algorithm proceeds iteratively, and at each iteration, it checks if there is any unvisited node $v \in Q$. If there is an unvisited node, the algorithm computes the noisy density of v. For this purpose, the Laplace mechanism of DP can be used [11]. The noisy density is determined as: $\hat{d}(v) = d(v) + Lap(\lambda)$, where $Lap(\lambda)$ is a Laplace random variable with mean 0 and scale λ. Afterwards, node v is checked regarding whether it satisfies the splitting conditions, i.e., its noisy density is higher than split threshold θ and depth of resulting children will not exceed max depth limit h^*. Indeed, if $\hat{d}(v) \geq \theta$ and $h(v) + 1 \leq h^*$, then v is split into four children, the children are inserted to Q, and they are marked as *unvisited*. Otherwise, v is not split and becomes a leaf node. At this point, v has been processed; it is marked as *visited* and the algorithm proceeds to the next iteration (next unvisited node in Q). When all nodes in Q eventually become visited, the algorithm terminates and returns Q.

It can be shown that this algorithm satisfies ε-DP in the centralized setting when $\lambda \geq h^*/\varepsilon$. To verify this, let a new user with an arbitrary location be inserted (removal of an arbitrary user is very similar). This insertion will impact the noisy densities of nodes residing in exactly one root-to-leaf path in Q; since by properties of quadtrees, nodes with the same depth do not have any intersection in their geographic coverages $g(\cdot)$. Then, since the number of nodes residing in one root-to-leaf path in Q is at most h^*, adding Laplace noise calibrated to h^*/ε is sufficient to achieve ε-DP.

Our baseline solution for building quadtrees with LDP adapts the aforementioned algorithm from the centralized DP literature to LDP. Two key modifications are needed in this adaptation. First, the above algorithm visits nodes one-by-one in arbitrary order, as long as they are unvisited. In contrast, our baseline solution visits nodes in breadth-first order, i.e., depth = 1 in the first iteration, depth = 2 in the second iteration, and so forth. Notice that this has no adverse impact on utility or privacy (the aforementioned algorithm can be trivially modified to act in breadth-first order), but it offers us an important convenience in LDP: It enables us to estimate node densities with LDP iteratively such that in the first iteration all nodes with depth = 1 are estimated, in the second iteration all nodes with depth = 2 are estimated, and so forth. The second modification we perform is that instead of adding Laplace noise, we execute an LDP protocol (OUE) to perform node density estimation. While Laplace noise addition is a de facto mechanism to achieve centralized DP, it is not directly applicable to LDP, therefore the usage of an LDP protocol becomes necessary.

3.2   Baseline Solution for Building Quadtrees Under LDP

Our baseline solution for building a quadtree under LDP is shown in Algorithm 1. Given the total privacy budget ε, on line 1, the algorithm computes $\hat{\varepsilon} = \varepsilon/(h^* - 1)$. Here, considering that the algorithm will traverse the quadtree depth by depth and h^* is the max depth parameter, $\hat{\varepsilon}$ is the privacy budget that the algorithm will spend at each depth. Since the density of the root node is always equal to $|\mathcal{U}|$ and the server can trivially know the size of the user population, no privacy budget is spent at depth

---

Algorithm 1. Baseline solution

Input : $\mathcal{U}, \Omega, \theta, h^*, \varepsilon$

Output: Quadtree Q

1 $\hat{\varepsilon} \leftarrow \varepsilon/(h^* - 1)$
2 Initialize quadtree Q with root node v_1
3 Set $g(v_1) = \Omega$
4 $i \leftarrow 1$ // current depth
5 **while** $i \leq h^*$ **do**
       // find densities at current depth
6      $nodes \leftarrow$ list of nodes in Q with depth $= i$
7   **if** $|nodes| == 1$ **then**
8   Set $d(nodes[1]) = |\mathcal{U}|$ // $i = 1$, root node only
9   **else**
10         $estimates \leftarrow$ GET_ESTIMATES($nodes, \mathcal{U}, \hat{\varepsilon}$)
11   **for** $j = 1$ *to* $|nodes|$ **do**
12   Set $d(nodes[j]) = estimates[j]$
       // for each node at current depth, determine if it should
          split or not
13   **for** $j = 1$ *to* $|nodes|$ **do**
14   **if** $d(nodes[j]) \geq \theta$ *and* $i + 1 \leq h^*$ **then**
15   Split $nodes[j]$ into its four children and add the children to Q
16   **else**
17   Do not split $nodes[j]$
18     $i \leftarrow i + 1$
19 **return** Q

$= 1$ (only the root node exists at depth $= 1$). Thus, dividing ε into $h^* - 1$ pieces is sufficient. On lines 2–3, the algorithm initializes the root node. Then, the main loop of the algorithm (lines 5–18) iterates depth-by-depth, and at each iteration, it estimates the densities of nodes at the current depth. The case where depth $= 1$ (only the root node exists) is handled between lines 7–8. At every other depth value, nodes' densities at that depth are computed with the help of the GET_ESTIMATES function (lines 10–12), which is explained below. GET_ESTIMATES satisfies $\hat{\varepsilon}$-LDP, and note that Algorithm 1 invokes it at most $h^* - 1$ times; thus, the overall algorithm satisfies ε-LDP by sequential composition. Finally, lines 13–17 are devoted to checking which nodes should split and which ones should not split. If and only if a node satisfies the splitting conditions, i.e., its noisy density is $\geq \theta$ and the height of its children will not exceed h^*, then the node will split.

The GET_ESTIMATES function, which is used by our baseline solution as well as our proposed solution, is described in Algorithm 2. Its inputs are the list of nodes $\mathcal{N}$, list of users $\mathcal{U}$, and privacy budget $\hat{\varepsilon}$. It returns a list called $estimates$, such that $estimates[j]$ is the estimated noisy density of node $\mathcal{N}[j]$. The execution of the GET-_ESTIMATES function can be broken down into three steps. First, the server sends $\mathcal{N}$ to each user. Second, on the user side, each user u_i constructs a bitvector B_i, where $|B_i| = |\mathcal{N}|$. For each position j, $B_i[j]$ is determined according to whether u_i's real

---

Algorithm 2. Get_Estimates function

Input : $\mathcal{N}, \mathcal{U}, \hat{\varepsilon}$
Output: *estimates*

      `// Server-side`
1 Server sends $\mathcal{N}$ to each user in $\mathcal{U}$
      `// User-side`
2 **foreach** $u_i \in \mathcal{U}$ **do**
3   u_i constructs his/her bitvector B_i with length $|\mathcal{N}|$ such that:

$$\forall j \in [1, |\mathcal{N}|] : \quad B_i[j] = \begin{cases} 1 & \text{if } l_i \in g(\mathcal{N}[j]) \\ 0 & \text{otherwise} \end{cases}$$

4   u_i perturbs B_i to satisfy $\hat{\varepsilon}$-LDP according to Equation 2
5   u_i sends resulting perturbed bitvector B_i' to server
      `// Server-side`
6 *estimates* $\leftarrow [\,]$ `// initialize empty`
7 **for** $j = 1$ *to* $|\mathcal{N}|$ **do**
8   Server computes reported count of position j as: $\widehat{C}(j) = \sum\limits_{i=1}^{|\mathcal{U}|} B_i'[j]$
9   Server computes estimate $\bar{C}(j)$ as: $\bar{C}(j) = \dfrac{2 \cdot \left((e^{\hat{\varepsilon}}+1) \cdot \widehat{C}(j) - |\mathcal{U}| \right)}{e^{\hat{\varepsilon}} - 1}$
10   Server appends $\bar{C}(j)$ to *estimates*
11 **return** *estimates*

---

location l_i falls within the geographic boundaries of node $\mathcal{N}[j]$. That is, if l_i falls within $g(\mathcal{N}[j])$ then the j'th position of B_i is set to 1, otherwise it is 0. After constructing the B_i, it must be perturbed probabilistically in order to satisfy $\hat{\varepsilon}$-LDP. To do so, the user-side perturbation process of the OUE protocol is executed, as shown in Eq. 2. The output of this process is the perturbed bitvector B_i', which is sent to the server. Finally, the third step begins after the server receives perturbed bitvectors from all users. The server initializes *estimates* as an empty list. Afterwards, for j between 1 and $|\mathcal{N}|$, the server first computes $\widehat{C}(j)$ and then uses $\widehat{C}(j)$ to compute $\bar{C}(j)$ according to the equations on lines 8–9. $\bar{C}(j)$ is appended to *estimates* in each iteration, and eventually, *estimates* is returned by Algorithm 2.

3.3 Proposed Solution for Building Quadtrees Under LDP

The main weakness of the baseline solution is that it divides the total ε privacy budget into $h^* - 1$ pieces, each to be used in one depth of estimation. Since the privacy budget used per estimation is smaller, higher noise gets added to satisfy privacy. This causes resulting node density estimations to contain large amounts of noise. Excessively noisy densities are also used in the decision to split or not split a node, further causing structural inaccuracies in the resulting quadtree, since a node that should not be split according to its real density ends up being split due its noisy density (or vice versa). Consequently, although ε-LDP is achieved, the quadtrees built using our baseline solution can have low similarity in terms of structure and node densities compared to a noise-free quadtree.

Algorithm 3. Proposed solution

Input : $\mathcal{U}, \Omega, \theta, h^*, \varepsilon$
Output: Quadtree Q

```
// Step 1: Construct initial tree
```
1 Initalize quadtree Q with root node v_1
2 Set $g(v_1) = \Omega$
3 **for** $i = 1$ *to* $h^* - 1$ **do**
4   **foreach** *node* v *in* Q *with* $h(v) = i$ **do**
5   Split v into its four children and add the children to Q
```
// Step 2: Density estimation for leaf nodes with LDP
```
6 *leaves* $\leftarrow$ list of nodes in Q with depth $= h^*$
7 *estimates* $\leftarrow$ GET_ESTIMATES(*leaves*, $\mathcal{U}, \varepsilon$)
8 **for** $j = 1$ *to* $|leaves|$ **do**
9   Set $d(leaves[j]) = estimates[j]$
```
// Step 3: Bottom-up propagation of densities
```
10 **for** $i = h^* - 1$ *to* 1 **do**
11   **foreach** *node* v *in* Q *with* $h(v) = i$ **do**
12   Initialize $d(v) \leftarrow 0$
13   **for** $v_{child} \in c(v)$ **do**
14             $d(v) \leftarrow d(v) + d(v_{child})$
```
// Step 4: Top-down correction
```
15 **for** $i = 1$ *to* $h^* - 1$ **do**
16   **foreach** *node* v *in* Q *with* $h(v) = i$ **do**
17   **if** $d(v) < \theta$ **then**
18   Remove all children $c(v)$ and all subtrees rooted at those children from Q
19 **return** Q

In order to address this problem, the key insight of our proposed solution is that instead of dividing ε into $h^* - 1$ pieces, it uses the whole ε in a single step. This single-step estimation is performed at the leaves of the quadtree (depth $= h^*$) and contains low noise, therefore the leaves contain high quality density estimates. Then, leaves' densities are propagated upwards (in bottom-up fashion) towards the root, to populate the densities of remaining nodes. Finally, in top-down fashion, corrections and refinements are made in the structure of the quadtree.

The pseudocode of our proposed solution is shown in Algorithm 3. Its inputs and outputs are same as the baseline solution. It can be observed from Algorithm 3 that the proposed solution consists of four main steps, which are explained below.

Step 1: Construct Initial, Balanced Quadtree with Height $= h^*$. We construct an initial quadtree Q that is fully-grown until height h^*. That is, we let each node in the quadtree split into its four children until h^* is reached. The resulting Q is fully balanced. Note that the θ threshold is not taken into account in constructing this initial Q.

Step 2: Density Estimation for Leaf Nodes with LDP. In the second step, we retrieve all leaf nodes in Q and obtain density estimates for each of them using the full privacy budget ε. This is achieved by a single invocation of the GET_ESTIMATES function with all leaves and full privacy budget ε. After this step is complete, for each leaf node $v \in Q$, its density $d(v)$ is determined.

Step 3: Bottom-up Propagation of Densities. While densities of the leaves have been determined in step 2, densities of all remaining nodes (non-leaf nodes) are unknown. In this step, densities of non-leaf nodes are determined in bottom-up fashion. First, all nodes with depth $h^* - 1$ are handled, then, all nodes with depth $h^* - 2$ are handled, ... until the root node. For each non-leaf node, recall from Eq. 6 that its density is equal to the sum of the densities of its four children.

Step 4: Top-down Correction. The initial quadtree Q constructed in step 1 is fully-balanced rather than taking into account the density threshold θ. As a result, it is possible that a node v which should not have children (because it fails the $d(v) \geq \theta$ condition) actually has children in Q. The goal of step 4 is to iterate through Q in top-down fashion and fix such situations. To do so, the algorithm starts at depth = 1 and moves down iteratively (depth = 2, depth = 3, ..., depth = $h^* - 1$). For each node at the current depth, if node v does not satisfy the $d(v) \geq \theta$ condition, its children along with the subtrees rooted at those children (i.e., if the child has any descendants) are removed from Q.

4   Experimental Evaluation

4.1   Experiment Setup

We implemented the baseline and proposed solutions in Python. We experimentally compare them under varying ε, θ, and h^* parameters using multiple evaluation metrics. We use four real-world location datasets in our experiments: Kaggle, Brightkite, Gowalla, and Foursquare.

Kaggle: The Kaggle dataset contains trips of 442 taxis driving in the city of Porto. The dataset was originally made public for the taxi service prediction competition in ECML-PKDD; we downloaded it from Kaggle [12]. While the dataset contains full taxi trips (multiple location reading per trip), we pre-processed it by keeping only the starting location of each trip, and treated the trip starting locations as the current locations of users in the user population. At the end of this processing, we ended up with 1,048,575 users and their latitude, longitude locations.

Brightkite: The Brightkite dataset contains users' location check-ins from a social network service provider called Brightkite [6]. From the full dataset, we extracted check-ins made in the United States, between longitudes -124.26 and -71.87 and latitudes 25.45 and 47.44.

Gowalla was also a location-based social network site where users contributed their data by sharing their locations [6]. Similar to Brightkite, we extracted check-ins made in the United States using the same latitude and longitude boundaries.

Foursquare: The Foursquare dataset contains location check-ins of users in Tokyo, between the time period from 12 April 2012 to 16 February 2013 [35]. We used this dataset without any pre-processing. It contains a total of 573,703 location check-ins. The minimum latitude is 35.51, maximum latitude is 35.87, minimum longitude is 139.47, and maximum longitude is 139.91.

4.2   Utility Metrics

Let Q denote the gold standard, noise-free quadtree that would be built without privacy protection. Let Q' denote the noisy quadtree built under ε-LDP. We use three utility metrics to measure the difference between Q and Q'. Higher the values of these metrics, higher the difference between Q and Q', and therefore higher the amount of utility loss.

Average Query Error (AQE): We generate $N = 100$ random queries and compute their answers on the actual quadtree Q and the noisy quadtree Q', denoted by ans_q and ans'_q respectively. Then, AQE measures the average error between ans_q and ans'_q across all queries as follows:

$$AQE = \frac{\sum\limits_{i=1}^{N} \frac{|ans_{q_i} - ans'_{q_i}|}{max\{ans_{q_i}, b\}}}{N}$$

where q_i denotes the i'th query and b denotes a sanity bound that mitigates the effect of queries with extremely high selectivities (extremely low answers) [4, 16, 39]. We set the value of b as: $b = 2\% \times |\mathcal{U}|$.

Tree Edit Distance (TED): TED measures the structural difference between Q and Q'. Consider that we want to measure TED between two subtrees rooted at nodes v and v', such that $g(v) = g(v')$. $TED(v, v')$ is defined recursively as follows:

$$TED(v, v') = \begin{cases} 0 & \text{if } |c(v)| = 0 \text{ and } |c(v')| = 0 \\ num\_desc(v) & \text{if } |c(v)| > 0 \text{ and } |c(v')| = 0 \\ num\_desc(v') & \text{if } |c(v)| = 0 \text{ and } |c(v')| > 0 \\ \sum\limits_{\substack{x \in c(v),\, x' \in c(v') \\ s.t.\ g(x) = g(x')}} TED(x, x') & \text{if } |c(v)| > 0 \text{ and } |c(v')| > 0 \end{cases}$$

where $num\_desc(v)$ denotes the number of descendent nodes that v has (excluding itself). The rationale is as follows: If both v and v' do not have any children, then they have zero TED (no structural difference). If one of them has children but the other does not, then all descendents must be counted as part of TED. If both v and v' has children, then their TED is computed recursively on pairs (x, x') where x and x' have matching geographical regions, i.e., x' in Q' is the noisy counterpart of x from Q.

Once TED between v and v' is defined as above, it can be used to measure TED between two quadtrees Q and Q' as: $TED(Q, Q') = TED(v_{root}, v'_{root})$ where v_{root} is the root node of Q and v'_{root} is the root node of Q'.

Node Density Difference (NDD): NDD measures the difference between Q and Q' by computing the differences between corresponding nodes' densities.

$$NDD(Q, Q') = \sum_{v \in Q} \varphi(v)$$

where:

$$\varphi(v) = \begin{cases} |d(v) - d(v')| & \text{if } \exists\, v' \in Q' \text{s.t. } g(v) = g(v') \\ d(v) & \text{otherwise} \end{cases}$$

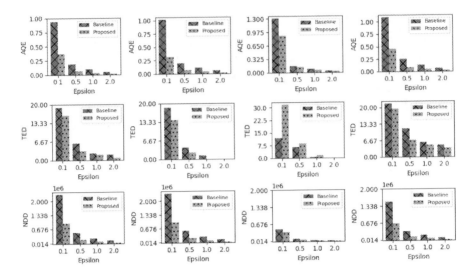

Fig. 2. Results with AQE, TED and NDD metrics (one metric each row) on Brightkite, Gowalla, Kaggle and Foursquare datasets (left to right).

In other words, NDD iterates over each node $v \in Q$ and checks if its counterpart exists in Q', i.e., $v' \in Q'$ with $g(v) = g(v')$. If it exists, then the difference between their densities is computed and added to NDD. However, due to structural differences between Q and Q', it is also possible that such a v' does not exist. In that case, $d(v')$ is assumed to be 0 and therefore $d(v)$ is added directly to NDD.

4.3   Results and Discussion

We first keep the h^* and θ parameters constant and vary the ε parameter to observe its impact. The results are reported in Fig. 2 ($h^* = 4$, $\theta = 10000$). Four popular (conventional) ε values are used: $\varepsilon = 0.1, 0.5, 1, 2$. Each experiment is repeated 10 times and their average results are reported.

Across all datasets and metrics, we observe that: (i) errors decrease as ε is increased, and (ii) the proposed solution yields lower errors than the baseline solution. The prior is an intuitive result because as ε increases, the noise caused by LDP decreases, therefore it becomes possible to build more accurate quadtrees. With regards to the latter, especially on Brightkite and Gowalla datasets, the proposed solution makes remarkable improvement in terms of the AQE and NDD metrics when ε is low. The difference between the two solutions is relatively lower in terms of the TED metric. Similar observation holds for the Foursquare dataset – while the difference between the baseline solution and proposed solution is high in terms of AQE and NDD metrics, it is relatively less pronounced in terms of the TED metric. The only exception in which the proposed solution yields higher error than the baseline solution is the Kaggle dataset and the TED metric. The reason behind this observation is the significant skew in the spatial distribution of the Kaggle dataset. Users' locations in this dataset are heavily accumulated

Table 1. AQE, TED and NDD of different heights h^* with threshold $\theta = 10000$.

			AQE				TED				NDD ($\times 10^4$)			
			$\varepsilon=0.1$	$\varepsilon=0.5$	$\varepsilon=1$	$\varepsilon=2$	$\varepsilon=0.1$	$\varepsilon=0.5$	$\varepsilon=1$	$\varepsilon=2$	$\varepsilon=0.1$	$\varepsilon=0.5$	$\varepsilon=1$	$\varepsilon=2$
Brightkite	$h^*=3$	Baseline	0.317	0.056	0.028	0.014	0.0	0.0	0.0	0.0	60.2	10.4	5.5	2.3
		Proposed	0.156	0.030	0.014	0.006	0.0	0.0	0.0	0.0	30.1	5.2	2.5	1.2
	$h^*=4$	Baseline	0.941	0.189	0.095	0.046	18.8	6.0	2.4	2.0	229.5	51.7	26.0	13.8
		Proposed	0.369	0.067	0.032	0.015	16.0	3.2	2.0	0.8	94.1	18.5	9.7	4.0
	$h^*=5$	Baseline	1.924	0.423	0.213	0.092	105.2	66.8	41.2	19.2	499.1	139.9	74.7	38.8
		Proposed	0.637	0.146	0.080	0.036	110.4	55.2	16.0	4.8	258.3	58.6	27.3	11.7
Gowalla	$h^*=3$	Baseline	0.292	0.053	0.026	0.011	0.0	0.0	0.0	0.0	50.7	10.4	4.8	2.4
		Proposed	0.140	0.022	0.013	0.005	0.0	0.0	0.0	0.0	24.8	4.8	2.5	1.1
	$h^*=4$	Baseline	1.015	0.201	0.108	0.057	18.4	4.0	1.2	0.0	234.2	56.5	28.4	14.0
		Proposed	0.313	0.069	0.039	0.016	14.0	2.4	0.0	0.0	95.9	20.9	9.5	4.3
	$h^*=5$	Baseline	2.076	0.436	0.215	0.094	118.4	68.8	40.0	17.6	554.0	151.7	80.5	42.3
		Proposed	0.850	0.172	0.074	0.032	122.4	49.2	17.6	7.6	285.5	62.1	29.6	13.0
Kaggle	$h^*=3$	Baseline	0.396	0.058	0.025	0.011	4.0	1.2	0.0	0.0	20.5	4.9	2.2	1.1
		Proposed	0.296	0.051	0.020	0.008	5.2	1.6	0.0	0.0	17.8	3.4	1.5	0.6
	$h^*=4$	Baseline	1.302	0.155	0.085	0.039	12.0	6.4	0.4	0.0	47.0	9.4	5.1	2.5
		Proposed	0.885	0.137	0.065	0.026	31.6	8.8	1.6	0.0	37.2	7.4	3.2	1.4
	$h^*=5$	Baseline	3.823	0.562	0.145	0.064	52.0	31.2	4.0	0.0	95.7	16.0	8.5	4.2
		Proposed	1.815	0.290	0.133	0.054	74.0	29.6	8.8	0.8	73.0	14.7	7.6	2.8
Foursquare	$h^*=3$	Baseline	0.373	0.062	0.038	0.019	0.0	0.0	0.0	0.0	38.5	7.3	3.9	1.8
		Proposed	0.154	0.033	0.017	0.008	0.0	0.0	0.0	0.0	19.5	3.5	1.8	0.8
	$h^*=4$	Baseline	1.085	0.249	0.128	0.060	21.6	11.6	6.0	4.8	149.5	36.0	20.1	9.8
		Proposed	0.462	0.084	0.045	0.024	19.6	6.8	4.8	3.6	65.8	14.4	8.0	3.8
	$h^*=5$	Baseline	2.334	0.455	0.207	0.098	94.8	58.4	44.0	22.4	275.3	68.7	37.8	19.5
		Proposed	0.883	0.195	0.087	0.046	109.2	56.0	25.6	17.2	146.2	38.4	17.7	8.9

within a small range of latitude and longitude coordinates, and much fewer location readings exist outside this range. Consequently, in the noise-free quadtree, there exist few branches with high depth whereas remaining branches are shallow. However, the proposed solution which constructs a fully balanced quadtree first and then performs top-down structural corrections in its final step has a higher tendency to end up with a more breadth-balanced quadtree than the noise-free version, thus causing high TED.

Next, we fix $\theta = 10000$ and vary the h^* and ε parameters. The results are shown in Table 1. We again observe that the proposed solution performs better than the baseline solution. For both solutions, it seems that as we increase h^*, errors tend to increase. For the baseline solution, this shows the ineffectiveness of splitting the original ε budget into $h^* - 1$ parts. Another interesting observation is that TED results are good when h^* is low, such as $h^* = 3$. This shows that for the first few levels of the quadtree (which are close to the root node), there is relatively small structural error. For example, when $h^* = 3$, TEDs are usually 0 meaning that our LDP quadtrees have identical structure to noise-free quadtrees. However, as we increase h^* to 4 and 5, there is an increasing amount of structural inequality as demonstrated by increasing TEDs. Overall, this shows that LDP quadtrees are more likely to have structural errors towards their leaf nodes whereas their structure close to the root node remains more accurate.

Table 2. AQE with privacy budget $\varepsilon = 1$, varying h^* and θ.

		Baseline				Proposed			
		$\theta = 1000$	$\theta = 5000$	$\theta = 10000$	$\theta = 20000$	$\theta = 1000$	$\theta = 5000$	$\theta = 10000$	$\theta = 20000$
Brightkite	$h^* = 3$	0.027	0.029	0.032	0.022	0.015	0.015	0.012	0.012
	$h^* = 4$	0.100	0.099	0.103	0.084	0.036	0.036	0.035	0.039
	$h^* = 5$	0.278	0.229	0.195	0.182	0.078	0.072	0.085	0.082
Gowalla	$h^* = 3$	0.025	0.025	0.026	0.030	0.012	0.013	0.014	0.013
	$h^* = 4$	0.097	0.106	0.100	0.108	0.034	0.028	0.036	0.041
	$h^* = 5$	0.257	0.221	0.214	0.175	0.084	0.067	0.076	0.085
Kaggle	$h^* = 3$	0.046	0.030	0.023	0.024	0.031	0.024	0.021	0.020
	$h^* = 4$	0.170	0.085	0.073	0.075	0.089	0.065	0.073	0.062
	$h^* = 5$	0.396	0.268	0.150	0.161	0.173	0.156	0.177	0.160
Foursquare	$h^* = 3$	0.035	0.035	0.035	0.028	0.016	0.018	0.018	0.017
	$h^* = 4$	0.134	0.130	0.134	0.098	0.046	0.044	0.042	0.043
	$h^* = 5$	0.318	0.294	0.210	0.135	0.096	0.095	0.083	0.088

Finally, in Table 2, we fix $\varepsilon = 1$ and vary the h^* and θ parameters. For low h^* such as $h^* = 3$, different values of θ do not seem to cause substantial changes in AQE on Brightkite, Gowalla and Foursquare datasets. However, for $h^* = 4$ and $h^* = 5$, changes to θ yield higher differences in terms of AQE. Usually, $\theta = 5000$ or 10000 seem to be the ideal choice when $h^* = 4$ and $h^* = 5$ for the proposed solution. In contrast, higher θ such as 10000 or 20000 seem to be better for the baseline solution. This is because increasing θ decreases the risk of creating erroneous nodes caused by LDP noise. When θ is higher, it is less likely that LDP noise causes node densities to erroneously increase to higher than θ and cause an erroneous split. Similarly, higher θ implies shorter quadtrees for the baseline solution, which eliminates the creation of deeper nodes that have higher risk of being dominated by LDP noise.

5   Related Work

LDP for Spatial Data. In recent years, LDP has emerged as an accepted privacy standard and it has also been successfully deployed in the industry [1,7,10,13,18,37]. With the popularity of LDP, there is rising interest in applying LDP to spatial data, considering the ubiquity of location-based services and sensitive nature of users' locations. Wang et al. [30] developed L-SRR to privately collect users' locations while they remain useful for LBS applications such as traffic density estimation and k-nearest neighbors. Hong et al. [20] proposed a perturbation mechanism designed to reduce the error of each perturbed location under LDP. Yang et al. [36] studied the problem of collecting individual trajectories under LDP. Cunningham et al. [9] proposed a technique which utilizes hierarchical n-grams for real-world trajectory sharing with LDP. Kim et al. [21] and Navidan et al. [25] applied LDP to indoor positioning data. Finally, Chen et al. [5] proposed a variant of LDP, called personalized LDP, for spatial data aggregation.

Spatial Decompositions Under DP. The above works apply LDP to spatial data, but they do not have the goal of building spatial decompositions. Although spatial decompositions have not been studied under LDP, they have been studied under centralized DP. Cormode et al. [8] proposed algorithms to build tree-based spatial decompositions such as quadtrees and kd-trees under DP. Later, the PrivTree algorithm developed by Zhang et al. [39] enabled constructing a DP spatial decomposition without requiring a pre-defined recursion limit (height). A popular alternative to tree-based decompositions is grid-based decompositions such as uniform and adaptive grids, as introduced by Qardaji et al. [27] and later used in other works [16, 17]. Hierarchical reference systems proposed by He et al. [19] employ hierarchically organized grids with different granularities, ordered from coarse to fine-grained.

More recently, Niknami et al. [26] proposed personalized DP and personalized noise addition for indexing geometric objects in spatial databases. Quadtrees and kd-trees are used as spatial indices. In the work of Li et al. [23], a data-dependent adaptive density grid decomposition is used at the first layer, and then a quadtree decomposition is adopted for further splitting. Yan et al. [34] proposed an unbalanced quadtree partitioning algorithm for improving query accuracy in publishing spatial data with DP. Similarly, Liu et al. [24] also proposed a quadtree algorithm for improving query accuracy under DP, by balancing noise error and uniformity error. A new decomposition structure called Homogeneous Tree Framework (HTF) was proposed by Shaham et al. [29], which shares similarities to kd-trees. All of these works operate under the assumptions of centralized DP rather than LDP, hence they are not comparable to our work.

6   Conclusion

In this paper we studied the problem of building quadtrees, a popular spatial decomposition method, while each user's location remains protected by LDP. We proposed two solutions to this problem: a baseline solution which adapts an iterative strategy inspired from the centralized DP literature, and a newly proposed solution which relies on a single LDP data collection step. We compared the baseline and proposed solutions using three metrics (AQE, TED, NDD) and four real-world spatial datasets. Results demonstrated the superiority of the proposed solution compared to the baseline solution across many settings and quadtree parameters. In future work, we plan to extend our solutions to other tree-based spatial decomposition methods such as k-dimensional trees and octrees.

Acknowledgements. We gratefully acknowledge the support by The Scientific and Technological Research Council of Türkiye (TUBITAK) under project number 121E303.

References

1. Apple - learning with privacy at scale (2020). https://machinelearning.apple.com/docs/learning-with-privacy-at-scale/appledifferentialprivacysystem.pdf
2. Bagdasaryan, E., Kairouz, P., Mellem, S., Gascón, A., Bonawitz, K., Estrin, D., Gruteser, M.: Towards sparse federated analytics: location heatmaps under distributed differential privacy with secure aggregation. Proc. Privacy Enhancing Technol. **4**, 162–182 (2022)
3. Bassily, R., Smith, A.: Local, private, efficient protocols for succinct histograms. In: Proceedings of the 47th Annual ACM Symposium on Theory of Computing, pp. 127–135. ACM (2015)

4. Chen, R., Acs, G., Castelluccia, C.: Differentially private sequential data publication via variable-length n-grams. In: Proceedings of the 2012 ACM Conference on Computer and Communications Security, pp. 638–649 (2012)
5. Chen, R., Li, H., Qin, A., Kasiviswanathan, S.P., Jin, H.: Private spatial data aggregation in the local setting. In: 2016 IEEE 32nd International Conference on Data Engineering (ICDE), pp. 289–300. IEEE (2016)
6. Cho, E., Myers, S.A., Leskovec, J.: Friendship and mobility: User movement in location-based social networks. In: Proceedings of the 17th ACM SIGKDD International Conference on Knowledge Discovery and Data Mining, pp. 1082–1090. Association for Computing Machinery, New York (2011)
7. Cormode, G., Jha, S., Kulkarni, T., Li, N., Srivastava, D., Wang, T.: Privacy at scale: Local differential privacy in practice. In: Proceedings of the 2018 International Conference on Management of Data, pp. 1655–1658. ACM (2018)
8. Cormode, G., Procopiuc, C., Srivastava, D., Shen, E., Yu, T.: Differentially private spatial decompositions. In: 28th IEEE International Conference on Data Engineering, pp. 20–31. IEEE (2012)
9. Cunningham, T., Cormode, G., Ferhatosmanoglu, H., Srivastava, D.: Real-world trajectory sharing with local differential privacy. Proc. VLDB Endowment **14**(11), 2283–2295 (2021)
10. Ding, B., Kulkarni, J., Yekhanin, S.: Collecting telemetry data privately. In: Advances in Neural Information Processing Systems, pp. 3571–3580 (2017)
11. Dwork, C., Roth, A., et al.: The algorithmic foundations of differential privacy. Found. Trends Theor. Comput. Sci. **9**(3–4), 211–407 (2014)
12. ECML/PKDD: Taxi trajectory prediction dataset. https://www.kaggle.com/c/pkdd-15-predict-taxi-service-trajectory-i/data
13. Erlingsson, Ú., Pihur, V., Korolova, A.: Rappor: randomized aggregatable privacy-preserving ordinal response. In: Proceedings of the 2014 ACM SIGSAC Conference on Computer and Communications Security, pp. 1054–1067. ACM (2014)
14. Gursoy, M.E., Liu, L., Chow, K.H., Truex, S., Wei, W.: An adversarial approach to protocol analysis and selection in local differential privacy. IEEE Trans. Inf. Forensics Secur. **17**, 1785–1799 (2022)
15. Gursoy, M.E., Rajasekar, V., Liu, L.: Utility-optimized synthesis of differentially private location traces. In: IEEE International Conference on Trust, Privacy and Security in Intelligent Systems and Applications (TPS-ISA), pp. 30–39. IEEE (2020)
16. Gursoy, M.E., Liu, L., Truex, S., Yu, L.: Differentially private and utility preserving publication of trajectory data. IEEE Trans. Mob. Comput. **18**(10), 2315–2329 (2018)
17. Gursoy, M.E., Liu, L., Truex, S., Yu, L., Wei, W.: Utility-aware synthesis of differentially private and attack-resilient location traces. In: Proceedings of the 2018 ACM SIGSAC Conference on Computer and Communications Security, pp. 196–211 (2018)
18. Gursoy, M.E., Tamersoy, A., Truex, S., Wei, W., Liu, L.: Secure and utility-aware data collection with condensed local differential privacy. IEEE Trans. Dependable Secure Comput. (2019)
19. He, X., Cormode, G., Machanavajjhala, A., Procopiuc, C.M., Srivastava, D.: Dpt: differentially private trajectory synthesis using hierarchical reference systems. Proc. VLDB Endowment **8**(11), 1154–1165 (2015)
20. Hong, D., Jung, W., Shim, K.: Collecting geospatial data with local differential privacy for personalized services. In: 2021 IEEE 37th International Conference on Data Engineering (ICDE), pp. 2237–2242 (2021)
21. Kim, J.W., Kim, D.H., Jang, B.: Application of local differential privacy to collection of indoor positioning data. IEEE Access **6**, 4276–4286 (2018)
22. Kuo, Y.H., Chiu, C.C., Kifer, D., Hay, M., Machanavajjhala, A.: Differentially private hierarchical count-of-counts histograms. Proc. VLDB Endowment **11**(11), 1509–1521 (2018)

23. Li, S., Geng, Y., Li, Y.: A differentially private hybrid decomposition algorithm based on quad-tree. Comput. Secur. **109**, 102384 (2021)
24. Liu, G., Tang, Z., Wan, B., Li, Y., Liu, Y.: Differential privacy location data release based on quadtree in mobile edge computing. Trans. Emerging Telecommun. Technol. **33**(6), e3972 (2022)
25. Navidan, H., Moghtadaiee, V., Nazaran, N., Alishahi, M.: Hide me behind the noise: local differential privacy for indoor location privacy. In: 2022 IEEE European Symposium on Security and Privacy Workshops (EuroS&PW), pp. 514–523. IEEE (2022)
26. Niknami, N., Abadi, M., Deldar, F.: A fully spatial personalized differentially private mechanism to provide non-uniform privacy guarantees for spatial databases. Inf. Syst. **92**, 101526 (2020)
27. Qardaji, W., Yang, W., Li, N.: Differentially private grids for geospatial data. In: 2013 IEEE 29th International Conference on Data Engineering (ICDE), pp. 757–768 (2013)
28. Samet, H.: The quadtree and related hierarchical data structures. ACM Comput. Surv. (CSUR) **16**(2), 187–260 (1984)
29. Shaham, S., Ghinita, G., Ahuja, R., Krumm, J., Shahabi, C.: Htf: homogeneous tree framework for differentially-private release of large geospatial datasets with self-tuning structure height. ACM Trans. Spatial Algorithms Syst. (2022)
30. Wang, H., Hong, H., Xiong, L., Qin, Z., Hong, Y.: L-srr: Local differential privacy for location-based services with staircase randomized response. In: Proceedings of the 2022 ACM SIGSAC Conference on Computer and Communications Security, pp. 2809–2823. Association for Computing Machinery, New York (2022)
31. Wang, S., Huang, L., Wang, P., Nie, Y., Xu, H., Yang, W., Li, X.Y., Qiao, C.: Mutual information optimally local private discrete distribution estimation. arXiv preprint arXiv:1607.08025 (2016)
32. Wang, T., Blocki, J., Li, N., Jha, S.: Locally differentially private protocols for frequency estimation. In: Proceedings of the 26th USENIX Security Symposium, pp. 729–745 (2017)
33. Wang, T., Li, N., Jha, S.: Locally differentially private frequent itemset mining. In: IEEE Symposium on Security and Privacy (SP). IEEE (2018)
34. Yan, Y., Gao, X., Mahmood, A., Feng, T., Xie, P.: Differential private spatial decomposition and location publishing based on unbalanced quadtree partition algorithm. IEEE Access **8**, 104775–104787 (2020)
35. Yang, D., Zhang, D., Zheng, V.W., Yu, Z.: Modeling user activity preference by leveraging user spatial temporal characteristics in lbsns. IEEE Trans. Syst. Man Cybernetics Syst. **45**(1), 129–142 (2015)
36. Yang, J., Cheng, X., Su, S., Sun, H., Chen, C.: Collecting individual trajectories under local differential privacy. In: 2022 23rd IEEE International Conference on Mobile Data Management (MDM), pp. 99–108. IEEE (2022)
37. Yang, M., Lyu, L., Zhao, J., Zhu, T., Lam, K.Y.: Local differential privacy and its applications: a comprehensive survey. arXiv preprint arXiv:2008.03686 (2020)
38. Ye, Q., Hu, H., Meng, X., Zheng, H.: Privkv: key-value data collection with local differential privacy. In: 2019 IEEE Symposium on Security and Privacy (SP), pp. 317–331. IEEE (2019)
39. Zhang, J., Xiao, X., Xie, X.: Privtree: a differentially private algorithm for hierarchical decompositions. In: Proceedings of the 2016 International Conference on Management of Data, pp. 155–170 (2016)

Privacy-Preserving Genomic Statistical Analysis Under Local Differential Privacy

Akito Yamamoto[(✉)] and Tetsuo Shibuya

Human Genome Center, The Institute of Medical Science, The University of Tokyo, Tokyo 108-8639, Japan
a-ymmt@ims.u-tokyo.ac.jp, tshibuya@hgc.jp

Abstract. As the amount of personal genomic information and privacy concerns in data publication have been growing, several studies have pointed out that the presence information of a particular individual could be revealed from the statistics obtained in large-scale genomic analyses. Existing methods for releasing genome statistics under differential privacy do not prevent the leakage of personal information by untrusted data collectors. In addition, the existing studies for statistical tests using a contingency table had restrictions on the number of cases and controls. Moreover, the methods for correcting for population stratification cannot protect genotype information. Thus, developing a more general and stronger method is desired. In this study, we present privacy-preserving methods for releasing key genome statistics. Our methods enhance the randomized response technique and guarantee individuals' privacy, even when untrusted data collectors exist. Moreover, our methods do not require any restrictions on the contingency tables, and they also guarantee the privacy of targeted genotype information for the analyses to correct for population stratification. The experimental results indicate that our methods can achieve comparable high accuracy to existing methods while preserving privacy more strictly from any data collectors. Furthermore, for statistical analysis using a contingency table, we consider the case where different privacy budgets are assigned to each of the row and column information, and present optimal methods in terms of privacy assurance for the entire table that outperform the existing method. Overall, this study is the first step toward genomic statistical analysis under local differential privacy. The Python implementation of our experiments and Supplementary Material are available at https://github.com/ay0408/LDP-genome-statistics.

Keywords: Local Differential Privacy · Randomized Response · Genome Statistics

Supported by JSPS KAKENHI Grant Numbers 20H05967, 21H05052, and 23H03345, and JSPS Grant-in-Aid for JSPS Fellows Grant Number 23KJ0649. The supercomputing resource was provided by Human Genome Center, the Institute of Medical Science, the University of Tokyo.

© IFIP International Federation for Information Processing 2023
Published by Springer Nature Switzerland AG 2023

V. Atluri and A. L. Ferrara (Eds.): DBSec 2023, LNCS 13942, pp. 40–48, 2023.
https://doi.org/10.1007/978-3-031-37586-6_3

1   Introduction

With the recent increase in the volume of genomic information and biomedical data, the utilization of genome data for personalized medicine has gained importance [17]. Simultaneously, privacy concerns regarding the release of large-scale data have been widely recognized [16,18]. For instance, several attack methods for identifying individuals against genome-wide association studies (GWAS) have been proposed [11,14]. To conduct genomic analysis while protecting privacy, various methods using cryptographic theory, such as homomorphic encryption and secret sharing [4–6,13] have been proposed. However, these methods do not guarantee the output privacy and require additional protection. Therefore, the concept of differential privacy [7] and its application have been widely considered for releasing genome statistics.

The essential statistics for large-scale genomic analyses such as GWAS include those in statistical tests using a contingency table, those in family-based association studies, and those considering correction for population stratification, and several differentially private methods [9,15,19,22–24] have been proposed for these statistics. However, these methods do not prevent attacks from them or their servers. In addition, the existing studies for statistical tests using a contingency table [9,24] have restrictions on the number of cases and controls. Moreover, the existing methods for correcting for population stratification [15,22] cannot protect genotype information.

Therefore, we propose new methods for releasing each genome statistic using the concept of local differential privacy [25], which can protect privacy even in the presence of untrusted data collectors. In this study, we employ the randomized response technique [21] to satisfy local differential privacy, because the data used to compute genome statistics can be regarded as attribute data, and in several studies [10,20], the randomized response yielded higher accuracy than the Laplace mechanism and other methods satisfying local differential privacy. The contributions of this study are as follows:

1. We propose privacy-preserving methods for releasing essential genome statistics for large-scale genomic analysis. Our methods utilize the randomized response and can protect individuals' privacy even from untrusted data collectors. Moreover, they do not require any restrictions on the contingency tables, and for correcting for population stratification, the proposed method can protect the privacy of the targeted genotype information in addition to that of the phenotype information. The experimental results indicate that our methods can output accurate statistics comparable to existing methods while providing stronger privacy guarantees.
2. For genomic analysis using a contingency table, we also consider the case where different privacy budgets are assigned to each of the row and column information. The existing randomized response technique for multiple-attribute data [20] considers perturbing each attribute information in turn by employing the Kronecker product. However, this approach provides only a weak privacy guarantee for the entire dataset. Therefore, we propose new

methods for 2×2 and 3×2 contingency tables that are optimal in terms of the privacy level of the entire table. Our methods can also be employed for the analyses to correct for population stratification.

In the Supplementary Material, we first review the related studies. We then describe the key statistical tests in GWAS and the existing studies to release the statistics under differential privacy. In addition, we describe the randomized response technique and the related studies. We then propose local differentially private methods for a transmission disequilibrium test (TDT) and EIGENSTRAT. We also present the theoretical proofs of our theorems and provide supplemental discussion on the proposed methods and all experimental results.

2   Methods

In this section, we present local differentially private methods for key statistical tests in large-scale genomic analyses: χ^2-tests for case-control studies using a contingency table, TDT for family-based studies, and EIGENSTRAT to correct for population stratification. The methods for the latter two are provided in the Supplementary Material. The proposed methods utilize the randomized response technique to satisfy differential privacy, referring to an existing study on hypothesis testing [10]. In particular, for the analyses using a contingency table, we consider the case where different privacy budgets are given to row and column attributes and show the optimal methods that provide the strongest privacy guarantee for the entire table.

2.1   Local Differentially Private Methods for Case-Control Studies

First, we propose methods for case-control studies. Unlike the existing methods, our methods do not require assumptions regarding the number of cases and controls and are applicable to all situations.

Case 1: ϵ for the entire table. In Case 1, we consider the case where the privacy budget for the entire contingency table is ϵ, without focusing on the privacy level of row and column attributes of the table.

2×2 *Contingency Table.* We consider statistical analyses using the following 2×2 contingency table containing N individuals:

		Disease Status		Total
		0	1	
Allele	0	a	b	$a+b$
	1	c	d	$c+d$
Total		$a+c$	$b+d$	$2N$

Because each allele of the individuals in the dataset belongs to one of a, b, c, or d in the above table, these positions can be taken as attribute values. Subsequently, by applying the randomized response with a 4×4 distortion matrix, we can generate a differentially private contingency table. To perturb the attribute values as minimally as possible, we should maximize the sum of the diagonal elements of the distortion matrix, and in accordance with existing work [20], we can use the following $\mathbf{P}$, s.t.

$$\mathbf{P}_{uv} = \begin{cases} \frac{e^\epsilon}{e^\epsilon + 3} & (u = v) \\ \frac{1}{e^\epsilon + 3} & (u \neq v) \end{cases}.$$

When using this distortion matrix, the privacy guarantees provided to row and column information are both $\log\left(\frac{e^\epsilon + 1}{2}\right)$.

After we perturb the original attribute values according to the matrix $\mathbf{P}$, we can obtain a private contingency table. Here, we let a', b', c', and d' be the values corresponding to a, b, c, and d in the original table, respectively. Then, we can conduct statistical analyses using these values. However, a', b', c', and d' are expected to be equalized compared to the original values, and the χ^2-statistics obtained from these values will become smaller. Therefore, we consider reconstructing the original a, b, c, and d to release statistically significant data more accurately. In the following, we show two reconstruction procedures: one using an inverse matrix and the other using an EM algorithm in accordance with several existing studies [3,8,12,20].

The first method for recovering a, b, c, and d uses the inverse matrix $\mathbf{P}^{-1}$; the recovered values $\tilde{a}$, $\tilde{b}$, $\tilde{c}$, and $\tilde{d}$ can be calculated by $\left(\tilde{a}, \tilde{b}, \tilde{c}, \tilde{d}\right)^\mathsf{T} = \mathbf{P}^{-1} \cdot (a', b', c', d')^\mathsf{T}$. We provide Theorem 1 about the expected values and variances of the recovered values. The proof is provided in the Supplementary Material.

Theorem 1. *The expected values of $\tilde{a}$, $\tilde{b}$, $\tilde{c}$, and $\tilde{d}$ are a, b, c, and d, and the variables of them are $\frac{2}{e^\epsilon - 1} a + \frac{2(e^\epsilon + 2)}{(e^\epsilon - 1)^2} N$, $\frac{2}{e^\epsilon - 1} b + \frac{2(e^\epsilon + 2)}{(e^\epsilon - 1)^2} N$, $\frac{2}{e^\epsilon - 1} c + \frac{2(e^\epsilon + 2)}{(e^\epsilon - 1)^2} N$, and $\frac{2}{e^\epsilon - 1} d + \frac{2(e^\epsilon + 2)}{(e^\epsilon - 1)^2} N$, respectively.*

The second method for recovering the original table uses an EM algorithm. The procedure is similar to that in the previous study [8], and the detail is provided in the Supplementary Material. Using the reconstructed values from these procedures, we can conduct the statistical tests under local differential privacy with no restriction on the number of cases and controls.

As in the case of the previous case, we can also consider the case of 3×2 contingency table. The detail is provided in the Supplementary Material.

Case 2: ϵ_1 for row and ϵ_2 for column. In Case 2, we discuss the case of assigning privacy budgets to each of the row and column information; for example, in a 2×2 contingency table, the privacy levels required for information on disease status and allele might be different. In such cases, we must regard the elements of row and column as having different attributes and guarantee differential privacy for each.

Our proposed methods can provide the strongest privacy guarantee among the randomized response techniques for data with two attributes, including the existing method that uses the Kronecker product [20].

2×2 *Contingency Table.* We consider the same contingency table as in Case 1. Here, we discuss the first column of the 4×4 distortion matrix $\mathbf{P}$: $(p_{00}, p_{10}, p_{20}, p_{30})^{\mathsf{T}}$, because $\mathbf{P}$ is expected to be a symmetric matrix. Among these four values, the largest is p_{00} and the smallest is p_{30}. Our goal is to maximize the privacy guarantee for the entire table; therefore, we should minimize the value of $\frac{p_{00}}{p_{30}}$.

Here, we let $A = \frac{p_{00}}{p_{30}}$, $B = \frac{p_{10}}{p_{30}}$, $C = \frac{p_{20}}{p_{30}}$, and $D = \frac{p_{30}}{p_{30}} = 1$. Given that the privacy levels for row and column are ϵ_1 and ϵ_2, A is minimized when

$$(A, B, C, D) = \begin{cases} \left(\frac{2e^{\epsilon_1+\epsilon_2}+e^{\epsilon_2}-1}{e^{\epsilon_2}+1}, \frac{2e^{\epsilon_1}-e^{\epsilon_2}+1}{e^{\epsilon_2}+1}, 1, 1 \right) & (\epsilon_1 \geq \epsilon_2) \\ \left(\frac{2e^{\epsilon_1+\epsilon_2}+e^{\epsilon_1}-1}{e^{\epsilon_1}+1}, 1, \frac{-e^{\epsilon_1}+2e^{\epsilon_2}+1}{e^{\epsilon_1}+1}, 1 \right) & (\epsilon_1 < \epsilon_2) \end{cases}.$$

Using these values, we can construct the optimal distortion matrix in terms of privacy assurance. The detailed discussion is provided in the Supplementary Material.

We illustrate the privacy levels (i.e., the values of ϵ) for the entire dataset when using our proposed distortion matrix and when using the existing method with the Kronecker-product in Fig. 1. Here, note that smaller ϵ values represent stronger privacy guarantees.

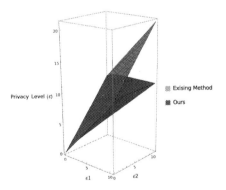

Fig. 1. Comparison of the privacy level for a 2×2 contingency table between the existing method (using the Kronecker-product) and ours. The x and y-axis represent the privacy budget given to row and column information, respectively. The z-axis represents the privacy level for the entire table.

Figure 1 implies that our technique can achieve a stronger privacy guarantee especially when the privacy budget given to each attribute information is large. In other words, even if we set some large ϵ_1 and ϵ_2, the privacy guarantee for the entire table remains high compared with the existing method. In addition, this figure indicates that when the entire privacy budget is fixed, we can distribute more privacy budgets to the row and column information.

The proposed distortion matrix perturbs data with two attributes collectively, in contrast to the existing method using the Kronecker-product [20], which perturbs row and column information sequentially. Besides the contingency tables focused on in this study, our idea could be enhanced to general $M \times N$ tables and even more multidimensional data. A future challenge is to develop a universal randomized response technique that can be utilized for statistical analysis using more general data beyond genomic analysis.

As for the case of a 3×2 contingency table, we can obtain an optimal 6×6 distortion matrix that provide the strongest privacy guarantee for the entire table when the privacy budgets are given to each of row and column information. The detailed discussion and result are provided in the Supplementary Material.

Furthermore, in the Supplementary Material, we proposed local differentially methods for TDT for family-based studies and EIGENSTRAT to correct for population stratification.

3   Experimental Results

3.1   Cochran–Armitage Trend Test

Here, we show the results on the Cochran–Armitage trend test [1] using a 3×2 contingency table. To evaluate the accuracy of our methods, we measured the absolute value of the difference between the original and differentially private statistic at each SNP while varying the privacy level ϵ for the entire table.

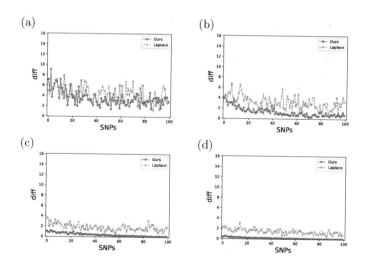

Fig. 2. Differences between original and differentially private χ^2-statistics for the Cochran–Armitage trend test on 100 SNPs when (a) $\epsilon = 2$, (b) $\epsilon = 3$, (c) $\epsilon = 5$, and (d) $\epsilon = 7$.

In this case, we compared our method to the existing method with the Laplace mechanism [24]. Note that the existing method is for a restricted situation in which the number of cases and controls are equal under central differential privacy. The results averaged over 20 runs are shown in Fig. 2. SNPs are ordered by the original χ^2-statistic in descending order, and details of the simulation data used in the experiments are provided in the Supplementary Material.

Figure 2 indicates that our method is as accurate as the existing Laplace mechanism even under local differential privacy. Given that local differential privacy can achieve equivalent privacy guarantees to central differential privacy with a larger ϵ [2] and our method requires no restriction on the number of cases and controls, it outperforms the existing method in terms of privacy assurance and utility. One unique characteristic of our method is that the differences become larger when the original χ^2-statistic is larger, whereas the Laplace mechanism does not depend on the statistic values. This might be because the variance of reconstructed elements increases as the original value increases (see our theorems). This characteristic might be desirable because false positives could decrease.

The results for other genomic statistical analyses and detailed discussion are provided in the Supplementary Material.

4   Conclusion

In this study, we proposed privacy-preserving methods for releasing essential genome statistics under local differential privacy. The proposed methods differ from existing ones in that they can protect individuals' privacy even from untrusted data collectors by using the randomized response technique. Moreover, our methods do not require any restrictions on the number of cases and controls in the contingency tables. They can also protect the privacy of targeted genotype information for the analyses to correct for population stratification. The experimental results indicate that our methods can output accurate statistics comparable to existing differentially private methods while providing stronger privacy guarantees. Furthermore, for statistical analyses using a contingency table, we considered the case where different privacy budgets are assigned to each of the row and column information, and we presented optimal methods in terms of privacy assurance for the entire table that outperform the existing method using the Kronecker product.

In future studies, we must consider more suitable randomized response methods and appropriate ϵ values for each genomic information. Thereafter, we might be able to develop more accurate methods for recovering the original data, including improvements to the EM algorithm and enhancement of other local differentially private methods. Then, we hope to advance more research on genome statistical analysis under local differential privacy, including the consideration of genomic dependencies. Furthermore, this study is expected to be enhanced in other research areas that are not limited to genome statistics, such as releasing data with multiple attributes and statistical analyses using an $M \times N$ table.

References

1. Armitage, P.: Tests for linear trends in proportions and frequencies. Biometrics **11**(3), 375–386 (1955)
2. Bernau, D., Robl, J., Grassal, P.W., Schneider, S., Kerschbaum, F.: Comparing local and central differential privacy using membership inference attacks. In: Data and Applications Security and Privacy XXXV: 35th Annual IFIP WG 11.3 Conference, DBSec 2021, Calgary, Canada, 19–20 July 2021, Proceedings, pp. 22–42 (2021)
3. Blair, G., Imai, K., Zhou, Y.Y.: Design and analysis of the randomized response technique. J. Am. Stat. Assoc. **110**(511), 1304–1319 (2015)
4. Blatt, M., Gusev, A., Polyakov, Y., Goldwasser, S.: Secure large-scale genome-wide association studies using homomorphic encryption. PNAS **117**(21), 11608–11613 (2020)
5. Bonte, C., Makri, E., Ardeshirdavani, A., Simm, J., Moreau, Y., Vercauteren, F.: Towards practical privacy-preserving genome-wide association study. BMC Bioinform. **19**, 537 (2018)
6. Cho, H., Wu, D.J., Berger, B.: Secure genome-wide association analysis using multiparty computation. Nat. Biotechnol. **36**, 547–551 (2018)
7. Dwork, C.: Differential privacy. In: Bugliesi, M., Preneel, B., Sassone, V., Wegener, I. (eds.) Automata, Languages and Programming, pp. 1–12 (2006)
8. Fanti, G., Pihur, V., Erlingsson, Ú.: Building a RAPPOR with the unknown: privacy-preserving learning of associations and data dictionaries. In: Proceedings on Privacy Enhancing Technologies (PoPETS), no. 3, 2016 (2016)
9. Fienberg, S.E., Slavkovic, A., Uhler, C.: Privacy preserving GWAS data sharing. In: IEEE 11th International Conference on Data Mining Workshops, pp. 628–635 (2011)
10. Gaboardi, M., Rogers, R.: Local private hypothesis testing: Chi-square tests. In: Dy, J., Krause, A. (eds.) Proceedings of the 35th International Conference on Machine Learning, vol. 80, pp. 1626–1635 (2018)
11. Jacobs, K.B., et al.: A new statistic and its power to infer membership in a genome-wide association study using genotype frequencies. Nat. Genet. **41**(11), 1253–1257 (2009)
12. Kairouz, P., Bonawitz, K., Ramage, D.: Discrete distribution estimation under local privacy. In: Proceedings of the 33rd International Conference on International Conference on Machine Learning, vol. 48, pp. 2436–2444 (2016)
13. Kockan, C., et al.: Sketching algorithms for genomic data analysis and querying in a secure enclave. Nat. Methods **17**, 295–301 (2020)
14. Sankararaman, S., Obozinski, G., Jordan, M.I., Halperin, E.: Genomic privacy and limits of individual detection in a pool. Nat. Genet. **41**(9), 965–967 (2009)
15. Simmons, S., Sahinalp, C., Berger, B.: Enabling privacy-preserving GWASs in heterogeneous human populations. Cell Syst. **3**(1), 54–61 (2016)
16. Su, J., Cao, Y., Chen, Y., Liu, Y., Song, J.: Privacy protection of medical data in social network. BMC Med. Inform. Decis. Mak. **21**, 286 (2021)
17. Urban, A., Schweda, M.: Clinical and personal utility of genomic high-throughput technologies: perspectives of medical professionals and affected persons. New Genet. Soc. **37**(2), 153–173 (2018)
18. Wan, Z., Hazel, J.W., Clayton, E.W., Vorobeychik, Y., Kantarcioglu, M., Malin, B.A.: Sociotechnical safeguards for genomic data privacy. Nat. Rev. Genet. **23**(7), 429–445 (2022)

19. Wang, M., et al.: Mechanisms to protect the privacy of families when using the transmission disequilibrium test in genome-wide association studies. Bioinformatics **33**(23), 3716–3725 (2017)
20. Wang, Y., Wu, X., Hu, D.: Using randomized response for differential privacy preserving data collection. In: Palpanas, T., Stefanidis, K. (eds.) Proceedings of the Workshops of the EDBT/ICDT 2016 Joint Conference, EDBT/ICDT Workshops 2016, Bordeaux, France, 15 March 2016, vol. 1558 (2016)
21. Warner, S.L.: Randomized response: a survey technique for eliminating evasive answer bias. J. Am. Stat. Assoc. **60**(309), 63–66 (1965)
22. Wei, J., Lin, Y., Yao, X., Zhang, J., Liu, X.: Differential privacy-based genetic matching in personalized medicine. IEEE Trans. Emerg. Top. Comput. **9**(3), 1109–1125 (2021)
23. Yamamoto, A., Shibuya, T.: Differentially private linkage analysis with TDT - the case of two affected children per family. In: 2021 IEEE International Conference on Bioinformatics and Biomedicine (BIBM), pp. 765–770 (2021)
24. Yamamoto, A., Shibuya, T.: More practical differentially private publication of key statistics in GWAS. Bioinform. Adv. **1**(1) (2021)
25. Yilmaz, E., Ji, T., Ayday, E., Li, P.: Genomic data sharing under dependent local differential privacy. In: Proceedings of the Twelfth ACM Conference on Data and Application Security and Privacy, pp. 77–88 (2022)

Secure Data Sharing

New Results on Distributed Secret Sharing Protocols

Alfredo De Santis and Barbara Masucci$^{(\boxtimes)}$

Dipartimento di Informatica, Università di Salerno, Fisciano, Italy
{ads,bmasucci}@unisa.it

Abstract. A *Distributed Secret Sharing Protocol* (*DSSP* for short) allows a dealer to share multiple secrets among a set of users by storing the shares on storage nodes distributed over a public insecure network. Users can later download the shares from the nodes they can access, in order to reconstruct the secrets (each user is allowed to reconstruct exactly one secret).

In this paper we propose three contributions: we first carefully analyze the security requirements for DSSPs and we show that if the shared secrets are statistically dependent, then no DSSP satisfying either the weak secrecy requirement or the perfect secrecy one can exist. Then, we propose two new definitions of security for DSSPs, which also take into account the statistical dependencies among the secrets. Afterwards, we consider DSSPs for a specific class of access structures, i.e., those which can be represented by a graph. In particular, we propose a protocol which can be used to share independent secrets having different sizes. The protocol can manage any kind of graph and generalizes previous protocols for secrets having the same sizes, while maintaining optimal storage requirements.

Keywords: Data Protection · Privacy · Distributed Secret Sharing · Graph-Based Secret Sharing · Information Theory

1 Introduction

A secret sharing scheme is a protocol that allows a *dealer* to distribute a secret among a set of users. This distribution is done in such a way that some qualified subsets of users, pooling together the pieces of information received by the dealer, called *shares*, can reconstruct the secret; whereas, other, forbidden, subsets of users have no information about the secret. The family of all subsets of users that are qualified to reconstruct the secret is called the *access structure* of the scheme. Since their introduction as a solution to the problem of secure information storage, secret sharing schemes have been widely employed in cryptography as a tool to construct more elaborated cryptographic primitives as well as several types of secure protocols, e.g., attribute-based encryption [1,2], threshold cryptography [3], secure multi-party computation [4–6], access control

© IFIP International Federation for Information Processing 2023
Published by Springer Nature Switzerland AG 2023
V. Atluri and A. L. Ferrara (Eds.): DBSec 2023, LNCS 13942, pp. 51–68, 2023.
https://doi.org/10.1007/978-3-031-37586-6_4

[7]. Usually, in a secret sharing scheme the distribution of the shares is done by means of a dedicated, secure, and reliable channel connecting the dealer to each user. However, in a more realistic scenario, a secure channel between the dealer and each user might be not available, since they could be connected through a large public network, such as the Internet. In such cases, the shares could be first stored into a set of storage nodes and later be downloaded by users, where each user might have access to a specific subset of storage nodes. Schemes of this kind are called *Distributed Secret Sharing Protocols (DSSP)* and have been first proposed by Soleymani and Mahdavifar [8], who considered DSSPs where each user i is allowed to reconstruct exactly a secret, denoted by s_i and called the *individual secret* of user i.

Distributed secret sharing might be useful in many real-life situations. For example, consider the Internet of Things (IoT) scenario, where the dealer assumes the role of an IoT gateway that controls a number of servers and each device can access only a subset of the controlled servers. Another scenario where the distributed secret sharing model might be useful is that of multiple access wireless networks, where the storage servers might be seen as resource elements in different time or frequency and each user can access only a subset of resource elements.

Soleymani and Mahdavifar [8] considered two security requirements for DSSPs: the first one, called *weak secrecy*, requires that each user i does not get any information about any other secret other than his individual secret s_i, whereas, the second one, called *perfect secrecy*, requires that each user i does not get any information regarding the collection of all the other secrets other than his individual secret s_i. Soleymani and Mahdavifar [8] first proposed a DSSP satisfying the perfect secrecy requirement but having huge storage overhead; afterwards, they considered DSSPs satisfying the weak secrecy requirement while offering optimal or nearly optimal storage requirements. In particular, their protocols work for (k, n)-threshold access structures, i.e., those in which there is a secret associated to each subset of exactly k out of n storage nodes. Recently, De Prisco et al. [9] have shown new protocols for (k, n)-threshold access structures; such protocols improve on those in [8], since they achieve both storage optimality and a faster encoding phase.

When each user is allowed to access exactly two storage nodes, the access structure can be described by an undirected graph, where the storage nodes are the vertices and a user corresponds to the edge that connects the two nodes that he can access. Such kind of structures, called *graph-based access structures*, have been analyzed in [10], where a complete characterization of DSSPs with respect to the storage overhead was given. In particular, De Prisco et al. [10] proposed different protocols that can handle any kind of graph, improving on the protocols in [8,9], that handle only complete graphs. Such protocols, as well as those in [8], assume that all secrets are chosen from the same set $\mathbb{Z}_q$, where q is an appropriate integer, and thus have the same size $\log q$. The problem of designing DSSPs for graph-based access structures where the secrets can be selected from different fields has been left as an open problem in [10].

1.1   Contributions

In this paper we first carefully analyze the security requirements for DSSPs proposed in [8] and we show that if the shared secrets are statistically dependent, then no DSSP satisfying either the *weak secrecy* requirement or the *perfect secrecy* one can exist. Motivated by the need to take into account the more general situation in which there could be statistical relationships between the secrets, we propose two new definitions of security for DSSPs, called *single-secret secrecy* and *multiple-secrets secrecy*. Such definitions generalize the ones proposed by [8] and represent a starting point for analyzing DSSPs for secrets chosen according to arbitrary probability distributions.

Afterwards, following the lines of [10], we consider DSSPs for graph-based access structures satisfying the weak secrecy requirement. We first provide a lower bound on the total amount of information distributed to the storage nodes in any weakly-secure graph-based DSSP. Our result generalizes the one shown in [10] for the particular case of tree-based access structures. Then, we propose a weakly-secure protocol which can be used to share (independent) secrets having different sizes. The protocol can manage any kind of graph and generalizes previous protocols for secrets having the same sizes [10], while maintaining optimal storage requirements.

1.2   Related Works

The seminal works by Blakley [11] and Shamir [12] first introduced the concept of secret sharing schemes. In particular, they analyzed the case when only subsets of at least k out of n users can reconstruct the secret, where $k \leq n$, but subsets of cardinality less than k have no information about the secret, regardless of the computation that they are able to perform on their shares. These schemes are called (k, n)-threshold schemes. Secret sharing schemes for general access structures were subsequently proposed by Ito, Saito, and Nishizeki [13] and Benaloh and Leichter [14]. An unified description of results about secret sharing schemes can be found in the survey articles by Simmons [15] and Stinson [16].

Many practical applications require the protection of more than one secret, thus, several models for sharing multiple secrets have been considered in the literature. In particular, Karnin, Greene and Hellman [17], as well Jackson, Martin, and O'Keefe [18], considered threshold access structures for multiple secrets. In [19] the problem of sharing more than one secret among a set of users has been generalized to the case where all the secrets are shared according to a fixed access structure. In the proposed model, any qualified set of users can recover all the secrets, whereas, any non qualified set of users has absolutely no information about each secret but, knowing some secrets, might have *some information* about the other secrets. Schemes of this kind have also been considered in [20, 21]. The problem of sharing many secrets according to different access structures has been considered in [22] and has been further investigated in [23–26].

1.3 Organization

The remainder of the paper is organized as follows: in Sect. 2 we recall the description of the distributed secret sharing model proposed in [8] and further analyzed in [10], by using an information-theoretic approach; in Sect. 3 we analyze existing security requirements for DSSPs and propose two new definitions of security; in Sect. 4 we consider graph-based DSSPs and provide a lower bound on the total storage overhead; in Sect. 5 we propose a protocol, satisfying the weak secrecy requirement, which can be used to share (independent) secrets having different sizes according to any graph-based access structure. Finally, in Sect. 6 concluding remarks are given.

2 The Distributed Secret Sharing Model

A *Distributed Secret Sharing Protocol* (*DSSP* for short) allows a dealer to share m secrets $s_1, \ldots, s_m$ among a set $M = \{1, \ldots, m\}$ of users, by computing t pieces of secret information $sh_1, \ldots, sh_t$, called *shares*, which are distributed among n storage nodes $D_1, \ldots, D_n$, also called *disks*. The distribution is done in such a way that each disk D_i receives from the dealer a subset of the shares, which can be later downloaded by all users which are allowed to access such a disk. More precisely, for each user $i \in M$, we denote by A_i the subset of the disks that user i can access. Such a set is called the *access set* for user i and the set $\mathcal{A} = \{A_1, \ldots, A_m\}$ of all access sets is called the *access structure* of the protocol. The goal of the protocol is to allow each user $i \in M$ to compute his *individual secret* s_i by using the shares which are stored on the disks in the access set A_i. Figure 1 shows an example, where $m = 6$, $n = 5$ and $t = 8$. The access structure $\mathcal{A}$ consists of the following sets: $A_1 = \{1, 4\}$, $A_2 = \{1, 2, 3\}$, $A_3 = \{3, 4\}$, $A_4 = \{1, 5\}$, $A_5 = \{2, 5\}$, and $A_6 = \{4, 5\}$.

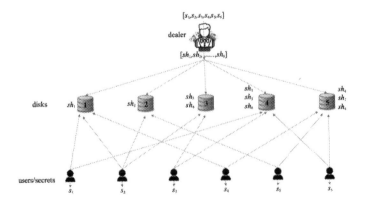

Fig. 1. The distributed secret sharing model.

In the following we formally define DSSPs by using an information-theoretic approach. Let $S_1 \times \cdots \times S_m$ be the set from which the secrets are chosen (the i-th secret to be shared is chosen from S_i), according to some probability distribution on such a set. Similarly, let $Sh_1 \times \cdots \times Sh_t$ be the set from which the shares are chosen (the j-th share is chosen from Sh_j), according to some probability distribution on such a set. The dealer stores in each disk D_i a subset of the shares. For any $i = 1, \ldots, n$, we denote by ShD_i the set of shares stored in disk D_i. Each user $j \in M$ is allowed to download the set of shares stored in all the disks in A_j, that is, the shares in $Sh_j = \cup_{i \in A_j} ShD_i$. To ease the notation, in the following we will use D_i to denote both the i-th disk and the set of shares ShD_i stored in it, the actual meaning will be clear from the context. Similarly, we will use A_j to denote both the access set for user j and the set of shares Sh_j.

In this paper with a boldface capital letter, say $\mathbf{X}$, we denote a random variable taking value on a set, denoted with the corresponding capital letter X, according to some probability distribution $\{Pr_{\mathbf{X}}(x)\}_{x \in X}$. The values such a random variable can take are denoted with the corresponding lower-case letter. Given a probability distribution $\{Pr_{\mathbf{X}}(x)\}_{x \in X}$ on a set X, we denote by $H(\mathbf{X})$ the Shannon *entropy* of $\mathbf{X}$, defined as

$$H(\mathbf{X}) = - \sum_{x \in X} Pr_{\mathbf{X}}(x) \log Pr_{\mathbf{X}}(x)$$

(all logarithms in this paper are to the base 2). The entropy function $H(\mathbf{X})$ measures the uncertainty associated with the random variable $\mathbf{X}$ and its value ranges from 0 to $\log |X|$ (for a complete treatment about the subject the reader is advised to consult [27]). Let d be an arbitrary positive integer and let $\mathbf{X}_1, \ldots, \mathbf{X}_d$ be d random variables taking values on the sets $X_1, \ldots, X_d$, respectively. For any subset $V = \{i_1, \ldots, i_v\} \subseteq \{1, \ldots, d\}$, with $i_1 \leq \ldots \leq i_v$, we denote with X_V the set $X_{i_1} \times \ldots \times X_{i_v}$ and with $\mathbf{X}_V$ the sequence of random variables $\mathbf{X}_{i_1}, \ldots, \mathbf{X}_{i_v}$.

Following the lines of [8,10], we formally define DSSPs by using the entropy function, mainly because this leads to a compact and simple description of the requirements they have to satify; moreover, the entropy approach takes into account all probability distributions on the secrets to be shared. In any DSSP for $\mathcal{A}$ with secrets chosen according to $\mathbf{S}_1 \ldots \mathbf{S}_m$, the following requirement holds:

Reconstruction: Each user i can compute his individual secret s_i by using the shares stored in his access set A_i. Formally, for any $i \in M$, it holds that $H(\mathbf{S}_i | \mathbf{A}_i) = 0$.

The reconstruction requirement is equivalent to saying that the values of the shares stored in the disks in the access set A_i correspond to a unique value of the secret s_i.

Soleymani and Mahdavifar [8] proposed two different definitions of security for DSSP, called *weak secrecy* and *perfect secrecy*, respectively.

Weak Secrecy: Each user i does not get any information about the individual secret associated to any other user $j \neq i$. Formally, for any $i \in M$ and any $j \neq i$, it holds that $H(\mathbf{S}_j | \mathbf{A}_i) = H(\mathbf{S}_j)$.

The above security requirement is equivalent to saying that the probability that the individual secret associated to user j is equal to s_j, given the values of the shares distributed to the disks in the access set A_i, is the same as the *a priori* probability that the secret is s_j, i.e., the random variables $\mathbf{S}_j$ and $\mathbf{A}_i$ are statistically independent. A DSSP satisfying the reconstruction requirement and the weak secrecy requirement is referred to as a *weakly secure* DSSP.

Perfect Secrecy: Each user i does not get any information about the individual secrets associated to all other users. *Formally, for any $i \in M$ it holds that* $H(\mathbf{S}_{M\setminus\{i\}}|\mathbf{A}_i) = H(\mathbf{S}_{M\setminus\{i\}})$.

The above security requirement is equivalent to saying that the probability that the $(m-1)$-tuple of individual secrets associated to all users other than i is equal to $(s_1,\ldots,s_{i-1},s_{i+1},\ldots,s_m)$, given the values of the shares stored in the disks in the access set A_i, is the same as the *a priori* probability that the $(m-1)$-tuple of secrets is equal to $(s_1,\ldots,s_{i-1},s_{i+1},\ldots,s_m)$, i.e., the random variables $\mathbf{S}_{M\setminus\{i\}}$ and $\mathbf{A}_i$ are statistically independent. A DSSP satisfying the reconstruction requirement and the perfect secrecy requirement is referred to as a *perfectly secure* DSSP.

The efficiency of a DSSP is measured mainly by the *storage overhead*, which is defined as

$$SO = \frac{\sum_{i=1}^{n} H(\mathbf{D}_i)}{\sum_{j=1}^{m} H(\mathbf{S}_j)}.$$

Clearly, it is desirable to keep the storage overhead as low as possible. Since the total amount of information distributed to the disks must be bigger than the total amount of the secrets, then $SO \geq 1$. A DSSP achieving the minimum possible value for SO is said to be a *storage-optimal* protocol.

3   On the Definitions of Security for DSSPs

In this section we carefully analyze the definitions of security proposed by Soley-mani and Mahdavifar [8]. We first notice that neither the weak secrecy nor the perfect secrecy requirements take into account the *statistical dependencies* among the secrets. It can be shown that if the secrets are statistically dependent, then no DSSP satisfying either the weak secrecy requirement or the perfect secrecy one can exist.

Indeed, assume that the secrets s_i and s_j associated to two different users i and j are statistically dependent. Then, according to the reconstruction requirement, user j reconstructs its secret s_j, but also gains some information about the secret s_i associated to user i, thus violating the weak secrecy requirement. Formally, the next theorem holds.

Theorem 1. *Let $\mathcal{A}$ be an access structure on a set of m users. In any weakly secure DSSP for $\mathcal{A}$, with secrets chosen according to $\mathbf{S}_1 \ldots \mathbf{S}_m$, it holds that $H(\mathbf{S}_j|\mathbf{S}_i) = H(\mathbf{S}_j)$, for any $j = 1,\ldots,m$ and any $i \neq j$.*

The previous theorem implies that if two secrets are dependent, then no weakly secure DSSP exists. Analogously, the perfect secrecy requirement implies that each secret is independent on all other secrets. Indeed, in a perfectly secure DSSP, user j can reconstruct s_j but has no information about the $(m-1)$-tuple of all other secrets $(s_1, \ldots, s_{j-1}, s_{j+1}, \ldots, s_m)$. If $(s_1, \ldots, s_{j-1}, s_{j+1}, \ldots, s_m)$ and s_j were dependent, then user j would learn something about the m-tuple of secrets $(s_1, \ldots, s_{j-1}, s_{j+1}, \ldots, s_m)$, thus violating the perfect secrecy requirement. Formally, the next result holds.

Theorem 2. *Let $\mathcal{A}$ be an access structure on a set of m users. In any perfectly secure DSSP for $\mathcal{A}$, with secrets chosen according to $\mathbf{S}_1 \ldots \mathbf{S}_m$, for any $i \in M$, it holds that $H(\mathbf{S}_{M\setminus\{i\}}|\mathbf{S}_i) = H(\mathbf{S}_{M\setminus\{i\}})$.*

The previous theorem implies that if a secret is dependent on the others, then no perfectly secure DSSP exists. Motivated by the need to take into account the more general situation in which there are statistical relationships between the secrets, we propose two new definitions of security for DSSP, called *single-secret secrecy* and *multiple-secrets secrecy*, respectively.

Single-Secret Secrecy: Each user i has no more information about the individual secret s_j associated to any other user $j \neq i$ other than the information given by his individual secret s_i. *Formally, for any $i \in M$ and any $j \neq i$ it holds that $H(\mathbf{S}_j|\mathbf{A}_i) = H(\mathbf{S}_j|\mathbf{S}_i)$.*

The above security requirement is equivalent to saying that the values of the shares stored in the disks in the access set A_i can reveal *some information* about the secret s_j. A DSSP satisfying the correctness requirement and the single-secret secrecy requirement is referred to as a *single-secret secure* DSSP.

Multiple-Secrets Secrecy: Each user i has no more information about the individual secrets associated to all other users other than the information given by his individual secret s_i. *Formally, for any $i = 1, \ldots, m$, it holds that $H(\mathbf{S}_{M\setminus\{i\}}|\mathbf{A}_i) = H(\mathbf{S}_{M\setminus\{i\}}|\mathbf{S}_i)$.*

The above security requirement is equivalent to saying that the values of the shares stored in the disks in the access set A_i can reveal *some information* about the $(m-1)$-tuple of secrets $(s_1, \ldots, s_{i-1}, s_{i+1}, \ldots, s_m)$. A DSSP satisfying the reconstruction requirement and the multiple-secrets secrecy requirement is referred to as a *multiple-secrets secure* DSSP.

The new definitions proposed above generalize the ones proposed by [8] and represent a starting point for analyzing DSSPs for secrets chosen according to arbitrary probability distributions.

4   Weakly-Secure Graph-Based DSSPs

In this section we consider the situation where each user has access to exactly two disks. The corresponding access structure can be depicted by an undirected graph $G = (V, E)$ where each node $i \in V$ represents a disk D_i and each edge represents both a user and the secret he can access. In such kind of access structures, called *graph-based access structures*, each user accessing two disks D_i and D_j can also be identified with the corresponding edge (i, j) and the associated secret can be referred to as $s_{i,j}$. For example, referring to Fig. 2, the edge connecting disks 1 and 2 corresponds to the secret $s_{1,2}$.

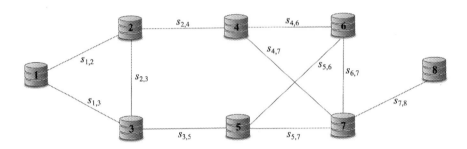

Fig. 2. A graph-based access structure.

Special cases of graph-based access structures are *paths*, *cycles*, and *trees*. Such structures have been analyzed in [10], where different protocols for DSSPs have been provided.

The following lemma, proven in [10], provides a lower bound on the size of the information stored in each internal node for any graph-based DSSP satisfying weak secrecy. For any node $j \in G$, we denote by $deg(j)$ its degree, i.e., the number of edges which are incident on it.

Lemma 1. *([10]) Let $G = (V, E)$ be a graph-based access structure and let $(i, j) \in E$ such that $deg(j) > 1$. Then, in any weakly-secure DSSP for G, it holds that*

$$H(\mathbf{D}_i) \geq H(\mathbf{S}_{i,j}).$$

Since Lemma 1 holds for any node j which is adjacent to i then we obtain the following result, which generalizes the one shown in [10] for the particular case where the graph corresponding to the access structure is a tree.

Lemma 2. *Let $G = (V, E)$ be a graph-based access structure. In any weakly-secure DSSP for G, for any node $i \in V$, it holds that*

$$H(\mathbf{D}_i) \geq \max_{(i,j) \in E \,:\, deg(j) > 1} H(\mathbf{S}_{i,j}).$$

Summing over all nodes in G, we obtain the following result, which holds for arbitrary graph-based access structures. A similar result has been shown in [10] for the particular case where the graph corresponding to the access structure is a tree.

Theorem 3. *Let $G = (V, E)$ be a graph-based access structure. In any weakly-secure DSSP for G, it holds that*

$$\sum_{i \in V} H(\mathbf{D}_i) \geq \sum_{i \in V} \max_{(i,j) \in E : deg(j) > 1} H(\mathbf{S}_{i,j}). \tag{1}$$

In the following we recall some results about DSSPs for paths, cycles and trees provided in [10]. In particular, the *Cycle Protocol* described below will be used to establish our main result in Sect. 5.

Paths. The access structure of a *path* P_{m+1}, where $m \geq 3$, on a set of $m + 1$ disks $D_1, \ldots, D_{m+1}$ has m access sets $A_1, \ldots, A_m$, where $A_1 = \{D_{i_1}, D_{i_2}\}$, $A_2 = \{D_{i_2}, D_{i_3}\}, \ldots, A_m = \{D_{i_m}, D_{i_{m+1}}\}$, and $i_1, i_2, \ldots, i_m, i_{m+1}$ are different values in $\{1, 2, \ldots, m + 1\}$. Without loss of generality, in the following we assume that $D_{i_j} = D_j$, for any $j = 1, \ldots, m + 1$, i.e., $A_1 = \{D_1, D_2\}$, $A_2 = \{D_2, D_3\}, \ldots, A_m = \{D_m, D_{m+1}\}$. Moreover, we denote by s_j the secret associated to the j-th edge of the path, for any $j = 1, \ldots, m$. This corresponds to the fact that user j has access to disks D_j and D_{j+1}. Consider a path P_{m+1}, where $m \geq 3$. Since for nodes D_1, D_2, D_m, and D_{m+1} there is only one adjacent node with degree greater than one, while for any other node D_i, where $i \in \{3, \ldots, m - 1\}$ there are two adjacent nodes with degree greater than one, then from Theorem 3 the following result holds.

Lemma 3. *([10]) Let P_{m+1} be a path-based access structure with $m \geq 3$. In any weakly-secure DSSP for P_{m+1}, it holds that*

$$\sum_{i=1,\ldots,m+1} H(\mathbf{D}_i) \geq H(\mathbf{S}_1) + H(\mathbf{S}_2) + H(\mathbf{S}_{m-1}) + H(\mathbf{S}_m)$$

$$+ \sum_{i=3,\ldots,m-1} \max\{H(\mathbf{S}_{i-1}), H(\mathbf{S}_i)\}.$$

Notice that the inequality of Lemma 3 does not hold for paths of length 2 and 3, i.e., when either $m = 1$ or $m = 2$. Indeed, for the case $m = 1$, Lemma 2 cannot be applied since there are no nodes with degree greater than one. On the other hand, for the case $m = 2$, Lemma 2 can be applied only to nodes D_1 and D_3, but not to node D_2, since there is no node adjacent to D_2 with degree greater than one. For these particular cases, De Prisco et al. [10] suggested the following simple protocols satisfying weak secrecy and achieving optimal storage (see Fig. 3):

- For $m = 1$, i.e., for a path having a single edge, the node D_1 receives the whole secret s_1, while the node D_2 receives nothing. Hence $H(\mathbf{D}_1) + H(\mathbf{D}_2) = H(\mathbf{S}_1)$, which implies $SO = 1$;
- For $m = 2$, i.e., for a path having two edges, the node D_2 receives nothing, while the nodes D_1 and D_3 receive the whole secrets s_1 and s_2, respectively. Hence $H(\mathbf{D}_1) + H(\mathbf{D}_2) + H(\mathbf{D}_3) = H(\mathbf{S}_1) + H(\mathbf{S}_2)$, which implies $SO = 1$.

Fig. 3. Example óf protocol for paths P_2 and P_3.

Cycles. Let $m \geq 3$. In the following we consider the access structure of a *cycle* $C_m = (i_1, \ldots, i_m)$ on a set of m disks, where $i_1, \ldots, i_m$ are values in $\{1, \ldots, m\}$ and $(i_1, i_2), (i_2, i_3), \ldots, (i_{m-1}, i_m), (i_m, i_1)$ are the edges of the cycle. Each edge of the cycle is associated to a secret, thus there are m secrets to be shared. The corresponding access sets are $A_1 = \{D_{i_1}, D_{i_2}\}$, $A_2 = \{D_{i_2}, D_{i_3}\}, \ldots, A_{m-1} = \{D_{i_{m-1}}, D_{i_m}\}$, $A_m = \{D_{i_m}, D_{i_1}\}$. De Prisco et al. [10] proposed the following protocol for cycle-based access structures:

The Cycle Protocol: Let C_m be a cycle of length $m \geq 3$ and let $s_1, \ldots, s_m$ be m secrets uniformly chosen at random from $\mathbb{Z}_q$, where $q \geq 3$ is an odd number. Each secret is split over the two disks connected by the edge corresponding to the secret. The protocol builds m shares, which are also elements of $\mathbb{Z}_q$ as follows:

$$sh_i = \sum_{j=1}^{m} s_j + \sum_{j=i}^{m} s_j, \quad \text{for } i = 1, \ldots, m.$$

For each $i = 1, \ldots, m$ the share sh_i is stored on disk D_i.

The *Cycle Protocol* satisfies both the reconstruction and the weak secrecy requirements. Moreover, it is storage-optimal, since $SO = 1$. Fig. 4 shows an example of the *Cycle Protocol* for $C_4 = (1, 2, 3, 4)$.

Trees. The access structure of a *tree* T, i.e., a connected acyclic graph, with n nodes has $m = n - 1$ access sets, corresponding to its edges. If the diameter d of T is greater than or equal to three (the diameter of a tree is the number of nodes in the longest path between any two leaves in the tree), then, for each node $i \in T$ in there exists at least an edge (i, j) such that $deg(j) > 1$. Thus, assuming that all secrets have the same entropy $H(\mathbf{S})$, we have that each node in the tree contributes with a term of $H(\mathbf{S})$ to inequality (1), and from Theorem 3 the following result holds.

Lemma 4. *([10]) Let T be a tree-based access structure with diameter $d \geq 3$. In any weakly-secure DSSP for T, it holds that $SO \geq 1 + 1/m$.*

De Prisco et al. [10] proposed the following protocol for tree-based access structures having diameter $d \geq 3$:

The Tree Protocol (TP): Let T be a tree with n nodes and let $s_1, \ldots, s_m$ be $m = n - 1$ secrets uniformly chosen at random from $\mathbb{Z}_q$, where $q \geq 2$. Without

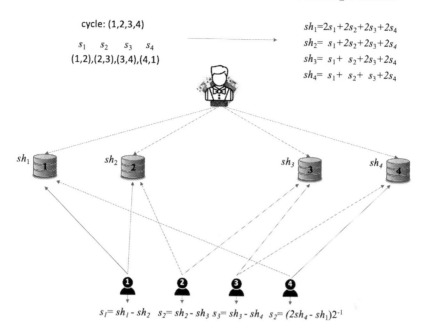

Fig. 4. Example of the *Cycle Protocol* for $C_4 = (1, 2, 3, 4)$.

loss of generality, let D_1 be the root of the tree, and for any node D_i, where $i \geq 2$, let P_i be the path from the root to D_i in T. The protocol builds n share, which are also elements of $\mathbb{Z}_q$ as follows, starting from a randomly chosen element $r \in \mathbb{Z}_q$: more precisely, the share for the root D_1 is the value r, whereas, for any other disk D_i, where $i \geq 2$, the share sh_i for disk D_i is the sum of r and of all other secrets in the path P_i from the root to D_i.

The *Tree Protocol* satisfies both the reconstruction and the weak secrecy requirements. Moreover, it is storage-optimal. The *Tree Protocol* also works if the access structure corresponds to a forest: it is enough to consider each tree of the forest separately.

Using the *Cycle Protocol* and the *Tree Protocol* as building blocks, it is possible to obtain protocols for arbitrary graphs [10]. The protocols proposed in [10], as well as those in [8], assume that all secrets are chosen from the same set $\mathbb{Z}_q$, where q is an appropriate integer, and thus have the same size $\log q$. The problem of designing DSSPs for graph-based access structures where the secrets can be selected from different fields has been left as an open problem in [10]. In Sect. 5 we will address such a problem by providing a protocol which can be used to share secrets of different sizes according to any graph-based access structure.

5   A Weakly-Secure Graph-Based DSSP for Secrets of Different Sizes

In this section we propose a protocol which can be used to share m secrets of different sizes according to a graph-based access structure. In our construction, referred in the following as the *Different Secrets Size Protocol*, we assume that the secrets are statistically independent. Moreover, we also assume that the secret $s_{i,j}$ associated to each edge (i, j) in the graph $G = (V, E)$ consists of $\ell_{i,j} \geq 1$ elements which are uniformly chosen at random from $\mathbb{Z}_q$, where $q \geq 3$ is an odd number, and we denote it by $s_{i,j} = (s_{i,j,1}, \ldots, s_{i,j,\ell_{i,j}})$.

The idea behind the *Different Secrets Size Protocol* is the following: we first distribute the shares for the secrets associated to the edges in G which are incident to at least a leaf. For each edge (i, j) such that $deg(j) = 1$, the share assigned to node j will be equal to the whole secret $s_{i,j}$, independently of the length of such a secret, whereas, the share assigned to node i will be empty. This can be seen as the *Step 0* of the *Different Secrets Size Protocol*.

Afterwards, we consider the reduced graph G' obtained by removing from G the leaf nodes and their incident edges, and distribute the shares for the remaining secrets to the nodes in G'. Such a process will involve ℓ_{max} steps of shares distribution, where $\ell_{max} = \max_{(i,j) \in E} \ell_{i,j}$, by using the *Subgraph Share Distribution Protocol* described below. More precisely, at *Step 1* of the *Different Secrets Size Protocol*, the *Subgraph Share Distribution Protocol* is used to distribute the secrets $s_{i,j,1}$ to the nodes of the graph G', whereas, at *Step h*, where $2 \leq h \leq \ell_{max}$, the *Subgraph Share Distribution Protocol* is used to distribute the secrets $s_{i,j,h}$ to the nodes of the graph G'_h, which is the subgraph of G' obtained after removing all edges corresponding to secrets of length at most $h - 1$.

Notice that at step h of the *Different Secrets Size Protocol*, where $h \geq 2$, the subgraph G'_h of G' contains only the edges corresponding to secrets having length at least h. Such a graph G'_h might be not connected, due to the edge removal operations; in this case, we consider its connected components. Figure 5 shows the graphs involved by the *Different Secrets Size Protocol*, starting on the graph G depicted on the top of the figure and for the secrets $s_{1,2} = (s_{1,2,1}, s_{1,2,2})$, $s_{2,3} = (s_{2,3,1}, s_{2,3,2}, s_{2,3,3})$, $s_{3,4} = (s_{3,4,1}, s_{3,4,2})$, $s_{1,4} = (s_{1,4,1}, s_{1,4,2}, s_{1,4,3})$, and $s_{4,5} = (s_{4,5,1}, s_{4,5,2})$. Notice that, while the reduced graph G' and the subgraph G'_2 are connected, G'_3 is not connected, but it can be seen as the union of two disjoint connected components.

We only need to clarify how to distribute the secrets $s_{i,j,h}$ to the nodes of the graph G'_h at each step $h \geq 1$ of the *Different Secrets Size Protocol*. Such a task will be done by using the *Subgraph Share Distribution Protocol*, described below, on each connected component of the subgraph G'_h with the relative secrets, where $G'_1 = G'$. Thus, at *Step h*, the *Subgraph Share Distribution Protocol* will be performed $comp\_conn(G'_h)$ times, where $comp\_conn(G'_h)$ denotes the number of connected components of the graph G'_h. In the following we will describe the *Subgraph Share Distribution Protocol* for a connected graph $J = (V_J, E_J)$ with associated secrets $x_{i,j}$, where $(i, j) \in E_J$.

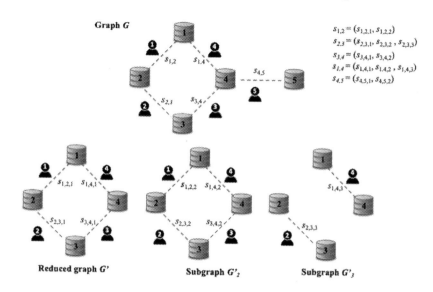

Fig. 5. The graphs involved in the different steps of the *Different Secrets Size Protocol.*

Subgraph Share Distribution Protocol

Input: A connected graph $J = (V_J, E_J)$ with associated secrets $\{x_{i,j}\}_{(i,j) \in E_J}$

If There is a cycle C in J
    then Distribute the secrets $x_{i,j}$, with $(i, j) \in C$ using the *Cycle Protocol*;
        Let $Z = (V_Z, E_Z)$ be the graph with nodes and edges of the cycle C;
    else Choose an edge $(i, j) \in E_J$;
        Uniformly choose a random $r_{i,j} \in \mathbb{Z}_q$, where $q \geq 3$ is an odd number;
        Store shares $r_{i,j}$ and $r_{i,j} + x_{i,j}$ on nodes i and j, respectively;
        Let $Z = (V_Z, E_Z)$ be the graph with nodes i and j and edge (i, j);
For each $(i, j) \in E_J \setminus E_Z$, where at least one between i and j is in V_Z
    do Assume that i has at least one share and let dsh_i be one of its shares;
        To share the secret $x_{i,j}$, store the share $dsh_i + x_{i,j}$ on node j;
        Add j to V_Z and (i, j) to E_Z;

Figure 6 shows the share distribution to the nodes of the graph G depicted on the top of Fig. 5, for *Step 0*, *Step 1*, and *Step 2*, whereas, Fig. 7 shows the share distribution for *Step 3*. In both figures, the share distributed to each node i at step h is denoted by sh_i^h. In particular, since the graph G_3' is not connected, the *Subgraph Share Distribution Protocol* is executed on each connected component of G_3'.

The next results, whose proofs are omitted due to space constraints, hold.

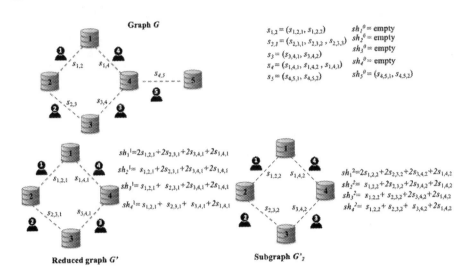

Fig. 6. Share distribution for *Step 0*, *Step 1*, and *Step 2* on the graph of Fig. 5.

Lemma 5. *Let* $G = (V, E)$ *be a graph-based access structure. The Different Secrets Size Protocol for* G *satisfies the reconstruction property.*

Lemma 6. *Let* $G = (V, E)$ *be a graph-based access structure. The Different Secrets Size Protocol for* G *satisfies the weak security property.*

Lemma 7. *Let* $G = (V, E)$ *be a graph-based access structure. The Different Secrets Size Protocol for* G *is optimal with respect to the size of the information distributed to each disk.*

In the following, we evaluate the storage overhead SO achieved by the *Different Secrets Size Protocol*. We first consider the case of a tree-based access structure T. Notice that if $diam(T) \leq 2$, then T contains only an internal node (the root of the tree), whereas, all other nodes are leaves. Therefore, only *Step 0* of the *Different Secrets Size Protocol* is executed. Hence, the next lemma holds.

Lemma 8. *Let* T *be a tree-based access structure with diameter* $d \leq 2$. *The Different Secrets Size Protocol for* T *has storage overhead* $SO = 1$.

The next lemma analyzes the case of a tree-based access structure T with diameter $d \geq 3$. Let $comp\_conn(T'_h)$ denote the number of connected components of the reduced tree T'_h, for any $h = 2, \ldots, \ell_{max}$, and let $comp\_conn(T) = \sum_{h=2}^{\ell_{max}} comp\_conn(T'_h)$.

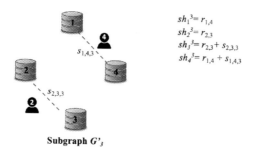

$$sh_1{}^3 = r_{1,4}$$
$$sh_2{}^3 = r_{2,3}$$
$$sh_3{}^3 = r_{2,3} + s_{2,3,3}$$
$$sh_4{}^3 = r_{1,4} + s_{1,4,3}$$

Subgraph G'_3

Fig. 7. Share distribution for *Step 3* on the graph of Fig. 5.

Lemma 9. *Let T be a tree-based access structure with diameter $d \geq 3$. The Different Secrets Size Protocol for T has storage overhead*

$$SO = 1 + \frac{comp\_conn(T)}{L},$$

where $L = \sum_{(i,j) \in G} \ell_{i,j}$.

Proof. Since T is a tree, also the reduced graph T' is a tree, and each node in T' receives a share. Thus, the number of shares distributed in *Step 1* of the *Different Secrets Size Protocol* is equal to $|\{(i,j) : \ell_{i,j} \geq 1\}| + 1$ (one for each node in T').

Consider the subgraph T'_h, where $h = 2, \ldots, \ell_{max} - 1$. After edge removal operations, T'_h might be not connected anymore; indeed, it might be the union of two of more disjoint connected tree components. Thus, the number of shares distributed in *Step h* is equal to $|\{(i,j) : \ell_{i,j} \geq h\}| + comp\_conn(T'_h)$. Finally, the number of shares distributed in *Step ℓ_{max}* is equal to $|\{(i,j) : \ell_{i,j} = \ell_{max}\}| + comp\_conn(T'_{\ell_{max}})$.

Hence, the total number of shares distributed to the nodes of T is equal to $\sum_{(i,j) \in T} \ell_{i,j} + comp\_conn(T)$. Therefore,

$$\sum_{i \in T} H(\mathbf{D}_i) = \sum_{(i,j) \in T} \ell_{i,j} \cdot \log q + comp\_conn(T) \cdot \log q.$$

Since $\sum_{(i,j) \in T} H(\mathbf{S}_{i,j}) = \sum_{(i,j) \in T} \ell_{i,j} \cdot \log q = L \cdot \log q$ the lemma follows. $\square$

Notice that, if all secrets have the same size $\log q$, then $L = \sum_{(i,j) \in T} \ell_{i,j} = m$ and $comp\_conn(T) = 1$, thus $SO = 1 + 1/m$. Hence, the value of the storage overhead SO reached by the *Different Secrets Size Protocol* generalizes the one achieved by the construction for trees in [10]. Following the lines of Lemma 9, we can prove the next result.

Lemma 10. *Let $G = (V, E)$ be a graph-based access structure containing a cycle. The Different Secrets Size Protocol for G has storage overhead*

$$SO = 1 + \frac{number\_tree(G)}{L},$$

where $L = \sum_{(i,j)\in G} \ell_{i,j}$, $number\_tree(G) = \sum_{h=2}^{\ell_{max}} tree\_comp\_conn(G'_h)$ and $tree\_comp\_conn(G'_h)$ denotes the number of connected components of the subgraph G'_h which are trees.

Notice that, if all secrets have the same size $\log q$, then $L = \sum_{(i,j)\in T} \ell_{i,j} = m$ and $number\_tree(G) = 0$, thus $SO = 1$. Hence, the value of the storage overhead SO reached by the *Different Secrets Size Protocol* generalizes the one achieved by the construction for arbitrary graphs in [10]. The next result follows from Lemmas 8, 9 and 10.

Theorem 4. *Let $G = (V, E)$ be a graph-based access structure. The Different Secrets Size Protocol for G is storage-optimal.*

To conclude, we have the following characterization with respect to the storage overhead for graph-based DSSPs: if the graph is a tree with diameter ≤ 2, then it is possible to achieve a storage overhead of 1; if the graph G is either a tree with diameter ≥ 3 or it contains a cycle, then the best possible storage overhead is $1 + number\_tree(G)/L$. This generalizes the characterization provided in [10] for graph-based DSSPs where all the secrets have the same size.

6   Conclusions

In this paper we have considered Distributed Secret Sharing Protocols (DSSPs). First, we have carefully analyzed the security requirements for DSSPs and we have shown that if the shared secrets are statistically dependent, then no DSSP satisfying either the weak secrecy requirement or the perfect secrecy one can exist. Motivated by the need to take into account the more general situation in which there could be statistical dependences between the secrets, we have proposed two new definitions of security for DSSPs. Afterwards, we have considered DSSPs for a specific class of access structures, i.e., those which can be represented by a graph. In particular, we have proposed a protocol, satisfying the weak secrecy requirement, which can be used to share (independent) secrets having different sizes. The protocol can manage any kind of graph and generalizes previous protocols for secrets having the same sizes, while maintaining optimal storage requirements.

We remark that our results for graph-based access structures concern DSSPs satisfying the *weak secrecy* requirement. It would be interesting to consider the other security requirement proposed in [8], as well as the two ones introduced in this paper, in order to provide lower bounds on the size of the stored information and to design storage-optimal constructions for DSSPs.

Acknowledgements. This work was partially supported by project *"SEcurity and RIghts in the CyberSpace (SERICS)"* (PE00000014) under the NRRP MUR program funded by the EU - NGEU.

References

1. Goyal, V., Pandey, O., Sahai, A., Waters, B.: Attribute-based encryption for fine-grained access control of encrypted data. In: Proceedings of the 13th ACM Conference on Computer and Communications Security - CCS 2006, pp. 89–98
2. Waters, B.: Ciphertext-policy attribute-based encryption: an expressive, efficient, and provably secure realization. In: Proceedings of Public Key Cryptography - PKC 2011, pp. 53–70
3. Desmedt, Y., Frankel, Y.: Shared generation of authenticators and signatures. In: Proceedings of Advances in Cryptology - CRYPTO '91, pp. 457–469
4. Michael Ben-Or, S.G., Wigderson, A.: Completeness theorems for non-cryptographic fault-tolerant distributed computation. In: Proceedings of the Twentieth Annual ACM Symposium on Theory of Computing - STOC '88, pp. 1–10
5. Chaum, D., Crépeau, C., Damgard, I.: Multiparty unconditionally secure protocols. In: Proceedings of the Twentieth Annual ACM Symposium on Theory of Computing - STOC '88, pp. 11–19
6. Ronald Cramer, D., Ivan, Maurer, U.: General Secure Multi-party Computation from any Linear Secret-Sharing Scheme. In: Proceedings of Advances in Cryptology - EUROCRYPT 2000, pp. 316–334
7. Naor, M., Wool, A.: Access control and signatures via quorum secret sharing. IEEE Trans. Parallel Distrib. Syst. $9(9)$, 909–922 (1998)
8. Soleymani, M., Mahdavifar, H.: Distributed multi-user secret sharing. IEEE Trans. Inf. Theory $67(1)$, 164–178 (2021)
9. De Prisco, R., De Santis, A., Palmieri, F.: Improved protocols for distributed secret sharing. IEEE Trans. Dependable Secur. Comput. (2022). https://doi.org/10.1109/TDSC.2022.3213790
10. De Prisco, R., De Santis, A., Palmieri, F.: Bounds and protocols for graph-based distributed secret sharing. IEEE Trans. Dependable Secur. Comput. (2023). https://doi.org/10.1109/TDSC.2023.3261239
11. Blakley, G.R.: Safeguarding Cryptographic Keys. In: Proceedings of AFIPS 1979 National Computer Conference, pp. 313–317 (1979)
12. Shamir, A.: How to share a secret. Commun. ACM $22(22)$, 612–613 (1979)
13. Ito, M., Saito, A., Nishizeki, T.: Multiple assignment scheme for sharing secret. J. Cryptol. 6, 15–20 (1993)
14. Benaloh, J., Leichter, J.: Generalized secret sharing and monotone functions. In: Goldwasser, S. (ed.) CRYPTO 1988. LNCS, vol. 403, pp. 27–35. Springer, New York (1990). https://doi.org/10.1007/0-387-34799-2_3
15. Simmons, G.J.: Introduction to shared secret and/or shared control schemes and their applications," Contemporary Cryptology, IEEE Press, pp. 441–497 (1991)
16. Stinson, D.R.: An Explication of Secret Sharing Schemes. Des. Codes Cryptography 2, 357–390 (1992)
17. Karnin, E.D., Greene, J.W., Hellman, M.E.: On secret sharing systems. IEEE Trans. Inf. Theory $29(1)$, 35–41 (1983)
18. Jackson, W.-A., Martin, K.M., O'Keefe, C.M.: A construction for multisecret threshold schemes. Des. Codes Cryptography $9(3)$, 287–303 (1996)
19. Blundo, C., De Santis, A., Vaccaro, U.: Efficient sharing of many secrets. In: Enjalbert, P., Finkel, A., Wagner, K.W. (eds.) STACS 1993. LNCS, vol. 665, pp. 692–703. Springer, Heidelberg (1993). https://doi.org/10.1007/3-540-56503-5_68
20. Jackson, W.-A., Martin, K.M., O'Keefe, C.M.: On sharing many secrets. In: Pieprzyk, J., Safavi-Naini, R. (eds.) ASIACRYPT 1994. LNCS, vol. 917, pp. 42–54. Springer, Heidelberg (1995). https://doi.org/10.1007/BFb0000423

21. De Santis, A., Masucci, B.: Multiple ramp schemes. IEEE Trans. Inf. Theory **45**(5), 1720–1728 (1999)
22. Blundo, C., De Santis, A., Di Crescenzo, G., Giorgio Gaggia, A., Vaccaro, U.: Multi-secret sharing schemes. In: Proceedings of Advances in Cryptology - CRYPTO '94, vol. 839, pp. 150–163
23. Blundo, C., Masucci, B.: Randomness in multi-secret sharing schemes. J. Univ. Comput. Sci. **5**(7), 367–389 (1999)
24. Di Crescenzo, G.: Sharing one secret vs sharing many secrets. Theoret. Comput. Sci. **295**(1–3), 123–140 (2003)
25. Masucci, B.: Sharing multiple secrets: models, schemes, and analysis. Des. Codes Crypt. **39**(1), 89–111 (2006)
26. Javier Herranz, A.R., Sáez, G.: New results and applications for multi-secret sharing schemes. Designs, Codes, and Cryptography, vol. 73, no. 3, pp. 841–864 (2014)
27. Cover, T.M., Thomas, J.A.: Elements of Information Theory (Wiley Series in Telecommunications and Signal Processing). Wiley-Interscience, USA (2006)

Probabilistic Fingerprinting Scheme for Correlated Data

Emre Yilmaz[1]([✉]) [iD] and Erman Ayday[2] [iD]

[1] University of Houston-Downtown, Houston, TX 77002, USA
yilmaze@uhd.edu
[2] Case Western Reserve University, Cleveland, OH 44106, USA
exa208@case.edu

Abstract. In order to receive personalized services, individuals share their personal data with a wide range of service providers, hoping that their data will remain confidential. Thus, in case of an unauthorized distribution of their personal data by these service providers, data owners want to identify the source of such data leakage. We show that applying existing fingerprinting schemes to personal data sharing is vulnerable to the attacks utilizing the correlations in the data. To provide liability for unauthorized sharing of personal data, we propose a probabilistic fingerprinting scheme that efficiently generates the fingerprint by considering a fingerprinting probability (to keep the data utility high) and publicly known inherent correlations between data points. To improve the robustness of the proposed scheme against colluding malicious service providers, we also utilize the Boneh-Shaw fingerprinting codes as a part of the proposed scheme. We implement and evaluate the performance of the proposed scheme on real genomic data. Our experimental results show the efficiency and robustness of the proposed scheme.

Keywords: Fingerprinting · Liability · Data sharing

1 Introduction

In today's data-driven world, individuals share vast amount of personal information with several service providers (SPs) to receive personalized services. During such data sharings, data owners usually do not want SPs to share their personal data with other third parties. Such issues are typically addressed via a consent (or data usage agreement) between a data owner and an SP to determine how much the SP gains the ownership of the user's data. However, user's data may often end up in the hands of unauthorized third parties since (i) SPs sometimes share (or sell) users' personal information without their authorization or (ii) databases of SPs are sometimes breached (e.g., due to insufficient or non-existing security measures). When such a leakage occurs, data owners would like to know the source of it to keep the corresponding SP(s) liable due to the leakage.

© IFIP International Federation for Information Processing 2023
Published by Springer Nature Switzerland AG 2023
V. Atluri and A. L. Ferrara (Eds.): DBSec 2023, LNCS 13942, pp. 69–90, 2023.
https://doi.org/10.1007/978-3-031-37586-6_5

Digital fingerprinting [15] is a technique to identify the recipient of a digital object by embedding a unique mark (called fingerprint) into the digital object. Fingerprinting techniques have been developed for different types of digital content, such as audio, video, and software. However, such techniques are not directly applicable for our scenario (sharing personal correlated data) because (i) they (especially for multimedia) utilize the high redundancy in the data, (ii) the embedded marks need to be large, which reduces the utility of shared data, and (iii) they do not consider the correlations between data points.

We propose a fingerprinting technique for sequential personal data having correlations between data points, such as genomic data or location data. We consider several different malicious behavior that can be launched by the malicious SPs against the proposed fingerprinting scheme including: (i) flipping data points, (ii) using a subset of the data points, (iii) utilizing the correlations in the data, and (iv) colluding SPs to identify and/or distort the fingerprint. Boneh-Shaw codes [4] and Tardos codes [14] are considered as the state-of-the-art fingerprinting codes to prevent collusion attacks. However, as we show in our experimental evaluation, they do not provide robustness against other attacks against a fingerprinting scheme which use data correlations. The proposed fingerprinting scheme essentially relies on adding controlled noise into particular data points in the original data and keeps the data utility high by controlling the fraction of fingerprinted data points. By building a correlation model, the proposed scheme guarantees that the fingerprint is consistent with the nature of the data. Furthermore, the proposed fingerprinting scheme utilizes Boneh-Shaw codes [4] to improve its collusion resistance while also providing robustness against other types of malicious behavior, such as flipping or utilizing correlations in the data (that are not considered by Boneh-Shaw codes).

We implement the proposed fingerprinting scheme for genomic data sharing using real-life datasets. Via simulations, we show the robustness of the proposed scheme for a wide-variety of attacks against a fingerprinting scheme and also compare it with the state-of-the-art. We show that the proposed scheme is efficient and scalable in terms of its running time.

The rest of the paper is organized as follows. We summarize the related work in Sect. 2. We describe the problem settings in Sect. 3. We propose the probabilistic fingerprinting scheme in Sect. 4 and explain how to utilize Boneh-Shaw codes to resist collusion attacks in Sect. 5. We present our experimental results in Sect. 6. Section 7 concludes the paper.

2   Related Work

Digital watermarking is the act of embedding an owner-specific mark into a digital object to prove the ownership of the object [6]. Watermarking techniques have been proposed for multimedia [3,8], text documents [5], graphs [16], and spatiotemporal datasets [9]. Digital fingerprinting can be seen as a personalized version of watermarking since embedded mark (i.e., fingerprint) is different in each copy of data with the objective to identify the recipient if data is disclosed to a third party without authorization of data owner. Fingerprinting schemes have been proposed for multimedia [15], relational databases [10], and sequential data [2]. Fingerprinting schemes for multimedia utilize the high redundancy in digital object, which are not applicable to personal data sharing (which typically includes less redundancy). Fingerprinting schemes for relational databases [10] do not consider correlations between attributes. Moreover, since databases consist of numerous tuples, the redundancy is much higher compared to personal data. In [2], authors proposed a fingerprinting algorithm for sequential data. Since this scheme solves an optimization problem at each step of the algorithm, it is not scalable. In addition, they minimize the probability of identifying the whole fingerprint in a collusion attack. However, the attackers can achieve their goal by modifying some of the fingerprinted points.

Since each fingerprinted copy of a data stream is different, malicious recipients can collude and detect fingerprinted points by comparing their copies. Boneh and Shaw proposed a general fingerprinting solution for binary data that is robust against collusion [4] by including overlapping fingerprints in each copy. However, fingerprint length needs to be significantly long to guarantee robustness against collusion, which reduces the utility of the shared data. Tardos also proposed probabilistic fingerprinting codes [14], which requires shorter codes than Boneh-Shaw by assigning a probability to each data point. However, the length of the fingerprint still needs to be high to provide robustness guarantees. The robustness of both schemes are guaranteed if the colluding SPs do not change the value of a data point when they all received the same value (i.e., marking assumption). In practice, colluding parties can behave randomly or use correlations in the data. Therefore, their theoretical analysis may not work in practice. Since we deal with correlations and probabilistic adversarial behavior, we choose to show the robustness statistically, with experimental evaluation in this work. Although there are some works relaxing marking assumption [7] or improving utility of Boneh-Shaw and Tardos codes [11,13], none of these schemes consider other attacks against a fingerprinting scheme, such as using correlations in the data for detecting fingerprinted points. Due to such limitations, directly using these codes for personal data sharing will result in low robustness and utility. In Sect. 6, we show how our proposed scheme provides higher robustness than Boneh-Shaw and Tardos codes against various attacks. As we explain in Sect. 5.2, we utilize Boneh-Shaw codes to improve the robustness of the proposed scheme against collusion attacks. We prefer to integrate Boneh-Shaw codes to improve the robustness of our scheme rather than Tardos codes, because our goal is to explicitly assign overlapping fingerprints as proposed by Boneh-Shaw codes. Therefore, we develop an efficient fingerprinting scheme which is robust against a wide-variety of attacks.

3   Problem Settings

In this section, we present our system model, threat model, and robustness measures. We describe the system and data models in a general way (i.e., without relying on a specific data type or size). In Sect. 6, we discuss and evaluate the use of the proposed fingerprinting scheme for genomic data.

3.1   System and Data Model

We show our system model in Fig. 1. We assume a data owner (Alice) with a sequence of data points $\mathcal{X} = [x_1, \ldots, x_l]$, where l is the length of the data and each x_i can have a value from the set $\mathcal{D} = \{d_1, \ldots, d_m\}$. Alice wants to share her data with multiple service providers (SPs) to receive a service from these SPs related to her data. Thus, we consider the scenario, in which the data owner shares her personal data (as a stream) with several service providers (SPs). We represent these SPs with a set $\mathcal{S}$ and each SP with an index such that $SP_i \in \mathcal{S}$. We assume Alice wants to detect the source of data leakage in the case of an unauthorized data sharing by any of these SPs. In other words, upon observing that her data is included in a leaked/breached dataset, the goal of the data owner is to statistically prove which specific SP leaked her data. Hence, for each $SP_i \in \mathcal{S}$, Alice creates a unique fingerprinted copy ($\mathcal{X}'_i = [x'_{i,1}, \ldots, x'_{i,l}]$) of $\mathcal{X}$ by changing the values of some data points. Note that the proposed fingerprinting scheme detects the source of data leakages; it does not provide guarantees to SPs about the correctness of data provided by Alice. Thus, similar to other fingerprinting schemes, we do not consider data credibility issues.

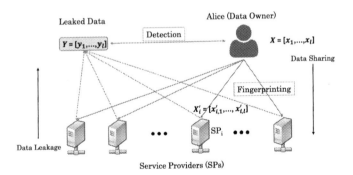

Fig. 1. The system model. Alice shares her data with several SPs after fingerprinting. In case of a data leakage, the goal of Alice is to identify the guilty SP (via the detection algorithm) that is responsible for this leakage.

Changing the states of more data points for fingerprinting increases the chance of Alice to detect the malicious SP(s) who leaks her data. However, fingerprinting naturally degrades the utility of shared data and one of our goals is to minimize this degradation while providing a robust fingerprinting scheme. We provide a general definition for the utility of a shared copy $\mathcal{X}'_i$ as $\mathcal{U}_i = \sum_{j=1}^{l} u_j D^i_j$, where u_j is the utility of data point x_j, $D^i_j = 1$ if $x_j = x'_{i,j}$, and $D^i_j = -1$ if $x_j \neq x'_{i,j}$.

We assume that data points are correlated and we mainly consider pairwise correlations between consecutive data points for clarity of presentation. The proposed mechanism can also be extended to consider more complex correlations, which may result in eliminating more possible values with low correlations. Thus, we let conditional probabilities (e.g., $P(x_{j+1} = d_\beta | x_j = d_\alpha)$ values) representing the correlations between data points be publicly available for any $j \in \{1, \ldots, l-1\}$ and $d_\alpha, d_\beta \in \mathcal{D}$. For different data types, such as location patterns and genomic data, data points may have pairwise correlations between each other. Therefore, a malicious SP may use such correlations to identify and exclude fingerprinted data points (e.g., the ones that are not compliant with the expected correlation model) in its unauthorized data sharing. Note that we do not expect the data owner to know and understand these correlations. We foresee that the system that will deploy the proposed algorithm to compute the correlations using public datasets and to use them in fingerprinting algorithm.

3.2 Threat Model

In this section, we present the attacks which may be performed by malicious SPs (attackers). We consider these attacks when developing the proposed scheme and we evaluate the robustness of the proposed scheme against these attacks in Sect. 6. In all of these attacks, the main goals of the attacker(s) are (i) to avoid being detected by the data owner and (ii) to share as many correct data points as possible. The attacker(s) needs to modify the values of some data points in its copy to distort the fingerprint. These modifications in the data mostly cause utility loss for the attacker(s). Let $\mathcal{Y} = [y_1, \ldots, y_l]$ be the leaked copy of Alice's data $\mathcal{X}$. Similar to the utility of shared data, we provide the general definition for the utility of the attacker(s) as $\mathcal{U}_\mathcal{Y} = \sum_{j=1}^{l} u_j D_j$, where u_j is the utility of x_j, $D_j = 1$ if $x_j = y_j$ and $D_j = -1$ if $x_j \neq y_j$. Flipping, subset, and majority attacks have already been introduced [10], whereas we propose correlation attack in the following and probabilistic majority attack in Sect. 5.1.

Flipping Attack. A malicious SP flips the values of some data points randomly to distort the fingerprint (before it does the unauthorized sharing). The malicious SP flips each data point with probability p_f. If it decides to flip, then it selects one of the remaining $(m-1)$ values (states) of the corresponding data point with equal probability and shares that state. While the probability of being detected by Alice becomes lower for higher p_f, the utility of shared data decreases as well.

Subset Attack. A malicious SP excludes (removes) some randomly chosen data points before leaking data, instead of flipping them. We denote the probability of excluding a data point as p_s. This attack is not as powerful as the flipping attack because flipping data points might create a fingerprint pattern that looks similar to some other SP's fingerprint pattern, and hence Alice may falsely accuse an innocent SP. However, to succeed in the subset attack, the malicious SP needs to exclude almost all of the fingerprinted data points.

Correlation Attack. As discussed, the correlations between consecutive data points are assumed to be publicly known. A malicious SP can use these correlations to degrade the robustness of the fingerprinting mechanism (we will define the robustness of the mechanism later). Assume the malicious SP_i receives $\mathcal{X}'_i = \{x'_{i,1}, \ldots, x'_{i,l}\}$ from Alice and let two data points in the received data be $x'_{i,j+1} = d_\beta$ and $x'_{i,j} = d_\alpha$. If $P(x_{j+1} = d_\beta | x_j = d_\alpha)$ is low, then the attacker infers that either $x'_{i,j}$ or $x'_{i,j+1}$ is fingerprinted with a high probability. After detecting such a pair, the malicious SP may change their values or exclude them before unauthorized sharing.

Since flipping attack can be more powerful (as discussed in Sect. 3.2), we assume the malicious SP combines correlation attack with flipping attack as follows: For two consecutive data points x_j and x_{j+1}, the malicious SP_i checks $P(x_{j+1} = x'_{i,j+1} | x_j = x'_{i,j})$. If this probability is less than a threshold τ_c, the malicious SP changes the value of $x'_{i,j+1}$ to a different value from the set $\mathcal{D}$ that provides the highest conditional probability (correlation) between $x'_{i,j}$ and $x'_{i,j+1}$. Otherwise, the malicious SP flips the value of $x'_{i,j+1}$ with probability p_f (as in the flipping attack). By doing so, the malicious SP (i) distorts the fingerprint with a high probability (by distorting the data points that are not compliant with the inherent correlations in the data) and (ii) adds random noise to the data to further reduce the chance of being detected by Alice. Following a similar strategy, the malicious SP checks all pairs up to $x'_{i,l-1}$ and $x'_{i,l}$. If the malicious SP does not combine correlation attack with flipping attack, Alice can perform a similar correlation attack on $\mathcal{X}'_i$ and obtain a similar result with the malicious SP. Thus, the randomness in the flipping attack makes it difficult for Alice to detect the malicious SP.

Collusion Attack. If multiple malicious SPs collude, by comparing their copies, they may detect and distort the fingerprinted data points. The goal of the colluding SPs is to share a single copy of $\mathcal{X}$ without being detected. One well-known collusion attack against fingerprinting schemes, called majority attack in the literature [10], is when colluding SPs compare all their received data points and choose to share the data value that is observed by the majority of the colluding SPs. However, doing such an attack alone cannot be successful for attackers if there is no randomness in the attack. Otherwise, Alice can simulate the majority attack of the colluding SPs (and identify the malicious SPs easily). Hence, in Sect. 5.1, we explain a more powerful collusion attack which also includes correlation and flipping attacks.

3.3   Robustness Measures

The attacks described in Sect. 3.2 may cause Alice to accuse an innocent SP due to the data leakage, and hence cause false positives in the fingerprint detection algorithm. A fingerprinting scheme is considered robust if it resists malicious attacks and allows the detection of the guilty SP that leaks the data after performing an attack. In this work, we assume that the detection algorithm always returns a guilty SP when Alice observes an unauthorized copy of her data. The proposed detection methods compute a score for each SP having a copy of Alice's data and identify the guilty SP based on these scores. In order to quantify the robustness of the proposed scheme, we use the accuracy (a) of the detection algorithm which is defined as the probability of detecting the guilty SP from the leaked data. In [10], misattribution false hit (fh^A) is defined as a robustness measure (defined as the probability of detecting an incorrect fingerprint from the leaked data). Therefore, a is equivalent to $(1 - fh^A)$. Similar to most collusion resistant fingerprinting schemes, such as Boneh-Shaw codes [4], we also define a as the probability of detecting one guilty SP from the leaked data in case of collusion attack.

4 Probabilistic Fingerprinting Scheme for Correlated Data

In this section, we propose our probabilistic fingerprinting scheme which considers correlations in data (considering the attack in Sect. 3.2). In Sect. 5, we will improve this scheme to also consider colluding malicious SPs.

4.1 Proposed Fingerprinting Algorithm

Assume data owner (Alice) has a sequence of data points $\mathcal{X} = [x_1, \ldots, x_l]$ and she wants to share her data with an SP_i as $\mathcal{X}'_i = [x'_{i,1}, \ldots, x'_{i,l}]$ after fingerprinting. Alice determines a fingerprinting probability p, which means on average $p \cdot l$ data points will be fingerprinted (i.e., their value will be changed) when sharing l data points with SP_i. Lower p values increase the utility of shared data by decreasing the robustness.

Under these settings, a naive algorithm fingerprints each data point with the same probability, without considering correlations in the data. Hence, each data point is shared correctly ($x'_{i,j} = x_j$) with probability $1 - p$ and incorrectly/fingerprinted ($x'_{i,j} \neq x_j$) with probability p. For each fingerprinted data point, the shared state is selected among $(m-1)$ states in $\mathcal{D}$ with equal probability. However, if this naive scheme is used, a malicious SP can detect some of the fingerprinted data points using the correlations and distort them via flipping, as discussed in Sect. 3.2.

In order to prevent such an attack, one needs to consider the correlations in the fingerprinting scheme. In our proposed probabilistic fingerprinting scheme, for each data point x_j, considering the correlations in the data, we assign a different probability for sharing each different state of this data point in $\mathcal{D}$. Let P_{x_j, d_k} be the probability of sharing data point x_j as d_k (i.e., $x'_{i,j} = d_k$). The proposed scheme assigns a P_{x_j, d_k} value for all $j \in \{1, \ldots, l\}$ and $k \in \{1, \ldots, m\}$. In the following, for simplicity, we describe the proposed fingerprinting algorithm by assuming pairwise correlations between consecutive data points and sequential order of processing of the data points for fingerprinting. However, the proposed system also works for different correlation models. We propose an iterative algorithm that starts from the first data point x_1 and assigns probabilities $P_{x_1,d_1}, \ldots, P_{x_1,d_m}$. Since we consider correlations between consecutive data points, for the first data point x_1, similar to the naive approach, Alice shares the correct value with probability $1 - p$ and each incorrect value with probability $p/(m-1)$. Based on these probabilities, the algorithm selects a value for $x'_{i,1}$ from the set $\mathcal{D}$. For the subsequent data points, the algorithm computes the fingerprinting probabilities by checking the correlation with the preceding data points.

Let the shared value of x_{j-1} (i.e., $x'_{i,j-1}$) be d_α. The algorithm checks the conditional probabilities $P(x_j = d_k | x_{j-1} = d_\alpha)$ for all $d_k \in \mathcal{D}$. If the algorithm decides to share x_j as d_k, and if $P(x_j = d_k | x_{j-1} = d_\alpha)$ is low, a malicious SP can detect that either $x'_{i,j-1}$ or $x'_{i,j}$ is fingerprinted. To eliminate such correlation attack, the proposed algorithm uses a threshold τ and sets $P_{x_j,d_k} = 0$ if $P(x_j = d_k | x_{j-1} = d_\alpha) < \tau$. Hence, the algorithm never selects d_k as the value of $x'_{i,j}$ if d_k is not consistent with the inherent correlations in the data. Let d_c be the actual value of x_j. If $P(x_j = d_c | x_{j-1} = d_\alpha) \geq \tau$, P_{x_j,d_c} is set to $1 - p$. All of the remaining probabilities ($P_{x_j,d_k}, k \neq c$) are assigned directly proportional to the value of $P(x_j = d_k | x_{j-1} = d_\alpha)$. After assigning all probabilities, the algorithm chooses one of the values from $\mathcal{D}$ based on the assigned probabilities and sets the value of $x'_{i,j}$ accordingly.

Since the proposed algorithm considers correlations, total number of fingerprinted points in the original data may significantly deviate from the expected number ($p \cdot l$). Considering correlations may cause fingerprinting significantly more (or fewer) data points than anticipated. To prevent this, we dynamically decrease (or increase) the fingerprinting probability p depending on number of currently fingerprinted data points. To keep the average number of fingerprinted data points as $p \cdot l$, the proposed algorithm divides the data points into blocks consisting of $\lceil 1/p \rceil$ data points. We expect (on the average) one fingerprinted data point in each block. Therefore, the algorithm keeps a count of the number of fingerprinted data points at the end of each block. If the ratio of fingerprinted data points is less than p, the algorithm sets the fingerprinting probability for the next block as $p \cdot (1 + \theta)$. Here, θ is a design parameter in the range $[0, 1)$ and we evaluate the selection of θ in Sect. 6. If the ratio of fingerprinted data points is greater than p, the algorithm sets the fingerprinting probability for the next block as $p \cdot (1 - \theta)$.

For each SP, Alice executes the same algorithm with a different seed value (i.e., starting point in generating random numbers) and stores the fingerprint pattern of each SP to use it in the detection in case her data is leaked. If the data size is large, Alice can just store the seed value for each SP as the key of the fingerprinting algorithm and seed value can be used to generate the same fingerprint.

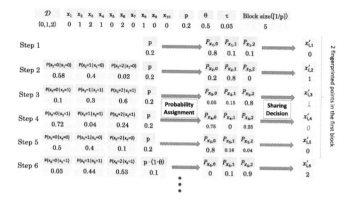

Fig. 2. A toy example showing the execution of the proposed algorithm. Input parameters of the algorithm are shown at the top as the original data $\mathcal{X}$, the fingerprinting probability p, probability adjustment parameter θ, correlation threshold τ, and the block size $\lceil 1/p \rceil$.

Figure 2 shows a toy example to illustrate the execution of the proposed algorithm. Each step shows one iteration for deciding the value of one data point. In the first step, probabilities are assigned just by using p. In the next steps, correlations are also used to determine the sharing probabilities. When the correlation is less than $\tau = 0.05$, the algorithm assigns 0 for the probability of selecting the corresponding value. At the end of the first block (a block includes 5 data points in the example), since the number of fingerprinted data points (2) is greater than the expected (1), the fingerprinting probability is adjusted as $p \cdot (1 - \theta) = 0.1$ for the second block.

4.2 Detecting the Source of Data Leakage

Let the leaked copy of Alice's data be $\mathcal{Y} = [y_1, \ldots, y_l]$. The goal of Alice is to detect the SP that leaks her data. Here, Alice can apply a probabilistic detection algorithm which was proposed in [12]. With some independence assumptions, their algorithm computes the probability of being guilty for each SP and returns the SP with the highest probability. We also propose to use the similarity between leaked data and fingerprinted copies in the following and compare the performance of probabilistic detection and similarity-based detection in terms of their accuracy to identify the guilty SP in Sect. 6.

Similarity-Based Detection. For an SP_i, Alice compares the leaked data $\mathcal{Y}$ with the copy $\mathcal{X}'_i$ and counts the matching data points in the fingerprint pattern. In other words, Alice checks the size of the following set: $\mathcal{M}_i = \{x_j \mid x_j \in \mathcal{X}, \; x_j \neq x'_{i,j}, \; x'_{i,j} = y_j\}$. Alice also counts the fingerprinted data points $\mathcal{F}_i = \{x_j \mid x_j \in \mathcal{X}, \; x_j \neq x'_{i,j}\}$ of SP_i. Eventually, the SP with the maximum $sim_i = |\mathcal{M}_i|/|\mathcal{F}_i|$ is identified as guilty.

5   Considering Colluding Service Providers

Here, we first present a strong attack against the proposed fingerprinting scheme (also against the existing fingerprinting schemes in general) by integrating colluding SPs, correlations in the data, and the flipping attack. Then, we propose utilizing Boneh-Shaw codes [4] to improve robustness against such a strong collusion attack.

5.1   Probabilistic Majority Attack

As discussed, the goal of the colluding SPs is to share (leak) a copy of the data without being detected by Alice. In a standard collusion attack, the colluding SPs compare their received values for each data point and select the most observed value to share. We propose an advanced collusion attack called "probabilistic majority attack" (to distinguish it from the standard majority attack), in which the colluding SPs decide the value of each leaked data point by considering (i) all observed values for that data point, (ii) correlation of that data point with the others, and (iii) the probability of adding a fingerprint to a data point (p). If the colluding SPs do not know the fingerprinting probability p, we assume they use an estimated probability p_e in their attack ($p_e = p$ if p is publicly known).

Let the set of colluding SPs be $\mathcal{C}$ and $|\mathcal{C}| = n$. The goal of the colluding SPs is to create a copy $\mathcal{Y} = [y_1, \ldots, y_l]$ to share and avoid being detected by Alice. In this attack, the colluding SPs decide the value of each data point y_j by computing a probability P_{y_j, d_k} for each possible state $d_k \in \mathcal{D}$ of y_j. Let c_{j,d_k} be the number of observations of d_k for data point j by n colluding SPs (in $\mathcal{C}$). In the standard majority attack, the colluding SPs choose d_k with the maximum c_{j,d_k} value as the value of y_j (assuming it is the original value of the data point) to avoid detection by Alice. However, it is possible (with lower probability) that other values with lower c_{j,d_k} may also be the original value of y_j.

As discussed in Sect. 3.2, correlations can be used to detect and distort fingerprinted data points by the attackers. Therefore, the attackers tend to select each leaked value that have high correlation with the previous shared (leaked) values. In order to integrate the correlations with the collusion attack, the conditional probabilities (due to correlations) are used as weights to determine the sharing probabilities of colluding SPs (P_{y_j, d_k}). The colluding SPs first compute the weighted probability values (referred as t_{j,d_k}) and then compute P_{y_j, d_k} by normalizing the weighted probability values. The weighted probability for d_k value of a data point j is computed as: $t_{j,d_k} = (1 - p_e)^{c_{j,d_k}} \cdot (\frac{p_e}{m-1})^{n-c_{j,d_k}} \cdot P(x_j = d_k | x_{j-1} = y_{j-1})$. Here, $(1 - p_e)^{c_{j,d_k}} \cdot (\frac{p_e}{m-1})^{n-c_{j,d_k}}$ is the probability of d_k to be the original value of data point j by assuming each data point is fingerprinted with probability p_e. The conditional probability is used as a weight. Then, t_{j,d_k} values are normalized as $P_{y_j, d_k} = t_{j,d_k}/(\sum_{k=1}^{n} t_{j,d_k})$. The colluding SPs decide on the value of each shared point y_j proportional to these probabilities. Thus, they do not necessarily select the value observed by the majority. By doing so, we allow the malicious SPs to further distort the fingerprint compared to the standard majority attack.

Furthermore, existing techniques to prevent collusion attacks (e.g., Boneh-Shaw codes) assign common fingerprints to multiple SPs, which allows data owner to detect colluding SPs with a high chance. However, to avoid such detection, the attackers may flip some random data points before they leak the data. Thus, in the probabilistic majority attack, we also let colluding SPs flip each y_j with probability p_f (as discussed in Sect. 3.2). A toy example to illustrate this attack is given in Appendix A.

5.2   Integrating Boneh-Shaw Codes

In order to provide robustness against collusion attacks, Boneh and Shaw proposed fingerprinting codes (B-S codes) for detecting one of the colluding SPs [4]. The effectiveness of their codes depends on the "marking assumption", which states that when the colluding SPs have the same value for the same data point j, they choose this value as y_j as the leaked data point. Hence, it is assumed that colluding SPs cannot detect the fingerprint if all of them have the same fingerprint. However, B-S codes do not consider correlation and flipping attacks, and hence their detection method is not successful when colluding SPs also utilize the correlations and the flipping attack.

In Boneh-Shaw (c,r)-codes, ith codeword consists of $(i-1)\cdot r$ zeros and $(c-i)\cdot r$ ones. In order to fingerprint data, some data points are selected from the original data and XOR'ed with the permuted codeword in order to prevent colluding SPs from detecting and distorting the fingerprint. The data points that are XOR'ed with ones in the codeword becomes fingerprinted. Therefore, the ones in the binary code represent fingerprints. Thus, increasing r decreases the error in detection, but it also decreases the utility by increasing the fingerprint length. We show how to utilize these codes in the proposed scheme in the following.

Using Boneh-Shaw Codes in the Proposed Scheme. The marking assumption of [4] does not consider the flipping attack and correlation attack which are included in the probabilistic majority attack. If the colluding SPs flip some of the bits randomly or based on correlations, the data owner may accuse an SP who is not involved in the collusion. Therefore, using B-S codes and their detection algorithm in our scenario directly results in low robustness against the correlation and flipping attacks. Instead, we utilize B-S codes to assign overlapping fingerprints between different SPs.

The fingerprints of two SPs may be the same for some random data points when Alice creates fingerprinted copy of each SP independently as described in Sect. 4. Here, we explicitly assign overlapping fingerprints using B-S codes to improve robustness against collusion attacks. When a data point is fingerprinted using B-S codes, the same value is also used as a fingerprint in the copies of other SPs if their codewords also include one for the same data point.

We integrate the B-S codes into our scheme as follows: Alice creates the first fingerprinted copy of her data $\mathcal{X}_1'$ as described in Sect. 4. Approximately $p\cdot l$ data points are fingerprinted in $\mathcal{X}_1'$. Let f be the number of fingerprinted data points for SP_1. We want to use some portion of these f data points as B-S codes. Then, Alice decides the value of c and r such that $(c-1) \cdot r \leq f$ to apply B-S codes for the next sharings. As mentioned, c and r are design parameters of B-S codes determining the length of codes and error in detection. We represent $(c-1) \cdot r$ as f_1, which is the length of B-S codeword. Here, c is the number of B-S codewords that Alice can create and r is the block size. If Alice wants to share her data with more than c SPs, she assigns the same B-S codewords in a similar order. SP_{c+1} receives the same codeword as SP_1, SP_{c+2} receives the same codeword as SP_2, and so on. In this way, although same B-S codewords are assigned to some SPs, since other parts of their fingerprints will be different, the proposed detection algorithm can still identify the guilty SP using the entire fingerprint. For higher f_1, the robustness against collusion attacks increases, however, the robustness against the attacks performed by single SP decreases. Hence, we set f_1 approximately equal to $f/2$ to detect the guilty SP regardless of whether the attack is performed by single SP or multiple SPs.

Alice randomly selects f_1 of f fingerprinted points in $\mathcal{X}'_1$. These f_1 fingerprinted data points are considered as the first codeword in B-S codes. For her next sharing with SP_2, Alice randomly selects $f_2 = f_1 - r$ of f_1 points to assign the same fingerprints to SP_2 (i.e., $x'_{2,j} = x'_{1,j}$ for these f_2 data points). Moreover, Alice assigns the original value for the remaining r points (i.e., $x'_{2,j} = x_j$ for these r data points). In other words, the B-S codeword of SP_2 consists of r zeros and $f_1 - r$ ones. In order to assign approximately $p \cdot l$ fingerprinted points to SP_2, the fingerprinting probability of SP_2 is selected as $\frac{p \cdot l - f_2}{l - f_1}$ since f_2 fingerprints are already assigned before running the probabilistic algorithm. Alice runs the proposed algorithm to sequentially add the remaining fingerprints. Also, since f_2 fingerprints and r original values are already assigned (as the B-S codeword of SP_2) before the algorithm, the algorithm will skip these points while adding fingerprints. Furthermore, when the algorithm is determining the probabilities for each possible value of a data point (i.e., inner loop of the algorithm), it also considers the correlations of the data points with the already assigned B-S codeword. The updated algorithm is shown in Algorithm C.1 in Appendix C , which includes these new conditions. For each SP_i, Alice repeats the same process by first adding f_i fingerprints and $f_1 - f_i$ original values (i.e., B-S codeword). Then, Alice runs Algorithm C.1 to determine the values of remaining points in $\mathcal{X}'_i$. We illustrate this process with a toy example in Appendix B.

5.3   Detection Algorithm

Here, we propose a detection algorithm for the proposed collusion-resilient fingerprinting scheme. In practice, when Alice realizes that a copy $\mathcal{Y}$ of her data is leaked without her consent, she cannot know whether $\mathcal{Y}$ is leaked by single SP (by performing flipping or correlation attack) or multiple SPs (by performing collusion attack). Thus, Alice cannot use the detection techniques in Sect. 4.2 or the detection technique of B-S codes directly. We propose a detection algorithm that utilizes both techniques. We describe the detection algorithm using similarity-based detection since it performs slightly better than probabilistic detection as we show in Sect. 6.

To detect a guilty SP, Alice initially computes a similarity score (sim_i) in the range $[0, 1]$ for each $SP_i \in \mathcal{S}$ as explained in Sect. 4.2. If there is a collusion of two SPs and the colluding SPs observe different values for a data point, they select either of these values with equal probabilities. Thus, we expect that they damage approximately half of the fingerprinted data points (this will be more if the collusion includes more than 2 SPs). Hence, we assume that there is an attack by single SP if the similarity score of an SP is greater than 0.5. In such a case, Alice identifies the SP with the highest similarity score as guilty. Otherwise, there is a collusion attack with high probability, and hence Alice identifies the suspects according to their similarity scores and returns one of them utilizing the detection technique of B-S codes.

Let the index of SP with maximum similarity score be max. Alice generates a suspect list by including $\lfloor 1/sim_{max} \rfloor$ SPs having highest similarity scores. Hence, if sim_{max} is greater than 0.5, there will be just one SP in the suspect list and the algorithm will return SP_{max} as guilty. If sim_{max} is less than or equal to 0.5, there will be more than one suspects, which means that a collusion attack is performed with high probability. In this case, the algorithm returns one of the suspects using the detection method of B-S codes [4] as follows: In B-S codes, it is expected that the colluding SPs create a copy consisting of several random values followed by all ones and the starting point of ones (a block with all ones) gives us one of the colluding SPs. Let B_R represents a block (consists of r data points) having at least one zero value and B_1 represents a block having all ones. Assuming the leaked copy created by colluding SPs is $[B_R, ..., B_R, B_1, ..., B_1]$, SP_i is identified as guilty if the first observed B_1 block is the ith block. However, as a result of probabilistic majority attack described in Sect. 5.1, some ones may turn into zeros and some zeros may turn into ones. Therefore, the detection algorithm may fail against such an attack. To avoid this, we define $\hat{B}_1$ as a block having majority of points as one and $\hat{B}_R$ as a block having majority of points as zero. Then, the algorithm checks all suspects in the suspect list starting from SP_{max}. If (max)th block is $\hat{B}_1$ and ($max - 1$)th block is $\hat{B}_R$, the algorithm returns SP_{max} as guilty. Otherwise, the algorithm continues with the other SPs in the suspect list in the order of decreasing similarity scores. For each SP_i in the suspect list, the algorithm returns it as guilty if the (i)th block is $\hat{B}_1$ and the ($i - 1$)th block is $\hat{B}_R$. When such an SP is found, the algorithm stops and returns the SP as guilty. If there is no such an SP, the algorithm returns SP_{max} as guilty. The steps of the proposed detection algorithm are also shown with an example in Appendix D.

6   Evaluation

To evaluate its robustness and utility, we implemented the proposed fingerprinting algorithm (in Sect. 5.2) and the detection algorithm (in Sect. 5.3). We implemented Tardos codes [14] as a state-of-the-art fingerprinting scheme for comparison. We also implemented B-S codes as a standalone fingerprinting scheme and observed that its robustness against the attacks is similar to Tardos codes. Hence, we here present the results of Tardos codes to show the superiority of our scheme to deal with correlation and flipping attacks.

6.1   Data Model and Settings

Nowadays, individuals can obtain their genome sequences easily and share their genomic data with medical institutions and direct-to-consumer service providers for various genetic tests or research purposes. Since genomic data contains sensitive personal information, such as the risk of developing particular diseases, sharing genomic data without the authorization of the data owner causes privacy violations. Hence, fingerprinting genomic data can be a solution or disincentive to prevent its unauthorized sharing. Furthermore, genomic data contains inherent pairwise correlations between point mutations (single nucleotide polymorphisms - SNPs), which makes genomic data an ideal usecase to evaluate the proposed scheme. SNP is the variation of a single nucleotide (from the set $\{A, T, C, G\}$) in the population. For each SNP position, only two different nucleotides can be observed: (i) major allele, which is observed in the majority of the population and (ii) minor allele, which is observed rarely. Each SNP consists of two nucleotides, one is inherited from the mother and the other from the father. Since each SNP is represented by the number of its minor alleles, $\mathcal{D} = \{0, 1, 2\}$ for genomic data.

The 1000 Genomes Phase 3 dataset [1] includes partial genomic records of 2504 individuals from 26 populations. Among these, we extracted the 5000 SNPs belonging to 99 people from the Utah residents with northern and western European ancestry (CEU) population of the HapMap project. Using this dataset, we computed the correlations between SNPs to build our correlation model. Unless stated otherwise, we set the data size $l = 1,000$, fingerprinting probability $p = 0.1$, and the correlation threshold of the algorithm $\tau = 0.05$. The threshold τ is used in the algorithm to prevent adding fingerprints causing low correlation. Note that the attacker has its own correlation threshold τ_c in its correlation attack. We choose the data size as 1,000 to show the robustness of the proposed scheme for a relatively small data. As we show via experiments later (in Sect. 6.4), robustness increases with the increasing data size because as data size increases, we obtain more fingerprinted data points for the same fingerprinting probability p. Hence, for larger data sizes, p can be selected much lower than 0.1 to provide the same level of fingerprint robustness. As expected, utility of the data owner (as introduced in Sect. 3.1) decreases linearly with increasing p. We observed that the average utility is 0.8 when p is 0.1 and u_j (utility of each data point) is $1/l$. To compare the robustness of the proposed scheme with Tardos codes, we allocated $2p$ of the data points for Tardos codes. Hence, when $p = 0.1$ is used in the proposed scheme, 20% of the data points are allocated for Tardos codes. Since approximately half of them are fingerprinted in probabilistic Tardos codes, 10% of the data points are fingerprinted in each copy, which provides approximately the same utility with the proposed scheme.

We expect to change the value of approximately $p \cdot l = 100$ data points as fingerprint for each SP, and (as discussed in Sect. 5.2) we used approximately half of the fingerprinted data points for B-S codes. We set the number of B-S codes (c) as 10 and the block size (r) as 5. Hence, $(c-1) \cdot r = 45$ fingerprinted data points of first SP were used for B-S codes. Another design parameter in the algorithm is θ can have any value in the range $[0, 1)$. It is used to dynamically adjust fingerprinting probability p to keep the number of fingerprinted data points close to $p \cdot l$. We set $\theta = 0.5$ in our experiments. We repeated all experiments 10 times for each individual in the dataset (totally 99 individuals), and hence all results are given as the average of 990 executions. We also provide a discussion about the complexity and practicality of the proposed scheme in Appendix E.2, which shows that the running times of both fingerprinting algorithm and detection algorithm grow linearly with the design parameters.

6.2 Flipping and Subset Attacks

We implemented flipping and subset attacks to compare these attacks as well as to compare similarity-based and probabilistic detection techniques. We present our results in Appendix E.1. From these results, we can conclude that (i) similarity-based detection provides slightly better accuracy than the probabilistic detection, (ii) flipping attack is more powerful than subset attack, (iii) the attacker needs to flip at least half of the data points in the proposed scheme to avoid being detected, and (iv) the proposed scheme is more robust than Tardos codes against flipping and subset attacks. For the rest of the experiments, we use the similarity-based detection algorithm described in Sect. 5.3.

6.3 Correlation Attack

We implemented the correlation attack described in Sect. 3.2 to evaluate the robustness of the proposed scheme. We set the total number of SPs to 1,000. As before, we set the correlation threshold of the algorithm (decided by data owner) as $\tau = 0.05$. Therefore, the fingerprinted copies did not include consecutive pairs of data points whose correlation is less than 0.05. Note however that the correlation threshold of the attack τ_c is determined by the attacker. We also implemented the naive fingerprinting scheme described in Sect. 4, in which each data point is fingerprinted with probability p. In correlation attack, data points whose correlation with the previous data point is less than τ_c is flipped and the remaining data points are flipped with probability p_f. Figure 3a shows the comparison of the proposed scheme with the naive approach and Tardos codes for different values of τ_c when $p_f = 0.2$. The proposed scheme provides 100% detection accuracy up to $\tau_c = 0.2$ and accuracy decreases to 98% when $\tau_c = 0.25$. However, as also shown in Fig. 3a, the utility of the attacker $(\mathcal{U}_y)$ reduces to 0.263 when $\tau_c = 0.25$. We also observed that both the naive approach and Tardos codes are not robust against correlation attacks and the attacker can easily prevent detection by utilizing the correlations in the data. This clearly shows the importance of considering correlations in the data within the fingerprinting algorithm.

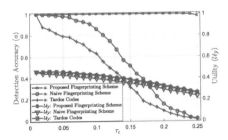

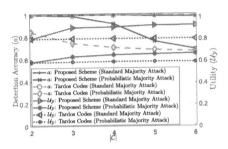

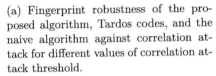

(a) Fingerprint robustness of the proposed algorithm, Tardos codes, and the naive algorithm against correlation attack for different values of correlation attack threshold.

(b) Fingerprint robustness of the proposed scheme and Tardos codes against standard majority attack and probabilistic majority attack for different values of n.

Fig. 3. Fingerprint robustness against different attacks.

6.4 Collusion Attack

We first compare the utility and robustness under standard and probabilistic majority attacks. We set $c = 10$ and $r = 5$. Hence, we can create 10 different B-S codewords with block size of 5. Note that c is the number of codewords and Alice can share her data more than c SPs in the proposed scheme by repeating codewords as we discussed before. We set the total number of SPs ($|\mathcal{S}|$) to 20, $\tau_c = 0.1$, and $p_f = 0.1$. We quantified both utility and fingerprint robustness for different values of number of colluding SPs (n). As shown in Fig. 3b, using probabilistic majority attack decreases the colluding SPs' probability of being detected by reducing the data utility. Since the probabilistic majority attack is more powerful than the standard one for the colluding SPs, we perform the probabilistic majority attack for the rest of the experiments.

As mentioned, both Tardos codes and B-S codes assume the colluding SPs decide the value of a data point randomly if they observe more than one value in their copies (i.e., marking assumption). Therefore, these codes do not provide guarantees against the probabilistic majority attack (including the flipping attack). In Fig. 3b, we showed the robustness of the Tardos codes against collusion attacks (we observed similar results for B-S codes). Although Tardos codes provide high robustness against standard majority attack, robustness of these codes against probabilistic majority attack is lower than our proposed scheme since Tardos codes do not consider correlations and random flipping in probabilistic majority attack. Moreover, to provide the robustness guarantees for Tardos codes and B-S codes, the number of fingerprinted points needs to be high. For instance, to provide 90% robustness guarantee against 3 colluding SPs performing standard majority attack, 2,700 fingerprinted data points are needed in Tardos codes regardless of the data size. Similarly, to create 10 B-S codes with the same guarantee, we need more than 10,000 fingerprinted data points. Fingerprinting such a high number of data points also decreases the utility of the data owner significantly. Thus, Tardos codes and B-S codes provide guarantees for only standard majority attack with high number of fingerprinted data points (we only use approximately $p \cdot l = 100$ data points for fingerprinting in our experiments and, as we show later, our scheme provides high robustness with smaller p when data size increases). Therefore, we conclude that Tardos codes and B-S codes do not provide robustness against the attacks utilizing correlations and random flipping. While our proposed scheme utilizes the B-S codes to increase its robustness against collusion attacks, Algorithm C.1 generates unique fingerprints to also provide robustness against correlation and flipping attacks.

One important parameter for the fingerprinting scheme is data size. In our experiments we used a data with 1,000 SNPs ($l = 1,000$). Therefore, we just changed the state of approximately 100 data points as a fingerprint when fingerprinting probability p was selected as 0.1. By keeping the same fingerprinting probability, increasing data size allows to change more data points as fingerprint. With more fingerprinted data points, the data owner can detect the colluding SPs with higher accuracy. To show the effect of data size (i.e., l) on robustness, we conducted experiments by increasing l (we kept $c = 10$ and increased r proportional to l). As shown in Table 1, Alice detects one of 3 colluding SPs among 100 SPs with 99.7% accuracy when $l = 5,000$ and $p_f = 0.1$. Our results show that the robustness of the proposed scheme significantly improves with increasing data size. Thus, when data size is larger, Alice can select a much lower fingerprint probability (p) to obtain the same robustness guarantees. For instance, when data size (l) is 5,000, decreasing p from 0.1 to 0.05 increases the utility of fingerprinted data from 0.8 to 0.9 while still providing 96.3% accuracy for 3 colluding SPs performing a probabilistic majority attack.

Table 1. Fingerprint robustness (a) of the proposed scheme for different l (data size) values. The number of SPs (that received data owner's data) is 100 and the number of colluding SPs (n) is 3. Flipping probability in the attack is 0.1.

l	1,000	2,000	3,000	4,000	5,000
a	0.759	0.914	0.973	0.993	0.997

7   Conclusion

We have proposed a probabilistic fingerprinting scheme that also considers the correlations in the data during fingerprint insertion. First, we have shown how to assign probabilities for the sharing decision of each data point that are consistent with the inherent correlations in the data. Then, we have described the integration of Boneh-Shaw codes into the proposed algorithm to improve fingerprint robustness against collusion attacks. Our experimental results on genomic data show that the proposed fingerprinting scheme is robust against a wide range of attacks. We plan to evaluate the proposed scheme on trajectory data in the future.

Acknowledgements. The work was partly supported by the National Library of Medicine of the National Institutes of Health under Award Number R01LM013429 and by the National Science Foundation (NSF) under grant numbers 2141622, 2050410, 2200255, and OAC-2112606.

A   Toy Example for the Probabilistic Majority Attack

To illustrate the probabilistic majority attack with a toy example, let $n = 4$ and $\mathcal{D} = \{0, 1, 2\}$. Assume 3 of the colluding malicious SPs have received value 0 for the first data point (x_1) and the other malicious SP has received value 1. Let the estimated fingerprinting probability $p_e = 0.1$. Colluding SPs compute $t_{1,0} = (0.9)^3 \cdot (0.1)^1 \cdot 1$, $t_{1,1} = (0.9)^1 \cdot (0.1)^3 \cdot 1$, and $t_{1,2} = (0.9)^0 \cdot (0.1)^4 \cdot 1$. Since x_1 is the first data point and we consider pairwise correlations between consecutive data points, here, conditional probabilities are all considered as 1. Then, colluding SPs choose a value (to share) from $\mathcal{D}$ with the following probabilities: $P_{y_1,0} = 0.0729/0.0739 = 0.987$, $P_{y_1,1} = 0.0009/0.0739 = 0.012$, and $P_{y_1,2} = 0.0001/0.0739 = 0.001$. Finally, the chosen value is flipped with probability p_f.

B   Toy Example for Using Boneh-Shaw Codes in the Proposed Algorithm

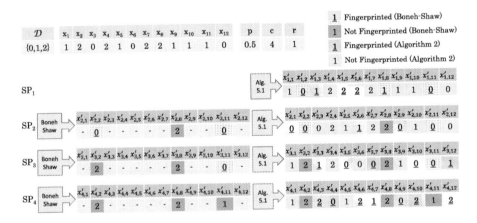

Fig. 4. An example execution of the proposed algorithm by integrating Boneh-Shaw codes.

Here, we describe the algorithm explained in Sect. 5.2 on a toy example, which is also illustrated in Fig. 4. Let the original data of Alice be $\mathcal{X} = [1, 2, 0, 2, 1, 0, 2, 2, 1, 1, 1, 0]$, where $l = 12$ and $\mathcal{D} = \{0, 1, 2\}$. Let p be 0.5 and Alice shares $\mathcal{X}_1' = [1, \underline{0}, \underline{1}, 2, \underline{2}, \underline{2}, 2, \underline{1}, 1, 1, \underline{0}, 0]$ with SP_1 after running Algorithm C.1, where underlined points represent fingerprinted data points.

C   The Fingerprinting Algorithm

In Algorithm C.1, we provide the algorithm discussed in Sect. 5.2.

D   Toy Example for the Proposed Detection Algorithm

The steps of the proposed detection algorithm (in Sect. 5.3) are also shown with an example in Fig. 5. After checking the similarity of leaked data with the fingerprinted data points of each SP, the algorithm adds $\lfloor 1/sim_{max} \rfloor = 2$ SPs into the suspect list. When the algorithm checks the 1st and the 2nd blocks of leaked data for SP_2, it does not return SP_2 as guilty since both blocks are $\hat{B}_R$. Then, it checks the 3rd and the 4th blocks of leaked data for SP_4 and returns SP_4 as guilty since the 4th block is $\hat{B}_1$ and the 3rd block is $\hat{B}_R$.

Algorithm C.1: Probabilistic fingerprinting scheme after assigning the Boneh-Shaw codeword to provide robustness against the collusion attack. Blue parts represent the difference with algorithm described in Section 4.

> **input** : Original data $\mathcal{X} = [x_1, x_2, \ldots, x_l]$, f_1 already assigned points in $\mathcal{X}'_i$ (f_i of them are fingerprinted), fingerprinting probability $\frac{p \cdot l - f_i}{l - f_1}$, probability adjustment parameter θ, block size $\lceil 1/p \rceil$, correlation threshold τ, pairwise correlations between data points.
>
> **output:** Fingerprinted copy $\mathcal{X}'_i = [x'_{i,1}, x'_{i,2}, \ldots, x'_{i,l}]$

1 $prob \longleftarrow \frac{p \cdot l - f_i}{l - f_1}$;
2 **forall** $j \in \{1, 2, \ldots, l\}$ **do**
3   **if** $x'_{i,j}$ *is not assigned* **then**
4   **forall** $k \in \{1, 2, \ldots, m\}$ **do**
5   **if** $j = 1$ & $x_j = d_k$ **then**
6                  $P_{x_j, d_k} \longleftarrow 1 - prob$;
7   **else if** $j = 1$ & $x_j \neq d_k$ **then**
8                  $P_{x_j, d_k} \longleftarrow prob/(m - 1)$;
9   **else if** $P(x_j = d_k | x_{j-1} = x'_{i,j-1}) < \tau$ **then**
10                  $P_{x_j, d_k} \longleftarrow 0$;
11   **else if** $x'_{i,j+1}$ *is assigned* & $P(x_{j+1} = x'_{i,j+1} | x_j = d_k) < \tau$ **then**
12                  $P_{x_j, d_k} \longleftarrow 0$;
13   **else if** $x_j = d_k$ **then**
14                  $P_{x_j, d_k} \longleftarrow 1 - prob$;
15   **end**
16   distribute the remaining probability (1 - (sum of assigned probabilities)) by assigning P_{x_j, d_k} directly proportional to the value of $P(x_j = d_k | x_{j-1} = x'_{i,j-1})$ if P_{x_j, d_k} is not assigned in the previous step;
17          $x'_{i,j} \longleftarrow$ random value from $\mathcal{D}$ using probability distribution $P_{x_j, d_1}, \ldots, P_{x_j, d_m}$;
18   **end**
19   **if** j *is multiple of* $\lceil 1/p \rceil$ **then**
20          $c \longleftarrow$ total number of fingerprinted data points;
21   **if** $c > p \cdot j$ **then**
22              $prob \longleftarrow p \cdot (1 - \theta)$;
23   **else if** $c < p \cdot j$ **then**
24              $prob \longleftarrow p \cdot (1 + \theta)$;
25   **else**
26              $prob \longleftarrow p$;
27   **end**
28   **end**
29 **end**

E   Experimental Results

E.1   Flipping and Subset Attacks

In this experiment, we compared the flipping and subset attacks in terms of their effect on the fingerprint robustness. Also, to compare the similarity-based and probabilistic detection techniques (which are the basic building blocks of the proposed detection algorithm in Sect. 5.3), we implemented them for this experiment. We set the total number of SPs to 1,000. Figure 6 shows the accuracy (a) of the both detection techniques for different values of p_f (probability of flipping a data point in flipping attack) and p_s (probability of removing a data point in subset attack).

E.2   Complexity and Practicality

In the proposed fingerprinting algorithm (Algorithm C.1), each data point sequentially decides on a probability for each possible value in set $\mathcal{D}$ and inserts

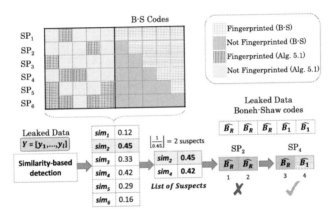

Fig. 5. An example execution of the detection algorithm.

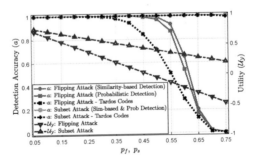

Fig. 6. Fingerprint robustness of the proposed scheme and Tardos codes against flipping and subset attacks for different values of p_f and p_s. Right y-axis is used to show the utility of the attacker.

the fingerprints accordingly. Hence, the complexity of fingerprinting algorithm is $\Theta(l \cdot m)$. To detect the guilty SP in case of data leakage, the data owner needs to compare all fingerprint patterns (given to all SPs) with the leaked data. Since the expected value of fingerprinted data points is $p \cdot l$ in each fingerprinted copy, the complexity of the detection algorithm is $\Theta(|\mathcal{S}| \cdot p \cdot l)$, where $|\mathcal{S}|$ is the number of SPs that received a fingerprinted copy. Note that this is also the storage complexity for Alice if she stores all the fingerprint patterns. As mentioned before, if Alice does not want to store all fingerprint patterns, she can just store the seed value for each SP, which slightly increases the complexity of detection algorithm since it requires Alice to run the fingerprinting algorithm along with the detection algorithm. Thus, we conclude that the running times of both fingerprinting algorithm and detection algorithm grow linearly with the design parameters.

Based on our implementation with Java using a computer with 1.8 GHz Dual-Core Intel Core i5 processor and 8 GB memory, we measured the average running time of fingerprinting algorithm to create one fingerprinted copy as 0.15 ms. and the average running time of detection algorithm as 3.11 ms. when $|\mathcal{S}| = 1000$, $l = 1000$, $p = 0.1$, and $m = 3$. These results also show the efficiency and practicality of the proposed scheme.

References

1. (2023). https://mathgen.stats.ox.ac.uk/impute/1000GP_Phase3.html. Accessed 10-January-2023
2. Ayday, E., Yilmaz, E., Yilmaz, A.: Robust optimization-based watermarking scheme for sequential data. In: 22nd International Symposium on Research in Attacks, Intrusions and Defenses ({RAID} 2019), pp. 323–336 (2019)
3. Bassia, P., Pitas, I., Nikolaidis, N.: Robust audio watermarking in the time domain. IEEE Trans. Multimed. **3**(2), 232–241 (2001)
4. Boneh, D., Shaw, J.: Collusion-secure fingerprinting for digital data. IEEE Trans. Inf. Theory **44**(5), 1897–1905 (1998)
5. Brassil, J., Low, S., Maxemchuk, N.: Copyright protection for the electronic distribution of text documents. Proc. IEEE **87**(7), 1181–1196 (1999)
6. Cox, I.J., Miller, M.L., Bloom, J.A., Honsinger, C.: Digital watermarking. Springer (2002)
7. Fodor, G., Schelkens, P., Dooms, A.: Fingerprinting codes under the weak marking assumption. IEEE Trans. Inf. Forensics Secur. **13**(6), 1495–1508 (2017)
8. Hartung, F., Girod, B.: Watermarking of uncompressed and compressed video. Signal Process. **66**(3), 283–301 (1998)
9. Jin, X., Zhang, Z., Wang, J., Li, D.: Watermarking spatial trajectory database. In: Zhou, L., Ooi, B.C., Meng, X. (eds.) DASFAA 2005. LNCS, vol. 3453, pp. 56–67. Springer, Heidelberg (2005). https://doi.org/10.1007/11408079_8
10. Li, Y., Swarup, V., Jajodia, S.: Fingerprinting relational databases: Schemes and specialties. IEEE Trans. Dependable Secure Comput. **2**(1), 34–45 (2005)
11. Nuida, K., et al.: An improvement of discrete tardos fingerprinting codes. Des. Codes Crypt. **52**(3), 339–362 (2009)
12. Papadimitriou, P., Garcia-Molina, H.: Data leakage detection. IEEE Trans. Knowl. Data Eng. **23**(1), 51–63 (2010)

13. Škorić, B., Katzenbeisser, S., Celik, M.U.: Symmetric tardos fingerprinting codes for arbitrary alphabet sizes. Des. Codes Crypt. **46**(2), 137–166 (2008)
14. Tardos, G.: Optimal probabilistic fingerprint codes. J. ACM (JACM) **55**(2), 1–24 (2008)
15. Wu, M., Trappe, W., Wang, Z.J., Liu, K.R.: Collusion-resistant fingerprinting for multimedia. IEEE Signal Process. Mag. **21**(2), 15–27 (2004)
16. Zhao, X., Liu, Q., Zheng, H., Zhao, B.Y.: Towards graph watermarks. In: Proceedings of the 2015 ACM on Conference on Online Social Networks, pp. 101–112. ACM (2015)

Optimized Stream-Cipher-Based Transciphering by Means of Functional-Bootstrapping

Adda-Akram Bendoukha[1]([⊠]), Pierre-Emmanuel Clet[2], Aymen Boudguiga[2], and Renaud Sirdey[2]

[1] Télécom SudParis, Institut Polytechnique de Paris, Evry, France
adda-akram.bendoukha@telecom-sudparis.eu
[2] Université Paris-Saclay, CEA-List, Gif-sur-Yvette, France
{pierre-emmanuel.clet,aymen.boudguiga,renaud.sirdey}@cea.fr

Abstract. Fully homomorphic encryption suffers from a large expansion in the size of encrypted data, which makes FHE impractical for low-bandwidth networks. Fortunately, transciphering allows to circumvent this issue by involving a symmetric cryptosystem which does not carry the disadvantage of a large expansion factor, and maintains the ability to recover an FHE ciphertext with the cost of extra homomorphic computations on the receiver side. Recent works have started to investigate the efficiency of TFHE as the FHE layer in transciphering, combined with various symmetric schemes including a NIST finalist for lightweight cryptography, namely Grain128-AEAD. Yet, this has so far been done without taking advantage of TFHE functional bootstrapping abilities, that is, evaluating any discrete function "for free" within the bootstrapping operation. In this work, we thus investigate the use of TFHE functional bootstrapping for implementing Grain128-AEAD in a more efficient base ($B > 2$) representation, rather than a binary one. This significantly reduces the overall number of necessary bootstrappings in a homomorphic run of the stream-cipher, for example reducing the number of bootstrappings required in the warm-up phase by a factor of ≈ 3 when $B = 16$.

Keywords: FHE · stream-ciphers · transciphering · functional bootstrapping

1 Introduction

Despite its privacy advantages in cloud services, Fully Homomorphic Encryption (FHE) has a notable drawback of expanding the size of encrypted data to

This work was supported by the France ANR project ANR-22-CE39-0002 EQUIHID (first author) and France 2030 ANR project ANR-22-PECY-003 SecureCompute (third and fourth authors).

A.-A. Bendoukha—This author's contribution to this work was done while at CEA List.

© IFIP International Federation for Information Processing 2023
Published by Springer Nature Switzerland AG 2023
V. Atluri and A. L. Ferrara (Eds.): DBSec 2023, LNCS 13942, pp. 91–109, 2023.
https://doi.org/10.1007/978-3-031-37586-6_6

a significant extent, which limits its practicality for low-bandwidth networks. However, transciphering provides a solution by using a symmetric cryptosystem that does not result in a large expansion factor and still allows the recovery of an FHE ciphertext with extra computation on the receiver's end.

Previous research [BBS22] has shown the effectiveness of TFHE [CGGI18] as the FHE layer in transciphering, combined with various symmetric schemes such as Grain128-AEAD [HJMM06], which is a finalist for NIST call for lightweight cryptography. The functional bootstrapping feature of TFHE allows the evaluation of any function with the bootstrapping operation, leading to a significant improvement in transciphering performance.

This work explores the utilization of TFHE's functional bootstrapping to implement the boolean operators which are required for updating the internal state of a stream-cipher. The approach involves representing the internal state of the stream-cipher using decomposition in a base B ($B > 2$) instead of a binary one. This results in reducing the necessary number of bootstrappings in a homomorphic run of the stream-cipher by a factor of $\log(B)$. As such, this approach is expected to provide a notable speedup on the server side.

1.1   Transciphering

Transciphering, also referred to as Proxy-reencryption, uses a symmetric cryptosystem as a way of securely *compressing* FHE ciphertexts prior to their transmission to the cloud. Regarding symmetric cryptosystems, the expansion factor is approximately equal to 1^1. Meanwhile, *decompressing* the ciphertext returns a full-size FHE ciphertext that will be used as input to the desired computation on the cloud side.

The main idea behind transciphering is to reduce the size of homomorphically encrypted data to be sent to the Cloud by encrypting it symmetrically instead, and preserving the ability to recover a homomorphic encryption of the initial data. To do so, a client encrypts his message m with a symmetric encryption scheme as: $\mathsf{SYM.Enc_{SYM.sk}}(m)$, and encrypts the symmetric key $\mathsf{SYM.sk}$ with a homomorphic cryptosystem as: $\mathsf{FHE.Enc_{FHE.pk}}(\mathsf{SYM.sk})$. At the reception of $(\mathsf{SYM.Enc_{SYM.sk}}(m), \mathsf{FHE.Enc_{FHE.pk}}(\mathsf{SYM.sk}))$, the Cloud server homomorphically runs the symmetric cryptosystem's decryption function. That is, he evaluates $\mathsf{SYM.Dec}$ using the FHE encryption of the symmetric key: $\mathsf{FHE.Enc_{FHE.pk}}(\mathsf{SYM.sk})$ to get $\mathsf{FHE.Enc_{FHE.pk}}(m)$.

With a stream-cipher, the client encrypts his message m with a keystream ks as: $m \oplus ks$, where $\oplus$ is the XOR operator. Then, he sends $m \oplus ks$ and the stream-cipher secret key $\mathsf{FHE.Enc_{FHE.pk}}(\mathsf{SYM.sk})$ to the Cloud server. The latter runs the stream-cipher warm-up homomorphically with $\mathsf{FHE.Enc_{FHE.pk}}(\mathsf{SYM.sk})$ to get: $\mathsf{FHE.Enc_{FHE.pk}}(ks)$. Then, he computes $m \oplus ks \oplus \mathsf{FHE.Enc_{FHE.pk}}(ks)$ to obtain: $\mathsf{FHE.Enc_{FHE.pk}}(m)$.

---

[1] Symmetric algorithms will usually lead to negligible or small overheads due to some padding rule.

The size of the plaintext m can be arbitrarily large, whereas the size of the symmetric key SYM.sk is constant and typically small enough to be homomorphically encrypted and transmitted only once. This results in compression, which comes at the expense of running the symmetric scheme's decryption function homomorphically on the server side.

In terms of security, as most practically-used symmetric encryption algorithms do not have formally established indistinguishability properties, it should be emphasized that using transciphering jeopardizes the IND-CPA property of the FHE scheme (FHE schemes can be at most IND-CCA1 and all the schemes presently used in practice are only IND-CPA). This should however not be considered an issue in practice, provided that symmetric encryption more often than not teams with provably-secure public-key encryption for efficiency reasons in practical scenarios, and FHE is no exception. Nevertheless, if we assume a perfect PRF on the symmetric side, the resulting construction would be IND-CPA [CCF+18a].

Yet, one important point is to choose the key size of the symmetric encryption algorithm consistently with the parameters of the FHE scheme. At present, common practice generally targets FHE security parameters λ of around 128 bits and not more as FHE performances significantly decreases in the parameter regimes of larger λ. As such, at present, transciphering should consider symmetric algorithms with 128 bits keys.

1.2   Related Work

In [CCF+18a] authors introduced transciphering using a stream-cipher, as a secure and efficient way of compressing FHE ciphertexts. They also provide the first FHE-friendly 80-bits-key stream-cipher, Trivium, which was later extended to Kreyvium [CCF+18b] that accommodates a 128-bits key.

With the advent of TFHE, and its fast bootstrapping operation, multiplicative depth is no longer the bottleneck in fast-bootstrapping-based FHE. Therefore, the possibility to homomorphically evaluate more sophisticated ciphers became reachable. In [HMR20] authors evaluate FiLip with third generation homomorphic schemes GSW [GSW13] and TFHE. [CHK+20] propose a stream-cipher dubbed HERA suited for a hybrid HE framework allowing switching from CKKS [CKKS16] to BFV [FV12]. On the other hand, [DGH+21] provides a framework to build transciphering schemes, as well as the a stream-cipher called PASTA, the last one of the RASTA family of ciphers. PASTA is well suited for HE schemes supporting batching such as BGV [BGV12] and BFV [FV12].

Homomorphic evaluations of block-ciphers also has been studied under both levelled and bootstrapping-based HE schemes. Low-MC [ARS+15] was designed as an attempt to provide a minimal multiplicative-depth yet secure block-cipher suited for levelled HE schemes. Other attempts to provide optimized FHE implementations of the advanced encryption standard AES were investigated [GHS12a] but remain unpractical for real-life client/server use-cases. Subsequent works attempting to design FHE-friendly ciphers investigate the design of generic smaller stream or block-cipher components such as reduced-multiplicative depth Sboxes [BP12] or boolean functions [CM19]. These components can then be integrated in the design of FHE-friendly ciphers, providing a reasonable security/FHE-friendliness tradeoff.

As for TFHE, in [GBA21], $\mathbb{Z}_B$ plaintext spaces of more than two elements were investigated. In addition, many novel techniques [GBA21, KS22, OKC20, CZB+22] investigated TFHE functional bootstrapping for evaluating discrete non-linear functions over integers represented by their digits decomposition in a base $B > 2$.

1.3   Contribution

Unlike previous works where the efforts were made to build FHE-friendly ciphers that accommodate an FHE scheme or a class of FHE schemes[2] we focus on existing and standardized symmetric schemes. We provide a generic technique which reduces the number of bootstrappings required to *transcipher* from a symmetric ciphertext to a TFHE one, that applies to a wide range of ciphers. We validate our approach by providing an efficient implementation of Grain128-AEAD with TFHE. Indeed, thanks to its bootstrapping, TFHE offers greater freedom in the choice of the symmetric cryptosystem used for transciphering, allowing to perform more operations and relaxing the constraints imposed by the multiplicative depth[3].

Overall, we improve the work of Bendoukha et al., [BBS22], in which the authors benchmarked implementations of transciphering with various stream-ciphers (Trivium, Kreyvium and Grain128-AEAD) with TFHE, using the straightforward representation of the internal states of stream-ciphers as arrays of TFHE encrypted bits. In this work, we investigate a digit representation of these stream-ciphers internal states in a sequence of k digits in base B.

For this purpose we redefine boolean operations in bases $B > 2$ making the most of TFHE's functional bootstrapping. Reducing the number of ciphertexts reduces the number of bootstrappings needed to update the internal state of a stream-cipher by a factor $\log_2(B)$. Since the bootstrapping is by far the most time-consuming operation in TFHE, this technique results in a significant speed-up of the decompression phase on the server side.

To illustrate the speed-up brought by this technique, we implement a NIST finalist for lightweight cryptography, Grain128-AEAD [HJMM06], using the TFHE library[4]. Our implementation is 40% faster than the one from [BBS22] with binary ciphertexts representation of cipher's internal state. The choice of Grain128-AEAD is motivated by the fact that besides (so far) unpractical attempts to run AES in the homomorphic domain [GHS12a], no other works

---

[2] Based on their approach: bootstrapping or levelled, and their plaintext-space: binary, real, or $\mathbb{Z}_q$.

[3] The multiplicative depth of a circuit is the maximum number of successive multiplications in the circuit.

[4] https://github.com/tfhe/tfhe.

investigates the use of a standard cipher in a transciphering construction. Therefore, our work aims at demonstrating the feasibility and practicality of standard
ciphers under TFHE. In addition, its lightweight design induces a small number of
gates which translates in a small number of homomorphic operations when using
TFHE (which is not subject to multiplicative depth constraints). Additionally, it
is also amenable to efficient x-bits implementations (e.g., as in [BLSK19]) which
represents a good starting point for using TFHE beyond gate-bootstrapping.
Grain128-AEAD provides also a MAC computation along with the encryption
procedure. This feature can be used complementarily to transciphering in order
to perform an oblivious integrity check on the server side as described in [BBS21].

1.4 Paper Organization

The remainder of this paper is organized as follows. After recalling the principle of transciphering as a generic framework in the introduction (in Sect. 1.1),
we review our target FHE cryptosystem TFHE in Sect. 2. Then, in Sect. 3, we
describe how to use TFHE functional bootstrapping for computing boolean operations efficiently in the homomorphic domain. Indeed, we specify boolean operations for encrypted digits, from bases 4 and 16. In Sect. 4, we apply our new
operations to transciphering with the stream-cipher Grain128-AEAD [HJM+21].
Finally, we discuss implementation details and performance results in Sect. 5
before concluding the paper.

2 TFHE

2.1 Notations

We refer to the real torus by $\mathbb{T} = \mathbb{R}/\mathbb{Z}$. $\mathbb{T}$ is the additive group of real numbers modulo 1 ($\mathbb{R}\ mod[1]$) and it is a $\mathbb{Z}$-module. $\mathbb{T}_N[X]$ denotes the $\mathbb{Z}$-module
$\mathbb{R}[X]/(X^N + 1)\ mod[1]$ of torus polynomials, where N is a power of 2. $\mathcal{R}$ is the
ring $\mathbb{Z}[X]/(X^N + 1)$ and its subring of polynomials with binary coefficients is
$\mathbb{B}_N[X] = \mathbb{B}[X]/(X^N + 1)$ ($\mathbb{B} = \{0, 1\}$). Finally, we denote respectively by $[x]_\mathbb{T}$,
$[x]_{\mathbb{T}_N[X]}$ and $[x]_\mathcal{R}$ the encryption of x over $\mathbb{T}$, $\mathbb{T}_N[X]$ or $\mathcal{R}$. The plaintext space
(prior to encoding as torus elements) with respect to the FHE encryption layer
is denoted $\mathcal{M}$.

We refer to vectors by bold letters. $\langle \boldsymbol{x}, \boldsymbol{y} \rangle$ is the inner product of two vectors
$\boldsymbol{x}$ and $\boldsymbol{y}$. We denote matrices by capital letters, and the set of matrices with m
rows and n columns with entries sampled in $\mathbb{K}$ by $\mathcal{M}_{m,n}(\mathbb{K})$. $x \xleftarrow{\$} \mathbb{K}$ denotes
sampling x uniformly from $\mathbb{K}$, while $x \xleftarrow{\mathcal{N}(\mu,\sigma^2)} \mathbb{K}$ refers to sampling x from $\mathbb{K}$
following a Gaussian distribution of mean μ and variance σ^2.

2.2 TFHE Structures

The TFHE encryption scheme was proposed in 2016 [CGGI16]. It introduces
the TLWE problem as an adaptation of the LWE problem to $\mathbb{T}$. TFHE relies on
three structures to encrypt plaintexts defined over $\mathbb{T}$, $\mathbb{T}_N[X]$ or $\mathcal{R}$:

- **TLWE Sample:** $(\boldsymbol{a}, b)$ is a valid TLWE sample if $\boldsymbol{a} \xleftarrow{\$} \mathbb{T}^n$ and $b \in \mathbb{T}$ verifies $b = \langle \boldsymbol{a}, \boldsymbol{s} \rangle + e$, where $\boldsymbol{s} \xleftarrow{\$} \mathbb{B}^n$ is the secret key, and $e \xleftarrow{\mathcal{N}(0, \sigma^2)} \mathbb{T}$.

- **TRLWE Sample:** a pair $(\boldsymbol{a}, b) \in \mathbb{T}_N[X]^k \times \mathbb{T}_N[X]$ is a valid TRLWE sample if $\boldsymbol{a} \xleftarrow{\$} \mathbb{T}_N[X]^k$, and $b = \langle \boldsymbol{a}, \boldsymbol{s} \rangle + e$, where $\boldsymbol{s} \xleftarrow{\$} \mathbb{B}_N[X]^k$ is a TRLWE secret key and $e \xleftarrow{\mathcal{N}(0, \sigma^2)} \mathbb{T}_N[X]$ is a noise polynomial.

  Let $\mathcal{M} \subset \mathbb{T}_N[X]$ (or $\mathcal{M} \subset \mathbb{T}$) be the discrete message space[5]. To encrypt a message $m \in \mathcal{M} \subset \mathbb{T}_N[X]$, we add $(\boldsymbol{0}, m) \in \mathbb{T}_N[X]^k \times \mathbb{T}_N[X]$ to a fresh TRLWE sample (or a fresh TLWE sample if $\mathcal{M} \subset \mathbb{T}$). In the following, we refer to an encryption of m with the secret key $\boldsymbol{s}$ as a T(R)LWE ciphertext noted $\boldsymbol{c} \in \text{T(R)LWE}_{\boldsymbol{s}}(m)$.

  To decrypt a sample $\boldsymbol{c} \in \text{T(R)LWE}_{\boldsymbol{s}}(m)$, we compute its *phase* $\phi(\boldsymbol{c}) = b - \langle \boldsymbol{a}, \boldsymbol{s} \rangle = m + e$. Then, we round to it to the nearest element of $\mathcal{M}$. Therefore, if the error e was chosen to be small enough while ensuring security, the decryption will be accurate.

- **TRGSW Sample:** a vector of $(k+1) \cdot l$ TRLWE samples is a TRGSW sample. To encrypt a message $m \in \mathcal{R}$, we add $m \cdot H$ to a TRGSW sample, where H is a gadget matrix[6] using an integer B_g as a basis for its decomposition. Chilotti et al., [CGGI18] defines an external product between a TRGSW ciphertext A encrypting $m_a \in \mathcal{R}$ and a TRLWE ciphertext $\boldsymbol{b}$ encrypting $m_b \in \mathbb{T}_N[X]$. This external product consists in multiplying A by the approximate decomposition of $\boldsymbol{b}$ with respect to H (Definition 3.12 in [CGGI18]). It yields an encryption of $m_a \cdot m_b$ i.e., a TRLWE ciphertext $\boldsymbol{c} \in \text{TRLWE}_{\boldsymbol{s}}(m_a \cdot m_b)$. Otherwise, the external product allows also to compute a controlled MUX gate (CMUX) where the selector is $C_b \in \text{TRGSW}_{\boldsymbol{s}}(b)$, $b \in \{0, 1\}$, and the inputs are $\boldsymbol{c}_0 \in \text{TRLWE}_{\boldsymbol{s}}(m_0)$ and $\boldsymbol{c}_1 \in \text{TRLWE}_{\boldsymbol{s}}(m_1)$.

2.3 TFHE Bootstrapping

TFHE bootstrapping relies mainly on three building blocks:

- **Blind Rotate:** rotates a plaintext polynomial encrypted as a TRLWE ciphertext by an encrypted position ($\boldsymbol{c}_p \in \text{TRLWE}_{\boldsymbol{s}}(p)$). It takes as inputs: a TRLWE ciphertext $\boldsymbol{c} \in \text{TRLWE}_{\boldsymbol{k}}(m)$, a rescaled and rounded vector of $\boldsymbol{c}_p$ represented by $(a_1, \ldots, a_n, a_{n+1} = b)$ where $\forall i$, $a_i \in \mathbb{Z}_{2N}$, and n TRGSW ciphertexts encrypting $(s_1, \ldots, s_n)$ where $\forall i$, $s_i \in \mathbb{B}$. It returns a TRLWE ciphertext $\boldsymbol{c}' \in \text{TRLWE}_{\boldsymbol{k}}(X^{\langle a, s \rangle - b} \cdot m)$. In this paper, we will refer to this algorithm by BlindRotate. With respect to independence heuristic[7] stated

---

[5] In practice, we discretize the Torus with respect to our plaintext modulus. For example, if we want to encrypt $m \in \mathbb{Z}_4 = \{0, 1, 2, 3\}$, we encode it in $\mathbb{T}$ as one of the following value $\{0, 0.25, 0.5, 0.75\}$.

[6] Refer to Definition 3.6 and Lemma 3.7 in TFHE paper [CGGI18] for more information about the gadget matrix H.

[7] The independence heuristic ensures that all the coefficients of the errors of TLWE, TRLWE or TRGSW samples are independent and concentrated. More precisely, they are σ-subgaussian where σ is the square-root of their variance.

in [CGGI18], the variance $\mathcal{V}_{BR}$ of the resulting noise after a BlindRotate satisfies the formula:

$$\mathcal{V}_{BR} < V_c + \mathcal{E}_{BR} \tag{1}$$

where $\mathcal{E}_{BR} = n \left((k+1)\ell N \left(\frac{B_g}{2} \right)^2 \vartheta_{BK} + \frac{(1+kN)}{4.Bg^{2l}} \right)$.

V_c is the variance of the noise of the input ciphertext c, and ϑ_{BK} is the variance of the error of the bootstrapping key. Note that the noise of the BlindRotate is independent from the noise of the encrypted position c_p.

- **TLWE Sample Extract:** takes as inputs both a ciphertext $c \in$ TRLWE$_k(m)$ and a position $p \in [\![0, N[\![$, and returns a TLWE ciphertext $c' \in$ TLWE$_k(m_p)$ where m_p is the pth coefficient of the polynomial m. In this paper, we will refer to this algorithm by SampleExtract. This algorithm does not add any noise to the ciphertext.

- **Public Functional Keyswitching:** transforms a set of p ciphertexts $c_i \in$ TLWE$_k(m_i)$ into the resulting ciphertext $c' \in$ T(R)LWE$_s(f(m_1, \ldots, m_p))$, where $f()$ is a public linear morphism from $\mathbb{T}^p$ to $\mathbb{T}_N[X]$. This algorithm requires 2 parameters: the decomposition basis B_{KS} and the precision of the decomposition t. In this paper, we will refer to this algorithm by KeySwitch. As stated in [CGGI18, GBA21], the variance $\mathcal{V}_{KS}$ of the resulting noise after KeySwitch follows the formula:

$$\mathcal{V}_{KS} < R^2 \cdot V_c + \mathcal{E}_{KS}^{n,N} \tag{2}$$

where $\mathcal{E}_{KS}^{n,N} = nN \left(t\vartheta_{KS} + \frac{base^{-2t}}{4} \right)$.

V_c is the variance of the noise of the input ciphertext c, R is the Lipschitz constant of f and ϑ_{KS} the variance of the error of the keyswitching key. In this paper and in most cases, $R = 1$.

TFHE specifies a gate bootstrapping to reduce the noise level of a TLWE sample that encrypts the result of a boolean gate evaluation on two ciphertexts, each of them encrypting a binary input. TFHE gate bootstrapping steps are summarized in Algorithm 1. The step 1 consists in selecting a value $\hat{m} \in \mathbb{T}$ which will serve later for setting the coefficients of the test polynomial $testv$ (in step 3). The step 2 rescales the components of the input ciphertext c as elements of $\mathbb{Z}_{2N}$. The step 3 defines the test polynomial $testv$. Note that for all $p \in [\![0, 2N[\![$, the constant term of $testv \cdot X^p$ is $\hat{m}$ if $p \in]\!] \frac{N}{2}, \frac{3N}{2}]\!]$ and $-\hat{m}$ otherwise. The step 4 returns an accumulator $ACC \in$ TRLWE$_{s'}(testv \cdot X^{\langle \bar{a}, s \rangle - \bar{b}})$. Indeed, the constant term of ACC is $-\hat{m}$ if c encrypts 0, or $\hat{m}$ if c encrypts 1 as long as the noise of the ciphertext is small enough. Then, step 5 creates a new ciphertext $\bar{c}$ by extracting the constant term of ACC and adding to it $(\mathbf{0}, \hat{m})$. That is, $\bar{c}$ either encrypts 0 if c encrypts 0, or m if c encrypts 1 (By choosing $m = \frac{1}{2}$, we get a fresh encryption of 1).

Since a bootstrapping operation is a BlindRotate over a noiseless TRLWE followed by a Keyswitch, the bootstrapping noise ($\mathcal{V}_{BS}$) satisfies:

$$\mathcal{V}_{BS} < \mathcal{E}_{BS}, \text{ where } \mathcal{E}_{BS} = \mathcal{E}_{BR} + \mathcal{E}_{KS}^{N,1} \tag{3}$$

Algorithm 1. TFHE gate bootstrapping [CGGI18]

Input: a constant $m \in \mathbb{T}$, a TLWE sample $c = (a, b) \in \text{TLWE}_s(x \cdot \frac{1}{2})$ with $x \in \mathbb{B}$,
a bootstrapping key $BK_{s \to s'} = (BK_i \in \text{TRGSW}_{S'}(s_i))_{i \in [\![1,n]\!]}$ where S' is the
TRLWE interpretation of a secret key s'
Output: a TLWE sample $\bar{c} \in \text{TLWE}_s(x.m)$
1: Let $\hat{m} = \frac{1}{2}m \in \mathbb{T}$ (pick one of the two possible values)
2: Let $\bar{b} = \lfloor 2Nb \rceil$ and $\bar{a}_i = \lfloor 2Na_i \rceil \in \mathbb{Z}, \forall i \in [\![1, n]\!]$
3: Let $testv := (1 + X + \cdots + X^{N-1}) \cdot X^{\frac{N}{2}} \cdot \hat{m} \in \mathbb{T}_N[X]$
4: $ACC \gets \text{BlindRotate}((\mathbf{0}, testv), (\bar{a}_1, \ldots, \bar{a}_n, \bar{b}), (BK_1, \ldots, BK_n))$
5: $\bar{c} = (\mathbf{0}, \hat{m}) + \text{SampleExtract}(ACC)$
6: return $\text{KeySwitch}_{s' \to s}(\bar{c})$

2.4   TFHE Functional Bootstrapping

Functional bootstrapping [CJP21, KS21, YXS+21, CLOT21, CZB+22] refers to TFHE ability of implementing a Look-Up Table (LUT) of any function through the bootstrapping. In particular, TFHE is well-suited for negacyclic function[8], as the plaintext space for TFHE is $\mathbb{T}$, where $[0, \frac{1}{2}[$ corresponds to positive values and $[\frac{1}{2}, 1[$ to negative ones, and the bootstrapping step 2 of the Algorithm 1 encodes elements from $\mathbb{T}$ into powers of X modulo $(X^N + 1)$, and $X^{\alpha+N} \equiv -X^\alpha mod[X^N + 1]$.

3   Functional-Bootstrapping-Defined Boolean Operators

TFHE was initially presented in [CGGI16] as a bit-oriented cryptosystem. The homomorphic operations in this setting are limited to boolean operations (homomorphic XOR and homomorphic AND). Addition and multiplication of integers are defined using their respective binary circuits, and a bootstrapping is performed after every boolean gate.

Representing the internal state of a stream-cipher as an array of ciphertexts encrypting two bits or more allows the computation of the round function of a given stream-cipher with less bootstrappings compared to the binary representation (where each bit is encrypted separately). A non-realistic, yet compelling illustration, is to represent the entire internal state as a single ciphertext, and to encode the round function of a stream-cipher in a test vector as a $\mathbb{Z}_q \to \mathbb{Z}_q$ function, where q is a large enough integer. Doing so, a single functional bootstrapping would be required to update the internal state. Unfortunately, achieving this is not practical in real-world scenarios, as it requires enormous parameters for TFHE, resulting in computation times that are not realistic.

Our work aims at reducing the number of ciphertexts encrypting the internal state of a stream-cipher, and consequently reduces the number of necessary bootstrappings per round of the stream-cipher. Boolean operators in higher bases

---

[8] Negacyclic functions are antiperiodic functions over $\mathbb{T}$ with period $\frac{1}{2}$, i.e., $f(x) = -f(x + \frac{1}{2})$.

(i.e., non-binary bases) have to be redefined using Look-Up Tables (LUTs), which perfectly complies with the functional bootstrapping supported by TFHE.

3.1 Bitwise Operators

We provide a generic approach to evaluate any $\mathbb{Z}_B^2 \to \mathbb{Z}_B$ boolean function over integer ciphertexts with $\mathcal{M} = \mathbb{Z}_B$, using TFHE functional bootstrapping and [GBA21] chaining idea.

We denote by Op the logic gate that we want to evaluate. We set:

$$g_i^{Op} : \begin{array}{ccc} \mathbb{Z}_B & \to & \mathbb{Z}_B \\ x & \mapsto & Op(x, i) \end{array}$$

and $G_i^{Op}(X) = \sum_{k=0}^{B-1} g_i^{Op}(k) X^k$ its polynomial representation.

The test vector of our functional bootstrapping is then constructed from the polynomial representation of the lookup table which is of degree $B^2 - 1$:

$$v(X) = \sum_{i=0}^{B-1} G_i^{Op}(X) \cdot X^{iB} \tag{4}$$

For two values x and $y \in [\![0, B-1]\!]$, we observe that the $(Bx+y)$-th coefficient of v is equal to $Op(x, y)$.

The test vector TV_B^{Op} of degree $(N-1)$ used in the corresponding functional bootstrapping procedure is constructed from v by repeating each coefficient $\frac{N}{B^2}$ times, as follows:

$$TV_B^{Op}(X) = \sum_{i=0}^{B} \sum_{j=0}^{B} \sum_{k=0}^{\frac{N}{B^2}-1} g_i^{Op}(j) X^{k+j \cdot \frac{N}{B^2} + i \cdot \frac{N}{B}} \tag{5}$$

Once the test vector constructed, running a bootstrapping on the TLWE encryption of the linear combination of $(Bx + y)$ and the input TRLWE ciphertext from TV_B^{Op}, outputs a TRLWE ciphertext encryption of $Op(x, y)$.

Fact. Let's consider two TLWE ciphertexts c_1 and c_2 encrypting respectively the integer values a and $b \in \mathbb{Z}_B$. Calling TFHE gate-bootstrapping on the TLWE sample $c_1 B + c_2$, with a test vector constructed from v as in Eq. 5 outputs a TLWE sample encrypting the value $Op(a, b)$ with probability[9]:

$$\mathbb{P}(success) = \mathbb{P}(Err(c_1 B + c_2) \le \frac{1}{4B^2}) = \text{erf}(\frac{1}{4B^2\sqrt{B^2 V_{c_1} + V_{c_2} + V_{rounding}} \cdot \sqrt{2}})$$

where:

- $\text{erf}(x) = \frac{2}{\sqrt{\pi}} \int_0^x e^{-t^2} dt$ is the Gaussian error function.
- V_{c_1} is the variance of the error of c_1.
- V_{c_2} is the variance of the error of c_2.
- $V_{rounding} = \frac{n+1}{48N^2}$ is the variance of the rounding operation after re-scaling in the bootstrapping algorithm (Line 2 of Algorithm 1).

---

[9] Please refer to [CZB+22] for a complete description on how to compute this probability.

3.2   Example: AND Gate with $B = 4$

We consider a message m in $[\![0, 3]\!]$ as the concatenation of two bits thanks to its binary decomposition. We describe in this example how to compute a bitwise AND gate between the ciphertexts c_1 and c_2 encrypting 2 messages m_1 and m_2.

We refer by AND_i to the truth table of the bitwise AND gate between a message m and i. Thus, we get:

$$\text{AND}_0 = (0, 0, 0, 0), \; \text{AND}_1 = (0, 1, 0, 1), \; \text{AND}_2 = (0, 0, 2, 2), \; \text{AND}_3 = (0, 1, 2, 3).$$

Then, we build a test vector TV_4^{AND}, as described in Eq. 5, from the polynomial

$$v(X) = X^5 + X^7 + 2X^{10} + 2X^{11} + X^{13} + 2X^{14} + 3X^{15}$$

Finally, we get, by applying a functional bootstrapping to $(c_1 + B \cdot c_2)$ with TV_4^{AND} as a test vector, an encryption of $\text{AND}(m_1, m_2)$ by selecting the element $\frac{N}{B^2} \cdot (m_1 + B \cdot m_2 + e)$ of the test vector where e is an error term.

Note that a similar procedure can be applied to any bitwise operator.

3.3   Byte Shifts

An 8-bit implementation of stream-cipher often requires the bytes of the internal state to be shifted left or right in order to align the bits to be operated according to the encryption/decryption specifications. When representing the internal state as base 2 ciphertexts, a byte shift is a literal shift (simply consisting of memory access and copy operations). However, when a byte is represented as k ciphertexts encrypting base B integers, operating a shift with a position that is not a multiple of $\log_2(B)$ will have the effect of propagating a *carry* to the next digit, and will require additional computation of the non-linear function that provides both the output of the shift from the digit and the carry to propagate to the next one. The best way to compute non-linear functions in TFHE is to use a functional bootstrapping. Hence, our technique performs $\log_2(B)$-times less bootstrappings to compute AND, OR, and XOR operations, but an additional number of bootstrappings is required to perform the shifts. Despite this drawback, our method succeeds in significantly reducing the overall number of bootstrappings. Table 1 gives an estimation of the number of bootstrappings per round for an 8-bits implementation of Grain128-AEAD in different bases representations.

Base 4. A base 4 ciphertext representation of a byte is composed of four digits $b = (d_0, d_1, d_2, d_3)$, encrypted as $c = (\text{TLWE}_{sk}(d_0), \text{TLWE}_{sk}(d_1), \text{TLWE}_{sk}(d_2), \text{TLWE}_{sk}(d_3))$. Shifting by an odd position $r = 2s + 1$ is performed as s direct shifts, followed by a shift by one position that implies a functional bootstrapping-based algorithm.

We would like to extract two elements from every digit in a sequential fashion: (1) the result of the shift on the current digit $res(d_i)$, and (2) the carry it will propagate to the next digit $carry(d_i)$. The carry cannot be obtained using a linear function, so we extract it by using a functional bootstrapping corresponding to the following look-up tables (LUTs):

$$v^+ = [0, 0, 1, 1] \text{ if } r > 0$$
$$v^- = [0, 1, 0, 1] \text{ if } r < 0$$

The TRLWE test vectors $TV^+(X)$ and $TV^-(X)$ of degree $(N-1)$ are afterwards generated by using the same method as in Eq. 5 for v^+ and v^-, respectively.

Once the carry from digit d_i is obtained, the next element to extract is the result of the shift over d_i, which is equal to $2 \cdot d_i \bmod 4$. TFHE provides a natural modulo $|\mathcal{M}|$ operation due to the circular nature of the torus, but any other homomorphic evaluation of a modulo with a different moduli smaller than $|\mathcal{M}|$ would require extra bootstrapping. In our case $|\mathcal{M}| = 2B^2 = 32$. However we observed that the required value can be obtained using the linear combination $res(d_i) = (2 \cdot d_i - 4 \cdot carry(d_i)) + carry(d_{i-1})$ if $r > 0$, and $res(d_i) = (2 \cdot d_i - 4 \cdot carry(d_i)) + carry(d_{i+1})$ otherwise. This provides a byte shift operation at the cost of (at most) 3 bootstrappings, and four linear of combinations. These steps are summarized in Algorithm 2. Note that the inserted s digits (at the beginning or at the end depending on the sign of r) are noiseless-trivial samples of 0^{10}. Thus, in subsequent computations, when evaluating a gate with an operand equal to a noiseless-trivial sample of 0, no bootstrapping is needed[11].

Base 16. A base 16 ciphertext representation of a byte is composed of two digits. $b = (d_0, d_1)$. The carry extraction only applies to d_0. To shift by a positive position $pos = 4s + r$, we perform s literal ciphertexts shifts (free in terms of bootstrappings) followed by $0 \le r \le 3$ shifts involving carry-handling operations.

The three possible values for r are handled using three lookup-tables C-LUT$_1^+$, C-LUT$_2^+$, and C-LUT$_3^+$ such that: C-LUT$_i^+[d]$ stores the carry value that corresponds to shifting the digit d by i positions. Once the carry is obtained from d, we run a second bootstrapping to extract the resulting ciphertext from the operation $(d >> r)$ using the same approach. Three look-up tables S-LUT$_1^+$ S-LUT$_2^+$ S-LUT$_3^+$ such that S-LUT$_i^+[d] = (d >> i)$ are used to extract the resulting digit from the shift operation. The carry is afterwards propagated to d_1 followed by an evaluation of the same shift lookup table. Therefore, (at most) three calls to TFHE functional bootstrappings are needed to shift a byte ciphertext representation in the internal state. Following the same reasoning as with base 4 byte shifts, in the case where $pos > 4$, $\lceil \frac{pos}{4} \rceil$ noiseless-trivial encryptions of 0 are inserted at the first digits resulting in bootstrapping-free operations over these digits in subsequent operations. The same mechanism is applied for backward byte shifts with respective S-LUT$_i^-$ and C-LUT$_i^-$ lookup tables. Algorithm 3 describes this procedure.

---

[10] $c = (\boldsymbol{a}, b)$ is a noiseless-trivial encryption of 0 if $a_i = 0 \ \forall i \in [n]$ and $b = 0$. In other words, it represents an encoding of 0 as TLWE or TRLWE sample.

[11] The output of OR and XOR gates when one of the two operands is a noiseless trivial sample of 0 is equal to the other operand, while the output of an AND gate is a noiseless-trivial encryption of 0. The same stands for subsequent shifts of such samples, both the carry and the results are set to noiseless trivial samples of 0.

Algorithm 2. Byte shift with base 4

Input: 4 TLWE samples encrypting a byte b in little-endian representation [12] $c = (c_0, c_1, c_2, c_3)$, an odd position $r = 2s + 1$, and a bootstrapping key $BK_{s \to s'} = (BK_i \in \text{TRGSW}_{S'}(s_i))_{i \in [\![1,n]\!]}$ where S' is the TRLWE interpretation of a secret key s'

Output: 4 TLWE samples $(\hat{c}_0, \hat{c}_1, \hat{c}_2, \hat{c}_3)$ encrypting b shifted by r positions in little-endian representation.

1: **if** $r > 0$ **then**   ▷ right shift
2:      **for** i = 0 to (3 - s) **do**
3:          $\hat{c}_{i+s} = c_i$
4:      carry(c_0) = FunctionalBootstrapping$(c_0, TV^+(X), BK)$
5:      $\hat{c}_0 = 2 \cdot c_0 - 4 \cdot carry(c_0)$
6:      **for** i = 1 to 2 **do**
7:          carry(c_i) = FunctionalBootstrapping$(c_i, TV^+(X), BK)$
8:          $\hat{c}_i = (2 \cdot c_i - 4 \cdot carry(c_i)) + carry(c_{i-1})$
9:      carry(c_3) = FunctionalBootstrapping$(c_3, TV^+(X), BK)$
10:     $\hat{c}_3 = 2 \cdot c3 - 4 \cdot carry(c_3)$
11: **if** $r < 0$ **then**   ▷ left shift
12:     **for** i = 0 to (3 - s) **do**
13:         $\hat{c}_i = c_{i+s}$
14:     carry(c_3) = FunctionalBootstrapping$(c_3, TV^-(X), BK)$
15:     $\hat{c}_3 = 2 \cdot c_3 - 4 \cdot carry(c_3)$
16:     **for** i = 2 to 1 **do**
17:         carry(c_i) = FunctionalBootstrapping$(c_i, TV^-(X), BK)$
18:         $\hat{c}_i = (2 \cdot c_i - 4 \cdot carry(c_i)) + carry(c_{i+1})$
19:     carry(c_0) = FunctionalBootstrapping$(c_0, TV^-(X), BK)$
20:     $\hat{c}_0 = 2 \cdot c_0 - 4 \cdot carry(c_0)$
    return $(\hat{c}_0, \hat{c}_1, \hat{c}_2, \hat{c}_3)$

3.4 Stream-Cipher Adaptation

Representing the internal state of a stream-cipher as base B integers will have the effect of producing the keystream as base B integers as well, but the plaintext space with respect to the TFHE encryption layer is of size $2B^2$. The encryption (resp. decryption) process must then be slightly adapted. In order to take advantage from the fact that the FHE encrypted keystream is added to a symmetrically encrypted data, which is a plaintext-ciphertext operation with respect to the FHE encryption layer, and such operations do not increase the noise. Thus, no bootstrapping is required in this step of transciphering.

---

[12] Most significant encrypted digit is c_3.

Algorithm 3. Byte shift with base 16

Input: 2 TLWE samples encrypting a byte b in little-endian representation [13]
$c = (c_0, c_1)$, a position $r = 4s + q$ with $|r| < 8$
a bootstrapping key $BK_{s \to s'} = (BK_i \in \mathrm{TRGSW}_{S'}(s_i))_{i \in [\![1,n]\!]}$ where S' is the
TRLWE interpretation of a secret key s'

Output: 2 TLWE samples $(\hat{c}_0, \hat{c}_1)$ encrypting b shifted by r positions in little-endian
representation.

  1: **if** $r > 0$ **then**   ▷ right shift
  2:     **if** $s == 1$ **then**
  3:         $\hat{c}_0 \leftarrow$ Noiseless Trivial sample of 0
  4:         $\hat{c}_1 = \mathrm{FunctionalBootstrapping}(c_0, \text{S-LUT}_q^+(X), BK)$
  5:     **else**
  6:         $\mathrm{carry}(c_0) = \mathrm{FunctionalBootstrapping}(c_0, \text{C-LUT}_q^+(X), BK)$
  7:         $\hat{c}_0 = \mathrm{FunctionalBootstrapping}(c_0, \text{S-LUT}_q^+(X), BK)$
  8:         $\hat{c}_1 = \mathrm{FunctionalBootstrapping}(c_1, \text{S-LUT}_q^+(X), BK)$
  9:         $\hat{c}_1 + = \mathrm{carry}(c_0)$
10: **if** $r < 0$ **then**   ▷ left shift
11:     **if** $s == 1$ **then**
12:         $\hat{c}_1 \leftarrow$ Noiseless Trivial sample of 0
13:         $\hat{c}_0 = \mathrm{FunctionalBootstrapping}(c_0, \text{S-LUT}_q^-(X), BK)$
14:     **else**
15:         $\mathrm{carry}(c_1) = \mathrm{FunctionalBootstrapping}(c_1, \text{C-LUT}_q^-(X), BK)$
16:         $\hat{c}_1 = \mathrm{FunctionalBootstrapping}(c_1, \text{S-LUT}_q^-(X), BK)$
17:         $\hat{c}_0 = \mathrm{FunctionalBootstrapping}(c_0, \text{S-LUT}_q^-(X), BK)$
18:         $\hat{c}_0 + = \mathrm{carry}(c_1)$
    return $(\hat{c}_0, \hat{c}_1)$

Instead of the classical XOR between the keystream and the message (resp. ciphertext), one makes an addition (respectively substraction) modulo $2B$ [14]. Indeed, it would require a functional bootstrapping to evaluate a modulo B addition of plaintext-ciphertext elements when the ciphertext lies in a greater set than $\mathbb{Z}_B$ (the keystream digits). This modification of the encryption/decryption process has no effect whatsoever on the security of the stream-cipher.

Plaintext Space Size Limitations. The bootstrapping operation as described in [BMMP18] stores all the elements of a plaintext space $\mathcal{M}$ as coefficients of the test vector. The potential lack of precision in the BlindRotate operation due to the noise of the input ciphertext is solved, up to a certain level, thanks to the redundancy of the coefficients in the test vector. Indeed, in practice, $|\mathcal{M}|$ divides N so every element in $\mathcal{M}$ is repeated consecutively $\frac{N}{|\mathcal{M}|}$ times in the TRLWE polynomial which will be rotated. Therefore, if the input ciphertext's noise and the rounding error make the BlindRotate operation fail to bring the target coefficient of the test vector to the constant term, then the added

---

[13] Most significant encrypted digit is c_1.

[14] The modulo operation is never performed per se since the sum of two elements of $\mathbb{Z}_B$ is at most equal to $2(B-1)$.

redundancy ensures that any adjacent coefficient by at most $\frac{N}{2|\mathcal{M}|} - 1$ positions, to the left or right, according to the sign of the error, is still equal to the target coefficient. Increasing the size of $\mathcal{M}$ reduces the redundancy factor, and thus, the precision of the (functional) bootstrapping. Increasing N allows to proportionally increase the size of $\mathcal{M}$ without loss of precision in the bootstrapping. However, this solution also increases the size of a TRLWE ciphertext, and the runtime of the bootstrapping operation, which is quasi-linear in the degree of the TRLWE polynomial encoding the test vector. A challenging task is to find the right balance between the size of $\mathcal{M}$, the desired precision, and a parameter set for TFHE which provides a reasonable ciphertext size, in order to still ensure a significant speedup on the server-end. To that end, we provide a set of three parameters-set for TFHE presented in Table 1.

4   Grain128-AEAD

Grain128-AEAD [HJM+21] is a widely-used stream-cipher that draws inspiration from Grain128a [ÅHJM11]. It is a finalist in the NIST competition on lightweight cryptography[15] and features slight modifications from its predecessor. Grain128-AEAD has an Authenticated Encryption with Associated Data (AEAD) mode, which allows for the encryption of a subset of plaintext bits using a mask d with the formula $c_i = m_i \oplus (ks_i \cdot d_i)$. Additionally, a larger 64-bit MAC is computed on the encrypted data. The internal state of Grain128-AEAD is 256 bits in length and consists of a 128-bit Non-linear Feedback Shift Register (NFSR) and a 128-bit Linear Feedback Shift Register (LFSR), along with two 64-bit accumulator and shift registers for MAC computation.

Once warmed up with 384 rounds, Grain128-AEAD can generate two streams of bits, namely the encryption keystream (ks) and the MAC keystream (ms), which are extracted from the main keystream using bit parity. Specifically, ks_i is calculated as y_{384+2i} and ms_i is calculated as $y_{384+2i+1}$, where y_{383} represents the last output bit from the warm-up phase of the cipher.

5   Experimental Results

We ran *single core* performance tests on an 12th Gen Intel(R) Core(TM) i7-12700H v6 @ 2.60 GHz and 22 GB RAM.

Table 1 shows the performance of transciphering after applying a base $B \geq 2$ representation of the internal state of Grain128-AEAD. The performance metrics are the number of bootstrappings needed to homomorphically evaluate the warm-up phase of Grain128-AEAD. The chosen set of parameters impacts the runtime of a single bootstrapping operation, and therefore the runtime of entire the warm-up operation.

With every parameter-set we aim at finding a good balance between the bootstrapping's runtime and its accuracy, under the constraint of a security level of

---

[15] https://csrc.nist.gov/Projects/lightweight-cryptography.

$\lambda = 128$ bits, and a circuit accuracy of $1 - 2^{-32}$. The runtime of the bootstrapping operation is quasi-linear in the TRLWE polynomial degree N as well as linear in the TLWE dimension n and the gadget decomposition parameter l[CGGI18]. As such, we aim to minimize these parameters for better performances. The security of the scheme is linked to the parameters n, N, and the standard deviations used to define the noise of TLWE ciphertexts and TRLWE ciphertexts. We use lattice-estimator [APS15] to find secure sets of parameters for relatively small values of n and N. The other parameters are chosen to optimize correctness of computations under the chosen security. The selected sets of parameters are presented in Table 1.

It is clear from Table 1 that our base 2 implementation slightly outperforms base 2 implementations from [BBS21] (around 10% with equivalent computational resources) thanks to the introduced optimization where noiseless trivial samples are inserted when a byte-shift is performed, resulting in bootstrapping-free operations. The base 4 (4 ciphertexts) implementation results in a noticeable speedup compared to base 2: 20% less bootstrappings, and 10% faster due to larger parameters, while base 16 provides a significant improvement of almost 65% less bootstrappings compared to [BBS21]. However, base 16 warm-up time is bigger than base 2 or base 4 times due to the use of huge parameters in order to respect the fixed security level ($\lambda = 128$) and the bound on the error rate (2^{-32}).

Table 1. Summary of the performance results.

		Base		
		2	4	16
TFHE Params	N	1024	2048	65536
	n	595	740	930
	$log_2(B_g)$	5	11	32
	l	4	3	1
	keyswitch standard-dev.	$1.26e^{-4}$	$9.17e^{-6}$	$3e^{-7}$
	bootstrapping standard-dev.	$5.6e^{-8}$	$9.6e^{-11}$	$1.0e^{-100}$
	security level λ	128	128	128
Runtime	# of bootstrappings (warm-up circuit)	18912	16608	7718
	runtime (a single bootstrapping)	13 ms	17 ms	92 ms
	runtime (warm-up circuit)	4.80 min	3.98 min	11.83 min
Error estimation	error probability (a single bootstrapping)	2^{-47}	2^{-46}	2^{-45}
	error probability (warm-up circuit)	2^{-31}	2^{-32}	$2^{-31.5}$

6   Conclusion

In this work we revisit transciphering with stream-ciphers using TFHE's functional bootstrapping by specifying a set of operators with inputs represented by digits in base B. Despite the small adaptations that have to be taken into account when using this technique, regarding plaintext-space size, the decryption procedure, and the careful choice of FHE parameters, these operators can be readily employed to implement a wide range of stream-ciphers, and often result in non-negligible improvements regarding the required number of bootstrappings as shown with a standard encryption algorithm Grain128-AEAD.

While the need for larger parameters in larger bases increases the runtime for a single bootstrapping operation, this work also aims at leveraging cloud hardware acceleration modules for FHE [BBTV23, MAM20, WSKB22] which enables efficient FHE (LWE, RLWE, and RGSW) operations with a significantly better accommodation of larger parameter-sets than software implementation.

We plan to extend this approach to the homomorphic evaluation of block-ciphers, and other cryptographic primitives such as hash functions as investigated in [BSS+23]. Subsequent works involve implementing non-homogeneous base representation of a byte, using two digits in base 4 and a single digit in base 8. This could potentially improve the accuracy/number of ciphertexts trade-off, and showcase the versatility of encrypted byte representations, not only for transciphering-related applications, but also for other use-cases of FHE. A further optimization would be to take advantage of the symmetric aspect of the lookup tables (from the fact that boolean operators are commutative) to reduce the plaintext space size from $2B^2$ to B^2 by providing a more compact way to homomorphically reference elements inside the boolean operations lookup tables.

References

[ÅHJM11]   Ågren, M., Hell, M., Johansson, T., Meier, W.: Grain-128a: a new version of grain-128 with optional authentication. IJWMC **5**, 48–59 (2011)

[APS15]   Albrecht, M.R., Player, R., Scott, S.: On the concrete hardness of learning with errors. Cryptology ePrint Archive, Paper 2015/046 (2015). https://eprint.iacr.org/2015/046

[ARS+15]   Albrecht, M.R., Rechberger, C., Schneider, T., Tiessen, T., Zohner, M.: Ciphers for MPC and FHE. In: Oswald, E., Fischlin, M. (eds.) EUROCRYPT 2015. LNCS, vol. 9056, pp. 430–454. Springer, Heidelberg (2015). https://doi.org/10.1007/978-3-662-46800-5_17

[BBS21]   Bendoukha, A.A., Boudguiga, A., Sirdey, R.: Revisiting stream-cipher-based homomorphic transciphering in the TFHE era. In: 14th International Symposium of Foundation and Practice of Security (2021)

[BBS22]   Bendoukha, AA., Boudguiga, A., Sirdey, R.: Revisiting stream-cipher-based homomorphic transciphering in the TFHE era. In: Aïmeur, E., Laurent, M., Yaich, R., Dupont, B., Garcia-Alfaro, J. (eds.) FPS 2021. LNCS, vol. 13291. Springer, Cham (2022). https://doi.org/10.1007/978-3-031-08147-7_2

[BBTV23]   Bertels, J., Van Beirendonck, M., Turan, F., Verbauwhede, I.: Hardware acceleration of FHEW. Cryptology ePrint Archive, Paper 2023/618 (2023). https://eprint.iacr.org/2023/618

[BGV12] Brakerski, Z., Gentry, C., Vaikuntanathan, V.: (Leveled) fully homomorphic encryption without bootstrapping. In: Proceedings of the 3rd Innovations in Theoretical Computer Science Conference, ITCS '12, pp. 309–325. Association for Computing Machinery, New York, NY, USA (2012)

[BLSK19] Boudguiga, A., Letailleur, J., Sirdey, R., Klaudel, W.: Enhancing CAN security by means of lightweight stream-ciphers and protocols. In: Romanovsky, A., Troubitsyna, E., Gashi, I., Schoitsch, E., Bitsch, F. (eds.) SAFECOMP 2019. LNCS, vol. 11699, pp. 235–250. Springer, Cham (2019). https://doi.org/10.1007/978-3-030-26250-1_19

[BMMP18] Bourse, F., Minelli, M., Minihold, M., Paillier, P.: Fast homomorphic evaluation of deep discretized neural networks. In: Shacham, H., Boldyreva, A. (eds.) CRYPTO 2018. LNCS, vol. 10993, pp. 483–512. Springer, Cham (2018). https://doi.org/10.1007/978-3-319-96878-0_17

[BP12] Boyar, J., Peralta, R.: A small depth-16 circuit for the AES S-box. In: Gritzalis, D., Furnell, S., Theoharidou, M. (eds.) SEC 2012. IAICT, vol. 376, pp. 287–298. Springer, Heidelberg (2012). https://doi.org/10.1007/978-3-642-30436-1_24

[BSS+23] Bendoukha, A.A., Stan, O., Sirdey, R., Quero, N., Freitas, L.: Practical homomorphic evaluation of block-cipher-based hash functions with applications. In: Jourdan, G.V., Mounier, L., Adams, C., Sèdes, F., Garcia-Alfaro, J. (eds.) FPS 2022. LNCS, vol. 13877. Springer, Cham (2023). https://doi.org/10.1007/978-3-031-30122-3_6

[CCF+18a] Canteaut, A., et al.: Stream ciphers: a practical solution for efficient homomorphic-ciphertext compression. J. Cryptol. 31(3), 885–916 (2018)

[CCF+18b] Canteaut, A., et al.: Stream ciphers: a practical solution for efficient homomorphic-ciphertext compression. J. Cryptol. 31, 01 (2018)

[CGGI16] Chillotti, I., Gama, N., Georgieva, M., Izabachène, M.: Faster fully homomorphic encryption: bootstrapping in less than 0.1 seconds. In: Cheon, J.H., Takagi, T. (eds.) ASIACRYPT 2016. LNCS, vol. 10031, pp. 3–33. Springer, Heidelberg (2016). https://doi.org/10.1007/978-3-662-53887-6_1

[CGGI18] Chillotti, I., Gama, N., Georgieva, M., Izabachène, M.: TFHE: fast fully homomorphic encryption over the torus. Cryptology ePrint Archive, Report 2018/421 (2018). https://eprint.iacr.org/2018/421

[CHK+20] Cho, J., et al.: Transciphering framework for approximate homomorphic encryption (full version). Cryptology ePrint Archive, Paper 2020/1335 (2020). https://eprint.iacr.org/2020/1335

[CJP21] Chillotti, I., Joye, M., Paillier, P.: Programmable bootstrapping enables efficient homomorphic inference of deep neural networks. In: Dolev, S., Margalit, O., Pinkas, B., Schwarzmann, A. (eds.) CSCML 2021. LNCS, vol. 12716, pp. 1–19. Springer, Cham (2021). https://doi.org/10.1007/978-3-030-78086-9_1

[CKKS16] Cheon, J.H., Kim, A., Kim, M., Song, Y.: Homomorphic encryption for arithmetic of approximate numbers. Cryptology ePrint Archive, Report 2016/421 (2016). https://eprint.iacr.org/2016/421

[CLOT21] Chillotti, I., Ligier, D., Orfila, J.-B., Tap, S.: Improved programmable bootstrapping with larger precision and efficient arithmetic circuits for TFHE. Cryptology ePrint Archive, Report 2021/729 (2021). https://ia.cr/2021/729

108   A.-A. Bendoukha et al.

[CM19]   Carlet, C., Méaux, P.: Boolean functions for homomorphic-friendly stream ciphers. Cryptology ePrint Archive, Paper 2019/1446 (2019). https://eprint.iacr.org/2019/1446

[CZB+22] Clet, P.-E., Zuber, M., Boudguiga, A., Sirdey, R., Gouy-Pailler, C.: Putting up the swiss army knife of homomorphic calculations by means of TFHE functional bootstrapping. Cryptology ePrint Archive, Paper 2022/149 (2022). https://eprint.iacr.org/2022/149

[DGH+21] Dobraunig, C., Grassi, L., Helminger, L., Rechberger, C., Schofnegger, M., Walch, R.: Pasta: a case for hybrid homomorphic encryption. Cryptology ePrint Archive (2021)

[FV12]   Fan, J., Vercauteren, F.: Somewhat practical fully homomorphic encryption. Cryptology ePrint Archive, Report 2012/144 (2012). https://eprint.iacr.org/2012/144

[GBA21] Guimarães, A., Borin, E., Aranha, D.F.: Revisiting the functional bootstrap in TFHE. IACR Trans. Cryptogr. Hardw. Embed. Syst. **2021**(2), 229–253 (2021)

[GHS12a] Gentry, C., Halevi, S., Smart, N.P.: Homomorphic evaluation of the AES circuit. In: Safavi-Naini, R., Canetti, R. (eds.) CRYPTO 2012. LNCS, vol. 7417, pp. 850–867. Springer, Heidelberg (2012). https://doi.org/10.1007/978-3-642-32009-5_49

[GSW13] Gentry, C., Sahai, A., Waters, B.: Homomorphic encryption from learning with errors: conceptually-simpler, asymptotically-faster, attribute-based. In: Canetti, R., Garay, J.A. (eds.) CRYPTO 2013. LNCS, vol. 8042, pp. 75–92. Springer, Heidelberg (2013). https://doi.org/10.1007/978-3-642-40041-4_5

[HJM+21] Hell, M., Johansson, T., Maximov, A., Meier, W., Yoshida, H.: Grain-128aeadv2: strengthening the initialization against key reconstruction. Cryptology ePrint Archive, Report 2021/751 (2021). https://ia.cr/2021/751

[HJMM06] Hell, M., Johansson, T., Maximov, A., Meier, W.: A stream cipher proposal: Grain-128. In: 2006 IEEE International Symposium on Information Theory, pp. 1614–1618 (2006)

[HMR20] Hoffmann, C., Méaux, P., Ricosset, T.: Transciphering, using FILIP and TFHE for an efficient delegation of computation. Cryptology ePrint Archive, Paper 2020/1373 (2020). https://eprint.iacr.org/2020/1373

[KS21]   Kluczniak, K., Schild, L.: FDFB: full domain functional bootstrapping towards practical fully homomorphic encryption. Cryptology ePrint Archive, Report 2021/1135 (2021). https://ia.cr/2021/1135

[KS22]   Kluczniak, K., Schild, L.: FDFB: full domain functional bootstrapping towards practical fully homomorphic encryption. IACR Tran. Cryptogr. Hardw. Embed. Syst. **2023**(1), 501–537 (2022)

[MAM20] Morshed, T., Al Aziz, Md.M., Mohammed, N.: CPU and GPU accelerated fully homomorphic encryption. In: 2020 IEEE International Symposium on Hardware Oriented Security and Trust (HOST), pp. 142–153 (2020)

[OKC20] Okada, H., Kiyomoto, S., Cid, C.: Integerwise functional bootstrapping on TFHE. In: Susilo, W., Deng, R.H., Guo, F., Li, Y., Intan, R. (eds.) ISC 2020. LNCS, vol. 12472, pp. 107–125. Springer, Cham (2020). https://doi.org/10.1007/978-3-030-62974-8_7

[WSKB22] Wang, Z., Sylvester, D., Kim, H.-S., Blaauw, D.: Hardware acceleration for third-generation FHE and PSI based on it (2022)

[YXS+21] Yang, Z., Xie, X., Shen, H., Chen, S., Zhou, J.: Tota: fully homomorphic encryption with smaller parameters and stronger security. Cryptology ePrint Archive, Report 2021/1347 (2021). https://ia.cr/2021/1347

Applications

Control is Nothing Without Trust a First Look into Digital Identity Wallet Trends

Zahra Ebadi Ansaroudi[1]([✉]) [ID], Roberto Carbone[1] [ID], Giada Sciarretta[1] [ID], and Silvio Ranise[1,2] [ID]

[1] Center for Cybersecurity, FBK, 38123 Trento, Italy
{zebadiansaroudi,carbone,g.sciarretta,ranise}@fbk.eu,
[2] University of Trento, 38123 Trento, Povo, Italy
silvio.ranise@unitn.it

Abstract. In recent years, user-centric digital identity wallets have become increasingly available, aiming to give individuals direct control over their personal data. The EU proposal in the context of the recently revised eIDAS and its EU digital identity wallet reflects the high ambitions in this field at the EU level. However, to the best of our knowledge, no research review on the core technologies used to implement various features of these wallet solutions has been proposed so far. Our work addresses this issue providing a systematic analysis of a selection of available digital identity wallets on the market in terms of the technologies used to establish trust and controlled sharing. Building on this overview and help providers (including companies and European Member States) in charge of developing secure and trustworthy wallet-based infrastructures, we propose a classification of wallet solutions along two main dimensions (namely trust establishment and controlled credential sharing) with the goal of assisting designers to make informed design decisions and guarantee security, privacy, and trustworthiness.

Keywords: Digital Identity · Identity Wallet · Trust

1 Introduction

The digital identity landscape has evolved over time, starting with the most basic isolated identity management (IdM) systems and progressing through several stages with the addition of other models such as centralized, federated, and user-centric IdM systems. The isolated model allows service providers (SPs) to serve as identity providers (IdPs) to their users, providing unique identifiers (IDs) and associated credentials such as passwords. In the centralized model, a single IdP is used by all SPs. The shift to the federated model enables a set of SPs to recognize user IDs provided by IdPs from other SPs within a federated domain, allowing users to authenticate once and access multiple SPs without the need for re-authentication [43,71]. The three models mentioned prioritize the IdP/SPs' viewpoint, giving those entities control over the system. However,

© IFIP International Federation for Information Processing 2023
Published by Springer Nature Switzerland AG 2023
V. Atluri and A. L. Ferrara (Eds.): DBSec 2023, LNCS 13942, pp. 113–132, 2023.
https://doi.org/10.1007/978-3-031-37586-6_7

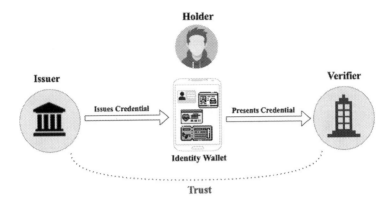

Fig. 1. Identity wallet role in a user-centric IdM system

a shift towards a user-centric model has occurred due to a growing awareness of privacy concerns and users' realization of the value of their data. This shift aims to address security and privacy issues present in the earlier models, such as data breaches resulting from IdPs aggregating large volumes of personal data [7]. User-centric IdM systems empower users with full control over their credentials, allowing them to store their credentials in storage they own or control, such as a digital identity wallet, and share them as desired [54].

A digital identity wallet is an application under the control of a user that allows the storage of multiple digital identities and related credentials. Users can use these identities to authenticate themselves online (and offline) with different levels of assurance (LoAs[1]). These identities can be obtained from government or private companies, as well as sovereign citizen documents like national identity cards and passports [47]. Figure 1 illustrates a user-centric IdM system, with a digital identity wallet at its core. The system involves three key roles: Issuer, Holder, and Verifier. The Issuer creates and issues credentials to the Holder, who receives and stores the credentials, and when required, shares them with the Verifier. The Verifier receives and verifies the credentials presented by the Holder. This system removes the need for a third-party IdP and supports a direct relationship between the Holder and an SP/Verifier, giving users full control over their data through the use of an identity wallet.

We can distinguish user-centric IdM systems based on the adopted trust model into two groups: DPKI-based and PKI-based. The former applies a decentralized public key infrastructure (DPKI) and may utilize a distributed ledger or a blockchain to create and manage decentralized identifiers (DIDs) in a decentralized manner. On the other hand, the latter employs a centralized PKI, relying on a hierarchy of trusted Certification Authorities (CAs). Our work considers both systems from a technical perspective and aims to fill the knowledge gap for designers and developers. We provide insights into the best approaches for

---

[1] A level of assurance refers to the certainty of a claimed identity being authentic.

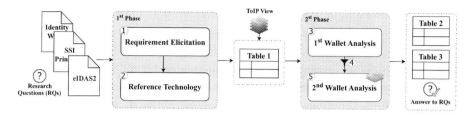

Fig. 2. Research Methodology

developing secure, private, and interoperable solutions for different use cases, based on the adopted trust model.

Organization of the Paper. First, Sect. 2 describes the research methodology employed in this study and presents the research questions. Next, Sect. 3 outlines the main requirements of digital identity wallets and the enabling technologies. This is followed by Sect. 4, which presents an analysis of a selected set of wallets in response to the research questions. Finally, Sect. 5 concludes the paper.

2   Research Methodology

The methodology we employed in this study is illustrated in Fig. 2. First of all, we pose two research questions in line with the purpose of the study which is to compare several digital identity wallet solutions made for user-centric IdM systems, based on their root of trust and the control they offer accordingly.

In the first phase: (1) we conduct a thorough literature review on digital identity wallets, eIDAS2, and SSI [35,57,60,63] to identify and extract the design requirements, both functional and non-functional, that these wallets are developed for, (2) we use next a reference technology architecture (specifically, ToIP [3]) to study the technological possibilities for these wallet solutions. As a result, we provide Table 1 with a list of non-functional requirements and the technologies that may be employed to meet them.

In the second phase, we proceed with the analysis of wallet solutions: (3) we conduct an internet search for digital identity wallets and define a set of reference wallets on the market, consisting of the first 32 wallets that provide sufficient documentation to ensure a comprehensive yet manageable analysis of the diverse landscape. We first analyze them for 6 basic differentiating features, including type (web vs mobile), use case, developer, code availability, maturity level, and supported trust model. The results of this first analysis are presented in Table 2. Then, in (4), from the reference wallets, we further narrow down our focus to a subset of 12 wallets, carefully selected to represent a fair ratio of solutions for the implemented trust models from various developers. Finally, in (5), we refer back to the ToIP and select only the technologies that address our research questions and review and study their technical specification accordingly. The results of this step are presented in Table 3 and further discussed as the answers to the research questions in Sect. 4.2.

2.1   Research Questions

We organize our analysis around two primary research questions outlined below:

RQ1. How is Trust Established? Is the Root of Trust Centralized or Decentralized? To address this question, we analyze reference wallet solutions, and mark them as centralized "PKI-based" or decentralized "DPKI-based".

RQ2. How are Credentials Shared in a Controlled Way? After understanding the trust model of the wallets, we analyze the selected solutions in terms of technologies used for controlled and trustworthy credential sharing. This analysis focuses on credential creation, management (including storage on mobile or web), sharing, and revocation.

3   Wallet Requirements and Technology Framework

Section 3.1 lists the general requirements necessary for realizing a digital identity wallet solution with a focus on the requirements of the recent European Digital Identity Wallet (EUDI Wallet) proposal in the context of electronic Identification and Authentication and trust Services 2 (eIDAS2) regulation[2] [20]. Section 3.2 then outlines the key technologies used to meet the wallet's requirements.

3.1   Requirements Elicitation

Functional Requirements. These requirements describe the functionalities that a digital wallet should implement. We conducted keyword research on digital wallets, particularly digital identity wallets, and identified that the main functional requirements for which they are developed are to store, manage, and share the identity or its related data. Manage (or controlling) the data includes removing and reviewing the data stored in the wallet and explicitly selecting what data to store/combine and share into/outside the wallet. Identity wallets also provide secure storage for cryptographic material associated with the data. The wallet may additionally have functionalities for recovery and back up [35,57,60]. The eIDAS2 regulation counts several functionalities as well for the EUDI Wallet in a recently published Architecture and Reference Framework (EUDI-ARF) [18]. The EUDI-ARF covers the aforementioned requirements along with other functionalities such as the creation of (qualified) electronic signatures/seals that demand the provision of interfaces to the services providing the functionality, requiring identification with an eIDAS high LoA.

Non-Functional Requirements. These requirements describe how a digital identity wallet satisfies a system's non-functional aspects [56]. Christopher Allen first in his paper [5] provided a comprehensive list of these requirements for a

---

[2] The eIDAS2 regulation aims to enhance the security and usability of electronic identification and trust services in the EU. The EUDI Wallet is expected to contribute to this objective by providing a standardized and interoperable digital identity solution.

user-centric wallet adhering to the Self-Sovereign Identity (SSI), referred to as SSI principles, including existence, control, access, and so on. The Sovrin working group provided later a rich list of these requirements in [65], which were categorized into three groups of "Agency", "Autonomy" and "Integrity". While there is some overlap between them, they are not identical. Both sets of principles emphasize the importance of control, access, transparency, and portability in SSI, but Sovrin's principles also prioritize equity, inclusion, and decentralization. See Table 1 for the definitions of each requirement. A user-centric digital identity wallet solution might fully or partially adhere to this list of requirements. The EUDI-ARF includes several aspects for the EUDI Wallet regarding these SSI principles as well and shows compliance with SSI, except for decentralization. This comes from the nature of trust in the context of eIDAS2. Although the eIDAS2 is technology-agnostic and supports both centralized and decentralized digital identities, acquiring qualified certifications for the services provided to the wallet from third-party providers or for the wallet itself is a limiting constraint [64].

3.2 Reference Technology Framework

The Trust over IP (ToIP) Foundation provides an open and collaborative platform for defining a complete architecture to establish digital trust between peers over the Internet or other networks. To achieve this, it combines available standards, protocols, and capabilities produced by standard development organizations and industry foundations such as the World Wide Web Consortium (W3C) and the Decentralized Identity Foundation (DIF) to fulfill the requirements of a digital trust architecture [23]. We based our evaluation of the technical foundation of the wallet solutions on the ToIP technology architecture or framework [3], which served as our inspiration. Additionally, we provide information in Table 1 on how and which technologies can be used to meet the non-functional requirements of digital identity wallets, along with a mapping of these requirements to the ToIP layers (find the layer numbers in the last column).

   ToIP Overview. ToIP has four layers: trust, agent, service, and application. The first two layers focus on establishing machine-to-machine trust, enabling secure and private communication between machines. Public key cryptography plays a crucial role in these layers, allowing entities to verify each other using their identifiers. These identifiers can be centralized or decentralized, and the trust establishment can be done with or without a root of trust and through peer-to-peer protocols.

   Layer 1 (trust) includes services designed to specifically support trust between peers in the upper layers, including trusted computing, secure storage of cryptographic materials, and trusted transport protocols such as HTTP(s), Bluetooth, NFC, and QR. The layer may also require support services that are outside the boundary of an application, such as trust registries, which offer functionality for discovering data about trustworthy entities (i.e., issuers and verifiers), applications, credentials (format, schema, and revocation mechanisms), identity assurance level, etc. These services can be implemented in various ways, using

Table 1. Non-functional requirements

	Requirement taken from [65]	Meaning	How it can be technically fulfilled	ToIP Mapping
Agency	Representation	Identity subjects must be able to be represented by any number of digital identities.	Subject identifiers, centralized Public Key Certificates (PKCs), or DIDs are used to achieve this principle. Identity subjects may also obtain multiple identifiers and build new identities when required. Additionally, they may prove their identity ownership in a one-way using zero-knowledge proofs, without including an identifier in the identity data (e.g., Attribute-based (or Anonymous) Credentials [63]).	1
Agency	Delegation (of control)/Provability	Identity subjects must have the ability to control how their identity data is used, and exert this control by employing and/or delegating to agents and guardians of their choice, including individuals, organizations, devices, and software.	This is done by using asymmetric cryptography authentication protocols, such as DID authentication occurring over the DIDComm messaging protocol [26], to prove control over a proof private key linked to subject identifiers.	1, 3
Agency	Equity and inclusion	Within a governance scope, identity subjects must not be subject to discrimination.	This is addressed by using an inclusive design approach to "all people regardless of their abilities, age, economic status, education, geographic location, language, etc. [76]," and by adapting user interfaces to satisfy the varied needs of different identity subjects [44].	4
Agency	Usability, accessibility, and consistency	Agents and other IdM system components must be as usable and accessible as possible for identity subjects, providing a consistent user experience.	Because they are always accessible, mobile wallets are ideal for constant accessibility. Careful design choices must also be made to improve usability using relevant technologies [46].	4
Autonomy	Participation (or consent)	Identity subjects cannot be made to participate against their will. They must have the option to opt out of giving their identity data for services where it is not required.	To guarantee that the identity system has the data subject's consent and conforms with legal requirements like the EU GDPR, careful design decisions must be made [19]. For example, personal data must not be written in a public ledger, as anybody can read the data kept in a public ledger. Alternatively, the data registry can be implemented using a private permissioned ledger.	3, 4
Autonomy	Decentralization	A subject's digital identity data must not be represented, controlled, or verified by an identity system that is dependent on a centralized system.	A decentralized trust paradigm is used to achieve this.	1
Autonomy	Interoperability	Digital identity data for a subject must be represented, exchanged, secured, protected, and verified in an interoperable manner.	This occurs on several levels, including technical interoperability, which enables interoperability between various user-centric IdM systems using open standards and protocols, as well as between existing conventional centralized or federated IdM systems. Semantic interoperability, and organizational interoperability that aims for, say, compatibility between various blockchains and user-centric ecosystems [81].	2
Autonomy	Portability	Identity subjects must be able to take their digital identity data anywhere (i.e., to the agents or systems of their choice).	Through the use of their private key, subjects are able to move their data between other devices and systems using distributed ledgers or blockchains [61].	2
Integrity	Security	Identity subjects must secure their identity data.	To protect data in transit and at rest, certain design considerations must be made, such as encrypted storage, signed transactions, and secure connections.	1-4
Integrity	Verifiability and authenticity	Identity subjects are required to provide verifiable proof of the authenticity of their digital identity information.	This is accomplished through the use of verifiable credentials and presentations.	1, 3
Integrity	Privacy and minimal disclosure	Identity subjects must protect the privacy of their digital identity data and share the minimum digital identity data required for any interaction.	User-centric IdM systems are privacy-oriented and provide the identity subject full control. The privacy features they give, however, differ depending on the credential types and proof they provide.	1-4
Integrity	Transparency	Identity subjects and all other stakeholders must have easy access to and verify information necessary to understand the incentives, rules, policies, and algorithms under which agents and other components of the ecosystems operate.	This is achieved by developing wallet solutions based on open protocols and open standards.	1, 3

distributed ledgers that host the registries or identity federations that treat only the members of the federation as trustworthy.

Layer 2 (agent) includes protocols that serve as a bridge between higher-level application-facing protocols and lower-level transport protocols. ToIP requires that these protocols define how to construct and format messages that can be verified to have certain properties, such as authenticity and integrity [2]. Examples of protocols that meet these requirements are OpenID for Verifiable Credentials (OpenID4VC) [31] and DIDComm messaging [26]. OpenID4VC protocols, for instance, satisfy these properties and define APIs for the issuance and presentation of credentials in the upper layer.

Layer 3 (service) is responsible for defining and executing the trust services required for establishing trust between different entities in the ToIP ecosystem. It includes functions such as verifying identities, establishing credentials, and authorizing access to resources. In our analysis, we focus on services related to the credentials lifecycle [75], including the issuance, request and presentation of credentials, as well as verification and revocation in this layer. We first explore the credentials-related type/data model, which mainly consists of metadata, claims (or identity attributes), and proofs under the relevant trust model. The relevant technologies often come in the form of libraries that implement different types of credentials, such as W3C VC [75], ABC [63], and mDOC [41].

Next, we explore the credential issuance or presentation protocols, which may run on top of Layer 2 protocols or use another service within this layer. For example, in the case of OpenID4VC, it occurs through specific protocols such as OpenID for Verifiable Credential Issuance (OpenID4VCI) [77] and OpenID for Verifiable Presentations (OpenID4VP) [78], or through DIDComm messaging [26], supporting Wallet and Credential Interaction (WACI) protocols such as the Issue Credential Protocol [29] and Present Proof Protocol [28], W3C Credentials Community Group VC APIs [73], Credential Handler API (CHAPI) [4], ISO mDOC Request and Response Protocol [42], and so on. Verification of credentials enables a wallet to verify and prove the authenticity and integrity of data in transmission by implementing asymmetric cryptography algorithms such as Digital Signatures (DSs) or Zero-Knowledge Proofs (ZKPs). Available technologies can be provided as a library, for example, Hyperledger Ursa [30] or Idemix [36], or as a service, such as an eIDAS trust service like an electronic signature [17].

Revocation allows for checking the validity of a credential before trusting it for authentication. Various revocation mechanisms are available, including Accumulator Value (AV) [14], Credential Status List [27], Validity attestations, and others.

We are also interested in identity-binding mechanisms. These mechanisms, such as token binding [62], are used to establish a connection between a credential subject and either the application or the credential itself. The authentication of binding parameters linked to the credentials allows the issuer (or verifier) to verify the credential subject and issue (or accept) the credentials. The authentication performed in this layer is separate from the public key authentication mentioned earlier in Layer 2. Its purpose is to verify that the current subject is indeed the intended recipient of the credentials. Biometric traits are one of the methods used for this purpose, as they offer individuals an immutable characteristic, thereby providing a high LoA authentication.

And finally, Layer 4 (application) facilitates the interaction between individuals (or credential subjects) and applications, allowing them to engage in trusted interactions that serve specific business, legal, or social purposes.

4   Wallet Analysis

First Wallet Analysis. We conducted a Google search using the terms "Digital identity wallet" or "SSI wallet" and found a significant number of wallets. As discussed in [45], these wallets were developed by various entities, including big tech companies such as Apple, public sectors such as the European Union, and independent wallet providers and startups like Evernym. These wallets vary in terms of their use cases, target audience, security, privacy, interoperability, and many other features as mentioned in Sect. 3.1, as well as the underlying technology stack. To account for these differences, we collected a set of 32 wallet solutions, called as "Reference Wallets" to form the basis of our study, and anlayzed them first based on six questions that arose during our search:

1. What kind of solution is it? Is it a WEB, or a mobile (MOB) solution?
2. What is the solution use case (UC)? Is it for personal (PERS) or business (BIZ) use cases? Personal ones are designed for individuals to manage their digital identity in a secure and convenient way. While the business ones on the other hand tend to have more specific features and requirements that are tailored to the needs of businesses and organizations, such as to store and manage employee data, such as HR records and payroll information.
3. Who is responsible for the wallet development? Is it a public (PUB) or private (PVT) solution? A public (or national) wallet is funded and developed by public sectors (or in partnership with a few private companies or organizations). A private wallet, on the other hand, is offered by one or more private sector (profit/non-profit) organizations, that are primarily in charge of wallet development.
4. Is the source code of the solution available online (OSS)?
5. What is the maturity level (MAT) of the solution? Is it a field product (FLD), a PILOT (tried with a small group of real users), a prototype PROTO (a working model of the solution with limited functionality), or a DEMO (a presentation of the solution)?
6. What is the employed trust model (TRU MDL) and if it uses a blockchain, which kind of blockchain is it?

Table 2 reports the reference wallets and their analysis.

Second Wallet Analysis. For the second analysis, we narrowed down the list of reference wallets to 12 (Connect.Me, KayTrust, Talao, Apple, IRMA, IDgov.pt, Open, mObywatel, IDEMIA, DIZME, Microsoft Authenticator, and Verse)-roughly 38% of them, based on their trust model, ensuring that the

Table 2. Reference wallets

No	Name	Type		UC		Developer	OSS	MAT	TRU MDL	Blockchain
		Web	MOB	PERS	BIZ					
1	Trinsic	Y[1]	Y	Y	Y		Y	FLD	DPKI	Sovrin, Indico (Indy networks)
2	Connect.Me	-	Y	Y	-		Y	FLD	DPKI	Sovrin
3	Lissi	-	Y	Y	-		Y	FLD	DPKI	Sovrin, IDUnion
4	esatus	-	Y	Y	Y		Y	FLD	DPKI	Sovrin, IDUnion
5	Jolocom SmartWallet	-	Y	Y	Y		Y	FLD	DPKI	Ethereum
6	Shocard	-	Y	-	Y		N	FLD	DPKI	Bitcoin
7	KayTrust	-	Y	-	Y	PVT	Y	FLD	DPKI	Alastria
8	SelfKey	-	Y	Y	-		Y	FLD	DPKI	Ethereum
9	Data	-	Y	Y			Y	FLD	DPKI	EBSI networks
10	Gataca	-	Y	Y	-		-	FLD	DPKI	Ethereum and EBSI networks
11	Talao	-	Y	Y	Y		Y	FLD	DPKI	Tezos, EBSI networks
12	AceID	-	Y	Y	Y		Y	FLD[2]	DPKI	AceBlock
13	Osma	-	Y	Y	Y		Y	FLD[3]	DPKI	Bitcoin, ION
14	DataKeeper	-	Y	Y	Y		N	FLD	DPKI	Ethereum Quorum
15	Microsoft Entra Verified ID	-	Y	Y	Y		Y	FLD	DPKI	Bitcoin
16	My Optus (Mastercard ID)	-	Y	Y	Y		-	PILOT[4]	DPKI	ID Network
17	Bloom	-	Y	Y	Y		Y	FLD	DPKI	Ethereum
18	DID	-	Y	Y	Y		Y	FLD	DPKI	AceBlock
19	ID Pocket	-	Y	Y	Y		N	FLD	DPKI	Ethereum
20	IDnow Online Ident	-	Y	-	Y		N	FLD	DPKI	IDUnion
21	IRMA	-	Y	Y	Y		Y	FLD	PKI	-
22	VIDwallet	-	Y	Y	Y		N	FLD	DPKI	Alastria, EBSI networks
23	Walt.id Wallet	Y	Y	Y	Y		Y	DEMO[5]	DPKI	Gaia-X/ Ocean, EBSI networks
24	DIZME	-	Y	Y	Y		Y	FLD	DPKI	Sovrin
25	Apple wallet	-	Y	Y	-		N	FLD[6]	PKI	-
26	ID Wallet	-	Y	Y	Y		Y	PILOT[7]	DPKI	Hyperledger Indy
27	Alastria ID	-	Y	Y	Y	PUB	Y	DEMO[3]	DPKI	Alastria networks
28	Open wallet	-	Y	Y	-		Y	PROTO	DPKI	Trustchain
29	IDEMIA (Mobile ID)	-	Y	Y	-		N	FLD	PKI	-
30	Veres[8]	Y	-	Y	Y		N	FLD	DPKI	EBSI networks
31	mObywatel	-	Y	Y	-		N	FLD	PKI	-
32	IDgov.pt	-	Y	Y	Y		N	FLD	PKI	-

[1] Trinisc Wallet SDK makes it possible to embed wallet functionalities into a web application.

[2] It has recently been removed from Google Play.

[3] Only the source code is available on GitHub.

[4] Currently launched in Australia (using My Optus wallet) and Brazil, see https://idwall.co/en/ for Brazil.

[5] Walt.id Wallet Kit enables re-branding, extending their web wallet[2], or building a new web or mobile wallet application.

[6] Currently, only the US states of Arizona, Colorado, and Maryland support IDs in the wallet.

[7] The ID wallet was temporarily removed from the App Store in September 2021 to improve it with respect to several aspects, such as the technical implementation and security of the wallet.

[8] Not accessible anymore.

included solutions either use a PKI or a DPKI model. As can be seen in Table 2, only 5 out of the 32 wallet solutions used PKI. We included all PKI-based solutions in the second analysis. From the DPKI-based solutions, we selected two from public solutions and the rest from private ones. This provides us with an approximate 40–60 percent rate for the trust models in developer types. If a DPKI-based solution with a blockchain in the system is present, we attempted to include various blockchains in the analysis. Find the selected wallet solutions highlighted as green in Table 2.

4.1   Wallets Description

DPKI-Based Wallet solutions:

- Connect.Me is the first SSI mobile wallet built by Evernym on the Sovrin network [66], which uses a public permissioned blockchain of Hyperledger Indy and will work with cheqd network in the future [12]. It can be adjusted to a variety of use cases, enabling access to both public and private services as well as the sharing of identity-related data in the form of Anonymous Credentials with the privacy features it offers.
- KayTrust is a mobile wallet developed by Everis and allows users to handle digital credentials for a variety of purposes, including diplomas, vaccination credentials, labor certificates, land registration documents, and any other digital accrediting document. The wallet improves the accreditation and certification process, combats document fraud, and ensures security, transparency, and digital truthfulness by allowing a credential to verify its authenticity, origin, and validity. At the same time, it seeks to improve the user experience, which will carry out real-time verification on the registration in the LACChain Ethereum network [6].
- Talao [10] is the first French mobile wallet adapted to the European market, developed by the Talao European startup. It is the first wallet to establish identity data in the format of the Tezos network [8]. Talao follows the recommendations of the European Self-Sovereign Identity Framework (ESSIF) to comply with the EU Digital Identity toolbox [18]. It enables users to collect various documents such as attestations, certificates, membership cards, permits, and identity passes, which serve as proof of identity and rights for accessing online services. User data is stored on the user's smartphone and exchanged in accordance with the GDPR [19]. This is achieved through the use of the DID web method, which does not require writing DIDs on a blockchain and hosts them and the related documents on a web domain [34]. Additionally, user consent is explicitly requested for certain actions.
- Open is a prototype wallet that was developed as part of an effort by the Dutch government to build an SSI system over the IPv8 peer-to-peer networking protocol [69], leveraging Trustchain [70]. It provides a REST API to retrieve and share identity data online or offline using Bluetooth, NFC, and QR technology. IPv8 also shares the data in a zero-knowledge way using three different protocols, namely Peng-Bao range proofs [59], Camenisch-Lysyanskaya (CL)

signatures, and an identity-based proof of plaintext [32] using Boneh's cryptosystem [11]. Additionally, the wallet stores identity data in an encrypted form, and its decryption necessitates passport facial recognition [68].

- DIZME (this is me) is a project by the Trust over IP Foundation aiming to fill the gap between SSI and eIDAS. This project details the governance and technology utilized to achieve certain LoA levels. DIZME achieves LoA levels up to substantial. DIZME combines the benefits of SSI, with the legal value and trust of a Qualified Trust Service Provider (QTSP), leveraging InfoCert [67], Italy's first certification authority, which issues and manages qualified digital signature certificates. InfoCert itself acts as a founding steward of the Sovrin trust framework. In brief, the Sovrin ledger is operated by Stewards, trusted organizations within the ecosystem who have agreed to abide by the requirements of the Sovrin trust framework and are responsible for operating the nodes that maintain the Sovrin distributed ledger. Interoperability between SSI and the trust services defined by the eIDAS regulation is made possible by the dual role of InfoCert, which acts not only as founding steward of the Sovrin network (as well as the DIZME governance authority) but also as a QTSP under the eIDAS regulation. DIZME supports both full-disclosure and ZKP formats. Besides depending on the credential LoA presented by the user, the verifier can issue a signature request (advanced or qualified) to obtain a digital signature (one-shot and eIDAS compliant) with which the user can confirm a specific transaction, fully guaranteeing legal compliance and value.
- Microsoft Authenticator was upgraded and transformed into an SSI mobile wallet as of August 2022. It enables its users to manage VCs through the Microsoft Entra Verified ID service [58]. A service that supports available SSI standards such as W3C VC [75], DIDs [74], and OpenID4VC [80]. The wallet obtains and presents the credentials using OpenID4VC protocols [80] in JSON Web Token (JWT) format with an Edwards-curve or elliptic curve digital signature. The signature is verified by resolving entities' DID documents recorded on Bitcoin (leveraging the ION Identity Overlay Network [25]) or a web domain. The ION is a Layer 2 open, permissionless network that relies on the Sidetree protocol to batch transactions together before recording them on the Bitcoin ledger. This resolves the problem of increasing transaction time on the ledger [21]. By batching, the network nodes can write a large number of DID documents to the Bitcoin ledger in a single transaction.
- Verse is an SSI web wallet that has emerged as a result of the EBSI4Austria project [9]. This project, funded by the Connecting Europe Facility (CEF), aims to set up, operate, and maintain Austria's EBSI node and pilot the diploma use case in the country. EBSI4Austria consists of three partners, namely two universities, the Graz University of Technology (TU Graz) and the Vienna University of Economics (WU Vienna), along with Danube Tech, a Vienna-based company specializing in SSI and distributed systems, which is actively involved in related standardization bodies. The Austrian EBSI node is set up and operated at the Department of the eGovernment Innovation Center (EGIZ), which is a part of the TU Graz.

PKI-Based Wallet Solutions

- IRMA is an SSI mobile wallet produced and maintained by the Privacy by Design Foundation (pbdf) [24]. It is used for identification and digital signing purposes. The IRMA SSI solution implements the Idemix cryptographic protocol [36] and issues Attribute-Based Credentials (ABCs). Instead of relying on a blockchain, the system trusts an IRMA server that hosts issuer public key information, which is operated by a verifier in the system. The wallet holder shares the ABC credentials in a zero-knowledge way by implementing the CL signature [15], see [40] for details.
- Apple has launched a collaboration with various US states to enable their residents to link their driver's license or state ID to the wallet on their iPhone and Apple Watch [39]. Arizona and Georgia were the first states to offer this technology to their citizens, followed by Connecticut, Iowa, Kentucky, Maryland, Oklahoma, and Utah. The Apple wallet adopts the International Standards Organization (ISO) 18013-5 standard[3] for Mobile Driving Licence (mDL) [42], which supports centralized PKI and guarantees privacy features such as selective disclosure.
- IDgov.pt is a mobile wallet launched by the Administrative Modernization Agency in Portugal. It stores and periodically updates (every 24 h) digital documents issued by the Portuguese State, such as citizen cards, driving licenses, and ADSE cards. This update occurs after successful user authentication with a Mobile Digital Key (CMD) through a national interoperability platform that makes the data available. Users can share their documents offline by generating a QR code that can be scanned by a similar wallet application and validated through an authentic source of data or by using a validity code via the government portal[4]. The wallet will adopt to the ISO 18013-5 standard and support the Bluetooth protocol in its future versions. Users can also generate a certified PDF that includes a Qualified Electronic Signature (QES) and share it via WhatsApp, email, etc.
- mObywatel is a mobile wallet launched by the Polish Ministry of Digital Affairs in 2018. It allows Polish citizens with a national ID card to access government services such as logging into the e-Tax Office, settling tax returns, storing confirmation of COVID-19 vaccination, verifying obtained driver's qualifications, checking driving license penalty points, and more (find a list of all the services in [48]). Different applications are used in conjunction with mObywatel to enable citizens to obtain their mobile documents. For example, to obtain mobile student ID cards (mLegitymacja [72]), university students need to use the Mobile USOS[5] which is the official university application for requesting

---

[3] Although ISO 18013-5 focuses on the mDL, it can be used to provide a variety of credentials.

[4] https://www.autenticacao.gov.pt.

[5] University Study-Oriented System (USOS) is a system that authorizes a student through the central authorization service (CAS) of the university, providing access to the student's educational information in the USOS database. Find more information at http://usos.edu.pl.

mobile student cards. The Mobile USOS forwards the request to the Ministry and displays a QR code and PIN to retrieve the information about the issued cards. The QR code and PIN are then copied and pasted into the mObywatel application to access the services. The credentials can be shared online via the login portal or using the mWeryfikatora application offline.

– Mobile ID is a user-centric mobile wallet by IDEMIA that allows American citizens to benefit from a government-issued trusted digital ID or mDL, enabling different services such as opening a bank account and filing taxes. Mobile ID adopts ISO 18013-5 [55] for mDL/ID and NIST SP 800-63-3 for IdM [55]. It enables identity verification online, offline, remote, and in-person [38]. NIST SP 800-63-3 specifies enrollment and identity proofing, as critical aspects for credential issuance, leveraging the Mobile ID wallet. This allows the wallet to derive and store identity data locally either from a governmental database or an eID document. The Mobile ID wallet integrates IDEMIA biometric check solutions (Capture SDK/Web Capture) that enable face verification, including liveness checks [37].

Mobile ID wallets have recently been developed in partnership with US state partners such as the Arizona Department of Transportation, Delaware Division of Motor Vehicles (DMV), Oklahoma, and Mississippi Department of Public Safety (DPS). Additionally, Mobile ID has also been developed for the state of Iowa and Colombia[6]. IDEMIA has recently collaborated with Microsoft Azure Active Directory to deliver a secure digital verified credentials solution, which is currently in public preview [1].

4.2   Answer to Research Questions

We provide a technical synopsis of the wallet solutions for Layer 1 (trust), remote support for that, and Layer 3 (credential) of ToIP found in Table 3, as our response to the research questions.

Answer to RQ1: How is Trust Established? Is the Root of Trust Centralized or Decentralized? There are several trust services available with hardware and software support at Layer 1. To make the analysis manageable, we have only considered the trust support for implementing the root of trust, as well as the trust registry service. Accordingly, Table 3 shows how trust is established for both user-centric PKI solutions using CAs and DPKI-based solutions using a blockchain in the system. The technological basis of user-centric PKI-based solutions is largely based on the ISO 18013-5 (mDL) standard, or it is being considered for future development. On the other hand, the DIDs and VCs standards have served as the basis for DPKI-based solutions, known as user-centric SSI, up until this point. Our study confirmed that utilizing SSI has primarily been associated with using a blockchain. However, SSI has a reputation for being blockchain-agnostic. DIDs can be used across different networks and

---

[6] No applications were found for Colombia.

Table 3. Technical specifications for the study wallets

ToIP Layer	Category		Tech Specs. / Wallet Name	1 Connect.Me	2 KeyTrust	3 Talao	4 IRMA	5 Open	6 DIZME	7 Verso	8 Microsoft	9 Apple	10 IDgov-pt	11 mObywatel	12 IDEMIA
Credential	Credential Type		VC [75]		✓	✓				✓	✓				
			ABC [63]	✓			✓	✓	✓						
			mDOC [42]									✓			✓
			PDF										✓		
			QR code										✓	✓	
	Encoding Scheme		JSON [52]		✓		✓	✓	✓	✓	✓				
			JSON-LD [51]	✓	✓	✓				✓	✓				
			CBOR [16]									✓			✓
	Exchange Protocol		DIDComm WACI	✓											
			OpenID4VCI/ OpenID4VP [77,78]		✓	✓				✓					
			CHAPI [4]							✓					
			RestAPI				IRMA protocol	✓						- No specific protocol	
			mDOC Request/ Response [42])									✓[1]	✓[2]		✓[1]
	Verification (or proof)	ZKP	ZKP-BBS+ [53]	✓		✓			✓						
			ZKP-CL [50]				✓	✓							
			ZKP- range & identity-based proof [32,59]					✓							
		DS	VC-JWT [75]		✓					✓	✓				
			VC-LD Signature [75]		✓					✓	✓				
			PoP PKI/MSO [42]									✓		✓	✓
	Revocation		AV [14]	✓			✓		✓						
			Credential status List [27]			✓			✓[3]		✓				
			Revocation status		✓										
			Out of scope												
	Authentication/ Binding		Biometric	FR[4]	UNLKG		UNLKG (OPT)	+ If rqd LivDet	LFR	In three LoAs[5]	-	FR & FPR	-	FR & FPR UNLKG	LPR (or 6-digit PIN)
			PIN		UNLKG		✓						CMD		
			Password							✓				✓	
			Email	ACTIV						✓			-		
			Phone									✓			✓
Trust	Trust Registry		Trusted issuer	-	✓	-	✓[6]		✓[7]	-	POSS	-			
			Trusted verifier							✓					
			Trusted application		- Holder				- Holder						
			Credential schema	✓	✓	-		✓	Schema URI (OPT)	✓	✓		✓		
			Revocation	✓	-	✓		✓[8]	-		✓	✓	✓[9]		
	Root of Trust	Blockchain-based	Sovrin	✓						✓					
			EBSI (Besu, Fabric)												
			Alastria (GoQuorum)		✓										
			Tezos (and Ethereum)			✓[10]									
			Trustchain						✓						
			ION (Bitcoin)								✓				
		Conventional/X.509 PKI					✓					✓	✓	✓	✓

FR: Facial Recognition, LFR: Live Facial Recognition, FPR: Fingerprint Recognition, UNLKG: Unlocking, ACTIV: Activation, OPT: Optional, POSS: Possible

[1] The credentials in Apple are derived from ID cards, while IDEMIA's credentials can be derived from ID cards or governmental datasets. Apple and IDEMIA applications only use the ISO-specific mDOC Request and Response protocol to present credentials to verifiers.

[2] Credentials can be shared over screen-camera communications by generating a QR code, or through a validity code via the government portal. Future versions are anticipated to adopt ISO 18013-5 and use the mDOC Request and Respond protocol over Bluetooth.

[3] Updated attestation status, presented by an attester (or issuer).

[4] In integration with iProov and Onfido.

[5] Authentication happens in three levels: 1) video selfie (and email or phone proof), 2) live photo (and ID card) and QES or 3) liveness assurance (remote or in person).

[6] Only the credential schema appears for trusted issuers in the GitHub repository of pbdf.

[7] All the entities must be registered in an AttestationCommunity, which provides a distributed dataset of their information.

[8] There is no specific revocation registry present. Revocation only happens by the holder and use of the IRMA keyshare server.

[9] By the use of the issuer Identity Hub API endpoint.

[10] Talao may also use a web domain.

platforms, offering better interoperability, enhanced security (no single point of failure), and no third-party control.

Answer to RQ2: How are Credentials Shared in a Controlled Way? This question explores how credentials are selectively shared or disclosed to meet specific requirements or predicates. Wallets employ various data disclosure protocols and cryptographic proofs to enable a controlled sharing of credentials. Table 3 provides an overview of the credential types, encoding schemes, exchange protocols, relevant proofs used for verification, and the revocation mechanisms applied to these credentials.

Table 3 shows credential types/data models mainly as W3C VCs and ABCs, or ISO 18013-5 mDOCs. ABCs are the most privacy-preserving credentials. They enable selectively disclosing data while preserving the privacy of the user using ZKPs[7] [33], and by avoiding any correlation between the credentials and their subjects. On the other hand, VCs are less privacy-preserving compared to ABCs and only a few proposal protocols exist to enable selective disclosure on them [22,79]. Find more detailed information on different types of VCs and their variations ABCs in [82]. ISO similarly offers an mDOC credential type with Concise Binary Object Representation (CBOR) or JavaScript Object Notation (JSON) encoding for sharing credentials offline or online, respectively. The mDOC credential includes a signed Mobile Security Object (MSO) as proof, supporting selective disclosure of the mDL credential. The MSO contains digests of each mDL attribute. The related public key of the signer/issuer, linked to its identity using X.509 PKC, must be maintained by a CA, which is a Verified Issuer Certificate Authority List (VICAL) provider in the mDL context [42]. Besides, the mDL credentials are linked to the holders' identifiers, typically their public keys associated with their wallets. This linkability enables the traceability of the mDLs back to their holders, which can potentially compromise their privacy.

Biometric authentication is a popular method employed by wallets for either binding credentials to individuals or for wallet authentication. For instance, ISO supports the biometric binding of mDL credentials by incorporating a user portrait within the credentials.

Revocation of a DPKI-based wallet credential is based on the data model and proof format, which, for instance, may use an accumulator value for those supporting a ZKP. On the other hand, ISO only adds a validity date to the credentials; revocation is not supported and may be implemented in practice through additional means outside the ISO standard.

User-centric PKI-based wallet agents predominantly exchange mDOC requests offline. However, ISO also defines OpenID or WebAPI protocols for online communications. On the other hand, the most significant credential exchange protocols in DPKI-based cases are DIDComm Messaging, which builds on the decentralized architecture of DIDs, and OpenID family protocols in the

---

[7] ZKPs enable a prover to persuade a verifier of the validity of a mathematical statement without revealing any further information.

context of VCs, namely OID4VCI and OID4VPs [77,78]. These OpenID protocols are credential-agnostic and also support the mDOC data model, allowing for alignment between the VC and the ISO-compliant mDL data models. This alignment presents interesting possibilities, particularly in the context of eIDAS2. Both technologies are included in the EUDI-ARF version 1.0.0, opening up new avenues for research in digital identity wallets. Notably, organizations like Spruce are actively working to align these standards, as mentioned in their work [13]. Furthermore, several solutions supporting technologies like OpenID Connect ensure interoperability with existing IdM systems. This concept has been explored in a study by Kuperberg et al. [49], which presents patterns and approaches for seamless integration between traditional IdM systems and associated applications with user-centric solutions.

5   Conclusion

In this paper, we have reviewed the technological trends of user-centric digital identity wallets, considering the trust models they employ and the control they provide. By formulating two research questions and adopting the ToIP layered technology framework, we have explored the most widely used technologies that address these questions. Each layer of the framework contributes in distinct ways to these dimensions, from the creation of tamper-proof digital credentials to enabling secure and selective credential exchange within the system. This investigation aims to assist designers in developing solutions that offer better functionalities including enhanced security, privacy, and interoperability to users, thereby promoting adoption. Nevertheless, identity wallets are still relatively new, and their adoption rates remain low. Future research in this area could focus on understanding the barriers to adopting these solutions, such as usability issues or lack of trust, and developing strategies to overcome these barriers.

Acknowledgements. This work has been partially supported by "Futuro Conoscenza Srl", jointly created by the FBK and Poligrafico e Zecca dello Stato Italiano (IPZS, the Italian Government Printing Office and Mint), as well as by project SERICS (PE00000014) under the MUR National Recovery and Resilience Plan funded by the European Union - NextGenerationEU.

References

1. Idemia collaborates with microsoft to deliver secure, digital verified credentials solution, 4 May 2021. https://www.idemia.com/press-release/idemia-collaborates-microsoft-deliver-secure-digital-verified-credentials-solution-2021-04-05
2. Trust over ip (toip) technology architecture specification. https://github.com/trustoverip/TechArch/blob/main/spec.md. Draft: 14 November, 2022
3. The toip trust spanning protocol (2023). https://trustoverip.org/blog/2023/01/05/the-toip-trust-spanning-protocol/
4. 3-Clause, B.: Credential handler api. https://github.com/credential-handler/chapi.io. Updated: January, 2023

5. Allen, C.: The path to self-sovereign identity (2016). http://www.lifewithalacrity. com/2016/04/the-path-to-self-soverereign-identity.html

6. Alliance, L.: Lacchain networks. https://lacnet.lacchain.net/overview/. Accessed: 1 February, 2023

7. Alpár, G., Hoepman, J.H., Siljee, J.: The identity crisis. security, privacy and usability issues in identity management. arXiv preprint arXiv:1101.0427 (2011)

8. Arthur Breitman, K.B.: Tezos network (2014). https://tezos.com/whitepaper.pdf

9. Austria, A.S.S.I.T.C.: Ebsi4austria. https://www.a-sit.at/ebsi4austria-at/. Accessed: June 2023

10. Barbe, R.: Talao wallet. https://apps.apple.com/app/talao-wallet/id1582183266? platform=ipad. Updated: 9 June, 2022

11. Boneh, D., Goh, E.-J., Nissim, K.: Evaluating 2-DNF formulas on ciphertexts. In: Kilian, J. (ed.) TCC 2005. LNCS, vol. 3378, pp. 325–341. Springer, Heidelberg (2005). https://doi.org/10.1007/978-3-540-30576-7_18

12. Burke, J.: The network for trusted data. https://cheqd.io. Accessed: 23 January, 2023

13. in Business, I.W.: Where the w3c verifiable credentials meets the iso 18013–5 mobile driving license. https://medium.com/@identitywoman-in-business/where-the-w3c-verifiable-credentials-meets-the-iso-18013-5-mobile-driving-license-2b0a6c992920, 12 September, 2022

14. Camenisch, J., Kohlweiss, M., Soriente, C.: An accumulator based on bilinear maps and efficient revocation for anonymous credentials. In: Jarecki, S., Tsudik, G. (eds.) PKC 2009. LNCS, vol. 5443, pp. 481–500. Springer, Heidelberg (2009). https:// doi.org/10.1007/978-3-642-00468-1_27

15. Camenisch, J., Lysyanskaya, A.: A signature scheme with efficient protocols. In: Cimato, S., Persiano, G., Galdi, C. (eds.) SCN 2002. LNCS, vol. 2576, pp. 268–289. Springer, Heidelberg (2003). https://doi.org/10.1007/3-540-36413-7_20

16. Carsten, B., Paul, H.: Rfc 8949 concise binary object representation (cbor), 16 July, 2020. https://www.w3.org/TR/json-ld/

17. Commission, E.: esignature: Create and verify electronic signatures in line with European standards (2023). https://ec.europa.eu/digital-building-blocks/wikis/display/digital/eSignature

18. Commission, E.: European digital identity architecture and reference framework, 23 February, 2022. https://digital-strategy.ec.europa.eu/en/library/european-digital-identity-architecture-and-reference-framework-outline

19. Commission, E.: General data protection regulation: Gdpr. Official Journal of the European Union, 27 April 2016

20. Content, E.C.D.C.N., Technology: Proposal for amending regulation (eu) no 910/2014: European digital identity framework (2021). https://www. europeansources.info/record/proposal-for-a-regulation-amending-regulation-eu-no-910-2014-as-regards-establishing-a-framework-for-a-european-digital-identity/

21. Daniel Buchner, Orie Steele, Troy Ronda (Eds.): Sidetree v1.0.0. https://identity. foundation/sidetree/spec/. Accessed: June, 2023

22. Fett, D., Kristina Yasuda, B.C.: Selective disclosure for jwts (sd-jwt)- ietf draft. https://datatracker.ietf.org/doc/draft-ietf-oauth-selective-disclosure-jwt/. Updated: 7 December, 2022

23. Davie, M., Gisolfi, D., Hardman, D., et al.: The trust over ip stack. IEEE Commun. Stand. Mag. **3**(4), 46–51 (2019)

24. by Design Foundation, P.: Donwload irma app/privacy by design foundation. https://privacybydesign.foundation. Accessed: 1 February, 2023

25. DIF: Ion. https://identity.foundation/ion/. Accessed: 30 January, 2023

26. DIF: Didcomm messaging v2.x editor's draft (2022). https://identity.foundation/didcomm-messaging/spec/

27. Draft, W.E.: Status list 2021, 8 January, 2023. https://w3c.github.io/vc-status-list-2021/

28. Foundation, D.I.: Present proof protocol 3.0. https://github.com/decentralized-identity/waci-didcomm/blob/main/present_proof/present-proof-v3.md. Updated: June, 2021

29. Foundation, D.I.: Issue credential protocol 3.0 (2020). https://github.com/decentralized-identity/waci-didcomm/blob/main/issue_credential/README.md

30. Foundation, H.: Hyperledger ursa: a shared cryptography library (2023). https://github.com/hyperledger/ursa

31. connect foundation, O.: Openid for verifiable credentials. https://openid.net/openid4vc/. Accessed: June 2023

32. Goldwasser, S., Kharchenko, D.: Proof of plaintext knowledge for the ajtai-dwork cryptosystem. In: Kilian, J. (ed.) TCC 2005. LNCS, vol. 3378, pp. 529–555. Springer, Heidelberg (2005). https://doi.org/10.1007/978-3-540-30576-7_29

33. Goldwasser, S., Micali, S., Rackoff, C.: The knowledge complexity of interactive proof-systems. In: Providing Sound Foundations for Cryptography: On the Work of Shafi Goldwasser and Silvio Micali, pp. 203–225 (2019)

34. Gribneau, C., Prorock, M., Steele, O., et al.: did:web method specification, 30 January, 2023. https://w3c-ccg.github.io/did-method-web/

35. Hassan, M.A., Shukur, Z.: Review of digital wallet requirements. In: 2019 International Conference on Cybersecurity (ICoCSec), pp. 43–48. IEEE (2019)

36. IBM: implementation of an anonymous identity stack for blockchain systems (2023). https://github.com/IBM/idemix

37. IDEMIA: Id&v solution in the context of nist sp 800-63a related to enrollment and identity proofing. https://experience.idemia.com/identity-proofing/develop/identity-proofing-verification/api-docs/1/nist/. Accessed: June 2023

38. IDEMIA: An idemia digital identity white paper: The importance of standards on the road to mobile id. https://pages.nist.gov/800-63-3/sp800-63-3.html (2019)

39. Inc., A.: Apple identity wallet: Add your driver's license or state id to apple wallet. https://support.apple.com/en-us/HT212940 (2022)

40. IRMA: Irma documentations. https://irma.app/docs/revocation/. Accessed: June 2023

41. ISO: Iso/iec dis 23220-1(en): Cards and security devices for personal identification, part 1, 1 August 2021. https://www.iso.org/obp/ui/fr/#iso:std:iso-iec:23220:-1:dis:ed-1:v1:en

42. ISO: Iso/iec 18013-5:2021 personal identification – iso-compliant driving licence – part 5: Mobile driving licence (mdl) application, September 2021. https://www.iso.org/standard/69084.html

43. Jøsang, A., Pope, S.: User centric identity management. In: AusCERT Asia Pacific Information Technology Security Conference, vol. 22, p. 2005. Citeseer (2005)

44. Joyce, A.: Inclusive design, 30 January, 2022. https://www.nngroup.com/articles/inclusive-design/

45. Kettunen, A.: Wallet wars? it's the war of ecosystems! (2023). https://identifinity.net/wallet-wars-its-the-war-of-ecosystems-1dc9261afaa9

46. Korir, M., Parkin, S., Dunphy, P.: An empirical study of a decentralized identity wallet: Usability, security, and perspectives on user control. In: Eighteenth Symposium on Usable Privacy and Security (SOUPS 2022), pp. 195–211 (2022)

47. Kostic, S., Poikela, M.: Do users want to use digital identities? a study of a concept of an identity wallet
48. Kowalski, R.: mobywatel- gov dla ciebie. https://ltqv7w.axshare.com/# id=sym1du&p=ux01_-_dashboard&sc=3&c=1. Accessed: Jan 2023
49. Kuperberg, M., Klemens, R.: Integration of self-sovereign identity into conventional software using established iam protocols: A survey. Open Identity Summit 2022 (2022)
50. Magdalena, B., Marian, M., Maximilian, R., et al.: Analysis of the anonymous credential protocol 'anoncreds 1.0' used in hyperledger indy, 27 March 2022. https://raw.githubusercontent.com/My-DIGI-ID/eesdi-docs/main/anoncreds%20analysis/Anonymous_Credential_protocol_in_Indy-5.pdf
51. Manu, S., Dave, L., Gregg, K., et al.: Json-ld 1.1, 16 July 2020. https://www.w3.org/TR/json-ld/
52. Michael, B.J., John, B., Nat, S.: Rfc 7519 json web token (jwt), 9 March 2019. https://datatracker.ietf.org/doc/rfc7519/
53. Michael, L., Dmitry, K.: Anonymous credentials 2.0., 26 February 2019. https://wiki.hyperledger.org/download/attachments/6426712/Anoncreds2.1.pdf
54. Naik, N., Jenkins, P.: uport open-source identity management system: an assessment of self-sovereign identity and user-centric data platform built on blockchain. In: 2020 IEEE International Symposium on Systems Engineering (ISSE), pp. 1–7. IEEE (2020)
55. NIST: Nist special publication 800-63: Digital identity guidelines, June 2017. https://pages.nist.gov/800-63-3/sp800-63-3.html. Updated: 2 February, 2020
56. Nokhbeh Zaeem, R., Chang, K.C., Huang, T.C., et al.: Blockchain-based self-sovereign identity: Survey, requirements, use-cases, and comparative study. In: IEEE/WIC/ACM International Conference on Web Intelligence and Intelligent Agent Technology, pp. 128–135 (2021)
57. O'Donnell, D., Eng, P.: The current and future state of digital wallets. Continuum Loop Inc., p. 83 (2019)
58. Patel, A.: Microsoft entra verified id. https://www.microsoft.com/en-us/security/business/identity-access/microsoft-entra-verified-id. Accessed: 28 May 2023
59. Peng, K., Bao, F.: An efficient range proof scheme. In: 2010 IEEE Second International Conference on Social Computing, pp. 826–833. IEEE (2010)
60. Podgorelec, B., Alber, L., Zefferer, T.: What is a (digital) identity wallet? a systematic literature review. In: 2022 IEEE 46th Annual Computers, Software, and Applications Conference (COMPSAC), pp. 809–818. IEEE (2022)
61. Poelman, M., Iqbal, S.: Investigating the compliance of the gdpr: processing personal data on a blockchain. In: 2021 IEEE 5th International Conference on Cryptography, Security and Privacy (CSP), pp. 38–44. IEEE (2021)
62. Popov, A., Nystroem, M., Balfanz, D., Hodges, J.: The token binding protocol version 1.0. Technical report (2018)
63. Rannenberg, K., Camenisch, J., Sabouri, A.: Attribute-based credentials for trust. Identity in the Information Society. Springer (2015)
64. Schwalm, S., Albrecht, D., Alamillo, I.: eidas 2.0: challenges, perspectives and proposals to avoid contradictions between eidas 2.0 and ssi. Open Identity Summit 2022 (2022)
65. Sovrin: Principles of ssi v3. https://sovrin.org/principles-of-ssi/. Accessed: November 2023
66. Sovrin: Sovrin networks. https://sovrin.org/overview/. Accessed: 1 Aug 2022
67. S.p.A., I.: Infocert offre una suite completa di prodotti dedicati al tuo mondo digitale. https://www.infocert.it/. Accessed: 1 Feb 2023

68. Speelman, T.: Self-sovereign identity: proving power over legal entities (2020)
69. Stokkink, Q., Ishmaev, G., Epema, D., Pouwelse, J.: A truly self-sovereign identity system. In: 2021 IEEE 46th Conference on Local Computer Networks (LCN), pp. 1–8. IEEE (2021)
70. Stokkink, Q., Pouwelse, J.: Deployment of a blockchain-based self-sovereign identity. In: 2018 IEEE International Conference on Internet of Things (iThings) and IEEE Green Computing and Communications (GreenCom) and IEEE Cyber, Physical and Social Computing (CPSCom) and IEEE smart data (SmartData), pp. 1336–1342. IEEE (2018)
71. Strüker, J., Urbach, N., Guggenberger, T., et al.: Self-sovereign identity: Grundlagen, anwendungen und potenziale portabler digitaler identitäten (2021)
72. System, E.U.I.: Eunis 2020 congress book of abstracts (2020). https://www.eunis.org/download/2020/EUNIS_Book-of-Abstract_2020.pdf
73. W3C: Vc api. https://github.com/w3c-ccg/vc-api. Updated: 7 March, 2022
74. (W3C), T.W.W.W.C.: Decentralized identifiers (dids) v1.0 (2022). https://www.w3.org/TR/did-core/
75. (W3C), T.W.W.W.C.: Verifiable credentials data model v1.1.(2022). https://www.w3.org/TR/vc-data-model/
76. (WAI), W.W.A.I.: Accessibility, usability, and inclusion. https://www.w3.org/WAI/fundamentals/accessibility-usability-inclusion/. Updated: 6 March, 2022
77. Workgroup, O.C.: Openid for verifiable credential issuance (2022). https://openid.net/specs/openid-4-verifiable-credential-issuance-1_0.html
78. Workgroup, O.C.: Self-issued openid provider v2 (2022). https://openid.net/specs/openid-connect-self-issued-v2-1_0.html
79. Yamamoto, D., Suga, Y., Sako, K.: Formalising linked-data based verifiable credentials for selective disclosure. In: 2022 IEEE European Symposium on Security and Privacy Workshops (EuroS&PW), pp. 52–65. IEEE (2022)
80. Yasuda, K., Lodderstedt, T., Chadwick, D., "et al.": Whitepaper: Openid for verifiable credentials (23 June, 2022)
81. Yildiz, H., Küpper, A., Thatmann, D., et al.: A tutorial on the interoperability of self-sovereign identities. arXiv preprint arXiv:2208.04692 (2022)
82. Young, K.: Verifiable credentials flavors explained. Linux Foundation Public Health, Linux Foundation Public Health (2021)

Impact of Using a Privacy Model on Smart Buildings Data for CO_2 Prediction

Marlon P. da Silva[1], Henry C. Nunes[1]([✉]), Charles V. Neu[2],
Luana T. Thomas[1], Avelino F. Zorzo[1], and Charles Morisset[2]

[1] Polytechnic School PUCRS, Porto Alegre, Brazil
Henry.Nunes@edu.pucrs.br
[2] School of Computing Newcastle University, Newcastle upon Tyne, UK

Abstract. There is a constant trade-off between the utility of the data collected and processed by the many systems forming the Internet of Things (IoT) revolution and the privacy concerns of the users living in the spaces hosting these sensors. Privacy models, such as the SITA (Spatial, Identity, Temporal, and Activity) model, can help address this trade-off. In this paper, we focus on the problem of CO_2 prediction, which is crucial for health monitoring but can be used to monitor occupancy, which might reveal some private information. We apply a number of transformations on a real dataset from a Smart Building to simulate different SITA configurations on the collected data and transformed that data with multiple Machine Learning (ML) techniques to analyse the performance of the models to predict CO_2 levels. Our results show that different SITA configurations do not make one algorithm perform better or worse than others; also, the temporal dimension was particularly sensitive, with scores decreasing up to 18.9% between the original and the transformed data. This shows the effect of different levels of data privacy on the data utility of IoT applications, and can also help to identify which parameters are more relevant for those systems so that higher privacy settings can be set while data utility is still preserved.

Keywords: Privacy · CO2 Prediction · Smart Buildings · Sensors Data

1 Introduction

The impact of the quality of an indoor environment on the well-being of its occupants is a relatively well-studied problem More than 20 years ago, Redlich *et al.* noted the increase of the Sick-Building Syndrome (SBS), which includes *"upper-respiratory irritative symptoms, headaches, fatigue, and rash"* [9]. Although they deemed CO_2 as *"an unlikely cause of SBS"*, a study widely covered in the general press, clearly indicates potential health risks associated with chronic exposure to

© IFIP International Federation for Information Processing 2023
Published by Springer Nature Switzerland AG 2023
V. Atluri and A. L. Ferrara (Eds.): DBSec 2023, LNCS 13942, pp. 133–140, 2023.
https://doi.org/10.1007/978-3-031-37586-6_8

environmentally relevant elevations in ambient CO_2, including *"inflammation, reductions in higher-level cognitive abilities and impact on different body organs"* [5]. There is, therefore, a clear need for precise and reactive monitoring of indoor CO_2, to detect and prevent dangerous situations.

On the one hand, smart buildings deploy IoT architecture usually including CO_2 and temperature sensors [14], intended to be used on new services that can be provided, many supported by Machine Learning (ML) techniques. Those services are intended to automatise management and optimise user comfort, security, and safety, quite often with a focus on occupancy measurement [3]. The need for CO_2 monitoring is likely to push an increasing deployment of such systems. On the other hand, this monitoring faces an increasing privacy concern related to ambient infrastructures. Naeini *et al.* for instance showed that although roughly half of the participants in a survey were comfortable or very comfortable with the collection of presence and temperature data, people nevertheless favour data collection in which they cannot be identified immediately and do not want inferences to be made from otherwise anonymous data [8].

Lately, new legislation has been introduced to support and regulate personal data usage and people's privacy preferences, e.g. GDPR (General Data Protection Regulation) in the EU/UK and LGPD (Lei Geral de Proteção de Dados) in Brazil. A common principle is that of *data minimisation*, which specifies that a system should not collect and process more data than needed for its purpose. There is also a clear concern that users must be involved in data collection and processing and their preferences must be considered. As a result, a data protection system must work out a difficult trade-off: minimise data collection to satisfy as much as possible user privacy preference while avoiding a loss to data utility, which might reduce the efficiency of processing, and as a consequence could impact the overall utility of the data to the provided services.

In this paper, we explore this trade-off in the context of a real-world smart building by evaluating how different ML methods perform to predict CO2 when different privacy levels are defined[1] We also evaluate how different levels of privacy impact data utility in comparison to when the whole data is available.

2   Background - Privacy Model and IoT Datasets

With the revolution of IoT devices, many smart buildings are emerging, especially in universities and business offices. They are responsible for collecting a huge amount of data from many people every day. Hence, there is a growing concern about data privacy.

In recent years there was an increase in demand for privacy techniques [11] [10]. This comes in line with an increase in awareness of society to how easily data is collected, distributed, and used in the information age. In IoT scenarios, data from sensors can be stored in datasets. A dataset can be useful for history, use in prediction models and pattern detection, forensics, and other cases. However, the

---

[1] All code and data used is available at https://github.com/conseg/SITA-CO2.

dataset can also be used in a malicious way. To reduce the chances of using this data for malicious purposes, legislation has been created in different jurisdictions that address this topic, GDPR and, LGPD are a few examples. This legislation tries to organise how data is treated and protected.

SITA [2] is a conceptual model divided into four dimensions: Spatial, referring to the user's location data; Identity, related to the user's personal identification data; Temporal, date and time information about user activity; Activity, sensitive data about user behavior, situational data, and preferences.

Each dimension can be assigned a level from zero to four. The level represents the amount of privacy for that dimension, where zero represents no access to the data and four represents full access. The values in-between allow controlling the shared data using aggregation, and obfuscation techniques to granularly control privacy, are application specific, and need to be created by the developer.

The embedded privacy control in most applications works binary, where a user can block or allow it to share all his data in the application. SITA proposes the use of different levels as a way to remediate this. The user can control how much information he is sharing, this, however, comes with a cost. Less information that is shared in the application can degrade an application service because of the lack of precise information. This trade-off is very common in privacy applications, known as the **privacy-utility trade-off**.

Even simple data such as CO_2 can be used to attack users' privacy. Here we present a simple model that can be used to exploit the CO_2 readings from a sensor, or its prediction if accurate, to determine which specific person is in a room. There is a number of studies that suggest that people who weigh more produce more CO_2 [7]. In this model, the potential difference of CO_2 emission between two individuals will change the CO_2 readings of the room, allowing it to be used to identify who is inside a room. The scenario for this model is a small closed room that is used by just two people. These two people have a significant difference in body composition and are of different sex. A third person wants to identify who is inside a room. This third person has background information about the room user's weight, historical and present CO_2 readings of the room.

The attacker can use a clustering ML algorithm to separate the historical CO_2 into three groups. The cluster group with less CO_2 values is when the room is empty. The remaining two groups are when someone is inside the room. The smallest CO_2 values from those two are when the smallest person is inside the room and the highest for the bigger person. Further readings can be compared to the clustered groups to identify who is inside the room.

3   Experiment

The objective of our experiment is to analyze the impact of the SITA privacy model in CO_2 predictions that use machine learning when one dimension of the configuration is changed. We briefly summarise the experiment conducted in the following sequence of steps.

The first step was the collection of the dataset for the prediction model. We used data publicly available from the Urban Sciences Building(USB) at Newcastle[2]. The second step was to transform the original dataset to better suit the SITA transformation. The third step was the creation of different datasets from different SITA configurations. We aim to analyze the isolated impact of each SITA dimension. Thus, for each dimension, we changed its level from 0 to 4 while keeping the others in a fixed state. The analysed configurations are X444, 44X4, and 444X, where X is a number between 0 and 4. Fourth step, prediction models are created using LR, RR, RF, GBR, and DTR. The selected techniques are based on the work of Wibisono *et al.* [15]. Each technique is used with all datasets previously generated. Fifth step, we analysed the impact on the prediction model using common ML metrics R^2 score, RMSE, and MAE. The chosen metrics are also based on the work of Wibisono *et al.* [15].

3.1 Dataset Scenario and Data Collection

We collected data from the USB. The building includes multiple IoT sensors that can be accessed online. An API is provided which allows to access the data in real-time, and historical data. The dataset has data from October 2018 to March 2020 from five sensors: humidity, temperature, occupancy, brightness, and CO_2, organised by rooms. The rooms differ in size, available sensors, and usage.

3.2 Data Transformation

To remove outliers, we defined a range of values for each feature. Thus CO_2 values are ranging from 0 to 1,000 ppm (ASHRAE limit for healthy environments[3]) and temperature values range from 0 °C to 50 °C. The relative humidity values ranged from 0% to 100% and the brightness values ranged from 0 lm to 2000 lm. This resulted in a new dataset with about 200,000 records.

The Identity dimension is not considered in our work, since there is no personal identification data used. The Spatial dimension is represented by data regarding the room and the zone of each entry; for the Temporal dimension, we took as input the datetime parameter; and for the Activity dimension, we considered the following attributes: CO_2, Temperature, Humidity, and Brightness. The data transformation was done using generalization and suppression techniques based on syntactic anonymity. For the experiment, a SITA configuration is applied to all the entries in the dataset. We will refer to a group of operations that changes the same dimension using X for the dimension that is changed (e.g., X444 refers to configurations 4444, 3444, 2444, 1444, and 0444).

3.3 Machine Learning Training

The ML models were trained using the Kaggle[4] platform, in a remote computing environment with 4 CPUs and 16 Gigabytes of RAM. The library used for the

---

[2] https://api.usb.urbanobservatory.ac.uk.

[3] https://www.ashrae.org/about/position-documents.

[4] https://www.kaggle.com and https://scikit-learn.org.

training was the scikit-learn version 1.0.2. Before the training, since the algorithms here studied only work with numerical data, we transformed all textual data into numerical over each dataset. After this, the datasets were split into training/testing in a proportion of 80/20 utilizing random sampling, with a random state of 10. Over these, we applied the *KFold()* method from scikit-learn, with ten splits and setting the parameter *shuffle* to *true*, to avoid overfitting the model. The machine learning algorithms used were the same as the previous work [3]. Each regressor method was then instantiated using their default implementations; the R^2, MAE, and RMSE scores were calculated using the function *cross_val_score()*, indicating in the *score* parameter the respective metric.

4   Results and Discussion

For every specific SITA configuration, we ran all five algorithms, and measured the results according to three parameters: the R^2 (Fig. 1), MAE (Fig. 2), and RMSE (Fig. 3) scores.

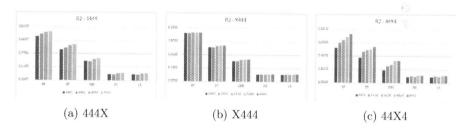

(a) 444X   (b) X444   (c) 44X4

Fig. 1. R^2 scores for machine learning algorithms in different SITA dimensions.

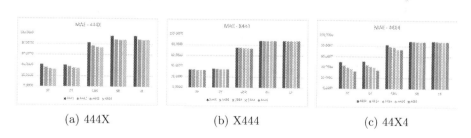

(a) 444X   (b) X444   (c) 44X4

Fig. 2. MAE scores for machine learning algorithms in different SITA dimensions.

Regarding the R^2 score, the Random Forest algorithm outperforms all other approaches, with an average value of 74.29% for the baseline data. When taking the Activity dimension as a variable, the minimum average score of this model is 66.05%. It is important to observe that we did not apply level 0 of SITA

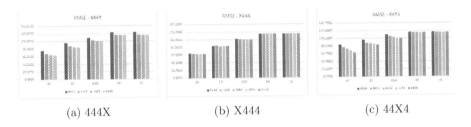

(a) 444X   (b) X444   (c) 44X4

Fig. 3. MAE scores for machine learning algorithms in different SITA dimensions.

transformations in that dimension since this operation would erase all CO_2 data, thus making it impossible to predict its levels. For the Temporal dimension, the minimum average score of RF is 51.80% for the Temporal privacy setting of 0 (*i.e.* all data deleted). This represents a performance decrease of 28.98% regarding the baseline. When considering the Spatial dimension, the RF model produces an average R^2 score of 71.86% when the privacy setting is at 0, 1.73% reduction from baseline.

Analyzing the MAE, the lowest score for the baseline was obtained running the Random Forest model, with a result of 32,40%. With the Activity dimension as variable, the maximum average score of such algorithm equals to 41,28% when privacy level = 1 for Activity. This represents an error increase of 27,38% regarding to the baseline. For the Temporal dimension, we have a maximum average score of 49,85% (level = 0), 53,50% higher than the baseline. The Spatial dimension has an MAE score of 33,63% on the strictest privacy level for the RF model. This represents an increase of 3,56%, considering the baseline.

Finally, we look at the RMSE metric. The lowest value was obtained again with the RF model, with a score of 62.99%. For the Activity dimension, the highest value was 75,47%, 13.83% higher than the baseline. When we set Temporal and Spatial domains as variables, their respective scores were 84.20% (an increase of 33.67%) and 64.31% (2.09% higher than the baseline).

Our results confirm the experimental data presented in [15], regarding the performance of the ML algorithms there analyzed. Linear Regression and Ridge Regression, being fairly simple algorithms , are expected to perform poorly than more sophisticated methods, especially on large datasets. The other algorithms used in our experiments can be seen as belonging to the same family, with Decision Tree being the basis for both Random Forest and Gradient Boosting. However, some careful tuning is necessary for the latter to achieve good results, which makes it harder to apply the method over different domains. We also show that RF is the only algorithm between those analyzed that produces R^2 scores over 70%. When analyzing the Mean Absolute Error, our results show that the performances of RF and DT algorithms are very close, but the RMSE values present a more significant difference between these two methods. This can be explained by the fact that RMSE has a tendency to be increasingly larger than MAE as the test sample size increases, thus exacerbating small differences in MAE values between the two approaches.

Another discussion can be made about the impact of applying our SITA implementation over the chosen dataset. Our results show that the dimensions present different sensibilities to more restrictive privacy settings. Taking the R^2 score, we show that the Spatial dimension is the least affected, and the Temporal dimension the most affected, with Activity being in an intermediate place. This can be used to better understand the importance of different variables in applying ML techniques. Also, by analysing the scores of each privacy setting, we observe that the Activity dimension has a score below 70% when the privacy setting is lower than 3; the same occurs for the Temporal dimension with privacy setting lower than 4 (reflecting the higher sensitivity of this dimension), and it is not observed in the Spatial dimension in any configuration. with this we demonstrate that it is possible, through different SITA settings, to improve the users' privacy and keep ML services functional.

5   Related Work

There are numerous works related to the prediction of CO_2 in IoT environments using machine learning algorithms. The CO_2 monitoring is an important component of controlling the air quality of a room, which when correctly managed provides well-being, controls general air pollution, and detects potential harms, such as fire. Creating a prediction model can be positive in cases presented by Kapoor *et al.* [6] where smart sensors are not available, also a model can be used to help in the building design. In his work, they present a model working with multiple machine learning algorithms and achieve a precise model. Other works are developed in a similar fashion using machine learning algorithms in an IoT scenario to create a prediction model for CO_2 [1] [12]. However, the use of such prediction models and privacy models as the one presented in Sect. 2 are not common. The readings of a CO_2 with other background information can be used in a linkage attack as presented in Sect. 2.

6   Final Consideration and Future Work

In this work, we analysed the trade-off between privacy and utility for CO_2 prediction on a real dataset in the context of smart buildings. Therefore, several transformations were implemented on the original data to simulate different privacy levels and generate new transformed datasets that were used as input to train five distinct machine learning models for CO_2 prediction.

The results show that the performance of Regression-based ML techniques is lower than decision Tree-based techniques. The use of the privacy model, as expected, deteriorated the performance of all algorithms. More aggressive SITA configurations resulted in worse performance and each dimension has a different impact on the prediction models. The highest impact was observed when higher privacy levels were simulated on the Temporal dimension.

As future research, our model could be improved by using Syntactic Anonymity [13] with SITA to increase the data privacy. To the best of our knowledge, there is no work of this kind yet. Also, the inclusion of Differential Privacy [4] is another possibility that could improve the privacy model, since it is a more powerful privacy definition than syntactic anonymity.

Acknowledgments. This work has been supported by: the PETRAS National Centre of Excellence for IoT Systems Cybersecurity, UK EPSRC grant EP/S035362/1, and by the Coordenação de Aperfeiçoamento de Pessoal de Nível Superior - Brasil (CAPES).

References

1. Data driven indoor air quality prediction in educational facilities based on IoT network. Energy Build. **236**, 110782 (2021)
2. Andersen, M.S., Kjargaard, M.B., Grønbæk, K.: The SITA principle for location privacy - conceptual model and architecture. In: 2013 International Conference on Privacy and Security in Mobile Systems (PRISMS), pp. 1–8 (2013)
3. Candanedo, L.M., Feldheim, V.: Accurate occupancy detection of an office room from light, temperature, humidity and co2 measurements using statistical learning models. Energy Build. **112**, 28–39 (2016)
4. Dwork, C.: Differential privacy: a survey of results. In: Proceedings of the 5th International Conference Conference on Theory and Applications Of Models of Computation (TAMC), pp. 1–19 (2008)
5. Jacobson, T.A., Kler, J.S., Hernke, M.T., Braun, R.K., Meyer, K.C., Funk, W.E.: Direct human health risks of increased atmospheric carbon dioxide. Nature Sustain. **2**(8), 691–701 (2019)
6. Kapoor, N.R., et al.: Machine learning-based CO_2 prediction for office room: a pilot study. Wire. Commun. Mobile Comput. **2022**, 9404807 (2022)
7. Magkos, F., et al.: The environmental foodprint of obesity. Obesity **28**(1), 73–79 (2019)
8. Naeini, P.E., et al.: Privacy expectations and preferences in an {IoT} world. In: Thirteenth Symposium on Usable Privacy and Security (SOUPS 2017), pp. 399–412 (2017)
9. Redlich, C.A., Sparer, J., Cullen, M.R.: Sick-building syndrome. The Lancet **349**(9057), 1013–1016 (1997)
10. Sarwar, K., Yongchareon, S., Yu, J., Ur Rehman, S.: A survey on privacy preservation in Fog-enabled internet of things. ACM Comput. Surv. **55**(1), 1–39 (2021)
11. Seliem, M., Elgazzar, K., Khalil, K.: Towards privacy preserving IoT environments: a survey. Wirel. Commun. Mob. Comput. **2018**, 1032761 (2018)
12. Sharma, P.K., De, T., Saha, S.: IoT based indoor environment data modelling and prediction. In: 2018 10th International Conference on Communication Systems & Networks (COMSNETS), pp. 537–539 (2018)
13. Sweeney, L.: Achieving k-anonymity privacy protection using generalization and suppression. Internat. J. Uncertain. Fuzziness Knowl.-Based Syst. **10**(05), 571–588 (2002)
14. Verma, A., Prakash, S., Srivastava, V., Kumar, A., Mukhopadhyay, S.C.: Sensing, controlling, and IoT infrastructure in smart building: a review. IEEE Sens. J. **19**(20), 9036–9046 (2019)
15. Wibisono, A., et al.: Dataset of short-term prediction of co2 concentration based on a wireless sensor network. Data Brief **31**, 105924 (2020)

Digital Twins for IoT Security Management

Philip Empl$^{(\boxtimes)}$ ⓘ, Henric Hager ⓘ, and Günther Pernul ⓘ

Department of Information Systems, University of Regensburg, Universitätsstraße 31,
93053 Regensburg, Germany
{philip.empl,henric.hager,guenther.pernul}@ur.de

Abstract. The proliferation of Internet of Things (IoT) devices has increased the risk of cyber threats to the confidentiality, integrity, and availability of data processed. In this context, proactive security management has emerged as a critical strategy for protecting assets and networks. However, managing the complex nature of IoT devices poses a significant challenge to effective IoT security management. Digital twins - virtual replicas of physical assets - offer a promising solution to address these challenges. By creating a digital twin of an IoT network, security analysts could continuously monitor and regulate the IoT network, detect potential problems before they escalate, and assess the impact of new configurations and updates without risking the physical ones. This paper proposes a concept that uses digital twins for proactive IoT security management. To this end, we implement a proof of concept to demonstrate the practical applicability of this approach for four different security use cases. Our results provide a starting point for further research to leverage digital twins for IoT security management.

Keywords: Internet of Things · Network · Cybersecurity · Security management · Digital twin · Digital twin network

1 Introduction

The pervasive use of Internet of Things (IoT) devices in our daily lives, ranging from smart home appliances to industrial automation systems, has led to significant threats to the availability, integrity, and confidentiality of data processed within IoT networks. The escalating growth of cybercrime is estimated to result in a staggering worldwide cost of $10.5 trillion by 2025, underscoring the importance of addressing security issues (i.e., insecure configurations or communication) in IoT networks [4,16]. In response, proactive security and automation have emerged as crucial strategies to safeguard assets and their associated networks [14,17]. By proactively identifying and addressing security risks, organizations can mitigate the likelihood of potential cyber-attacks, protecting sensitive data and ensuring the privacy of their networks [7]. In light of these

ⓒ IFIP International Federation for Information Processing 2023
Published by Springer Nature Switzerland AG 2023
V. Atluri and A. L. Ferrara (Eds.): DBSec 2023, LNCS 13942, pp. 141–149, 2023.
https://doi.org/10.1007/978-3-031-37586-6_9

developments, proactive network security management has become a relevant and necessary area of focus for protecting the security of organizational networks.

However, effective network security management in IoT has become an increasingly daunting task due to the intricate nature of IoT devices [1]. These devices exhibit diverse hardware, operating systems, and communication protocols, rendering them challenging to secure using traditional network security management. Furthermore, IoT devices are often tailored to specific use cases and are constrained by their processing power and memory, compounding network management's difficulty. To address these challenges, digital twins offer a promising solution for leveraging the security of IoT networks [7]. They are often considered as they provide a precise and comprehensive virtual representation of the physical IoT network, making IoT devices visible, which are usually hidden when performing IP network scans. By creating a digital twin of an IoT network, security analysts could continuously monitor the IoT network, detect potential issues before they escalate, and evaluate the effects of new configurations and updates without jeopardizing the physical network. To our knowledge, digital twins have not yet been considered for IoT security management.

This paper leverages digital twins to address the pressing need for proactive security management in IoT networks. Given the increasing threat landscape and the inherent complexity of IoT, traditional network management techniques have proven insufficient, necessitating alternative and more sophisticated solutions. Digital twins are an ideal solution as they allow for proactive network monitoring, analysis, and optimization to enhance security. Thus, this paper's research question is formulated as follows: *"How can digital twins enable IoT security management?"*. The contribution of this paper is twofold: firstly, we design a concept for leveraging digital twins in the context of proactive IoT security management. Secondly, we implement a proof of concept, demonstrating this concept's practical applicability through four different security use cases.

The remainder of this paper is structured as follows. Section 2 provides a detailed exposition of the background on IoT network management and digital twins. Section 3 presents our concept showing the use of digital twins to manage IoT networks. In Section 4, we validate our proposed concept by implementing a proof of concept considering four security use cases and measuring the performance outcomes of each. Finally, in Section 5, we conclude the paper by summarizing our research.

2   Background

2.1   IoT Network Management

Network management refers to *monitoring* and *optimizing* a computer network using methods like network verification [15], or testing [8]. Following the network management cycle is crucial to automate tasks, starting from measurement, moving towards decision-making, action strategy, verification, and execution [3].

According to the International Standard Organization (ISO), traditional network management encompasses five fundamental aspects, commonly referred to as fault, configuration, accounting, performance, and security management (FCAPS) [13]. *Fault management (F)* deals with detecting, isolating, and correcting faults or errors in the network. *Configuration management (C)* deals with maintaining accurate and up-to-date information about the network's configuration, e.g., hardware, software, topology, or policies. *Accounting management (A)* deals with tracking network resource usage, including bandwidth, storage, and CPU cycles. *Performance management (P)* monitors and manages the network's performance. *Security management (S)* aims to protect the network from unauthorized access, data theft, and other security threats.

Although these aspects have been specifically designed for computer networks, they apply to IoT as well [1]. The idea behind IoT is based on many heterogeneous devices that are identifiable and interconnected through dedicated communication networks [2]. As defined by the IEEE 802.15.4 standard, such devices are termed reduced functional devices, with a narrower range of functionalities than full functional devices. The German Federal Office for Information Security (BSI) categorizes IoT devices as controllable when operating within a sensor network or addressable when communicating within a TCP/IP network [11]. In this paper, we adopt the definition provided by the BSI.

2.2   Digital Twin Network

A digital twin is a virtual representation of a physical asset used for simulation, replication, or analytics [5]. It maintains bidirectional communication with its physical counterpart. Digital twins are used for many security operations, e.g., cyber ranges [18] or security simulations [6]. A digital twin network addresses the complexities of real-world networks by establishing mappings between multiple digital twins [19]. It incorporates various network metrics, such as topology, routing, and traffic, enabling comprehensive modeling [9,10]. Digital twin networks facilitate "what-if" analyses based on periodic configuration and real-time data collection [12].

3   Digital Twin-Based IoT Security Management

We propose a concept that combines the network management cycle methodology [3] with digital twins to enable security management in IoT networks, as depicted in Fig. 1. This concept addresses the challenges posed by IoT devices' heterogeneity and their networks' dynamic nature. Digital twins play a crucial role in modeling IoT devices, making them visible, providing security recommendations, and facilitating verification and optimization. Our proposed concept comprises three interconnected components: the real world, virtual representation, and network management.

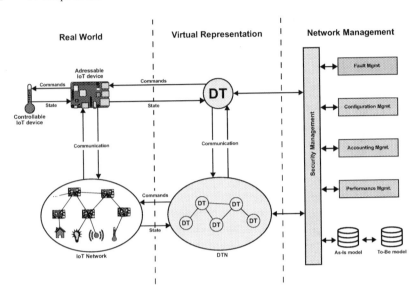

Fig. 1. Digital twin-based IoT security management.

The real world encompasses IoT devices such as laptops, sensors, actuators, controllers, and wearables. Addressable IoT devices serve as coordinators and define access control policies, while controllable IoT devices are limited nodes communicating with coordinators. The IP networks define the primary networks in the network topology, and controllable IoT networks become subnets if an addressable IoT device functions as a coordinator. The network represents the communication relationships between addressable and controllable IoT devices.

The virtual representation models the dependencies of the real world and employs digital twins. Digital twins realistically represent IoT devices and networks, including information about addressable and controllable IoT devices. Digital twins enable bidirectional communication with physical assets and orchestrate commands in the real world. A digital twin network captures the relationships between digital twins and replicates the communication links in the real world. This combination of real-world information and digital twins facilitates subsequent IoT security management.

Network management utilizes digital twins and their networks to monitor and optimize IoT devices in the real world. It encompasses all aspects of FCAPS, focusing on security management, and is coordinated by a central manager. The As-Is model represents the current state of the virtual representation, while the To-Be model outlines the desired objectives regarding FCAPS. Security issues and possible optimizations can be identified by comparing these two models. Recommendations for optimizations are based on the To-Be model, but the final decision lies with the security analyst on whether to deploy them.

4   Proof of Concept

This section will validate the presented concept using four security use cases. These use cases are designed to improve the overall security posture of the IoT network using digital twins in analytics mode. We begin by detailing the security use cases that influence the experimental setting.

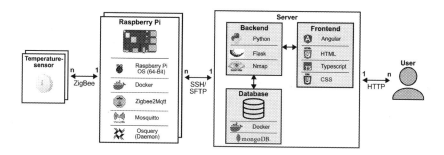

Fig. 2. Experimental setting detailing on the proof of concept.

4.1   Security Use Cases

In the realm of IoT, various security threats can compromise the confidentiality, integrity, and availability of data. We focus on addressable and controllable IoT devices, evaluating our concept against four security threats. *Open ports* (1) on addressable IoT devices can serve as gateways for attackers. To preserve device and network security, closing insecure network ports and leaving essential ones open is crucial. *Malicious USB dongles* (2) present another attack vector. To maintain network security, monitoring USB ports and implementing appropriate measures closely is essential. *Weak access controls* (3) pose significant risks to network confidentiality. Strict access control lists must be enforced to mitigate these risks. *Insecure configurations* (4) allow unauthorized devices access to the network, which should be optimized.

4.2   Experimental Setting

Our experimental setting, as shown in Fig. 2, addresses the security use cases in IoT networks. A digital twin is represented by the network's data stored in the database, while bidirectional communication aims at collecting data and optimizing IoT devices. The experiments were conducted using a Raspberry Pi 3B+ model running Raspberry Pi OS, and a CC2531 flashed ZigBee dongle. A MacOS machine with six cores, 16 GB RAM, and a 256 GB SSD acts as the server. Bidirectional communication between the server and the Raspberry Pi occurs via SSH and SFTP protocols. The Raspberry Pi hosts two critical containerized microservices: Zigbee2MQTT and Mosquitto. Zigbee2MQTT manages the ZigBee network, which includes controllable devices like Xiaomi temperature sensors. The controllable IoT network data is routed from the Zigbee network to the MQTT broker, creating an event-driven architecture. We use osquery, an open-source tool that provides a unified interface to different operating systems, analyzing and optimizing the Zigbee network. In addition to controllable IoT devices, we integrate multiple IP addressable devices, including routers and smartphones, expanding the scope of addressable IoT devices beyond the Raspberry Pi. Our proof of concept is available on GitHub[1].

Table 1. Security use cases, problem statements, and recommendations.

Use case	Problem statement	Recommendation
Open ports	Number of ports exceeds max	Terminate open ports
USB dongle	Unknown USB dongle	Unplug USB dongle
Weak access control	ACL inconsistency	Replace the ACL
Insecure config.	permit_join flag differs	Set permit_join flag

4.3   Results

We present our experimental results based on the optimization process by Arzo et al. [3]. We have findings for the different phases of the process and results related to the performance. In the *security assessment* phase, we extract data from IoT networks to create digital twins and a network representing the As-Is model. We develop an algorithm to strategically identify controllable IoT devices in IP networks, as they cannot be discovered solely through IP network scans. We successfully identify addressable and controllable IoT devices, storing the data in a MongoDB database. This data reflects the respective digital twins. Additional information, such as device logs and configuration files, is gathered for our pre-defined security use cases. All the data is automatically collected.

Optimization Process. During the *To-Be-model comparison* phase, the digital twins compare the respective network model (As-Is model) with the To-Be model. Analysts manually define the To-Be model, so we set the maximum number of open ports and establish secure configurations. The digital twin network emphasizes deviations between those two models as potential security issues. Last, we run the *optimization, test,* and *deployment* phases. Table 1 outlines the security use cases, their problem statements, and recommended optimizations. The digital twin network provides recommendations to analysts, who can verify and deploy optimizations to the real network.

---

[1] https://github.com/Ric1234567/DigitalTwinsForIoTSecurityManagement.

Performance Evaluation. We conduct a performance evaluation to assess the time required for monitoring and optimizing the IoT network (see Fig. 3). The evaluation reveals varying times for different security use cases, with USB dongle monitoring being the shortest and port monitoring being the longest. We successfully resolved all security use cases within the expected time frame, utilizing automation and the guidance of the digital twin network.

Limitations. We must consider the limitations of our research results in the context of IoT security management. Our proof of concept concentrates only on the digital twin in analytics mode and IoT networks' periodic monitoring and optimization. Therefore, we do not employ simulation, e.g., "what-if" analysis, and replication modes that could have aided in a more detailed optimization and verification throughout the process. Our proof of concept may also account for software-defined networks, which could be valuable in managing addressable and controllable IoT devices. However, this should not call into question the concept.

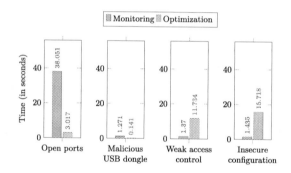

Fig. 3. Performance evaluation based on the four security use cases.

5   Conclusion

The heterogeneous nature of IoT networks poses significant challenges to traditional network management approaches, rendering them inadequate. To address this issue, we propose using digital twin networks to uncover controllable IoT devices that remain undetected through IP network scans. We illustrate the potential of digital twins and networks to enhance IoT security management. Our proof of concept showcases initial steps towards digital twins for IoT security management. Open challenges remain in developing more sophisticated digital twins, ensuring scalability, and enhancing data availability. Nevertheless, we maintain that digital twins possess immense potential to enable IoT security management, which should be further researched in future.

References

1. AboubDakar, M., Kellil, M., Roux, P.: A review of IoT network management: current status and perspectives. J. King Saud Univ. Comput. Inf. Sci. **34**(7), 4163–4176 (2022). https://doi.org/10.1016/j.jksuci.2021.03.006
2. Al-Fuqaha, A.I., Guizani, M., Mohammadi, M., Aledhari, M., Ayyash, M.: Internet of things: A survey on enabling technologies, protocols, and applications. IEEE Commun. Surv. Tutor. **17**(4), 2347–2376 (2015). https://doi.org/10.1109/COMST.2015.2444095
3. Arzo, S.T., Naiga, C., Granelli, F., Bassoli, R., Devetsikiotis, M., Fitzek, F.H.P.: A theoretical discussion and survey of network automation for IoT: challenges and opportunity. IEEE Internet Things J. **8**(15), 12021–12045 (2021). https://doi.org/10.1109/jiot.2021.3075901
4. Ventures, C.: 2021 report: Cyberwarfare in the C-suite. Tech. rep, Cybersecurity Ventures (2021)
5. Dietz, M., Pernul, G.: Digital twin: empowering enterprises towards a system-of-systems approach. Bus. Inf. Syst. Eng. **62**(2), 179–184 (2020). https://doi.org/10.1007/s12599-019-00624-0
6. Dietz, M., Vielberth, M., Pernul, G.: Integrating digital twin security simulations in the security operations center. In: Proceedings of the 15th. International Conference on Availability, Reliability and Security (ARES 2020). Association for Computing Machinery (2020). https://doi.org/10.1145/3407023.3407039
7. Empl, P., Schlette, D., Zupfer, D., Pernul, G.: SOAR4IoT: securing IoT assets with digital twins. In: Proceedings of the 17th. International Conference on Availability, Reliability and Security (ARES 2022), Vienna, Austria, 23–26 August 2022, pp. 1–10. ACM (2022). https://doi.org/10.1145/3538969.3538975
8. Fayaz, S.K., Yu, T., Tobioka, Y., Chaki, S., Sekar, V.: BUZZ: testing context-dependent policies in stateful networks. In: Proceedings of the 13th. USENIX Symposium on Networked Systems Design and Implementation (NSDI 2016), pp. 275–289 (2016)
9. Galmés, M.F., Cheng, X., Shi, X., Xiao, S., Barlet-Ros, P., Cabellos-Aparicio, A.: FlowDT: a flow-aware digital twin for computer networks. In: Proceedings of the IEEE International Conference on Acoustics, Speech and Signal Processing, (ICASSP 2022), pp. 8907–8911. IEEE (2022). https://doi.org/10.1109/ICASSP43922.2022.9746953
10. Galmés, M.F., et al.: Building a digital twin for network optimization using graph neural networks. Comput. Networks **217**, 109329 (2022). https://doi.org/10.1016/j.comnet.2022.109329
11. German Federal Office for Information Security (BSI): Allgemeines zum Einsatz von IoT-Geräten. BSI Grundschutz-Kompendium, Module SYS 4.4, German Federal Office for Information Security (2021)
12. Hui, L., Wang, M., Zhang, L., Lu, L., Cui, Y.: Digital twin for networking: a data-driven performance modeling perspective. IEEE Network, pp. 1–8 (2022). https://doi.org/10.1109/MNET.119.2200080
13. ISO/IEC: Information technology - open systems interconnection - basic reference model: management framework (1989). https://www.iso.org/standard/14258.html. ISO/IEC 7498-4
14. Juniper Networks: the 2020 state of network automation report. Tech. rep. (2020)
15. Li, Y., et al.: A survey on network verification and testing with formal methods: approaches and challenges. IEEE Commun. Surv. Tutor. **21**(1), 940–969 (2019). https://doi.org/10.1109/comst.2018.2868050

16. Networks, N.: OT/IoT security report: cyber war insights, threats and trends, recommendations. Tech. rep, Nozomi Networks (2022)
17. NTT Ltd.: 2022–23 global network report (2022). https://services.global.ntt/zh-cn/insights/2022-23-global-network-report
18. Vielberth, M., Glas, M., Dietz, M., Karagiannis, S., Magkos, E., Pernul, G.: A digital twin-based cyber range for SOC analysts. In: Barker, K., Ghazinour, K. (eds.) DBSec 2021. LNCS, vol. 12840, pp. 293–311. Springer, Cham (2021). https://doi.org/10.1007/978-3-030-81242-3_17
19. Wu, Y., Zhang, K., Zhang, Y.: Digital twin networks: a survey. IEEE Internet Things J. **8**(18), 13789–13804 (2021). https://doi.org/10.1109/jiot.2021.3079510

Privacy

Data Distribution Impact on Preserving Privacy in Centralized and Decentralized Learning

Bakary Dolo[1]([✉]) [iD], Faiza Loukil[2]([✉]) [iD], and Khouloud Boukadi[1]([✉]) [iD]

[1] Mir@cl Laboratory, Sfax University, Sfax, Tunisia
`bakary.dolo@fsegs.usf.tn`, `khouloud.boukadi@fsegs.usf.tn`
[2] LISTIC, Univ. Savoie Mont Blanc, Annecy-le-Vieux, France
`faiza.loukil@univ-smb.fr`

Abstract. Since its inception, Federated Learning (FL) has successfully dealt with various challenges, such as facilitating training across multiple clients without compromising raw data, preserving individual data privacy, and establishing secure collaboration environments across different devices. Despite its potential benefits, FL still faces privacy and security obstacles, including data leakage, model poisoning, and compliance risks. To address these privacy concerns, the FL domain has widely employed the technique of differential privacy, which involves introducing noise to client data without significantly altering the statistical properties of query results. However, the use of differential privacy can potentially impact the data's utility by reducing model accuracy. To overcome this problem, we propose a novel approach called Distribution Invariant Local Differential Privacy for Federated Learning (DILDP-FL). DILDP-FL is based on the distribution-invariant privatization method known as DIP. It transforms and perturbs the data while employing suitable transformations to achieve query results similar to those obtained from the original data. Our experimental findings demonstrate that the proposed DILDP-FL technique, when applied to local clients in the FL context, outperforms the conventional Differentially Private Stochastic Gradient Descent. Additionally, we have observed that DILDP-FL performs at least as well as, if not better than, traditional machine learning techniques.

Keywords: Federated Learning · Local Differential Privacy · Distribution Invariant · Stochastic Gradient Descent · Machine Learning

1 Introduction

Federated learning is a machine learning approach that allows models to be trained on distributed data sources, such as mobile or Internet of Things (IoT)

© IFIP International Federation for Information Processing 2023
Published by Springer Nature Switzerland AG 2023
V. Atluri and A. L. Ferrara (Eds.): DBSec 2023, LNCS 13942, pp. 153–164, 2023.
https://doi.org/10.1007/978-3-031-37586-6_10

devices. This approach offers several potential advantages, including enhanced efficiency, improved accuracy, and decreased concerns regarding data privacy. Nonetheless, federated learning brings about several privacy issues. These issues stem from the fact that the data sources utilized in federated learning are frequently delicate and include confidential information regarding individuals. Researchers have developed several techniques to address these privacy problems, including perturbation techniques, which involve adding noise or randomness to the original data to mask sensitive information and preserve privacy [17]. These techniques allow the statistical information calculated from the perturbed data to be statistically indistinguishable from the original data and maintain a trade-off between statistical accuracy and the degree of privacy preserved. At the same time, adding noise to a data distribution can have various impacts depending on the type and level of noise added. Adding noise can increase the variability or randomness of the data, making it harder to identify patterns or relationships between variables. It can lead to inaccuracies in statistical analysis or modeling results. This is especially true when the noise is large or systematic. Adding noise can introduce bias into the data, leading to incorrect conclusions or decisions. Finally, adding noise to a data distribution can prevent the overfitting of models by making it harder for the models to fit the noise. This can lead to more generalizable models that perform better on new data.

To overcome all these impacts and contribute to the state-of-the-art, we propose a distribution invariant local differential privacy technique for federated learning (DILDP-FL) based on DIP technique [3] to preserve privacy and high accuracy without altering the distribution of initial data significantly after adding noise. DIP technique transforms and perturbs the data and then uses appropriate transformations to obtain the same query results as if the original data were used. According to the nature of the data distribution, Laplace or Gaussian mechanisms are proposed to privatize the data. DILDP-FL shows better accuracy compared to Differentially Private Stochastic Gradient Descent (DP-SGD) for FL [1] and has similar or better accuracy when compared to the Federated Averaging (FEDAVG) technique [10] and several machine learning techniques, such as Logistic Regression [4], Decision Trees [6], Random Forest [5]. This paper aims to propose an efficient technique for FL based on data privacy and data distribution invariance preservation. This paper promotes distribution invariant differential privacy, which is ϵ-differentially private, where the privatized sample follows the original distribution O asymptotically when O is unknown.

Therefore, the rest of this paper is organized as follows. Section 2 introduces some FL key concepts and differential privacy techniques categories in FL, especially local differential privacy techniques and distribution invariant differential privacy techniques. Section 3 presents the related studies based on local federated learning and differential privacy techniques used to guarantee data privacy. Section 4 describes our proposed privacy-preserving local federated learning technique called DILDP-FL. In Sect. 5, we discuss the implementation details and the performance evaluation of the proposal. Finally, Sect. 6 concludes the paper with possible future directions.

2   Background

This section provides a brief overview of federated learning and privacy-preserving techniques for federated learning. It emphasizes the concepts of local, global differential privacy and distribution invariant differential privacy.

Federated learning [10], is a machine-learning approach that enables multiple parties to collaborate on model creation without sharing their raw data. It addresses challenges related to privacy, data security, and centralization. Figure 1 depicts the centralized-server approach of federated learning where a central server sends a model to each party, and each party trains the model on its local data. Only the model updates are shared with the central server, which aggregates them to create a new model. This iterative process continues until an optimal model is obtained.

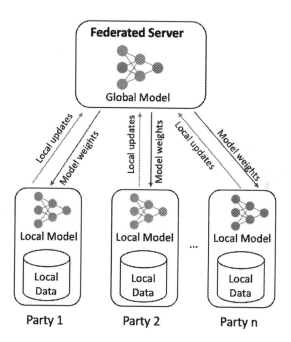

Fig. 1. A centralized-server approach of federated learning.

Although federated learning protects the raw data, privacy concerns still exist. For example, when Federated learning keeps data on local devices, there is still a risk of data leakage during the training process. During model updates, there may be opportunities for adversaries to infer information about the training data on the local devices, potentially compromising privacy. Then, malicious participants can attempt to poison the federated model by intentionally providing incorrect or manipulated updates. This can lead to the creation of a compromised global model that may negatively impact privacy. In some cases, individual users can be identified based on their unique data patterns, even if the data itself is not directly exposed. Aggregating local updates to create a global model may unintentionally reveal information about specific users, leading to privacy concerns. Thus, Privacy remains a significant challenge in federated learning, leading to the development of privacy-preserving techniques.

PPFL (Privacy-Preserving Federated Learning) combines federated learning with privacy-preserving mechanisms to balance data privacy and utility. Different categories of techniques, such as encryption [7], perturbation [8], anonymization [12], and hybrid methods [16], can be employed in PPFL.

Differential Privacy (DP), which is perturbation-based PPFL is widely adopted to safeguard the privacy of data. DP is a concept and framework for privacy protection in data analysis. It provides a rigorous mathematical definition of privacy guarantees that ensures individuals' sensitive information remains protected even when their data is used for analysis. DP focuses on preventing the disclosure of individual-level information by introducing controlled randomness or noise into the analysis process. The main idea behind DP is to limit the impact that an individual's data has on the overall outcome of the analysis. By doing so, DP aims to provide privacy guarantees that hold regardless of any auxiliary information or background knowledge an adversary may possess. This means that the presence or absence of any individual's data should not significantly affect the final results or enable the identification of specific individuals. DP offers two main categories: Local Differential Privacy (LDP) and Global Differential Privacy (GDP)

Local Differential Privacy (LDP) is a specific category of differential privacy tailored to scenarios where data is processed locally on individual devices before sharing or analysis. It is a privacy-preserving mechanism designed to protect individual data points while allowing statistical analysis. It perturbs each data point independently, adding noise based on a privacy budget parameter. LDP ensures that no individual data point can be inferred from the aggregated data. The composition theorem states that privacy guarantees hold when multiple computations are performed on the same data set. LDP offers strong privacy guarantees, allows for flexible data analysis, and is computationally efficient. However, it may not be suitable for all types of data analysis and requires careful consideration of the privacy budget and noise levels.

In contrast, Global Differential Privacy (GDP) is a privacy-preserving mechanism that aims to protect the privacy of individuals' data in a centralized setting. Unlike Local Differential Privacy (LDP), which perturbs data locally on individual devices, GDP focuses on preserving privacy when data is collected and analyzed by a central server. In GDP, a central server collects data from multiple individuals or sources and applies privacy-preserving mechanisms to ensure that the privacy of each individual's data is maintained. The server aggregates the data and performs computations or analyses while minimizing the risk of revealing sensitive information about any individual in the dataset.

However, in real-world scenarios, the distribution of data may be unknown, diverse, or subject to change. This can potentially compromise the privacy guarantees offered by GDP and LDP when an attacker possesses prior knowledge about the data distribution.

Distribution Invariant Differential Privacy (DIDP) emerges as a solution that overcomes these limitations. It provides stronger privacy guarantees when the data distribution is unknown or changes over time. It ensures that privacy holds regardless of the underlying data distribution. DIDP achieves this by extending the concept of differential privacy and introducing a distribution-invariant privatization (DIP) mechanism. DIP transforms the data, including adding noise and using a function to preserve the original distribution asymptotically. DIDP guarantees privacy even when an attacker has prior knowledge of the data distribution. It achieves superior statistical accuracy. However, it's important to note that DIP requires sample-splitting, which reduces the size of the released sample. Despite this drawback, the DIP mechanism performs as if non-private data were used, addressing the challenge of distribution invariance in privacy-preserving federated learning. The main goal of our paper is to propose and evaluate a Federated Learning Algorithm using DIDP locally on the client's side during the training process.

3   Related Work

Reading through the related work, we summarize the related proposals as follows.

A local differential privacy mechanism has been extensively used in many federated learning techniques. Wang et al.in [15] presented a framework for industrial-grade text mining based on local differential privacy in which they demonstrated that both data privacy and model accuracy can be ensured.

Kim et al. [9] provided a noise variance bound that guarantees a given LDP level after multiple rounds of weight updates. Their method has been applied to a FedSGD model with a Gaussian LDP mechanism. The obtained results guarantee a significantly larger utility and a smaller transmission rate as compared to existing privacy accounting methods.

Bhowmick et al. [2] proposed a federated learning method using local differential privacy to defend against reconstruction attacks. In a client-side computation, each sample was protected by the local differential privacy mechanism. In addition, in the server-side computation, the local differential privacy was also used to guarantee the privacy preservation of the global model update.

Truex et al. [14] proposed a federated learning solution with Local Differential Privacy (LDP-FL) designed in two steps. First, it enables participants to customize their LDP privacy budget locally according to their own preferences. Second, LDP-Fed implements a novel privacy-preserving collaborative training approach towards utility-aware privacy perturbation to prevent uncontrolled noise from overwhelming the FL training technique in the presence of large, complex model parameter updates.

By using local differential privacy, the aforementioned papers showed several limitations. First, there is a tradeoff between privacy and utility when using local differential privacy. The more noise that is added to the data, the more private it becomes, but the less useful it is for analysis. Second, statistical analyses performed on LDP-protected data may yield inaccurate or biased results. Another limitation of LDP is that it requires a large amount of data to be effective. LDP works by adding random noise to individual data points, which helps to obscure individual values and make it more difficult to identify individual data points. However, this noise needs to be large enough to be effective, which means that LDP requires a large amount of data to work well.

Local differential privacy can also distort the distribution of the data. LDP adds random noise to individual data points in order to protect privacy, but this noise can also affect the overall distribution of the data.

To solve all these problems concerning LDP, authors in [3] proposed a novel privatization method called DIP, which preserves the original data's distribution while satisfying differential privacy. Their study demonstrates that DIP mitigates the trade-off between differential privacy and statistical accuracy, protects the structure of high-dimensional graphical networks, and is differentially private even if the underlying data have unbounded support or unknown distributions. They also propose to explore how to generalize this concept to local differential privacy, which provides further privacy protection for data in a local device or server. However, the DIP has not been applied yet to federated learning. Accordingly, we propose a new technique that implements distribution-invariant local differential privacy based on the DIP mechanism for federated learning.

One of the challenges of LDP is finding the right balance between privacy and accuracy. Adding too much noise can make it difficult to extract meaningful insights from the data while adding too little noise can compromise individual privacy. Distribution invariant local differential privacy solves this problem by proposing an equitable addition of portion noise to the entire dataset. Finally, every client got ϵ-differentially private data following initial distribution.

4   Our Proposal

In this section, we present a new technique called Distribution Invariant Local Differential Privacy for Federated Learning (DILDP-FL), which is an extension of DIP applied in the Federated Learning domain. The DIP method ensures both differential privacy and the preservation of the original data distribution.

Our technique aims to ensure both data utility and data privacy by incorporating local differential privacy and preserving the data distribution after adding noise, thus maintaining statistical analysis performances.

By combining local differential privacy with federated learning, we enhance data privacy protection, and by preserving the initial distribution, we can achieve better privacy preservation for FL models.

DILDP-FL is specifically designed to provide individual-level privacy guarantees. It offers robustness against changes in data distribution, making it particularly useful when data is collected from various sources with varying distributions.

Our technique can be applied in federated learning to provide privacy guarantees for each individual node's data. In this approach, each node adds random noise to its local data before sharing them with a central server for aggregation. The noise added by each node is chosen based on the node's local data distribution, ensuring that the noise added is appropriate for the shared data.

To achieve distribution-invariant local differential privacy, the privacy mechanism must satisfy two main requirements :

- ϵ-differential privacy: The mechanism must adhere to the standard ϵ-differential privacy definition, which bounds the probability of two adjacent datasets generating the same output by a factor of ϵ.
- Post-processing invariance: The privacy guarantee should remain intact even if the output of the mechanism undergoes further processing or transformation by an attacker. This ensures that the privacy guarantee is not weakened if an attacker gains access to the mechanism's output.

The process involving the DILDP-FL technique consists of four main steps: data split, uniform distribution, noise addition, and original distribution restoration.

Data Split Step: The initial dataset held by each party is divided into two independent subsets: a hold-out subset and a to-be-privatized subset. The hold-out subset is securely retained and should not be accessed, altered, queried, or released. The choice of the portion split, p, is important as it determines the extent of privatization and the number of samples obtained.

Uniform Distribution Step: The to-be-privatized subset's distribution is transformed into a sample of the uniform distribution using a technique called QuantileTransformer. This transformation reduces the impact of outliers and ensures equal variance among features. By transforming the data distribution to a uniform one, biased results due to non-uniform distributions in the original data can be avoided.

Noise Addition Step: After transforming the subset into a uniform distribution, random Laplace or Gaussian noise is added to perturb and mask the data. The choice of Laplace or Gaussian noise depends on whether the data is discrete/categorical or continuous/normally distributed, respectively. Laplace noise provides differential privacy and is more suitable for discrete data, while Gaussian noise preserves statistical properties and is more suitable for continuous data.

Original Distribution Restoration Step: The obfuscated data obtained after adding noise is transformed using an appropriate function to approximate the original data distribution. This step, known as data de-obfuscation or unmasking, can involve statistical analysis or reverse engineering techniques depending on the level of obfuscation applied.

5   Performance Evaluation

We propose an experimental setup to evaluate the efficacy of our technique. Firstly, we define the two used datasets. Next, we explain how to apply DILDP-FL. Finally, we present the experimental results of our comparative study.

5.1   Used Datasets

Two datasets are used to evaluate our technique, including the "Portuguese bank marketing campaign data" dataset [13] and the "Hotel booking demand datasets" [11].

Portuguese Bank Marketing Campaign Data [13]: This dataset relates to direct marketing initiatives run by a Portuguese banking organization, which focused on contacting potential customers over the phone. The primary goal of the dataset is to categorize whether or not a client will sign up for a term deposit given by the bank. The binary classification result is represented by the variable 'y'. Each of the 41,188 samples in the dataset "bank-additional-full.csv" has 20 inputs and is arranged chronologically from May 2008 to November 2010.

Hotel Booking Demand Datasets [11]: These two sets, one for a resort hotel (H1) and the other for a city hotel, both contain information on hotel demand (H2). The sets are identically organized, and 31 variables are used to describe 79,330 observations of H2 and 40,060 observations of H1. Each observation corresponds to a hotel reservation made between July 1, 2015, and August 31, 2017, including both confirmed reservations and cancellations. All identifying information has been removed from the data to preserve the privacy of hotel visitors and customers.

5.2   DILDP-FL Application

Preprocessing is done on datasets to get rid of any identifiable information like name, address, etc. Any incorrect or missing data points, such as incorrect values or incomplete records, are removed or corrected. The "hotel booking demand datasets" will be combined into a single, unified format utilizing data integration, often using a common identifier or key variable. Continuous variables will be scaled or normalized, and categorical variables will be encoded, as part of the data transformation process. We next proceed with the privatization phase described in Sect. 4 after distributing data among all devices (clients). In order to get an asymptotically initial distribution, each client of the federated learning process will first partition the data into a range between 0.5 and 0.75, uniformize the to-be-privatized data distribution, add noise, and then re-transform the data using hold-out samples. Every client has distribution-invariant local private data at the end of this application that satisfies differential privacy criteria and is asymptotically similar to the initial data distribution.

5.3   Experiment Configuration

We performed a series of experiments with the value of $\epsilon=1$ to see the impact of privacy and utility on DILDP-FL and DP-SGD. The number of clients, rounds, and learning rate are all set as 200, 10, and 0,01 respectively. Because of the characteristics of our dataset, we decided to use the Gaussian noise mechanism in this experiment. For our classification challenge, we build a three-layer MLP model. We present the findings as accuracy and loss. After that, we evaluate the effectiveness of DILDP-FL by measuring privacy loss and utility loss. Privacy loss is measured using the ϵ-DP metric, which is the maximum change in the probability of a particular output due to the presence or absence of any individual's data in the dataset. The utility loss is measured using the accuracy of a sparse categorical cross-entropy task on the dataset.

5.4   Comparative Study Analysis

We present below the experimental results of our proposed technique. We evaluated our approach on the two aforementioned datasets. We compare the performance of DILDP-FL with Federated Averaging (FedAvg) [10], Differential Privacy Stochastic Gradient Descent (DP-SGD), and ML techniques, such as Logistic Regression [4], Decision Trees [6], Random Forest [5].

For the Bank Dataset (Portuguese bank marketing campaign data), the results showed that DILDP-FL with $\epsilon=1$, p=0.5 and p=0.75 achieved respectively an accuracy rate of 91.34% and 91.27%, which is higher than Decision Trees (90.89%) and Logistic regression (91.05%) accuracies. We can conclude that DILDP-FL performs as well as ML techniques for the "Portuguese bank marketing campaign data" dataset.

With the second dataset (Hotel booking demand datasets), we observe a similar reality when comparing DILDP-FL accuracy (82.56%) to Decision Trees (76.32%) and Logistic regression (81.04%). DILDP-FL comparison with ML techniques is shown in Table 1.

Table 1. DILDP-FL shows better or similar accuracy than ML techniques.

Techniques	Bank Dataset	Hotel Dataset
Logistic Regression	0.9105	0.8104
Decision Trees	0.9089	0.7632
Random Forest	0.9143	0.8591
DILDP-FL(p=0.5 - ϵ=1)	0.9134	0.8256
DILDP-FL(p=0.75 - ϵ=1)	0.9127	0.8241

We also note the impact of portion choice p on the global results. A portion of 0.5 produces better results than a higher portion of 0.75. This observation

could be explained by the added noise factor when the to-be-privatized dataset
has a larger portion of the initial dataset. Under a portion of 0.5, the hold-out
subset size is smaller than the to-be-privatized subset. The smaller the hold-
out subset, the further away we are from the original distribution of the data
when we apply reverse engineering techniques. So it is important to choose the
ideal portion p-value when using DILDP-FL. We find that the ideal p-value is
around 0.5 in our experiment. But we do not exclude the hypothesis that the
relationship between data points in a dataset can influence and vary the choice
of the p-value.

Regarding the case of federated learning techniques, the global observations
show that DILDP-FL shows better or similar accuracy, lower loss, and strong
privacy compared to FedAvg and DP-SGD FL techniques. Figure 2 and Fig. 3
show details about federated learning techniques' performances in terms of accuracy for the two chosen datasets with portions of p=0.5. Indeed, Fig. 2 illustrates
federated learning techniques applied in the "Bank Dataset" in terms of accuracy
and loss metrics when $\epsilon=1$ and portion p=0.5. Figure 3 illustrates DILDP-FL
applying in the "Hotel Dataset" in terms of accuracy and loss metrics combined
when $\epsilon=1$ and portion p=0.5.

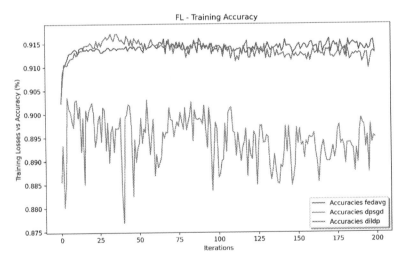

Fig. 2. Comparison of FedAvg, DP-SGD, and DILDP-FL accuracy metric for the
"Bank dataset".

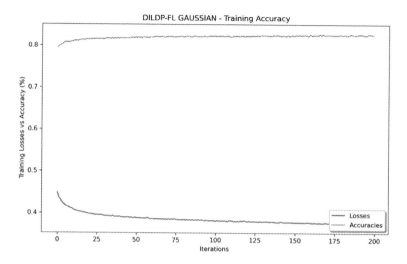

Fig. 3. Comparison of DILDP-FL combined accuracy and loss metrics for the "Hotel Dataset".

6   Conclusion

Although federated learning holds considerable potential advantages, it also introduces several privacy concerns that require resolution. To ensure the safe and secure utilization of federated learning while safeguarding individuals' privacy and their data, it is essential to develop and implement appropriate privacy protection strategies. This paper proposes a technique called Distribution Invariant Local Differential Privacy (DILDP-FL) for federated learning, which builds upon the DIP technique. The objective of this approach is to protect data privacy by maintaining strong privacy guarantees while preserving the original data's distribution, which can be compromised by the traditional method of adding noise in differential privacy. The research findings indicate that DILDP-FL performs significantly better or comparably to baseline techniques in terms of accuracy and privacy.

These findings illustrate the potential of the DILDP-FL technique as a valuable tool for balancing data utility and stringent privacy requirements. The technique's performance can be further explored across different datasets and scenarios by adjusting factors, such as dataset size, composition, data preprocessing, and hyperparameter selection. Overall, the combination of federated learning and distribution invariant differential privacy presents an intriguing area of research that could significantly impact the advancement of machine learning and data privacy in the future. However, additional research is necessary to gain a deeper understanding of the challenges associated with this approach and to develop practical techniques for its effective implementation.

References

1. Abadi, M., et al.: Deep learning with differential privacy. In: Proceedings of the 2016 ACM SIGSAC Conference on Computer and Communications Security, pp. 308–318 (2016)
2. Bhowmick, A., Duchi, J., Freudiger, J., Kapoor, G., Rogers, R.: Protection against reconstruction and its applications in private federated learning. arXiv preprint arXiv:1812.00984 (2018)
3. Bi, X., Shen, X.: Distribution-invariant differential privacy. J. Econometr. **235**, 444–453 (2022)
4. Bisong, E., et al.: Building machine learning and deep learning models on Google cloud platform. Springer (2019). https://doi.org/10.1007/978-1-4842-4470-8
5. Breiman, L.: Bagging predictors. Machine Learn. **24**, 123–140 (1996)
6. Fürnkranz, J.: Decision Tree. In: Sammut, C., Webb, G.I. (eds.) Encyclopedia of Machine Learning. Springer, MA (2010). https://doi.org/10.1007/978-0-387-30164-8_204
7. Gao, D., Liu, Y., Huang, A., Ju, C., Yu, H., Yang, Q.: Privacy-preserving heterogeneous federated transfer learning. In: 2019 IEEE international conference on big data (Big Data), pp. 2552–2559. IEEE (2019)
8. Geyer, R.C., Klein, T., Nabi, M.: Differentially private federated learning: a client level perspective. arXiv preprint arXiv:1712.07557 (2017)
9. Kim, M., Günlü, O., Schaefer, R.F.: Federated learning with local differential privacy: Trade-offs between privacy, utility, and communication. In: ICASSP 2021– 2021 IEEE International Conference on Acoustics, Speech and Signal Processing (ICASSP), pp. 2650–2654. IEEE (2021)
10. McMahan, B., Moore, E., Ramage, D., Hampson, S., y Arcas, B.A.: Communication-efficient learning of deep networks from decentralized data. In: Artificial intelligence and statistics, pp. 1273–1282. PMLR (2017)
11. Mostipak, J.: Hotel booking demand (2020). https://www.kaggle.com/datasets/jessemostipak/hotel-booking-demand
12. Song, M., et al.: Analyzing user-level privacy attack against federated learning. IEEE J. Sel. Areas Commun. **38**(10), 2430–2444 (2020)
13. Sui, A.: Kaggle (2019). https://www.kaggle.com/datasets/yufengsui/portuguese-bank-marketing-data-set
14. Truex, S., Liu, L., Chow, K.H., Gursoy, M.E., Wei, W.: LDP-Fed: federated learning with local differential privacy. In: Proceedings of the Third ACM International Workshop on Edge Systems, Analytics and Networking, pp. 61–66 (2020)
15. Wang, Y., Tong, Y., Shi, D.: Federated latent Dirichlet allocation: a local differential privacy based framework. In: Proceedings of the AAAI Conference on Artificial Intelligence, vol. 34, pp. 6283–6290 (2020)
16. Xu, G., Li, H., Liu, S., Yang, K., Lin, X.: VerifyNet: secure and verifiable federated learning. IEEE Trans. Inf. Forensics Secur. **15**, 911–926 (2019)
17. Yin, X., Zhu, Y., Hu, J.: A comprehensive survey of privacy-preserving federated learning: a taxonomy, review, and future directions. ACM Comput. Surv. (CSUR) **54**(6), 1–36 (2021)

On the Utility Gain of Iterative Bayesian Update for Locally Differentially Private Mechanisms

Héber H. Arcolezi[✉][iD], Selene Cerna[iD], and Catuscia Palamidessi[iD]

Inria and École Polytechnique (IPP), Palaiseau, France
{heber.hwang-arcolezi,selene-leya.cerna-nahuis,
catuscia.palamidessi}@inria.fr

Abstract. This paper investigates the utility gain of using Iterative Bayesian Update (IBU) for private discrete distribution estimation using data obfuscated with Locally Differentially Private (LDP) mechanisms. We compare the performance of IBU to Matrix Inversion (MI), a standard estimation technique, for seven LDP mechanisms designed for one-time data collection and for other seven LDP mechanisms designed for multiple data collections (*e.g.*, RAPPOR). To broaden the scope of our study, we also varied the utility metric, the number of users n, the domain size k, and the privacy parameter ϵ, using both synthetic and real-world data. Our results suggest that IBU can be a useful post-processing tool for improving the utility of LDP mechanisms in different scenarios without any additional privacy cost. For instance, our experiments show that IBU can provide better utility than MI, especially in high privacy regimes (*i.e.*, when ϵ is small). Our paper provides insights for practitioners to use IBU in conjunction with existing LDP mechanisms for more accurate and privacy-preserving data analysis. Finally, we implemented IBU for all fourteen LDP mechanisms into the state-of-the-art `multi-freq-ldpy` Python package (https://pypi.org/project/multi-freq-ldpy/) and open-sourced all our code used for the experiments as tutorials.

Keywords: Expectation-Maximization · Iterative Bayesian Update · Local Differential Privacy · Distribution Estimation

1 Introduction

The widespread availability of Big Data has led to the development of new methods for extracting valuable insights from large datasets. However, the increased capacity to collect and analyze data also raises significant concerns about privacy, particularly in cases where sensitive information about individuals is involved. Thus, the direct collection and storage of users' raw data on a centralized server should be avoided as these data are subject to illegal access [21] or internal fraud [28], for example. To address this issue, recent works have proposed several mechanisms satisfying Differential Privacy (DP) [12,13], in the distributed setting, referred to as Local DP (LDP) [19].

© IFIP International Federation for Information Processing 2023
Published by Springer Nature Switzerland AG 2023
V. Atluri and A. L. Ferrara (Eds.): DBSec 2023, LNCS 13942, pp. 165–183, 2023.
https://doi.org/10.1007/978-3-031-37586-6_11

One of the strengths of LDP is its simple trust model: since each user sanitizes their data locally, user privacy is protected even if the server is malicious. However, the increased privacy of the local DP model comes at the cost of reduced utility. That is, as each user's data is obfuscated, several lower bounds exist on the error of these LDP mechanisms. This strongly differentiates the local DP model from the central DP model. [8]. To address this issue, one line of research has largely explored the issue of improving the utility of LDP distribution estimation mechanisms [7,16,18,24,25,30], in which the data collector estimates the number of users for each possible value based on the sanitized data of the users. Distribution estimation is a primary objective of LDP [29], as it is a building block for more complex tasks (*e.g.*, heavy hitter estimation [7], marginal estimation [9,17,20,23], and distribution monitoring [3,6,16]).

Two commonly used estimators for distribution estimation under LDP are [29]: Matrix Inversion (MI), which is based on simple linear algebra techniques, and Iterative Bayesian Update (IBU) [1,2], which is based on the well-known Expectation-Maximization [10] algorithm. Thus, another line of research has explored how to improve the estimation at the server side through post-processing techniques [14,15,22,26]. For instance, to improve the utility of the MI estimator, in [18], the authors evaluate two post-processing techniques, namely, normalization (also adopted in this paper) and projection on the simplex. More recently, Wang *et al.* [26] revisited and introduced, in total, ten post-processing techniques for the MI estimator. Regarding IBU, ElSalamouny & Palamidessi [14,15] investigated a generalization of IBU for personalized LDP and, in [22], the authors improved IBU considering small number of users.

Main Contributions. While the aforementioned works have explored how to improve the estimation of LDP mechanisms on the server side through post-processing techniques, no study has compared the performance of MI and IBU estimators for more than three LDP mechanisms. This paper aims to fill this research gap by conducting an in-depth empirical analysis of the utility gain by using IBU instead of MI for *fourteen state-of-the-art LDP mechanisms*. More precisely, we have experimentally assessed seven state-of-the-art LDP distribution estimation mechanisms, namely, Generalized Randomized Response (GRR) [18], Binary Local Hashing (BLH) [7], Optimal Local Hashing (OLH) [25], Symmetric Unary Encoding (SUE) [16], Optimal Unary Encoding (OUE) [25], Subset Selection (SS) [24,30], and Thresholding with Histogram Encoding (THE) [25]. In addition, we also extended the analysis to seven state-of-the-art memoization-based LDP mechanisms, namely, Longitudinal GRR (L-GRR) [3], four Longitudinal Unary Encoding (L-UE) [3,16] mechanisms, and two Longitudinal Local Hashing (L-LH) [6] mechanisms. To further broaden the scope of our study, we have evaluated two popular utility metrics by varying the number of users n, the privacy guarantee ϵ, and the domain size k, with both synthetic and real-world datasets. Finally, this paper open-sources the implementation of IBU for all aforementioned LDP mechanisms into the `multi-freq-ldpy` Python package [4], as well as the code used for our experiments in the form of tutorials.

In summary, the three main contributions of this paper are:

- We present an in-depth analysis of the utility gain of IBU over MI for seven state-of-the-art LDP mechanisms designed for one-time data collection;
- To the authors' knowledge, we are the first to extend IBU and conduct a detailed analysis of its utility gain over MI for seven state-of-the-art longitudinal LDP mechanisms designed for multiple data collections;
- We open-sourced the IBU implementation for all aforementioned LDP mechanisms into `multi-freq-ldpy` [4], facilitating future research in the area and making it easier for researchers to replicate and build upon our findings.

Outline. The rest of this paper is organized as follows. Section 2 introduces the notation, the problem, and the metrics, and briefly reviews LDP and the two estimators, *i.e.*, MI and IBU. In Sect. 3, we present all LDP distribution estimation mechanisms analyzed in this paper. Next, Sect. 4 details the experimental setting and main results before discussing related work in Sect. 5. Finally, we conclude this work indicating future perspectives in Sect. 6.

2   Preliminaries

In this section, we present the notation, the problem, the utility metrics, the LDP privacy model, and both MI and IBU estimators, used in this paper.

2.1   Notations and Problem Statement

The main notation used throughout this paper is summarized in Table 1. This paper considers a distributed setting with n users and one untrusted server. Each user holds a value $v \in V$, where V ranges on a finite domain $\mathcal{D}$ of size k. The distribution of V is represented by $\mathbf{f} = \{f(v)\}_{v \in \mathcal{D}} \in [0,1]^k$, *i.e.*, $\mathbf{f}(v)$ is the probability of $v \in \mathcal{D}$. To satisfy LDP, each user i, for $i \in [1..n]$, will apply an obfuscation mechanism $\mathcal{M}_{(\epsilon)}$ to their value v^i to obtain an output $y^i = \mathcal{M}_{(\epsilon)}(v^i)$ from a finite set Y ranging on $\mathcal{D}$. The obfuscation mechanism $\mathcal{M}_{(\epsilon)}$ maps $v \in \mathcal{D}$ to $y \in \mathcal{D}$ through a channel matrix A_{vy}, *i.e.*, the probability that $\mathcal{M}_{(\epsilon)}$ yields y from v. Upon collecting the obfuscated data of all users, the server computes the observed distribution of y^i denoted as $\tilde{\mathbf{f}} = \{\tilde{f}(v)\}_{v \in \mathcal{D}} \in [0,1]^k$, where $\tilde{\mathbf{f}}(v)$ is the probability of $v \in \mathcal{D}$ and is calculated by counting the number of times that v is observed in Y and divided by n. The server's goal is to estimate $\mathbf{f}$ by calculating $\tilde{\mathbf{f}}$ and with the knowledge of the obfuscation mechanism $\mathcal{M}_{(\epsilon)}$. We denote the estimated distribution of $\mathbf{f}$ by $\hat{\mathbf{f}} = \{\hat{f}(v)\}_{v \in \mathcal{D}}$.

As utility metrics, we use the Mean Squared Error (MSE) and the Mean Absolute Error (MAE) to measure the difference between the original distribution $\mathbf{f}$ and estimated distribution $\hat{\mathbf{f}}$, which are formally defined as:

- **MSE.** Given $\mathbf{f}$ and $\hat{\mathbf{f}}$, the MSE is an expectation of the squared error:

$$\text{MSE} = \frac{1}{k} \sum_{v \in \mathcal{D}} (f(v) - \hat{f}(v))^2.$$

Table 1. Notations

Symbol	Description
$\mathcal{D}$	Data domain
k	Domain size $k = \|D\|$
n	Number of users
V	Discrete set of original data $\{v^1, v^2, v^3, \dots, v^n\}$, ranging on $\mathcal{D}$
Y	Discrete set of obfuscated data $\{y^1, y^2, y^3, \dots, y^n\}$, ranging on $\mathcal{D}$
$\mathbf{f}$	Distribution of original data, where $\mathbf{f} = \{f(v)\}_{v \in \mathcal{D}} \in [0,1]^k$
$\tilde{\mathbf{f}}$	Distribution of obfuscated data, where $\tilde{\mathbf{f}} = \{\tilde{f}(v)\}_{v \in \mathcal{D}} \in [0,1]^k$
$\hat{\mathbf{f}}$	Estimated distribution of $\mathbf{f}$, where $\hat{\mathbf{f}} = \{\hat{f}(v)\}_{v \in \mathcal{D}}$
$\mathcal{M}_{(\epsilon)}$	ϵ-LDP obfuscation mechanism, $\mathcal{M}_{(\epsilon)} : V \to Y$
A_{vy}	Channel matrix, probability that $\mathcal{M}_{(\epsilon)}$ yields $y \in \mathcal{D}$ from $v \in \mathcal{D}$
Γ	Utility gain of IBU over MI defined in Eq. (1)
$[a, b]$	Set of all real numbers $\geq a$ and $\leq b$
$[1..a]$	Set of integers $\{1, 2, 3, \dots, a\}$
$\mathbf{a}_i$	i-th coordinate of vector $\mathbf{a}$

– **MAE.** Given $\mathbf{f}$ and $\hat{\mathbf{f}}$, the MAE is an expectation of the absolute error:

$$\text{MAE} = \frac{1}{k} \sum_{v \in \mathcal{D}} |f(v) - \hat{f}(v)|.$$

In this paper, we are interested in comparing the two main statistical estimators for $\hat{\mathbf{f}}$, namely, MI and IBU. Based on the two popular metrics MSE and MAE, we define the utility gain Γ of IBU over MI as follows:

$$\Gamma(\%) = 100 \cdot \max\left(\frac{\text{Metric}_{\text{MI}} - \text{Metric}_{\text{IBU}}}{\text{Metric}_{\text{MI}}}, 0\right), \tag{1}$$

that is, the utility gain is clipped to zero to represent no gain.

2.2   Local Differential Privacy (LDP)

In this paper, we use LDP [19] as the privacy model considered, formalized as:

Definition 1 (ϵ-Local Differential Privacy). *A randomized mechanism $\mathcal{M}$ satisfies ϵ-LDP, where $\epsilon > 0$, if for any input $v, v' \in \mathcal{D}$, we have:*

$$\forall y \in \mathcal{D}: \quad \Pr[\mathcal{M}(v) = y] \leq e^{\epsilon} \cdot \Pr[\mathcal{M}(v') = y].$$

Proposition 1 (Post-Processing [13]). *If $\mathcal{M}$ is ϵ-LDP, then for any function g, the composition of $\mathcal{M}$ and g, i.e., $g(\mathcal{M})$ satisfies ϵ-LDP.*

The parameter ϵ controls the privacy-utility trade-off. Note that lower values of ϵ result in tighter privacy protection and vice versa. Moreover, an LDP mechanism is called "pure LDP" if it satisfies the following definition [25].

Definition 2 (Pure LDP [25]). *An ϵ-LDP mechanism is pure if there are two probability parameters $0 < q^* < p^* < 1$ such that for all $v \in \mathcal{D}$,*

$$\Pr[\mathcal{M}(v) \in \{y | v \in S(y)\}] = p^*,$$
$$\forall v \neq v' \in \mathcal{D} \quad \Pr[\mathcal{M}(v') \in \{y | v \in S(y)\}] = q^*,$$

where $S(y)$ is the set of items that y supports. That is, $S(y)$ maps each possible output y to a set of input values that y "supports".

2.3 Matrix Inversion (MI) Estimator

All obfuscation mechanisms we analyze in this paper are pure LDP (*cf.* Definition 2), which makes their analysis advantageous. For instance, for any pure LDP mechanism, the server estimates the distribution $\hat{\mathbf{f}} = \{\hat{f}(v)\}_{v \in \mathcal{D}} \in \mathbb{R}^k$ as [25]:

$$\forall v \in \mathcal{D}, \quad \hat{f}(v) = \frac{\sum_{i=1}^n \mathbb{1}_{S(y^i)}(v^i) - nq^*}{n(p^* - q^*)}, \qquad (2)$$

in which y^i represents the obfuscated data provided by each user (for $i \in [1..n]$), and the function $\mathbb{1}_{S(y^i)}(v^i)$ equals 1 if y^i supports the value v^i, and 0 otherwise. However, when the number of users is small, many elements estimated with Eq. (2) can be negative. Therefore, we clip the negative estimates to 0 and re-normalize the estimated frequencies so that they sum up to 1, ensuring that they constitute a valid probability distribution. Another way to write Eq. (2) is: $\hat{\mathbf{f}} = \tilde{\mathbf{f}} A_{vy}^{-1}$, in which $\tilde{\mathbf{f}}$ is the observed distribution and A_{vy}^{-1} is the inverse of A_{vy} [14,18,22]. For any pure LDP mechanism, we observed that the channel matrix A_{vy} is a square matrix with values p^* in the diagonal and q^* otherwise.

2.4 Iterative Bayesian Update (IBU) Estimator

The IBU estimator [1,2,14] is based on the Expectation Maximization (EM) [10] method, which is a powerful method for obtaining parameter estimates when part of the data is missing. IBU estimates the distribution of $\mathbf{f}$ as follows. Let $\tilde{\mathbf{f}}$ be the observed distribution on Y, A_{vy} be the channel matrix, which represents the probability of obtaining y from v, and $\hat{\mathbf{f}}$ be the estimated distribution on V. IBU starts with a full-support distribution $\hat{\mathbf{f}}^0$ on V (*e.g.*, the uniform distribution). Next, it iteratively generates new distributions by updating Eq. (3), where $(*)$, $(\cdot)$, and $(/)$ represent the element-wise product, dot product, and element-wise division, respectively. Finally, it converges until a specified tolerance is reached.

$$\hat{\mathbf{f}}^{t+1} = \tilde{\mathbf{f}} \cdot \frac{\hat{\mathbf{f}}^t * A_{vy}}{\hat{\mathbf{f}}^t \cdot A_{vy}}. \qquad (3)$$

3   LDP Distribution Estimation Mechanisms

In this section, we briefly review fourteen state-of-the-art LDP distribution estimation mechanisms, *i.e.*, seven for one-time collection (Sect. 3.1) and seven for multiple collections (Sect. 3.2).

3.1   LDP Mechanisms for One-Time Data Collection

Algorithm 1 exhibits the general procedure for one-time discrete distribution estimation under pure LDP. The five following subsections briefly present state-of-the-art pure LDP mechanisms.

Algorithm 1. General pure LDP procedure for distribution estimation.

   Input : Original data of users, privacy parameter ϵ, mechanism $\mathcal{M}_{(\epsilon)}$.
   Output : Estimated discrete distribution.
   # User-side
1: **for** each user $i \in [1..n]$ with input data $v^i \in V$ **do**
2:    Encode(v^i) into a specific format (**if needed**);
3:    Obfuscate(v^i) as $y^i = \mathcal{M}_{(\epsilon)}(v^i)$;
4:    Transmit y^i to the aggregator.
5: **end for**
   # Server-side
6: Obtain the support set $S(y)$ and probabilities p^* and q^* for $\mathcal{M}_{(\epsilon)}$.
7: ~~Estimate~~ Aggregate the obfuscated data y^i ($i \in [1..n]$) to estimate $\{\hat{f}(v)\}_{v \in \mathcal{D}}$.
8: **return** : Estimated discrete distribution $\hat{\mathbf{f}}$ (*i.e.*, a k-bins histogram).

Generalized Randomized Response (GRR). The GRR [18] mechanism generalizes the Randomized Response (RR) surveying technique proposed by Warner [27] for $k \geq 2$ while satisfying ϵ-LDP.

Encode. GRR [18] uses no particular encoding, *i.e.*, $\text{Encode}_{\text{GRR}}(v) = v$.

Obfuscate. Given the user's personal data v, GRR outputs v with probability p, and any other randomly chosen value $v' \in \mathcal{D} \setminus \{v\}$ otherwise. More formally:

$$\forall y \in \mathcal{D}: \quad \Pr[\mathcal{M}_{\text{GRR}(\epsilon,k)}(v) = y] = \begin{cases} p = \frac{e^\epsilon}{e^\epsilon + k - 1}, & \text{if } y = v, \\ q = \frac{1}{e^\epsilon + k - 1}, & \text{otherwise,} \end{cases} \quad (4)$$

in which y is the obfuscated value sent to the server.

Estimate. For aggregation at the server side, it is important to obtain the support set $S(y)$ and the probabilities p^* and q^*. For GRR, an obfuscated value y only supports itself, *i.e.*, $S_{\text{GRR}}(y) = \{y\}$. Given the support set and with $p^* = p$ and $q^* = q$, the server can estimate item frequencies using Eq. (2) for MI and Eq. (3) for IBU.

Local Hashing (LH). LH mechanisms [7,25] can handle a large domain size k by using hash functions to map an input data to a smaller domain of size g, for $2 \leq g \ll k$, and then applying GRR to the hashed value. Let $\mathscr{H}$ be a universal hash function family such that each hash function $\text{H} \in \mathscr{H}$ hashes a value $v \in \mathcal{D}$ into $[1..g]$, *i.e.*, $\text{H}: \mathcal{D} \to [1..g]$. There are two variations of LH mechanisms:

- **Binary LH (BLH)** [7]. A simple case that just sets $g = 2$;
- **Optimal LH (OLH)** [25]. An optimized version that selects $g = \lfloor e^\epsilon + 1 \rfloor$.

Encode. $\texttt{Encode}_{\text{LH}}(v) = \langle H, H(v) \rangle$, in which $H \in \mathscr{H}$ is selected at random.

Obfuscate. LH mechanisms only obfuscate the hash value $H(v)$ with GRR and does not change H. In particular, the LH reporting mechanism is:

$$\mathcal{M}_{\text{LH}(\epsilon)}(v) := \langle H, \mathcal{M}_{\text{GRR}(\epsilon,g)}(H(v)) \rangle,$$

in which $\mathcal{M}_{\text{GRR}(\epsilon,g)}$ is given in Eq. (4), while operating on the new domain $[1..g]$. Each user reports, the hash function and obfuscated value $\langle H, y \rangle$ to the server.

Estimate. The support set for LH mechanisms is $S_{\text{LH}}(\langle H, y \rangle) = \{v | H(v) = y\}$, *i.e.*, the set of values that are hashed into the obfuscated data y. LH mechanisms are pure with probabilities $p^* = p$ and $q^* = \frac{1}{g}$ [25]. Thus, the server can estimate item frequencies using Eq. (2) for MI and Eq. (3) for IBU.

Unary Encoding (UE). UE mechanisms [16,25] interpret the user's input data $v \in \mathcal{D}$, as a one-hot k-dimensional vector and obfuscate each bit independently.

Encode. $\texttt{Encode}_{\text{UE}}(v) = \mathbf{v} = [0, \ldots, 0, 1, 0, \ldots, 0]$ is a binary vector with only the bit at the position corresponding to v set to 1 and the other bits set to 0.

Obfuscate. The obfuscation function of UE mechanisms randomizes the bits from $\mathbf{v}$ independently to generate $\mathbf{y}$ as follows:

$$\forall i \in [1..k]: \quad \Pr[\mathbf{y}_i = 1] = \begin{cases} p, & \text{if } \mathbf{v}_i = 1, \\ q, & \text{if } \mathbf{v}_i = 0, \end{cases} \tag{5}$$

in which $\mathbf{y}$ is sent to the server. There are two variations of UE mechanisms:

- **Symmetric UE (SUE)** [16]. Also known as Basic One-Time RAPPOR, SUE selects $p = \frac{e^{\epsilon/2}}{e^{\epsilon/2}+1}$ and $q = \frac{1}{e^{\epsilon/2}+1}$ in Eq. (5), such that $p + q = 1$;
- **Optimal UE (OUE)** [25]. OUE selects $p = \frac{1}{2}$ and $q = \frac{1}{e^\epsilon+1}$ in Eq. (5).

Estimate. An obfuscated vector $\mathbf{y}$ supports an item v if and only if the v-th bit of $\mathbf{y}$, denoted as $\mathbf{y}_v$, equals to 1. Formally, we have $S_{\text{UE}}(\mathbf{y}) = \{i | \mathbf{v}_i = 1\}$, for $i \in [1..k]$. UE mechanisms are pure with $p^* = p$ and $q^* = q$. Thus, the server can estimate item frequencies using Eq. (2) for MI and Eq. (3) for IBU.

Subset Selection (SS). The SS [24,30] mechanism was proposed for the case where the obfuscation output is a subset of values Ω of the original domain V. The user's true value $v \in \mathcal{D}$ has higher probability of being included in the subset Ω, compared to the other values in $\mathcal{D} \setminus \{v\}$. The optimal subset size that minimizes the MSE is $\omega = \lfloor \frac{k}{e^\epsilon+1} \rfloor$.

Encode. $\text{Encode}_{SS}(v) = \Omega = \emptyset$ is an empty subset.

Obfuscate. Given the empty subset Ω, the true value v is added to Ω with probability $p = \frac{\omega e^{\epsilon}}{\omega e^{\epsilon} + k - \omega}$. Finally, it adds values to Ω as follows:

- If $v \in \Omega$, then $\omega - 1$ values are sampled from $\mathcal{D} \setminus \{v\}$ uniformly at random (without replacement) and are added to Ω;
- If $v \notin \Omega$, then ω values are sampled from $\mathcal{D} \setminus \{v\}$ uniformly at random (without replacement) and are added to Ω.

Afterward, the user sends the subset Ω to the server.

Estimate. An obfuscated subset Ω supports an item v if and only if $v \in \Omega$. Formally, we have $S_{SS}(\Omega) = \{v | v \in \Omega\}$. The SS mechanism is pure with $p^* = p$ and $q^* = \frac{\omega e^{\epsilon}(\omega - 1) + (k - \omega)\omega}{(k-1)(\omega e^{\epsilon} + k - \omega)}$. Thus, the server can estimate item frequencies using Eq. (2) for MI and Eq. (3) for IBU.

Thresholding with Histogram Encoding (THE). In Histogram Encoding (HE) [25], an input data $v \in \mathcal{D}$ is encoded as a one-hot k-dimensional histogram and each bit is obfuscated independently with the Laplace mechanism [12]. For any two input data $v, v' \in \mathcal{D}$, the L1 distance between the two vectors is $\Delta = 2$.

Encode. $\text{Encode}_{HE(v)} = \mathbf{v} = [0.0, \ldots, 0.0, 1.0, 0.0, \ldots, 0.0]$, where only the v-th component is 1.0 and the other bits are set to 0.0.

Obfuscate. HE outputs $\mathbf{y}$ such that $\mathbf{y}_i = \mathbf{v}_i + \text{Lap}\left(\frac{2}{\epsilon}\right)$, in which $\text{Lap}(\beta)$ is the Laplace distribution where $\Pr[\text{Lap}(\beta) = x] = \frac{1}{2\beta}e^{-|x|/\beta}$.

Estimate. Since Laplace noise with zero mean is added to each bit independently, a simple aggregation method is to sum the noisy counts for each bit. However, this aggregation method does not provide a support function and is not pure (a.k.a. SHE in [25]). Wang et $al.$ [25] proposed THE such that the user reports (or the server computes) the support set as $S_{THE}(\mathbf{y}) = \{v \mid \mathbf{y}_v > \theta\}$, $i.e.$, each noise count that is $> \theta$ supports the corresponding value. According to [25], the optimal threshold value θ that minimizes the MSE $= \frac{2e^{\epsilon\theta/2} - 1}{(1 + e^{\epsilon(\theta - 1/2)} - 2e^{\epsilon\theta/2})^2}$ is within $(0.5, 1)$. THE is pure with $p^* = 1 - \frac{1}{2}e^{\frac{\epsilon}{2}(\theta - 1)}$ and $q^* = \frac{1}{2}e^{-\frac{\epsilon}{2}\theta}$. Thus, the server can estimate item frequencies using Eq. (2) for MI and Eq. (3) for IBU.

3.2   LDP Mechanisms for Multiple Data Collections

The LDP mechanisms presented in Sect. 3.1 consider a one-time data collection. In this section, we consider the server is interested in multiple collections throughout time. More precisely, for longitudinal data ($i.e.$, data that is monitored over time $t \in [\tau]$), all major LDP mechanisms make use of an internal memoization mechanism [16]. Memoization was designed to enable longitudinal collections through memorizing an obfuscated version of the true value v as

$y = \mathcal{M}_{\epsilon_\infty}(v)$, and consistently reusing y as the input to a second step of obfusca-tion in time $t \in [\tau]$. Algorithm 2 exhibits the general procedure for longitudinal discrete distribution estimation under LDP guarantees.

Without loss of generality, we consider $\tau = 1$ (one-time collection) in this paper, which will allow us to compare all LDP mechanisms under the same privacy guarantees: (i) ϵ_∞-LDP, which is the privacy guarantees of the first obfuscation step and the upper bound when $\tau \to \infty$; (ii) ϵ_1-LDP, which is the privacy guarantees of the first report by chaining two LDP mechanisms (i.e., the lower bound when $\tau = 1$). Naturally, $\epsilon_1 \leq \epsilon_\infty$ and, in practice, we want $\epsilon_1 \ll \epsilon_\infty$.

The three following subsections briefly present state-of-the-art longitudinal LDP mechanisms [3,6,16], which are based on GRR, LH, and UE mechanisms, i.e., same encoding, perturbation, and aggregation methods. Therefore, we focus on presenting the composition of two LDP mechanisms (i.e., $\mathcal{M}_1 \circ \mathcal{M}_2$) and both p^* and q^* parameters that are based on the privacy guarantees $\epsilon_\infty, \epsilon_1$.

Algorithm 2. Memoization-based procedure for longitudinal distribution esti-mation under LDP guarantees [3,6,16].

Input : Original data of users, privacy parameters $\epsilon_\infty, \epsilon_1$, mechanisms $\mathcal{M}_1, \mathcal{M}_2$.
Output : Estimated discrete distribution $\hat{\mathbf{f}}$ at each $t \in [\tau]$.

\# User-side
1: **for** each user $i \in [1..n]$ with input data $v^i \in V$ **do**
2:    Encode(v^i) into a specific format (**if needed**);
3:    Obfuscate(v^i) as $y^i = \mathcal{M}_{1(\epsilon_\infty)}(v^i)$;   ▷ First obfuscation step: p_1^* and q_1^*
4:    Memoize(y^i) for v^i.
5:    **for** each time $t \in [\tau]$ **do:**
6:        Obfuscate(y^i) as $y_t^i = \mathcal{M}_{2(\epsilon)}(y^i)$;   ▷ Second obfuscation step: p_2^* and q_2^*
7:        Transmit y_t^i to the aggregator.
8:    **end for**
9: **end for**
\# Server-side
10: Obtain the support set $S(y)$ and probabilities p_1^*, q_1^*, p_2^*, and q_2^* for $\mathcal{M}_{1(\epsilon)}, \mathcal{M}_{2(\epsilon)}$.
11: **for** each time $t \in [\tau]$ **do:**
12:    Estimate Aggregate the obfuscated data y_t^i ($i \in [1..n]$) to estimate $\{\hat{f}(v)\}_{v \in \mathcal{D}}$.
13: **end for**

Longitudinal GRR (L-GRR). The L-GRR [3] mechanism chains GRR in both obfuscation steps of Algorithm 2 (i.e., GRR ∘ GRR).

L-GRR Parameters:

– First obfuscation step: $p_1^* = \frac{e^{\epsilon_\infty}}{e^{\epsilon_\infty}+k-1}$ and $q_1^* = \frac{1-p_1}{k-1}$;

– Second obfuscation step: $p_2^* = \frac{e^{\epsilon_\infty+\epsilon_1}-1}{-ke^{\epsilon_1}+(k-1)e^{\epsilon_\infty}+e^{\epsilon_1}+e^{\epsilon_1+\epsilon_\infty}-1}$ and $q_2^* = \frac{1-p_2}{k-1}$.

– Aggregation: $p^* = p_1^* p_2^* + q_1^* q_2^*$ and $q^* = p_1^* q_2^* + q_1^* p_2^*$.

Longitudinal UE (L-UE) Mechanisms. Arcolezi *et al.* [3] analyzed all four combinations between OUE and SUE in both obfuscation steps, *i.e.*, L-SUE (SUE ∘ SUE, a.k.a. Basic RAPPOR [16]), L-SOUE (SUE ∘ OUE), L-OUE (OUE ∘ OUE), and L-OSUE (OUE ∘ SUE). Without loss of generality, we present the parameters of L-OSUE only and refer the readers to [3] and to `multi-freq-ldpy` [4] to access the parameters of the other L-UE mechanisms.

L-OSUE Parameters:

- First obfuscation step: $p_1^* = \frac{1}{2}$ and $q_1^* = \frac{1}{e^{\epsilon_\infty}+1}$;
- Second obfuscation step: $p_2^* = \frac{e^{\epsilon_\infty}e^{\epsilon_1}-1}{e^{\epsilon_\infty}-e^{\epsilon_1}+e^{\epsilon_\infty+\epsilon_1}-1}$ and $q_2^* = 1 - p_2$.
- Aggregation: $p^* = p_1^*p_2^* + (1 - p_1^*)q_2^*$ and $q^* = q_1^*p_2^* + (1 - q_1^*)q_2^*$.

Longitudinal LH (L-LH). Arcolezi *et al.* [6] extended LH mechanisms for two obfuscation steps. More specifically, L-LH mechanisms use a hash function $H \in \mathscr{H}$ to map a value $v \in \mathcal{D} \to [1..g]$ and use L-GRR to obfuscate the hash value $H(v)$ in the new domain $[1..g]$. There are two variations of L-LH:

- L-BLH: A simple case that just sets $g = 2$;
- L-OLH: Let $a = e^{\epsilon_\infty}$ and $b = e^{\epsilon_1}$, this optimized version selects $g = 1+\max\left(1, \left\lfloor \frac{1-a^2+\sqrt{a^4-14a^2+12ab(1-ab)+12a^3b+1}}{6(a-b)} \right\rfloor\right)$.

L-LH Parameters:

- First obfuscation step: $p_1^* = \frac{e^{\epsilon_\infty}}{e^{\epsilon_\infty}+g-1}$ and $q_1^* = \frac{1}{g}$;
- Second obfuscation step: $p_2^* = \frac{e^{\epsilon_\infty+\epsilon_1}-1}{-ge^{\epsilon_1}+(g-1)e^{\epsilon_\infty}+e^{\epsilon_1}+e^{\epsilon_1+\epsilon_\infty}-1}$ and $q_2^* = \frac{1-p_2}{g-1}$.
- Aggregation: $p^* = p_1^*p_2^* + q_1^*q_2^*$ and $q^* = p_1^*q_2^* + q_1^*p_2^*$.

4   Experimental Evaluation

In this section, we present the setting of our experiments and our main results.

4.1   Setup of Experiments

Environment. All algorithms are implemented in Python 3 and run on a local machine with 2.50 GHz Intel Core i9 and 64 GB RAM. The codes we develop for all experiments are available in the *tutorials* folder of the `multi-freq-ldpy` GitHub repository (https://github.com/hharcolezi/multi-freq-ldpy) [4].

IBU Parameters. We fix the # iterations to 10000 and the tolerance to 10^{-12}.

Data Distribution. For ease of reproducibility, we generate synthetic data following five well-known distributions and use one real-world dataset.

- **Gaussian.** We generate n samples following the Gaussian distribution with parameters $\mu = 1000$ and $\sigma^2 = 100$ and bucketize to a k-bins histogram;

- **Exponential.** We generate n samples following the Exponential distribution with parameters $\lambda = 1$ and bucketize to a k-bins histogram;
- **Uniform.** We generate n samples following the Uniform distribution in range $[100, 10000]$ and bucketize to a k-bins histogram;
- **Poisson.** We generate n samples following the Poisson distribution with parameters $\lambda = 5$ and bucketize to a k-bins histogram;
- **Triangular.** We generate n samples following the Triangular distribution with parameters $a = 100$ (right), $c = 4500$ (center), and $b = 10000$ (left) and bucketize to a k-bins histogram;
- **Real.** We query for n samples of the Income dataset, which is retrieved with the folktables [11] Python package. We only use the "PINCP" numerical attribute and set the parameters: survey_year='2018', horizon='5-Year', survey='person'. Afterward, we bucketize to a k-bins histogram.

Varying Parameters. When generating our data, we considered different:

- **Domain size.** We varied the domain size k of attributes as $k \in \{2, 50, 100, 200\}$;
- **Number of users.** We varied the number of users n as $n \in \{20000, 100000\}$.

Methods Evaluated. We assessed the following LDP mechanisms for:

- **One-time collection.** All seven pure LDP mechanisms from Sect. 3.1, *i.e.*, GRR, SUE, OUE, SS, THE, BLH, and OLH;
- **Multiple collections.** All seven longitudinal pure LDP mechanisms from Sect. 3.2, *i.e.*, L-GRR, L-SUE, L-SOUE, L-OUE, L-OSUE, L-BLH, and L-OLH.

Stability. As LDP protocols and the synthetic data generation procedure are randomized, we report average results over 20 runs.

Metrics. We evaluated the privacy-utility trade-off of all fourteen LDP mechanisms according to:

- **Utility metrics.** We measured the utility gain of IBU over MI following Eq. (1) for both MSE and MAE metrics;
- **Privacy guarantees.** We varied ϵ of LDP mechanisms for one-time collection as $\epsilon \in \{1, 2, 4\}$, representing high, medium, and low privacy regimes, respectively. Besides, we varied the privacy guarantees ϵ_∞ and ϵ_1 of longitudinal LDP mechanisms for multiple collections as $\epsilon_\infty \in \{2, 4, 8\}$ and $\epsilon_1 = \frac{\epsilon_\infty}{2}$. That is, the first report has the same privacy guarantees as one-time LDP mechanisms, and, thus, similar results are expected for LDP mechanisms with both one-time and longitudinal versions (*e.g.*, GRR and L-GRR).

4.2   Main Results

First, considering the real data distribution and the MSE metric, Fig. 1 (one-time LDP mechanisms) and Fig. 2 (longitudinal LDP mechanisms) illustrate the IBU utility gain calculated as in Eq. (1), by fixing $n = 20000$, $k = 100$, and varying $\epsilon \in \{1, 2, 4\}$ (resp. $\epsilon = \epsilon_1$). These two figures also illustrate the Average Gain (AvgGain) considering all LDP mechanisms within the same subplot. From Fig. 1, one can notice that IBU consistently and considerably outperformed MI for all LDP mechanisms in the medium ($\epsilon = 2$) and low privacy regimes ($\epsilon = 4$). For $\epsilon = 1$, IBU was only better for GRR, OUE, SS, and OLH, while achieving similar results for SUE and THE, and unsatisfactory results for BLH. Similar behavior can be noticed on the left-side plot of Fig. 2 in which IBU did not improve over MI for L-SUE and L-BLH. This is because both privacy guarantees are equal for both one-time and longitudinal LDP mechanisms, i.e., $\epsilon_1 = \epsilon$, and thus, similar results will occur, on expectation, when running more iterations for stability. Overall, for both Figs. 1 and 2, the higher AvgGain occurs in the medium privacy regime, followed by low and high privacy regimes, respectively.

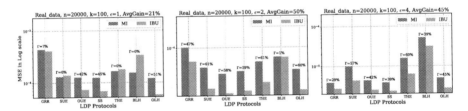

Fig. 1. IBU utility gain in % (*cf.* Eq. (1)) for each one-time pure LDP mechanism with the MSE metric, the real distribution, $n = 20000$, $k = 100$, and $\epsilon \in \{1, 2, 4\}$. AvgGain indicates the average gain considering all LDP mechanisms in the same subplot.

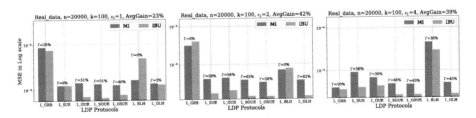

Fig. 2. IBU utility gain in % (*cf.* Eq. (1)) for each longitudinal pure LDP mechanism with the MSE metric, the real distribution, $n = 20000$, $k = 100$ $\epsilon_\infty \in \{2, 4, 8\}$, and $\epsilon_1 = \frac{\epsilon_\infty}{2}$. AvgGain indicates the average gain considering all LDP mechanisms in the same subplot.

Second, in Fig. 3 (one-time LDP mechanisms) and Fig. 4 (longitudinal LDP mechanisms), we compare the IBU utility gain in different types of distributions (including real data) by varying ϵ (left-side plots), n (centered plots), and k

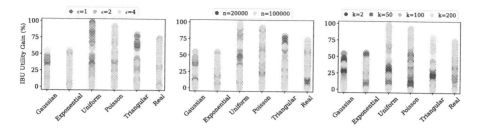

Fig. 3. IBU utility gain is in %. Each subplot shows all gains obtained by distribution type when the privacy level (ϵ), number of users (n), and domain size (k) are varied, respectively from left to right. We computed all gains with all one-time pure LDP mechanisms considered and the MSE metric.

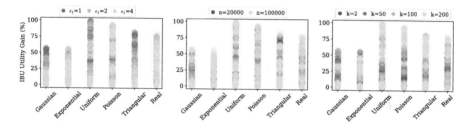

Fig. 4. IBU utility gain is in %. Each subplot shows all gains obtained by distribution type when the privacy level (ϵ), number of users (n), and domain size (k) are varied, respectively from left to right. We computed all gains with all longitudinal pure LDP mechanisms considered and the MSE metric.

(right-side plots). In both figures, we observed that the uniform distribution presented the highest gain, while the Gaussian and Exponential distributions obtained the lowest gains. This is due to the fact that more values close or equal to zero are generated in Gaussian and Exponential distributions, which makes estimation difficult not only for IBU but also for MI. When analyzing the variation of ϵ in both figures, we noticed that the lower ϵ (high privacy regime), the higher the IBU gain, which is desirable in practice. Furthermore, when examining the variation of the number of users n, we noticed that the gains obtained considering all LDP mechanisms for all data distributions present a better performance when n is higher, especially with longitudinal mechanisms. This is because longitudinal mechanisms have a higher variance and require more samples to reduce their estimation error [3, 6, 16]. Last, when analyzing the behavior of the domain size k, in both figures, it is shown that IBU outperforms MI, as the domain grows, *i.e.*, IBU supports data with high dimensionality, which better reflects real-world data collections.

Finally, Table 2 (one-time LDP mechanisms) and Table 3 (longitudinal LDP mechanisms) exhibit the averaged utility gain of IBU for all LDP mechanisms, all data distributions, and both MSE and MAE metrics by considering $k \in \{2, 50, 100, 200\}$, $n \in \{20000, 100000\}$, and $\epsilon \in \{1, 2, 4\}$ (resp. $\epsilon_1 = \epsilon$). From these tables, one can gather the averaged gain for each utility metric (MSE and MAE) by LDP mechanism considering all data distributions (*i.e.*, last row). For instance, in Table 2, while the THE mechanism is the one which presented the higher utility gain followed by the SUE mechanism, GRR presented the lowest utility gain. Similar results can be observed in Table 3, *i.e.*, the L-SUE mechanism presented the higher utility gain and L-GRR the lowest one. In [14], the authors also remarked that the IBU utility gain for GRR was not substantial. Indeed, while in Table 3 L-UE mechanisms showed higher utility gain than L-LH mechanisms, in Table 2, both UE and LH present similar results. Additionally, from Table 2 and Table 3, one can also gather the averaged gain for each utility metric (MSE and MAE) by data distribution considering all LDP mechanisms (*i.e.*, last two columns). For example, for both tables, the higher utility gain was observed for the Poisson distribution followed by the real data distribution. The lower utility gain considering all LDP mechanisms was for the Gaussian distribution followed by the Triangular distribution.

Table 2. Averaged IBU utility gain in % (*cf.* Eq. (1)) for all one-time pure LDP mechanisms and all data distributions (Dist.), considering $k \in \{2, 50, 100, 200\}$, $n \in \{20000, 100000\}$, and $\epsilon \in \{1, 2, 4\}$. Results highlighted in **bold font** represent the two highest utility gains, on average.

Dist.	GRR		SUE		OUE		SS		THE		BLH		OLH		Avg.	
	MSE	MAE	MSE	MAE	MSE	MAE	MSE	MAE	MSE	MAE	MSE	MAE	MSE	MAE	MSE	MAE
Gauss.	1	1	13	7	10	6	3	1	13	7	16	9	11	7	9	5
Exp.	16	11	26	15	27	16	19	11	26	15	16	10	27	16	22	13
Unif.	0	0	29	21	20	14	14	10	31	22	57	43	18	12	24	17
Poiss.	39	28	41	26	44	28	41	27	41	27	14	6	46	30	**38**	**24**
Triang.	0	0	21	13	15	9	10	6	23	14	36	21	15	9	17	10
Real	31	21	40	23	42	25	34	19	42	25	21	11	44	27	**36**	**21**
Avg.	14	10	**28**	**17**	26	16	20	12	**29**	**18**	26	16	26	16	24	15

Table 3. Averaged utility gain in % of IBU over MI (*cf.* Eq. (1)) for all longitudinal pure LDP mechanisms and all data distributions (Dist.), considering $k \in \{2, 50, 100, 200\}$, $n \in \{20000, 100000\}$, $\epsilon_\infty \in \{2, 4, 8\}$, and $\epsilon_1 = \frac{\epsilon_\infty}{2}$. Results highlighted in **bold font** represent the two highest utility gains, on average.

Dist.	L-GRR		L-SUE		L-OUE		L-SOUE		L-OSUE		L-BLH		L-OLH		Avg.	
	MSE	MAE	MSE	MAE	MSE	MAE	MSE	MAE	MSE	MAE	MSE	MAE	MSE	MAE	MSE	MAE
Gauss.	14	5	13	8	9	5	10	7	12	7	2	0	7	4	9	5
Exp.	4	1	27	16	26	15	27	16	27	16	4	2	20	12	19	11
Unif.	36	25	31	22	12	8	16	11	18	13	54	43	21	16	26	19
Poiss.	5	2	43	28	48	32	49	32	44	29	11	6	42	30	**34**	**22**
Triang.	28	17	24	15	11	7	13	9	16	10	26	14	14	9	18	11
Real	4	1	43	25	43	27	44	27	43	25	9	4	34	22	**31**	**18**
Avg.	15	8	**30**	**19**	24	15	**26**	**17**	26	16	17	11	23	15	23	14

```
# Multi-Freq-LDPy functions for GRR protocol
from multi_freq_ldpy.pure_frequency_oracles.GRR import GRR_Client,
    GRR_Aggregator_IBU

# NumPy library
import numpy as np

# Parameters for simulation
eps = 1 # privacy guarantee
n = int(1e6) # number of users
k = 5 # attribute's domain size

# Simulation dataset following Uniform distribution
dataset = np.random.randint(k, size=n)

# Simulation of client-side data obfuscation
rep = [GRR_Client(user_data, k, eps) for user_data in dataset]

# Simulation of server-side aggregation
GRR_Aggregator_IBU(rep, k, eps, nb_iter=10000, tol=1e-12, err_func="max_abs")
>>> array([0.199, 0.201, 0.199, 0.202, 0.199])
```

Listing 1.1. Code snippet for performing distribution estimation using IBU [1,2] with data obfuscated through the GRR [18] mechanism.

Implementation Details. The `multi-freq-ldpy` Python package [4] is function-based and simulates the LDP data collection pipeline of n users and one server. Thus, for each solution and/or mechanism, there is always a *client* and an *aggregator* function. As `multi-freq-ldpy` had only aggregator functions based on MI, our implementation of IBU contributes with another aggregator function for LDP mechanism in both `pure_frequency_oracle` and `long_freq_est` modules. For example, the complete code to execute one-time distribution estimation using IBU [1,2] with data obfuscated through the GRR [18] mechanism is illustrated in Listing 1.1 with the resulting estimated frequency for a given set of parameters and a randomly generated dataset. One can notice that the `GRR_Aggregator_IBU` function receives as input: the set of obfuscated data (rep), the domain size k, the privacy guarantee ϵ, the # iterations (nb_iter), and a small tolerance value (tol) that works along with an error function (err_func). The three last parameters 'nb_iter', 'tol', and 'err_func' are stopping criteria for IBU to terminate, and the values in Listing 1.1 are the default parameters.

5 Related Work

The literature on the local DP model [29] has largely explored the issue of minimizing the utility loss of LDP mechanisms. On the one hand, some works [7,16,18,24,25,30] focused on designed new encoding and perturbation functions, often leading to new privacy-utility trade-offs as well as robustness to privacy attacks [5]. On the other hand, recent research works [14,15,18,22,26] focused on improving the estimation method on the server side through post-processing techniques for the MI estimator and using IBU. For instance, the authors in [18] investigated distribution estimation with GRR and SUE by using two post-processing approaches for MI, namely, a method that clips negative elements of $\hat{\mathbf{f}}$ to 0 and re-normalizes $\hat{\mathbf{f}}$ so that its sum is 1, and a method that projects $\hat{\mathbf{f}}$ onto the probability simplex. Wang *et al.* [26] studied and proposed, in total 10 post-processing approaches for MI ranging from methods that enforce only non-negativity of elements in $\hat{\mathbf{f}}$ or that $\hat{\mathbf{f}}$ sums to 1, and other methods that enforce both. Experiments in [26] were performed with the OLH mechanism. Regarding IBU [1,2], recent works have proposed and investigated its performance for discrete distribution estimation [14,15,22] and for joint distribution estimation [17,23]. More precisely, ElSalamouny & Palamidessi [14,15] proposed a generalization of IBU for personalized LDP, *i.e.*, considering different privacy guarantees ϵ_i ($i \in [1..n]$) and different LDP mechanisms (*i.e.*, GRR and SUE).

While the aforementioned research works [14,15,18,22,26] answer interesting questions experimenting only with the GRR [18], SUE [16], and OLH [25] mechanisms, we consider in this work fourteen ϵ-LDP mechanisms, *i.e.*, seven for one-time data collection and seven for multiple data collections. In our analysis we varied the utility metrics (*i.e.*, MSE and MAE), the data distribution (*i.e.*, synthetic data following standard distribution and one real-world data), the number of users n, the domain size k, and the privacy guarantees ϵ. Last, we have also open-sourced the IBU implementation into `multi-freq-ldpy` [4], thereby enabling researchers to easily use and expand upon our results.

6   Conclusion and Perspectives

In conclusion, this paper presents an in-depth investigation into the effectiveness of Iterative Bayesian Update (IBU) as a post-processing technique for improving the utility of LDP mechanisms used for private discrete distribution estimation. Based on our experiments on both synthetic and real-world data, we compared the performance of IBU to Matrix Inversion (MI), a standard estimation technique. We assessed the utility gain of IBU over MI for seven state-of-the-art LDP mechanisms designed for one-time collection [7,16,18,24,25,30] and for seven state-of-the-art longitudinal LDP mechanisms [3,6,16] designed for multiple data collections. On average, both THE [25] and SUE (a.k.a. Basic One-Time RAPPOR) [16] mechanisms showed the highest IBU utility gain in our experiments, which involved varying n, k, ϵ, and the data distribution. Regarding longitudinal LDP mechanisms, L-UE mechanisms [3,16] presented higher IBU utility gain, on average, than L-GRR [3] and L-LH [6] mechanisms. Overall, our results show that IBU can significantly improve the utility of LDP mechanisms for certain data distributions (*e.g.*, Poisson) and specific settings (*cf.* Table 2 and Table 3).

Based on the findings of this paper, there are several areas that could be explored for future work. Some potential avenues for further research include investigating the performance of IBU on non-pure LDP mechanisms as well as for high-dimensional data, *e.g.*, $k \gg 200$. Additionally, we plan to investigate different settings for the IBU initialization and stopping criteria, *i.e.*, considering non-uniform initial distributions and different tolerance calculation functions.

Finally, we also aim to implement GIBU (Generalized IBU) [14] and the estimation methods proposed in [15] for personalized LDP, into `multi-freq-ldpy` [4].

Acknowledgements. This work was supported by the European Research Council (ERC) project HYPATIA under the European Union's Horizon 2020 research and innovation programme. Grant agreement n. 835294.

References

1. Agrawal, D., Aggarwal, C.C.: On the design and quantification of privacy preserving data mining algorithms. In: Proceedings of the Twentieth ACM SIGMOD-SIGACT-SIGART Symposium on Principles of Database Systems. ACM (2001). https://doi.org/10.1145/375551.375602
2. Agrawal, R., Srikant, R., Thomas, D.: Privacy preserving OLAP. In: Proceedings of the 2005 ACM SIGMOD International Conference on Management of Data. ACM (2005). https://doi.org/10.1145/1066157.1066187
3. Arcolezi, H.H., Couchot, J.F., Bouna, B.A., Xiao, X.: Improving the utility of locally differentially private protocols for longitudinal and multidimensional frequency estimates. Digit. Commun. Netw. (2022). https://doi.org/10.1016/j.dcan.2022.07.003
4. Arcolezi, H.H., Couchot, J.F., Gambs, S., Palamidessi, C., Zolfaghari, M.: Multi-Freq-LDPy: multiple frequency estimation under local differential privacy in python. In: Atluri, V., Di Pietro, R., Jensen, C.D., Meng, W. (eds.) Computer Security - ESORICS 2022. Lecture Notes in Computer Science, vol. 13556, pp. 770–775. Springer, Cham (2022). https://doi.org/10.1007/978-3-031-17143-7_40
5. Arcolezi, H.H., Gambs, S., Couchot, J.F., Palamidessi, C.: On the risks of collecting multidimensional data under local differential privacy. Proc. VLDB Endow. **16**(5), 1126–1139 (2023). https://doi.org/10.14778/3579075.3579086
6. Arcolezi, H.H., Pinzón, C.A., Palamidessi, C., Gambs, S.: Frequency estimation of evolving data under local differential privacy. In: Proceedings of the 26th International Conference on Extending Database Technology, EDBT 2023, Ioannina, Greece, 28 - 31 March 2023, pp. 512–525. OpenProceedings.org (2023). https://doi.org/10.48786/EDBT.2023.44
7. Bassily, R., Smith, A.: Local, private, efficient protocols for succinct histograms. In: Proceedings of the Forty-Seventh Annual ACM Symposium on Theory of Computing, pp. 127–135. STOC 2015, Association for Computing Machinery, New York, NY, USA (2015). https://doi.org/10.1145/2746539.2746632
8. Cheu, A.: Differential privacy in the shuffle model: a survey of separations. arXiv preprint arXiv:2107.11839 (2021)
9. Costa Filho, J.S., Machado, J.C.: Felip: A local differentially private approach to frequency estimation on multidimensional datasets. In: Proceedings of the 26th International Conference on Extending Database Technology, EDBT 2023, Ioannina, Greece, 28 - 31 March 2023, pp. 671–683. OpenProceedings.org (2023). https://doi.org/10.48786/EDBT.2023.56
10. Dempster, A.P., Laird, N.M., Rubin, D.B.: Maximum likelihood from incomplete data via the EM algorithm. J. Roy. Stat. Soc.: Ser. B (Methodol.) **39**(1), 1–22 (1977). https://doi.org/10.1111/j.2517-6161.1977.tb01600.x
11. Ding, F., Hardt, M., Miller, J., Schmidt, L.: Retiring adult: new datasets for fair machine learning. In: Advances in Neural Information Processing Systems 34 (2021)

12. Dwork, C., McSherry, F., Nissim, K., Smith, A.: Calibrating noise to sensitivity in private data analysis. In: Halevi, S., Rabin, T. (eds.) TCC 2006. LNCS, vol. 3876, pp. 265–284. Springer, Heidelberg (2006). https://doi.org/10.1007/11681878_14

13. Dwork, C., Roth, A., et al.: The algorithmic foundations of differential privacy. Found. Trends® Theoret. Comput. Sci. **9**(3–4), 211–407 (2014)

14. ElSalamouny, E., Palamidessi, C.: Generalized iterative Bayesian update and applications to mechanisms for privacy protection. In: 2020 IEEE European Symposium on Security and Privacy (EuroS&P). IEEE (2020). https://doi.org/10.1109/eurosp48549.2020.00038

15. ElSalamouny, E., Palamidessi, C.: Reconstruction of the distribution of sensitive data under free-will privacy. arXiv preprint arXiv:2208.11268 (2022)

16. Erlingsson, U., Pihur, V., Korolova, A.: RAPPOR: randomized aggregatable privacy-preserving ordinal response. In: Proceedings of the 2014 ACM SIGSAC Conference on Computer and Communications Security, pp. 1054–1067. ACM, New York, NY, USA (2014). https://doi.org/10.1145/2660267.2660348

17. Fanti, G., Pihur, V., Erlingsson, Ú.: Building a RAPPOR with the unknown: Privacy-preserving learning of associations and data dictionaries. Proceed. Priv. Enhan. Technol. **2016**(3), 41–61 (2016). https://doi.org/10.1515/popets-2016-0015

18. Kairouz, P., Bonawitz, K., Ramage, D.: Discrete distribution estimation under local privacy. In: International Conference on Machine Learning, pp. 2436–2444. PMLR (2016)

19. Kasiviswanathan, S.P., Lee, H.K., Nissim, K., Raskhodnikova, S., Smith, A.: What can we learn privately? In: 2008 49th Annual IEEE Symposium on Foundations of Computer Science, pp. 531–540 (2008). https://doi.org/10.1109/FOCS.2008.27

20. Liu, G., Tang, P., Hu, C., Jin, C., Guo, S.: Multi-dimensional data publishing with local differential privacy. In: Proceedings of the 26th International Conference on Extending Database Technology, EDBT 2023, Ioannina, Greece, 28 - 31 March 2023, pp. 183–194. OpenProceedings.org (2023). https://doi.org/10.48786/edbt.2023.15

21. McCandless, D., et al.: World's biggest data breaches & hacks (2021). https://www.informationisbeautiful.net/visualizations/worlds-biggest-data-breaches-hacks/. Accessed 11 Mar 2023

22. Murakami, T., Hino, H., Sakuma, J.: Toward distribution estimation under local differential privacy with small samples. Proceed. Priv. Enhan. Technol. **2018**(3), 84–104 (2018). https://doi.org/10.1515/popets-2018-0022

23. Ren, X., et al.: LoPub: high-dimensional crowdsourced data publication with local differential privacy. IEEE Trans. Inf. Forensics Secur. **13**(9), 2151–2166 (2018). https://doi.org/10.1109/TIFS.2018.2812146

24. Wang, S., et al.: Mutual information optimally local private discrete distribution estimation. arXiv preprint arXiv:1607.08025 (2016)

25. Wang, T., Blocki, J., Li, N., Jha, S.: Locally differentially private protocols for frequency estimation. In: 26th USENIX Security Symposium (USENIX Security 17), pp. 729–745. USENIX Association, Vancouver, BC (2017)

26. Wang, T., Lopuhaa-Zwakenberg, M., Li, Z., Skoric, B., Li, N.: Locally differentially private frequency estimation with consistency. In: Proceedings 2020 Network and Distributed System Security Symposium. Internet Society (2020). https://doi.org/10.14722/ndss.2020.24157

27. Warner, S.L.: Randomized response: a survey technique for eliminating evasive answer Bias. J. Am. Stat. Assoc. **60**(309), 63–69 (1965). https://doi.org/10.1080/01621459.1965.10480775

28. Wong, J.C.: Facebook to be fined $5bn for cambridge analytica privacy violations - reports (2019). https://www.theguardian.com/technology/2019/jul/12/facebook-fine-ftc-privacy-violations. Accessed 11 Mar 2023
29. Xiong, X., Liu, S., Li, D., Cai, Z., Niu, X.: A comprehensive survey on local differential privacy. Secur. Commun. Netw. **2020**, 1–29 (2020). https://doi.org/10.1155/2020/8829523
30. Ye, M., Barg, A.: Optimal schemes for discrete distribution estimation under locally differential privacy. IEEE Trans. Inf. Theory **64**(8), 5662–5676 (2018). https://doi.org/10.1109/TIT.2018.2809790

Differentially Private Streaming Data Release Under Temporal Correlations via Post-processing

Xuyang Cao[1]([✉]), Yang Cao[1], Primal Pappachan[2], Atsuyoshi Nakamura[1],
and Masatoshi Yoshikawa[3]

[1] Graduate School of IST, Hokkaido University, Sapporo, Japan
xuyang.cao@ist.hokudai.ac.jp
[2] Portland State University, Portland, OR, USA
[3] Faculty of Data Science, Osaka Seikei University, Osaka, Japan

Abstract. The release of differentially private streaming data has been extensively studied, yet striking a good balance between privacy and utility on temporally correlated data in the stream remains an open problem. Existing works focus on enhancing privacy when applying differential privacy to correlated data, highlighting that differential privacy may suffer from additional privacy leakage under correlations; consequently, a small privacy budget has to be used which worsens the utility. In this work, we propose a post-processing framework to improve the utility of differential privacy data release under temporal correlations. We model the problem as a maximum posterior estimation given the released differentially private data and correlation model and transform it into nonlinear constrained programming. Our experiments on synthetic datasets show that the proposed approach significantly improves the utility and accuracy of differentially private data by nearly a hundred times in terms of mean square error when a strict privacy budget is given.

Keywords: Differential Privacy · Data Correlations · Time-series Stream · Continual Data Release · Post-processing

1 Introduction

Data collection and analysis in many real-world scenarios are performed in a streaming fashion, such as location traces [21], web page click data [12], and real-time stock trades. However, releasing data continuously may result in privacy risks. To this end, *differentially private streaming data release* have been thoroughly studied [3,4,7,8,11–15,22]. The curator of the database can use a differentially private mechanism, such as Laplace Mechanism (LM), that adds noises to the query results at each time point for satisfying a formal privacy guarantee called ϵ-Differential Privacy (ϵ-DP) [9], where ϵ is the parameter (i.e., privacy budget) controlling trade-off between privacy protection and utility of data release. A small ϵ indicates a high level of privacy and thus requires adding a larger amount of noise. Taking location traces as an example to elaborate, Fig. 1

© IFIP International Federation for Information Processing 2023
Published by Springer Nature Switzerland AG 2023
V. Atluri and A. L. Ferrara (Eds.): DBSec 2023, LNCS 13942, pp. 184–200, 2023.
https://doi.org/10.1007/978-3-031-37586-6_12

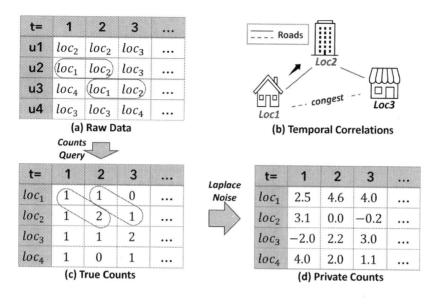

Fig. 1. Scenario: Differentially Private Streaming Data Release.

(a) (c) (d) illustrate how differentially private location statistics are released using LM at each time point where (a) represent real-time location raw data sets (i.e., values of longitude and latitude of residence, company, shopping mall respectively) of users in a database D collected by devices with GPS sensors (i.e., GPS, GNSS) [21], (c) are the true counts of each location computed by a count query function $f(D)$ and (d) what will be released and sent to the public are streaming private counts through a differentially private mechanism such as Laplace Mechanism (LM) [10].

However, recent studies [5,6,17,23,26,27] reveal that, when the data are correlated, more noises have to be added to prevent leakages which deteriorates the utility. They point out that differential privacy algorithms suffer extra privacy leakage on correlated data and develop techniques to enhance differential privacy with a smaller ϵ. In the context of streaming data release, a Markov chain could be used to model the temporal correlations. For example, as shown in Fig. 1 (b), temporal correlation is manifested as the transition probabilities between different locations, which can be obtained through public information such as road networks or traffic data. Based on the temporal correlation presented in Fig. 1(b), we have the probability of users proceeding from location $loc1$ to $loc2$ will be $Pr(l^{t+1} = loc2|l^t = loc1) = 1$ if we have the knowledge that another road is congested. Cao et al. [5,6] quantified such a private leakage and proposed a special privacy definition on temporal correlated data named α-DP_T, to calibrate a smaller privacy budget in order to cover the extra privacy leakage caused by temporal correlations. Song et al. [23] proposed Wasserstein Mechanism for Pufferfish privacy (i.e., a privacy notion that generalizes differential privacy) and Markov Quilt Mechanism specifically when correlation between data is described by a Bayesian Network or a Markov chain. Similar to [5,6], they calculate an

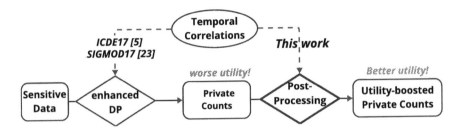

Fig. 2. Existing studies [5,23] propose approaches for enhancing DP on temporally correlated data; however, these methods sacrifice utility. This work tackles this problem by utilizing temporal correlations as prior knowledge about the data for post-processing purposes.

enlarged ϵ to enhance the privacy but sacrifice more utility. Hence, the challenge is how to boost the utility of differentially private streaming data release on temporally correlated data.

Our approach to addressing the aforementioned issue involves capitalizing on the existing temporal correlations as prior knowledge about the original data through post-processing. Although *post-processing* [16,18,20,25] has been extensively researched as a means to enhance the utility of differential privacy, current methods are ill-equipped to deal with temporal correlations. Post-processing primarily aims to refine differentially private (noisy) results by enforcing them to comply with certain ground-truth constraints or prior knowledge about the data. For instance, *deterministic* consistency constraints between data points are frequently employed in previous studies to represent inherent properties of the data (e.g., released counts in histograms should be integers). In this study, we apply the post-processing technique to improve the utility of differentially private streaming data release in the presence of temporal correlations. By accounting for temporal correlations along with other consistency constraints, we strive to obtain the most accurate current counts which could be estimated from previous private counts while approximating the true current counts.

In this study, we formulate post-processing as a nonlinear optimization problem within the Maximum A Posteriori (MAP) framework, accounting for both probabilistic constraints of temporal correlations and deterministic consistency constraints. Similar to [5,6,23], we assume that temporal correlations are public knowledge and are expressed by a transition matrix. As illustrated in Fig. 2, our approach leverages the transition matrix to enhance the utility of differentially private counts. Thus, we pose the problem of determining the most plausible counts that satisfy the constraints (both probabilistic and deterministic) and exhibit the least distance from the released private data. To model this probabilistic distribution, we employ the knowledge of Laplace noise distribution and introduce a Markov chain model to calculate the distribution of true counts. Finally, extensive experiments demonstrate and validate the effectiveness of our methods.

To summarize, our contributions are as follows:

- To the best of our knowledge, this paper presents the first attempt to enhance the utility of differentially private data release under temporal correlations. We propose a post-processing framework using maximum a posteriori estimation, which incorporates both probabilistic correlations and deterministic constraints.
- We implement the post-processing framework for temporal correlations in the differentially private continual data release. Specifically, we formulate this problem as constrained nonlinear programming, which can be solved using off-the-shelf optimization software.
- Our experiments on synthetic data demonstrate the effectiveness of the proposed approach. We show that the utility of differentially private data is significantly improved, with nearly a 100-fold reduction in mean square error under a strict privacy budget, while preserving temporal correlations between data.

We would like to note that this work is an extension of our previous poster paper [2], in which we briefly presented the idea without delving into technical details. This paper provides a clearer and more in-depth exploration of our previous work, offering a comprehensive understanding of the proposed MAP-based post-processing framework.

2   Related Work

Several well-studied methods exist to enhance the utility of differentially private data, as post-processing is an effective tool. In this section, we review related works on improving the utility of private data through post-processing.

One of the most widely studied approaches for utility enhancement is the utilization of *consistency constraints* [16,18] in data (e.g., the *sum* of the released data should be a fixed number, or the released values should be *integer* in the case of counting queries). In our location traces scenario, these consistency constraints can be expressed by the sum of location records or the total number of users as a fixed value (e.g., n) for each time point, with counts always being integers. Previous works formulate the problem as a least squares estimation (LSE) problem [16] or a maximum likelihood estimation (MLE) problem [18], demonstrating the effectiveness of such post-processing approaches.

Hay et al. [16] focused on improving the accuracy of private histograms through post-processing, solving an LSE problem given consistency constraints such as *sum*, *sorted*, and *positive* to find the 'closest' private histograms that also satisfy these constraints. Furthermore, Lee et al. [18] considered noise distribution (Laplace distribution in their scenario) to boost the utility of private query results. They formulated their post-processing problem as an MSE problem and employed the ADMM algorithm to solve the programming problem.

However, when publishing statistics continually, the data points are often temporally correlated. The post-processing methods mentioned above only focus on single-time data release and cannot efficiently capture probabilistic temporal correlations. Moreover, it remains unclear how to formulate *probabilistic* correlations as constraints, as existing works assume *deterministic* constraints as prior knowledge about the data. We also observe that many existing works on differentially private streaming data release neither provide a formal privacy guarantee under temporal correlations [3,4,7,11–15,22] nor offer reasonable utility for private outputs. Therefore, our study represents the first attempt to enhance the utility of DP with formal privacy under temporal correlations.

3   Preliminaries

3.1   Differential Privacy

Informally, the DP notion requires any single element in a dataset to have only a limited impact on the output. Namely, if D and D' are two *neighboring* databases, the difference in outputs of executing a randomized algorithm on these databases should be minimal [19].

Definition 1. *(ϵ-DP) A randomized mechanism $\mathcal{M}$ is said to satisfy ϵ-DP, where $\epsilon \geq 0$, if and only if for any neighboring datasets D and D' that differ on one element, we have*

$$\forall T \subseteq Range(\mathcal{M}) : Pr(\mathcal{M}(D) \in T) \leq e^{\epsilon} Pr(\mathcal{M}(D') \in T)$$

where $Range(\mathcal{M})$ represents the set of all possible outputs of the algorithm of mechanism $\mathcal{M}$, the parameter ϵ represents the privacy budget.

3.2   The Laplace Mechanism

The Laplace Mechanism [10] is the first and probably most widely used mechanism for DP. It satisfies ϵ-DP by adding noise to the output of a numerical function [19].

Definition 2. *(Global sensitivity) Let $D \approx D'$ denote that D and D' are neighboring. The global sensitivity of a query function f, denoted by Δ, is given below*

$$\Delta = \max_{D \approx D'} |f(D) - f(D')|$$

According to the definition of DP, the probability density function of the noise should have the property that if one moves no more than Δ units, the probability should increase or decrease no more than e^{ϵ}. The distribution of noise that naturally satisfies this requirement is $Lap(\frac{\Delta}{\epsilon})$ [19], which denotes a Laplace distribution with location 0 and scale $\frac{\Delta}{\epsilon}$.

Theorem 1. *(Laplace Mechanism, LM) For any function f, the Laplace mechanism A_f that adds i.i.d noise to each function output f satisfies ϵ-DP.*

$$A_f(D) = f(D) + Lap\left(\frac{\Delta}{\epsilon}\right).$$

Commonly, we denote the scale parameter using $\lambda = \frac{\Delta}{\epsilon}$.

Table 1. Notations

D	A bounded database
Loc	Value domain of locations of all users
l_i^t	The location information of $user_i$ at time t, $user_i \in U$, $l_i^t \in$ **Loc**
$\mathcal{M}$	A differential privacy mechanism over D
$\mathbf{R}$	The set of real continual time-series query outputs
$\tilde{\mathbf{R}}$	The set of added-noise continual time-series query outputs
R^t	The set of query outputs at time t, $R^t \subseteq \mathbf{R}$
r_l^t	A specific query output at time t and location l, $l \in$ **Loc**, $r_l^t \in R^t$
$\mathcal{T}$	The transition matrix of locations
$\mathbf{P^t}$	The possibility of locations for a single user at time t
$Pr(\hat{\mathbf{R}})$	The joint distribution of possible private counts

4   Problem Statement

This section will introduce and formulate the primary issue we aim to address. First, below we present the notations used throughout this paper. We use D to represent a *bounded database* consisting of n users. We prefer to use bold letters to indicate vectors. We use r_l^t to denote a specific query output at a given time point t and location l. $\mathcal{T}$ represents a transition matrix modeling temporal correlations between data. More detailed notations are in Table 1.

Temporally Correlated Stream Data. In our scenario of location traces mentioned above, we assume that n people (labeled from 1 to n) staying at m locations (labeled from 1 to m) respectively at single time point t (shown in Fig. 1 (a)). Let **Loc** denote the sets of locations. Naturally, the data at each time point are temporally correlated: for each user, her current location depends on the previous location in the form a transition matrix $\mathcal{T}$. Without loss of generality, we assume the transition matrix is the same for all users and is given in advance since it can be learned from public information such as road networks. This assumption follows existing works [5,23].

Differentially Private Stream Data Release. A server collects users' real-time locations l^t at time t in a database D, and aims to release differentially private query results over D. In particular, we consider a query function $f : D \to \mathbf{N}^m$ that counts the total number of people at each location over the entire publishing time T, denoted as $f(D)$. The query outputs are represented by $\mathbf{R} = (R^1, \ldots, R^t, \ldots, R^T)$ and $R^t = (r_1^t, \ldots, r_m^t)$. Many existing works, such as [3,4,7,11–15,22], have considered a similar problem setting as ours. However,

Table 2. Transition Matrix

$Pr(l^{t+1}|l^t)$	Loc1	Loc2	Loc3
Loc1	0.33	0.33	0.34
Loc2	0.80	0.10	0.10
Loc3	0.05	0.90	0.05

due to temporal correlations, increased noise is added to the true answers to preserve strict privacy [5,23], which reduces the utility of the released private counts. Our question is: *can we leverage the temporal correlations to improve the utility of differentially private data via post-processing* (while preserving the enhanced privacy as [5,23])?

5 Methodology

In this section, we will explain how to formulate the post-processing problem for streaming data release under temporal correlations. To address the above-mentioned challenge, we use post-processing, allowing us to refine the private counts using publicly known prior knowledge.

Intuition. Our core idea is that the temporal correlations can be seen as probabilistic constraints on the data. We can formulate the problem as determining the most probable query outputs $\hat{\mathbf{R}}$ that satisfy such constraints when given $\tilde{\mathbf{R}}$, leveraging the knowledge of $\mathcal{T}$ as shown in Fig. 1 (b). Specifically, we aim to solve the programming problem of maximizing $Pr(\hat{\mathbf{R}}|\tilde{\mathbf{R}})$, subject to the *transition matrix* and other *consistency constraints*. Our method will demonstrate that the estimation depends on the noise distribution and the joint distribution of true counts, which are determined by the mechanism used and the inherent correlations within the raw data.

5.1 Maximum a Posterior Estimation Framework for Correlated Data

Firstly, we propose a Maximum A Posterior (MAP) Estimation framework to assist formulating probabilistic post-processing problem.

Definition 3. *(MAP Framework) Let D be a bounded database with n records. A post-processing approach is feasible under a framework $\mathcal{F}(\mathcal{M}, \mathcal{C})$ if for all noisy query results $\tilde{Q} \in \mathcal{O}$ through a given privacy mechanism $\mathcal{M}$, we have*

$$P(\hat{Q}|\tilde{Q}) = \frac{P(\tilde{Q}|\hat{Q})P(\hat{Q})}{P(\tilde{Q})}, \tag{1}$$

$$\hat{Q}^* = \arg\max_{\hat{Q}} P(\tilde{Q}|\hat{Q})P(\hat{Q}) \tag{2}$$

where $\mathcal{C}$ represents correlations between data for all true query results Q, $\mathcal{O}$ is denoted as all possible output set of $\mathcal{M}(D)$, $\hat{Q}$ and $\hat{Q}^*$ are variable and our desired 'closest' query result which also meets correlation $\mathcal{C}$ respectively.

We apply MAP Framework to solve post-processing problem of streaming data release under temporal correlations. Given a mechanism $\mathcal{M}$(i.e., Laplace Mechanism here) and temporal correlations $\mathcal{C}$ between data, the 'closest' private counts $\hat{\mathbf{R}}$ is tended to be obtained by calculating the maximum of the posterior possibility under MAP framework $\mathcal{F}(\mathcal{M}, \mathcal{C})$

$$Pr(\hat{\mathbf{R}}|\tilde{\mathbf{R}}) = \frac{Pr(\tilde{\mathbf{R}}|\hat{\mathbf{R}})Pr(\hat{\mathbf{R}})}{Pr(\tilde{\mathbf{R}})} \tag{3}$$

subjecting to the correlations $\mathcal{C}$ and other constraints if exist. For convenience, the logarithm form of the above formula is applied

$$\ln Pr(\hat{\mathbf{R}}|\tilde{\mathbf{R}}) = \ln Pr(\tilde{\mathbf{R}}|\hat{\mathbf{R}}) + \ln Pr(\hat{\mathbf{R}}) - \ln Pr(\tilde{\mathbf{R}}) \tag{4}$$

Therefore, the objective 'closest' query outputs (achieve the maximum of (3)) after post-processing will be

$$\hat{\mathbf{R}}^* = \arg\max_{\hat{\mathbf{R}}}\{\ln Pr(\tilde{\mathbf{R}}|\hat{\mathbf{R}}) + \ln Pr(\hat{\mathbf{R}})\} \tag{5}$$

when the private counts $\tilde{\mathbf{R}}$ is given.

In essence, the first term and the second term of right side of (5) come from $\mathcal{M}$ and $\mathcal{C}$ respectively. What makes it different from prior works is that we focus on calculating the joint distribution of private counts $Pr(\hat{\mathbf{R}})$ which are simply viewed as a uniform distribution, namely a constant, in most of previous works. We point out that it cannot be omitted when there are correlations between data especially under temporal correlations.

5.2   Calculation of Terms of Objective Equation

The next steps are how to calculate the left two terms in the right side of (5).

Calculation of the First Term. For this term, it tells us that noises should be considered while improving accuracy and [18] also points out that we are able to formulate it into a L_1 function if the noises come from LM[1]. Thus, we formulate the first term of (5) in the following

$$\ln Pr(\tilde{\mathbf{R}}|\hat{\mathbf{R}}) = -\frac{1}{\lambda}||\tilde{\mathbf{R}} - \hat{\mathbf{R}}||_{L_1} + Const. \tag{6}$$

---

[1] Please note that our method can be applied to other mechanisms. However, for the duration of this article, we have temporarily chosen to default to the Laplace Mechanism.

Calculation of the Second Term. A *Markov Chain* model is introduced to calculate the possibilities of single user's locations released in continual time-series stream because the possibility of present location only relies on previous one. With the transition matrix and a prior distribution of locations of single user at $t = 1$, we are able to calculate user's probability distribution of location at any time. We introduce two policies to obtain the prior distribution: (a) the first one is to use the normalized frequency of private counts at $t = 1$, $\tilde{R}^1$ (*frequency p-d*); (b) another is to simply use a uniform distribution (*uniform p-d*) instead. Consequently, we can derive all the possibilities of moving next locations at each time t, $\mathbf{P}^t$, expressed as below:

$$\mathbf{P}^t = \mathbf{P}^{t-1}\mathcal{T} \tag{7}$$

for each $t \in \{2, \ldots, T\}$. However, a joint distribution of users' locations should be calculated when given a bounded database containing data of n users.

Note that all of n users are independent here which means their next actions will not be influenced by others. With the probability distribution of location of single user at each time, therefore, the joint distribution of all location counts at specific time point can be expressed by a *multinomial distribution*

$$Pr(R^t) = n! \prod_l \frac{(\mathbf{P}^t_l)^{r^t_l}}{r^t_l!} \tag{8}$$

for each $R^t \subseteq \mathbf{R}$ where n represents total number of users.

Recall the *Stirling's Approximation*

$$\ln x! \approx \frac{\ln 2\pi x}{2} + x \ln \frac{x}{e} \tag{9}$$

We apply the approximation (9) to mitigate our calculation

$$\ln Pr(R^t) \approx \ln n! + \sum_l (r^t_l \ln \mathbf{P}^t_l - \frac{\ln 2\pi r^t_l}{2} - r^t_l \ln \frac{r^t_l}{e}) \tag{10}$$

Naturally, our 'closest' query answer $\hat{\mathbf{R}}$ also obeys this multinomial distribution the same as true query answer.

5.3   Nonlinear Constrained Programming

We conclude our method of formulating this post-processing problem under temporal correlations into a nonlinear constrained programming problem. By calculating the minimum estimation of $-\ln Pr(\hat{\mathbf{R}}|\tilde{\mathbf{R}})$ and combining with (6) (10), we finally transform (5) into a nonlinear constrained programming as below

$$\text{Minimize } \frac{1}{\lambda} ||\tilde{\mathbf{R}} - \hat{\mathbf{R}}||_{L_1}$$

$$- \sum_{t=1}^{T} \sum_{l} (r_l^t \ln \mathbf{P}_l^t - \frac{\ln 2\pi r_l^t}{2} - r_l^t \ln \frac{r_l^t}{e})$$

$$\text{Subject to } \sum r_l^t = n, \text{ for each } t \in \{1, 2, \ldots, T-1, T\}$$

$$r_l^t \geq 0, \text{ for each } t \in \{1, 2, \ldots, T-1, T\}$$

where $\hat{\mathbf{R}} = ((\hat{r}_1^1, \ldots, \hat{r}_m^1), \ldots, (\hat{r}_1^T, \ldots, \hat{r}_m^T))$.

Then, we point out that this nonlinear constrained programming is solvable. By introducing augmented *Lagrangian* to our objective function (O.F.), there are many convergence results proved in the literature (e.g. *ADMM* [1]) where we could prove the O.F. will finally converge as dual variables converge. Also, variables r_l^t must satisfy $\sum r_l^t = n$ and $r_l^t \geq 0$ simultaneously. Thus, the boundary of r_l^t is $n \geq r_l^t \geq 0$.

Asymptotical Analysis. As shown in derived objective function, there are two terms which represent the contribution from Mechanism applied to true counts and Correlations between true counts respectively. As ϵ approaches zero, the first term, namely $\frac{1}{\lambda}||\tilde{\mathbf{R}} - \hat{\mathbf{R}}||_{L_1}$ will also approach to zero because of coefficient λ. In other words, the second term

$$- \sum_{t=1}^{T} \sum_{l} (r_l^t \ln \mathbf{P}_l^t - \frac{\ln 2\pi r_l^t}{2} - r_l^t \ln \frac{r_l^t}{e})$$

will matter the most to objective function when a stricter privacy budget ϵ is given. Also, we'd like to analyze what the objective function will perform if a 'weak' level correlation is given (note that we will provide a mathematical definition of levels of correlations in our Experiments part) such that probabilities of proceed to the next location from previous ones is a fixed value, namely $\mathbf{P}_l^t$ is a uniform distribution. Then, the second term is able to be 'ignored' and the first term

$$\frac{1}{\lambda}||\tilde{\mathbf{R}} - \hat{\mathbf{R}}||_{L_1}$$

will thus matter the most to solutions. We should point out that our framework will result in an MLE problem such that post-processing problem mentioned by [18] if there is no correlations amount original data.

6   Experiments

In this section, we present experimental results that demonstrate the effectiveness of our proposed MAP framework for post-processing continuous data release under temporal correlations. To validate our method, we apply it to both synthetic and real-world datasets, and evaluate its performance in terms of accuracy and utility. Furthermore, we have made our code available on GitHub[2], enabling other researchers to reproduce our experiments and extend our work. For statistical significance, all experiments are performed 50 times and the mean values are reported as the final results.

Environment. The experiments were executed on CPU: $Intel(R)Core(TM)$ $i7 - 11370H$ @3.30GHz with *Python* version 3.7.

Nonlinear Programming Solver. The solver used for solving nonlinear constrained programming is *Gurobi Optimizer version* 10.0.1 API for *Python*.

Level of Temporal Correlations. To evaluate the performance of our post-processing method under different temporal correlations, we introduce a method to generate transition matrix in different *levels*. To begin with, we default a transition matrix indicating the "strongest" correlations which contains probability 1.0 in its diagonal cells. Then, we utilize *Laplacian smoothing* [24] to uniform the possibilities of $n \times n$ transition matrix $\mathcal{T}^S$ of 'strongest' correlations. Next, let p_{ij} denote the element at the ith row and jth column of $\mathcal{T}^S$. The uniformed possibilities $\hat{p}_{i,j}$ can be generated from (11), where s ($0 \le s < \infty$) is a positive parameter that controls the levels of uniformity of probabilities in each row. That's, a smaller s means stronger level temporal correlations. Also, We should note that, different s are only comparable under the same n.

$$\hat{p}_{i,j} = \frac{p_{ij} + s}{\sum_{j=1}^{n}(p_{ij} + s)} \tag{11}$$

6.1   Utility Analysis

In this subsection, we conduct a utility analysis using the objective function of the nonlinear constrained programming approach described above. The objective function consists of two parts: the noise distribution and the joint distribution of query answers under temporal correlations. The key to the effectiveness of our post-processing method in achieving high utility lies in its ability to recover the correlations between data that are blurred by incremental noise added to the original query answers. For example, it enables the preservation of the correlation that 'the current number of people staying at $loc1$ must equal the previous number of people staying at $loc2$' by solving the relevant nonlinear constrained programming problem. As a result, the similarity between the post-processing query answers and the original query answers is improved significantly.

Moreover, we introduce MSE and *Possibility* as metrics to measure the utility of optimal counts instead of MSE solely for supporting the validation of our MAP post-processing method. For instance, synthetic streaming binary counts, such that total number of locations is $n_{loc} = 3$, total number of users is $n_{user} = 1$, are going to be released under ϵ−DP. And the temporal correlations are known to the public which can be expressed by transition matrix $\mathcal{T} =$

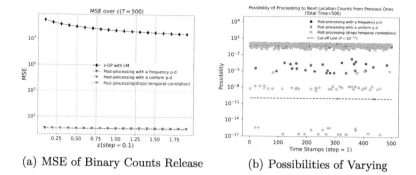

(a) MSE of Binary Counts Release   (b) Possibilities of Varying

Fig. 3. a) Scenario: Streaming Binary Counts Released under Temporal Correlations; b) Possibility of Proceeding to Current Counts from Prior Counts of Post-processing Results (under 1−DP) (Color figure online)

$$\left\{ \begin{array}{ccc} 0.0 & 0.0 & 1.0 \\ 0.5 & 0.0 & 0.5 \\ 0.0 & 1.0 & 0.0 \end{array} \right\}$$ which also represents the basic temporal correlation used for generating synthetic datasets. Then, we post-process and release optimal counts using post-processing methods of MLE with a ADMM algorithm [18] and our MAP framework respectively illustrated by Fig. 3(a). The red line of Fig. 3(a) represents optimal results that drop temporal correlations obtained by calculating MLE problem while the greed and blue lines represent the optimal results obtained from our method of MAP framework under two different strategies. The details of them will be revealed in the following subsections. When calculating the possibilities of achieving current counts from previous counts (shown in Fig. 3(b)), however, we note that many possibilities of post-processing points of dropping temporal correlations are lower than cut-off line (10^{-10}) which will be seen as 'impossible events' if possibility is smaller than 10^{-10}. It proves that our MAP framework is able to preserve the probabilistic properties owned by original data, namely temporal correlations, compared with prior post-processing methods.

We will now explore the tradeoff between privacy and utility. The objective function reveals that the privacy budget ϵ is a weight parameter affecting the noises' part, but it has no impact on the correlations' part. This means that the correlations' part is dominant when the privacy budget is strict, while the noises' part replaces it when the budget is lax. As a result, the utility is always preserved under any given privacy budget, since the method always preserves known correlations when calculating the 'closest' private counts.

6.2 Synthetic Datasets

To thoroughly examine the feasibility and effectiveness of our MAP framework and related post-processing methods, we conduct an evaluation on various synthetic datasets. This evaluation aims to provide a comprehensive understanding of the performance of our approach under different scenarios and to validate its potential for practical applications.

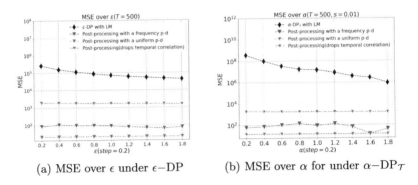

(a) MSE over ϵ under ϵ–DP   (b) MSE over α for under α–DP$_\mathcal{T}$

Fig. 4. a) MSE over ϵ under ϵ–DP; total release time is $T = 500$, total number of users is $n_{user} = 200$ and level of correlations is $s = 0$. b) MSE over α for under α–DP$_\mathcal{T}$; total release time is $T = 500$, total number of users is $n_{user} = 200$ and level of correlations is $s = 0.01$.

MSE vs Privacy Budget ϵ or α

Here, we compare the performance of our post-processing method by varying privacy budget ϵ or α from 0.2 to 2.0 (with $step = 0.2$) at a given total publishing time T in different mechanisms, $\epsilon - DP$ and $\alpha - DP_\mathcal{T}$, respectively. Note that we must choose a prior distribution(p-d) for P^1 when $t = 1$, and our strategy is to use the frequency of $\tilde{R}^1$ or a uniform distribution to substitute for it. And the results, shown in Fig. 4 (a) and Fig. 4 (b), illustrate that our post-processing method significantly improves the utility and accuracy of outputs while achieving a desired privacy budget both in $\epsilon - DP$ and $\alpha - DP_\mathcal{T}$.

The red line which represents prior method of MLE using ADMM only considers utilizing public knowledge of mechanisms instead of both mechanisms and correlations to boost utility of released counts. The blue line and green line are the results after our post-processing given two different policy to choose p-d. As shown in figure, MSE become smaller while increasing privacy budget ϵ. And our methods perform better than MLE method by decreasing MSE nearly hundred times at any given fixed ϵ.

MSE vs Total Release Time

We vary the total publishing time T from 100 to 200 ($step = 10$) to examine the performance of our post-processing method under both ϵ-DP and α-DP$_\mathcal{T}$, using the same methods for generating the synthetic datasets as described above. We use default privacy budgets of $\alpha, \epsilon = 1.0, 1.0$.

The results of our experiments, as shown in Fig. 5, indicate that the mean squared error (MSE) values of ϵ-DP and α-DP$_\mathcal{T}$ increase significantly as the total release time is extended. However, our post-processing method demonstrates a

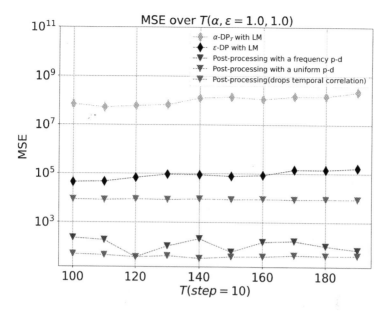

Fig. 5. MSE over Total Release Time under $\alpha-\mathrm{DP}_{\mathcal{T}}$ and $\epsilon - DP$; privacy budget is $\alpha = 1.0$, $\epsilon = 1.0$ and level of correlations is $s = 0.01$.

remarkable boost in utility, as both of its policies consistently yield lower MSE values than the method that drops temporal correlations. These findings underscore the effectiveness of our post-processing method in preserving the correlations between raw data, and the importance of considering temporal correlations when designing and evaluating different data release mechanisms.

MSE vs Different Temporal Correlations

In this subsection, we finally check the performance of our post-processing method upon different intensities of temporal correlations. We default the privacy budget and total publishing time as $\alpha = 1.0$ and $T = 500$ respectively. Note that it will have relatively higher temporal correlations if users have a higher possibility from present location to the next specific location (e.g., $Pr(l_i^t|l_i^{t-1}) = 1.0$). Therefore, we firstly generate a transition matrix $\mathcal{T} = \begin{Bmatrix} 0.0\ 0.0\ 1.0 \\ 0.5\ 0.0\ 0.5 \\ 0.0\ 1.0\ 0.0 \end{Bmatrix}$. Then, we apply (11) to generate different level degree of correlations, weak correlations, medium correlations and strong correlations corresponding to $s = 1$, $s = 0.1$, $s = 0.01$ respectively.

And the results, shown in Fig. 6, reveal validation of this post-processing method by giving prominent improvement in accuracy. We also compare a special post-processing method that drops temporal correlations which means that the joint distribution of query results $Pr(R)$ is a constant. And the results show that the post-processing method with temporal correlations will achieve higher utility with a lower MSE.

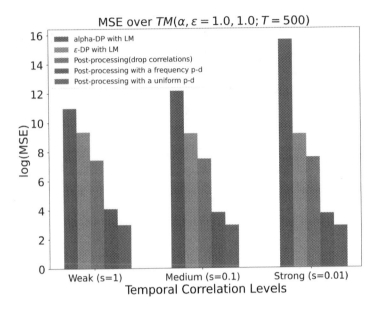

Fig. 6. MSE over Different Levels of Temporal Correlations under $\alpha-DP_\mathcal{T}$ and $\epsilon-DP$; privacy budget is $\alpha = 1.0$ and $\epsilon = 1.0$, total number of users is $n_{user} = 200$ and total release time is $T = 500$.

These experiments also highlight the essential role of the MAP framework, demonstrating that correlations between raw data can significantly impact the results and cannot be disregarded in both the mechanism design and post-processing stages.

7   Conclusion

In this paper, we have shown that temporal correlations are often present in differential privacy data releases and proposed a MAP framework to address the post-processing problem in this context. Our experiments demonstrate the effectiveness of incorporating temporal correlations into the post-processing step, resulting in significant improvements in accuracy and utility.

Furthermore, our work suggests that the MAP framework can be a useful tool for addressing other post-processing problems involving correlated data, such as Bayesian DP and Pufferfish Privacy Mechanisms. While our approach assumes independence between users, this may not always hold true in practice. Future work could explore how to extend our framework to address post-processing for streaming data releases under temporal correlations when users are correlated.

Overall, our work contributes to advancing the state of the art in differential privacy data releases by providing a new perspective on post-processing under temporal correlations and opens up new avenues for future research in this area.

Acknowledgments. This work was partially supported by JST CREST JPMJ CR21M2, JST SICORP JPMJSC2107, JSPS KAKENHI Grant Numbers 19H04215, 21K19767, 22H03595 and 22H00521. Additionally, Xuyang would like to express appreciation to tutor for his meticulous instruction, as well as to his family and friend Yuchan Z. for their encouraging support in his research endeavors.

References

1. Boyd, S., Parikh, N., Chu, E., Peleato, B., Eckstein, J.: Distributed optimization and statistical learning via the alternating direction method of multipliers. Found. Trends® Mach. Learn. **3**(1), 1–122 (2011)
2. Cao, X., Cao, Y., Yoshikawa, M., Nakamura, A.: Boosting utility of differentially private streaming data release under temporal correlations. In: 2022 IEEE International Conference on Big Data (Big Data), pp. 6605–6607 (2022)
3. Cao, Y., Yoshikawa, M.: Differentially private real-time data release over infinite trajectory streams. In: 2015 16th IEEE International Conference on Mobile Data Management (MDM), vol. 2, pp 68–73, June 2015
4. Cao, Y., Yoshikawa, M.: Differentially private real-time data publishing over infinite trajectory streams. IEICE Trans. Inf. Syst. **E99–D**, 163–175 (2016)
5. Cao, Y., Yoshikawa, M., Xiao, Y., Xiong, L.: Quantifying differential privacy under temporal correlations. In: 2017 IEEE 33rd International Conference on Data Engineering (ICDE), pp. 821–832, April 2017
6. Cao, Y., Yoshikawa, M., Xiao, Y., Xiong, L.: Quantifying differential privacy in continuous data release under temporal correlations. IEEE Trans. Knowl. Data Eng. **31**(7), 1281–1295 (2019)
7. Chen, Y., Machanavajjhala, A., Hay, M., Miklau, G.: PeGaSus: data-adaptive differentially private stream processing. In: Proceedings of the 2017 ACM SIGSAC Conference on Computer and Communications Security, CCS 2017, Dallas, TX, USA, 30 October–03 November 2017, pp. 1375–1388 (2017)
8. Cunningham, T., Cormode, G., Ferhatosmanoglu, H., Srivastava, D.: Real-world trajectory sharing with local differential privacy. Proc. VLDB Endowment **14**(11), 2283–2295 (2021)
9. Dwork, C.: Differential privacy: a survey of results. In: Agrawal, M., Du, D., Duan, Z., Li, A. (eds.) TAMC 2008. LNCS, vol. 4978, pp. 1–19. Springer, Heidelberg (2008). https://doi.org/10.1007/978-3-540-79228-4_1
10. Dwork, C., McSherry, F., Nissim, K., Smith, A.: Calibrating noise to sensitivity in private data analysis. In: Halevi, S., Rabin, T. (eds.) TCC 2006. LNCS, vol. 3876, pp. 265–284. Springer, Heidelberg (2006). https://doi.org/10.1007/11681878_14
11. Dwork, C., Naor, M., Pitassi, T., Rothblum, G.N.: Differential privacy under continual observation. In: Proceedings of the 42nd ACM Symposium on Theory of Computing, STOC 2010, Cambridge, Massachusetts, USA, 5–8 June 2010, pp. 715–724 (2010)
12. Erlingsson, Ú., Pihur, V., Korolova, A.: RAPPOR: randomized aggregatable privacy-preserving ordinal response. In: Proceedings of the 2014 ACM SIGSAC Conference on Computer and Communications Security, CCS 2014, pp. 1054–1067 (2014)
13. Fan, L., Xiong, L., Sunderam, V.: FAST: differentially private real-time aggregate monitor with filtering and adaptive sampling. In: Proceedings of the 2013 ACM SIGMOD International Conference on Management of Data, SIGMOD 2013, pp. 1065–1068 (2013)

14. Friedman, A., Sharfman, I., Keren, D., Schuster, A.: Privacy-preserving distributed stream monitoring. In: NDSS (2014)
15. Kellaris, G., Papadopoulos, S., Xiao, X., Papadias, D.: Differentially private event sequences over infinite streams. Proc. VLDB Endow. **7**, 1155–1166 (2014)
16. Hay, M., Rastogi, V., Miklau, G., Suciu, D.: Boosting the accuracy of differentially-private queries through consistency. In: 36th International Conference on Very Large Databases (VLDB) (2010)
17. Kifer, D., Machanavajjhala, A.: Pufferfish: a framework for mathematical privacy definitions. ACM Trans. Database Syst. **39**, 31–336 (2014)
18. Lee, J., Wang, Y., Kifer, D.: Maximum likelihood postprocessing for differential privacy under consistency constraints. In: Proceedings of the 21th ACM SIGKDD International Conference on Knowledge Discovery and Data Mining, KDD 2015, pp. 635–644, New York, NY, USA, 2015. Association for Computing Machinery
19. Li, N., Lyu, M., Dong, S., Yang, W.: Differential privacy: from theory to practice. In: Synthesis Lectures on Information Security, Privacy, and Trust, vol. 8, no. 4, pp. 1–138 (2016)
20. McKenna, R., Sheldon, D., Miklau, G.: Graphical-model based estimation and inference for differential privacy. In: International Conference on Machine Learning, pp. 4435–4444. PMLR (2019)
21. Mehta, H., Kanani, P., Lande, P.: Google maps. Int. J. Comput. Appl. **178**(8), 41–46 (2019)
22. Mir, D., Muthukrishnan, S., Nikolov, A., Wright, R.N.: Pan-private algorithms via statistics on sketches. In: Proceedings of the Thirtieth ACM SIGMOD-SIGACT-SIGART Symposium on Principles of Database Systems, PODS 2011, pp. 37–48 (2011)
23. Song, S., Wang, Y., Chaudhuri, K.: Pufferfish privacy mechanisms for correlated data. In: Proceedings of the 2017 ACM International Conference on Management of Data, pp. 1291–1306 (2017)
24. Sorkine, O., Cohen-Or, D., Lipman, Y., Alexa, M., Rössl, C., Seidel, H.-P.: Laplacian surface editing. In: Proceedings of the 2004 Eurographics/ACM SIGGRAPH Symposium on Geometry Processing, SGP 2004, pp. 175–184, New York, NY, USA. Association for Computing Machinery (2004)
25. Wang, Z., Reiter, J.P.: Post-processing differentially private counts to satisfy additive constraints. Trans. Data Privacy **14**, 65–77 (2021)
26. Yang, B., Sato, I., Nakagawa, H.: Bayesian differential privacy on correlated data. In: Proceedings of the 2015 ACM SIGMOD international conference on Management of Data, pp. 747–762 (2015)
27. Zhu, T., Xiong, P., Li, G., Zhou, W.: Correlated differential privacy: hiding information in non-IID data set. IEEE Trans. Inf. Forensics Secur. **10**(2), 229–242 (2015)

Access Control and Vulnerability Assessment

Assurance, Consent and Access Control for Privacy-Aware OIDC Deployments

Gianluca Sassetti[1,2]✉ ⓘ, Amir Sharif[1]✉ ⓘ, Giada Sciarretta[1]✉ ⓘ, Roberto Carbone[1]✉ ⓘ, and Silvio Ranise[1,2]✉ ⓘ

[1] Fondazione Bruno Kessler, Trento, Italy
{asharif,g.sciarretta,carbone,gsassetti,ranise}@fbk.eu
[2] University of Trento, Trento, Italy

Abstract. The large amount of personal data that is shared in the digital age has proportionally increased the risks of user privacy violations. The same privacy risks are reflected in OpenID Connect, which is one of the most widespread protocols used for identity management to access both private and public administration services. Since personal data is collected and shared via OpenID Connect, appropriate technologies to protect user privacy should be adopted as suggested by data protection guidelines and regulations (e.g., the General Data Protection Regulation). Unfortunately, it is difficult to make the privacy-enhancing technology suggestions in such documents actionable and available to IT professionals who are required to configure them within their OpenID Connect deployments. To overcome this problem, we present a practical approach to improving user privacy in OpenID Connect-based solutions by identifying a set of privacy-preserving features extracted from the available OpenID Connect specifications. We conduct a privacy compliance analysis on popular private and governmental OpenID Providers to determine how widely these privacy best practices are used in the wild. The findings indicate that different OpenID Providers grant varying levels of assurance and address different aspects of privacy, failing to provide full support for data protection principles.

Keywords: OpenID Connect · Digital Identity · Privacy · GDPR

1 Introduction

Online privacy has become increasingly important because of the growing number of digital transactions that require processing personal data. Multi-party applications [55] are a common configuration in which service providers trust identity providers to authenticate users and then make access decisions based on the authentication information provided. Such information includes personal data comprising name, email, address and more. This requires the deployment of appropriate controls to support the privacy of users.

One of the most widely used identity management solutions in multi-party applications is OpenID Connect (OIDC) [53], which is implemented for services supported by both private organizations and public administrations [6,54].

ⓒ IFIP International Federation for Information Processing 2023
Published by Springer Nature Switzerland AG 2023
V. Atluri and A. L. Ferrara (Eds.): DBSec 2023, LNCS 13942, pp. 203–222, 2023.
https://doi.org/10.1007/978-3-031-37586-6_13

Notable examples of the former are financial and banking applications, while national and international digital identity infrastructures are the most important instances of the latter and are used to allow citizens to access a wide range of online services of the public administration. In both cases, large volumes of highly sensitive personal data are processed and exchanged among identity and service providers, and the disclosure or unauthorized modification of this data may have serious consequences for end users, clients and citizens. As a result, it is crucial to guarantee that OIDC deployments are privacy-preserving and comply with data protection laws, such as the European General Data Protection Regulation (GDPR) [12].

Unfortunately, it is unclear what the current state of the art is for OIDC deployments with respect to the degree of privacy they offer. The problem is twofold. First, there is a lack of a coherent set of Best Current Practices (BCPs) to help in configuring and implementing privacy-aware OIDC deployments. Instead, considerations and suggestions to use data protection mechanisms are scattered in several official OIDC specifications or are emerging as de facto standards while being adopted by a large number of OIDC Providers (OP). The second issue is a lack of privacy compliance analysis for private and public sector OPs to determine how much they use the privacy-enhancing features available in various OIDC specifications.

To address these issues, our work takes a pragmatic approach and considers compliance with existing data protection regulations by using the GDPR principles to characterize the notion of privacy and proposes: (i) a well-defined set of BCPs derived from OIDC specifications and current practices adopted by OPs; (ii) a study of the adoption of the identified set of BCPs in current OIDC deployments used by both private and public online services; this allows us to understand the level of privacy and assurance offered by OPs. The BCPs can serve as a reference for developers to deploy privacy-preserving OPs. Furthermore, they can be used in services that analyze the degree of assurance that various OPs grant. As a matter of fact, this work can provide the main building block to automate the process of detecting BCPs adoption, paving the way for a large-scale analysis of OPs.

Paper Structure. Section 2 presents some notions needed to understand this work. Section 3 details some relevant previous work that deals with privacy issues in OIDC. In Sect. 4, we provide the list of features analyzed for this work alongside our recommended privacy BCPs to provide privacy-preserving OPs' implementations. We present our privacy BCP compliance analysis results for popular private and eIDAS OPs in Sect. 5 and discuss some interesting observations in Sect. 6.

2   Background

We characterize privacy w.r.t. five goals extracted from the GDPR [12] (Sect. 2.1) and provide a concise description of OAuth and OIDC (Sect. 2.2).

2.1   Privacy Principles

We take a pragmatic approach to decomposing privacy with respect to the privacy goals identified in the GDPR [12]. From Article 5 of the GDPR, we recall the following principles, by focusing on those aspects that are more relevant to the privacy of OIDC deployments.

Data Minimization: the parties involved in data exchanges should use and
   share only the minimum amount of user data necessary for their functions;
Confidentiality: personal data shall be protected from unauthorized, unlawful disclosure. Here we focus on the aspects of confidentiality related to the controlled disclosure of personal information.
Data Accuracy: data shall be exact and correct; the party collecting the data should have a minimum degree of confidence in the correctness of the data;
Transparency: the party collecting data shall clearly state the purpose of the data acquisition and allow the user to opt-in to the processing of their data. Also, the parties with which personal data will be shared need to be communicated to the user.

We also define one more privacy principle which is not explicitly included in Art. 5 of the GDPR, but can be directly derived from it:

Unlinkability: the user should not be identifiable and traceable across different platforms, without giving explicit consent. User data should be stored and shared in a way that would not allow other parties to identify the user and link their actions to a single account, thus granting a minimum level of anonymity. Unlinkability should hold even when colluding parties unlawfully share data.

These privacy principles are the ones that can be supported by OIDC implementations. Principles such as accountability, storage limitation, and lawfulness, which are also defined in the GDPR, are outside the scope of this work. OIDC does neither specify how parties store and keep data nor the data processing policies that are put in place. Although confidentiality is a broad concept, that needs to be ensured at different levels of the implementation stack, we work under the assumption that other security mechanisms [48] have been put in place and consider only the mechanisms to access and disclose user data.

Unlinkability is a pragmatic transposition of purpose limitation, for which data shall be collected and processed only for its explicit and legitimate purpose, as stated in Art. 5 par. 1 lit. b of the GDPR. Any unauthorized party that is able to identify the user extracts an additional quantity of data from the user's activity. Thus, it violates the principles of confidentiality and transparency, as the user has not acknowledged and agreed to the use of their data. Given that this scenario is particularly relevant for OIDC, we have included unlinkability as a privacy principle. For ease of reference, we report in Table 1, a summary of the five privacy principles introduced here.

2.2   OAuth and OIDC

We present here an introduction to OAuth and OIDC that is not meant to be exhaustive. Rather, its aim is to illustrate the main concepts and elements of the protocol, with a focus on the features that will be discussed in the following. OAuth is an authorization framework with which an application, called Relying Party (RP), can be granted access to user resources by first asking for consent from the user. OIDC is an identity protocol that adds authentication to the OAuth framework. Authentication is possible by distributing user-identifying data called claims.

OIDC flows start with an authorization request sent by the RP to the OP. Authorization requests include various parameters, but most importantly the `scope` parameter, with which the user's resources are requested. The RP's accesses are limited to the resources listed in `scope`, and thus the parameter is pivotal to enable access control. The list of parameters supported by the authorization request depends on the OP. Distinct OPs may choose to refer to different OIDC specifications and add new parameters. However, all OPs implement a set of mandatory parameters, amongst which `scope`. The OP prompts the user to sign in after processing the authorization request. The user is then directed to an authorization, or consent, page. The authorization page informs the user of what `scope` has been requested and allows the user to consent to share their resources (it is the main way to ensure transparency). Once the user consent has been granted, the OP sends an authorization code back to obtain an Identity (ID) Token and Access Token. The ID Token is a security data structure consisting of a unique user identifier, user claims, and authentication context data. The Access Token can be used to access the user resources and obtain claims on the authenticated user.

3   Related Work

In the past, the security of OAuth and OIDC protocols has been widely studied, both theoretically and practically. The research has been mostly focused on concrete attacks to the protocols [38,40,41], and a number of solutions and mitigations have been proposed to tackle their vulnerabilities [37,46,59]. Despite that, little effort has been put into studying how OPs protect user privacy by integrating privacy-by-design principles within their implementations. In the following, we summarize some of the available works in the literature that deal with privacy issues of OIDC protocol.

Fett et al., proposed a privacy-preserving Single-Sign-On (SSO) system for the web called "SPRESSO" [39] that decouples the direct communication between RP and OP by using a forwarder agent at the user's side with the aim to avoid user linkability by the OP at various RPs. Asghar et al. in [33] introduced a privacy-preserving solution that is a modified version of the cryptographic construction presented in Oblivion [34]. Their solution decouples the interaction between the OP and RP by separating the credential issuance by the OP from its usage by the user at RP. Navas and Beltrán provide a comprehensive threat model for the OIDC in [51] that highlights the following privacy threats: lack of control over required personal data, personal data leakage, user profiling, and location tracking. The authors also proposed mitigations that include encryption to minimize the risk of personal data leakage and using flow-specific user identifiers to avoid user profiling. In 2020, Apple introduced its SSO solution based on OIDC called "Sign In with Apple" [28] that uses randomized (per RP) identifiers in place of a user email address to avoid user linkability across RPs. Zhang et al. proposed a privacy-preserving system based on OIDC called "EL PASSO" [58] that implements anonymous credentials to enable selective disclosure and avoid user linkability. Hammann et al. [44] and Li et al. [45] proposed solutions to address the problem of user linkability by decoupling the interaction between the OP and RP in obtaining and using credentials. Most recently, Morkonda et al. described a browser extension called "SSOPrivateEye" [50] that provides a privacy comparison where users have multiple choices of OPs to login into an RP. Exploiting this information, users can choose the one that shares less amount of personal data with RPs. This solution provides some privacy insights only for Google, Facebook, and Apple as OPs.

Most of the aforementioned research works demand either major changes to the OIDC protocol or the installation of a browser plugin within the user's device to partially increase the user's privacy. Indeed, none of them provide some easy-to-implement privacy-preserving features by leveraging the features already available in OIDC [47,49,53]. Furthermore, no study has assessed the privacy of solutions that are provided by eIDAS solutions. Given that, our work can be used to complement and enhance plug-in-based solutions by providing more informative data, e.g. privacy principles satisfied by each OP that make the users more aware of the privacy level of the OP. In addition, our research work can be integrated into a stand-alone tool to automate the procedure of privacy compliance analysis. A good candidate for a stand-alone tool can be illustrated by extending our already developed tool for security analysis of OIDC deployments called "Micro-ID Gym" [35].

4   OIDC Privacy Best Current Practices

We have selected three OIDC specifications taken from the official list published by the OpenID Foundation [43]: OIDC core, OIDC for Identity Assurance and OIDC iGov profile [47,49,53]. Besides OIDC Core, which introduces the protocol, the other specifications seek to increase the baseline privacy and assurance of OIDC. With OIDC for Identity Assurance, OPs can issue trustworthy user claims by providing evidence of a verification process. The iGov profile introduces assurance requirements suitable for public, governmental identity services. The other available specifications have not been considered because they are outside the scope of this paper. Either they introduce features to support use cases that are not covered in OIDC Core, such as native applications or wireless network operators, or they do not include privacy considerations.

We have extracted a set of features whose deployment supports our recommended privacy BCPs. A first group (OIDC features) has been extracted from the selected OIDC specifications, whereas a second group (non-OIDC features) is not specified in OIDC standards, but is commonly implemented by OPs. Each feature contributes to one or more of the privacy principles introduced in Sect. 2.1, and can be easily implemented by OPs without making any change to the OIDC protocol. We have not considered non-OIDC features that cover aspects of privacy that are not already within the scope of OIDC, such as policies for data storage, data integrity, and handling breaches.

The analysis has been conducted by surveying the implementation of our BCPs in two groups of OPs: one developed by private companies, from here on called private OPs, and one of eIDAS OPs, developed for European public infrastructures. The analyses carried out on the two groups of OPs use the same set of features, yet they yield different results.

4.1 Privacy-Supporting Features

We propose a set of privacy-supporting features for OIDC deployments, whose adoption constitutes our suggested BCPs. They are depicted in Fig. 1, together with their connection to the privacy goals of Sect. 2.1, also summarized in Table 1, and the sources from which they were extracted. Table 2 provides a short description of the aforementioned features. Below, we discuss them according to the fact that they are parameters in the authorization request, supported subject identifiers, or non-OIDC features (recall the description in Sect. 2.2).

We first discuss the features in the authorization request.

scope: Through this parameter, the RP can request access to user-owned resources. Scopes are identifiers for sets of resources or permissions, and thus they are used for access control. The parameter supports data minimization, as all user resources are requested through it. Although it is used in AC policies, the parameter does not directly support confidentiality because it can only be used to specify resources. scope was introduced in OIDC Core [53], and is a mandatory parameter in authorization requests; it has to contain the value openid. As an example of usage, an RP can include scope=openid profile email address in the authorization request. Later on, the RP can obtain the data related to the user's profile, email and address by querying the UserInfo endpoint.

claims: Through this parameter, the RP can request specific claims to be returned in the ID Token or from the UserInfo endpoint after successful user authentication. If the parameter is missing, the OP will provide a default set of claims. claims can be used to request only the necessary resources, thus limiting the sharing of user data. The parameter is included in OIDC Core [53] and is defined as mandatory in the iGov profile [49] because of its importance for data minimization.

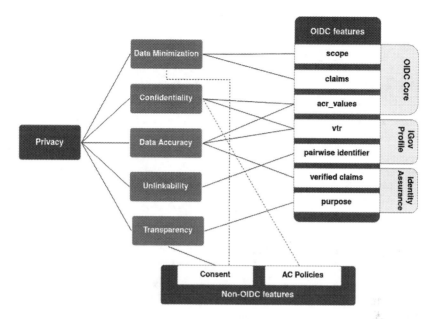

Fig. 1. Summary of our BCPs and their connection to privacy principles

purpose: This is a subfield of the `claims` parameter that was introduced in
OIDC for Identity Assurance [47]. With it, the RP can specify a reason for
requesting the claim. Purposes are displayed to the user on the consent page.
If the OP does not implement `claims` it cannot implement `purpose`.
The responsibility of making the consent transparent usually falls on the OP
alone. The OP would normally add to the consent page a list of the scopes
and claims that have been requested, along with a short description for each.
The implementation of the `purpose` parameter creates a new way for RPs to
specify their purpose, thus directly contributing to transparency.

verified_claims: This is a new parameter introduced in OIDC for Identity
Assurance [47] that allows requesting a set of verified user claims. On the
OP side, user claims are associated with a verification method and a trust
framework which they refer to. An example of such a framework is eIDAS, or
a national eID scheme. The verification process usually happens upon regis-
tering the user's claims, e.g., via an electronic identity card. After successful
authorization, user claims are returned alongside metadata containing evidence of the verification process. A higher level of assurance is guaranteed for
the requested claims that are returned in the ID Token. By providing trusted
information, the parameter contributes to data accuracy.

acr_values: This parameter allows the RP to request strong authentication
methods. It defines a set of scalar values representing the minimum levels
of identity proofing asserted during authentication. Depending on the value
that the RP requests, the OP enforces different authentication methods. For
instance, the first level is usually associated with a simple username and
password login. Other levels may require Multi-Factor Authentication instead.

Table 1. Summary of the privacy principles

Principle	Description
Data Minimization	Use and collect only the minimum amount of data
Confidentiality	Grant access only to authorized parties
Data Accuracy	Information provided has to be correct
Unlinkability	User accounts cannot be traced across services
Transparency	Clearly state the purpose for collecting and processing user data

Table 2. Summary of privacy-supporting features

Feature	Description	Source
scope	Request user resources	Core [53]
claims	Request specific user claims	Core, iGov [49,53]
purpose	State the purpose of a claim request	Id. Assurance [47]
verified_claims	Request specific user claims along with evidence of the verification process	Id. Assurance [47]
acr_values	Request stronger authentication	Core, iGov [49,53]
vtr	Request stronger authentication, define the authentication context	iGov [49]
pairwise	User cannot be identified with the subject type	Core, iGov [49,53]
Consent	Transparent, informative consent page, implementation of selective disclosure	Common practices
AC Policies	Controlled disclosure of user data	Common practices

acr_values allows to increase the authentication requirements; therefore, it contributes to privacy by providing greater data accuracy and confidentiality.

vtr: Vectors of Trust (also VoT) is a parameter introduced in the iGov profile [49] that has the same purpose as acr_values. It allows requesting a minimum identity proofing level. vtr is a vector of scalar values, each of which defines a certain aspect of the authentication context. It is, therefore, more precise and flexible than acr_values [52]. It provides data accuracy and confidentiality.

We now describe the features related to subject identifiers. The subject_type defines how to generate the sub field, or subject identifier, a mandatory parameter of the ID Token that uniquely identifies the user. subject_type can have two values: public and pairwise, both defined in OIDC Core [53]. With public all the RPs under the same OP receive the same identifier for a fixed user. Instead, with pairwise, the same user will have a different identifier for each RP. The purpose of pairwise is to minimize the risk of linkability between RPs. The implementation of pairwise identifiers for unlinkability has been questioned in the past [44,45]. As a matter of fact, pairwise identifiers grant unlinkability only if sub is the only identifying information contained in the ID Token. If data such as email or name is returned by the OP, RPs can easily identify and trace the user just by sharing the ID Token. There are available solutions in the wild that tackle this problem. However, except for the use of pseudonymization, the other solutions (e.g., Blind broker architecture [36] or Zero-Knowdlege Proofs [44]) demand either major changes to the OPs or to the OIDC protocol. Despite that, the iGov profile [49] stresses the importance of `pairwise` identifiers and makes their implementation mandatory. We stand by this privacy guideline because `pairwise` identifiers are a necessary step to grant unlinkability.

Finally, we explain the non-OIDC features that are commonly implemented by OPs.

Consent page: We check for the presence of a descriptive consent page, where the data collected is transparently communicated. Moreover, we check for the implementation of selective disclosure, a feature of consent pages that allows the user to select which resources, among those requested, to grant access to. Selective disclosure helps make the user aware of which personal data is being processed while contributing to transparency and data minimization.

Access Control (AC) Policies for sensitive scopes: This feature includes any kind of policy for accessing high-risk or sensitive resources (e.g., users' health records, biometric data). Through said policies, RPs may have their access restricted or limited in case they request sensitive resources through `scope` or `claims`. An example of said policies would be to initiate multi-factor authentication when sensitive resources are requested. Another option would be to restrict access to some scopes only to a subset of specifically authorized RPs. In general, we take into consideration any policy that enforces access control on requested resources.

Access control policies are ouside the scope of OIDC. We investigate them as they impact the security of user data and confidentiality. Despite being a security mechanism, the feature falls under our definition of confidentiality. We consider the AC policies that are enforced on requested scopes, and that concern the access and disclosure of user data.

OIDC for Identity Assurance and iGov profile [47,49] make up for the lack of privacy considerations in OIDC Core [53] by addressing data minimization, accuracy, confidentiality, transparency and unlinkability. Each specification contributes to different aspects of privacy, with some overlaps. Our BCPs connect the contributions of each specification, thus providing a complete and well-rounded set of recommendations. Moreover, the privacy principles, as well as the BCPs that enforce them, are interlinked. The risks deriving from the violation of any privacy principle impact negatively all the others. We argue that our BCPs should be implemented altogether to minimize the overall risk to privacy and grant the highest degree of assurance to users.

4.2   BCPs for Assurance, Consent and Access Control

In digital identity management, assurance is the ability to trust that an electronic credential belongs to the user. Higher assurance levels allow for regulated scenarios like government, finance, and healthcare. Privacy goals vary by use case, and Fig. 1 helps determine the necessary features to achieve the desired privacy posture of OPs. We observe that tuning the level of assurance can be seen as a prerequisite for establishing a suitably strong trust relationship between an OP and RPs deployed in a certain use case scenario. In other words, Fig. 1 can be considered a high-level map to orient designers in the adoption of privacy features capable of yielding the right level of assurance and trustworthiness for the ecosystem (comprising OPs and RPs) supporting a certain use case scenario. Needless to say, we are assuming that other security measures, such as those extensively discussed in various OIDC specification documents, are put in place as an obvious and much-needed complement to the BCPs described in Fig. 1. As a final remark, we observe that—despite not being included in the OIDC standard—the Consent and Access Control features seem to be crucial in providing adequate support for assurance and trustworthiness as they support the controlled sharing of personal data among OPs and RPs, thereby helping to achieve three of the five privacy goals in Sect. 2.1 (namely Data Minimization, Confidentiality and Transparency) and comply with the GDPR.

5   BCPs in the Wild

We now want to understand how well OIDC deployments support privacy-preserving features. We do this by checking whether the privacy BCPs identified in Sect. 4.1 are implemented by a significant set of OPs. We decompose our evaluation w.r.t. private and eIDAS OPs and the identified privacy principles. We now explain how the OPs were selected and how we performed the analysis. Our findings are summarized in Fig. 2 and Table 3.

We have analyzed 14 private and 13 eIDAS OPs. The private OPs have been selected from the lists of OIDC-certified providers available at [42], and based on their popularity according to their Alexa rank. Only the OPs that have a developer console accessible without a subscription have been considered for this study.[1]

The 13 eIDAS OPs[2] that have been selected are European-notified and pre-notified solutions of EU Member States. They have been taken from the list of (pre-)notified eIDAS solutions available at the EU Commission official website [56]. Since the eIDAS regulation is not binding as for the choice of technologies, OPs implement mainly either SAML 2.0 or OIDC [27,53]. From the list, we have selected only those OPs that already implement OIDC or are in the process of implementing OIDC within their solutions.

Our analysis relies on the official documentation provided by OPs. Whenever possible, we have tested each feature of each OP either through publicly available

---

[1] Despite Alexa rank ending its service in May 2022, we have used the data available as of April 2022, which we considered reasonably updated.

[2] NHS Login is not currently an eIDAS solution due to international political developments, but was developed as such. We have included it since it complies with the specification.

demos, by deploying the OP server locally, or, by creating test applications on their platforms and interfacing with their API. In total, we have tested all private OPs and 12 eIDAS OPs.

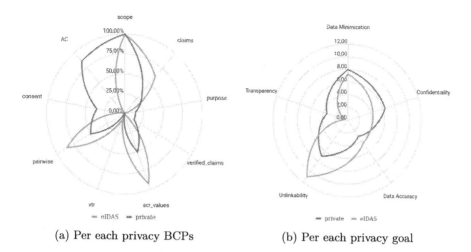

(a) Per each privacy BCPs   (b) Per each privacy goal

Fig. 2. Implementation rate of the privacy-supporting features for private and eIDAS OPs

Table 3. Summary of the supported BCPs for private and eIDAS OPs

OP	scope	claims	purpose	verified_claims	acr_values	vtr	pairwise	consent	AC policies
Authlete [3]	●	●	●	●	●		●		
ForgeRock [9]	●	●		●		●			●
Connect2id [7]	●	●	●	●	●		●	●	●
Cloudentity [5]	●	●			●		●	●	●
WSO2 [31]	●	●			●			●	●
IBM [14]	●							●	●
Google [13]	●							●	●
Facebook [8]	●					●			●
Yahoo [32]	●								
Amazon [4]	●								●
Microsoft [17]	●						●		●
Ping [24]	●				●	●			●
OKTA [23]	●								●
Auth0 [2]	●				●				●
itsme (BE) [16]	●	●			●		●		
MitID (DN) [18,20]	●	●			●		●		
NemID (DN) [18,20]	●	●			●		●		
FC (FR) [10]	●				●		●		
FC+ (FR) [10,11]	●	●			●		●		
P.S.C. (FR) [25]	●				●		●		
SMART-ID (ES) [29]	●				●				
SPID (IT) [30]	●	●			●		●		
CIE (IT) [30]	●	●			●		●		
ID Austria (AT) [1]	●						●		
ID-Porten(NO) [15]	●	●			●		●		
NHS (UK) [21]	●						●	●	
MojeID (CZ) [19]	●	●			●			●	●

5.1   Private OPs

Regarding data minimization, `scope` has been implemented by all OPs since it is mandatory for OIDC. Instead, `claims` has been implemented only in 5 out of 14 (35%) cases. The fact that `claims` cannot be used for AC and that it can be replaced by returning a default set of user claims associated with the requested scopes can be the reason for its low implementation rate.

The analysis of confidentiality features yields diverging results. Despite having the same purpose, and the flexibility and precision granted by `vtr`, `acr_values` has been implemented in 7 (50%) OPs, whereas `vtr` in no OP. Moreover, the results for AC policies show that OPs implement a wide range of solutions.

In the wild, each OP adopts its own specific solution to manage RP accesses, which makes it difficult to categorize policies. Nevertheless, during our study, we have found a very significant trend in private OPs. 10 (71%) OPs allow the customization of AC policies, that are also enforced on scopes. There is a clear trend for OPs to deliver AC as part of their service and grant developers a high level of customizability. The purpose of customizing AC policies is to share claims and grant scopes only to a subset of RPs, or only under certain conditions, such as a higher authentication context. Some OPs give the possibility to create AC policies from scratch, while others allow to modify default policies. As part of their service, OPs may allow to change the list of claims that are returned for each scope. Or also to create new scopes and return claims based on the RP or the authentication context.

An example of AC policy customization would be to allow developers to flag scopes with security levels, and then define for each security level a set of authentication requirements. The OP would then match the highest authentication level among the requested scopes before granting access to the resources. Some OPs allow managing users with user groups. When that is the case, AC policies could define different authentication requirements and accessible resources for each user group.

The example above introduces step-up authentication [57]. That is the request for stronger authentication, also through Multi-Factor Authentication, upon accessing protected resources. We have found that all the OPs that implement AC customization allow step-up authentication, which highlights the importance of this feature. Just like in the example above, this feature is often integrated as part of AC customization. This means that developers define which resources start the step-up process. Although, it can also be the case that sensitivity levels cannot be changed by developers and a default set of scopes will always start the step-up flow. This would limit the degree of customization but ensure a baseline security level.

Another viable solution for OPs is to make developers submit their RP for review. In this case, a dedicated team checks the RP activity and purpose. Only once it is deemed conforming to the provider rules, the RP is allowed to access protected scopes and API resources. This solution is often adopted by OPs that allow to quickly create and set up RPs. Thus, developers can easily access basic functionalities, while sensitive scopes are protected by granting access only to verified RPs. Nevertheless, this solution suffers from a lack of scalability and flexibility and is therefore adopted only in 2 (14%) cases.

For data accuracy, we have already considered the results of `acr_values` and `vtr`. We only add that also `verified_claims` saw little implementation: only in 2 (14%) OPs.

As for unlinkability, `pairwise` identifiers have been implemented in 7 (50%) OPs. In order to find a trend in the implementation of `subject_types`, we have also surveyed the implementation of `public` identifiers. Since `sub` is a mandatory field, the OPs that have not implemented `pairwise` have instead implemented `public` identifiers. Also, 5 (35%) OPs implement both `sub` types. That is usually the case for OPs that want to allow RPs greater flexibility. Interestingly, there are 2 (14%) OPs, Google and Microsoft, that allow only the use of `pairwise`. This should be considered a privacy-preserving design choice.

The features that support transparency have seen little implementation. `purpose` has been implemented only in 2 (14%) OPs, and consent page with selective disclosure capability in 5 (35%) OPs. Despite that, OPs show in the consent pages short descriptions of the requested `claims` and `scope`. In this case, OPs still meet an adequate level of transparency.

5.2   eIDAS OPs

Some of the trends seen in private OPs are confirmed in eIDAS OPs as well. The results differ the most for unlinkability, confidentiality and data accuracy. In general, eIDAS OPs show a tendency to grant higher assurance to both users and RPs and have better privacy-preserving designs.

For data minimization, `claims` has been implemented in 8 out of 13 (61%) cases, which marks a sharp increase in comparison with private OPs.

The results for the features that enforce confidentiality reflect the higher assurance requirements of eIDAS OPs. `acr_values` has been implemented in 12 (92%) cases, almost all OPs, which is a steep increase w.r.t. the implementation rate in private OPs. Despite that, the trend of preferring `acr_values` to `vtr` is confirmed, since the latter was implemented only 1 (7%) time. Unfortunately, we haven't been able to test the AC policies enforced by eIDAS OPs and we have no results in that regard. That is because eIDAS OPs' demos often do not allow for the creation of testing RPs but rather only offer a test flow.

The higher implementation rate of `acr_values` leverages the overall higher support for data accuracy. That being said, another trend of private OPs is confirmed since `verified_claims` was never implemented.

As for unlinkability, `pairwise` has been implemented in 11 (84%) cases, compared to 50% of private OPs. Interestingly, we can see a change in the implementation rate of `public` too. `public` has been implemented 6 (46%) times. Although the number of OPs that implement public only, without pairwise, decreased to 2 (14%), compared to 50% of private OPs. At the same time, the number of OPs implementing only `pairwise` has increased to 6 (46%). However, the number of OPs that implement both identifiers stays the same. The results

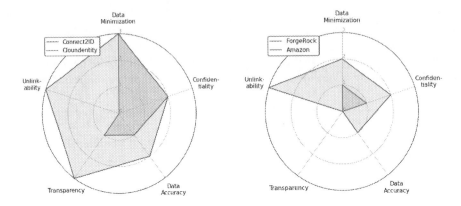

Fig. 3. Comparison of the assurance level of different private OPs

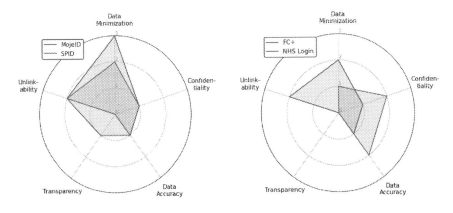

Fig. 4. Comparison of the assurance level of different eIDAS OPs

could derive from the emphasis given to `pairwise` identifiers in the OIDC iGov profile, their relevance for unlinkability, as well as the higher privacy assurance requirements that are fulfilled by eIDAS OPs.

Transparency has been mostly overlooked since `purpose` has never been implemented and consent page with selective disclosure has been in only 1 (7%) OP. Interestingly, while 4 (30%) OPs presented a normal, static consent screen with short `scope` descriptions, 6 (46%) OPs skipped the consent page. So the user, after logging in, would be redirected to the RP with the access code right away. This behaviour can be explained with the following: (*i*) the eIDAS regulation [26] defines the minimum set of user data that can be shared with RPs and that is needed for user accountability; (*ii*) since it is required to share at least the minimum set of data with the RPs to access their services, the user is not left with the choice of sharing the aforementioned data. The user would consent to sharing said set of data upon logging in. We would like to highlight that this is possible only with eIDAS OPs, private OPs would otherwise violate the principles of transparency and purpose specification.

6   Discussion, Conclusions and Future Work

The results show that 6 out of 14 (42%) private OPs implement half or more of our BCPs, whereas the rate rises to 8 out of 13 (61%) for eIDAS OPs. The difference between the two groups is further highlighted if we consider only the OIDC features. In this case, 6 (42%) private OPs implement at least half of the features, whereas 11 (84%) eIDAS OPs do. We can also see that a subset of OIDC features, namely `purpose`, `verified_claims` and `vtr` were implemented by almost no OPs from both the private and eIDAS groups. Interestingly, a subset of OPs have implemented only the mandatory features that are required to be certified by the OpenID Foundation. The features in question are `scope` and `public` identifiers, without implementing `pairwise`. The results show that 5 (35%) private OPs fall under this category, whereas no eIDAS OP does.

Our study shows a very low adoption rate of the OIDC for Identity Assurance specification, which was implemented only in 2 private OPs, and in no eIDAS OPs. This result could be explained by the novelty of the specification, which was released only recently. Also the requirements of the iGov profile, which are the implementation of `claims, acr_values, vtr` and `pairwise`, were satisfied by no OPs. Although, the reader should mind that a larger group of OPs complies partially with the iGov profile. If we do not take into account `vtr`, which has the lowest support rate overall, 5 (35%) private OPs and 8 (61%) eIDAS OPs comply with the other requirements of the iGov profile. Interestingly, new specifications for public infrastructures have been derived from the iGov profile, such as the Netherlands Gov Assurance Profile [22].

The OPs from both groups have shown to have different priorities for the privacy goals. As shown in Fig. 2(b), data minimization and unlinkability are the most widely supported goals in both groups, with unlinkability having a higher priority in eIDAS OPs. Confidentiality is the third most supported privacy goal for all OPs. Instead, transparency and data accuracy are the least supported privacy goals in both groups.

Moreover, to make clear the importance that the two groups give to different privacy goals, for each goal we have analyzed the number of OPs that implement at least one feature that contributes to that goal. We have found that a minimal level of confidentiality is supported by 13 OPs (92%) in both groups. Without considering the `scope` parameter, which is mandatory, 7 private OPs (50%) and 9 eIDAS OPs (69%) support data minimization. Unlinkability is supported in 6 private OPs (42%) and 12 eIDAS OPs (92%). Data accuracy has a minimum level of support in 7 (50%) private OPs and 12 (92%) eIDAS OPs. Transparency is supported in 6 (42%) private OPs and only in 1 (7%) eIDAS OP.

The previous results for data minimization, unlinkability and transparency are confirmed, although we can see that many eIDAS OPs support at least one feature for confidentiality and data accuracy. We can see that the biggest differences between the two groups are in their support for data accuracy, transparency and unlinkability. Specifically, eIDAS OPs prioritized the development of features for data accuracy and unlinkability with the aim to enhance the assurance level for users and RPs, whereas private OPs developed transparency-enhancing features more often. We would like to clarify that the lack of support for transparency derives from two main reasons: the low implementation rate of OIDC for Identity Assurance and the possibility for eIDAS OPs to skip the consent page (Sect. 5.2). That does not mean no compliance with the GDPR requirements for transparency and purpose specification.

The results presented up to this point show the differences between private and eIDAS OPs. We can safely state that eIDAS OPs provide on average a higher degree of assurance, for both users and RPs. That is understandable, as they are designed to handle sensitive information. To grade the general level of assurance that each OP grants, we have scored each OP for each privacy principle based on the number of features that it supports, according to Fig. 1. The results of some selected OPs are shown in Fig. 3 and 4. We have then included the entire survey in our Drive folder[3]. The results show homogeneity in the assurance level of eIDAS OPs, caused by their similar requirements, and a greater diversity for private OPs, which often do not refer to the same set of requirements. This is true also for the features' implementation, Table 3. We can see that eIDAS OPs adopt a similar set of features, whereas private OPs are more diverse. Moreover, we can differentiate between two groups of private OPs, one of which implements way more features than the other. Instead, we cannot make such a distinction for eIDAS OPs.

The BCPs that we have provided and the extracted features can serve as a reference for developers to deploy privacy-preserving OPs. Furthermore, they can be used in services that analyze the degree of assurance that various OPs grant. As a matter of fact, most of the analyses on OIDC features in this work can be automated. As future work, we are planning on extending the functionalities of a tool to perform security analysis of OIDC deployments called "Micro-Id-Gym" [35]. We will integrate the privacy BCPs into the tool to extend the metrics that are already present and to automatically perform compliance analysis on any OP to provide the level of privacy satisfied by the OP w.r.t. privacy goals. Another possible future route would be to improve existing browser plug-in-based solutions to provide more information, such as the privacy goals satisfied by the OP. Our aim is to assist users in making an informed decision when choosing among different OPs based on the level of assurance and privacy granted.

Acknowledgements. This work was partially supported by project SERICS (PE00000014) under the MUR National Recovery and Resilience Plan funded by the European Union - NextGenerationEU, by "Futuro & Conoscenza S.r.l.", jointly created by the FBK and the Italian National Mint and Printing House (IPZS), Italy and by the project "METAfora: Metodologie e tecnologie di rappresentazione per il metaverso" (CUP code B69J23000190005), proposed by BIT4ID S.r.l.

---

[3] https://drive.google.com/drive/folders/1SVKA9ti2-0Rt6Lu_bIX2jaWxjsN5cVfP.

References

1. AUSTRIA ID OIDC documentation. https://eid.egiz.gv.at/wp-content/uploads/2021/10/ID-Austria-Technisches-Whitepaper-fuer-Service-Owner-1.pdf. Accessed 28 Nov 2022
2. Auth0 API documentation. https://auth0.com/docs/api/authentication. Accessed 28 Nov 2022
3. Authlete API documentation. https://docs.authlete.com/en/shared/2.2.19. Accessed 28 Nov 2022
4. AWS Cognito OIDC documentation. https://docs.aws.amazon.com/cognito/latest/developerguide/cognito-userpools-server-contract-reference.html. Accessed 28 Nov 2022
5. Cloudentity API documentation. https://cloudentity.com/developers/api/authorization_apis/oauth2/. Accessed 28 Nov 2022
6. Cnil dossier thématique dédié à l'identité numérique. https://www.cnil.fr/sites/default/files/atoms/files/cnil_dossier-thematique_identite-numerique.pdf. Accessed 4 Mar 2023
7. Connect2Id API documentation. https://connect2id.com/products/server/docs/api. Accessed 28 Nov 2022
8. Facebook OIDC documentation. https://developers.facebook.com/docs/facebook-login/guides/advanced/manual-flow/. Accessed 28 Nov 2022
9. ForgeRock API documentation. https://backstage.forgerock.com/docs/am/7.1 . Accessed 28 Nov 2022
10. FranceConnect identity provider documentation. https://partenaires.franceconnect.gouv.fr/fcp/fournisseur-identite. Accessed 28 Nov 2022
11. FranceConnect+ OIDC documentation. https://github.com/france-connect/Documentation-FranceConnect-Plus/blob/main/fs/docs-fs.md. Accessed 28 Nov 2022
12. General data protection regulation. https://eur-lex.europa.eu/legal-content/EN/TXT/HTML/?uri=CELEX:32016R0679&from=EN. Accessed 25 Nov 2022
13. Google Identity API documentation. https://developers.google.com/identity/openid-connect/openid-connect. Accessed 25 Nov 2022
14. IBM Oidc documentation. https://www.ibm.com/docs/en/sva/9.0.7?topic=methods-openid-connect-oidc-authentication. Accessed 25 Nov 2022
15. ID-Porten OIDC documentation. https://docs.digdir.no/docs/idporten/oidc/oidc_guide_english. Accessed 25 Nov 2022
16. itsme API documentation. https://belgianmobileid.github.io/slate/login.html. Accessed 25 Nov 2022
17. Microsoft OIDC documentation. https://connect2id.com/products/server/docs/api. Accessed 25 Nov 2022
18. MitID and NemID service provider documentation. https://broker.signaturgruppen.dk/application/files/7415/8763/0084/Nets_MitID_Broker_Technical_reference_v._0.9.5.pdf. Accessed 25 Nov 2022
19. MojeID OIDC documentation. https://www.mojeid.cz/documentation/html/ImplementacePodporyMojeid/OpenidConnect/index.html. Accessed 25 Nov 2022
20. NemID identity provider documentation. https://broker.signaturgruppen.dk/application/files/6616/5166/7106/Nets_eID_Broker_Identity_Providers_v.1.2.6.pdf. Accessed 25 Nov 2022
21. NHS Login OIDC OIDC documentation. https://developer.nhs.uk/library/systems/eis/. Accessed 25 Nov 2022

22. NL Gov Assurance Profile OIDC documentation. https://logius.gitlab.io/oidc/#authorization-endpoint. Accessed 25 Nov 2022

23. OKTA Api documentation. https://developer.okta.com/docs/reference/api/oidc/. Accessed 28 Nov 2022

24. PING Federation SSO documentation. https://docs.pingidentity.com/bundle/pingone/page/gbj1632772285136.html. Accessed 28 Nov 2022

25. Pro Santé Connect OIDC documentation. https://industriels.esante.gouv.fr/produits-services/pro-sante-connect/documentation-technique. Accessed 28 Nov 2022

26. Regulation on electronic identification and trust services for electronic transactions. https://eur-lex.europa.eu/legal-content/EN/TXT/HTML/?uri=CELEX:32014R0910&from=EN. Accessed 25 Nov 2022

27. Security assertion markup language (saml) v2.0 technical overview. http://docs.oasis-open.org/security/saml/Post2.0/sstc-saml-tech-overview-2.0.html. Accessed 4 Mar 2023

28. Sign in with apple. https://developer.apple.com/sign-in-with-apple/. Accessed 23 Dec 2022

29. SMART-ID OIDC documentation. https://e-gov.github.io/TARA-Doku/TechnicalSpecification. Accessed 28 Nov 2022

30. SPID Oidc documentation. https://docs.italia.it/AgID/documenti-in-consultazione/lg-openidconnect-spid-docs/it/bozza/index.html. Accessed 28 Nov 2022

31. WSO2 Identity Server documentation. https://is.docs.wso2.com/en/latest/guides/before-you-start/. Accessed 28 Nov 2022

32. Yahoo OIDC documentation. https://developer.yahoo.com/oauth2/guide/openid_connect/. Accessed 28 Nov 2022

33. Asghar, M.R., Backes, M., Simeonovski, M.: Prima: Privacy-preserving identity and access management at internet-scale. In: 2018 IEEE International Conference on Communications (ICC), pp. 1–6. IEEE (2018)

34. Simeonovski, M., Bendun, F., Asghar, M.R., Backes, M., Marnau, N., Druschel, P.: Oblivion: mitigating privacy leaks by controlling the discoverability of online information. In: Malkin, T., Kolesnikov, V., Lewko, A.B., Polychronakis, M. (eds.) ACNS 2015. LNCS, vol. 9092, pp. 431–453. Springer, Cham (2015). https://doi.org/10.1007/978-3-319-28166-7_21

35. Bisegna, A., Carbone, R., Pellizzari, G., Ranise, S.: Micro-id-gym: a flexible tool for pentesting identity management protocols in the wild and in the laboratory. In: Saracino, A., Mori, P. (eds.) Emerging Technologies for Authorization and Authentication, pp. 71–89. Springer International Publishing, Cham (2020)

36. Boysen, A.: Decentralized, self-sovereign, consortium: the future of digital identity in Canada. Front. Blockchain 11 (2021)

37. Calzavara, S., Focardi, R., Maffei, M., Schneidewind, C., Squarcina, M., Tempesta, M.: WPSE: Fortifying web protocols via Browser-Side security monitoring. In: 27th USENIX Security Symposium (USENIX Security 18), Baltimore, MD, pp. 1493–1510. USENIX Association, August 2018. https://www.usenix.org/conference/usenixsecurity18/presentation/calzavara

38. Chari, S., Jutla, C., Roy, A.: Universally composable security analysis of oauth v2.0. Cryptology ePrint Archive, Paper 2011/526 (2011). https://eprint.iacr.org/2011/526

39. Fett, D., Küsters, R., Schmitz, G.: Spresso: a secure, privacy-respecting single sign-on system for the web. In: Proceedings of the 22nd ACM SIGSAC Conference on Computer and Communications Security, pp. 1358–1369 (2015)

40. Fett, D., Küsters, R., Schmitz, G.: A comprehensive formal security analysis of oauth 2.0. In: Proceedings of the 2016 ACM SIGSAC Conference on Computer and Communications Security. CCS 2016, pp. 1204–1215, New York, NY, USA. Association for Computing Machinery (2016). https://doi.org/10.1145/2976749.2978385, https://doi.org/10.1145/2976749.2978385

41. Fett, D., Küsters, R., Schmitz, G.: The web sso standard openid connect: In-depth formal security analysis and security guidelines. In: 2017 IEEE 30th Computer Security Foundations Symposium (CSF), pp. 189–202. IEEE (2017)

42. Foundation, O.: Certified openid providers, https://openid.net/certification/. Accessed 23 Nov 2022

43. Foundation, O.: List of openid specifications (2023). https://openid.net/developers/specs/. Accessed 6 Mar 2023

44. Hammann, S., Sasse, R., Basin, D.: Privacy-preserving openid connect. In: Proceedings of the 15th ACM Asia Conference on Computer and Communications Security. ASIA CCS 2020, New York, NY, USA, pp. 277–289. Association for Computing Machinery (2020). https://doi.org/10.1145/3320269.3384724, https://doi.org/10.1145/3320269.3384724

45. Li, W., Mitchell, C.J.: User access privacy in oauth 2.0 and openid connect. In: 2020 IEEE European Symposium on Security and Privacy Workshops (EuroS&PW), pp. 664–6732. IEEE (2020)

46. Li, W., Mitchell, C.J., Chen, T.: Oauthguard: protecting user security and privacy with oauth 2.0 and openid connect. In: Proceedings of the 5th ACM Workshop on Security Standardisation Research Workshop. SSR 2019, New York, NY, USA, pp. 35–44, Association for Computing Machinery (2019). https://doi.org/10.1145/3338500.3360331, https://doi.org/10.1145/3338500.3360331

47. Lodderstedt, T., Fett, D., Haine, M., Pulido, A., Lehmann, K., Koiwai, K.: Openid connect for identity assurance 1.0. https://openid.net/specs/openid-connect-4-identity-assurance-1_0.html. Accessed 23 Nov 2022

48. Lodderstedt, T., Bradley, J., Labunets, A., Fett, D.: OAuth 2.0 Security Best Current Practice. Internet-Draft draft-ietf-oauth-security-topics-21, Internet Engineering Task Force, September 2022. https://datatracker.ietf.org/doc/draft-ietf-oauth-security-topics/21/. work in Progress

49. Varley, M., Grassi, P.: International government assurance profile (igov) for openid connect 1.0. https://openid.bitbucket.io/iGov/openid-igov-profile-id1.html

50. Morkonda, S.G., Chiasson, S., van Oorschot, P.C.: Ssoprivateeye: timely disclosure of single sign-on privacy design differences. arXiv preprint arXiv:2209.04490 (2022)

51. Navas, J., Beltrán, M.: Understanding and mitigating openid connect threats. Comput. Secur. **84**, 1–16 (2019)

52. Richer, J., Johansson, L.: Vectors of trust. RFC 8485, RFC Editor, October 2018. https://www.rfc-editor.org/info/rfc8485

53. Sakimura, N., Bradley, J., Jones, M., De Medeiros, B., Mortimore, C.: Openid connect core 1.0. The OpenID Foundation, p. S3 (2014)

54. Sharif, A., Ranzi, M., Carbone, R., Sciarretta, G., Marino, F.A., Ranise, S.: The eidas regulation: a survey of technological trends for European electronic identity schemes. Appl. Sci. **12**(24) (2022). https://doi.org/10.3390/app122412679

55. Sudhodanan, A., Carbone, R., Compagna, L., Dolgin, N., Armando, A., Morelli, U.: Large-scale analysis & detection of authentication cross-site request forgeries. In: 2017 IEEE European Symposium on Security and Privacy (EuroS&P), pp. 350–365. IEEE (2017)

56. eID User Community: Overview of pre-notified and notified eid schemes under eidas (2019). https://ec.europa.eu/digital-building-blocks/wikis/display/EIDCOMMUNITY/Overview+of+pre-notified+and+notified+eID+schemes+under+eIDAS . Accessed 23 Nov 2022

57. Wilson, Y., Hingnikar, A.: Solving Identity Management in Modern Applications: Demystifying OAuth 2.0, OpenID connect, and SAML 2.0. Springer, Berkeley (2019). https://doi.org/10.1007/978-1-4842-5095-2

58. Zhang, Z., Król, M., Sonnino, A., Zhang, L., Rivière, E.: El passo: privacy-preserving, asynchronous single sign-on. arXiv preprint arXiv:2002.10289 (2020)

59. Zhou, Y., Evans, D.: SSOScan: automated testing of web applications for single Sign-On vulnerabilities. In: 23rd USENIX Security Symposium (USENIX Security 14), San Diego, CA, pp. 495–510. USENIX Association, August 2014. https://www.usenix.org/conference/usenixsecurity14/technical-sessions/presentation/zhou

Maintain High-Quality Access Control Policies: An Academic and Practice-Driven Approach

Sascha Kern[1]([⊠])([iD]), Thomas Baumer[1]([iD]), Ludwig Fuchs[1],
and Günther Pernul[2]([iD])

[1] Nexis GmbH, Franz-Mayer-Straße 1, Regensburg 93053, Bavaria, Germany
sascha.kern@nexis-secure.com
[2] University of Regensburg, Universitätsstraße 31, Regensburg 93053,
Bavaria, Germany
https://nexis-secure.com/,
http://www.ur.de/informatik-data-science/wi-pernul/startseite

Abstract. Organizations encounter great difficulties in maintaining high-quality Access Control Policies (ACPs). Policies originally modeled and implemented with good quality deteriorate over time, leading to inaccurate authorization decisions and reduced policy maintainability. As a result, security risks arise, delays prevent users from carrying out tasks, and ACP management becomes more expensive and error-prone. In contrast to the initial modeling of ACPs, their long-term maintenance has been addressed scarcely by existing research. This work addresses this research gap with three contributions: First, we provide a detailed problem analysis based on a literature survey and six real-world practitioner expert interviews. Second, we propose a framework that supports organizations in implementing and performing ACP maintenance. Third, we present a maintenance case study in which we implemented maintenance capabilities for a real-world ACP dataset that allowed us to significantly improve its quality.

Keywords: Identity management · Access control · Access control policies · Data quality · Policy maintenance · Security management

1 Introduction

Authorizing users' access to protected resources is a cornerstone of every modern IT security framework. While technologies to enforce well-defined authorizations exist, organizations still struggle with their management: Numerous scientific studies and industry reports highlight major difficulties in adhering to the Principle of Least Privilege (PoLP) [35,47] and point out the high frequency of related IT security vulnerabilities, such as attacks through malicious insiders or hijacking of privileged identities [1,9]. The basis for the definition of IT

The research leading to these results was supported by the German Federal Ministry of Education and Research as part of the DEVISE project (https://devise.ur.de).

© IFIP International Federation for Information Processing 2023
Published by Springer Nature Switzerland AG 2023
V. Atluri and A. L. Ferrara (Eds.): DBSec 2023, LNCS 13942, pp. 223–242, 2023.
https://doi.org/10.1007/978-3-031-37586-6_14

authorizations are Access Control Policies (ACPs). These machine-processable rules define the user's access to resources. The high-quality modeling of new ACPs has received significant interest in research realms such as policy mining and policy engineering. However, policy modeling is not a one-off effort: Changes within an organization or its IT infrastructure, incorrect policy updates and a common practice of granting permissions too freely [47] cause ACPs to deteriorate and lose quality over time [23,45]. This decay leads to inaccurate authorizations, which create security risks or prevent users from accessing resources, and a reduction in ACP maintainability, which reduces the work efficiency of policy engineers and increases their proneness to further errors [6]. Unlike their initial modeling, maintaining the quality of existing ACPs over time has received little research attention.

This work offers three contributions to address this research gap: (i) We conduct a detailed problem analysis for ACP maintenance, building on a literature survey and six expert interviews with Identity and Access Management (IAM) experts. We identify five fundamental problems relevant during ACP maintenance. (ii) We propose a framework for ACP maintenance that addresses the identified problems. It provides an Access Control Model (ACM)-independent high-level structure for maintenance activities that span from the definition of goals over the implementation of a maintenance environment to the execution of a maintenance process. (iii) We conduct a case study on ACP maintenance that instantiates the proposed framework in a real-world enterprise environment. It evaluates the proposed framework and makes ACP maintenance tangible. The remainder of this work is structured as follows: Chap. 2 introduces preliminaries and related work. Chapter 3 presents the problem analysis which characterizes the identified research gap and underlines its relevance. Chapter 4 presents the proposed framework that contributes to closing this research gap. Chapter 5 presents the case study that shows the framework's general validity. Chapter 6 discusses the results and concludes this work.

2   Background

2.1   Basic Definitions and Assumptions

Identity and Access Management (IAM) deals with the management of (digital) identities and the control of user access to resources. Authorizations must be defined here in order to determine which resources a user may or may not access. IAM relies on *Access Control Policies (ACPs)* [37], machine-processable rules which are automatically evaluated by an access control mechanism to make authorization decisions. The data structure of ACPs is defined by *Access Control Policies (ACPs)*, with Discretionary Access Control (DAC) [39], Role-Based Access Control (RBAC) [13,38] and Attribute-Based Access Control (ABAC) [25] being among the most common. The authorizations granted by ACPs of different ACMs can be represented as an access matrix, which relates all covered subjects (users) with all covered objects (permissions) and contains the respective authorization decisions (permit or deny) as binary values. In condensed form, an access matrix can be expressed as a set of *User Permission Assignments*

(UPAs), which contains the sum of all effective permission grants defined by the ACP set as user-permission pairs. For an access control mechanism to make correct authorization decisions, ACPs must be modeled and maintained. The *IAM team* of an organization is the group of people who are responsible for their modeling and maintaining. Depending on the organization, the IAM team can be located differently, e.g. in IT operations, risk management, IT security management, or a specialized IAM department. Besides the IAM team, there may be *policy owners* who are formally responsible for specific ACPs, e.g. because they have formal responsibility for the affected users of permissions (e.g. department heads or application administrators). In addition to owners, there are *domain experts*, i.e. people who have specific knowledge necessary for understanding and managing specific ACPs, like effects of specific permissions or required activities of employees fulfilling their work. Many established regulatory frameworks and IT security standards oblige organizations to ensure current authorizations in accordance with the principle of least privilege [3,28,34]. This may include that policy owners periodically (e.g. annually) check the correctness of existing UPAs. To do this, organizations carry out *access reviews*, a largely manual process in which responsible persons check all effective UPAs of an ACP set and try to find excessive authorizations which are then revoked [29].

2.2   Related Work

Numerous publications address the initial modeling of high-quality policies. While policy engineering approaches aim to create policies from scratch in a top-down procedure [11,44], policy mining algorithms evaluate existing permission assignments to generate new policies based on them [32,48]. Hybrid approaches try to combine the advantages of both types [17]. Policy modeling approaches of both types provide valuable assistance in the initial creation of policies. However, they do not aim to assist in maintaining or improving the quality of existing policies. Several publications propose process models or frameworks that aim to assist in ACP maintenance: Fuchs et al. propose a process model which aims to maintain high-quality roles [15]. It defines four phases in which an existing role model is assessed and updated with operations such as role shrinking, UPA cleansing, role expansion, role modeling, and hierarchy optimization. The authors have a clear organizational focus and incorporate issues such as distributed expert knowledge and maintenance priorities. However, the proposed maintenance process is limited to a "pure" RBAC. It does not guide the strategic derivation of maintenance goals or the operational involvement of domain experts. Benedetti and Mori propose a process model to include access logs into role maintenance, and a Max-SAT algorithm that evaluates them to improve role quality [7]. They specifically focus on identifying and adding missing permission assignments to the role model while keeping its complexity low. A subsequent publication extends its approach also to handle excessive permission assignments [8]. Similarly, Hummer et al. propose a process model for including access logs into policy management activities [27]. They propose to use this data to identify authorization inaccuracies in a policy set and find invalid policies automatically.

Their approach does not go into the details of the subsequent maintenance activities. Instead, it suggests that policies recognized as invalid are re-mined fully automatically and recommended to a responsible human for confirmation. El Hadj et al. propose a framework that uses access logs to validate and maintain ABAC policies [20]. Their framework defines five modules that process policies and apply specific update operations to reduce complexity and remove conflicts and redundancies. Hu et al. propose a tool-based framework to support role updating [24]. The tool accepts desired UPA states as input. It generates possible role-permission and role-role relation updates that a policy administrator can apply to achieve the desired UPA state. Besides these frameworks, several ACP update algorithms were proposed [4,30]. ACP update algorithms aim to improve the quality of existing policies for a defined quality target while keeping the structure of the improved policies largely intact. They can help automate parts of ACP maintenance within a clearly defined scope but do not aim to support its technical or organizational implementation. To the best of our knowledge, no framework has been proposed to guide the maintenance of ACPs holistically in a real-world organization.

3   Problem Analysis

At the beginning of the research process we carried out a problem analysis. For this we researched common policy maintenance problems. The analysis of these problems served to better define the research gap and identify requirements for the developed framework. In the first part of the problem analysis, scientific IAM literature was examined in a structured literature survey with a scope for problems mentioned in the quality maintenance of ACPs. This grounding was then expanded with six expert interviews, in which IAM experts were asked about the procedure and known problems in ACPs maintenance. The knowledge body obtained in this way was then analyzed. Both the scientific literature and the expert interviews revealed a large number of problem aspects and examples that are difficult to survey in their entirety. We abstracted these and identified five overarching problems that have been mentioned repeatedly in literature and interviews and have a high level of validity. Table 1 shows analyzed literature that describes at least one of these problems. Table 2 shows in which expert interviews these problems were described. The remainder of this chapter describes details of the expert interviews and the five identified overarching problems.

3.1   Expert Interviews

The six expert interviews were conducted according to the semi-structured interview methodology proposed by Adams [2]. We formulated a catalogue of 13 questions which were walked through with the interviewees in natural conversations, which are listed in Table 5. When relevant problems or details about the maintenance practice were mentioned, we deviated from this catalogue in order to pursue them more deeply. The results were transcribed and evaluated, and if

Table 1. Considered literature.

Literature	P1	P2	P3	P4	P5
L1: Jaferian et al. [29]	X	X	X	X	
L2: Puchta et al. [36]	X	X		X	X
L3: Parkinson and Khan [35]	X	X			
L4: Servos and Osborn [40]	X	X		X	X
L5: Smetters and Good [41]	X	X			
L6: Fuchs et al. [15]	X	X			
L7: Hummer et al. [27]	X	X			X
L8: Groll et al. [18]	X	X	X	X	
L9: Hill [22]		X		X	
L10: Benedetti and Mori [8]		X	X	X	
L11: Hu et al. [24]	X		X		
L12: Strembeck [42]		X			
L13: Xu et al. [47]	X				
L14: Xiang et al. [46]		X	X		
L15: Bauer et al. [5]	X	X			
L16: Kunz et al. [31]	X	X			X
L17: Kern et al. [30]	X	X			X

anything was unclear, the interviewees were asked for clarification afterwards. In the remainder, the interviewees remain anonymous due to their employers' company policies. This enabled them to provide insight into their current challenges and issues in respect to ACPs. However, we are going to give a general classification of their employing organizations by highlighting the approximate number of employees and managed digital identities. These numbers do not deviate from the actual numbers by more than 20%.

Expert Interview (EI)1 was conducted with an IAM governance officer of a banking group (approx. 5,000 employees and 10.000 digital identities). EI2 was conducted with an IAM governance officer of a pharmaceutics company (approx. 15,000 employees and 30.000 digital identities). EI3 was conducted with an IAM governance officer and an IAM engineer working for an insurance company (approx. 5,000 employees and digital identities). EI4 was conducted with an IAM governance officer and an IAM engineer working for a retail company (approx. 50,000 employees and 20,000 digital identities). EI5 was conducted with the Chief Information Security Officer (CISO) of a software and consulting company (approx. 50 employees and digital identities). EI6 was conducted with two senior IAM consultants of the same company who approximated that they had completed IAM projects for a combined total of 60 customer companies. Note that some companies manage more digital identities than they have employees since they also manage access for their organizational network, like external contractors or suppliers.

Table 2. Participants of the Expert Interviews (EIs).

Expert Interviews (EI)	Sector	P1	P2	P3	P4	P5
EI1: IAM officer	Banking	X	X	X	X	
EI2: IAM officer	Pharmaceutics	X	X	X	X	X
EI3: IAM officer, IAM engineer	Insurance	X	X	X	X	X
EI4: IAM officer, IAM engineer	Retail	X	X	X	X	X
EI5: CISO	Software & Consulting		X	X	X	
EI6: 2 IAM consultants	Software & Consulting	X	X	X	X	X

All companies considered by interviews EI1-5 used RBAC as their basic authorization model. In parallel to RBAC, however, there have always been manual direct permission assignments without an intermediary role. The IAM consultants from EI6 emphasize that a pure RBAC is de facto absent in practice and is also not desirable due to the role explosion problem [14]. Moreover, all companies used automation mechanisms for basic authorizations. These mechanisms permit or deny authorizations on the basis of a person's position in the company's organizational structure, logic-based or attribute-based assignment rules. Similarly, all companies use mechanisms to assign roles automatically to employees based on employee attributes. In addition, Segregation of Duty (SoD) rules exist with varying degrees of complexity: They range from simple 1-to-1 exclusions of two permissions over SoD matrices to very complex logic-based rule structures. Overall, the authorization structures could not be limited to a single ACM in any case. In addition, the authorization structures within a data schema were subdivided semantically: For example, roles were divided into hierarchy levels using multi-level concepts, and permissions were treated differently based on their application affiliation.

The five companies perform regular maintenance processes in the form of access reviews. In addition, reactive maintenance is carried out. The most frequently named reason are changes to the company's organizational structure; e.g., because departments are merged or subcompanies are acquired. This typically leads to changes in the entitlement structures that are directly linked to organizational affiliation (e.g. department roles). Proactive maintenance is only carried out to a limited extent. Interviewees EI1-5 reported that isolated cases, e.g. outdating of obsolete permissions, can be conducted relatively easily, i.e. without any organizational resistance. However, they were reluctant to make changes to more complex entitlement structures, e.g. roles that could not easily be attributed to a well-defined user or permission group, due to the involved work effort and fear of errors. The IAM consultants from EI6 underlined that proactive ACP maintenance in their experience is scarce and often not carried out at all. Despite this reluctance, all interviewees emphasized that it pays off to improve entitlement structures if it can be done with a manageable amount of effort. The most frequently mentioned motivation are efficiency gains, as simpler entitlement structures allow for easier permission assignments and speed up employee onboarding, and improve entitlement maintainability. Another important motivation was maintenance decentralization, since simpler authorization structures can be better maintained by policy owners in departments without deeper IT or IAM knowledge. Possible improvements in authorization accuracy were also often considered valuable. It also became clear, however, that compliance with regulatory requirements or supplier requirements from customers are no less important than internal motivations. Such compliance requirements in fact often represent the decisive reason for performing ACP maintenance, especially for access reviews.

3.2 Identified Problems

P1. Amount and Complexity of Policies: The amount of ACPs in their various forms is too large to keep track of and update manually. For this reason, tool support is necessary for entitlement data overview and maintenance. This complexity was made particularly clear in the example of access reviews: Several interviewees explained that responsible policy owners often perceive this manual review of permission assignments as a "penalty work", and that it would not be enforceable without external compliance pressure. In the worst case, policy owners would blindly confirm all existing permission assignments, resulting in uncontrolled proliferation of authorizations [18]. The underlying IAM infrastructure's complexity also hampers entitlement data overview. The basic task of implementing a unified IAM data view is a nontrivial challenge because the managed permissions reside scattered in a large number of application systems. While provisioning engines and meta-data views aim to tackle this complexity, they represent only an abstraction of the underlying entitlement structures and cannot eliminate their complexity. For example, one interviewee highlighted, that their organization operates a parallel structure of in-house and cloud applications, which leads to intended redundancies in entitlement data. Specially customized meta-database views, which are supposed to provide an overview of the effective permission assignments of a user (so-called "reports"), are complex to comprehend and error-prone. Another interviewee explained that deployed data synchronization tools have malfunctioned in the past, causing errors in the entitlement data that remained unnoticed for a while. This interviewee also mentioned the problem of shadow IT, which occurs when departments set up IT applications bypassing the central IT operations: The IAM team then is not aware of the authorizations managed there and cannot maintain them [16].

P2. Distributed Knowledge: The knowledge needed to manage ACPs is typically spread across an organization. IAM or IT security officers have an overview of the rough structure but find it hard assessing the effects of permissions within the applications or determining the required permissions for a specific employee. The knowledge for this typically lies with IT experts (e.g., application administrators) or domain experts (e.g., department heads). For this reason, the IAM team cannot keep authorization structures up to date on their own but rely on the cooperation with these knowledge bearers. In two interviews, experts reported that they have handed over some of their responsibility for role maintenance to IT or domain experts. Another two have stated this as a future goal. Several interviewees emphasized that it can be difficult for both, the IAM team and IT or domain experts to understand the semantic meaning behind existing permissions or ACPs. This starts with low-level problems, e.g., when permission naming is not related to any semantics (e.g. using numbers) or when descriptions documenting the business meaning are absent. The experts also highlighted an occasional absence of defined contact persons for further questions, e.g., to determine the security criticality of permissions. Great emphasis was placed on the semantic meaningfulness of authorization objects. One interviewee stated that one should be able to explain in one sentence what the content of a role or SoD rule is. Another interviewee emphasized that comprehensible entitlement structures are the central prerequisite for involving domain experts outside the IAM team in policy maintenance.

P3. Importance of Business Facilitation: At all interviewed companies, uninterrupted business operations are the top priority. As a result, IAM teams act very carefully not to revoke too many permissions from users, potentially causing negative business impact. When in doubt, they are often willing to put up with excess rights rather than prevent employees from doing their jobs [29, 47]. For example, one interviewee reported the following typical behavior during their mover processes: When users change departments, they often execute tasks from their old department during a transition period, meaning that they might still need some permissions associated with their old department. The removal of known outdated UPAs is thus problematic and only carried out after such a transition period. The high importance of business facilitation is an obstacle to the maintenance of authorization structures and favors their proliferation.

P4. Organizational and Regulatory Restrictions: The interviewees unanimously reported formal hurdles in the maintenance of ACPs. These can be due to internal organizational requirements, for example, due to existing processes or "company politics" [16, 26], or because of external regulations (often referred to as *regulatory compliance*). Such restrictions make it necessary to define ACP owners, for example, for all permissions within an application or for every role. Granting permissions to users or changing the structure of ACPs often requires the approval of these owners. This represents a hurdle for the maintenance of ACPs, especially if formally defined owners do not actually have the knowledge to assess a given change in a qualified manner. In addition, regulations often make more complex entitlement structures necessary. In the interviews, it was noticeable that heavily regulated financial service companies defined a larger amount and more complex SoD rules than those from less heavily regulated sectors. The IAM consultants from EI6 reported instances where additional layers were modeled into role or permission hierarchies only to accommodate responsibilities.

P5. Attribute Quality: Accuracy, integrity, and timeliness of attributes of IAM-relevant data play a major role for ACP maintenance. In addition to the comprehensibility-relevant attributes of ACPs themselves, data records of users and departmental structures (e.g., HR records), as well as user accounts and permissions within individual applications, are elementary as a source of information [31]. Incorrect or outdated attributes in these data, e.g., the wrong department assignment of an employee, therefore lead to incorrect policy updates or to a complete lack of necessary maintenance if the trust in the master data is missing. The IAM consultants from EI6 emphasized that sufficient master data quality is always a prerequisite for further data analyses and must therefore be ensured before attempting larger IAM projects (e.g., role modeling).

4   Proposed ACP Maintenance Framework

In the following we propose a framework for the maintenance of ACPs. It was developed and evaluated using the design science methodology [21] and builds on the previously presented problem analysis. The proposed framework describes activities that are necessary for the maintenance of ACPs and their successful integration in an organizational context. It defines four domains to which the maintenance activities are assigned: Governance, the IAM team, IT & domain experts and the maintenance environment. The governance domain is responsible for defining strategic goals, from which IAM maintenance activities are derived, and for reviewing the achievement of these goals. The IAM team has the operational responsibility for ACP maintenance. The IT & domain experts domain includes people with contextual knowledge that assists during ACP maintenance, as well as policy owners who must be included in maintenance activities. The maintenance environment is a collection of tools and software components that support the analysis and updating of the ACPs. Figure 1 gives a schematic overview of the four domains and the associated maintenance activities. Note that the framework in its entirety is not designed as a business process. The policy updating activities are short-term periodic tasks that are well-suited to be implemented as a process. The definition of strategic goals and quality objectives, and the implementation of analysis and updating capabilities are executed over a longer period and hence better suited for project-type organization. The remainder of this chapter presents the activities of the proposed framework.

4.1   Defining Strategic IAM Goals and ACP Quality Objectives

The governance domain defines strategic goals which serve as work basis for the IAM team. Strategic IAM goals commonly involve compliance, business facilitation, risk reduction and quality-related goals [26]. Risk reduction and business facilitation are directly related to the accuracy of ACPs, i.e. the amount of excessive and missing UPAs defined by them [6]. They are addressed by identifying which UPAs a given user *should* have, and updating the existing ACPs to correct deviations. Quality-related strategic goals, such as data quality, software quality or process quality, aim to ensure an efficient operability of IT and enable high-quality work results. The quality of ACPs significantly influences these goals: Beside accuracy, ACP quality includes maintainability, which affects administrative effort and error proneness through factors such as complexity, understandability or redundancy; as well as evaluation efficiency, which is a performance

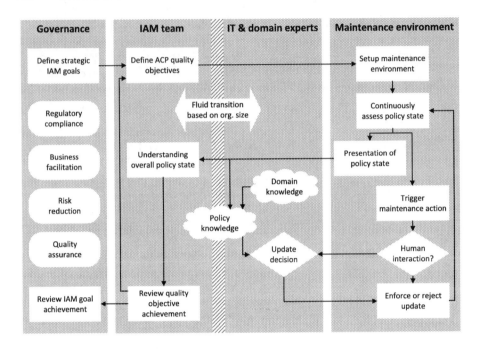

Fig. 1. Schematic overview of the proposed ACP Maintenance Framework.

bottleneck if ACPs are evaluated in real-time [30]. Compliance goals typically overlap with the aforementioned, and may also include adherence to the principle of least privilege, implementation of SoD policies, definition and adherence to formal responsibilities, and comprehensive change logs and reporting capabilities to verify compliance with these requirements. Based on the formulated strategic goals, the IAM team evaluates the available resources and defines ACP quality objectives that can be achieved in a given period (e.g., 6 months). These quality objectives serve as basis for the ACP maintenance process and must be checked and reviewed periodically. Since maintenance capabilities must be implemented and evolved over time, the initial quality objectives must be formulated at a low level. As the maintenance process matures, they can then be gradually increased until a satisfactory ACP quality level is reached and can be maintained over the long term. The IAM team reports to the governance domain using appropriate key performance indicators so that the governance domain can monitor the achievement of the formulated strategic goals.

4.2   Implementing the ACP Maintenance Environment

The ACP maintenance is supported by a maintenance environment. This can include, for example, data analysis and visualization tools, workflow tools, IAM-specific tools or in-house developments. At the beginning of the implementation, an understanding of the existing entitlement structures must be achieved. Since the IAM-relevant data is typically distributed in a heterogeneous form in a large number of applications (e.g. target systems, IAM systems, supplementary data sources such as human resource systems and directories), an integrated IAM data view must first be implemented. This data view bundles and normalizes the managed ACPs and associated data in an appropriate data model (e.g. [31]). The larger and more complex an IT infrastructure is, the more important it is to obtain a sufficient understanding of the managed data before the actual maintenance, e.g. through appropriate ACP visualization methods [10,12,43]. On this basis, the IAM team needs to build an overview of the total amount of ACPs managed in an organization and possible quality issues. IT and domain experts can support the IAM team by bringing in their domain knowledge when reviewing policies that affect their line of work. In return, the IAM team must enable IT and domain experts to understand the meaning of their policies and the possible consequences of changes. Once a high-level overview of the entitlement structures has been obtained, metrics can be defined to determine the ACP quality and monitor its development throughout the maintenance process.

The maintenance process can be implemented as soon as the required data has been developed. First, subsets of the ACP data must be defined whose quality is of interest and should be maintained. It is helpful to separate ACP subsets based on their data structure (e.g., different ACMs) as well as their semantic meaning (e.g., different layers in a role model, or different maintenance priorities of ABAC policies). Quality checks must then be implemented for the defined ACP subsets. A quality check comprises two elements: A check condition and a maintenance action. A check condition defines an automatically identifiable quality problem or opportunity for quality improvement. Examples of this can be a metric indicating low ACP quality, a constraint such as an SoD quality being violated, an ACP exceeding a defined timeliness (e.g. one year passed since the last review), or detectable events like the creation of a new department or IT application. Check conditions are evaluated periodically and fully automated. When need for maintenance is identified, a corresponding maintenance action is triggered.

4.3   Executing the ACP Maintenance Process

A quality check's maintenance action can be defined and implemented by the IAM team according to their maintenance goals. There are numerous possibilities for quality improvement and they depend on the identified quality problem and the affected ACPs: For example, a quality check that identifies excessive UPAs can trigger a permission withdrawal. The violation of an SoD rule can lead to a review of the violating ACPs, or a quality optimization algorithm can attempt to resolve identified conflicts or redundancies between multiple rules. We propose three prototypical grades of automation: Informing, recommending, and fully automated. (i) The simplest case is a purely informational request to check the identified quality problem. Such a request can be delegated to a responsible IT or domain expert who can decide based on this to manually update the affected policies or accept the quality issue. (ii) In the second level of automation, possible policy updates are generated automatically (e.g. by a quality optimization algorithm) and recommended to responsible IT or domain experts. The experts now have the option of accepting or rejecting the recommendation. It is important that the IT and domain experts understand the recommendation, i.e. its reason and its concrete effect. Tool support can enable IT and domain experts to make a qualified decision, e.g. by providing data visualization techniques or low-threshold contact options with the IAM team. If an expert decides to accept the recommendation, the update is performed and the ACP state is updated. If the decision is rejected, the rejected recommendation must be logged so that it is not proposed again. (iii) The third level is full automation. This level is limited to policies for which no human approval is required, e.g. because they are not subject to such regulations or because their security criticality is low enough. Fully automated ACP updates also require trust in the correctness of the recommendation, which must grow over time. Just like changes initiated externally, a successful maintenance action leads to an update of the ACP state and thus to an update of the measured ACP quality. The IAM team monitors the ACP quality and, based on this, adjusts existing quality checks or implements new ones.

Note that the roles of the IAM team and domain experts cannot always be clearly separated: In small organizations, the persons responsible for IAM tasks often take on the function of domain experts themselves. As the organization grows, these tasks can no longer be managed by the IAM team due to the work quantity and distributed content knowledge and must be consistently outsourced to IT and domain experts. It cannot be expected that a full ACP maintenance capability will be built immediately. The initial implementation focus should be on creating a data overview and analysis options that improve understanding of the ACPs and possible quality problems. Over time, new quality checks can be implemented sequentially in order to increase the coverage of considered quality problems and the degree of automation of the maintenance capabilities. For all updates made, complete logging of the changes to ACPs is helpful for traceability and external accountability. In addition, recording the quality development over time helps to check the success of the maintenance and offset it against the invested resources.

5   Evaluation with Real-World Enterprise Data

To evaluate the proposed framework, it was instantiated in a case study. For this purpose, we worked with IAM practitioners of a large financial service provider, who gave us read access to the centrally managed entitlement data of their productive IT infrastructure. Our practice partners assumed the function of the governance domain, while we filled out the IAM team domain. First, we obtained an overview of the existing entitlement structures. The company uses an RBAC model with two semantic types of roles: Organization-driven *business roles* and application-specific *system roles*. In addition, there are manual permission assignments, and proprietary rules for automated permission assignment. There are also constraints that must be observed when updating the entitlement structure, including an SoD matrix that defines mutually exclusive permissions, and application-specific restrictions for the assignment of permissions. After understanding the basic data model, we defined maintenance priorities in consultation with the practice partners. They were interested in improving the data overview and eliminating unnecessary complexity. The identification of excess authorizations and the improvement of master data quality were also of interest. At the same time, restrictions applied: First, any ACP updates had to comply with the defined constraints. Second, we had no access to domain experts or policy owners, as this would go beyond the resources provided for the case study. Third, no access logs were available, which could have provided a data basis for automated identification of excessive authorizations. Based on the available data and resources, we formulated the maintenance objective of reducing the complexity and redundancy of the ACPs. We decided to use two metrics to verify maintenance success: The WSC defines the complexity of ACPs by summing up all contained data elements [33]. We decided to use a neutral configuration of (1, 1, 1, 1, 1). Redundancy was defined as the ratio of redundant UPAs among all UPAs [19].

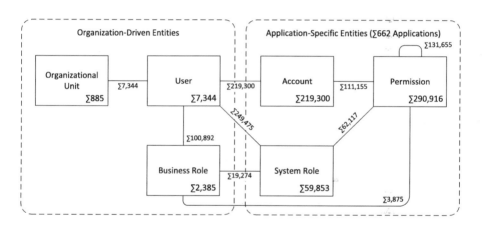

Fig. 2. Assumed data model of the case study with initial entity counts.

After agreeing on maintenance objectives and metrics we implemented the maintenance environment. Herefore we created a relational database and implemented an integrated IAM data view in accordance with [31]. It comprised the managed users, their organizational unit affiliations, user accounts and permissions, roles and the relations between these entities. Entity attributes contained rules for automatic permission assignment, SoD classes and roles and permissions, application-specific assignment constraints, and context information such as job descriptions, policy ownership definitions or security criticality flags. Figure 2 summarizes the integrated data model. In order to keep the data complexity manageable in the context of the case study, we excluded some known exceptional cases from the imported data, such as authorization assignments to external employees without a domain account, orphan accounts, or applications without centrally managed permissions. In a productive maintenance project, these exceptional cases would be considered once maintenance was established for the basic ones.

We then proceeded to implement analysis and maintenance capabilities. The data analysis capabilities included a tool-based data browsing interface, a graphic filter for the analysis of data subsets, a grid visualization for entitlement data, and quality metric calculations for selected data sets. A workflow engine enabled us to bundle data changes into change requests and delegate them to selected deciders via E-Mail. While we did not have permission to query actual domain experts, we did a proof-of-concept configuration that used ownership attributes from the imported permission data to include domain experts in the maintenance process. We then defined three subgroups within the imported ACP data subject to quality considerations: 2,385 business roles, 59,853 system roles, and 111,115 manual account-permission assignments. First quality measurements showed that the ACP set realized a total of 3,666,181 UPAs, out of which 1,134,596 (30.95%) were redundant. The initial WSC was 1,031,597. Since the business roles accounted for 62.99% of the UPAs, but only 10.01% of the complexity, we decided to minimize direct permission and system role assignments in favor of the well-maintainable business roles.

Table 3. The six quality checks implemented for the case study.

ACP Subset	Check	Condition	Maintenance action
Business roles	C1	Role without employee	Delete role
	C2	Role without permission	Delete role
	C5	All employees inherit the same system role	Assign system role to business role
	C6	All employees inherit the same permission	Assign permission to business role
System roles	C3	Redundant assignment	Revoke assignment
Manual p. ass	C4	Redundant assignment	Revoke assignment

With the analysis capabilities in place, we proceeded to implement quality checks in two cycles. Table 3 lists all implemented checks. The first two checks were trivial: *C1* identified business roles that are assigned to no users, and *C2* identified business roles that inherit no permissions or child roles. Such "empty" roles are leftovers from past updates that bloat the ACP set and can be deleted. The checks identified 524 roles assigned to no users and 146 without permissions or child roles, with an intersection of 80 roles. Since we were surprised by the high number of results, we contacted our practice partners, who confirmed their correctness. The 590 empty business roles where hence deleted, reducing their amount to 1,795. Check *C3* identified redundant assignments of system roles to users: If a user already inherits a system role through a (well-maintainable) business role, any direct assignment of this role was considered redundant and would be revoked. Similarly, *C4* revoked manual permission assignments if they were identified as redundant. $C3$ and $C4$ resulted in the deletion 24,573 direct system role assignments and 25 manual permission assignments. After the first check implementation cycle, the redundancy ratio was reduced to 25.81% and the WSC by 3.16% to 999,039.

Table 4. Quality development during the maintenance process.

	Σ UPAs	Redundant	Ratio	WSC
Initial state	3,666,181	1,134,596	30.85%	1,031,597
1st reduction	3,412,097	880,512	25.81%	999,039
2nd reduction	3,412,097	880,512	25.81%	932,991
Quality improv.		22.39%	5.14%	9.56%

The subsequently implemented checks $C5$ and $C6$ identified opportunities for structural improvement. $C5$ generated recommendations to create new role hierarchy relations: If all employees of a business role inherit the same system role, the system role should be assigned to the business role as a child. By the same logic, $C6$ recommended to assign permissions to a business role, unless it was already inherited by a system role with an open recommendation from $C5$. Both $C5$ and $C6$ omitted recommendations that would violate SoD or application-specific constraints by evaluating respective attributes of all related roles and permissions. Since $C5$ and $C6$ changed the structure of existing roles, we defined that the responsible role owners had to confirm these recommendations. However, since we could not contact the real role owners, we simulated this process in the workflow engine by configuring an automatic decision with an assumed acceptance probability of 80%. In the end, $C5$ created 2,447 new role hierarchy relations and $C6$ created 6,537 role-permission assignments, which increased the UPA coverage of the business roles. Afterwards, $C3$ identified and revoked 55,282 direct user - system role assignments, and $C4$ revoked 16,498 manual permission assignments, which had become redundant through these updates. At the end of the second implementation cycle, the WSC was reduced to 932,991 (-9.56% compared to the initial value) while the redundancy ratio remained at 25.81%. Table 4 summarizes the quality development. We discussed these result with the practice partners and concluded that the maintenance objectives of a substantial reduction in redundancy and complexity had been be achieved. The implemented maintenance environment remains functional and can react to future changes in the underlying ACP set by triggering ACP updates with a high degree of automation. Our practice partners received the maintenance implementation and a protocol for the conducted checks and quality improvements.

6   Discussion and Conclusion

At the beginning of this work, we carried out a detailed analysis of the problem of ACP maintenance. Rigor and relevance were ensured through a structured literature search and six expert interviews. Based on this, we proposed a framework that offers guidance for the maintenance of ACPs and thus contributes to closing this research gap. The framework is not limited to a particular ACM, but provides a high-level structure for maintenance activities, spanning from the definition of quality and maintenance objectives, over the implementation of a maintenance environment, to the execution of an ACP maintenance process. We instantiated the framework in cooperation with practice partners from a large financial services company: After defining maintenance objectives and metrics, we implemented a maintenance environment and used it to significantly improve the quality of a real-world ACP data set. Due to the open structure, the proposed framework can address arbitrary quality issues with many different maintenance approaches. While the quality checks implemented for the evaluation were intentionally kept simple, they could be supplemented by more sophisticated checks to address further quality objectives or expand the maintenance for existing ones. It should be noted that the leaps in quality achieved during the evaluation can only be expected when new quality checks are carried out for the first time. Continuous execution should instead stabilize the level of quality achieved.

This work also has limitations: First, the proposed framework can only offer guidance for the identified problems $P1$-4. $P5$ (insufficient attribute quality) must be addressed by data quality management measures, which are not within the scope of ACP maintenance. Due to its high level of abstraction, the framework cannot define concrete quality improvements (unlike quality optimization algorithms, for example), but serves as a template for structuring ACP maintenance in the context of an organization. During the evaluation, we could only simulate the involvement of domain experts, which limits its general validity. In addition, some constellations of the real-world ACP data set (e.g. proprietary rules for automated permission assignment) were ignored due to limited resources. Overall, we were able to show that the proposed framework has a high degree of general validity and is suitable for guiding the maintenance of ACP in a real-world environment.

Future work can address open research questions that became apparent in the course of this work. First, there are few approaches to measure or improve the human intelligibility of ACPs, which has a strong impact on their maintainability. Another open question is how excessive UPAs can be identified effectively when no access logs are available. The integration of domain experts in ACP maintenance also represents a major difficulty, for which little assistance has been provided so far. We are also not aware of any empirical data that would provide information about real ACP quality developments, for example to investigate the extent to which users accumulate excess authorizations over time.

A   Appendix

Table 5. Question catalogue for the semi-structured expert interviews

	Interview Question
Q1:	Which ACMs are used in your organization?
Q2:	Who is responsible for maintaining ACPs in daily operations?
Q3:	Who in your organization understands meaning & effect of selected ACPs?
Q4:	Do you perform access reviews? If yes, what exactly is being reviewed?
Q5:	What motivation and goals would speak for improving existing ACP structures?
Q6:	Which efforts do you make to improve ACP structure?
Q7:	(How) do you prioritize which ACPs to improve?
Q8:	How regularly does structural improvement take place?
Q9:	How clearly is this structured and documented?
Q10:	Which components of structural improvement are currently automated?
Q11:	What degree of automation would be desirable or realistic?
Q12:	Are there examples of specific problems encountered during maintenance or optimization of existing ACP structures?
Q13:	What are the major structural challenges in ACP maintenance?

References

1. Owasp foundation.: Owasp top ten project (2021). https://owasp.org/Top10/. Accessed Apr 10 2023
2. Adams, W.C.: Conducting semi-structured interviews. Handbook of practical program evaluation, pp. 492–505 (2015)
3. Basel Committee on Banking Supervision: Basel accords (1988–2004). https://www.bis.org/basel_framework/index.htm. Accessed Apr 10 2023
4. Batra, G., Atluri, V., Vaidya, J., Sural, S.: Incremental maintenance of abac policies. In: Proceedings of the Eleventh ACM Conference on Data and Application Security and Privacy, pp. 185–196 (2021)
5. Bauer, L., Cranor, L.F., Reeder, R.W., Reiter, M.K., Vaniea, K.: Real life challenges in access-control management. In: Proceedings of the SIGCHI Conference on Human Factors in Computing Systems, CHI 2009, pp. 899–908. Association for Computing Machinery, New York (2009). https://doi.org/10.1145/1518701.1518838,https://doi.org/10.1145/1518701.1518838
6. Beckerle, M., Martucci, L.A.: Formal definitions for usable access control rule sets from goals to metrics. In: Proceedings of the Ninth Symposium on Usable Privacy and Security, pp. 1–11 (2013)
7. Benedetti, M., Mori, M.: Parametric rbac maintenance via max-sat. In: Proceedings of the 23nd ACM on Symposium on Access Control Models and Technologies, SACMAT 2018, pp. 15–25. Association for Computing Machinery, New York (2018). https://doi.org/10.1145/3205977.3205987. https://doi.org/10.1145/3205977.3205987

8. Benedetti, M., Mori, M.: On the use of max-SAT and PDDL in RBAC maintenance. Cybersecurity **2**(1), July 2019. https://doi.org/10.1186/s42400-019-0036-9. https://doi.org/10.1186/s42400-019-0036-9

9. Beyond Identity: Former employees admit to using continued account access to harm previous employers, February 2022. https://www.beyondidentity.com/blog/great-resignation-impact-on-company-security

10. Colantonio, A., Di Pietro, R., Ocello, A., Verde, N.V.: Visual role mining: a picture is worth a thousand roles. IEEE Trans. Knowl. Data Eng. **24**(6), 1120–1133 (2011)

11. Das, S., Mitra, B., Atluri, V., Vaidya, J., Sural, S.: Policy engineering in rbac and abac. From Database to Cyber Security: Essays Dedicated to Sushil Jajodia on the Occasion of His 70th Birthday, pp. 24–54 (2018)

12. Das, S., Sural, S., Vaidya, J., Atluri, V., Rigoll, G.: VisMAP: visual mining of attribute-based access control policies. In: Garg, D., Kumar, N.V.N., Shyamasundar, R.K. (eds.) ICISS 2019. LNCS, vol. 11952, pp. 79–98. Springer, Cham (2019). https://doi.org/10.1007/978-3-030-36945-3_5

13. Ferraiolo, D.F., Sandhu, R., Gavrila, S., Kuhn, D.R., Chandramouli, R.: Proposed nist standard for role-based access control. ACM Trans. Inf. Syst. Secur. **4**(3), 224–274 (2001). https://doi.org/10.1145/501978.501980. https://doi.org/10.1145/501978.501980

14. Fuchs, L., Pernul, G., Sandhu, R.: Roles in information security - a survey and classification of the research area. Computers & Security **30**(8), 748–769 (2011) 10.1016/j.cose.2011.08.002, https://www.sciencedirect.com/science/article/pii/S016740481100099X

15. Fuchs, L., Kunz, M., Pernul, G.: Role model optimization for secure role-based identity management. In: European Conference on Information Systems (ECIS), pp. 1–15, Juni 2014. https://epub.uni-regensburg.de/30394/

16. Fuchs, L., Pernul, G.: Supporting compliant and secure user handling - a structured approach for in-house identity management. In: The Second International Conference on Availability, Reliability and Security (ARES'07), pp. 374–384 (2007). https://doi.org/10.1109/ARES.2007.145

17. Fuchs, L., Pernul, G.: HyDRo – hybrid development of roles. In: Information Systems Security, pp. 287–302. Springer, Heidelberg (2008). https://doi.org/10.1007/978-3-540-89862-7_24. https://doi.org/10.1007/978-3-540-89862-7_24

18. Groll, S., Kern, S., Fuchs, L., Pernul, G.: Monitoring access reviews by crowd labelling. In: Fischer-Hübner, S., Lambrinoudakis, C., Kotsis, G., Tjoa, A.M., Khalil, I. (eds.) TrustBus 2021. LNCS, vol. 12927, pp. 3–17. Springer, Cham (2021). https://doi.org/10.1007/978-3-030-86586-3_1

19. Guarnieri, M., Arrigoni Neri, M., Magri, E., Mutti, S.: On the notion of redundancy in access control policies. In: Proceedings of the 18th ACM Symposium on Access Control Models and Technologies, pp. 161–172 (2013)

20. Hadj, M.A.E., Erradi, M., Khoumsi, A., Benkaouz, Y.: Validation and correction of large security policies: A clustering and access log based approach. In: 2018 IEEE International Conference on Big Data (Big Data), pp. 5330–5332 (2018). https://doi.org/10.1109/BigData.2018.8622610

21. Hevner, A., Chatterjee, S., Hevner, A., Chatterjee, S.: Design science research in information systems. Design research in information systems: theory and practice, pp. 9–22 (2010)

22. Hill, L.: How automated access verification can help organizations demonstrate HIPAA compliance: a case study. J. Healthc. Inf. Manag. **20**(2), 116–122 (2006)

23. Hu, H., Ahn, G.J., Kulkarni, K.: Anomaly discovery and resolution in web access control policies. In: Proceedings of the 16th ACM Symposium on Access Control Models and Technologies, pp. 165–174 (2011)

24. Hu, J., Zhang, Y., Li, R.: Towards automatic update of access control policy. In: Proceedings of the 24th International Conference on Large Installation System Administration, LISA 2010, pp. 1–7. USENIX Association, USA (2010)

25. Hu, V.C., et al.: Guide to attribute based access control (ABAC) definition and considerations. Tech. rep., U.S. Department of Commerce (Jan 2014). https://doi.org/10.6028/nist.sp.800-162. https://doi.org/10.6028/nist.sp.800-162

26. Hummer, M., Groll, S., Kunz, M., Fuchs, L., Pernul, G.: Measuring identity and access management performance - an expert survey on possible performance indicators. In: Proceedings of the 4th International Conference on Information Systems Security and Privacy, pp. 233–240. SCITEPRESS - Science and Technology Publications (2018). https://doi.org/10.5220/0006557702330240. https://doi.org/10.5220/0006557702330240

27. Hummer, M., Kunz, M., Netter, M., Fuchs, L., Pernul, G.: Adaptive identity and access management - contextual data based policies. EURASIP J. Inf. Secur. 2016(1), August 2016. https://doi.org/10.1186/s13635-016-0043-2. https://doi.org/10.1186/s13635-016-0043-2

28. International Organization for Standardization: Iso/iec 27000:2013 - information technology - security techniques - information security management systems - overview and vocabulary (2013). https://www.iso.org/standard/54534.html. Accessed Apr 10 2023

29. Jaferian, P., Rashtian, H., Beznosov, K.: To authorize or not authorize: helping users review access policies in organizations. In: Proceedings of the Tenth USENIX Conference on Usable Privacy and Security, SOUPS 2014, pp. 301–320. USENIX Association, USA (2014)

30. Kern, S., Baumer, T., Groll, S., Fuchs, L., Pernul, G.: Optimization of access control policies. J. Inf. Secur. Appl. 70, 103301 (2022) https://doi.org/10.1016/j.jisa.2022.103301. https://www.sciencedirect.com/science/article/pii/S2214212622001533

31. Kunz, M., Puchta, A., Groll, S., Fuchs, L., Pernul, G.: Attribute quality management for dynamic identity and access management. J. Inf. Secur. Appl. 44, 64–79 (2019). https://doi.org/10.1016/j.jisa.2018.11.004. https://www.sciencedirect.com/science/article/pii/S2214212618301467

32. Mitra, B., Sural, S., Vaidya, J., Atluri, V.: A survey of role mining. ACM Comput. Surv. (CSUR) 48(4), 1–37 (2016)

33. Molloy, I., et al.: Mining roles with semantic meanings. In: Proceedings of the 13th ACM Symposium on Access Control Models and Technologies, pp. 21–30 (2008)

34. One Hundred Seventh Congress of the United States of America: Sarbanes-oxley act of 2002 (2002). https://www.govinfo.gov/content/pkg/PLAW-107publ204/pdf/PLAW-107publ204.pdf. Accessed 10 Apr 2023

35. Parkinson, S., Khan, S.: A survey on empirical security analysis of access-control systems: a real-world perspective. ACM Comput. Surv. 55(6) (2022). https://doi.org/10.1145/3533703. https://doi.org/10.1145/3533703

36. Puchta, A., Böhm, F., Pernul, G.: Contributing to current challenges in identity and access management with visual analytics. In: Foley, S.N. (ed.) DBSec 2019. LNCS, vol. 11559, pp. 221–239. Springer, Cham (2019). https://doi.org/10.1007/978-3-030-22479-0_12

37. Samarati, P., de Vimercati, S.C.: Access control: policies, models, and mechanisms. In: Focardi, R., Gorrieri, R. (eds.) FOSAD 2000. LNCS, vol. 2171, pp. 137–196. Springer, Heidelberg (2001). https://doi.org/10.1007/3-540-45608-2_3

38. Sandhu, R.S.: Role-based access control. portions of this chapter have been published earlier in sandhu et al. (1996), sandhu (1996), sandhu and bhamidipati (1997), sandhu et al. (1997) and sandhu and feinstein (1994). In: Zelkowitz, M.V. (ed.) Advances in Computers, Advances in Computers, vol. 46, pp. 237–286. Elsevier, online (1998). https://doi.org/10.1016/S0065-2458(08)60206-5. https://www.sciencedirect.com/science/article/pii/S0065245808602065

39. Sandhu, R.S., Samarati, P.: Access control: principle and practice. IEEE Commun. Mag. **32**(9), 40–48 (1994)

40. Servos, D., Osborn, S.L.: Current research and open problems in attribute-based access control. ACM Comput. Surv. **49**(4) (2017). https://doi.org/10.1145/3007204. https://doi.org/10.1145/3007204

41. Smetters, D.K., Good, N.: How users use access control. In: Proceedings of the 5th Symposium on Usable Privacy and Security. SOUPS 2009. Association for Computing Machinery, New York (2009). https://doi.org/10.1145/1572532.1572552. https://doi.org/10.1145/1572532.1572552

42. Strembeck, M.: Scenario-driven role engineering. IEEE Secur. Privacy **8**(1), 28–35 (2010). https://doi.org/10.1109/MSP.2010.46

43. Sun, W., Su, H., Xie, H.: Policy-engineering optimization with visual representation and separation-of-duty constraints in attribute-based access control. Future Internet **12**(10), 164 (2020)

44. Verde, N.V., Vaidya, J., Atluri, V., Colantonio, A.: Role engineering: from theory to practice. In: Proceedings of the Second ACM Conference on Data and Application Security and Privacy, pp. 181–192 (2012)

45. Xia, H., Dawande, M., Mookerjee, V.: Role refinement in access control: model and analysis. INFORMS J. Comput. **26**(4), 866–884 (2014)

46. Xiang, C., et al.: Towards continuous access control validation and forensics. In: Proceedings of the 2019 ACM SIGSAC Conference on Computer and Communications Security, CCS 2019, pp. 113–129. Association for Computing Machinery, New York (2019). https://doi.org/10.1145/3319535.3363191. https://doi.org/10.1145/3319535.3363191

47. Xu, T., Naing, H.M., Lu, L., Zhou, Y.: How do system administrators resolve access-denied issues in the real world? In: Proceedings of the 2017 CHI Conference on Human Factors in Computing Systems, CHI 2017, pp. 348–361. Association for Computing Machinery, New York (2017). https://doi.org/10.1145/3025453.3025999. https://doi.org/10.1145/3025453.3025999

48. Xu, Z., Stoller, S.D.: Mining attribute-based access control policies. IEEE Trans. Dependable Secure Comput. **12**(5), 533–545 (2014)

SMET: Semantic Mapping of CVE to ATT&CK and Its Application to Cybersecurity

Basel Abdeen[1(✉)], Ehab Al-Shaer[2], Anoop Singhal[3], Latifur Khan[1], and Kevin Hamlen[1]

[1] University of Texas at Dallas, Richardson, TX, USA
basel.abdeen@utdallas.edu
[2] Carnegie Mellon University, Pittsburgh, PA, USA
[3] National Institute of Standards and Technology, Gaithersburg, MD, USA

Abstract. Cybercriminals relentlessly pursue vulnerabilities across cyberspace to exploit software, threatening the security of individuals, organizations, and governments. Although security teams strive to establish defense measures to thwart attackers, the complexity of cyber defense and the magnitude of existing threats exceed the capacity of defenders. Therefore, MITRE took the initiative and introduced multiple frameworks to facilitate the sharing of vital knowledge about vulnerabilities, attacks, and defense information. The Common Vulnerabilities and Exposures (CVE) program and ATT&CK Matrix are two significant MITRE endeavors. CVE facilitates the sharing of publicly discovered vulnerabilities, while ATT&CK collects and categorizes adversaries' Tactics, Techniques, and Procedures (TTP) and recommends appropriate countermeasures.

As CVE yields a low-level description of the vulnerability, ATT&CK can complement it by providing more insights into that vulnerability from an attacking perspective, thereby aiding defenders in countering exploitation attempts. Unfortunately, due to the complexity of this mapping and the rapid growth of these frameworks, mapping CVE to ATT&CK is a daunting and time-intensive undertaking. Multiple studies have proposed models that automatically achieve this mapping. However, due to their reliance on annotated datasets, these models exhibit limitations in quality and coverage and fail to justify their decisions. To overcome these challenges, we present SMET—a tool that automatically maps CVE entries to ATT&CK techniques based on their textual similarity. SMET achieves this mapping by leveraging ATT&CK BERT, a model that we trained using the SIAMESE network to learn semantic similarity among attack actions. In inference, SMET utilizes semantic extraction, ATT&CK BERT, and a logistic regression model to map CVE entries to ATT&CK techniques. As a result, SMET has demonstrated superior performance compared to other state-of-the-art models.

ⓒ IFIP International Federation for Information Processing 2023
Published by Springer Nature Switzerland AG 2023
V. Atluri and A. L. Ferrara (Eds.): DBSec 2023, LNCS 13942, pp. 243–260, 2023.
https://doi.org/10.1007/978-3-031-37586-6_15

1   Introduction

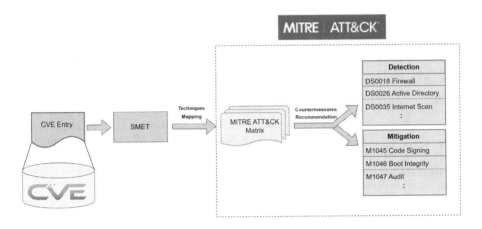

Fig. 1. CVE to ATT&CK mapping importance

The amount, robustness, and impact of cyber attacks have significantly increased in the past few years. The cost of cybercrime was estimated to be around $8.4 trillion globally in 2022, and it is predicted to reach $23.84 trillion annually by 2027 [14]. As organizations and governments strive to combat cybercrime, their efforts are being met with increasingly complex attacks and hindered by the prevalence of software vulnerabilities. A notable example of such an attack is WannaCry, a malware that leveraged a vulnerability in the Windows system to spread globally and cause an estimated financial loss of $4 billion [12].

A vulnerability is a software design or implementation flaw that attackers can exploit to adversely impact confidentiality, integrity, or availability. Efforts have been made to counter vulnerability threat, primarily by identifying vulnerabilities in public software and sharing critical information about them. MITRE has led these efforts and introduced a list of publicly disclosed vulnerabilities known as Common Vulnerabilities and Exposures (CVE). Each entry of CVE consists of a unique ID number and a description of a discovered vulnerability alongside other critical information. Furthermore, the National Institute of Standards and Technology (NIST) introduced the National Vulnerability Database (NVD), which enriches CVE entries with more information, such as an estimation of the vulnerability's severity and classification of the vulnerability type. CVE is leveraged by organizations to monitor newly discovered vulnerabilities and ensure the security of their systems and networks.

In addition to CVE, multiple comprehensive knowledge bases and ontologies have been constructed by various organizations to aid security analysts in understanding and categorizing information regarding attackers' behaviors and objectives. ATT&CK is another knowledge base developed by MITRE that categorizes attack techniques that adversaries have been observed using in the real world. ATT&CK categorizes attack techniques into different tactics, where each tactic represents a goal that the attacker tries to achieve, such as initial access, execution, or defense evasion. A tactic contains multiple techniques that an attacker can each of which includes a textual description of the attacker's behaviors and examples of real-world uses of the technique by known malicious groups and software. Moreover, each technique contains detection and mitigation recommendations to aid security teams in countering the technique. ATT&CK's high-level attack categorization and practical defense recommendation made it a useful resource for security analysts to secure their systems and networks.

As CVE and ATT&CK offer distinct perspectives on threat information, linking them enriches both frameworks and enables defenders to gain more insight into vulnerabilities and leverage information from ATT&CK to set their defense measures accordingly, as shown in Fig. 1. However, achieving this link is a difficult task that requires experts with a thorough understanding of both frameworks. Moreover, as the size of CVE grows daily, manually mapping all of its entries to techniques becomes an infeasible task. Previous studies have tackled this problem and introduced machine learning models that automatically map a CVE entry to an ATT&CK technique [6,16,20,23]. In these studies, researchers utilized an annotated dataset of CVE-ATT&CK mapping and trained a text classification model to classify entries to a limited number of techniques using the entry's description. However, the performance and coverage of these models are constrained by the annotated dataset that they rely on and cannot adapt to the dynamic nature of these frameworks. Moreover, these approaches lack explainability due to the black-box nature of deep learning models.

Unlike previous studies, SMET maps CVE to ATT&CK techniques without relying on any annotated dataset. SMET maps a CVE entry to techniques by first leveraging a semantic role labeling (SRL) model to extract attack vectors from the entry description. Attack vectors are textual descriptions of malicious actions that an attacker can perform. Some examples of attack vectors include "exploit a vulnerability to gain access to a network," "execute code on a victim machine," or "send data to a C2 server." SMET then extracts the embedding of these attack vectors using our developed ATT&CK BERT model. ATT&CK BERT is a transformer model that we fine-tuned using the SIAMESE network over ATT&CK Matrix data. As a result, ATT&CK BERT extracts a semantically meaningful embedding of attack vectors. Thus, extracted embeddings of similar attack vectors are close in the embedding space. Finally, SMET uses a logistic regression model trained using the ATT&CK Matrix to estimate the probability of an attack vector belonging to each ATT&CK technique and rank techniques based on the estimated probability. SMET[1] is publicly available on GitHub.

In this paper, we made the following contribution. First, we studied the relationship between CVE and ATT&CK and identified criteria to map any CVE entry to a corresponding ATT&CK technique. Second, we introduced a dataset that we manually annotated based on our criteria. We only used this dataset for evaluation purposes. Third, we developed SMET, a tool that maps any CVE entry to ATT&CK techniques. This paper is organized as follows.

---

[1] https://github.com/basel-a/SMET.git.

Section 2 presents the motivation and the problem statement. Section 3 presents previous related work. Section 4 introduces SMET. Section 5 evaluates SMET. Section 6 contains the conclusion and future work.

Mitigations

ID	Mitigation	Description
M1048	Application Isolation and Sandboxing	Application isolation will limit what other processes and system features the exploited target can access.
M1050	Exploit Protection	Web Application Firewalls may be used to limit exposure of applications to prevent exploit traffic from reaching the application.
M1030	Network Segmentation	Segment externally facing servers and services from the rest of the network with a DMZ or on separate hosting infrastructure
M1026	Privileged Account Management	Use least privilege for service accounts will limit what permissions the exploited process gets on the rest of the system.
M1051	Update Software	Update software regularly by employing patch management for externally exposed applications.
M1016	Vulnerability Scanning	Regularly scan externally facing systems for vulnerabilities and establish procedures to rapidly patch systems when critical vulnerabilities are discovered through scanning and through public disclosure.

Fig. 2. The exploitation for privilege escalation technique mitigation from ATT&CK

2   Motivation and Problem Statement

2.1   Motivation

Whenever a CVE entry for publicly used software is published, security analysts in organizations must be alerted and take appropriate measures to ensure the security of their system against the newly discovered vulnerability. Although the best defense against a vulnerability is applying its patch, patches take time to implement, during which, the software remains vulnerable, threatening organizations' systems and networks. Moreover, some vulnerabilities are never patched due to cost and complexity. Therefore, security analysts must take other measures to counter the vulnerability. Here is when ATT&CK proves helpful. When a vulnerability is linked to an ATT&CK technique, it can be studied from an attacker's perspective, as ATT&CK sheds insight into how an attacker can exploit the vulnerability, what an attacker can gain from the exploitation, and what mitigation and detection measures can be taken to counter the attacks. An example of mitigation measures recommended by ATT&CK to mitigate the exploitation for privilege escalation technique is shown in Fig. 2.

Previous studies have proposed models that automatically map a CVE to an ATT&CK. In these approaches, experts first annotate a dataset by manually mapping a number of CVE entries to ATT&CK techniques. They then train a supervised machine learning model to link entries to techniques using the annotated data. The process of annotation is both time-consuming and labor-intensive, which leads to datasets that have limited quality and coverage. Consequently, models trained on such datasets suffer from performance limitations and are unable to accommodate the dynamic nature of both CVE and ATT&CK. In contrast, in this paper, we tackle the problem of mapping a CVE entry to an ATT&CK technique in an unsupervised manner by leveraging the textual description similarity between a CVE entry and an ATT&CK technique.

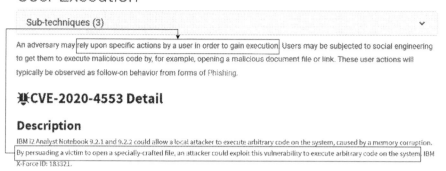

Fig. 3. Text similarity between the user execution technique description and a CV-2020-4553 description

2.2 Problem Statement

Our proposed approach achieves unsupervised mapping by leveraging text similarities between CVE and the descriptions of techniques. An example of similar text can be seen in Fig. 3, where a CVE-2020-4553 description states that an attacker can exploit it by persuading the victim to open a crafted file. This attack behavior is represented in the user execution technique from ATT&CK. Identifying sentences' semantic similarities is a challenging and active area of research. Although researchers have introduced several deep learning models to extract sentence similarity, no research has investigated sentence similarity in the cybersecurity domain. The complexity of text similarity in cybersecurity stems from the lack of annotated data and the semantic gap between low-level and high-level attack vectors. For example, the sentence "An attacker runs a script in a machine" is semantically similar to "A malicious actor executes code on a system," as they represent a similar objective. However, the two sentences have no words in common. On the other hand, the two sentences "An attacker reads a file" and "An attacker deletes a file" share almost all words but are semantically different, as each attack vector corresponds to different attack objectives. Table 1 shows examples of semantically similar attack vectors.

2.3 CVE-ATT&CK Association Analysis

The description of an ATT&CK technique contains several attack vectors that the attacker performs to achieve the technique. These attack vectors can range from low-level behaviors, such as "create file" or "read registry," to high-level behaviors, such as "compromise system" or "steal information." Each ATT&CK technique consists of mainly two attack vectors: an action that an attacker takes and the objective of that action. For example, in the exploitation for client execution technique, an attacker exploits software vulnerability in client applications (action) to execute code (objective). Actions are usually lower-level attack vectors, while objectives are higher-level attack goals and can represent the tactic

Table 1. Semantically Similar Attack Vectors

Similar Attack Vectors
<Execute code, Run a script in the system >
<Read file, Retrieve the content of a file>
<Disable security tools, Delete Antivirus files >
<Identify the OS version, Collect system information >
<Crash the system, Cause machine termination >
<Take a screenshot, Capture the desktop screen >

of the attack. The action and objective can be identified for all techniques from the first sentence in the technique description.

ATT&CK techniques cover all stages of an attack life cycle, from reconnaissance and initial access to the compromising of confidentiality, integrity, and availability. Therefore, techniques can be linked to a CVE entry through various means. We investigated the CVE-ATT&CK association and identified two types of techniques for classifying a CVE entry that are inspired by [9]. First, a CVE entry can be mapped to techniques that describe an exploitation method, more specifically, a technique that an attacker needs to perform to exploit a vulnerability, such as exploiting a web browser vulnerability or tricking a user into performing an action. Second, CVEs can be mapped to techniques that describe the consequences of exploiting a vulnerability or the objectives that an attacker can accomplish after exploiting the vulnerability, such as code execution, privilege escalation, or data manipulation. In other words, one technique enables an attacker to exploit a vulnerability, and a vulnerability enables an attacker to achieve other techniques. We refer to these techniques as pre-exploit and post-exploit techniques, respectively.

We studied various ATT&CK techniques and identified techniques that correspond to each mapping type. Pre-exploit techniques are mostly part of the initial access tactic, such as drive-by compromise, exploit public-facing applications, user execution, and valid accounts. In the drive-by compromise technique, an attacker uses websites to exploit a vulnerability in users' web browsers. In the exploit public-facing application technique, an attacker exploits a website or any public-facing application, such as databases or standard services that use crafted input. In the user execution technique, the attacker depends on an action by the user to exploit a vulnerability. Finally, in the valid accounts technique, an attacker needs to compromise an account first in order to exploit the vulnerability.

Post-exploit techniques can be part of any tactic. The execution, privilege escalation, and credential access tactics all involve a technique of an adversary exploiting a vulnerability to achieve the tactic. The techniques are: exploitation for client execution, exploitation for privilege escalation, and privilege escalation for credential access, respectively. In addition, the lateral movement tactic contains a technique—exploitation of remote services—where an attacker exploits a vulnerability in remote services to gain access to systems. Moreover, the impact tactic contains various techniques where an attacker aims to compromise the system or data's availability or integrity. One example is the application or system exploitation sub-technique, which describes the attack technique where an attacker exploits a vulnerability to compromise availability. CVE can also be mapped to other techniques that are not limited to vulnerability exploitation but describe the attacker's goals, such as data manipulation or system shutdown/reboot. In conclusion, the ATT&CK framework contains various techniques related to CVE. Some techniques focus specifically on vulnerability exploitation, while other general techniques can be achieved after exploitation.

3   Related Work

Since the ATT&CK Matrix became a vital resource for security analysts to understand and counter cyber threats, researchers have proposed multiple algorithms to automatically map various cyber information resources to ATT&CK techniques. For example, multiple studies have proposed models to map Cyber Threat Intelligence (CTI) reports to ATT&CK techniques [8,18,21,22]. Other studies have proposed models to map CVE entries to ATT&CK techniques [6,16,20,23]. Moreover, researchers have proposed models to map malware behavior, Linux shell commands, and threat data from smart grid systems to ATT&CK [7,19,25]. Other studies have focused on enriching CVE by automatically mapping it to the Common Weaknesses Enumeration (CWE) or Common Attack Pattern Enumeration and Classification (CAPEC) frameworks [5,10]. Researchers have also proposed domain-specific language models for cybersecurity that can be applied to a wide range of downstream tasks [2,4].

In one study, researchers studied the performance of various traditional machine learning models (e.g., Naive Bayes and SVC) and advanced deep learning models (e.g., CNN, BERT, SciBERT, and SecBERT) in linking CVE entries to the ATT&CK matrix using supervised learning [16]. They also studied the impact of data augmentation methods that help enrich the training set. They used the dataset introduced by MITRE Engenuity [13] for training and testing and enriched it with their own labeled data. In their evaluation, they only considered mapping to 31 ATT&CK techniques.

In another study, researchers proposed a neural network architecture—Multi-Head Joint Embedding Neural Network—that automatically maps CVE to ATT&CK techniques [20]. To create a training dataset, they introduced an unsupervised labeling technique with which they extracted CVE information from publicly available threat reports. Their labeling technique was able to map CVE entries to 17 ATT&CK techniques. Moreover, researchers have proposed CVET, a transformer-based model that has mapped CVE entries to 10 ATT&CK tactics [6]. CVET was trained using the self-knowledge distillation approach over the BRON dataset [17].

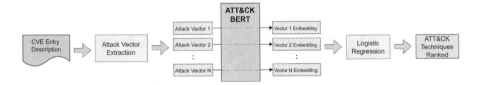

Fig. 4. SMET overview

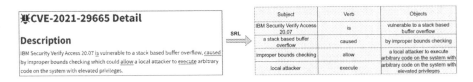

Fig. 5. Semantic role labeling (SRL) example

The aforementioned proposed models map CVE to a limited number of ATT&CK techniques due to their reliance on a manually annotated dataset. However, in a CTI mapping research, researchers introduced a tool—AttacKG—that maps CTI reports to all ATT&CK techniques [22]. AttacKG converts CTI reports and ATT&CK techniques into structured attack behavior graphs and maps reports by aligning their graphs to the techniques' template graphs. In the alignment phase, AttacKG uses character-level similarity to align nodes instead of semantic similarity. Unfortunately, character-level similarity is limited and cannot align text with similar meanings but different wording.

4   Approach

4.1   SMET Overview

SMET consists of three components: an attack vector extraction component, an attack vector representation model (ATT&CK BERT), and a logistic regression model. First, we used a semantic role labeling (SRL) model to extract attack vectors from a CVE entry description. The CVE entry description contains attack vectors alongside other vulnerability details that are irrelevant to our task. Therefore, we designed a few rules using SRL to identify attack vectors while discarding irrelevant information. Second, we proposed an attack vector embedding model—ATT&CK BERT—that extracts a semantic vector representation of attack vectors. Using ATT&CK BERT extraction, the extracted embedding of similar attack vectors are close in the embedding space. Thus, they have a high cosine similarity, while unrelated attack vectors have a low cosine similarity. Third, we used a logistic regression model to estimate the probability of CVE belonging to techniques and ranked all techniques by the estimated probability. Figure 4 shows an overview of the SMET architecture.

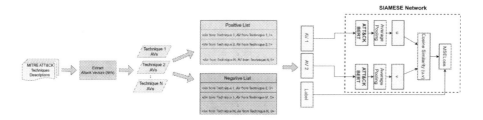

Fig. 6. ATT&CK BERT fine-tuning

4.2   Attack Vector Extraction

A CVE entry textual description contains different types of information regarding the CVE, including software name, affected versions, vulnerability type, vulnerability description, actions that an attacker can take to exploit the vulnerability, and objectives that an attacker can gain from the exploitation. Unfortunately, CVE entries do not follow a predefined structure, and not all of the information mentioned above exists for all CVE entries. Therefore, the attack vector extraction component aims to automatically identify attack vectors from the CVE description. To achieve this extraction, we leveraged an Allenlp SRL model, a state-of-the-art semantic extraction model that extracts semantic frames from unstructured text [15]. A semantic frame consists of a verb linked to its neighboring words/phrases that are tagged by their semantic relationship to the verb, such as a subject, patient, location, manner, or purpose. Figure 5 shows an example of semantic frames extracted from the CVE-2021-27032 description. For simplicity, we combined all roles other than subject and verb and assigned them an "objects" tag in the table.

Semantic frames can represent various types of information. For example, the first semantic frame in Fig. 5 represents an attribute of the software using the verb "is," while the second semantic frame represents a causal relationship between "buffer overflow" (subject) and "improper bound checking" (objects) using the verb "caused." The last semantic frame represents an attack vector identified by the subject "local attacker." SMET considers a semantic frame to be an attack vector if one of these conditions is met. First, the words attacker, adversary, vulnerability, or user exist in the subject, as these subjects indicate that the frame contains an action that an attacker can do. Second, the verb is either allow, lead, or result. Our CVE analysis shows that these verbs precede an attack vector even if the subject is not an attacker. An example can be shown in the third semantic frame, where the verb is "allow," and the object is an attack vector.

4.3   ATT&CK BERT

Semantic similarity between sentences is a multifaceted concept that requires a clear definition based on the research goals at hand. In our study, we observed

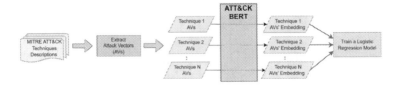

Fig. 7. Logistic regression training

that attack vectors can exhibit similarities in various aspects. For example, "create a file" and "create a registry key" are similar in the sense that both represent adding a storage unit in the system, while "create a file" and "delete a file" are similar in the sense that both apply an action to a file. Other dimensions of similarity can encompass the location of attack vectors (e.g., system or network) or privileges needed (e.g., administrator or user). Since we aim to map attack vectors to ATT&CK techniques, we consider two attack vectors similar only if they share the same objective and help achieve the same technique. For example, the three attack vectors "delete system file," "delete anti-virus file," and "delete log files" are different, although they all represent deleting a file from the system. "Delete system file "aims to interrupt the availability of the system; "delete anti-virus file" aims to disable defensive mechanisms; and "delete log files" aims to cover attack actions.

To extract semantic embedding, we propose ATT&CK BERT. ATT&CK BERT is a transformer model that aims to represent attack vectors in a semantically meaningful embedding where the embedding of attack vectors with similar meanings are close in the embedding space and thus, have high cosine similarity. Text embedding has been an active research challenge for a long time. The evolution of the transformer model, researchers have introduced multiple transformer-based sentence embedding models. One of the best-performing recent models is Sentence BERT (SBERT) [24]. SBERT introduced a method to train the BERT model using SIAMESE network architecture by taking two sentences as input, extracting each sentence embedding using BERT, and then optimizing the network weights to maximize the similarity of the two embeddings if the sentences are semantically similar and minimize it otherwise.

Since the original SBERT is trained on a general entitlement dataset, its performance on cybersecurity text is limited. However, preparing a dataset of pairs of sentences that cover all attack life cycle information and annotating them is an infeasible task. To overcome this challenge, we propose an approach to fine-tune SBERT using the ATT&CK framework as follows. First, we extract all attack vectors from each ATT&CK technique description and procedure examples using the Allenlp SRL model. Second, we create two lists that we denote as positive and negative lists. The positive list contains pairs of attack vectors that are extracted from the same technique, while the negative list contains pairs of attack vectors where each is extracted from a different technique. Finally, we train SBERT to maximize the cosine similarity between pairs from the positive

Fig. 8. SMET ATT&CK mapping

list and minimize the cosine similarity between pairs from the negative list. This approach is shown in Fig. 6.

Specifically, the dataset was prepared as follows. From each technique, we extracted all attack vectors and combined each two extracted attack vectors in a list of pairs. We randomly selected 40 pairs from the list if the list size was more than 40. All selected pairs from all techniques were combined in the positive list. For each technique, we paired its attack vectors with at most six attack vectors from each other technique. We randomly sampled 160 pairs from the resulting pairings and added them to the negative list. This resulted in 38,396 pairs—7,356 positives and 31,040 negatives. We fine-tuned the pre-trained all-mpnet-base-v2 model using our dataset. We used the Adam optimizer with a 2e−05 learning rate and fine-tuned the model for one epoch.

4.4   ATT&CK Mapping

Leveraging ATT&CK BERT, we trained a logistic regression model as follows. First, we collected all attack vectors from each technique and labeled each attack vector by its corresponding technique. We then used ATT&CK BERT to extract all attack vectors' embedding and trained a multinomial logistic regression model using this training set. This training approach is shown in Fig. 7. We used logistic regression instead of a more complex model to avoid overfitting due to our dataset's high number of classes (185 techniques) and the small number of samples per class (52 median). Moreover, we used the class weights mechanism, where weights are adjusted inversely proportional to class frequencies during training to overcome the class imbalance.

When mapping a CVE entry to techniques, SMET runs the trained logistic regression model over each attack vector extracted from the entry and the entire entry description. Each run will return a probability score for each technique, representing how likely the attack vector belongs to the corresponding technique. SMET then combines all results by setting the probability score of each technique to the maximum score across all attack vectors. For example, if a CVE has two attack vectors, AV1 and AV2, we would run logistic regression three times—one time over each attack vector and a third over the entire entry text. For example, assume a technique T with probability scores of 0.2, 0.3, and .01 for AV1, AV2, and full description, respectively. SMET sets the probability score of T to 0.3. SMET does the same for all techniques and then ranks them based on the final probability scores.

Table 2. SMET and baselines' results

Model	Coverage Error	Ranking Loss	LRAP	R@5
SMET(our)	**13.96**	**0.05**	**53.77%**	**67.71%**
SBERT	32.66	0.126	24.58%	31.05%
TF-IDF	32.28	0.12	23.71%	30.90%
LLM chatbot	129.00	0.605	20.97%	33.60%

As ATT&CK BERT extracts semantic embedding of attack vectors, SMET explains its mapping by identifying the most similar attack vectors from the mapped technique's description or procedure examples. This explanation helps security analysts understand SMET's decision and gain insight into its mapping criteria. Figure 8 shows an example of SMET's mapping of CVE-2021-27032. The middle step presents a list of attack vectors extracted by SMET, and the last step shows SMET's two highest ranked techniques and the most similar attack vector from each technique to the CVE.

5   Evaluation

5.1   Dataset

To evaluate SMET, we collected 1,813 CVE entries published from 2014 to 2022 and gathered by existing research [9,16]. We annotated the entries by mapping each entry to appropriate ATT&CK techniques. To ensure an accurate and justifiable mapping, we divide the mapping into two tasks. First, we identified attack vectors from the entry description. Second, we identified the most similar attack vector from ATT&CK for each extracted attack vector and mapped the entry to the corresponding technique. Each attack vector in an entry can be mapped to different techniques, so an entry can also be mapped to multiple techniques. Figure 3 shows an example of mapping CVE-2020-4553 to the user execution technique.

We mapped 303 CVE entries to 41 techniques from ATT&CK Matrix version 12.0. Figure 9 shows the number of CVE entries mapped to each technique. For example, the exploitation for the client execution technique had the most entries mapped to it, as many CVE entries in our dataset allow an attacker to execute code. Moreover, the four techniques with the most entry mappings all focus on vulnerability exploitation, whereas other techniques are more general.

5.2   Results

When evaluating a ranking model, we aim to rank the ground truth labels as low as possible. We evaluated SMET ranking using four multi-label ranking metrics: coverage error, label ranking loss, label ranking average precision (LRAP), and recall@k. LRAP calculates what percentage of the higher-ranked labels are true

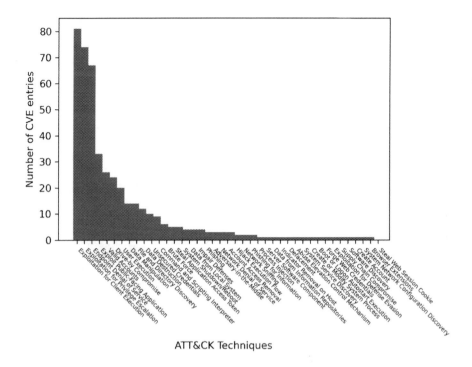

Fig. 9. Histogram of Ground Truth Techniques

labels. LRAP values range from 0 to 1, excluding 0, and the best LRAP value is 1. Coverage error represents the average number of top-scored predictions required so that the predictions include all ground truth labels. The best coverage error value equals the average number of labels. Label ranking loss represents the average number of incorrectly ordered label pairs with respect to the number of correctly ordered labels. Label ranking loss's best value is 0. recall@K calculates the proportion of ground truth labels found in the top-k predictions. We set k to 5 to correspond with the top 2.55% of the predicted labels (185 techniques).

Below are the formulas of the first three metrics as defined by the scikit-learn python library [1], where $y \in \{0,1\}^{n_{\text{samples}} \times n_{\text{labels}}}$ is the ground truth labels and $\hat{f}$ is the score associated with each class.

$$\text{LRAP}(y, \hat{f}) = \frac{1}{n_{\text{samples}}} \sum_{i=0}^{n_{\text{samples}}-1} \frac{1}{\|y_i\|_0} \sum_{j:y_{ij}=1} \frac{|\mathcal{L}_{ij}|}{\text{rank}_{ij}}$$

$$\mathcal{L}_{ij} = \left\{ k : y_{ik} = 1, \hat{f}_{ik} \geq \hat{f}_{ij} \right\}, \text{rank}_{ij} = \left| \left\{ k : \hat{f}_{ik} \geq \hat{f}_{ij} \right\} \right|$$

$$\text{ranking\_loss}(y, \hat{f}) = \frac{1}{n_{\text{samples}}} \sum_{i=0}^{n_{\text{samples}}-1} \frac{1}{\|y_i\|_0 (n_{\text{labels}} - \|y_i\|_0)}.$$

$$\left| \left\{ (k, l) : \hat{f}_{ik} \leq \hat{f}_{il}, y_{ik} = 1, y_{il} = 0 \right\} \right|$$

$$\text{coverage}(y, \hat{f}) = \frac{1}{n_{\text{samples}}} \sum_{i=0}^{n_{\text{samples}} - 1} \max_{j:y_{ij}=1} \text{rank}_{ij}$$

We first compared SMET performance to the following two unsupervised text similarity models: SBERT, and TF-IDF. SBERT is a sentence embedding model introduced by [24], where they used the SIAMESE network to train transformer models on natural language inference datasets. In our experiments, we used the pre-trained all-mpnet-base-v2 model, which was trained on over 1 billion training pairs and designed for general-purpose text similarity. The all-mpnet-base-v2 model achieves the highest average score on over 20 NLP datasets [3].

TF-IDF is a traditional information retrieval model that computes the similarity of documents based on a statistical analysis of word distribution across documents. TF-IDF's robustness and simplicity make it the first go-to method in text similarity tasks.

In each case, we extracted the embeddings of ATT&CK technique descriptions and CVE entries and then ranked all techniques based on their cosine similarity to the entry. As shown in Table 2, our tool greatly outperforms all baselines in all metrics. We attribute the superior performance of SMET to three main reasons. First, instead of using the entries and technique descriptions for mapping, SMET uses attack vectors as a key feature, which reduces noise by eliminating irrelevant information. Second, SMET uses ATT&CK BERT, which we fine-tuned using the ATT&CK matrix and can thus extract embedding that better represents attack vectors. Third, instead of cosine similarity, SMET uses a logistic regression model that we trained to predict attack vectors' techniques.

LLM Chatbots. Recently, large language models (LLMs) chatbots have been used to solve various NLP tasks. These chatbots have knowledge of the web and can answer complicated questions regarding various topics without any fine-tuning. We studied the performance of one of the most popular chatbots in mapping CVE to ATT&CK by providing it with a CVE entry description and asking it to map that description to techniques. Due to government policy, we are unable to reveal the name of the chatbot. We conducted three experiments by providing the chatbot with the following three prompts:

1. Please identify MITRE ATT&CK techniques that can be associated with the CVE description below: "cve_des". Please return a list of identified ATT&CK techniques IDs.
2. Please identify what MITRE ATT&CK techniques an attacker can perform using the CVE description below: "cve_des". Please return a list of identified ATT&CK techniques IDs.
3. Please identify MITRE ATT&CK techniques that are mentioned in the CVE description below: "cve_des". Please return a list of identified ATT&CK techniques IDs.

We used regular expressions to extract technique IDs from each response.

Table 3. SMET components analysis

Modification	Model	Coverage Error	Ranking Loss	LRAP	R@5
–	SMET	**13.96**	**0.05**	**53.77%**	**67.71%**
Extraction Component	LLM chatbot	15.24	0.55	48.59%	61.61%
Embedding Model	MPNET	15.84	0.058	46.93%	61.36%
	SecBERT	29.51	0.115	34.22%	44.31%
	$BERT_{Base}$	30.38	0.117	33.31%	43.41%

Although the chatbot showed a basic understanding of ATT&CK, its mapping performance was inferior. Although the prompts were semantically similar, the chatbot showed inconsistent behavior and responded with a different set of techniques for each prompt. For example, the number of techniques the chatbot extracted across all responses were 976, 993, and 486 techniques for the first, second, and third prompts, respectively. In only six instances, all three prompts provided the same techniques, and in 41 instances, the three prompts agreed on at least one technique.

To compare the chatbot to SMET, we combined the prediction of the three prompts by making each prompt vote for its predicted techniques and ranked the techniques based on the number of votes. Techniques with the same number of votes were ranked randomly. We presented the results in Table 2. The chatbot performance was inferior in all metrics except R@5, where it performed slightly better than the TF-IDF and SBERT models. We attribute these results to the fact that the chatbot is not a ranking model. Even though we ranked techniques based on prompt voting, most techniques had no votes and were ranked randomly. However, R@5 is a classification metric that gives a more accurate indication of the chatbot's performance.

5.3 SMET Component Analysis

We investigated the performance of SMET after replacing its components with other existing alternatives from the literature. In the first experiment, we replaced the attack vector extraction model with a LLM chatbot by using the following prompt: "Please identify actions that can be done by an attacker from the following description inclusively: "cve_des." Return each action along with all its objects in a line with the format subject—verb—objects." We then used a regular expression to extract the attack vectors from the chatbot's responses. In the second experiment, we replaced ATT&CK BERT with different transformer models introduced by researchers. We used $BERT_{Base}$, which was introduced by the original BERT paper [11]. Moreover, we used the sentence transformer model all-mpnet-base-v2, which was trained on over 1 billion training pairs to achieve meaningful semantic embedding. Lastly, we used SecBERT, a domain-specific transformer model trained over cybersecurity data, such as CTI reports, articles, and databases [2].

As shown in Table 3, SMET achieved the highest score across all metrics. On average, $BERT_{Base}$ exhibited the weakest performance, as BERT is not a domain-specific model, and its embedding is not semantically meaningful. Although SecBERT is a domain-specific model, its performance was comparable to BERT's, as its embedding is not semantically meaningful either. MPNET (all-mpnet-base-v2) achieved a higher performance as it was trained on a text similarity task. Thus, its embedding is semantically meaningful. Finally, SMET achieved the highest performance as it uses ATT&CK BERT, which was trained on cybersecurity data (ATT&CK Matrix), and its embedding is semantically meaningful.

When we used the LLM chatbot for extraction, the performance of SMET decreased. As discussed in the previous section, the chatbot output is inconsistent and sensitive to prompts. Moreover, unlike SRL models, the chatbot responds with unstructured text, which requires further processing using regular expressions to extract attack vectors. This unstructured response introduces noise that might affect the quality of extracted attack vectors. More investigation needs to be conducted to study the possibility of using LLM chatbots to accurately extract attack vectors from unstructured text. We leave this challenge for future work.

6   Conclusion and Future Work

In this paper, we introduced SMET—a tool that automatically maps CVE to ATT&CK to assist security analysts in understanding vulnerabilities and gaining more insight into appropriate countermeasures. SMET utilizes a semantic extraction model to identify information regarding attack actions from CVE and ATT&CK descriptions and leverages ATT&CK BERT, a model that we propose to extract semantically meaningful embedding of unstructured attack description text. We evaluated SMET using a ground truth that we manually created based on our analysis of the CVE-ATT&CK association. SMET achieved a robust performance compared to existing state-of-the-art models. Moreover, we studied the importance of SMET's components by replacing them with existing alternatives from the literature. Although this paper focused on CVE mapping, SMET has the potential to be applied to other forms of cybersecurity resources (e.g., CTI reports, data breach reports, cybersecurity articles and news). Mapping these sources to ATT&CK can also be very helpful to security analysis in understanding current attack trends and applicable countermeasures. We leave this challenge to future work due to the complexity of processing such unstructured documents and the need for additional robust components to achieve accurate mapping.

Disclaimer. Certain equipment, instruments, software, or materials are identified in this paper in order to specify the experimental procedure adequately. Such identification is not intended to imply recommendation or endorsement of any product or service by NIST, nor is it intended to imply that the materials or equipment identified are necessarily the best available for the purpose.

References

1. 3.3. metrics and scoring: Quantifying the quality of predictions. https://scikit-learn.org/stable/modules/model_evaluation.html#multilabel-ranking-metrics
2. Jackaduma/secbert · hugging face. https://huggingface.co/jackaduma/SecBERT
3. Pretrained models. https://www.sbert.net/docs/pretrained_models.html
4. Aghaei, E., Niu, X., Shadid, W., Al-Shaer, E.: SecureBERT: a domain-specific language model for cybersecurity. In: Li, F., Liang, K., Lin, Z., Katsikas, S.K. (eds.) SecureComm 2022. LNICS, SITE, vol. 462, pp. 39–56. Springer, Cham (2023). https://doi.org/10.1007/978-3-031-25538-0_3
5. Aghaei, E., Shadid, W., Al-Shaer, E.: ThreatZoom: hierarchical neural network for CVEs to CWEs classification. In: Park, N., Sun, K., Foresti, S., Butler, K., Saxena, N. (eds.) SecureComm 2020. LNICSSITE, vol. 335, pp. 23–41. Springer, Cham (2020). https://doi.org/10.1007/978-3-030-63086-7_2
6. Ampel, B., Samtani, S., Ullman, S., Chen, H.: Linking common vulnerabilities and exposures to the Mitre ATT&CK framework: a self-distillation approach. arXiv preprint arXiv:2108.01696 (2021)
7. Andrew, Y., Lim, C., Budiarto, E.: Mapping Linux shell commands to Mitre ATT&CK using NLP-based approach. In: 2022 International Conference on Electrical Engineering and Informatics (ICELTICs), pp. 37–42. IEEE (2022)
8. Ayoade, G., Chandra, S., Khan, L., Hamlen, K., Thuraisingham, B.: Automated threat report classification over multi-source data. In: 2018 IEEE 4th International Conference on Collaboration and Internet Computing (CIC), pp. 236–245. IEEE (2018)
9. Center-for-Threat-Informed-Defense: Center-for-threat-informed-defense/attack_to_cve: A methodology for mapping Mitre ATT&CK techniques to vulnerability records to describe the impact of a vulnerability. https://github.com/center-for-threat-informed-defense/attack_to_cve
10. Das, S.S., Halappanavar, M., Tumeo, A., Serra, E., Pothen, A., Al-Shaer, E.: VWC-BERT: scaling vulnerability-weakness-exploit mapping on modern ai accelerators. In: 2022 IEEE International Conference on Big Data (Big Data), pp. 1224–1229. IEEE (2022)
11. Devlin, J., Chang, M.W., Lee, K., Toutanova, K.: BERT: pre-training of deep bidirectional transformers for language understanding. arXiv preprint arXiv:1810.04805 (2018)
12. Editor, C.C., Cooper, C., Editor, C., the AuthorCharles CooperConsulting EditorCharles Cooper has covered technology, A., business for more than 25 years. He is now assisting Symantec with our blog writing, managing our editorial team., Author, A.T.: Wannacry: Lessons learned 1 year later. https://symantec-enterprise-blogs.security.com/blogs/feature-stories/wannacry-lessons-learned-1-year-later
13. Engenuity, M.: MAPPING ATT&CK to CVE: Threat-informed defense project, January 2023. https://mitre-engenuity.org/blog/2021/10/21/mapping-attck-to-cve-for-impact/
14. Fleck, A., Richter, F.: Infographic: cybercrime expected to skyrocket in coming years, December 2022. https://www.statista.com/chart/28878/expected-cost-of-cybercrime-until-2027/
15. Gardner, M., et al.: AllenNLP: a deep semantic natural language processing platform (2017)

16. Grigorescu, O., Nica, A., Dascalu, M., Rughinis, R.: CVE2ATT&CK: BERT-based mapping of CVEs to Mitre ATT&CK techniques. Algorithms **15**(9), 314 (2022)
17. Hemberg, E., et al.: Linking threat tactics, techniques, and patterns with defensive weaknesses, vulnerabilities and affected platform configurations for cyber hunting. arXiv preprint arXiv:2010.00533 (2020)
18. Husari, G., Al-Shaer, E., Ahmed, M., Chu, B., Niu, X.: Ttpdrill: automatic and accurate extraction of threat actions from unstructured text of CTI sources. In: Proceedings of the 33rd Annual Computer Security Applications Conference, pp. 103–115 (2017)
19. Izzuddin, A.B., Lim, C.: Mapping threats in smart grid system using the Mitre ATT&CK ICS framework. In: 2022 IEEE International Conference on Aerospace Electronics and Remote Sensing Technology (ICARES), pp. 1–7. IEEE (2022)
20. Kuppa, A., Aouad, L., Le-Khac, N.A.: Linking CVE's to Mitre ATT&CK techniques. In: Proceedings of the 16th International Conference on Availability, Reliability and Security, pp. 1–12 (2021)
21. Legoy, V., Caselli, M., Seifert, C., Peter, A.: Automated retrieval of ATT&CK tactics and techniques for cyber threat reports. arXiv preprint arXiv:2004.14322 (2020)
22. Li, Z., Zeng, J., Chen, Y., Liang, Z.: ATTACKG: constructing technique knowledge graph from cyber threat intelligence reports. In: Atluri, V., Di Pietro, R., Jensen, C.D., Meng, W. (eds.) ESORICS 2022. LNCS, vol. 13554, pp. 589–609. Springer, Cham (2022). https://doi.org/10.1007/978-3-031-17140-6_29
23. Mendsaikhan, O., Hasegawa, H., Yamaguchi, Y., Shimada, H.: Automatic mapping of vulnerability information to adversary techniques. In: The Fourteenth International Conference on Emerging Security Information, Systems and Technologies SECUREWARE2020 (2020)
24. Reimers, N., Gurevych, I.: Sentence-BERT: sentence embeddings using Siamese BERT-networks. arXiv preprint arXiv:1908.10084 (2019)
25. Sajid, M.S.I., Wei, J., Abdeen, B., Al-Shaer, E., Islam, M.M., Diong, W., Khan, L.: Soda: a system for cyber deception orchestration and automation. In: Annual Computer Security Applications Conference, pp. 675–689 (2021)

Machine Learning

Classification Auto-Encoder Based Detector Against Diverse Data Poisoning Attacks

Fereshteh Razmi⬤ and Li Xiong$^{(\boxtimes)}$⬤

Emory University, Atlanta, GA 30322, USA
{frazmim,lxiong}@emory.edu

Abstract. Poisoning attacks are a category of adversarial machine learning threats in which an adversary attempts to subvert the outcome of the machine learning systems by injecting crafted data into training data set, thus increasing the resulting model's test error. The adversary can tamper with the data feature space, data labels, or both, each leading to a different attack strategy with different strengths. Various detection approaches have recently emerged, each focusing on one attack strategy. The Achilles heel of many of these detection approaches is their dependence on having access to a clean, untampered data set. In this paper, we propose CAE, a Classification Auto-Encoder based detector against diverse poisoned data. CAE can detect all forms of poisoning attacks using a combination of reconstruction and classification errors without having any prior knowledge of the attack strategy. We show that an enhanced version of CAE (called CAE+) does not have to rely on a clean data set to train the defense model. The experimental results on three real datasets (MNIST, Fashion-MNIST and CIFAR-10) demonstrate that our defense model can be trained using contaminated data with up to 30% poisoned data and provides a significantly stronger defense than existing outlier detection methods. The code is available at https://.github.com/Emory-AIMS/CAE

Keywords: Data Poisoning · Anomaly Detection · Autoencoder

1 Introduction

Poisoning attacks are attacks at *training time* [6] in which an attacker manipulates a small fraction of the training data in order to corrupt the model. Consequently, the model may learn a significantly different decision boundary, resulting in drastic test error. Poisoning attacks are acquiring increasing importance in emerging crowd-based systems that collect data from outside sources [12,13,37]. In crowd-sourcing platforms, the attacker can cause massive damages without having a direct access to the system, but rather by poisoning the collected data from her. A few examples are autonomous driving cars, health systems, online

This work was funded by National Science Foundation (NSF) CNS-2124104.

© IFIP International Federation for Information Processing 2023
Published by Springer Nature Switzerland AG 2023

V. Atluri and A. L. Ferrara (Eds.): DBSec 2023, LNCS 13942, pp. 263–281, 2023.
https://doi.org/10.1007/978-3-031-37586-6_16

review systems, and malware/spam detection systems. Also, recently poisoning attacks have been widespread in federated learning systems [32,33,36].

The most recognized poisoning attacks are *label flipping* and *optimal attacks* [7,41]. In these types of attacks, according to the attacker's goal and his accessibility to the data, he may change the labels of some training samples or distort the feature space of the samples, usually in an optimal way to diverge the training from its regular path. Another class of poisoning attacks is backdoor attacks in which the attacker only targets a group of test data that include a specific backdoor trigger [8,16]. Backdoor attacks are not explored in this paper, but they can be considered as future work.

Several defense methods have been recently developed to address flipping or optimal poisoning attacks. Most of them consider poisoned points as outliers and utilize outlier detection techniques. They can be based on k-Nearest Neighbor (kNN) algorithms that consider a point with contrasting label with nearby samples as a poison [30]. They can determine whether a point is poisoned by comparing its distance to a nearby point or other data points in its cluster [22,29]. However, they have several limitations. First, they may only work for a particular type of attacks (optimal or flipping) as the detection is based on the change of either labels or features. Second, they rely on purely clean data to learn the patterns of normal points. Training on tainted data is plausible only when the fraction of the anomalous data is negligible. Also they usually rely on a threshold to determine an outlier.

A potential solution for outlier detection that has not been explored for data poisoning attacks is auto-encoder based method [4,38] which learns the data representation in an unsupervised way. It has been utilized for generating poisoning attacks [10,14,45], anomaly detection [31,49], and adversarial example detection [26]. While promising, utilizing auto-encoders for detecting poisoned points under poisoning attacks present several challenges. First, existing methods train auto-encoders using clean data while there is no guarantee of purely clean data under poisoning attacks [11,24]. Second, existing methods typically select a threshold by allowing certain percentage of clean points to pass (e.g., 90% clean data) but there is no access to such clean data under poisoning attacks. Finally, existing methods for detecting adversarial examples during inference time only utilize feature space (adversarial examples do not have labels). Thus, if directly applied for detecting poisoning attacks, they overlook some essential aspects of the attacks, i.e., the labels of the poisoned data (they may be flipped).

Contributions. In this paper, we develop a Classification Auto-Encoder based detector (CAE) that utilizes both feature space and label (class) information to defend against diverse poisoned data. We use a Gaussian Mixture Model for discriminating poisoned points from clean data so that it does not require any explicit threshold. We further propose an enhanced version of our method (CAE+) which does not require purely clean data for training. We elaborate our contributions as follows:

- We develop a classification auto-encoder based detector (CAE) to defend against diverse data poisoning attacks, including flipping and optimal attacks.

The key idea is to utilize two components, an auto-encoder based reconstruction for learning the representation of the data from the feature space and an auxiliary classifier for incorporating the label (class) information into the data representation so it can better detect the poison points.

- We further propose an enhanced model CAE+ so that it can be trained even on partially poisoned data. The key idea is to add a reconstruction auto-encoder (RAE) with CAE to form a joint auto-encoder architecture combined with early stopping of CAE so that it does not overfit the poisoned data while still learning useful representations of the clean data.

- We evaluate our method using three large and popular image datasets and show its resilience to poisoned data and advantage compared to existing state-of-the-art methods. Our defense model can be trained using contaminated data with up to 30% poisoned data and still works significantly better than existing outlier detection methods.

2   Background and Related Work

2.1   Poisoning Attacks

Assume distribution R on $\mathcal{X} \times \mathcal{Y}$ where $\mathcal{Y} = \{-1, 1\}$. For a clean training dataset $D_{tr} = \{(x_i, y_i) \subseteq R\}_{i=0}^{n_{tr}}$, the goal of a binary classification task $\mathcal{M}$ parameterized by $\boldsymbol{w}$ is to minimize objective loss function $\mathcal{L}(D_{tr}, \boldsymbol{w})$, w.r.t its parameters $\boldsymbol{w}$. In a poisoning attack, the attacker's goal is to produce n_p poisoned data points $D_p = \{(x_i, y_i) \subseteq R\}_{i=0}^{p}$ so that using new training data $D'_{tr} = D_{tr} \cup D_p$ by the learner results in attacker's goal or objective function. This goal can be maximizing the loss on the entire clean test dataset (untargeted attacks) or on a subset or class of them (targeted attacks). As a result the classification accuracy of the entire clean test data or a subset of them will drop drastically.

Poisoning attacks have different manifestations depending on which part of the data is manipulated during the attack [39]. Each of them can have a different impact on attacker's objective function and different attack strength. In *Label flipping attacks* or in short flipping attacks, only class labels of poisoned data are flipped, and the adversary usually has a limited budget for the number of samples it is allowed to change their labels [30, 41, 43, 46].

Optimal attacks are based on optimizing the poisons to maximizing the degradation of the model's performance. These attacks are stronger compared to other poisoning attacks, since both feature space and labels can be changed. For classification problems [7, 27, 42], the rule of thumb is to initialize poisons with real samples from training data set and flip their labels. Since labels are not differentiable, they only optimize the feature space. For image datasets, the input space refers to the pixels comprising the image.

In this paper, we also introduce *Semi-optimal attacks* which keep the original labels of the points without flipping them and only optimize the feature space. This attack can be realistic when the attacker has no control over the labeling process. The distinction between the different attacks are shown in Table 1.

Table 1. Various types of poisoning attacks based on tampering different input domains of the initial candidate poisoning points.

Domain	Attack		
	Flipping	Semi-optimal	Optimal
$\mathcal{X}$	-	✓	✓
$\mathcal{Y}$	✓	-	✓

2.2   Defense Against Poisoning Attacks

Outlier Detectors. Outlier detection methods are common to defend against poisoning attacks. These methods are based on the fact that poisoned data deviates from normal points or underlying data generation mechanism. Paudice et al. [29] suggest distanced-based outlier detection methods to mitigate the effect of optimal attacks, assuming they have access to a trusted dataset to train the outlier detector. Steinhardt et al. [35] use a centroid-based outlier detector and estimates a data-dependent upper-bound on the objective loss for poisoning attacks, offering a certified defense. Chen et al. [11] benefit from combining Generative Adversarial Network (GAN) based models, namely cGAN and WGAN-GP, to create augmented clean samples from a trusted dataset and mimic the original model. It then compares the training data against a threshold calculated by the augmented clean data to detect the poisoned samples. Outliers can also be detected by clustering based methods [34]. Laishram and Phoha [22] consider clustering in the combination of feature and label space to defend against optimal attacks and showed that the poisoned points are more separated from the rest of their cluster compared to using features alone. K-nearest neighbor algorithm is proposed to combat flipping attacks [30]. They assume samples close together share a common label; otherwise, the sample's label is highly likely flipped.

As we discussed, the existing outlier detection based methods have several limitations. They typically focus on one type of attacks and rely on purely clean data to train the detector and a threshold to determine outliers and hence are not very effective or robust. Furthermore, a recent work [20] considers a new attack method that generates adjacent poisoned samples. In this case, proximity-based outlier detection algorithms such as K-nearest neighbor fail to recognize poisoned data.

Contribution-Based Methods. Another type of defense methods are based on how and to what extent each point contributes to or influences the resulting model. In the context of regression problems, Jagielski et al. [18] retrain the model multiple times and removes points with high residuals as poisonous points. RONI [28] is another defense method that tests the impact of each data point on training performance and discards those points that have a negative contribution. Baracaldo et al. [5] takes a similar approach but reduces computational expenses by examining the impact of entire group of points on the model in order to find manipulated groups. [19] is another work that attempts to find the high impact samples in a less costly process using influence functions. Hong et al. [17] shows poisoned data impact the magnitude and orientation of gradients during the training. They use DP-SGD [1], a training method for achieving differential privacy [48], to add noise to the gradients and limit their sensitivity to mitigate the impact of poisoned samples. In summary, while showing promising results without approximation, the contribution-based methods have the main drawback of high computation cost due to enumerative retraining, which makes it impractical, especially for settings where potentially poisonous data are being continuously acquired. Also, for the differentially private defense methods, they suffer from a decrease in model utility [17].

2.3   Auto-Encoders in Anomaly Detection

Auto-encoders [4,38] are neural networks that learn data representation in an unsupervised way. Auto-encoders reconstruct input x into output x' by minimizing reconstruction error usually on an L_p-norm distance:

$$RE(x) =\| x - x' \|_p \tag{1}$$

If auto-encoders are trained with only benign data, they learn to capture only the main characteristics of these data. So when the reconstruction error of a sample exceeds a threshold, it is considered an anomaly [2,31]. Nevertheless most anomalies are recognized as samples with observable differences from the real data [3], which are not effective for poisoned data that have very small perturbations.

Auto-encoders have been proposed to detect adversarial examples at inference time by Magnet [26]. In addition to considering reconstruction error between the input and output, they also feed them to the target classifier and compare the corresponding softmax layer outputs to boost the detection power. However, in the context of poisoning attacks, a pre-trained trusted classifier does not exist. Instead the defender has access to an extra piece of information which is the associated label of the poisoned point.

When used for both outlier detection and adversarial example detection, the auto-encoders need to be trained with pure clean data to capture shared properties amongst normal data [2,26]. Even in some works [3,47] that considered anomalous data in the training process of the auto-encoders, the percentage of anomalies in the dataset is insignificant. In the setting of poisoning attacks, the assumption of having a clean dataset for training the defense method is not realistic. By utilizing a joint architecture, we show that our defensive model can remain resilient to poisoning attacks even up to 30% poisoned points.

3   Classification Auto-Encoder Based Detector

As a baseline solution, we can train an auto-encoder on feature space as in existing outlier detection methods. For a clean sample $s_c = (x_c, y_c)$, and a poisoned

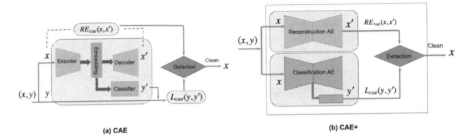

Fig. 1. Auto-encoders Structure: (a) The structure of Classification Auto-encoder (CAE). If trained on pure clean dataset it provides a high success defense against all poisoning attacks. (b) The structure of CAE+. Both Reconstruction Auto-encoder (RAE) and Classification Auto-encoder (CAE) work together to combat against poisons. This joint structure makes the defense method more robust even if trained on a contaminated dataset.

sample $s_p = (x_p, y_p)$, the reconstruction error $RE(x_p)$ can be used to discriminate x_c and x_p:

$$RE(x_c) \ll RE(x_p) \tag{2}$$

According to (2) any data point with significantly large reconstruction error (greater than certain threshold) can be considered as a poison. The limitation of this approach is that it will only capture the changes in the feature space. Hence it will address only semi-optimal attacks which only change the features.

3.1 Classification Auto-Encoder (CAE)

To defend against all types of poisoning attacks, we need a method that incorporates both labels and features in detection process. In other words, the latent encoding of the auto-encoder needs to reflect the label information.

Classification Auto-Encoder. We propose Classification Auto-Encoder (CAE) which has an auxiliary classifier fed by the latent representation z of the encoder (as shown in Fig. 1(a)). If RE_{cae} indicates the reconstruction error, and L_{cae} indicates the auxiliary classifier's loss on representation layer z, CAE is trained to minimize $\sum_{x_i}(RE_{cae}(x_i) + L_{cae}(x_i)))$ on training dataset $D_c = \{x_i, y_i\}_{i=0}^n$. As a result, z is learned in such a way that the classifier is able to predict the label, and the decoder can reconstruct the associated input. To boost the connection between these two tasks, we train the auxiliary classifier and the decoder simultaneously. It contrasts with previous works that utilize classification auto-encoders for predictive or classification objectives. They employ a two-stage training process which trains the pair of encoder-decoder and then uses the low-dimensional representation for training the classifier [15,44].

Detection Criteria. Once the CAE is trained, given a data point, we can use the combined reconstruction error and classification loss as a detection criteria for poisoned data (e.g., if it is greater than certain threshold), since it considers deviations in both feature space and label space.

$$Error(x) = \alpha.RE_{cae}(x) + (1 - \alpha).L_{cae}(x) \qquad (3)$$

The first term $RE_{cae}(x)$ is the reconstruction error of CAE and the second term $L_{cae}(x)$ is the loss of the CAE auxiliary classifier. α and $1 - \alpha$ are weights to control the effect of each term. Since $RE(x)$ is indicative of changes in x, and $L(x)$ reflects the classification loss, the combined metric $Error(x)$ can detect both changes in feature space and labels and hence defend against the different types of attacks.

In general, a threshold can be defined based on *a guess on the number of possible poisoned points K* [18]. Tuning K is a difficult job that makes the detector very sensitive to the actual fraction of poisoned data. Instead, we use a clustering approach and cluster all points based on $Error(x)$ into two clusters using a Gaussian Mixture Model (GMM). We show that the error is so distinct between clean and poisoned points that GMM can separate it very well into two clusters, each representing clean or poisoned data.

3.2 Enhanced Classification Auto-Encoder (CAE+)

CAE requires clean data for training the auto-encoder so it can learn the structure of the normal data and detect any deviation from that. Since we assume the training data is poisoned, we need to add a mechanism that is robust to contaminated data. We do so by leveraging a combination of early stopping and a replicate reconstruction auto-encoder.

Early Stopping. Since we assume there is no access to purely clean data for training the detector, to prevent CAE to learn patterns from poisoned data, we use the early stopping method. Early stopping leads the auto-encoder to focus on reconstructing the pattern of the majority of data, and avoids overfitting on anomalies. The auxiliary classifier is a single dense layer and can usually catch all the class information quickly, especially in binary-class problems. Selecting a small number of neurons in this layer does not provide sufficient parameters for the classification task, and leads to missing even the general patterns of the training dataset. On the other hand, large number of neurons makes the classifier more complex and may overfit the poisonous data. To capture all the information and avoid underfitting, we can select a fairly large number of neurons and address the overfitting problem using early stopping.

By using this approach, CAE can be very robust to the poisoned data. However, at the stop point of the training process, z has captured those patterns of the data that help mostly with classification, but not the reconstruction (which takes longer to learn). Hence we propose a joint auto-encoder architecture to address this challenge by using a parallel reconstruction auto-encoder (RAE).

Reconstruction Auto-encoder. The Reconstruction Auto-Encoder (RAE) is a replicate of the encoder-decoder part of CAE without the auxiliary classifier (as shown in Fig. 1(b)). RAE is trained to minimize the reconstruction error only. By having these two auto-encoders, for an input $\{x, y\}$ we calculate the following combined error:

$$Error(x) = \alpha.RE_{rae}(x) + (1 - \alpha).L_{cae}(x) \tag{4}$$

This is a modification to (3), in which the reconstruction error has been replaced with reconstruction error of RAE ($RE_{rae}(x)$).

This extra auto-encoder helps us adjust the training process for RAE separately so that while RAE can be trained to full capacity, CAE with early stopping is not overfitting the poisonous data. In comparison to the classifier of CAE, RAE with high capacity (especially with convolutional layers) can be trained with a high number of epochs without overfitting the poisoned data. We call this joint structure of CAE and RAE, CAE+, since it is enhancing the CAE functionality.

In practice, the training data may be poisoned, so using CAE+ and Eq. 4 is required. In Sect. 4, we investigate potential scenario of having a clean training dataset D_c and compare CAE vs. CAE+. In the case of clean training data, since the concern of overfitting poisoned data does not exist, CAE can be trained until both the classification layer and decoder converge. We show that CAE can be effective under this circumstance. In contrast, when training data is poisoned, we show that CAE+ is much more robust.

Overview. Combining all the previously mentioned information, the overview of the detection mechanism can be summarized as follows: Initially, we train the CAE+ detector using the available poisoned data. Subsequently, we utilize the output of this detector to create two separate clusters for GMM: one for normal data and the other for poisoned data. Afterwards, we input the suspected points to the combined models of the trained CAE+ and GMM. If a point falls within the clean cluster, it is utilized for training the target classifier.

4   Experiments

In Sect. 4.1, we describe the details of our experimental settings, including the datasets, the attacker's target model, the architecture of our detectors, the comparison methods, and the attributes of the attacks. We also evaluate mixed attacks that combine all types of poisoning attacks to show the strength of CAE+ against diverse attacks. Furthermore, we clarify how we used the periodic update of the model to mimic real scenarios wherein poisoning attacks occur.

In Sect. 4.2, we depict the impact of each type of attack on the poisoned data under different defense methods, the prominence of the Gaussian Mixture Model (GMM) over threshold selection, and the effect of the different auto-encoders employed in the CAE+. Then an ablation study reveals the benefit of CAE+ over CAE and RAE. To confirm the superiority of CAE+, it is compared to the other state-of-the-art detectors in the literature on multiple datasets, including MNIST, Fashion-MNIST, and CIFAR-10. Finally, we evaluate the robustness of CAE+ and CAE under a hypothetical setting in contrast to the previous experiments, when there is a trusted training dataset for training CAE.

4.1   Experimental Setup

Datasets. First, we evaluate the performance of CAE+ using the MNIST dataset [23], and more challenging Fashion-MNIST dataset [40] on binary sub-problem classes: MNIST 9 vs. 8 and 4 vs. 0, and Fashion-MNIST Sandal vs. Sneaker and Top vs. Trouser. It is common practice to apply binary setting for data poisoning attacks [7,19]. Second, we conduct experiments on a more complex dataset CIFAR-10 [21] for two randomly chosen classes Airplane vs. Automobile. All datasets are normalized within the interval [0, 1]. These three datasets are frequently employed in the literature to evaluate poisoning attacks [7,9] and offer varying levels of complexity.

Attacks. Support Vector Machines (SVM) are known to be subject to strong poisoning attacks [7,41]. In contrast to complicated models and neural networks [27], poisoning attacks can achieve a high success in dropping the accuracy of SVM. As we will show in Fig. 6, the accuracy of optimal attacks on the SVM model drops to 60% with 10% of poisons. Hence, we use poisoning attacks against SVMs in the experiments to better demonstrate and evaluate the effectiveness of different defense methods. We use linear kernel for MNIST and Fashion-MNIST and RBF kernel for CIFAR-10. We note that our methods work on poisoning attacks against any target models such as neural networks.

We compare four types of attacks; flipping, optimal, semi-optimal, and mixed attacks, then assess our defense model against them. In a mixed attack, the attacker selects 1/3 of the poisons from each of the aforementioned attack types. This way, we can challenge the defender's ability to detect diverse poison simultaneously, despite their different characteristics. The optimal attack is conducted based on [25] with some modifications.

Setup. A common paradigm for training machine learning models in real world is the periodic update [22] in which the data is acquired continuously. In this scenario, data is provided by users and buffered until sufficient data is obtained to retrain the model. To implement such a periodic update setting for SVM classifier, we consider 60 rounds of SVM updates. Each round represents a new batch of data which consists of 500 data points divided into a training set, a validation set, and a test set of 100, 200, and 200 samples, respectively. Based on different attack types, the attacker generates poisoned points for each round and adds them into the training data for that round. At the next step, we assume that the defender has access to the recent 50 rounds of buffered data. By aggregating the contaminated buffered data of those 50 runs, we train our defense model. Then for evaluation purposes, we use the remaining 10 rounds of updates for testing the defense methods, namely 10 times the buffered data is fed to the detector and the data passing through it is used for model assessment. Every result reported in this paper is the average of these 10 test runs. Maintaining a ratio of 5/1 between training and testing the defense method guarantees a sufficient amount of data is available to evaluate the effectiveness of the defense method.

Note that for each of the attacks unless otherwise specified, up to 10% of the clean data are poisoned. In practical scenarios, attackers typically have limited access to data, usually restricted to a small percentage. Therefore, exceeding 10% may not be realistic [7,20,22]. We believe this is high enough to validate the robustness of CAE+ against poisonous data. To further show the impact of the percentage of the poisoned data, we conduct the experiment on CIFAR-10 with a higher poisoning rate (up to 30%).

Implementation Details. The structure of CAE reconstruction component and RAE is inspired by the auto-encoders introduced in Magnet [26] with some modifications. Our reconstruction auto-encoders, for MNIST and Fashion-MNIST dataset, consist of 3×3 convolutional layers in the encoder, each composed of 3 filters of size 3×3 with 1×1 strides and sigmoid activations. Between these two convolutional layers a MaxPooling 2×2 is located. At the decoder, the structure of convolutional layers are the same as the encoder. The only difference is that the MaxPooling layer is replaced with a 2D UpSampling layer. As the last layer of the decoder we have a third 3×3 convolutional layer with only one filter (compatible to number of channels in MNIST and Fashion-MNIST) to reconstruct an output image with the same size as the input image. Also, as [26] suggests, we use a slightly different architecture for CIFAR-10, by utilizing only one convolutional layer in the encoder and one in the decoder with the mentioned parameters. For the auxiliary classifier, the encoder's output is flattened and fed to a dense classification layer with size 128. We experimentally found out that dropping out the data with rates 0.25 and 0.5 before and after the dense layer serves the best in training the model and reduces the overfitting. For each dataset, we train CAE for 100 epochs and the RAE for 300 epochs with a batch size of 256 using the Adam optimizer. The aggregated error $Error(x)$ is calculated based on Equation (4) on weighted sum of the normalized L_1-norm reconstruction error and the auxiliary classifier's cross entropy loss.

Comparison Methods. Distance-based outlier detectors are state-of-the-art methods in defending against poisoning attacks [20,29]. One of their interesting properties is that they are more robust against poisoned data and do not require to be trained on a purely clean dataset compared to other outlier detection based methods. So, similar to [29], we select **centroid-based Outlier Detectors (OD)** as the baseline. It first finds the centroids of each class in the training dataset and then discards the points that are distant from their respective class centroid.

Furthermore, we compare our method to a modified Magnet, a state-of-the-art auto-encoder based detector designed for adversarial examples [26]. We note that there are more recent detection approaches against adversarial examples, however, our goal is not to defend against adversarial examples, but rather

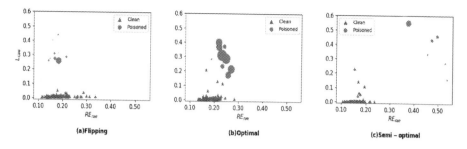

Fig. 2. The effect of different attack types on the reconstruction error and auxiliary classification loss for poisoned MNIST-4-0 dataset. Triangles and circles represent clean and poisoned points, respectively. The poisons' size represents their impact on degrading the SVM accuracy (larger circles indicate higher impact).

to adapt the auto-encoder based detector as a potential solution for poisoning attacks as a comparison. We make the following modifications in order to make it compatible with poisoning attacks under our setting. We train Magnet on the same poisonous data as the other defense methods. It contrasts with the original paper in which the authors train Magnet on a thoroughly clean dataset. The assumption of access to a clean dataset is valid under adversarial example attacks at inference time, but not under the poisoning attacks during training time. We use the same structure as the original paper suggests [26], the only hyperparameter we change is the number of epochs for a better adaptation to poisoning attacks (from 100 epochs to 300 epochs). In addition to the detector, we also evaluate the performance of Magnet detector paired with a reformer [26]. In this case, after Magnet detector filters out poisons, it passes the remaining data through the reformer, which is another auto-encoder. The reformer's reconstructed output will replace the original input and then be fed to the classifier.

4.2   Results

Effect of Different Attacks. As we discussed in Sect. 3, each type of poisoned data can have a different impact on CAE+ components. Figure 2 illustrates this fact by showing the classification error L_{cae} and reconstruction error RE_{rae} of the different poisoning attacks on MNIST-4-0. Blue triangles and orange circles represent the clean and poisoned points, respectively. Clean data is the same for all three plots. For the poisoned data, the size of circles indicates their importance in degrading the SVM classification results. Larger circles imply that the insertion of those poisons to the SVM clean training dataset drops more accuracy.

For the flipping attack, the reconstruction error RE_{rae} cannot differentiate the poisoned samples from the rest of the data since the feature space of the poisons is intact, while the classification loss L_{cae} is much larger for the poisoned data. Under the optimal and semi-optimal attacks, the transformations that occur in the feature space discriminate the clean data and the poisons through RE_{rae}. It is more noticeable for the semi-optimal attack because the features

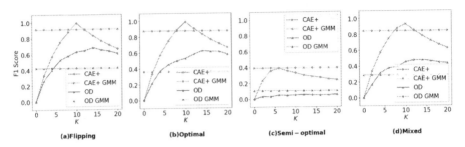

Fig. 3. Changes on MNIST-4-0 F1-score over different thresholds for CAE+ and OD. Thresholds are guesses on the probable number of poisoned data within the training dataset.

alter more drastically than in the optimal attack. This discrepancy between the poisons' features and the clean space impacts their classification results and increases the loss L_{cae}. Therefore, as Eq. 4 suggests, a mixture of both reconstruction and classification errors is required to detect diverse attacks in the context of an attack-agnostic defense.

Threshold vs. GMM. According to Sect. 3.1, we pass the detectors' output to a GMM for clustering the data into poisoned and clean data, so that we do not need to specify a threshold of possible poisoned points K for filtering poisons. We compare our GMM-based approach with the baseline threshold approach when a fixed number of training data is poisoned (about 10% of the training data, i.e., 10 poisons). We report **F1-score** for the detection, which is the harmonic mean of the precision and recall with the best value at 1. F1-score is indicative of how successful a detector is in filtering poisons and passing clean data. An ideal detection algorithm can identify all and only poison data, which means a perfect F1-score.

Figure 3 depicts how the detectors' F1-scores change with different threshold of K for MNIST-4-0 (solid lines). For flipping, optimal and mixed attacks, the F1-score of CAE+ hits almost 1 at $K = 10$. In other words, it can accurately detect all ten poisoned points with very few false positives. The V shape of CAE+ plots depicts its sensitivity to an accurate threshold K. Before threshold 10 there are naturally some false negatives, and after that point, false positives are emerging. In contrast, we do not need to specify any threshold in the unsupervised GMM method (dashed line) for CAE+. We can see that it competes very closely with the best guess on K in the threshold-based method.

For the semi-optimal attacks, the scenario is slightly different. The majority of the poisoned points in semi-optimal attacks get stuck in local maxima and do not change their feature space; hence they have little impact on the attack. For the same reason, they do not harm the accuracy even though they can not be filtered out. This fact is illustrated in Fig. 2. Some of the low-impact attacked points (shown with small circles) are placed at the bottom left corner of the plot, where the majority of the clean data points are located. As a result, in Fig. 3,

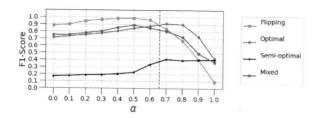

Fig. 4. CAE+ F1-score for different values of α (Eq. 4)

F1-score for semi-optimal attacks is not high; but we show later that CAE+ can detect all the high impact attack points and achieve the original SVM's accuracy.

In all the attacks, for both threshold-based and GMM methods, CAE+ yields significantly better F1-scores than OD. For linear SVM, overlooking poisoned points can be much more harmful than filtering out clean data. So despite the high false-positive rate, OD can still partially enhance the SVM accuracy. OD completely fails to operate as a detector if the system is sensitive to clean data removal. In the remaining experiments, we leverage GMM for all the detection approaches (including the baseline OD) to have a fair comparison of how they boost SVM accuracy.

Impact of Alpha. There are four types of attacks. Each of the CAE+ reconstruction or classification auto-encoders is suitable to address different attack types. Coefficient α in Eq. 4 can be adjusted to meet this goal. Since the attacker's attack type is not known to the defender, α should be pre-adjusted considering all the attack types. Figure 4 demonstrates how different values of α affect F1-score. Reconstruction error has a significant impact on semi-optimal attacks, and as a result, higher α boosts the F1-score. In flipping attacks and optimal attacks, classification error gains more importance. In particular, in optimal attacks, there is a trade-off between reconstruction error and classification error. The vertical dashed line shows α=0.66 in which every attack sustains high F1-socre. According to Eq. 4, at this value the coefficient of $RE(x)$ is twice as the coefficient of $L(x)$.

Ablation Study. In this section we show the contribution of each component in CAE+ (recall Fig. 1). We train two additional models for comparison: 1) CAE that is not combined with the RAE (the bottom auto-encoder in Fig. 1(b)) and has the error function in Eq. 3; 2) RAE that is a stand-alone reconstruction auto-encoder (the top auto-encoder in Fig. 1(b)) and uses reconstruction error as defined in Eq. 1.

The error for CAE is calculated based on Eq. 3, and for RAE, it is limited to just reconstruction error. Note that all these methods are trained with 10% contaminated data and paired with GMM. Figure 5 shows the effectiveness of these detectors based on F1-score. Since RAE considers only feature space, it is effective on semi-optimal attacks and, to a less extent, on optimal attacks.

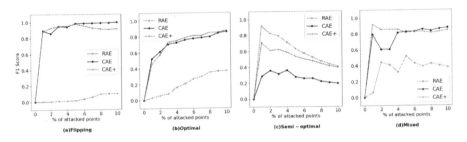

Fig. 5. Ablation study between CAE+, CAE and RAE on MNIST 4-0

However, flipping attacks can evade it. On the other hand, CAE relies on classification and reconstruction errors with more emphasis on classification loss. So it fails on semi-optimal attacks. CAE+ has the advantage of using both CAE classification error and RAE reconstruction error, and as a result, it gains a better F1-score on average. Since the attack is not known in advance, CAE+ is the best detector among these three.

Comparison. In this experiment, we compare the performance of CAE+ in terms of accuracy of the resulting model with state-of-the-art defense methods. We feed the learner's training data into detectors and filter suspicious poisoned points using GMM. The rest of the points are used to retrain the SVM classifier. A perfect filter leaves us with the entire clean data, excluding all poisons, which results in a high SVM accuracy.

Figure 6 illustrates the resulting accuracy on different percentages of poisoned training datasets. The plots on the first row (a to d), second row (e to h) and third row (i to l) belong to MNSIT-4-0, Fashion-MNIST-Sandal-Snkear and CIFAR-10 Airplane-Automobile, respectively, with original accuracies of 99%, 88% and 73% on clean unpoisoned datasets. In each row, all plots have the same scale. Each plot indicates one type of attack and corresponding detection methods.

In each plot, we show the accuracy without any detection (attack), and the accuracy with CAE+, in comparison with other three detection methods (OD, Magnet, and Magnet+reformer). We first elaborate on the results of the first row, for MNIST-4-0 dataset. Considering each plot individually, for all the attack types, CAE+ constantly achieves almost the original accuracy (blue lines), and outperforms other detectors. As expected, optimal attacks are the strongest among all four types of attacks.

Magnet does not consider label flipping, so it fails on flipping attack scenarios. When the feature space changes are significant (mostly semi-optimal attacks), its performance is comparable to CAE+. Magnet's sensitivity to perturbation size has been explored in [26] for evasion attacks under multiple adversarial example distortion rate ϵ. Adding the reformer enhances Magnet's results significantly. It gives us the insight that using the reformer along with CAE+ can boost its performance, which can be a direction for future work. The Fashion-MNIST and CIFAR-10 results are similar to MNIST.

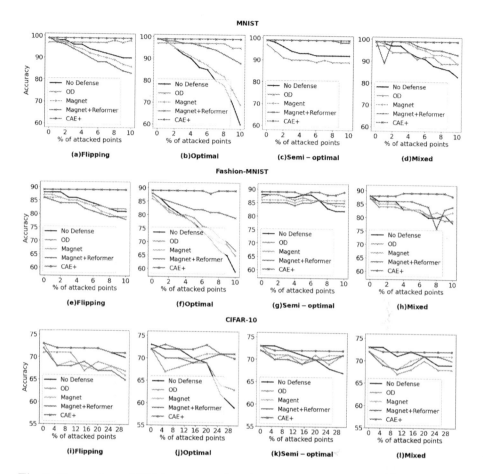

Fig. 6. Comparison of SVM accuracy after filtering suspicious points by CAE+, OD, and Magnet over different percentages of poisons. The first row represents MNIST-4-0, the second row is Fashion-MNIST Sandal-Sneaker and the third row belongs to CIFAR-10 Airplane-Automobile.

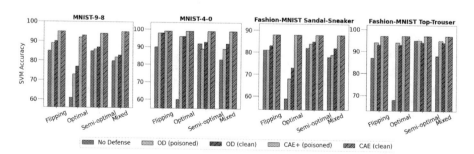

Fig. 7. Comparison of SVM accuracy using detectors trained on clean vs. poisoned data

Note that MNIST and Fashion-MNIST were tested for up to 10% of poisoned data, and CIFAR-10 is tested for up to 30% of poisons. Although it is not practical for an attacker to inject this high number of poisons into the system in real world, this is a good stress test to show CAE+ is robust to even higher poison rates.

Robustness. Given the assumption of having access to only an untrusted (contaminated) dataset, CAE+ was chosen over CAE in all the previous experiments. However, if clean data is available, we can simply use CAE. Therefore, to verify the impact of this assumption on the detectors' performance, we train a stand-alone CAE on clean data, utilizing Equation (3) and on a large number of epochs (300). In this experiment, we end up with two new detectors; a clean CAE and a clean OD.

We use a training dataset with 10% poisoned data to train SVM, then apply both clean and poisoned versions of CAE(+) and OD on this data to see how they filter poisoned points and recover SVM accuracy. The result of this comparison on four datasets MNIST 9-8, 4-0, Fashion-MNIST Sandal-Snkear, and Top-Trousers are represented in Fig. 7. The original SVM accuracies on trusted data for these datasets are 95%, 99%, 88%, and 97%, respectively. We observe that OD is susceptible to contaminated data as clean OD usually surpasses its contaminated version. We note that when the defender has access to a clean dataset, it is adequate to train CAE directly without CAE+. Also, CAE+ and CAE always outperform OD, especially in optimal attacks.

5   Conclusion

This paper utilized auto-encoders to defend against various types of poisoning attacks for the first time. We proposed CAE, a novel two-component auto-encoder that utilizes an auxiliary classifier to boost detection performance. We enhanced the structure of CAE by introducing CAE+. The enhanced version is a joint auto-encoder detector that has a high robustness against contaminated data. Experiments demonstrated the detection power of CAE+ against diverse poisoning attacks including optimal, semi-optimal and label-flipping attacks and showed that it surpasses the state-of-the-art distance-based outlier detector and Magnet detector. In all these cases, CAE+ is trained on a dataset that is corrupted with a high rate of poisoned data and still preserved its performance.

Directions for future work include demonstrating the results of such detectors on non-convex target models. Studies can also explore the influence of these defensive approaches on multi-classification problems. Besides, it is worth extending current work on backdoor attacks since they are carried out during training and share many characteristics with poisoning attacks.

References

1. Abadi, M., et al.: Deep learning with differential privacy. In: Proceedings of the 2016 ACM SIGSAC Conference on Computer and Communications Security, pp. 308–318 (2016)
2. An, J., Cho, S.: Variational autoencoder based anomaly detection using reconstruction probability. Special Lecture on IE 2(1) (2015)
3. Aytekin, C., Ni, X., Cricri, F., Aksu, E.: Clustering and unsupervised anomaly detection with l 2 normalized deep auto-encoder representations. In: 2018 International Joint Conference on Neural Networks (IJCNN), pp. 1–6. IEEE (2018)
4. Baldi, P.: Autoencoders, unsupervised learning, and deep architectures. In: Proceedings of ICML Workshop on Unsupervised and Transfer Learning, pp. 37–49 (2012)
5. Baracaldo, N., Chen, B., Ludwig, H., Safavi, J.A.: Mitigating poisoning attacks on machine learning models: a data provenance based approach. In: Proceedings of the 10th ACM Workshop on Artificial Intelligence and Security, pp. 103–110 (2017)
6. Biggio, B., Fumera, G., Roli, F.: Security evaluation of pattern classifiers under attack. IEEE Trans. Knowl. Data Eng. 26(4), 984–996 (2013)
7. Biggio, B., Nelson, B., Laskov, P.: Poisoning attacks against support vector machines. arXiv preprint arXiv:1206.6389 (2012)
8. Borgnia, E., et al.: Strong data augmentation sanitizes poisoning and backdoor attacks without an accuracy tradeoff. In: ICASSP 2021–2021 IEEE International Conference on Acoustics, Speech and Signal Processing (ICASSP), pp. 3855–3859. IEEE (2021)
9. Carnerero-Cano, J., Muñoz-González, L., Spencer, P., Lupu, E.C.: Regularisation can mitigate poisoning attacks: a novel analysis based on multiobjective bilevel optimisation. arXiv preprint arXiv:2003.00040 (2020)
10. Chan, A., Tay, Y., Ong, Y.S., Zhang, A.: Poison attacks against text datasets with conditional adversarially regularized autoencoder. In: Proceedings of the 2020 Conference on Empirical Methods in Natural Language Processing: Findings, pp. 4175–4189 (2020)
11. Chen, J., Zhang, X., Zhang, R., Wang, C., Liu, L.: De-Pois: an attack-agnostic defense against data poisoning attacks. IEEE Trans. Inf. Forensics Security 16, 3412–3425 (2021)
12. Estellés-Arolas, E., González-Ladrón-de Guevara, F.: Towards an integrated crowdsourcing definition. J. Inf. Sci. 38(2), 189–200 (2012)
13. Fang, M., Sun, M., Li, Q., Gong, N.Z., Tian, J., Liu, J.: Data poisoning attacks and defenses to crowdsourcing systems. In: Proceedings of the Web Conference 2021, pp. 969–980 (2021)
14. Feng, J., Cai, Q.Z., Zhou, Z.H.: Learning to confuse: generating training time adversarial data with auto-encoder. Adv. Neural. Inf. Process. Syst. 32, 11994–12004 (2019)
15. Geng, J., Fan, J., Wang, H., Ma, X., Li, B., Chen, F.: High-resolution SAR image classification via deep convolutional autoencoders. IEEE Geosci. Remote Sens. Lett. 12(11), 2351–2355 (2015)
16. Gu, T., Liu, K., Dolan-Gavitt, B., Garg, S.: Badnets: evaluating backdooring attacks on deep neural networks. IEEE Access 7, 47230–47244 (2019)
17. Hong, S., Chandrasekaran, V., Kaya, Y., Dumitraş, T., Papernot, N.: On the effectiveness of mitigating data poisoning attacks with gradient shaping. arXiv preprint arXiv:2002.11497 (2020)

18. Jagielski, M., Oprea, A., Biggio, B., Liu, C., Nita-Rotaru, C., Li, B.: Manipulating machine learning: poisoning attacks and countermeasures for regression learning. In: 2018 IEEE Symposium on Security and Privacy (SP), pp. 19–35. IEEE (2018)

19. Koh, P.W., Liang, P.: Understanding black-box predictions via influence functions. In: Proceedings of the 34th International Conference on Machine Learning, vol. 70, pp. 1885–1894. JMLR. org (2017)

20. Koh, P.W., Steinhardt, J., Liang, P.: Stronger data poisoning attacks break data sanitization defenses. Mach. Learn., 1–47 (2022)

21. Krizhevsky, A., Hinton, G., et al.: Learning multiple layers of features from tiny images (2009)

22. Laishram, R., Phoha, V.V.: Curie: a method for protecting SVM classifier from poisoning attack. arXiv preprint arXiv:1606.01584 (2016)

23. LeCun, Y., Haffner, P., Bottou, L., Bengio, Y.: Object recognition with gradient-based learning. In: Shape, Contour and Grouping in Computer Vision. LNCS, vol. 1681, pp. 319–345. Springer, Heidelberg (1999). https://doi.org/10.1007/3-540-46805-6_19

24. Madani, P., Vlajic, N.: Robustness of deep autoencoder in intrusion detection under adversarial contamination. In: Proceedings of the 5th Annual Symposium and Bootcamp on Hot Topics in the Science of Security, pp. 1–8 (2018)

25. Melis, M., Demontis, A., Pintor, M., Sotgiu, A., Biggio, B.: SECML: a python library for secure and explainable machine learning (2019). arXiv preprint arXiv:1912.10013

26. Meng, D., Chen, H.: Magnet: a two-pronged defense against adversarial examples. In: Proceedings of the 2017 ACM SIGSAC Conference on Computer and Communications Security, pp. 135–147 (2017)

27. Muñoz-González, L., et al.: Towards poisoning of deep learning algorithms with back-gradient optimization. In: Proceedings of the 10th ACM Workshop on Artificial Intelligence and Security, pp. 27–38 (2017)

28. Nelson, B., et al.: Exploiting machine learning to subvert your spam filter. LEET **8**, 1–9 (2008)

29. Paudice, A., Muñoz-González, L., Gyorgy, A., Lupu, E.C.: Detection of adversarial training examples in poisoning attacks through anomaly detection. arXiv preprint arXiv:1802.03041 (2018)

30. Paudice, A., Muñoz-González, L., Lupu, E.C.: Label sanitization against label flipping poisoning attacks. In: Alzate, C., et al. (eds.) ECML PKDD 2018. LNCS (LNAI), vol. 11329, pp. 5–15. Springer, Cham (2019). https://doi.org/10.1007/978-3-030-13453-2_1

31. Sakurada, M., Yairi, T.: Anomaly detection using autoencoders with nonlinear dimensionality reduction. In: Proceedings of the MLSDA 2014 2nd Workshop on Machine Learning for Sensory Data Analysis, pp. 4–11 (2014)

32. Shejwalkar, V., Houmansadr, A.: Manipulating the byzantine: optimizing model poisoning attacks and defenses for federated learning. In: NDSS (2021)

33. Shejwalkar, V., Houmansadr, A., Kairouz, P., Ramage, D.: Back to the drawing board: a critical evaluation of poisoning attacks on production federated learning. In: IEEE Symposium on Security and Privacy (2022)

34. Shen, S., Tople, S., Saxena, P.: Auror: defending against poisoning attacks in collaborative deep learning systems. In: Proceedings of the 32nd Annual Conference on Computer Security Applications, pp. 508–519 (2016)

35. Steinhardt, J., Koh, P.W.W., Liang, P.S.: Certified defenses for data poisoning attacks. In: Advances in Neural Information Processing Systems, pp. 3517–3529 (2017)

36. Sun, J., Li, A., DiValentin, L., Hassanzadeh, A., Chen, Y., Li, H.: FL-WBC: enhancing robustness against model poisoning attacks in federated learning from a client perspective. In: Advances in Neural Information Processing Systems, vol. 34 (2021)

37. Tahmasebian, F., Xiong, L., Sotoodeh, M., Sunderam, V.: Crowdsourcing under data poisoning attacks: a comparative study. In: Singhal, A., Vaidya, J. (eds.) DBSec 2020. LNCS, vol. 12122, pp. 310–332. Springer, Cham (2020). https://doi.org/10.1007/978-3-030-49669-2_18

38. Vincent, P., Larochelle, H., Lajoie, I., Bengio, Y., Manzagol, P.A.: Stacked denoising autoencoders: learning useful representations in a deep network with a local denoising criterion. J. Mach. Learn. Res. 11(Dec), 3371–3408 (2010)

39. Wang, Z., Ma, J., Wang, X., Hu, J., Qin, Z., Ren, K.: Threats to training: a survey of poisoning attacks and defenses on machine learning systems. ACM Comput. Surv. **55**(7), 1–36 (2022)

40. Xiao, H., Rasul, K., Vollgraf, R.: Fashion-MNIST: a novel image dataset for benchmarking machine learning algorithms. arXiv preprint arXiv:1708.07747 (2017)

41. Xiao, H., Xiao, H., Eckert, C.: Adversarial label flips attack on support vector machines. In: ECAI, pp. 870–875 (2012)

42. Xiao, H., Biggio, B., Brown, G., Fumera, G., Eckert, C., Roli, F.: Is feature selection secure against training data poisoning? In: International Conference on Machine Learning, pp. 1689–1698 (2015)

43. Xiao, H., Biggio, B., Nelson, B., Xiao, H., Eckert, C., Roli, F.: Support vector machines under adversarial label contamination. Neurocomputing **160**, 53–62 (2015)

44. Xing, C., Ma, L., Yang, X.: Stacked denoise autoencoder based feature extraction and classification for hyperspectral images. J. Sens. 2016 (2016)

45. Yang, C., Wu, Q., Li, H., Chen, Y.: Generative poisoning attack method against neural networks. arXiv preprint arXiv:1703.01340 (2017)

46. Zhao, M., An, B., Gao, W., Zhang, T.: Efficient label contamination attacks against black-box learning models. In: IJCAI, pp. 3945–3951 (2017)

47. Zhou, C., Paffenroth, R.C.: Anomaly detection with robust deep autoencoders. In: Proceedings of the 23rd ACM SIGKDD International Conference on Knowledge Discovery and Data Mining, pp. 665–674 (2017)

48. Zhu, T., Li, G., Zhou, W., Yu, P.S.: Differential Privacy and Applications. AIS, vol. 69. Springer, Cham (2017). https://doi.org/10.1007/978-3-319-62004-6

49. Zong, B., et al.: Deep autoencoding gaussian mixture model for unsupervised anomaly detection (2018)

CodeGraphSMOTE - Data Augmentation for Vulnerability Discovery

Tom Ganz[1]([✉]), Erik Imgrund[1], Martin Härterich[1], and Konrad Rieck[2]

[1] SAP Security Research, Walldorf, Germany
{tom.ganz,erik.imgrund,martin.harterich}@sap.com
[2] Technische Universität Berlin, Berlin, Germany
rieck@tu-berlin.de

Abstract. The automated discovery of vulnerabilities at scale is a crucial area of research in software security. While numerous machine learning models for detecting vulnerabilities are known, recent studies show that their generalizability and transferability heavily depend on the quality of the training data. Due to the scarcity of real vulnerabilities, available datasets are highly imbalanced, making it difficult for deep learning models to learn and generalize effectively. Based on the fact that programs can inherently be represented by graphs and to leverage recent advances in graph neural networks, we propose a novel method to generate synthetic code graphs for data augmentation to enhance vulnerability discovery. Our method includes two significant contributions: a novel approach for generating synthetic code graphs and a graph-to-code transformer to convert code graphs into their code representation. Applying our augmentation strategy to vulnerability discovery models achieves the same originally reported F1-score with less than 20% of the original dataset and we outperform the F1-score of prior work on augmentation strategies by up to 25.6% in detection performance.

Keywords: Vulnerability Discovery · Data Augmentation · Graph Neural Networks

1 Introduction

The research in the field of automatic vulnerability discovery has made remarkable progress recently but is still far from complete. Traditional rule-based tools suffer from high false negative or false positive rates in their detection performance. Consequently, advances in deep learning spark interest in the development of learning-based vulnerability discovery models. For instance, recent models borrow techniques from natural language processing using recurrent neural networks (RNNs), in particular, long short-term memorys (LSTMs), where the source code is processed as a flat sequence of code tokens [6,30,31,38]. Even more recent approaches use graph neural networks (GNNs) thereby leveraging code graphs as a compact structure to represent the syntactic and semantic properties

© IFIP International Federation for Information Processing 2023
Published by Springer Nature Switzerland AG 2023
V. Atluri and A. L. Ferrara (Eds.): DBSec 2023, LNCS 13942, pp. 282–301, 2023.
https://doi.org/10.1007/978-3-031-37586-6_17

of programs [6,10,43,55]. Graph learning is still a young field with a big room for improvement, but a promising technique to foster further research, especially in software security [15].

However, one major obstacle in learning-based vulnerability discovery, is obtaining enough representative code samples since most datasets available are either too small, unrealistic or imbalanced [6,34,44]. While clean code samples are vastly available and can be gathered easily, vulnerable samples, on the other hand, are scarce [2]. GNNs architectures suffer under that shortage the most, as they tend to overfit very easily and hence need balanced labels for training. Chakraborty et al. [6] report that models trained on inappropriate and imbalanced datasets are less transferable and have disadvantageous detection capabilities. The question arises then, on how to apply vulnerability discovery models to projects that lack a large history of vulnerabilities.

In traditional machine learning domains, data augmentation techniques are commonplace: For image data, random crops, offsets and rotations generate slightly different images with the same underlying meaning [40]. In tabular data, Synthetic Minority Oversampling Technique (SMOTE) is used to interpolate between minority samples and thus generate new samples [7]. Natural language processing uses techniques, such as synonym replacement, random word swaps, deletions or back translation [39]. While graph-based deep learning provides a unified method for neural networks on grids, groups, geodesics and gauges, no augmentation method for full graphs and even less so for code graphs exists.

Although augmentation techniques for node-level [54] and edge-level [52] tasks are available, techniques for graph classification are still unexplored [51]. The graph-specific augmentation methods that have been developed so far, either only perturb graphs [32,51], cannot generate new graphs with node attributes of the target domain [21] or only perturb the node attributes [26]. Even worse, these augmentation strategies are disconnected from the underlying vulnerability discovery task, causing the generated samples to be neither syntactically nor semantically correct rendering them effectively uninterpretable.

More promising approaches like Graph2Edit [50], SequenceR [9] or Hoppity [12] can generate new vulnerable samples by learning semantic edits applied to clean code samples [34]. Although they are better suited for balancing vulnerability datasets than random graph perturbations, they already require a large number of vulnerable samples for training, which is the problem we are trying to solve in the first place. Furthermore, Nong et al. [34] observe that neural code editing approaches for vulnerability injection only yield significant improvements if the generated samples are assessed and selected and thus require extensive manual labor. Hence, we need data augmentation strategies explicitly tailored for vulnerability discovery which do not require large amounts of vulnerable training data and produce human-readable code. We present Code-GraphSMOTE, a novel method to augment code graph samples for vulnerability discovery models. It generates new vulnerable samples for the minority class in a dataset by porting SMOTE to the graph domain, specifically for code graphs. It does so by interpolating in the latent space of a variational autoencoder.

Our approach focuses on interpretable and sound sample generation. In essence, the contributions we present are:

1. A novel method to generate sound and interpretable synthetic code graphs.
2. A graph-to-code transformer to translate code graphs back to source code.
3. An evaluation demonstrating the practicability of our method.

Moreover, we publish our implementation of this method to foster further research in this direction[1]. In the rest of this paper, we review Related Work in Sect. 2. Then we lay down the preliminaries for vulnerability discovery in Sect. 3 and for data augmentation in Sect. 4. We proceed to thoroughly describe our method in Sect. 5, then present our experimental evaluation in Sect. 6 and end with the Conclusion in Sect. 7.

2   Related Work

Some graph-specific data augmentation methods perturbing the given samples have been developed, while graph data augmentation methods that are extending the dataset by generating new graphs are heavily underdeveloped.

DropEdge [37] reduces overfitting and over-smoothing by removing random edges from the graph at training time, and several improvements over DropEdge have been made by choosing the dropped edges in a biased way [16,41]. Other methods are based on adding and removing edges [8,53], masking node attributes [56], sampling a random subset of the nodes [13,20] and cropping subgraphs [45]. DeepSMOTE interpolates images in the latent space of an autoencoder instead of the original pixel space.

This greatly improves downstream classification performance for imbalanced datasets by generating synthetic minority samples and works better than generating new samples based on generative adversarial networks [11]. The same idea is applied to graphs to generate new nodes for imbalanced node classification tasks in [54]. There, a GAE is trained to reconstruct the adjacency matrix, while simultaneously learning latent features of the edges. The nodes are then oversampled using SMOTE in the latent space obtained by the GAE, which is also used to generate edges connecting the new nodes with the rest of the graph. This method achieves better accuracy in the task of imbalanced node classification. However, no adaptation of this method has been published, that interpolates between graphs to be used in graph classification. Chakraborty et al. [6] already apply SMOTE on graph embeddings before using a vulnerability classifier, this was found to increase detection performance. However, their method is generally, hardly applicable since it uses intermediate representations from another vulnerability discovery model and does not reconstruct interpolated graphs let alone the underlying source code.

Other approaches have been proposed from different research branches. Neural code editing uses deep learning to generate syntactically and semantically

---

[1] https://github.com/SAP-samples/security-research-codegraphsmote.

valid code samples. Different approaches, for instance, Hoppity [12], SequenceR [9] and Graph2Edit [50] have been developed. A recent study found out, that these approaches do not work well for augmenting vulnerability datasets [34]. Furthermore, the generated additional samples by Graph2Edit were found to be unrealistic but still helpful as additional training data for a vulnerability discovery downstream task. Lastly, Evilcoder [36] allows for automatically inserting bugs using rule-based code modifications, for instance, modified/removed buffer checks. However, this method produces vulnerable code samples that are too trivial to distinguish from clean samples and hence not suitable for machine learning.

3   Vulnerability Discovery

The preliminary materials for our method concerning learning-based vulnerability discovery, program representations and representation learning on code graphs are discussed in this section.

3.1   Learning-Based Static Analyzer

We start by formalizing the vulnerability discovery task in the following section: Given a particular representation of a program, a static vulnerability discovery method is a decision function f that maps a code snippet x to a label $y \in \{\text{VULNERABLE}, \text{CLEAN}\}$.

Learning-based methods for vulnerability discovery build on such a decision function $f = f_\Theta$ parameterized by weights Θ that are obtained by training on a dataset of vulnerable and non-vulnerable code [18]. Compared to classical static analysis tools, learning-based approaches do not have a fixed rule set and can therefore adapt to the characteristics of different vulnerabilities in the training data. Current learning-based approaches differ in the program representation used as input and the inductive bias, that is, the way f depends on the weights Θ.

3.2   Program Representations

Different representations for programs have been used as a basis for vulnerability discovery models in the past. Popular natural language processing-based approaches represent a program as the natural token sequence that appears in the source code [38]. Since programs can be modeled inherently as directed graphs [1], more recent approaches make use of graph representations [10,43,55] for source code instead of flat token sequences achieving state-of-the-art performances [38]. We refer to the resulting program representation as a *code graph* and denote the underlying directed graphs as $G = G(V, E)$ with vertices V and edges $E \subseteq V \times V$. Moreover, for $v \in V$, we define $N(v)$ as the set of its neighboring nodes.

Code graphs differ in the syntactic and semantic features they capture. Recent works, for instance, rely only on syntactic features using the abstract syntax tree (AST) [1], while newer approaches also capture the semantic properties, as for instance using the control flow graph (CFG), which connects statements with edges in the order they will be executed or the data flow graph

(DFG) connecting the usages of variables. Based on these classical representations, combined graphs have been developed. A popular one is the code property graph (CPG) [49], which resembles a combination of the AST, CFG and program dependence graph (PDG). Other approaches use different combinations [5,46]. All these representations are denoted CPGs, however, to distinguish them from the original CPG proposed by Yamaguchi et al. [49], we formally define a code graph in Definition 1 as an attributed and combined graph structure representing programs.

Definition 1. *A code graph is an attributed graph $G = (V, E, X_V, X_E)$ derived from source code and providing a syntactic or semantic view of the program.*

Naturally, code graphs have attributes, for instance, a node could have code tokens or AST labels attached. Since deep learning algorithms expect input features to be numeric, recent works embed these attributes into vector spaces [6,10,43,55]. Hence a code graph extends the pair (V, E) by node attributes $X_V \in \mathbb{R}^{|V| \times d_V}$ of dimensionality d_V and edge attributes $X_E \in \mathbb{R}^{|E| \times d_E}$ of dimensionality d_E [47].

3.3 Learning on Code Graphs

Vulnerability discovery using code graphs as input representation is a graph classification task. Building on a set of labels y and a set of attributed code graphs G it aims to learn a function $f_\Theta : G \mapsto y$. A set $\mathcal{G}_{\text{train}}$ of training graphs with known labels for each of those is given through which the parameters Θ of the function are optimized.

To build a graph neural network for code graphs, a convolutional and a global pooling block are needed [3]. Many graph convolutional blocks have been developed, the simplest of which is the graph convolutional network (GCN) [25]. The GCN can be formulated based on:

$$X' = \widehat{D}^{-1/2} \hat{A} \widehat{D}^{-1/2} X \Theta, \tag{1}$$

where $\hat{A} = A + I$ is the adjacency matrix with added self-loops, $\widehat{D}_{ii} = \sum_j \hat{A}_{ij}$ is the degree matrix and X the initial node feature matrix. Other types of convolutional blocks might be a gated graph neural network (GGNN) [29] or a graph isomorphism network (GIN) [48], where the former uses gated recurrent units instead of a feed-forward network and the latter has a separate optimizable parameter for the weights applied to the self-loops. In vulnerability discovery, however, we often lack a representative amount of vulnerable samples and, in consequence, have to deal with imbalanced graph classification [22].

4   Data Augmentation

Since there are few examples of vulnerabilities in the wild and the datasets for vulnerability discovery are unbalanced, as a remedy, we discuss the basics of data augmentation in this section.

4.1   SMOTE

The Synthetic Minority Oversampling Technique (SMOTE) [7] extends a dataset by generating new samples for all minority classes based on feature-space interpolation in the input domain. This way, the imbalance ratio of the dataset can be reduced and generalization to minority classes improved. New samples are generated by randomly selecting a sample and choosing a second sample from a random subset of the k nearest neighbors of the same class. New samples are generated by linearly interpolating between the features of the two selected nodes, yielding a new feature vector $\tilde{x} = \lambda x_1 + (1 - \lambda)x_2$, where x_1, x_2 are the features of the original samples and $\lambda \in [0, 1]$ is a uniformly random number.

4.2   Graph Autoencoder

Due to their discrete nature, SMOTE is not readily applicable to code graphs. It is not directly evident how one would interpolate between two graphs with both having, e.g., different numbers of nodes or edges. Some recent works apply SMOTE on the compressed latent space representation learned by an autoencoder in the computer vision domain [11], which learns to generate meaningful latent variables for samples from a data distribution [23] consisting of an encoder and a decoder. Moreover, the encoder of a variational autoencoder infers a probability distribution of the latent representation, by choosing a parametric probability distribution as the prior distribution for the latent variables. During training, the encoder infers the parameters of that distribution. For example, a variational autoencoder with a Gaussian distribution as the prior for the latent space would have two encoders $e_\mu(x) = z_\mu$ and $e_{\sigma^2}(x) = z_{\sigma^2}$. Then the latent representation needs to be decoded by sampling from $z \sim \mathcal{N}(z_\mu, z_{\sigma^2})$. This way, the decoder can still operate on a continuous latent representation, where it then tries to reconstruct the original input [24].

Graph autoencoders (GAEs) take this idea to the domain of graphs. They encode a graph into a latent space representation and decode it back into a graph. The latent space can be structured as a node- or graph-wise latent representation. The latter implies a single constant-sized vector for the complete graph, while the former latent space representation consists of a vector per node. Furthermore, the reconstruction target can be the adjacency matrix [24], the node or edge feature matrix [28]. Just like for the classical autoencoder, a variational variant exists, called variational graph autoencoder (VGAE).

5   CodeGraphSMOTE

CodeGraphSMOTE is applied on code graphs since not only do they provide state-of-the-art performance results on vulnerability discovery but also retain semantic and syntactic information in a compressed structure. Moreover, Code-GraphSMOTE is also equipped with a transformer to convert graphs back to source code representations. In particular, it consists of an autoencoder, interpolation method and graph-to-code transformation model. Figure 1 shows an overview of those blocks and their interplay.

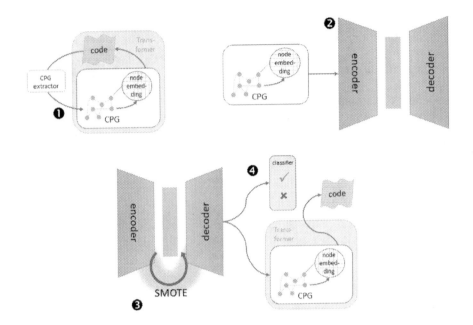

Fig. 1. Overview of the building blocks of CodeGraphSMOTE for training on imbalanced graph datasets.

5.1 Overview

The method has multiple training stages: The first stage is training a transformer model to convert code graphs to their original source code (1). The learned intermediate token embeddings of the transformer can then be used in the following stage to provide aggregated node embeddings for the VGAE. The second stage consists of training an autoencoder model to reconstruct code graphs in an unsupervised fashion (2). In the third stage, new samples can be generated by applying classic SMOTE to the VGAE latent representation (3). The last stage consists of training a vulnerability discovery model on an augmented version of the original dataset (4).

To augment the dataset, first, all code graphs of the original dataset are encoded by the autoencoder. Next, a balanced dataset is created by generating interpolated samples for the minority class. Lastly, the interpolated and original latent space representations are decoded by the autoencoder to generate new graphs for the vulnerability discovery downstream task. We proceed to explain our VGAE architecture and then provide insights into our transformer model.

5.2 Code Graph Generation

The input to the VGAE is a code graph, while the learning task is to pertain to as much information in the latent space as needed to reconstruct the original code graph. This ensures a semantically structured latent representation of vulnerable and clean code samples.

Encoder. To produce latent space representations on the level of code graphs, a node-level autoencoder is implemented, where the intermediate node embeddings are calculated by applying a GNN to the input code graph. Conventional GNNs, such as GCNs, are low-pass filters and thus remove high-frequency features [35]. As it could be detrimental to decoding performance to smooth out the high-frequency features of the graph, an alternative architecture is used. The deconvolutional autoencoder [28] aims to preserve features of all components of the frequency spectrum by using more terms of the approximated eigendecomposition. Hence, a deconvolutional network with three layers and graph normalization [4] is used as the architecture for the encoder.

Decoder. The decoder needs to decode not only the edge and node features but also the graph's topology. For the node level decoder, we use a GNN from Li et al. [28] which employs an approximate inverse convolution operation, restoring high-frequency features and consequently alleviating the problem of GCNs being mostly low-pass filters [35]. Since the node feature decoder depends on the graph's topology, we first reconstruct the adjacency matrix using a topology decoder.

The most prominent topology decoder is the inner product decoder which connects two distinct nodes with latent representations X'_i and X'_j by an edge with probability $\sigma(X'_i X'^T_j)$. Therefore, we can sample edges given these probabilities or, in a deterministic setting, draw an edge iff $\sigma(X'_i X'^T_j) > p_0$ (usually $p_0 = 0.5$), or in other words iff

$$X'_i X'^T_j > t \tag{2}$$

for some threshold t (usually $t = 0$). Note that increasing t leads to fewer edges.

During the reconstruction of the adjacency matrix, nodes with similar features tend to have a very high probability of an edge between them. As a solution, we decode the node features and topology separately, by splitting the latent representation of each node in half and using only one part for each decoder. The topology decoder is then trained to reconstruct the adjacency matrix using a weighted binary cross-entropy loss due to the natural sparsity of adjacency matrices.

Another problem arises since decoders based on the inner product can only reconstruct undirected graphs due to their inherent symmetry. Hence, we implement an asymmetric inner-product-based decoder, by splitting the adjacency matrix into two halves by its diagonal. One half of the topology decoder's latent space is used for the upper and one for the lower part of the adjacency matrix.

Finally, a third problem with inner-product-based decoders stems from the random node embeddings causing the expected average degree to increase proportionally with the number of nodes. This is problematic since the average

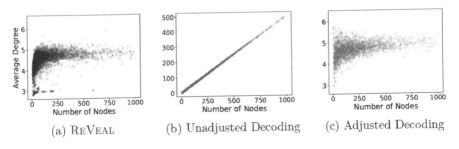

(a) REVEAL   (b) Unadjusted Decoding   (c) Adjusted Decoding

Fig. 2. Average degree compared against the number of nodes for code graphs, decoded naively and decoded with our correction.

degree will be higher for larger graphs, while in reality, code graphs have the property that their average node degree is independent of the number of nodes, which is illustrated in Fig. 2a and Fig. 2b.

The number of reconstructed edges for a particular graph can be seen as a random variable

$$|E| \sim B(p, |V|^2 - |V|) \tag{3}$$

with p the binomial probability to decode a particular edge among the possible $|V|^2 - |V|$ edges. Note that we consider directed edges but no loops. Hence, we obtain $\mathbb{E}(|E|) = p \cdot (|V|^2 - |V|)$. Assuming a deterministic sampling, edges are decoded, when their similarity as defined by the inner product is above a certain threshold t. Adjusting the threshold by incorporating the expected average embedding distance of the closest embeddings reduces the effect of the proportionally increasing average degree as depicted in Fig. 2c. The derivation of this adjustment can be found in Appendix A.1.

Interpolation Method. To augment the code graph datasets, new samples need to be generated given a set of selected graphs. To do that, we propose a method to select and interpolate code graphs in their latent space representations.

A sample denotes an embedding matrix $X' \in \mathbb{R}^{|V| \times d_V}$ for a fixed latent space dimension d_V and number of nodes $|V|$. Since this matrix has different sizes for graphs with different numbers of nodes, no common distance metric can be applied to calculate the nearest neighbors. To mitigate this issue, the graphs are padded with zero vectors for non-existing nodes to the size of the largest graph in the dataset. Additionally, this same issue is found when interpolating the samples and solved in the same way. The interpolated embedding matrix

$$\hat{X}' = \lambda X'_a + (1 - \lambda)X'_b \tag{4}$$

for two chosen code graphs G_a, G_b and a uniformly random $\lambda \in [0, 1]$ is truncated to a number of nodes interpolated in the same way: $|\hat{V}| = \lambda|V_a| + (1-\lambda)|V_b|$ with the same λ. This interpolation method is not permutation-equivariant, thus the node ordering affects the results. Since we use the same method in the nearest

```
void truncate(char *src, int size) {
  char *dest = malloc(size);
  if (!dest) return;
  memcpy(dest, src, size);
  memcpy(src, dest, sizeof(dest));
  free(dest);
}
```

```
void truncate(char *src, int size)
{
    char *dest = malloc(size);
    if (!dest) return;
    strcpy(dest, src);
    memcpy(src, dest, sizeof(dest));
    free(dest);
}
```

```
void truncate_type(char *dest, char *src, int *size)
{
    char *dest = malloc(size);
    if (!dest)
        return;

    memcpy(dest, src, sizeof(src));
    memcpy(src, dest, size);
    free(dest);
}
```

Fig. 3. An interpolated sample in its code representation.

neighbor search, however, this results in the corresponding nodes already being close to each other.

Finally, new latent space representation samples are generated, which can then be decoded using the decoder. To train a graph vulnerability discovery model on the augmented code graphs, we have to reconstruct both, edges and nodes. The node features are recovered using the node decoder's output which is trained using a cosine embedding loss. The adjacency matrices need to be discretized by sampling from a Bernoulli distribution with a probability conforming to the edge probability in the reconstructed adjacency matrix.

5.3 Graph to Code Transformation

The ability to transform code graphs back to source code adds three beneficial properties to our method: First, we can produce human-readable samples, second, we are no longer limited to GNNs and third, we can use the latent node embeddings as a fixed size vector for each node in the VGAE. Thus, we train a transformer [42] to decode non-interpolated graphs and eventually apply it to interpolated samples.

Similar to the variational autoencoder (VAE), a transformer model consists of an encoder and a decoder comprising multiple blocks each. A single block consists of two components, namely a bidirectional multi-head self-attention mechanism and a feed-forward neural network. The attention mechanism generates an attention vector for each code token providing a weight on how much one token affects the other.

We propose an auto-regressive transformer model with a BART-like architecture consisting of six encoder and decoder layers, a width of 128 and only two heads per layer [27]. The code graph is linearized by sequentially extracting the tokens through a depth-first traversal of the AST and embedded using the pre-trained byte-pair tokenizer by Nijkamp et al. [33]. As each node consists of a variable number of tokens, the transformer has to learn a fixed-size token-level embedding of dimension $\mathbb{R}^{|N| \times d_V}$. To this end, an additional transformer encoder layer is trained jointly, that learns a normalized and pooled node vector. This way, inter-dependencies of the tokens are encoded in a token-level representation for the node-level features for the code graphs in the GAE training.

Figure 3 shows a generated synthetic sample at the bottom. We take the graph representation from the upper two samples and interpolate between both latent representations. Then we translate the resulting graph to its code representation using the transformer model.

Both source methods truncate a string but run into buffer overflows due to potential size mismatches between src, dest and size. Note, that the upper samples are taken from two real vulnerabilities. The resulting generated function has a different name and signature, but its body is similar: It is obvious, that the resulting method is also an example of string truncation with a buffer overflow. The unused parameter char *dest in the signature may be erroneously caused by either the generation of the graph or the conversion of the graph to code but may be negligible due to the nature of data augmentation.

6   Evaluation

This section introduces the experiments designed to tackle three research questions, in particular, we describe our experimental setting and provide empirical results answering the following questions:

RQ1 *Does CodeGraphSMOTE provide a sound latent representation?*
RQ2 *Can CodeGraphSMOTE improve detection performance when we lack data?*
RQ3 *Do the augmented datasets yield better model transferability?*

6.1   Experimental Setting

We rely on Fraunhofer-CPG [46] as a tool to generate code graphs and preprocess them using networkx [19]. We use the GNN implementations from Pytorch Geometric [14] and train them on AWS EC2 g4dn instances. All experiments are conducted using 10-fold cross-validation and our VGAE consists of 2 encoder and 2 decoder layers for topology and node features respectively with a dimension of 384. We use an Adam and AdamW optimizer for the VGAE and the transformer with learning rates of 0.0005 and 0.001 respectively.

Datasets and Models. For our experimental evaluation, we use the following three datasets from recent publications around learning-based vulnerability discovery. All three datasets consist of a corpus of vulnerable and clean samples from C and C++ code repositories.

1. Chromium+Debian. The Chromium+Debian dataset consists of 1924 vulnerable and 17294 clean samples. Thus, the imbalance ratio is 10.01%. The dataset has been extracted from the Debian and Chromium bug tracker and hence contains C++ code samples [6].
2. FFmpeg+Qemu. The FFmpeg+Qemu dataset is nearly balanced with a ratio of 45.96% having 11466 and 9751 samples respectively for the clean and vulnerable class. The code was extracted using security-related keywords that have been matched against commits in the Github project repositories from Qemu and FFmpeg [55].
3. *PatchDB*. Finally, we utilize PatchDB [44], which consists of patches extracted from the national vulnerability database (NVD) for multiple C and C++ open-source projects. Vulnerable samples are labeled by their common weakness enumerations (CWEs). Overall, it has 3441 vulnerable and 30149 clean samples resulting in an imbalance ratio of 10.24%.

As ML models for the downstream vulnerability discovery task, we use REVEAL and Devign [6,55]. They both rely on GGNNs and a pooling layer followed by a feed-forward neural network prediction head. We train the transformer, VGAE and downstream classifier on the same training set and test on a disjoint separate dataset containing only real samples.

Metrics. We use two metrics recommended especially for imbalanced learning tasks to provide a comprehensive evaluation of the model's performance. By comparing these scores before and after augmentation, we can assess whether the augmentation has improved the model's performance.

1. *F1-score.* The F1-score is a commonly used metric to evaluate the performance of a classification model. It's a measure of the model's ability to correctly predict both positive and negative classes. The F1-score is calculated as the harmonic mean of precision (P) and recall (R).
2. *Balanced accuracy.* The second is balanced accuracy, which takes into account both, the true positive rate and true negative rate, and is calculated as the average of these two rates.

Baselines. To compare our method for plausibility and practicability, we benchmark against four commonly used augmentation strategies for graphs in general and vulnerability discovery models in particular.

1. *SARD enrichment.* The software assurance reference dataset (SARD) is a synthetic vulnerability corpus containing about 30k vulnerable and 30k clean samples. The vulnerable samples are pattern generated, and consequently, ML models tend to overfit [6]. We use vulnerable samples from this dataset to enrich their original dataset as proposed by Nong et al. [34].
2. *Graph Perturbation.* Borrowed from the graph domain, we can augment the dataset by randomly dropping nodes and edges. This graph perturbation

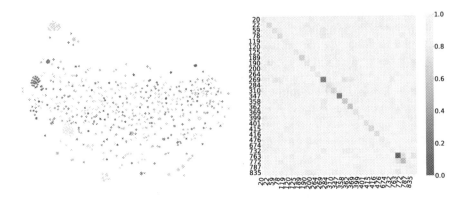

Fig. 4. Average normalized inter- and intra-cluster distance per CWE on PatchDB.

technique can be applied to vulnerable samples to augment the dataset. However, this technique will most likely break the code graph's semantics and generate unintelligible samples.

3. *Graph2Edit.* According to an empirical study [34], Graph2Edit [50] is currently state-of-the-art in neural code generation for vulnerability discovery. It uses a GGNN to learn graph and node embeddings and a LSTM network to predict edit actions on the AST. It is trained to convert ASTs of clean samples to vulnerable ones.

4. *Downsampling.* A naive approach is to downsample the majority class. That is, we remove clean samples until we have an imbalance ratio of 50%.

6.2   Results

The discussion of the experimental results is organized along the three research questions posed at the beginning of this section, which we try to answer in the following.

RQ1 — *Does CodeGraphSMOTE provide a sound latent representation?* First, we want to assess whether the learned latent space from the VGAE in Code-GraphSMOTE represents important features from the code graph and in particular for vulnerability discovery. The scatter plot on the left-hand side of Fig. 4 shows a two-dimensional t-SNE embedding of the VGAE latent representation per vulnerable code graph of the training set from PatchDB. Each sample is colored by its CWE. We can reason about the quality of the interpolated vulnerable samples since it correlates with the quality of the cluster. At least five clusters are clearly visible, including CWE-269 (improper privilege management), CWE-347 (improper verification of cryptographic signature) and CWE-763 (release of invalid pointer or reference). The right-hand side of Fig. 4 shows the average inter- and intra-cluster distances between the CWEs. The matrix is diagonal-dominant suggesting that the learned representation places samples from the

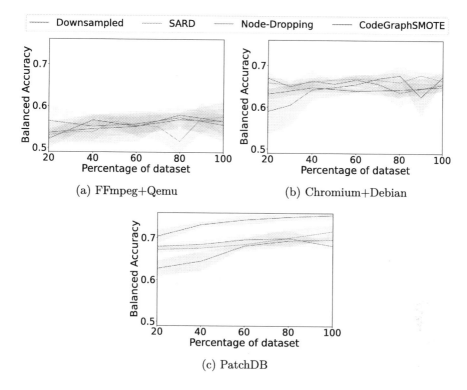

Fig. 5. Dataset augmentation strategies by replacement.

same type of vulnerability closer together. Overall, we can conclude that the latent representation encodes crucial information about the semantics of the code and vulnerability. Since SMOTE selects neighbors that are close to each other as interpolation candidates, it is safe to assume that it will automatically interpolate between vulnerabilities of the same type.

> The latent space representation learned by the VGAE clusters code graphs by their vulnerability type, making it suitable for SMOTE on vulnerability datasets.

RQ2 — *Can CodeGraphSMOTE improve detection performance when we lack data?* We evaluate our method against simple downsampling, SARD enrichment and node-dropping. We simulate smaller datasets, by removing a partition of vulnerable samples from the original FFmpeg+Qemu, Chromium+Debian and PatchDB datasets and re-balance them by augmenting the remaining. Figure 5 shows the performance of the Chromium+Debian model measured in their balanced accuracy. The x-axis denotes the percentage of real samples remaining from the original datasets, while 100% corresponds to the original

Table 1. Cross dataset evaluation presenting the F1-score. *C+D* and *F+Q* denote the Chromium+Debian and FFmpeg+Qemu datasets respectively.

Model	Training	Testing	Downsampling	Graph2Edit	SARD	CodeGraphSMOTE
ReVeal	C+D	F+Q	31.86%	36.94%	15.16%	**41.37%**
	F+Q	C+D	19.31%	**21.31%**	20.07%	18.26%
Devign	C+D	F+Q	5.25%	7.11%	5.70%	**62.97%**
	F+Q	C+D	16.83%	**19.31%**	18.58%	18.20%

dataset re-balanced using the specific method. On PatchDB, the most realistic dataset, CodeGraphSMOTE achieves an overall area under balanced accuracy score of 73.9%, compared against 68.9%, 65.5% and 63.5% for SARD, Node-Dropping and Downsampling respectively. Hence CodeGraphSMOTE yields a significantly stronger improvement compared to the other approaches with nearly 24% improvement against simple downsampling. This is particularly interesting because PatchDB has the most diverse and realistic dataset containing samples from multiple projects collected directly from the NVD. Although no augmentation strategy is a clear winner on the FFmpeg+Qemu dataset and the overall performance is only slightly above 55% as already shown by Chakraborty et al. [6] and Ganz et al. [15], we can still see that SARD is slightly worse than the other methods. Other observations are not statistically significant due to their large standard deviations.

For the Chromium+Debian datasets all augmentation strategies have less influence on the model as depicted by the large standard deviation compared to their effect on PatchDB. There is no augmentation strategy that dominates another with statistical significance. Thus, no method provides a statistically significant improvement over another except for downsampling. Downsampling is the worst method on every dataset while simple graph perturbation is the second best approach.

> Our method provides an improvement of up to 21% balanced accuracy against simple downsampling on realistic datasets and keeps the model performance constant at only 20% of the original dataset.

RQ3 — *Do the augmented datasets yield better model transferability?* Finally, we evaluate whether a pre-trained instance of CodeGraphSMOTE can be used to enhance vulnerability discovery when applied to different datasets that lack labeled or vulnerable samples. Despite recent publications showing that the Devign dataset (FFmpeg+Qemu) and model are unrealistic and underperforming [6,15], we still include both to stay comparable with Graph2Edit.

In contrast, we excluded PatchDB, which contains over 300 C and C++ projects, to demonstrate the usability of CodeGraphSMOTE on small individual projects.

Table 1 shows the average F1-score for the models REVEAL and Devign using four different augmentation strategies to re-balance the datasets. While the models have been trained and tested on disjoint datasets, our results, as shown in Table 1 and Fig. 5, indicate that training on the FFmpeg+Qemu dataset did not yield noteworthy detection capabilities. However, with F1-scores of 18.26% and 18.20%, respectively, CodeGraphSMOTE can be considered comparable to Graph2Edit with its F1-scores of 21.31% and 19.31%. Furthermore, the models trained on the Devign+Qemu dataset did not provide any transferability, highlighting the challenges associated with this dataset.

In contrast, training on the Chromium+Debian dataset reveals that CodeGraphSMOTE significantly improves detection capabilities by a factor of nearly 9 for Devign and 12% for REVEAL, as compared to the state-of-the-art method Graph2Edit. Interestingly, the Chromium+Debian dataset, with a higher degree of class imbalance than the FFmpeg+Qemu dataset, demonstrates the superior performance of CodeGraphSMOTE with increasing class imbalance.

> CodeGraphSMOTE significantly improves model transferability by up to 800% measured by the F1-score. The performance enhancement scales with increasing class imbalance.

7   Conclusion

This work introduces CodeGraphSMOTE, a novel augmentation method designed to address imbalanced attributed code graph datasets. Our approach employs a variational graph autoencoder to interpolate between code graph samples in the latent space, and a transformer model to convert these graphs back to their source code representation. On the way, we also address several common issues with graph autoencoders in general, particularly in topology reconstruction. Through experimental evaluation, we demonstrate that our method not only achieves comparable vulnerability discovery performance with fewer data but also improves the models' generalizability and transferability to new datasets.

Acknowledgment. This work has been funded by the German Federal Ministry of Education and Research (BMBF) in the project IVAN (FKZ: 16KIS1165K).

A   Appendix

A.1   Derivation of the Threshold Adjustment

Our goal is to adjust the threshold t in Equation (2) such that the average degree of a vertex in the reconstructed graph equals a given degree deg. Using

$\mathbb{E}(|E|) = p(|V|^2 - |V|)$, since we consider directed edges but no loops, this is the case if $p(|V|^2 - |V|) = deg\,|V|$ or

$$p = \frac{deg}{|V| - 1} \quad .$$

Now $p = P(X_i' X_j'^T > t)$ where X_i' and X'_j are d-dimensional latent representations of two nodes which (due to the targeted latent distribution of the VAE) we assume to be independent and identically distributed according to the standard normal distribution $\mathcal{N}(\mathbf{0}_d, \mathbf{I}_d)$. Hence the correct adjusted choice of t is given by

$$t = \mathrm{CDF}_Z^{-1}\left(1 - \frac{deg}{|V| - 1}\right) \tag{5}$$

where CDF_Z is the cumulative distribution function of the product $Z = XY$ of two i.i.d. vectors X and Y as above. By symmetry, we may assume that Y is parallel to the first coordinate axis and then X can be marginalized to this axis without affecting the inner product. Thus, we assume w.l.o.g. $d = 1$.

The density of $Z = XY = \frac{1}{4}\left((X + Y)^2 + (X - Y)^2\right)$ (a.k.a. variance gamma distribution) is known to be given by $\mathrm{PDF}_Z(z) = \frac{1}{\pi}K_0(z)$ where $K_0(z)$ is a modified Bessel function of the second kind (see [17]).

Finally, we use numerical integration to get $\mathrm{CDF}_Z(z) = \frac{1}{\pi}\int^z K_0(z)dz$ and solve numerically for t as in Equation (5).

References

1. Allamanis, M., Brockschmidt, M., Khademi, M.: Learning to represent programs with graphs. ArXiv abs/1711.00740 (2017)
2. Arp, D., et al.: Dos and don'ts of machine learning in computer security. In: 31st USENIX Security Symposium (USENIX Security 22), pp. 3971–3988, USENIX Association, Boston, MA (2022). ISBN 978-1-939133-31-1
3. Bronstein, M.M., Bruna, J., Cohen, T., Velivckovi'c, P.: Geometric deep learning: Grids, groups, graphs, geodesics, and gauges (2021)
4. Cai, T., Luo, S., Xu, K., He, D., yan Liu, T., Wang, L.: GraphNorm: a principled approach to accelerating graph neural network training (2020)
5. Cao, S., Sun, X., Bo, L., Wei, Y., Li, B.: Bgnn4vd: constructing bidirectional graph neural-network for vulnerability detection. Inf. Softw. Technol. **136**, 106576 (2021)
6. Chakraborty, S., Krishna, R., Ding, Y., Ray, B.: Deep learning based vulnerability detection: are we there yet? IEEE Trans. Softw. Eng. TBD, 1 (2020)
7. Chawla, N.V., Bowyer, K.W., Hall, L.O., Kegelmeyer, W.P.: Smote: synthetic minority over-sampling technique. J. Artif. Int. Res. **16**(1), 321–357 (2002). ISSN 1076–9757
8. Chen, D., Lin, Y., Li, W., Li, P., Zhou, J., Sun, X.: Measuring and relieving the over-smoothing problem for graph neural networks from the topological view (2019)
9. Chen, Z., Kommrusch, S., Tufano, M., Pouchet, L., Poshyvanyk, D., Monperrus, M.: Sequencer: sequence-to-sequence learning for end-to-end program repair. IEEE Trans. Softw. Eng. **47**(09), 1943–1959 (2021), ISSN 1939–3520

10. Cheng, X., Wang, H., Hua, J., Xu, G., Sui, Y.: DeepWukong: statically detecting software vulnerabilities using deep graph neural network. ACM Trans. Softw. Eng. Methodol. **30**(3) (2021)

11. Dablain, D., Krawczyk, B., Chawla, N.: DeepSMOTE: fusing deep learning and smote for imbalanced data. IEEE Trans. Neural Netw. Learn. Syst., 1–15 (2022). https://doi.org/10.1109/TNNLS.2021.3136503

12. Dinella, E., Dai, H., Li, Z., Naik, M., Song, L., Wang, K.: Hoppity: learning graph transformations to detect and fix bugs in programs. In: International Conference on Learning Representations (2020)

13. Do, T.H., Nguyen, D.M., Bekoulis, G., Munteanu, A., Deligiannis, N.: Graph convolutional neural networks with node transition probability-based message passing and DropNode regularization. Expert Syst. Appl. **174**, 114711 (2021)

14. Fey, M., Lenssen, J.E.: Fast graph representation learning with PyTorch Geometric. In: ICLR Workshop on Representation Learning on Graphs and Manifolds (2019)

15. Ganz, T., Härterich, M., Warnecke, A., Rieck, K.: Explaining graph neural networks for vulnerability discovery. In: Proceedings of the 14th ACM Workshop on Artificial Intelligence and Security, pp. 145–156, AISec '21, New York, NY, USA (2021)

16. Gao, Z., Bhattacharya, S., Zhang, L., Blum, R.S., Ribeiro, A., Sadler, B.M.: Training robust graph neural networks with topology adaptive edge dropping (2021)

17. Gaunt, R.E.: Products of normal, beta and gamma random variables: stein operators and distributional theory. Brazilian J. Probab. Stat. **32**(2), 437–466 (2018)

18. Grieco, G., Grinblat, G.L., Uzal, L., Rawat, S., Feist, J., Mounier, L.: Toward large-scale vulnerability discovery using machine learning. In: Proceedings of the Sixth ACM Conference on Data and Application Security and Privacy, pp. 85–96, CODASPY '16, New York, NY, USA (2016)

19. Hagberg, A., Swart, P., S Chult, D.: Exploring network structure, dynamics, and function using networkx (1 2008)

20. Hamilton, W.L., Ying, R., Leskovec, J.: Inductive representation learning on large graphs. In: NIPS (2017)

21. Han, X., Jiang, Z., Liu, N., Hu, X.: G-mixup: graph data augmentation for graph classification. In: Chaudhuri, K., Jegelka, S., Song, L., Szepesvari, C., Niu, G., Sabato, S. (eds.) Proceedings of the 39th International Conference on Machine Learning, Proceedings of Machine Learning Research, vol. 162, pp. 8230–8248, PMLR (17–23 Jul 2022)

22. Johnson, J.M., Khoshgoftaar, T.M.: Survey on deep learning with class imbalance. J. Big Data **6**(1), 27 (2019)

23. Kingma, D.P., Welling, M.: Auto-encoding variational Bayes. CoRR abs/1312.6114 (2014)

24. Kipf, T.N., Welling, M.: Variational graph auto-encoders. In: NIPS Workshop on Bayesian Deep Learning (2016)

25. Kipf, T.N., Welling, M.: Semi-supervised classification with graph convolutional networks. In: International Conference on Learning Representations (ICLR) (2017)

26. Kong, K., et al.: Robust optimization as data augmentation for large-scale graphs. In: Proceedings of the IEEE/CVF Conference on Computer Vision and Pattern Recognition (CVPR), pp. 60–69 (June 2022)

27. Lewis, M., et al.: BART: denoising sequence-to-sequence pre-training for natural language generation, translation, and comprehension. In: Proceedings of the 58th Annual Meeting of the Association for Computational Linguistics, pp. 7871–7880, Association for Computational Linguistics, Online (Jul 2020)

28. Li, J., Li, J., Liu, Y., Yu, J., Li, Y., Cheng, H.: Deconvolutional networks on graph data. In: Beygelzimer, A., Dauphin, Y., Liang, P., Vaughan, J.W. (eds.) Advances in Neural Information Processing Systems (2021)

29. Li, Y., Tarlow, D., Brockschmidt, M., Zemel, R.S.: Gated graph sequence neural networks. In: Bengio, Y., LeCun, Y., (eds.) 4th International Conference on Learning Representations, ICLR 2016, San Juan, Puerto Rico, May 2–4, 2016, Conference Track Proceedings (2016)

30. Li, Z., Zou, D., Xu, S., Jin, H., Zhu, Y., Chen, Z.: Sysevr: a framework for using deep learning to detect software vulnerabilities. IEEE Trans. Depend. Secure Comput. 19(4), 2244–2258 (2022)

31. Li, Z., Zou, D., Xu, S., Ou, X., Jin, H., Wang, S., Deng, Z., Zhong, Y.: Vuldeepecker: a deep learning-based system for vulnerability detection. In: 25th Annual Network and Distributed System Security Symposium, NDSS 2018, San Diego, California, USA, February 18–21, 2018, The Internet Society (2018)

32. Luo, Y., McThrow, M., Au, W.Y., Komikado, T., Uchino, K., Maruhashi, K., Ji, S.: Automated data augmentations for graph classification (2022)

33. Nijkamp, E., et al.: Codegen: an open large language model for code with multi-turn program synthesis. In: The Eleventh International Conference on Learning Representations (2023)

34. Nong, Y., Ou, Y., Pradel, M., Chen, F., Cai, H.: Generating realistic vulnerabilities via neural code editing: an empirical study, pp. 1097–1109, ESEC/FSE 2022, New York, NY, USA (2022)

35. NT, H., Maehara, T.: Revisiting graph neural networks: all we have is low-pass filters (2019)

36. Pewny, J., Holz, T.: Evilcoder: automated bug insertion. In: Proceedings of the 32nd Annual Conference on Computer Security Applications, pp. 214–225, ACSAC '16, New York, NY, USA (2016)

37. Rong, Y., Huang, W., Xu, T., Huang, J.: Dropedge: towards deep graph convolutional networks on node classification. In: ICLR (2020)

38. Russell, R., et al.: Automated vulnerability detection in source code using deep representation learning, pp. 757–762 (2018)

39. Sennrich, R., Haddow, B., Birch, A.: Improving neural machine translation models with monolingual data. CoRR abs/1511.06709 (2015)

40. Shorten, C., Khoshgoftaar, T.M.: A survey on image data augmentation for deep learning. J. Big Data 6(1), 60 (Jul 2019), ISSN 2196–1115

41. Spinelli, I., Scardapane, S., Hussain, A., Uncini, A.: Biased edge dropout for enhancing fairness in graph representation learning (2021)

42. Vaswani, A., et al.: Attention is all you need. In: Guyon, I., et al., (eds.) Advances in Neural Information Processing Systems, vol. 30, Curran Associates, Inc. (2017)

43. Wang, H., et al.: Combining graph-based learning with automated data collection for code vulnerability detection. IEEE Transactions on Information Forensics and Security 16, 1943–1958 (2021), ISSN 15566021

44. Wang, X., Wang, S., Feng, P., Sun, K., Jajodia, S.: Patchdb: a large-scale security patch dataset. In: 2021 51st Annual IEEE/IFIP International Conference on Dependable Systems and Networks (DSN), pp. 149–160 (2021)

45. Wang, Y., Wang, W., Liang, Y., Cai, Y., Hooi, B.: Graphcrop: subgraph cropping for graph classification. CoRR abs/2009.10564 (2020)

46. Weiss, K., Banse, C.: A language-independent analysis platform for source code (2022)

47. Wu, Z., Pan, S., Chen, F., Long, G., Zhang, C., Yu, P.S.: A comprehensive survey on graph neural networks. IEEE Trans. Neural Netw. Learn. Syst. **32**(1), 4–24 (2021). https://doi.org/10.1109/tnnls.2020.2978386
48. Xu, K., Hu, W., Leskovec, J., Jegelka, S.: How powerful are graph neural networks? In: International Conference on Learning Representations (2019)
49. Yamaguchi, F., Golde, N., Arp, D., Rieck, K.: Modeling and discovering vulnerabilities with code property graphs. In: 2014 IEEE Symposium on Security and Privacy, pp. 590–604 (2014)
50. Yao, Z., Xu, F.F., Yin, P., Sun, H., Neubig, G.: Learning structural edits via incremental tree transformations. In: 9th International Conference on Learning Representations, ICLR 2021, Virtual Event, Austria, May 3–7, 2021, OpenReview.net (2021)
51. Zhao, T., Liu, G., Gunnemann, S., Jiang, M.: Graph data augmentation for graph machine learning: a survey (2022)
52. Zhao, T., Liu, G., Wang, D., Yu, W., Jiang, M.: Counterfactual graph learning for link prediction. CoRR abs/2106.02172 (2021)
53. Zhao, T., Liu, Y., Neves, L., Woodford, O.J., Jiang, M., Shah, N.: Data augmentation for graph neural networks. In: AAAI (2021)
54. Zhao, T., Zhang, X., Wang, S.: GraphSMOTE: imbalanced node classification on graphs with graph neural networks. In: Proceedings of the 14th ACM International Conference on Web Search and Data Mining (2021)
55. Zhou, Y., Liu, S., Siow, J., Du, X., Liu, Y.: Devign: effective vulnerability identification by learning comprehensive program semantics via graph neural networks. In: Wallach, H., Larochelle, H., Beygelzimer, A., d'Alché-Buc, F., Fox, E., Garnett, R. (eds.) Advances in Neural Information Processing Systems, vol. 32, Curran Associates, Inc. (2019)
56. Zhu, Y., Xu, Y., Yu, F., Liu, Q., Wu, S., Wang, L.: Graph contrastive learning with adaptive augmentation. In: Proceedings of the Web Conference 2021, ACM (2021)

An Autoencoder-Based Image Anonymization Scheme for Privacy Enhanced Deep Learning

David Rodriguez[✉] and Ram Krishnan[✉]

Electrical and Computer Engineering Department,
University of Texas at San Antonio, San Antonio, TX 78249, USA
david.rodriguez3@my.utsa.edu, ram.krishnan@utsa.edu

Abstract. The development of deep learning (DL) technology is dependent on the availability of large-scale image datasets to train deep neural networks (DNNs) for image classification. However, many raw image datasets contain sensitive identity feature information that prohibit entities from disclosing data due to privacy regulations. For example, an image dataset may include age or gender information that could be used to identify an individual. Furthermore, medical images may include additional disease information that could lead to patient re-identification. To address this problem, we propose an image transformation scheme using a convolutional autoencoder and multi-output classification model for privacy enhanced deep learning. The proposed scheme obfuscates image visual information while retaining useful attribute features that are required for model utility. Additionally, the proposed method enhances privacy by generating encoded images that exclude sensitive identity feature information. First, we train a multi-output convolutional neural network (CNN) to classify identity features and image attributes. Second, we use the pre-trained multi-output classifier for regularization in training a standard convolutional autoencoder to generate obfuscated versions of the original images that exclude identity feature information and preserve attribute features that are useful for classification. Our results on CelebA and Cifar-100 datasets illustrate that the proposed method successfully degrades classification accuracy of sensitive image data while maintaining model utility for non-sensitive data features.

Keywords: deep neural networks · convolutional neural networks · convolutional autoencoder · privacy · utility

1 Introduction

Cloud-based services have become an extremely popular option for data owners to outsource large computationally expensive deep learning tasks due to flexibility and cost saving [1]. Cloud providers offer a full range of services including

Research supported in part by NSF CREST Grant HRD-1736209 (RK) and NSF CAREER Grant CNS-1553696 (RK).

© IFIP International Federation for Information Processing 2023
Published by Springer Nature Switzerland AG 2023
V. Atluri and A. L. Ferrara (Eds.): DBSec 2023, LNCS 13942, pp. 302–316, 2023.
https://doi.org/10.1007/978-3-031-37586-6_18

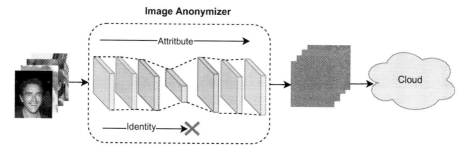

Fig. 1. Image anonymization overview.

storage, servers, virtual desktops, full applications and development platforms. Many organizations have access to large amounts of data but very limited computational resources and storage which prevent them from performing feature extraction tasks locally. Therefore, a large amount of data owners have opted for cloud services to allocate resources as needed for the given task at hand [2]. Typically, an entity will send its raw data such as images to a machine learning as a service (MLaaS) provider for the purpose of developing a DL algorithm directly using the raw images. However, image data may contain sensitive information that the data owner wishes keep private while preserving model utility.

There are several privacy risks that accompany the disclosure of raw image data containing sensitive information. Raw images consist of features that are useful for a specific classification task such as classifying facial attributes which may include if an individual is smiling or wearing glasses, etc. On the other hand, raw images may also include additional feature information that is not useful for the specific classification task such as gender or age which could be used to reveal the identity of an individual. For example, previous work [3] has shown that person identification can be accomplished with as little as a human ear, so given a dataset of raw human faces an attacker could gain access to a victims personal identity by simply possessing an image of the human ear. Furthermore, [4] demonstrated that DNNs could be trained to recover patient identity from chest X-ray data by identifying if two frontal chest X-ray images belong to the same individual even if they were taken years apart. Attackers could potentially leak patient information or analyze the identified images to gain access to additional sensitive information. Consequently, we aim to increase the privacy and security of sensitive data by transforming the original images such that identity information or sensitive attributes are excluded from encoded versions while maintaining classification accuracy.

Several visual information protection methods have been proposed to preserve privacy of image data such as pixelation, blurring and P3 [5]. Visual information protection methods encrypt data such that visible feature information of an image is concealed while making sure that the transformed version remains useful for classification [6–10]. However, these methods do not exclude identity feature information from the encoded version of the original image. Our proposed method not only transforms the image such that it is longer recognizable to humans but it also excludes specific sensitive feature information from the encoded data.

One of the major challenges in developing algorithms to anonymize sensitive image data is known as the trade-off between privacy and utility [11–13]. The goal is to anonymize image data such that an attacker could not learn any sensitive identity feature information while authorized users could perform useful statistics. Eliminating the entire dataset provides perfect privacy but this is not useful. On the other hand, publishing raw unaltered data is statistically useful but may be detrimental to the privacy of sensitive data. We propose to publish transformed versions of the original data that maintain model utility by retaining useful attribute features that are beneficial for classification while increasing privacy by removing sensitive identity features from the data. An overview of the image anonymization process is depicted in Fig. 1.

In this paper, we propose an image data anonymization scheme using a DL approach to increase data privacy while maintaining model utility. Specifically, we train a multi-output DL model to increase classification accuracy of identity feature information and image attributes. Then we train an anonymization network consisting of a convolutional autoencoder attached to the input of a pre-trained multi-output classifier to generate obfuscated versions of the original images. The encoded images exclude identity feature information and preserve attribute features that are useful for classification. In our results, we demonstrate that our image anonymization method increases data privacy while maintaining model utility using CelebA [14] and Cifar-100 [15] datasets.

In summary our contributions are as follows:

- We develop an autoencoder-based image anonymization method for privacy enhanced deep learning.
- We increase privacy of image identity feature information while maintaining model utility.

The remainder of this paper is organized as follows. In Sect. 2, we review related works of privacy protection methods in machine learning. In Sect. 3, the proposed image data anonymization method formulation and loss function are discussed. In Sect. 4, the dataset, network architecture and training procedure are described. In Sect. 5, we evaluate our image anonymization method by assessing the trade-off between privacy-utility and robustness to attacks. Finally, we discuss and conclude our paper in Sects. 6 and 7, respectively.

2   Related Works

Privacy protection in machine learning typically address the privacy of a model's input, the privacy of the model, or the privacy of the model's output. Several privacy preserving techniques have been proposed in the literature, some of which utilize secure multi-party computation, homomorphic encryption, federated learning, visual image protection and learnable image encryption. Secure multi-party computation is a set of cryptographic protocols that allow multiple parties to evaluate a function to perform computation over each parties private data such that only the result of the computation is released among participants while all other information is kept private [16]. Secure multi-party computation methods have been applied in machine learning among multiple parties by computing model parameters using gradient descent optimization without revealing any information beyond the computed outcome [17–20]. Our proposed method does not require multiple parties to perform gradient descent individually but instead allows all users to anonymize private data individually and share the transformed images.

Homomorphic encryption is a type of encryption that allows multiple parties to perform computations on its encrypted data without having access to the original data. It provides strong privacy but is computationally expensive requiring significant overhead to train machine learning models [21–26]. Our proposed encoding scheme does not require expensive encryption operations or specialized primitives for the training process.

Federated learning allows multiple parties to train a machine learning model without sharing data [27–29]. For example, in centralized federated learning a central server sends a model to multiple parties to train locally using their own data, then each participant sends it's own model update back to the central server to update the global model which is again sent to each party to obtain the optimal model without access to the local data by iterating through this process [30]. Essentially, federated learning builds protection into the model. Nevertheless, federated learning suffers from the privacy-utility trade-off [31]. Our proposed encoding scheme enables entities to share encoded data which do not reveal sensitive feature information and maintain model accuracy.

Visual image protection methods transform original images to unrecognizable versions of the image while maintaining the ability to perform useful statistics. A few examples of visual image protection methods are pixelation, blurring, P3 [5], InstaHide [32] and NueraCrypt [33] which aim at preserving privacy and utility—a model trained on an encoded dataset should be approximately as accurate as a model trained on the original dataset [34,35]. InstaHide mixes multiple images together with a linear pixel blend and randomly flips the pixel signs. NeuraCrypt encodes data instances through a neural network with random weights and adds position embeddings to keep track of image structure then shuffles the modified output in blocks of pixels. Our proposed encoding scheme removes the unnecessary complexity of NeuraCrypt's positional embeddings and permutations while maintaining privacy and utility.

Learnable image encryption methods encrypt images such that the encoded versions are useful for classification [6–10]. However, in some cases network adjustments are required to process learnable image encryptions such as blockwise adaptation [6]. Our method does not require any special modifications to the network and excludes identity information from the obfuscated samples while maintaining usability for classification. Our work is most closely related to [36] which removes user identity information from mobile sensor data while training a network to classify user activities. In our work, we develop a deep learning classification model using image attribute features while removing image identity features.

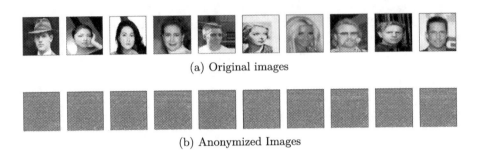

(a) Original images

(b) Anonymized Images

Fig. 2. Examples of anonymized images from Celeba dataset using the proposed scheme. The bottom row are the corresponding anonymized images of the top row.

3   Image Data Anonymization

Our goal is to transform image data such that all visual feature information is unrecognizable to humans as depicted in Fig. 2 but remains useful for classification. Additionally, we aim to remove identity feature information from the transformed images while preserving attribute features. Our method enables entities to share encoded versions of the original data that exclude sensitive feature information while maintaining model utility. We consider identity features that can be collected from an image as sensitive data. On the other hand, we consider attribute features in a given image as non-sensitive data. We wish to preserve attribute features in the transformed images while removing sensitive identity features. Additionally, we aim to maintain similar attribute classification performance on the transformed images as the original images.

3.1   Formulation

Our goal is to anonymize image data by removing identity feature information while preserving attribute features for model utility. Let $\mathcal{X}$ be the set of all possible 8-bit images in the data domain, $X_a \subseteq \mathcal{X}$ is the data owner's private subset and Y_a is the corresponding label set. Given the private image dataset $\{x_{a_i}\}_{i=1}^{N}$ where $x_{a_i} \in X_a$, the data owner encodes all images using a private image anonymization function $z_a = E(x_a)$ and shares the encoded set $\{z_{a_i}\}_{i=1}^{N}$ and corresponding attribute labels $\{y_{a_i}\}_{i=1}^{N}$ where $y_{a_i} \in Y_a$ with a third party cloud service provider without revealing sensitive identity feature information. The proposed image anonymization function is similar to [36] but instead of anonymizing mobile sensor data we develop our encoding function to anonymize image data. The proposed method consists of a multi-output classifier to distinguish between attribute and identity features. In addition, the network consists of an autoencoder to anonymize images. The objective of training the network is to obtain the image anonymizer E^* which transforms raw images into anonymized images.

In the multi-output classification model training phase, a resnet50 model is trained to classify identity features and attribute features using the same input images $\{x_{a_i}\}_{i=1}^N$ with their respective class labels. Our objective function for the multi-output classification model has two loss terms: identity loss for classifying identity features; and attribute loss for classifying attribute features. We aim to classify identity features and attribute features of a given image with high classification accuracy for the multi-output network. After training, the multi-output classification model is used to develop the anonymization network for the purpose of transforming original images into anonymized images. Our anonymization objective function also contains two loss terms: identity suppression loss for removing identity features; and attribute preservation loss for preserving attribute features. We aim to degrade the identity feature classification accuracy while preserving the attribute feature classification accuracy.

3.2   Multi-Output Classification Loss Function

The multi-output network is trained using a multi-objective loss function for image classification which consists of an identity and attribute loss function. The identity loss is used to minimize the error between the true identity and identity classifier's predicted identity. The attribute loss is used to minimize the error between the true attribute and the attribute classifier's predicted attribute. The aim is to classify identity features and attribute features with high classification accuracy.

Identity Loss. The identity loss function L_i uses cross-entropy to measure the performance of identity classifier $I(\cdot)$ which is trained to classify image identity features.

$$L_i(I, X, Y) = -\frac{1}{N} \sum_{i=1}^{N} Y_i log(I(x_i)) \tag{1}$$

where x_i is the ith image and Y_i is the corresponding ground truth identity label. $I(x_i)$ is the identity classifier's predicted output for the ith image.

Attribute Loss. The attribute loss function L_a uses categorical cross-entropy to measure the performance of the attribute classifier $A(\cdot)$ which is trained to classify image attribute features.

$$L_a(A, T, X) = -\frac{1}{N} \sum_{i=1}^{N} T_i log(A(x_i)) \tag{2}$$

where T_i is the ground truth N-dimensional one hot encoded vector attribute label for the ith image and $A(x_i)$ is the attribute classification function predicted softmax output which is an N-dimensional vector consisting of the attribute label probabilities for the ith image.

3.3 Multi-output Classification Objective

Our multi-output classification objective is:

$$L(I, A) = L_a(A, T, X) + L_i(I, X, Y) \qquad (3)$$

we aim to solve:

$$I^*, A^* = \underset{I,A}{\operatorname{argmin}} L(I, A) \qquad (4)$$

3.4 Image Anonymization Loss Function

The image anonymization network is trained using a multi-objective loss function for image classification which consists of an identity suppression and attribute preservation loss function. The aim is to remove identity features while preserving attribute features that are useful for classification.

Identity Suppression Loss. The identity suppression loss function L_s uses mean squared error to remove identity feature information from sensitive data.

$$L_s(\xi, I^*, E) = -\frac{1}{N} \sum_{i=1}^{N} (\xi - I^*(E(x_i)))^2 \qquad (5)$$

where E is the anonymization function and I^* is a pre-trained identity classification function. ξ is a positive value between 0–1. We maximize the difference between the predicted identity label and the true identity label by minimizing the mean squared error between ξ and the predicted identity label given the ith encoded image. The anonymization network is penalized if the transformed image contains identity feature information.

Attribute Preservation Loss. The attribute preservation loss function L_p uses categorical cross-entropy to preserve attribute feature information.

$$L_p(A^*, E) = -\frac{1}{N} \sum_{i=1}^{N} T_i log(A^*(E(x_i))) \qquad (6)$$

where A^* is the pre-trained attribute classification function. The aim is to minimize the preservation loss given the ith encoded image. We minimize the difference between the predicted attribute label and the true attribute label by minimizing the crossentropy between T_i and the predicted attribute label.

3.5   Image Anonymization Objective

Our image anonymization objective is:

$$L(\xi, I^*, A^*, E) = \lambda_1 L_p(A^*, E) + \lambda_2 L_s(\xi, I^*, E) \tag{7}$$

where the regularization parameters λ_1 and λ_2 are positive values that regulate the trade-off between privacy and utility.

we aim to solve:

$$E^* = \underset{E}{\mathrm{argmin}}\, L(\xi, I^*, A^*, E) \tag{8}$$

Our anonymization function E^* generates encoded images that retain useful attribute features by penalizing the autoencoder network using crossentropy if the output does not contain attribute features. In addition, the autoencoder network is penalized using mean squared error if the output contains identity features. Thus our objective is used to preserve attribute features by applying L_p while removing identity features by applying L_s.

4   Methods

4.1   Dataset

In this work, we use the publicly available CelebA [14] and Cifar-100 [15] image datasets to develop anonymization networks. The CelebA dataset is a large-scale face attribute dataset that consists of approximately 200K celebrity face images. It includes gender and 40 attributes per image with a variety of poses and backgrounds. However, in our experiments we select images of 4 mutually exclusive attribute labels consisting of pale skin, smiling, eye glasses and wearing hat. Increasing the number of attributes significantly reduces the amount images per class. Consequently, we include 10K images per attribute label. Our goal is to train the anonymization network to generate encoded images that include attribute label features while removing gender label features. The Cifar-100 dataset consists of 60,000 32×32 color images. It consists of 100 classes containing 600 images each which are referred to as the fine label set. It is also available with 20 superclasses containing 3,000 images each which are referred to as the coarse label set. We consider the fine label set to be private. Thus we aim to remove image features associated with the fine label set. Our goal is to train the anonymization network to generate encoded images that include coarse label feature while removing fine label features.

4.2   Anonymization Network Architecture

The anonymization network architecture depicted in Fig. 3 consists of two parts: a multi-output Resnet50 for image classification and a standard convolutional autoencoder (CAE) for image transformation. Resnets are large state-of-the-art

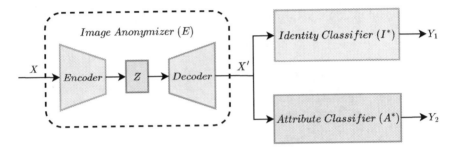

Fig. 3. Proposed anonymization model architecture.

DL architectures that consist of several blocks of residual modules and skip connections [37]. The multi-output architecture consists of one resnet50 feature extraction network with two separate classifiers at the output. The CAE encoder network consists of three convolution layers with 32, 64 and 128 filters, respectively. The kernel size is 3×3 with a stride of 2 and a latent space of 128. Each convolution layer consists of a leaky relu activation function with alpha 0.2 followed by a batch normalization layer. The decoder network consists of three transposed convolution layers with 128, 64 and 32 filters, respectively. The kernel size is 3×3 with a stride of 2 and output size of $224 \times 224 \times 3$. Each transposed convolution layer consists of a leaky relu activation function with alpha 0.2 followed by a batch normalization layer.

4.3   Training Procedure

Our training procedure consists of a feature extraction phase for classification and an identity removal phase for anonymization. First, in the feature extraction phase we train a multi-output resnet50 model from randomly initialized parameters for two different classification tasks given the same images. We train one classifer to predict the gender identity for a given image using binary crossentropy loss function for the CelebA dataset. In our Cifar-100 experiments we train the identity classifier using the fine label set which includes 100 classes. Simultaneously, we train another classifier to predict the attribute of the same image using categorical crossentropy loss function. In our Cifar-100 experiments we train the attribute classifier using the coarse label set which includes 20 classes. The coarse label set is the superclass of the fine label set, e.g., the fish label is the superclass of aquarium fish, flatfish, ray, shark, trout. We wish to classify fine label features and coarse label features for a given image set.

Second, in the identity removal phase we randomly initialize the CAE parameters and attach its output to the previously trained multi-output resnet50 classification model input. We freeze the resnet50 classifier model parameters to ensure that the weights do not change during CAE training for the identity removal phase. During training we aim to learn a CAE that retains useful attribute feature information to reconstruct an unrecognizable version of the

Table 1. Image Classification Accuracy of identity and attribute classifier for CelebA and Cifar-100 datasets

Encryption	Identity Acc (%)		Attribute Acc (%)	
	CelebA	Cifar-100	CelebA	Cifar-100
Plain Images	95.85	82.96	87.02	88.13
Proposed Scheme	50.33	20.71	85.96	83.45

original image for classification while removing the identity feature information. To remove identity feature information we optimize the identity classifier with a modified version of the mean absolute error loss function. To assure that the anonymized images retain attribute feature information we continue training the attribute classifier with the categorical crossentropy loss function.

Both networks were trained using the adam optimizer with a batch size of 128. Check points were used to save the model with the highest validation accuracy during the training procedure. All images were resized to 224×224 and normalized between 0 and 1. The dataset was randomly shuffled and split to generate the train, test and validation set. Minor data augmentation was applied during training using keras image data generator which include zoom range 0.2 and horizontal flip. All training was completed using a tesla v100 graphical processing unit.

5   Evaluation

5.1   Evaluating the Privacy/Utility Trade-Off

We train the anonymization network using the proposed method and examine the trade-off between privacy and utility, i.e. we measure the change in identity and attribute classification accuracy. First, we transform the original images using our anonymization method. Second, we compare the identity and attribute classification accuracy of original images and the transformed images.

The identity classification accuracy of anonymized images significantly decreased compared to original images. Additionally, the attribute classification accuracy of anonymized images is similar to original images. To quantify the trade-off between privacy and utility we measure the reduction in identity and attribute classification accuracy for the anonymized dataset compared to original dataset. In our experiments, we demonstrate that the proposed image anonymization method enables us to maintain high image attribute classification accuracy of 85.96% & 83.45% for CelebA and Cifar-100 datasets, respectively, which is similar to original images. It also enables us to reduce image identity classification accuracy from 95.85% & 82.96% to 50.33% & 20.71% for CelebA and Cifar-100 datasets, respectively, as shown in Table 1.

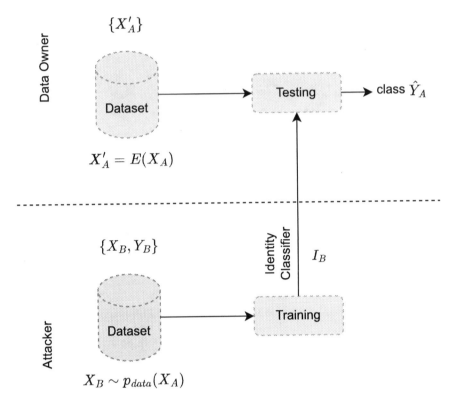

Fig. 4. Classifier transfer attack diagram. Where X'_A is the data owner's encoded dataset and X_B, Y_B are the attackers raw image dataset and identity labels which follows the probability distribution of the data owner's original dataset. I_B is the attacker's identity classifier. The attacker trains I_B with X_B, Y_B and uses the classifier to predict the identity label of the data owner's encoded dataset.

5.2 Evaluating Robustness to Attacks

Classifier Transfer Attack. We evaluate the robustness of our image anonymization approach against attacks that aim to learn an identity feature classifier and transfer it onto the data owners encoded set for classification. We conduct experiments on CelebA and Cifar-100 datasets using gender and coarse labels, respectively. We assume that the attacker is able to construct a dataset that follows a similar probability distribution as the data owner's original dataset and corresponding labels. First, the attacker trains his own identity classifier using the constructed dataset to achieve high classification accuracy. Then he attempts to classify the data owners encoded set using his pre-trained identity classifier. An overview of the classifier transfer attack is depicted in Fig. 4.

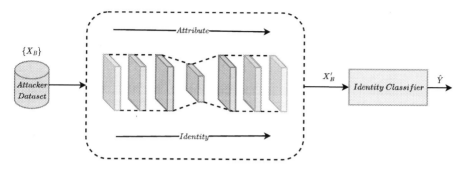

Fig. 5. Encoding transfer attack diagram. Where X_B is the attacker's dataset which follows the probability distribution of the data owner's original dataset. X'_B is the attacker's encoded dataset which consists of attribute features and identity features. The data owners identity classifier is used to predict the identity label of the attacker's encoded dataset to verify if X'_B captures the data owner's identity features.

We evaluate the performance of the attacker's pre-trained identity classifier using the data owner's encoded set. The goal of the attack is to classify identity features given the data owner's encoded dataset. Our experimental results demonstrate that the proposed method is resistant against classifier transfer attacks as shown in row 1 of Table 2 the classification accuracy is 23.49% and 17.01% for CelabA and Cifar-100, respectively.

Encoding Transfer Attack. We also consider the scenario where the attacker aims to learn a representation of the data owner's encoded set to classify identity features. Again, we assume the attacker constructs a dataset that follows a similar distribution as the data owner's original dataset and corresponding labels. First, the attacker trains a multi-output classification model for identity and attribute features similar to the proposed method. Then a randomly initialized autoencoder is trained to generate encoded samples such that identity and attribute information are both preserved. This is accomplished by freezing the weights of the pre-trained identity and attribute classifier and updating the autoencoder parameters based on the gradients of the classification loss. The attacker's modified anonymization network is trained to maintain high classification accuracy for both the identity and attribute classifiers. The encoding transfer attack is depicted in Fig. 5.

Finally, we evaluate the effective of the proposed method against encoding transfer attacks by assessing the performance of the data owner's identity classifier given the attacker's generated encoded set. The goal of the attack is to generate encoded images that include exploitable identity features. The data owner's identity classifier is used to verify if identity features are present in the attackers encoded set. Our experimental results show that the proposed method is resistant to encoding transfer attacks as shown in row 2 of Table 2, the classification accuracy is poor 25.59% and 20.58% for CelebA and Cifar-100, respectively.

Table 2. Classifier and encoding transfer attack performance on CelebA and Cifar-100 datasets

Attack Scheme	Identity Acc. (%)	
	CelebA	Cifar-100
Classifier Transfer	23.49	17.01
Encoding Transfer	25.59	20.58

6   Discussion

In this work, we train an attribute and identity classification model on raw image data and use the network to update a convolutional autoencoder to generate anonymized image data. In our experiments, we evaluate the trade-off between privacy and utility of our image anonymization method by measuring the identity and attribute classification accuracy before and after encoding the dataset. Our results show that the attribute classification accuracy remains high for the transformed images while the identity classification accuracy is significantly reduced for the transformed images. Also, we evaluate the robustness to attacks against the proposed method. In our experiments, we demonstrate that the classifier transfer attack and encoding transfer attack are unsuccessful at inferring the identity of the original images. The identity suppression loss function could be modified as an extension to our proposed method by minimizing the error between the incorrect class and the predicted label using cross-entropy, which we leave for future work. Also, we suspect that the autoencoder's encoder latent space may be sufficient to develop a DL classification model for attribute features while excluding identity features as compared to our proposed method in which we develop our anonymization network with obfuscated reconstructed images (decoder output), we leave this for future work.

7   Conclusion

We proposed an image anonymization method using a standard convolutional autoencoder and multi-ouput resnet50 model to enhance the privacy of raw image data. The images were transformed into unrecognizable versions of the original input data. Highly relevant feature information that is useful for classification was captured in the encoded images. Additionally, we increase privacy through the reduction of identity classification accuracy using the transformed images. In this paper, we demonstrated that the proposed method was able to protect raw data features in the original images and enhance privacy of identity feature information while maintaining model utility with high attribute classification accuracy. In our experiments, we evaluated the effectiveness of our image anonymization method by measuring the reduction of attribute and identity classification accuracy. The experimental results confirm that our proposed method not only enables us to maintain high image attribute classification accuracy but also to reduce image identity classification accuracy.

References

1. Atallah, M.J., Pantazopoulos, K.N., Rice, J.R., Spafford, E.E.: Secure outsourcing of scientific computations. Adv. Comput. **54**, 215–272 (2002)
2. Yuan, X., Wang, X., Wang, C., Squicciarini, A., Ren, K.: Enabling privacy-preserving image-centric social discovery. In: Proceedings of the 2014 IEEE 34th International Conference on Distributed Computing Systems, ser. ICDCS '14. USA: IEEE Computer Society, pp. 198–207 (2014). https://doi.org/10.1109/ICDCS.2014.28
3. Wu, Z., Huang, Y., Wang, L., Wang, X., Tan, T.: A comprehensive study on cross-view gait based human identification with deep CNNs. IEEE Trans. Pattern Anal. Mach. Intell. **39**(2), 209–226 (2016)
4. Packhäuser, K., Gündel, S., Münster, N., Syben, C., Christlein, V., Maier, A.: Is medical chest x-ray data anonymous? arXiv preprint arXiv:2103.08562 (2021)
5. McPherson, R., Shokri, R., Shmatikov, V.: Defeating image obfuscation with deep learning. arXiv preprint arXiv:1609.00408 (2016)
6. Tanaka, M.: Learnable image encryption. In: 2018 IEEE International Conference on Consumer Electronics-Taiwan (ICCE-TW), pp. 1–2 (2018)
7. Sirichotedumrong, W., Maekawa, T., Kinoshita, Y., Kiya, H.: Privacy-preserving deep neural networks with pixel-based image encryption considering data augmentation in the encrypted domain. In: 2019 IEEE International Conference on Image Processing (ICIP), pp. 674–678 (2019)
8. Sirichotedumrong, W., Kinoshita, Y., Kiya, H.: Pixel-based image encryption without key management for privacy-preserving deep neural networks. IEEE Access **7**, 177:844–177:855 (2019)
9. Sirichotedumrong, W., Kiya, H.: A gan-based image transformation scheme for privacy-preserving deep neural networks (2020). https://arxiv.org/abs/2006.01342
10. Chen, Z., Zhu, T., Xiong, P., Wang, C., Ren, W.: Privacy preservation for image data: a Gan-based method. Int. J. Intell. Syst. **36**(4), 1668–1685 (2021)
11. Rastogi, V., Suciu, D., Hong, S.: The boundary between privacy and utility in data publishing. In: Proceedings of the 33rd International Conference on Very Large Data Bases, pp. 531–542 (2007)
12. Li, T., Li, N.: On the tradeoff between privacy and utility in data publishing. In: Proceedings of the 15th ACM SIGKDD International Conference on Knowledge Discovery and Data Mining, pp. 517–526 (2009)
13. Yonghao, G., Weiming, W.: A quantifying method for trade-off between privacy and utility. In: IET International Conference on Information and Communications Technologies (IETICT 2013). IET, pp. 270–273 (2013)
14. Liu, Z., Luo, P., Wang, X., Tang, X.: Deep learning face attributes in the wild. In: Proceedings of International Conference on Computer Vision (ICCV) (2015)
15. Krizhevsky, A.: Learning multiple layers of features from tiny images (2009)
16. Yao, A.C.: Protocols for secure computations. In: 23rd Annual Symposium on Foundations of Computer Science (SFCS 1982), pp. 160–164. IEEE (1982)
17. Chase, M., Gilad-Bachrach, R., Laine, K., Lauter, K., Rindal, P.: Private collaborative neural network learning. Cryptology ePrint Archive (2017)
18. Mohassel, P., Zhang, Y.: Secureml: a system for scalable privacy-preserving machine learning. In: 2017 IEEE Symposium on Security and Privacy (SP), pp. 19–38 (2017)
19. Wagh, S., Gupta, D., Chandran, N.: Securenn: 3-party secure computation for neural network training. Proc. Priv. Enhancing Technol. **2019**(3), 26–49 (2019)

20. Nikolaenko, V., Weinsberg, U., Ioannidis, S., Joye, M., Boneh, D., Taft, N.: Privacy-preserving ridge regression on hundreds of millions of records. In: 2013 IEEE Symposium on Security and Privacy, pp. 334–348 (2013)

21. Aono, Y., Hayashi, T., Trieu Phong, L., Wang, L.: Scalable and secure logistic regression via homomorphic encryption. In: Proceedings of the Sixth ACM Conference on Data and Application Security and Privacy, pp. 142–144 (2016)

22. Bonte, C., Vercauteren, F.: Privacy-preserving logistic regression training. BMC Med. Genomics **11**(4), 13–21 (2018)

23. Crawford, J.L.H., Gentry, C., Halevi, S., Platt, D., Shoup, V.: Doing real work with FHE: the case of logistic regression. Cryptology ePrint Archive, Paper 2018/202 (2018). https://eprint.iacr.org/2018/202

24. Graepel, T., Lauter, K., Naehrig, M.: ML confidential: machine learning on encrypted data. In: Kwon, T., Lee, M.-K., Kwon, D. (eds.) ICISC 2012. LNCS, vol. 7839, pp. 1–21. Springer, Heidelberg (2013). https://doi.org/10.1007/978-3-642-37682-5_1

25. Kim, M., Song, Y., Wang, S., Xia, Y., Jiang, X., et al.: Secure logistic regression based on homomorphic encryption: design and evaluation. JMIR Med. Informat. **6**(2), e8805 (2018)

26. Nandakumar, K., Ratha, N., Pankanti, S., Halevi, S.: Towards deep neural network training on encrypted data. In: Proceedings of the IEEE/CVF Conference on Computer Vision and Pattern Recognition Workshops (2019)

27. Li, T., Sahu, A.K., Talwalkar, A., Smith, V.: Federated learning: challenges, methods, and future directions. IEEE Sig. Process. Mag. **37**(3), 50–60 (2020)

28. Bonawitz, K., et al.: Towards federated learning at scale: system design. Proc. Mach. Learn. Syst. **1**, 374–388 (2019)

29. Zhao, Y., Li, M., Lai, L., Suda, N., Civin, D., Chandra, V.: Federated learning with non-iid data. arXiv preprint arXiv:1806.00582 (2018)

30. Konečný, J., McMahan, H.B., Yu, F.X., Richtárik, P., Suresh, A.T., Bacon, D.: Federated learning: strategies for improving communication efficiency (2016). https://arxiv.org/abs/1610.05492

31. Kairouz, P., et al.: Advances and open problems in federated learning. Found. Trends® Mach. Learn. **14**(1–2), pp. 1–210 (2021)

32. Huang, Y., Song, Z., Li, K., Arora, S.: InstaHide: instance-hiding schemes for private distributed learning. In: Proceedings of the 37th International Conference on Machine Learning, Ser. Proceedings of Machine Learning Research, H. D. III and A. Singh, Eds., vol. 119. PMLR, 13–18 Jul, pp. 4507–4518 (2020). https://proceedings.mlr.press/v119/huang20i.html

33. Yala, A., et al.: Neuracrypt: hiding private health data via random neural networks for public training (2021). https://arxiv.org/abs/2106.02484

34. Carlini, N., et al.: Is private learning possible with instance encoding? (2020). https://arxiv.org/abs/2011.05315

35. Raynal, M., Achanta, R., Humbert, M.: Image obfuscation for privacy-preserving machine learning (2020). https://arxiv.org/abs/2010.10139

36. Malekzadeh, M., Clegg, R.G., Cavallaro, A., Haddadi, H.: Mobile sensor data anonymization. In: Proceedings of the International Conference on Internet of Things Design and Implementation, pp. 49–58 (2019)

37. He, K., Zhang, X., Ren, S., Sun, J.: Deep residual learning for image recognition (2015). https://arxiv.org/abs/1512.03385

Mobile Applications

Security and Privacy of Digital Mental Health: An Analysis of Web Services and Mobile Applications

Aishwarya Surani$^{(\boxtimes)}$ ⓘ, Amani Bawaked ⓘ, Matthew Wheeler ⓘ,
Braden Kelsey ⓘ, Nikki Roberts ⓘ, David Vincent ⓘ, and Sanchari Das ⓘ

University of Denver, Denver, CO 80208, USA
{aishwaryaumesh.surani,amani.bawaked,matthew.wheeler,braden.kelsey,
nicolette.roberts,david.vincent,sanchari.das}@du.edu

Abstract. In the wake of the COVID-19 pandemic, a rapid digital transformation has taken place in the mental healthcare sector, with a marked shift towards telehealth services on web and mobile platforms. This transition, while advantageous in many ways, raises critical questions regarding data security and user privacy given the sensitive nature of the information exchanged. To evaluate these concerns, we undertook a rigorous security and privacy examination of 48 web services and 39 mobile applications specific to mental healthcare, utilizing tools such as MobSF, RiskInDroid, AndroBugs, SSL Labs, and Privacy Check. We also delved into privacy policies, manually evaluating how user data is acquired, disseminated, and utilized by these services. Our investigation uncovered that although a handful of mental healthcare web services comply with expert security protocols, including SSL certification and solid authentication strategies, they often lack crucial privacy policy provisions. In contrast, mobile applications exhibit deficiencies in security and privacy best practices, including underdeveloped permission modeling, absence of superior encryption algorithms, and exposure to potential attacks such as Janus, Hash Collision, and SSL Security. This research underscores the urgency to bolster security and privacy safeguards in digital mental healthcare services, concluding with pragmatic recommendations to fortify the confidentiality and security of healthcare data for all users.

Keywords: Security and Privacy Analysis · Web Services · Mobile Applications · Mental Healthcare · Telehealth

1 Introduction

Mental healthcare services constitute a highly data-intensive field, generating, disseminating, storing, and accessing large volumes of data daily, particularly in the realm of telehealth services [14]. The data produced by mental healthcare services has become one of the most valuable assets in today's digital age [58]. Despite the growth of telehealth services, especially in mental healthcare services,

© IFIP International Federation for Information Processing 2023
Published by Springer Nature Switzerland AG 2023
V. Atluri and A. L. Ferrara (Eds.): DBSec 2023, LNCS 13942, pp. 319–338, 2023.
https://doi.org/10.1007/978-3-031-37586-6_19

which the pandemic has exacerbated, concerns about patient data security and privacy persist [51]. Technological advancements in this sector have led to several consequences concerning user privacy and data security [28]. Laws and regulations, such as the General Data Protection Regulation (GDPR) in the European Union, focus primarily on user data protection [1], while the Health Insurance Portability and Accountability Act (HIPAA) aims to protect user healthcare information [39]. Nonetheless, when patients receive consultations via mobile applications or web services, sometimes it is necessary to document their issues, such as symptoms or medical history, for treatment purposes [46,59]. These services may store not only symptoms but also personal details like name, age, user location, and gender-specific information or make them accessible to third parties [32].

Given the sensitive nature of the data in mental healthcare services, privacy and security issues persist within online applications and web services. This research aims to bridge this gap by examining the security and privacy aspects of mental healthcare applications and web services. To address these concerns, we conducted a security evaluation of 48 mental healthcare web services and 39 mental healthcare mobile applications to understand how these services are developed and implemented concerning security and privacy. We employed tools such as MobSF [36], Riskindriod [49], Androbugs [2] to assess mental healthcare mobile applications, and SSL Labs [54] and Privacy Check [41] to study mental healthcare web services. Furthermore, we manually analyzed privacy policies to understand how user data is collected, stored, used, and shared by the web services.

On a positive note, our findings revealed that more than half of the mental healthcare web services adhere to best practices in terms of certificate implementation, upgrading to the latest SSL and TLS protocols, using RSA 2048 public key size, and preventing downgrade attacks. However, they should consider improving privacy aspects by incorporating some of the missing privacy policies, such as information on users' Personally Identifiable Information (PII) data like Social Security Number (SSN), email address, policy on data collection and sharing with third parties, whether web services track user location, notification procedures in case of a data breach, and most importantly, if the web services provide users the ability to control how their data is stored, analyzed, or used.

2   Related Work

The healthcare sector, particularly mental healthcare, has been increasingly leveraged by patients online due to the COVID-19 pandemic, as they can access services from anywhere and at any time without needing to travel [16,43,47,48].

2.1   Mental Healthcare Web Services

Timely medical assistance is crucial in mental healthcare [26]. The COVID-19 pandemic has made these services more readily available to patients online through web services. Sorkin et al. conducted a survey study in the United States to examine the rise of mental healthcare tools during the COVID-19 pandemic, with results showing increased usage of mental healthcare tools as people sought more mental health support during the pandemic [53]. Oh et al. compared online and in-person mental health services and found that youth preferred online services, as they felt more comfortable sharing their issues with the system rather than medical professionals [44]. Derr conducted a systematic literature review to analyze the use of mental healthcare web services among immigrants in the United States. The study revealed a lower usage rate among immigrants compared to non-immigrants, despite the lack of mental healthcare support for immigrants who are away from family and friends [11]. Considering the various use cases of mental healthcare services and their increased usage, it is essential to study the security and privacy aspects to determine how these web services are technically implemented.

2.2   Mental Healthcare Mobile Applications

In addition to web services, mental healthcare services are also offered through mobile applications, facilitating easy online connections for users [8,20]. Wang et al. reviewed the use of mental healthcare applications during the COVID-19 pandemic, finding a surge in usage due to increased psychological needs during this time [61]. Grist et al. conducted a study to review mental healthcare applications for children, examining the practicality and safety of these applications [17]. Lui et al. focused on the practicality of mental health mobile applications in terms of psychological help, showing that users carefully use these applications considering the required medical assistance [27]. Luxton et al. introduced how healthcare can be implemented in smartphones to leverage technology for providing mental healthcare services online [29].

Lattie et al. conducted a mixed-method study with users and clinicians of a mental healthcare organization to understand their views on the technological aspects of mental healthcare services. Surprisingly, clinicians were more than happy to use technology for mental healthcare services, but users had concerns as they struggled with accessing services using technology [25]. Previous studies on mental healthcare mobile applications have focused on the vital role of technology in increasing online usage. However, an essential outcome of using these services is the potential invasion of digital privacy, such as patient confidentiality and the storage and sharing of data by application developers or third-party applications.

2.3   Security and Privacy Concerns in Mental Healthcare

The most critical concern when dealing with healthcare data is user data security and privacy [50]. Trust also plays an essential role from the user's perspective. When users communicate with the system, website and mobile application providers must ensure that the data is not compromised or shared, as it contains personal health-related information. As a result, it is necessary to have security and privacy laws and regulations between the users and the system for effective functioning [30]. In terms of mental healthcare websites, it is essential to study the communication protocols used over the internet and how the data is stored and used, as it might be stolen or disclosed to third parties [32]. Kramer et al. focused on the legal and regulatory aspects, such as proof of credentials, licensing, and security of mental healthcare mobile applications. The study presents a secure framework to mitigate security risks while communicating with mental healthcare mobile applications [23].

Given the rise of technology in these services, it is crucial to explore the security and privacy aspects for users to communicate with the system without hesitation. Security and privacy are vital when using mental healthcare services, whether in the form of websites or applications. Thus to understand further, we analyzed the mental healthcare web services (48) and mobile applications (39) from security and privacy perspective.

3   Methodology

We conducted the security assessment of 87 mental healthcare services over the period of one and a half years. We initiated our research by collecting mental healthcare web services and applications available to users in the United States. To locate and compile these services, we employed Google's search engine. We ensured that each service was available in English and operated by providers based in the United States. Our primary list included 48 web-based mental healthcare services and 39 mental healthcare mobile applications designed for the Android operating system, totaling 87 services and applications for evaluation. Our work is inspired by the previous security evaluation analysis done by [21,40].

3.1   Web-Services Evaluation

After assembling our primary list of mental healthcare web services, we concentrated on the various security tools and frameworks available for evaluating these services. We selected Qualys SSL Labs for web service evaluation because it examines how SSL is deployed and configured for web services and websites. The analysis delves into certificate configurations, downgrade attack prevention, session resumption, and TLS protocol usage, as well as potential vulnerabilities. Besides security analysis, we also focused on the privacy aspects of these web services, so we chose Privacy Check, a data mining tool developed by the University of Texas, Austin [41], to assess the privacy policies of the mental healthcare web services. This tool scans privacy policies and categorizes them into User Control and GDPR sections, assigning scores accordingly. We manually analyzed the privacy policies of all 48 web services to determine their adherence to regulations such as GDPR, HIPAA, CCPA, and others. Additionally, we scrutinized their privacy policies to understand if they addressed data retention, collection, storage, processing, and sharing of users' mental health data.

SSL Labs is an online service that evaluates a server's certificate, configurations, and TLS security, assigning a letter grade based on its findings. The analysis includes verifying the legitimacy of a certificate, examining protocol, key exchange, and cipher support, and reviewing server configuration. If any exploitable vulnerabilities are discovered or a particular patch is missing, letter grades are adjusted downward [38]. In certain cases, SSL Labs Server Test may not provide a letter grade; for example, if a site's certificate is not trusted, the test will issue a grade of T, or a grade of M if there is a certificate name mismatch. It is crucial to note that if a trust certificate is missing or there is a certificate name mismatch, the actual security grade is irrelevant since active network attackers can compromise secure connections [38].

To evaluate privacy aspects, we used Privacy Check, a Google Chrome extension created by the University of Texas, Austin [41], which scans the entire privacy policy page of a web service or website, focusing on User Control and General Data Protection Regulation (GDPR) aspects. The tool assigns a percentage score between 0 and 100 to each category, as well as individual scores of 0, 5, and 10 to the policies within each category. A score of 0 indicates an absence of a policy, while a score of 5 signifies that the policy is only for intended purposes and services. A score of 10 implies that essential policies are covered by the web service.

Security and Privacy Analysis. We assessed mental healthcare web services to determine their security levels, protocol usage, and other security aspects. SSL Labs identified three types of protocols: Hypertext Transfer Protocol (HTTP) [15], Transport Layer Security protocol (TLS) [12], and Secure Socket Layer (SSL) [12,13]. In web services, information transmitted between a user's browser and a web server can be intercepted and exploited by an attacker who can access the data sent between them [13]. Both TLS and SSL protocols aim to ensure the authenticity and confidentiality of online communications, as well as the integrity of transmissions [52,55]. We also examined the SSL version numbers and TLS version numbers, as older versions are more vulnerable to known security issues. During the evaluation, we focused on the usage of SSL/TLS and the oldest supported version [55]. Except for SSL 2.0 and SSL 3.0, no known security problems exist with newer TLS versions, provided that the server and client are correctly configured. The examination and usage of these protocols will be discussed further in Sect. 4. Another security aspect we considered is authentication and key exchange using public key infrastructure (PKI) [10,12,18].

We assessed privacy policies by running Privacy Check on each mental healthcare web service to identify the most critical policies that should be mentioned on a web service privacy policy page. The tool evaluates ten User-related policies, such as Email Address security, PII security, SSN data provision by users, Targeted Advertising, Location Tracking, COPPA Compliance, Law enforcement,

Privacy Policy opt-out, Data Control, and Data Aggregation. It also evaluates GDPR-related policies based on Site Transfer (whether the web service shares data with other services), Company Location (where PII data is stored and analyzed), the right to be forgotten (whether the web service offers the right to be forgotten when a user deletes an account), data retention notification (whether users are notified if their data is still used for legal purposes after being forgotten), PII usage rejection (whether users can reject the use of PII data), under-16 protection (whether the web service uses PII data for users below 16 years of age), data encryption, data processing content, data protection principles, and breach notification [41].

3.2   Mobile Application Evaluation

To assess mental healthcare applications, we employed three distinct tools to analyze specific features such as vulnerabilities, permissions, encryption algorithms, and certificates. We utilized MobSF for static analysis of mobile applications concerning permissions, shared libraries, vulnerabilities, and certificates. We further evaluated permissions using the RiskInDroid tool, which applies machine learning techniques and reverse engineering. Additionally, we employed Androbugs to identify critical vulnerabilities in the mobile applications, apart from those reported by MobSF.

MobSF features an interactive Graphical User Interface (GUI) that assists security researchers in visualizing the results more effectively [24]. This tool enables the analysis of various application components, validates certificates if present, and performs code analysis [24]. It is also useful for checking for malware [19]. Using this tool, we can analyze Android manifest files to verify permissions and identify potential risks. Code analysis can help detect hard-coded data, cryptographic keys, and SQL query parsing errors, which could lead to SQL injection [22].

Vulnerabilities pose a threat to applications, as they can compromise internal system controls and modify security procedures. Hence, in addition to MobSF, we used the Androbugs framework to scan for vulnerabilities, particularly security-related ones in the applications [3]. We also employed the RiskInDroid tool for quantitative analysis of applications. This tool utilizes the scikit-learn library in Python to calculate an overall risk score for applications based on permissions. It not only scans declared permissions in the application but also performs reverse engineering to categorize permissions into four groups: Declared (permissions declared in the application), Exploited (permissions declared and used), Ghost (permissions not declared but used in the application), and Useless (permissions declared but not used) [33].

Security and Privacy Analysis. We evaluated the security measures of mental healthcare applications to understand their performance concerning permissions, certificates, vulnerabilities, malware, and libraries using the MobSF tool. In terms of vulnerabilities, MobSF reported Janus and Hash Collision vulnerabilities with high, warning, and low severity levels in the report [4]. To further analyze the vulnerabilities, we employed the Androbugs tool, which provided five critical vulnerability categories: command, hacker, implicit intent, keystore, SSL security, and webview. In our study, we also sought to evaluate how mental healthcare applications handle permissions. Permissions are crucial, as they define access controls within the application and with third-party applications. Sharing location, camera, and audio permissions can be considered dangerous, so we assessed permissions using MobSF and the RiskInDroid tool. Furthermore, to evaluate different encryption algorithms, we used MobSF, which highlighted SHA1, SHA256 with RSA, and MD5 hash, among others [34]. Additionally, MobSF reports on the signature schemes and key sizes used by encryption algorithms. V1 signature is the traditional one based on signing the jar but has security issues, as it cannot protect certain parts of the code. V2 and V3 signatures are more effective and secure than V1. V2 can help identify all updates in the APK file, while V3 is similar to V2 but adds more information related to SDK versions [5].

4 Findings and Discussion

In this section, we present the findings of mental healthcare web services and mobile applications from SSL labs, Privacy Check, MobSF, RiskInDroid, and Androbugs tools.

4.1 Web-Services Security

The first measure we focused on to examine the security of the websites is the total letter grade. Grading is based on several factors that are evaluated with the help of the SSL Lab tool to determine if the SSL protocol is configured properly in the server. The evaluation process includes the following steps:

- 1: Verifying the validity and trustworthiness of a certificate
- 2: Examining the server configuration in three different categories: Protocol support, Key exchange support, and Cipher support.
- 3: Adding each category score to an overall score that is determined by a number between 0 and 100. A score of zero in any category will result in a total score of zero. As a reward for the exceptional configuration of the web services, some of them received a grade of A+.

A grade of A+ signifies that the website exhibits a strong configuration, no warnings, and HTTP Strict Transport Security support with a minimum age of 6 months. We found that 20 web services were given a rating of A+, while 17 of them were rated B, and the remaining 11 received an A rating.

We also examined the signature algorithms employed by these web services and discovered that 93.75% of the mental healthcare web services use SHA256 with RSA, while only 6.25% use SHA256 with ECDSA. Furthermore, we analyzed the key sizes utilized by these signature algorithms. We observed that web services do not use RSA 1024 bits, but the majority use RSA 2048 bits, followed by RSA 4096 and EC 256 bits. Additionally, 14.58% of these mental healthcare web services have DNS Certification Authority Authorization (CAA), indicating that domain name owners of these web services can be trusted to issue digital certificates to their host names; however, 85.42% are not permitted to do so.

We also investigated session resumption, which is an adaptive, performance-optimized technique that saves the results of expensive cryptographic operations and makes them available for reuse. When the session resumption mechanism is disabled or nonfunctional, a significant performance hit may be experienced. We discovered that 77.08% of the mental healthcare web services support session resumption through caching. Furthermore, we found that 68.75% of the web services did not have any certificate chain issues, while 27.08% encountered issues with adding both intermediate and root CA when only intermediate needed to be added, as the client will have the root CA, and 4.17% had problems related to incorrect order and extra certificates. We also analyzed the different TLS protocol versions supported by mental healthcare web services as reported by SSL Labs. TLS 1.3 support has been observed in 36% of the web services, and 90% of the web services support TLS 1.2. TLS 1.0 is not supported in 88% of the web services. The results also showed that HSTS support was observed in 64.58% of the web services. We also determined that 56.25% of the web services support the prevention of the downgrade attack with TLS_FALLBACK SCSV. For the remaining 43.75% of the web services, SSL labs were unable to determine the presence or lack of a downgrade attack prevention method. Forward secrecy, sometimes referred to as perfect forward secrecy, is a protocol feature that allows for secure communications independent from the private keys of the server. Our results showed that 79.17% of the mental healthcare web services support forward secrecy protocol with most browsers, while 8.33% support the protocol only with modern browsers.

4.2   Privacy Policies of Mental Healthcare Web Services

We also focused on the privacy policies employed by these web services. Privacy Check tool provided a list of scores for User and GDPR related privacy policies. User-related policies focused more on the presence of policies such as the use of PII data, COPPA compliance, data control, and the right to be forgotten policies, whereas GDPR-related policies focused on data retention, breach notifications, data encryption, and the way data is stored and sold to third parties. Figure 1 shows the scores of all the 20 privacy policies listed by the Privacy Check tool. We noticed that almost all of the mental healthcare web services do not have a breach notification policy, which means that in case of a security breach, none of the users of mental healthcare web services will be notified. Around 45% of the mental healthcare web services do not mention the right to be forgotten policy. The policy ensures that once the user is not associated with a particular organization or web service, the data should be deleted from the web service. This is alarming, as this policy should be present in all the mental healthcare web services, as these services deal with sensitive data. Also, around 41% of the mental healthcare web services neglect the under 16 protection policy, which ensures that no PII data should be used for those below 16 years of age. One of the policies that stand out positively is the way SSN is used or stored, and analysis shows that 77% of the mental healthcare web services do not ask for SSN, and only 12.5% of them use it for intended purposes only, with no web services sharing it with third-party web services or applications.

Additionally, we found that 91% of the web services share the data collection process in their privacy policy. The policies also mention how they intend to use the information collected for their internal processing, targeted advertising, and sharing it with third-party applications. Aetna web service policy page mentions:

We want you to know what personal information we may collect about you. Some examples of the personal information we may collect about you include: Contact information including your name, address, email address, telephone number, and certain personal device information Your password, if you create an account Demographic information, such as your age and date of birth, sex and/or gender Language preferences Driver's license information or Social Security number Information collected automatically through your device, such as web browser information, server log files, cookies, pixel tags, and web beacons, and other tracking information.

Apart from the data collection process and its use, we found 14 web services mentioning regulations such as GDPR, HIPAA, CCPA (California Consumer Privacy Act), and a few state-wide regulations in their privacy policies. Anthem Health mentions HIPAA in their privacy policy as:

Our Notice of Privacy Practices explains how your health information may be used and/or disclosed and how to access this information in accordance with HIPAA, an important federal privacy law. The notice reflects our obligations under federal and individual state regulations. By law, we're required to send our fully-insured health plan members a notice with those details.

In addition to HIPAA, we found web services including CCPA in their privacy policies. CCPA is a California-based act which is used to protect the way users' data is collected, processed, or stored for California residents. K Health includes CCPA in their privacy policy as:

Under the CCPA, if a business sells Personal Information, it must allow California residents to opt out of the sale of their Personal Information. However, we do not "sell" and have not "sold" Personal Information for purposes of the CCPA in the last 12 months. For example, and without limiting the foregoing, we do not sell the Personal Information of minors under 16 years of age.

We also found only one web service named Zocdoc, which includes Virginia, California, and Colorado state regulations in their privacy policy. Apart from regulations specific to the United States, BCBSM Online Visits web service mentions how the international users' data is treated when they use the web service:

We maintain information in the United States of America and in accordance with the laws of the United States, which may not provide the same level of protection as the laws in your jurisdiction. By using the website and providing us with information, you understand and agree that your information may be transferred to and stored on servers located outside your resident jurisdiction and, to the extent you are a resident of a country other than the United States, that you consent to the transfer of such data to the United States for processing by us in accordance with this Privacy Policy.

From a security perspective, out of 48 mental healthcare web services, 19 web services are considered the best in terms of key bit sizes, public key cryptography, preventing downgrade attacks, having certificate transparency, SSL secure renegotiation, and using the latest TLS protocol version. All of these web services are using RSA 2048-bit key size, except one using EC 256 bits. In terms of cryptography, SHA256 with RSA is observed in more than half of the best-performing web services, followed by SHA256 with ECDSA. Prevention of downgrade attacks and implementing secure SSL renegotiation are additional security features that we observed in these web services. The top three web services that adhere to the above-mentioned security standards and protocols are Nurx, SimplePractice, and Spruce Health. However, based on the privacy policy analysis, we found that all the web services share users' data with third-party services or applications for advertising and other purposes. We also noticed that very few web services include existing regulations such as GDPR, HIPAA, CCPA, and other state-wide regulations in their privacy policies. We also found a lack of clarity on how the data of children less than 13 years old is used or shared. However, data retention, encryption, transparency in how the data is used, collected, and shared, are some of the categories discussed in the privacy policies of all the web services.

4.3 Mobile Application Security and Privacy

We evaluated a total of 39 mental healthcare mobile applications to analyze their current security and privacy aspects. We employed MobSF, Androbugs, and RiskInDroid tools to assess the applications in various categories:

Security Score and Application Grades. After analyzing individual reports for each application, MobSF calculates an overall security score out of 100 based on permissions, vulnerabilities, and weak algorithms identified in the applications. We provided a list of security scores along with grades for each mental healthcare application. Sixteen applications received scores less than 40, while only two applications obtained security scores greater than 60. Heal application received the highest security score of 73, considering the signature algorithm and scheme version, key bit size, vulnerabilities, and permissions. The lowest score of 20 was given to three applications: Diabetes:M, Samsung Health, and Aetna Health, which are considered high-risk security applications. Only 5% of the applications (Heal and What's Covered) received an A rating. 53% of the total mental healthcare applications received a B rating. The average percentage score of the 39 mental healthcare applications was 41.6%. 12.8% of the applications received an F rating. The majority of the applications had a B rating, which is good from a security standpoint. However, five applications had an F rating due to poor security scores. The general trend of all applications with F ratings had very high severity risks and moderate medium severity risks.

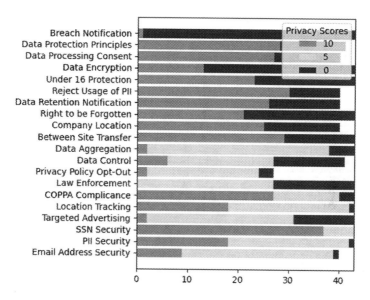

Fig. 1. Privacy Scores of Mental Healthcare Web Services as reported by Privacy Check where a score of 0 indicates absence of the policy, score of 5 indicates that the policy is only for intended purposes and services, and score of ten indicates that essential policies are mentioned in the web services.

Certificates and Permissions. Every website and mobile application needs a certificate for maintaining security and for identifying the traffic over the internet. We focused on how certificates are implemented in mental healthcare mobile applications and found that 23 applications use SHA 256 with RSA to encrypt and decrypt the certificates. All of them are signed, and the key bit size for 11 applications is RSA 2048, while 12 applications use a key bit size of RSA 4096. Additionally, 11 applications use a key bit size of RSA 1024.

We identified different types of software, hardware, and tools in mobile applications that need permissions, such as Internet access, network access, Wifi, boot startup access, read/write access to external storage, and location access through maps, among others. While analyzing the permissions scanned by MobSF, we identified four permission levels - Normal, Dangerous, Unknown, and Signature. Normal and unknown status permissions are not vulnerable to the application and can be treated as secure, as they denote that the applications do not access private data. Signature status is for devices to communicate with third parties.

The most severe permission level is Dangerous, as it implies that some permissions cannot be considered secure and may provide access to private and sensitive data. Table 1 shows the ranking of the most dangerous permissions used by the mobile applications overall. The highest-ranked permission is storage, where the majority of the applications have given full access to external or internal storage. Camera is the second largest permission that needs to be validated, as attackers accessing the camera can be considered a breach of privacy. Location access comprises 50% of applications, which is alarming.

Table 1. Table showing Janus, Hash Collision vulnerabilities along with Dangerous Permissions with percentage found in Mental Healthcare Mobile Applications as reported by MobSF

Janus Vulnerability	Percentage of Apps
High	2.5%
Warning	82.5%
None	15%
Hash Collision Vulnerability	
High	5%
Warning	37.5%
None	57.5%
Dangerous Permissions	
Storage	80%
Camera	70%
Location	50%
Phone State	40%
Audio Recording	32.5%
Account Related	17.5%
Contact Access	15%
System Alert Window	17.5%
Activity Recognition	12.5%
Use Credentials	10%
Body Sensors	2.50%
SMS	2%

In addition to MobSF, we also scanned our mental healthcare mobile applications through RiskInDroid. The tool provided an overall risk score for each application, with Kardia receiving the highest score of 44, followed by MyCigna with a score of 41 and Amazon Care with a score of 36. After analyzing the individual permissions for the top three (Kardia, MyCigna, and Amazon Care) applications, we noticed that the majority of the permissions have been declared in the application itself, with only a few remaining in the required but not used category. Although there are a few permissions like READ PROFILE, MANAGE ACCOUNTS, AUTHENTICATE ACCOUNTS, WRITE SETTINGS that are not required in these applications, they are still used according to the RiskInDroid tool. FollowMyHealth and Workit are the applications that received the lowest scores of 8 and 9, respectively. READ PHONE STATE, USE CREDENTIALS, CHANGE WIFI STATE, BLUETOOTH, ACCESS FINE LOCATION, SEND SMS are a few of the many permissions that are used in these applications. All the mental healthcare mobile applications need ACCESS NETWORK STATE permission, which provides network access to applications to avoid crashing while making calls. RECEIVE is the second largest permission required for authorization, followed by FOREGROUND SERVICE and REFERRER SERVICE permissions and WRITE EXTERNAL STORAGE.

Vulnerabilities. During our MobSF analysis, the two vulnerabilities found in the majority of the applications were Janus and Hash Collision. Janus is a type of vulnerability that can inject code into the application and can run any malware in the system. Table 1 shows that 15% of the applications do not have Janus vulnerability, but 82.5% of the applications have received a warning. The application named "mySymptoms food diary and symptom tracker" is the only application that is vulnerable to Janus vulnerability. Another critical vulnerability found was Hash Collision, and the results show that 57.5% of the applications do not have this vulnerability, but it is still vulnerable to 5% of the applications (myCigna and Doctor on Demand). We also used Androbugs to scan our mental healthcare mobile applications for any vulnerabilities apart from those reported by the MobSF tool. The most concerning critical vulnerability reported in every application is SSL Security. SSL Security vulnerability is a result of incorrect configuration of SSL in the domain server and is found in all the 39 mental healthcare applications. WebView is another critical vulnerability present in 20 applications, where it allows users to view web pages as part of any activity. 14 applications have found Implicit Intent vulnerability, where it provides access for attackers to access internal controls of the application and perform malicious activities. All of these vulnerabilities are identified as critical by Androbugs, and mental healthcare mobile applications need to work on resolving this.

Attacks on Vulnerabilities. Janus vulnerability was first found in the v1 signature scheme and was patched in 2017. However, it is concerning to report this vulnerability in mental healthcare applications. Even though Janus was initially found to be vulnerable to the v1 scheme, it is vulnerable to the v2 or v3 signing schemes used by the mobile applications [6,60]. On the other hand, we found hash collision as another popular vulnerability in mobile applications. MD5 and SHA-1 are the hash algorithms vulnerable to this vulnerability. MD5 hashes can result in more collisions, which means that multiple inputs could lead to the same hash, causing a collision attack [9]. We found that 17 mental healthcare applications are using SHA-1, which is vulnerable to hash collision attacks.

Our evaluation of mental healthcare mobile applications reveals significant security and privacy issues. Many applications have vulnerabilities such as Janus and Hash Collision, and the majority of them require permissions that can potentially compromise user privacy. SSL Security and WebView vulnerabilities are widespread, and there is a need for the developers of these applications to address these security concerns. Users should also be aware of the risks associated with using these applications and take appropriate precautions to safeguard their data.

5   Implications

Our findings highlight several security concerns related to data protection in mental healthcare web services and mobile applications. In this section, we provide recommendations to address these concerns.

5.1   Adopting Latest TLS Protocol Versions

We found that some web services use the RC4 cipher, which is a significant security flaw. Known for its weakness in SSL, RC4 stream ciphers should be disabled for all SSL and TLS versions if a web service does not use TLS1.2 or higher [62]. Approximately a quarter of mental healthcare websites use TLS versions older than 1.2. These versions lack the cryptographic protocols and algorithms recommended by the industry. Given the sensitive nature of the data in the mental healthcare field, we highly recommend that websites upgrade to at least TLS 1.2 and drop support for older versions [37].

5.2   Implementing Forward Secrecy Encryption

We recommend that web services closely monitor which versions of web security protocols they update to stay ahead of most cyber attacks. We suggest more comprehensive support for forward secrecy. Forward Secrecy is a protocol ensuring session keys are protected during secure key exchange [45]. With 8.33% of browsers supporting forward secrecy with only modern browsers, 8.33% supporting forward secrecy with a weak key exchange, and 4.17% supporting it with some browsers, there is concern for users who utilize uncommon browsers. While developing mental healthcare web services, organizations need to account for a diverse group of users, as various health issues affect every human at some point. As a result, there will likely be various browsers utilized by users, necessitating server-end security support for these browsers.

5.3   Enhancing User-Centered Privacy Policies

Privacy Policies are legal documents used by mental healthcare web services to state how the data is collected, stored, analyzed, or shared with any third-party web services or applications. Our analysis reveals that mental healthcare web services have poor privacy policies, which should be improved from a user's privacy standpoint. We recommend that mental healthcare web services include data breach notification, data control, and data encryption policy in their web services for efficient governing of user data. We also recommend including user-specific policies like Targeted Advertising and law enforcement, which control how user data should be used. Concerning GDPR-related privacy policies, we recommend that mental healthcare web services add the right to be forgotten and third-party transfer-related policies that protect user privacy and data.

5.4   Refining Permission Management in Mobile Applications

In mental healthcare applications, the primary focus should be on defining and implementing permissions. The list of dangerous permissions reported by MobSF along with Exploited and Ghost permissions reported by RiskInDroid is alarming. Access to storage, camera, location, accounts, phone contacts, body sensors, managing accounts, accessing user profiles, and reading phone state are some of the permissions that should be considered when developing applications [46].

5.5   Mitigating Vulnerabilities and Enhancing Security

We recommend that applications detected with Hash collision and Janus vulnerabilities resolve them as soon as possible. The Janus vulnerability is severe because it updates the APK file and can insert malicious code into the application. The Hash Collision vulnerability is also severe, as digital signatures become vulnerable once the hash function is known to the attackers [35]. Some recommendations for fixing SSL Security vulnerability include upgrading to the latest TLS protocol, avoiding expired certificates, and choosing the best encryption algorithm based on the use case [57]. To address the WebView vulnerability, we recommend not loading data from untrusted websites [7]. Applications detected with Implicit Intent vulnerability should analyze the functionalities needed for their application and determine if there is any use case that requires interaction with other applications. If there is no interaction with other applications, we recommend avoiding using implicit intent. However, if third-party applications are required, applications need to check for certificates and signatures for verification.

5.6   Upgrading to More Secure Encryption Algorithms

We observed that 42.5% of the mental healthcare applications use SHA1 with RSA, which can be considered a risk and increases the chances of hash collision attacks. Therefore, we recommend using SHA256 with RSA, which is much safer than SHA1 [56]. Additionally, 27.5% of the mental healthcare applications use a key bit size of 1024, which can enable attackers to quickly attack the application if the encryption algorithm is SHA1 with RSA. As a result, we recommend using a key bit size of RSA 2048 or RSA 4096 to enhance overall security [31].

6   Limitations and Future Work

This paper presents a comprehensive security and privacy evaluation for 87 mental healthcare services, including web and mobile applications. Although we used the Privacy Check tool to analyze the privacy policies of mental healthcare web services, the tool's accuracy is 60% [42]. We addressed this by conducting a manual analysis of the policies of the web services. However, one of our primary goals for future work is to perform manual analysis on privacy policies of mobile applications and also expand the list of healthcare services with a particular focus on countries where policies such as HIPAA do not apply. As a future extension, we aim to study the communication channels and investigate the vulnerabilities of sensors and hardware devices integrated into healthcare services and connected to different web servers and mobile applications in the healthcare industry.

7   Conclusion

Mental healthcare services, such as psychological counseling, prescription medication, group therapy, and others, can be accessed online through web services and mobile applications. We conducted an evaluation of 87 mental healthcare services, including 48 web services and 39 mobile applications. We utilized the SSL Labs tool to assess the security aspects of mental healthcare web services, Privacy Check tool in addition to manual analysis of the privacy policies of mental healthcare web services, and MobSF, RiskInDroid, and Androbugs to evaluate mental healthcare mobile applications. We then focused on specific security and privacy measures to assess the security and data protection in each electronic mental healthcare service, emphasizing authentication protocols, access control measures, data protection policies and compliance, and other technical aspects. Our analysis revealed that mental healthcare websites adhere to some basic security protocols, such as SSL/TLS, and take precautions against well-known website vulnerabilities, such as TLS 1.0 and TLS 1.1. However, these web services lack essential privacy policies, such as data breach notification, right to be forgotten, data control, and data encryption policies. In the case of mental healthcare mobile applications, there is a larger gap regarding data control permissions, encryption algorithms used for certificates, and addressing critical vulnerabilities. We recommend that mental healthcare mobile applications fix these vulnerabilities by upgrading to the latest TLS protocol and renewing expired certificates in a timely manner.

Acknowledgements. We would like to thank the Inclusive Security and Privacy focused Innovative Research in Information Technology (InSPIRIT) Laboratory at the University of Denver. The authors appreciate the reviewers' anonymous suggestions and criticisms. Any opinions, findings, conclusions, or recommendations expressed in this material are solely those of the authors and not of the organization or the funding agency.

References

1. Albrecht, J.P.: How the GDPR will change the world. Eur. Data Prot. L. Rev. **2**, 287 (2016)
2. Androbugs: Androbugs framework. https://github.com/AndroBugs/AndroBugs_Framework
3. Aydin, U.: Expanding the vulnerability detection of androbugs considering the recent changes in the android system. Ph.D. thesis, University of Groningen (Rijksuniversiteit Groningen) (2022)
4. Beaman, C., Redbourne, M., Mummery, J.D., Hakak, S.: Fuzzing vulnerability discovery techniques: survey, challenges and future directions. Comput. Secur. 102813 (2022)
5. Camenisch, J., Stadler, M.: Efficient group signature schemes for large groups. In: Kaliski, B.S. (ed.) CRYPTO 1997. LNCS, vol. 1294, pp. 410–424. Springer, Heidelberg (1997). https://doi.org/10.1007/BFb0052252
6. Chatzoglou, E., Kambourakis, G., Smiliotopoulos, C.: Let the cat out of the bag: popular android IoT apps under security scrutiny. Sensors **22**(2), 513 (2022)
7. Chin, E., Wagner, D.: Bifocals: analyzing webview vulnerabilities in android applications. In: Kim, Y., Lee, H., Perrig, A. (eds.) WISA 2013. LNCS, vol. 8267, pp. 138–159. Springer, Cham (2014). https://doi.org/10.1007/978-3-319-05149-9_9
8. Connolly, S.L., et al.: Veterans' attitudes toward smartphone app use for mental health care: qualitative study of rurality and age differences. JMIR Mhealth Uhealth **6**(8), e10748 (2018)
9. Crussell, J., Gibler, C., Chen, H.: AnDarwin: scalable detection of semantically similar android applications. In: Crampton, J., Jajodia, S., Mayes, K. (eds.) ESORICS 2013. LNCS, vol. 8134, pp. 182–199. Springer, Heidelberg (2013). https://doi.org/10.1007/978-3-642-40203-6_11
10. Das, S., Wang, B., Tingle, Z., Camp, L.J.: Evaluating user perception of multi-factor authentication: a systematic review. In: Proceedings of the Thirteenth International Symposium on Human Aspects of Information Security and Assurance (HAISA 2019) (2019)
11. Derr, A.S.: Mental health service use among immigrants in the united states: a systematic review. Psychiatr. Serv. **67**(3), 265–274 (2016)
12. Dierks, T., Allen, C., et al.: The TLS protocol version 1.0 (1999)
13. Eldewahi, A.E., Sharfi, T.M., Mansor, A.A., Mohamed, N.A., Alwahbani, S.M.: SSL/TLS attacks: analysis and evaluation. In: 2015 International Conference on Computing, Control, Networking, Electronics and Embedded Systems Engineering (ICCNEEE), pp. 203–208. IEEE (2015)
14. Esposito, C., De Santis, A., Tortora, G., Chang, H., Choo, K.K.R.: Blockchain: a panacea for healthcare cloud-based data security and privacy? IEEE Cloud Comput. **5**(1), 31–37 (2018)
15. Fielding, R., et al.: Rfc2616: hypertext transfer protocol-http/1.1 (1999)
16. Figueroa, C.A., Aguilera, A.: The need for a mental health technology revolution in the COVID-19 pandemic. Front. Psych. **11**, 523 (2020)
17. Grist, R., Porter, J., Stallard, P., et al.: Mental health mobile apps for preadolescents and adolescents: a systematic review. J. Med. Internet Res. **19**(5), e7332 (2017)
18. Hadan, H., Serrano, N., Das, S., Camp, L.J.: Making IoT worthy of human trust. In: TPRC47: The 47th Research Conference on Communication, Information and Internet Policy (2019)

19. Henchiri, M.M.H.: Handles for pentesting modern secure coding: bypassing mobile security. Int. J. Eng. Inf. Syst. (IJEAIS) 3(4) (2019)

20. Hilty, D.M., Chan, S., Hwang, T., Wong, A., Bauer, A.M.: Advances in mobile mental health: opportunities and implications for the spectrum of e-mental health services. Focus 16(3), 314–327 (2018)

21. Kishnani, U., Noah, N., Das, S., Dewri, R.: Privacy and security evaluation of mobile payment applications through user-generated reviews. In: Proceedings of the 21st Workshop on Privacy in the Electronic Society, pp. 159–173 (2022)

22. Kohli En, N., Mohaghegh, M.: Security testing of android based COVID tracer applications. In: 2020 IEEE Asia-Pacific Conference on Computer Science and Data Engineering (CSDE), pp. 1–6. IEEE (2020)

23. Kramer, G.M., Kinn, J.T., Mishkind, M.C.: Legal, regulatory, and risk management issues in the use of technology to deliver mental health care. Cogn. Behav. Pract. 22(3), 258–268 (2015)

24. Lamalva En, G., Schmeelk, S.: MobSF: mobile health care android applications through the lens of open source static analysis. In: 2020 IEEE MIT Undergraduate Research Technology Conference (URTC), pp. 1–4. IEEE (2020)

25. Lattie, E.G., Nicholas, J., Knapp, A.A., Skerl, J.J., Kaiser, S.M., Mohr, D.C.: Opportunities for and tensions surrounding the use of technology-enabled mental health services in community mental health care. Admin. Policy Mental Health Mental Health Serv. Res. 47(1), 138–149 (2020)

26. Lipson, S.K., Lattie, E.G., Eisenberg, D.: Increased rates of mental health service utilization by us college students: 10-year population-level trends (2007–2017). Psychiatr. Serv. 70(1), 60–63 (2019)

27. Lui, J.H., Marcus, D.K., Barry, C.T.: Evidence-based apps? A review of mental health mobile applications in a psychotherapy context. Prof. Psychol. Res. Pract. 48(3), 199 (2017)

28. Lustgarten, S.D., Garrison, Y.L., Sinnard, M.T., Flynn, A.W.: Digital privacy in mental healthcare: current issues and recommendations for technology use. Curr. Opin. Psychol. 36, 25–31 (2020)

29. Luxton, D.D., McCann, R.A., Bush, N.E., Mishkind, M.C., Reger, G.M.: mhealth for mental health: integrating smartphone technology in behavioral healthcare. Prof. Psychol. Res. Pract. 42(6), 505 (2011)

30. Mahapatra, B., Krishnamurthi, R., Nayyar, A.: Healthcare models and algorithms for privacy and security in healthcare records. In: Security and Privacy of Electronic Healthcare Records: Concepts, Paradigms and Solutions, p. 183 (2019)

31. Mahto, D., Yadav, D.K.: RSA and ECC: a comparative analysis. Int. J. Appl. Eng. Res. 12(19), 9053–9061 (2017)

32. Martinez-Martin, N., Kreitmair, K., et al.: Ethical issues for direct-to-consumer digital psychotherapy apps: addressing accountability, data protection, and consent. JMIR Mental Health 5(2), e9423 (2018)

33. Merlo, A., Georgiu, G.C.: RiskInDroid: machine learning-based risk analysis on android. In: De Capitani di Vimercati, S., Martinelli, F. (eds.) SEC 2017. IAICT, vol. 502, pp. 538–552. Springer, Cham (2017). https://doi.org/10.1007/978-3-319-58469-0_36

34. Michail, H.E., Athanasiou, G.S., Theodoridis, G., Gregoriades, A., Goutis, C.E.: Design and implementation of totally-self checking Sha-1 and Sha-256 hash functions' architectures. Microprocess. Microsyst. 45, 227–240 (2016)

35. Mitra, J.: A security & privacy analysis of us-based contact tracing apps. arXiv preprint arXiv:2207.08978 (2022)

36. MobSF: Mobsf/mobile-security-framework-mobsf: Mobile security framework (mobsf) is an automated, all-in-one mobile application (android/ios/windows) pentesting, malware analysis and security assessment framework capable of performing static and dynamic analysis. https://github.com/MobSF/Mobile-Security-Framework-MobSF

37. Moriarty, K., Farrell, S.: Deprecating tls 1.0 and tls 1.1. Internet Engineering Task Force, RFC 8996 (2021)

38. Müthing, J., Brüngel, R., Friedrich, C.M., et al.: Server-focused security assessment of mobile health apps for popular mobile platforms. J. Med. Internet Res. **21**(1), e9818 (2019)

39. Nass, S.J., Levit, L.A., Gostin, L.O.: Beyond the HIPAA privacy rule: enhancing privacy, improving health through research. PubMed (2009)

40. Noah, N., Shearer, S., Das, S.: Security and privacy evaluation of popular augmented and virtual reality technologies. In: Proceedings of the 2022 IEEE International Conference on Metrology for eXtended Reality, Artificial Intelligence, and Neural Engineering (IEEE MetroXRAINE 2022) (2022)

41. Nokhbeh Zaeem, R., et al.: Privacycheck v3: empowering users with higher-level understanding of privacy policies. In: Proceedings of the Fifteenth ACM International Conference on Web Search and Data Mining, pp. 1593–1596 (2022)

42. Nokhbeh Zaeem, R., et al.: Privacycheck v2: a tool that recaps privacy policies for you. In: Proceedings of the 29th ACM International Conference on Information and Knowledge Management, pp. 3441–3444 (2020)

43. Nouri, S., Khoong, E.C., Lyles, C.R., Karliner, L.: Addressing equity in telemedicine for chronic disease management during the COVID-19 pandemic. NEJM Catalyst Innov. Care Deliv. **1**(3) (2020)

44. Oh, E., Jorm, A.F., Wright, A.: Perceived helpfulness of websites for mental health information. Soc. Psychiatry Psychiatr. Epidemiol. **44**, 293–299 (2009)

45. Park, D.G., Boyd, C., Moon, S.-J.: Forward secrecy and its application to future mobile communications security. In: Imai, H., Zheng, Y. (eds.) PKC 2000. LNCS, vol. 1751, pp. 433–445. Springer, Heidelberg (2000). https://doi.org/10.1007/978-3-540-46588-1_29

46. Parker, L., Halter, V., Karliychuk, T., Grundy, Q.: How private is your mental health app data? an empirical study of mental health app privacy policies and practices. Int. J. Law Psychiatry **64**, 198–204 (2019)

47. Patil En, H.K., Seshadri, R.: Big data security and privacy issues in healthcare. In: 2014 IEEE International Congress on Big Data, pp. 762–765. IEEE (2014)

48. Power, J.: Us telehealth satisfaction study. SM, JD Power (2019)

49. riskindroid: Claudiugeorgiu.riskindroid. https://github.com/ClaudiuGeorgiu/RiskInDroid

50. Schueller, S.M., Washburn, J.J., Price, M.: Exploring mental health providers' interest in using web and mobile-based tools in their practices. Internet Interv. **4**, 145–151 (2016)

51. Siddiqui, S., Khan, A.A.: Challenges and privacy concerns related to use of information technology in mental healthcare. In: Mittal, M., Goyal, L.M. (eds.) Predictive Analytics of Psychological Disorders in Healthcare. LNDECT, vol. 128, pp. 285–303. Springer, Singapore (2022). https://doi.org/10.1007/978-981-19-1724-0_15

52. Sirohi, P., Agarwal, A., Tyagi, S.: A comprehensive study on security attacks on SSL/TLS protocol. In: 2016 2nd International Conference on Next Generation Computing Technologies (NGCT), pp. 893–898. IEEE (2016)

53. Sorkin, D.H., et al.: Rise in use of digital mental health tools and technologies in the united states during the COVID-19 pandemic: survey study. J. Med. Internet Res. **23**(4), e26994 (2021)
54. ssllabs: Qualys SSL labs. https://www.ssllabs.com/
55. Suga, Y.: Status survey of SSL/TLS sites in 2018 after pointing out about 'search form" issues. In: 2018 Sixth International Symposium on Computing and Networking Workshops (CANDARW). IEEE, November 2018
56. Sury, O.: Use of the Sha-256 algorithm with RSA, digital signature algorithm (DSA), and elliptic curve DSA (ECDSA) in SSHFP resource records. Technical report, CZ.NIC (2012)
57. Tang, J., Li, J., Li, R., Han, H., Gu, X., Xu, Z.: Ssldetecter: detecting SSL security vulnerabilities of android applications based on a novel automatic traversal method. Secur. Commun. Netw. **2019** (2019)
58. Terry, N.: Existential challenges for healthcare data protection in the United States. Ethics, Med. Publ. Health **3**(1), 19–27 (2017)
59. Torous, J., Nicholas, J., Larsen, M.E., Firth, J., Christensen, H.: Clinical review of user engagement with mental health smartphone apps: evidence, theory and improvements. Evid. Based Ment. Health **21**(3), 116–119 (2018)
60. Wang, H., Liu, H., Xiao, X., Meng, G., Guo, Y.: Characterizing android app signing issues. In: 2019 34th IEEE/ACM International Conference on Automated Software Engineering (ASE), pp. 280–292. IEEE (2019)
61. Wang, X., Markert, C., Sasangohar, F.: Investigating popular mental health mobile application downloads and activity during the COVID-19 pandemic. Hum. Fact. 0018720821998110 (2021)
62. Weerasinghe, T., Disanayake, C.: A research study: usage of rc4 stream cipher in SSL configurations of web servers used by Sri Lankan financial institutes. Int. J. Cyber Secur. Digit. Forensics **7**(2), 111–119 (2018)

Android Code Vulnerabilities Early Detection Using AI-Powered *ACVED* Plugin

Janaka Senanayake[1,2]([✉]) [ID], Harsha Kalutarage[1] [ID], Mhd Omar Al-Kadri[3] [ID], Andrei Petrovski[1] [ID], and Luca Piras[4] [ID]

[1] School of Computing, Robert Gordon University, Aberdeen AB10 7QB, UK
{j.senanayake,h.kalutarage,a.petrovski}@rgu.ac.uk
[2] Faculty of Science, University of Kelaniya, Kelaniya, Sri Lanka
janakas@kln.ac.lk
[3] School of Computing and Digital Technology, Birmingham City University,
Birmingham B5 5JU, UK
omar.alkadri@bcu.ac.uk
[4] Department of Computer Science, Middlesex University, London NW4 4BT, UK
l.piras@mdx.ac.uk

Abstract. During Android application development, ensuring adequate security is a crucial and intricate aspect. However, many applications are released without adequate security measures due to the lack of vulnerability identification and code verification at the initial development stages. To address this issue, machine learning models can be employed to automate the process of detecting vulnerabilities in the code. However, such models are inadequate for real-time Android code vulnerability mitigation. In this research, an open-source AI-powered plugin named **A**ndroid **C**ode **V**ulnerabilities **E**arly **D**etection (ACVED) was developed using the LVDAndro dataset. Utilising Android source code vulnerabilities, the dataset is categorised based on Common Weakness Enumeration (CWE). The ACVED plugin, featuring an ensemble learning model, is implemented in the backend to accurately and efficiently detect both source code vulnerabilities and their respective CWE categories, with a 95% accuracy rate. The model also leverages explainable AI techniques to provide source code vulnerability prediction probabilities for each word. When integrated with Android Studio, the ACVED plugin can provide developers with the vulnerability status of their current source code line in real-time, assisting them in mitigating vulnerabilities. The plugin, model, and scripts can be found on GitHub, and it receives regular updates with new training data from the LVDAndro dataset, enabling the detection of novel vulnerabilities recently added to CWE.

Keywords: Android application security · code vulnerability · labelled dataset · artificial intelligence · plugin

© IFIP International Federation for Information Processing 2023
Published by Springer Nature Switzerland AG 2023
V. Atluri and A. L. Ferrara (Eds.): DBSec 2023, LNCS 13942, pp. 339–357, 2023.
https://doi.org/10.1007/978-3-031-37586-6_20

1   Introduction

As of March 2023, the Google Play Store sees an average of 87,000 new Android mobile apps released each month, and Android dominates the market with a 70.93% share [23,24]. However, due to the lack of adherence to secure coding practices and standards, some of these apps have source code vulnerabilities that are attractive to hackers [26]. Therefore, the security of Android apps may always not be guaranteed. Hence, it is important to mitigate vulnerabilities promptly. It is worth noting that delaying bug fixing until later stages in the Software Development Life Cycle (SDLC) is 30 times more expensive than fixing them early on [9].

Without proper mechanisms in place, developers may not consider potential vulnerabilities of the source code. However, developers should pay attention to this as identifying source code weaknesses at an early stage can make the software less vulnerable. Therefore, it is essential to support Android app developers to continuously prioritise and apply security best practices. Developers find supportive tools, frameworks, and plugins beneficial in automating the coding process. However, there is a shortage of automated supportive tools that follow security best practices and address code vulnerabilities during application development [19].

Despite a few available tools that use conventional methods, Machine Learning (ML) methods and Deep Learning (DL) methods with static, dynamic, and hybrid analysis to identify Android app vulnerabilities [7,21], several limitations such as fewer detection capabilities and low performances, exist. Additionally, these tools cannot perform real-time detection during coding, and they can only identify vulnerabilities by analysing either Android Application Package (APK) files or the entire source code of an Android project.

To address such limitations, this paper makes the following contributions:

- An Artificial Intelligence (AI) based model that employs ensemble learning techniques to detect Android source code vulnerabilities with high accuracy. The LVDAndro dataset [20] was used to train this model.
- A plugin named ACVED, which employs the trained model and Explainable AI (XAI) techniques in its backend. The plugin can be integrated with Android Studio and can assist developers in identifying potential vulnerabilities in the source code and recommend appropriate mitigating approaches based on the reasoning behind the predictions.
- The plugin and model are publicly available as a GitHub Repository[1] along with source code and essential instructions for improvement to address the latest potential vulnerabilities.

The following is the organisation of the paper: In Sect. 2, background and related work are discussed, while the development process of the vulnerability detection model is explained in Sect. 3. The application of the ACVED Plugin is described in Sect. 4. The conclusion and future works are discussed in Sect. 5.

---

[1] https://github.com/softwaresec-labs/ACVED.

2   Background and Related Work

In this section, the foundation for the study is established by examining several topics and exploring related studies on source code vulnerabilities, techniques, tools and frameworks for vulnerability scanning and analysis, datasets used for machine learning (ML)-based vulnerability detection models, and the use of XAI to understand predictions. Additionally, how assistive tools can support Android developers in their work is also discussed.

2.1   Source Code Vulnerabilities

Reducing vulnerabilities in the source code is crucial for promoting secure software development practices, as highlighted in [16,27]. However, without proper mechanisms, developers may overlook potential vulnerabilities. Therefore, organisations and the community have identified various vulnerabilities documented in repositories such as Common Weakness Enumeration (CWE) [3] and Common Vulnerabilities and Exposures (CVE) [4], which are widely used. These repositories contain software and hardware-related vulnerabilities that can be identified across many platforms, making them a valuable resource for mobile application developers to mitigate security loopholes by identifying patterns in their source code. If automated tool support based on CWE and CVE details were available, the Android app development process could be completed efficiently by minimising vulnerable source code.

2.2   Application Analysis and Vulnerability Scanning

To identify source code vulnerabilities in Android apps, the first step involves analysing and scanning the completed app or the source code. Two approaches are available for scanning Android apps for source code vulnerabilities: 1) scanning the code by reverse-engineering the developed APKs, and 2) scanning the source code simultaneously as the code is being written [17]. Since the first approach requires a pre-built application, it cannot be applied in the early stages of the software development life cycle (SDLC) [1]. Although the second approach is more valuable to developers as it focuses on early detection, it is not widely practised due to the limited availability of tools and frameworks.

To analyse applications, static, dynamic, and hybrid analysis techniques can be employed. Static analysis methods can identify code issues without executing the application or the source code. Two types of static analysis techniques are available: Manifest analysis and code analysis. Manifest analysis can extract features for analysis by identifying package names, permissions, activities, services, intents, and providers. In contrast, code analysis can provide more insights into the source code by analysing features such as API calls, information flow, native code, taint tracking, clear-text analysis, and opcodes [8]. Conversely, dynamic analysis requires a runtime environment to execute the application for scanning. Five feature extraction methods for dynamic analysis have been identified: code instrumentation, system resources analysis, system call analysis, network traffic analysis, and user interaction analysis [6]. The hybrid analysis combines the features of both static and dynamic analysis. By performing a hybrid analysis, a mix of static and dynamic features can be extracted [6].

2.3 Tools and Frameworks for Vulnerability Scanning

There are several tools available for vulnerability scanning of Android applications, as discussed in [19]. Some widely used free tools include Qark, MobSF, AndroBugs, DevKnox, and JAADAS, and these can be utilised by app developers to detect source code vulnerabilities using application scanning techniques. Additionally, tools such as Guardsquare, AppSweep, DeepSource, Copilot and SonarQube are available, offering similar services, but they are not free to use. Previous research has suggested the application of ML-based and non-ML-based methods for this purpose, with a recent trend of using ML-based methods [7]. The accuracy and performance of ML models can be enhanced through dataset improvements and parameter tuning, as seen in experiments conducted in various studies, including [5,10,18,28]. These studies used ML algorithms such as Decision Tree (DT), Naive Bayes (NB), AdaBoost (AB), ID3, C4.5, J48, K-Star, Random Forest (RF), Gradient Boosting (GB), Extreme Gradient Boosting (XGB), Logistic Regression (LR), Support Vector Machine (SVM), and Multi-Layer Perception (MLP). However, none of these methods proposed a real-time Android code vulnerability detection approach.

2.4 Datasets for ML-Based Vulnerability Detection

ML-based models can be developed by training ML algorithms on properly labelled datasets. Several datasets have been proposed primarily related to application vulnerabilities. For instance, Ghera [12] is an open-source benchmark repository that captures 25 known vulnerabilities in Android apps. It also outlines some common characteristics of vulnerability benchmarks and repositories. The National Vulnerability Database (NVD) [15] is another dataset used to reference vulnerabilities. The AndroVul repository [14] contains Android security vulnerabilities, including high-risk shell commands, security code smells, and dangerous permission-related vulnerability details. LVDAndro [20], an Android code vulnerability dataset, contains vulnerable and non-vulnerable source code labelled with CWE categories. The proof-of-concept demonstrates that the LVDAndro is applicable in training ML models to detect Android code vulnerabilities.

2.5 Understanding ML-Based Vulnerability Predictions with XAI

ML models often function as a black box, providing only the output predictions and not the reasoning behind them. This lack of transparency can make it difficult for developers to identify the underlying causes of vulnerabilities and devise appropriate mitigation strategies. To better understand the reasons behind these predictions, additional effort outside of app development is often necessary [22]. XAI can help with this by generating algorithms that are both accurate and explainable [11]. Various Python-based frameworks, such as Shapash, Dalex, ELI5, Lime, SHAP, and EBM, can provide the probability of predictions in binary or multi-class classification models [2]. These frameworks can be selected based on specific requirements, such as Lime's applicability for text or image classification-related predictions.

2.6   Tools for Assisting Android Developers

The study in [13] suggests that code issues can arise due to human errors like a lack of focus and concentration. To address this, software developers use various strategies like self-concentration, process checklists, and integrated tools during development. To improve efficiency, developers often rely on Integrated Development Environments (IDEs) that assist with code writing, application building, validation, and integration. IDEs have built-in features and plugins that enhance the development process without altering its functionalities. Android Studio, which is the official IDE for Android app development and built on Jet-Brain's IntelliJ IDEA, is an example of an IDE that supports third-party plugins developed by external vendors [25].

The ACVED plugin is designed to address the limitations of real-time code vulnerability detection methods by employing an accurate ensemble learning approach. As a result, it can be integrated into Android Studio to provide tool support for detecting vulnerabilities in real-time.

3   Development of Vulnerability Detection Model

The dataset selection process, the process of building the model and web API, how to use XAI in conjunction with prediction probabilities, and model enhancements are discussed in this section. The entire process of model development is illustrated in Fig. 1.

3.1   Dataset Selection

The first step in developing a vulnerability detection model is to select an appropriate dataset. For this purpose, the LVDAndro dataset [20], which is properly labelled based on CWE-IDs, was chosen to train the AI-based model. The LVDAndro dataset was created by combining the capabilities of MobSF and Qark vulnerability scanners, leveraging the strengths of both tools. An analysis was carried out on the LVDAndro dataset to determine its characteristics. Table 1 displays the fields that are included in the dataset. Although the processed code, vulnerability status, and CWE-IDs are essential for detecting vulnerabilities, other fields such as severity level and vulnerability category can also provide

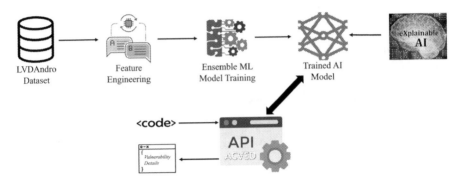

Fig. 1. Overall Model Development Process

Table 1. Fields in LVDAndro

Field Name	Description
Index	Auto-generated identifier
Code	Original source code line
Processed_code	Source code line after preprocessing
Vulnerability_status	Vulnerable(1) or Non-vulnerable(0)
Category	Category of the vulnerability
Severity	Severity of the vulnerability
Type	Type of the vulnerability
Pattern	Pattern of the vulnerable code
Description	Description of the vulnerability
CWE_ID	CWE-ID of the vulnerability
CWE_Desc	Description of the vulnerable class
CVSS	Common vulnerability scoring system value
OWSAP_Mobile	Open web application security project for mobile apps details
OWSAP_MASVS	OWASP Mobile application security verification standard
Reference	CWE reference URL for the vulnerability

additional predictive information. Table 2 provides statistics on the dataset, and the CWE distribution of the LVDAndro dataset is depicted in Fig. 2.

The number of non-vulnerable source code samples generally exceeds the number of vulnerable samples in the datasets generated from real applications. This data imbalance issue was addressed by down-sampling the non-vulnerable examples in the dataset. Vulnerable code examples consist of code lines for 23 CWE-IDs as shown in Fig. 2. However, for certain CWE-IDs such as CWE-79, CWE-250, CWE-295, CWE-297, CWE-299, CWE-327, CWE-330, CWE-502, CWE-599, CWE-649, CWE-919, CWE-926, and CWE-927, there are limited examples of vulnerable code. To handle this, a new class named *Other* was introduced and used to reassign the labels for these source code samples.

Table 2. Statistics of the LVDAndro Dataset

Characteristic	Value
No. of Used APKs	15,021
No. of Vulnerable Code Lines	6,599,597
No. of Non-Vulnerable Code Lines	14,689,432
No. of Distinct CWE-IDs	23

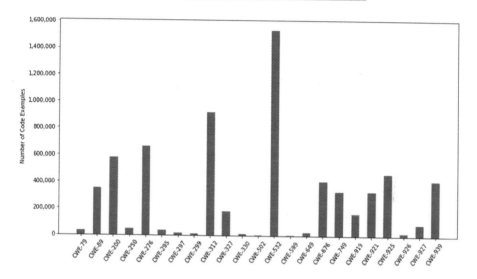

Fig. 2. CWE-ID Distribution

3.2   Model Building

When constructing the model, the LVDAndro dataset was divided into 75% for training and 25% for testing. Since the model needs to predict both the vulnerability status and the vulnerability category based on CWE, two classification tasks were performed: binary and multi-class classification as a continuation of the previous work in [18]. To create the feature vectors for these tasks, the n-gram technique with ngram_range = 1,3 and a minimum document frequency (min_df) of 100 and maximum document frequency (max_df) of 40 was used to generate two feature vectors. For the binary classification, the feature vector was created using the processed_code and vulnerability_status, while for the multi-class classification, the feature vector was created using the processed_code and CWE-ID.

To determine which classifiers perform well in both binary and CWE-based multi-class classification, widely used learning classifiers including NB, LR, DT, SVM, RF, GB, XGB, and MLP were analysed [19]. Then an ensemble learning model was built using the Stacking classifier from Scikit-learn, and the previously analysed learning classifiers were used as estimators. The ensemble model was evaluated using five-fold cross-validation, and prediction probability, decision function, and predictions were evaluated for each estimator.

The performance of each individual classifier and the proposed ensemble model was compared based on F1-scores and accuracies for both binary and multi-class classification. The results of the comparison of accuracies and the macro averages of precision, recall, and F1-score are presented in Table 3.

Table 3. Performance Comparison of Learning Models

Model	Binary Classification				Multi-class Classification			
	Accuracy	Precision	Recall	F1-Score	Accuracy	Precision	Recall	F1-Score
NB	91%	0.91	0.91	0.91	88%	0.86	0.89	0.87
LR	94%	0.94	0.94	0.94	94%	0.92	0.92	0.92
DT	94%	0.94	0.94	0.94	92%	0.90	0.90	0.90
SVM	89%	0.89	0.88	0.88	89%	0.88	0.87	0.88
RF	94%	0.94	0.94	0.94	93%	0.91	0.90	0.90
GB	91%	0.92	0.91	0.91	92%	0.92	0.91	0.91
XGB	94%	0.94	0.94	0.94	93%	0.92	0.92	0.92
MLP	93%	0.93	0.93	0.93	92%	0.91	0.90	0.90
Ensemble Model	95%	0.95	0.95	0.95	95%	0.94	0.93	0.93

Table 3 reveals that the proposed ensemble model achieves high accuracy, precision, recall, and F1-score combinations in both binary and multi-class classifications. This result is likely due to the fact that the ensemble stacking classifier combines the capabilities of all the other classifiers. The trained ensemble model has an accuracy of 95% for both binary and multi-class classification, and F1-scores of 0.95 and 0.93 for binary and multi-class classification, respectively. The precision, recall, and F1-score values for each CWE-ID in the multi-class classification can be found in Table 4.

Table 4. F1-Score for each CWE-ID with Ensemble Model

CWE-ID	Precision	Recall	F1-Score	Number of Examples
CWE-89	1.00	1.00	1.00	2,036
CWE-200	0.94	0.96	0.95	5,665
CWE-276	0.97	0.98	0.97	6,382
CWE-312	0.93	0.95	0.94	7,649
CWE-532	0.98	0.99	0.99	9,254
CWE-676	1.00	1.00	1.00	2,378
CWE-749	0.65	0.90	0.76	1,898
CWE-921	0.95	0.90	0.93	1,914
CWE-925	0.99	0.99	0.99	3,392
CWE-939	0.92	0.71	0.80	2,961
Other	0.96	0.90	0.93	4,467

3.3   Web API

Two pickle files were saved for each trained model, one for the classifier and one for the vectorizer. These files correspond to the trained ensemble model for both binary and multi-class classifications. They were used as inputs to the backend of a Flask-based web API developed using Python.

The web API receives a source code line from the user via a GET request and checks it for vulnerabilities. The code line is processed using the same techniques as those used in LVDAndro [20]. Specifically, the code replaces all user-defined string values with "user_string," except for string values containing IP addresses and encryption algorithms (AES, SHA-1, and MD5) due to the potential for vulnerabilities such as CWE-200 (exposure of sensitive information to unauthorised actors) and CWE-327 (use of a broken or risky cryptographic algorithm). Additionally, all comments are replaced with "//user_comment."

Upon initialisation of the web API, the pre-trained binary and multi-class model pickle files are loaded. When a user request is received, the vectorizer from the binary classification is used to transform the processed source code line. The transformed code is then passed to the binary model to obtain the vulnerability status. If the code line is predicted to be vulnerable, the code line is transformed using the loaded multi-class classification vectorizer and then passed to the multi-class learning model to predict the CWE-ID.

3.4   Prediction Probabilities with XAI

After predicting the vulnerability status and the CWE-ID, the processed source code is passed to the Lime package in Python, which supports XAI, to obtain prediction probabilities and explanations for both binary and multi-class models. The Lime package provides the contributions of each word in the processed source code line for both vulnerability prediction and vulnerable category prediction probabilities. Finally, the prediction results are returned to the user in the form of JSON responses, as shown in Fig. 3 and Fig. 4.

The Python Lime library's *show_in_notebook* function can provide visual aids for interpreting XAI prediction probabilities. Figure 5 demonstrates how Lime-based XAI predictions can highlight vulnerable source code, using the example of a line that writes to a log file: *"Log.e("Login Failure for username :", "user123");"*. This code is associated with CWE-532, which the model correctly predicted with a 0.99 probability. Additionally, the model identified "Log" as the most significant contributor to the prediction with a 0.53 probability. In multi-class classification, the prediction probability for CWE-532 was 0.99, and the contribution of "Log" to this was 0.96. This underscores the need for developers to exercise caution when using log statements in production-level applications, as attackers may exploit loopholes in the application by checking the log file. Encryption processes can be employed to generate log files in an encrypted form instead of plain text. Figure 6 demonstrates how can be represented graphically if there are no any vulnerabilities in a given code line.

348   J. Senanayake et al.

```
{
    "code": "Log.e(\"Login Failure for username :\", \"user123\");",
    "processed_code": "Log.e(\"user_str\", \"user_str\");",
    "code_vulnerability_status": "Vulnerable Code",
    "code_vulnerability_probability": "0.99425936",
    "probability_breakdown_of_vulnerable_code_words": "[('Log', 0.5418730074669474),
    ('user_str', 0.26238023912651687), ('e', 0.10409289309093726)]",
    "cwe_id": "CWE-532",
    "predicted_cwe_id_probability": "0.99",
    "probability_breakdown_of_cwe_related_vulnerable_code_words": "[('Log',
    0.9622543437900251), ('e', -0.0034988003499266235), ('user_str',
    -0.0002970462877947457)]",
    "description": "Information written to log files can be of a sensitive nature and give
    valuable guidance to an attacker or expose sensitive user information.",
    "mitigation": "Try to avoid inserting any confidential information in log statements.
    Minimise using log files in production-level apps.",
    "cwe_reference": "https://cwe.mitre.org/data/definitions/532.html"
}
```

Fig. 3. API Responses Example for Vulnerable Code

```
{
    "code": "String app_name=\"MyApp\"",
    "processed_code": "String app_name=\"user_str\"",
    "code_vulnerability_status": "Non-Vulnerable Code",
    "code_vulnerability_probability": "0.45635873",
    "probability_breakdown_of_vulnerable_code_words": "",
    "cwe_id": "",
    "predicted_cwe_id_probability": "0",
    "probability_breakdown_of_cwe_related_vulnerable_code_words": "",
    "description": "Non-vulnerable code",
    "mitigation": "Non-vulnerable code",
    "cwe_reference": "Non-vulnerable code"
}
```

Fig. 4. API Responses Example for Non-vulnerable Code

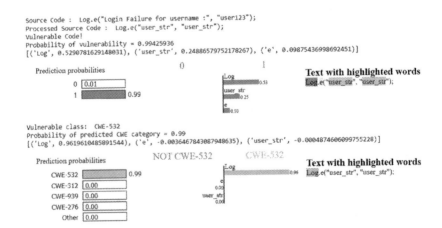

Fig. 5. Vulnerable Code

Fig. 6. Non-vulnerable Code

3.5 Continuous Model Enhancements

To keep pace with evolving threats and achieve optimal performance, the model must continuously evolve to detect new vulnerabilities and enhance its capabilities. Regular updates are essential to identify the most current source code vulnerabilities. As a result, the back-end model can improve by receiving updates to the LVDAndro training dataset.

If an update to the LVDAndro dataset is available, the model must undergo training. Otherwise, the pre-trained model can be used with the ACVED plugin. During re-training, if any classification metrics are better than those of the existing model, the new model will be employed for subsequent predictions within the plugin. The duration of model training typically relies on the available machine resources and the dataset size. In this case, the initial model was constructed using a machine equipped with an Intel Core i5 processor and 16GB of memory, taking approximately 55 min.

4 Application of ACVED Plugin

This section outlines how to use the ACVED plugin after integrating it with Android Studio. Furthermore, it includes a comparison of the performance of both the model and the plugin. The process of the ACVED plugin is illustrated in Fig. 7.

Fig. 7. Process of ACVED Plugin

4.1 Plugin Integration and Usage

The ACVED plugin, which functions as an Android Studio plugin, was created utilising IntelliJ IDEA. This plugin is capable of receiving requests (in the form of source code) from Android Studio and returning responses as notifications containing results generated by the web API.

In order to use the newly developed plugin, it must first be integrated into the Android Studio IDE. The plugin is available for download in the form of a jar file from the ACVED GitHub repository. To install the plugin into the latest version of Android Studio, simply follow the standard procedure for installing a third-party plugin. For older versions of Android Studio, the version number can be adjusted in the plugin.xml file to accommodate the appropriate version[2]. Once the plugin has been successfully installed, suggestions for resolving vulnerabilities can be retrieved as a balloon notification (see Appendix A). The ACVED plugin provides two options to detect vulnerabilities.

- **Quick Check**: Scan the whole source code file to detect the presence of vulnerable source code.
- **Detailed Check**: Detect if any vulnerability is associated with a particular code line.

When conducting a quick search, the developer will receive a balloon notification indicating whether vulnerable code is present in the source file. If no vulnerable code is found, that also will be notified. However, if no vulnerable code is detected, a notification will be displayed that specifies the vulnerable code lines and their corresponding CWE-IDs.

Upon conducting a detailed check, a notification will be received indicating the vulnerability status of the source code. If the code being focused on by the cursor is found to be vulnerable, a balloon notification will be displayed, containing a description of the vulnerability as well as a suggestion for mitigating it. The notification will also provide the binary classification prediction for vulnerability status, the associated CWE-ID, and the prediction probability for the CWE category in the multi-class classification prediction. Furthermore, the contribution of each word to the probability in both the binary and multi-class classification approaches will be indicated. The severity of the vulnerability will determine the type of notification (information or warning). To provide more detailed information about the vulnerability, ACVED offers suggestions for overcoming it by referencing the CWE repository [3].

The ability to re-perform the vulnerability check allows developers to examine how the probabilities vary when specific code lines are altered. This feature can be particularly useful in situations where 100% mitigation is not possible. For instance, in some cases, it may be necessary to maintain log file records for bug-fixing purposes, even in production-level applications.

---

[2] https://plugins.jetbrains.com/docs/intellij/android-studio-releases-list.html.

4.2 Plugin Performance

The ACVED plugin's accuracy and efficiency were evaluated by benchmarking it against the MobSF and Qark scanners, which were used to construct the LVDAndro dataset. To compare the accuracy of the detection of vulnerable code for new data, a total of 2,216 source code lines were utilised. This set included 604 examples of vulnerable code lines obtained from the CWE repository and 1,612 lines of well-known non-vulnerable code from real-world applications. These code lines were integrated into an Android app project, which was then scanned using both the MobSF and Qark scanners. The same code lines were then passed to the developed API by parsing them using the Quick Check option of the ACVED plugin. The accuracy, precision, recall, and F1-Score of each tool were compared and summarised in Table 5.

Table 5. Comparison of Accuracy, Precision, Recall and F1-Score of ACVED with MobSF and Qark

Performance Metrics	MobSF	Qark	ACVED
Accuracy	91%	89%	**94%**
Precision	0.92	0.92	**0.94**
Recall	0.95	0.93	**0.97**
F1-Score	0.93	0.92	**0.95**

Upon comparison, ACVED outperformed MobSF and Qark in predicting vulnerabilities in unseen code samples, achieving a high accuracy rate of 94%, along with a precision of 0.94, recall of 0.97, and F1-Score of 0.95. Additionally, ACVED was able to significantly decrease the false negative rate, indicating its effectiveness in reducing potential security risks associated with its predictions. Moreover, when compared with MobSF and Qark, ACVED stands out as the sole method capable of detecting code vulnerabilities during development.

In order to compare the efficiency of vulnerability detection methods, fifty open-source Android projects were downloaded from GitHub and scanned them using the ACVED plugin (integrated with Android Studio), MobSF, and Qark. The apps were categorised based on size, with five apps per category. The average analysis times for each method were measured for each category, and the experiments were conducted on a Windows OS environment with a Core i5 processor and 16GB RAM. The results, as shown in Table 6, indicate that ACVED is faster at detecting vulnerabilities, taking only 206.1s compared to MobSF's 344.8s and Qark's 419.9s. It is worth noting that this performance comparison was conducted for completed applications due to existing vulnerability scanner limitations. However, the ACVED plugin's main strength is that it does not require building the entire application.

The usage of the ACVED plugin in the Android Studio IDE does not disrupt the standard coding process. Developers can continue coding in their usual way. Once a quick or detailed check has been performed, a balloon notification containing vulnerability prediction results is displayed to the developer. The results

Table 6. Comparison of Average Time Taken to Analyse apps

App Categorise	MobSF	Qark	ACVED
$Size < 1\,\mathrm{MB}$	163 s	123 s	**100 s**
$1\,\mathrm{MB} \leq Size < 2\,\mathrm{MB}$	181 s	129 s	**115 s**
$2\,\mathrm{MB} \leq Size < 4\,\mathrm{MB}$	200 s	165 s	**122 s**
$4\,\mathrm{MB} \leq Size < 6\,\mathrm{MB}$	277 s	235 s	**132 s**
$6\,\mathrm{MB} \leq Size < 8\,\mathrm{MB}$	342 s	372 s	**162 s**
$8\,\mathrm{MB} \leq Size < 10\,\mathrm{MB}$	397 s	497 s	**228 s**
$10\,\mathrm{MB} \leq Size < 12\,\mathrm{MB}$	438 s	543 s	**259 s**
$12\,\mathrm{MB} \leq Size < 15\,\mathrm{MB}$	451 s	654 s	**301 s**
$15\,\mathrm{MB} \leq Size < 20\,\mathrm{MB}$	478 s	729 s	**313 s**
$20\,\mathrm{MB} \leq Size$	521 s	752 s	**329 s**
Average	**344.8 s**	**419.9 s**	**206.1 s**

obtained from the detailed check option can be utilised to modify the code and eliminate vulnerabilities. The detailed check option also includes a clear vulnerability description, allowing developers to easily comprehend it. Additionally, by following the link provided in the notification, developers can study the vulnerability in greater depth. The ACVED plugin is capable of delivering a prediction for one code line in less than 300 ms. The plugin's performance was evaluated in an Android Studio Chipmunk - 2021.2.1 version in a Windows OS environment with a Core i5 processor and 16 GB RAM. However, initiating the ACVED API took between 3 to 10 s in the same environment before executing the ACVED plugin. As a result, app developers do not need to devote any additional time or effort to obtain these real-time prediction results.

The plugin's performance was evaluated through a survey in which 63 developers were requested to rate their satisfaction levels in various aspects including Accuracy of Prediction, Efficiency of Prediction, Ease of Integration and Configuration, Ease of Use, Usefulness of Mitigation Suggestions, Look and Feel, and Overall Satisfaction using a 5-point Likert scale. The feedback collected was represented visually in Fig. 8.

The survey results showed that the majority of app developers, 87%, were highly satisfied with the accuracy and efficiency of the predictions made by the plugin. Most developers, 89%, also found the mitigation recommendations to be useful. However, the plugin's usability, integration, and look and feel aspects received lower satisfaction ratings, with only 22% being highly satisfied with usability and integration, and 57% not being highly satisfied with the look and feel. This feedback can be used to improve the plugin's features, such as integrating mitigation suggestions in a manner similar to how syntax errors are indicated. Nevertheless, the overall satisfaction rate was high, with 79% of developers being highly satisfied and 21% satisfied. The plugin has the potential for broader use to address Android source code vulnerabilities with further development.

Fig. 8. Survey Results - Satisfaction of the plugin

5 Conclusion and Future Work

With numerous mobile applications available on Google Play and other Android marketplaces, it is not uncommon for developers to overlook security best practices, leaving their applications vulnerable to attacks. To bridge this gap and assist Android app developers in mitigating source code vulnerabilities in real-time, an AI-powered plugin called ACVED was introduced in this study. An ensemble learning model was trained using the LVDAndro dataset and integrated into the ACVED plugin, which is equipped with an API to detect source code vulnerabilities. The model achieved 95% accuracy in both binary classification and CWE-based multi-class classification, with F1-Scores of 0.95 and 0.93, respectively. The ACVED plugin provides XAI-based reasons for predictions to help developers quickly address vulnerabilities by considering the prediction probabilities of each word in the code line. All necessary instructions and source code for the dataset, model, API, and ACVED plugin are freely available on GitHub. In order to improve the prediction model's performance, it is feasible to incorporate expert knowledge from app developers. This integration would enable the plugin suggestions to provide regular developers with advanced security recommendations to effectively address vulnerabilities. Another potential improvement is to fine-tune the model to identify intricate vulnerability patterns supported with generative pre-trained transformer models. Additionally, one can consider utilising federated learning methods, which would allow the distribution of the model to individual entities, such as app development companies, to retrain the model while safeguarding the confidentiality of the protected code bases. By implementing this approach, it is anticipated that the number of detectable vulnerabilities of ACVED will also experience additional growth.

Acknowledgment. We thank Robert Gordon University - UK and the Accelerating Higher Education Expansion and Development grant (AHEAD) of Sri Lanka, University of Kelaniya - Sri Lanka for their support.

A   Appendix

Once the plugin has been integrated (as in Fig. 9), to activate the quick check feature, the user can navigate to *Tools - Check Source Vulnerability* or use the shortcut key *CTRL+ALT+E* within the Android Studio. This feature provides a rapid search for identifying vulnerabilities, notifying the developer of the specific lines of vulnerable code and their corresponding CWE-IDs as depicted in Fig. 10 and Fig. 11.

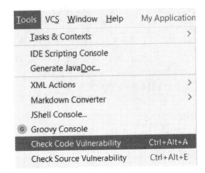

Fig. 9. Android Studio Tools Menu after Integrating ACVED

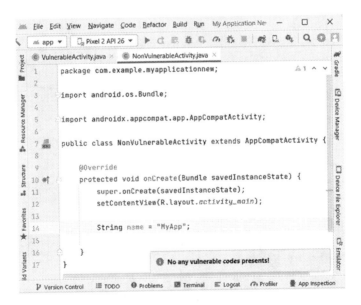

Fig. 10. Quick Check Notifications - No Any Vulnerable Code Lines

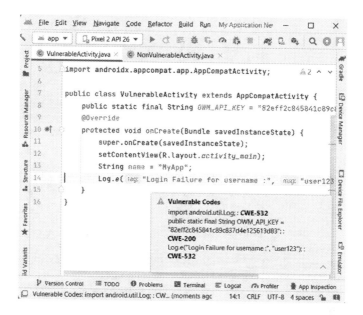

Fig. 11. Quick Check Notifications - Contain Vulnerable Code Lines

Alternatively, the detailed check feature can be activated by selecting *Tools - Check Code Vulnerability* or by using the shortcut key *CTRL+ALT+A* while the cursor is focused on a particular code line. Figure 12 presents an example of a detailed check executed on a vulnerable code line where the cursor is positioned on the statement *Log.e("Login Failure for username :", "user123");*.

Fig. 12. Detailed Check - Balloon Notification

References

1. Albakri, A., et al.: Survey on reverse-engineering tools for android mobile devices. Math. Probl. Eng. **2022** (2022). https://doi.org/10.1155/2022/4908134
2. Bhatnagar, P.: Explainable AI (XAI) - a guide to 7 packages in Python to explain your models (2021). https://towardsdatascience.com/explainable-ai-xai-a-guide-to-7-packages_in-python-to-explain-your-models-932967f0634b. Accessed 03 Feb 2023
3. Corporation, M.: Common weakness enumeration (CWE) (2023). https://cwe.mitre.org/. Accessed 01 Feb 2023
4. Corporation, M.: CVE details (2023). https://www.cvedetails.com/. Accessed 01 Feb 2023
5. Gajrani, J., Tripathi, M., Laxmi, V., Somani, G., Zemmari, A., Gaur, M.S.: Vulvet: vetting of vulnerabilities in android apps to thwart exploitation. Digit. Threats Res. Pract. **1**(2), 1–25 (2020). https://doi.org/10.1145/3376121
6. Garg, S., Baliyan, N.: Android security assessment: a review, taxonomy and research gap study. Comput. Secur. **100**, 102087 (2021). j.cose.2020.102087
7. Ghaffarian, S.M., Shahriari, H.R.: Software vulnerability analysis and discovery using machine-learning and data-mining techniques: a survey. ACM Comput. Surv. **50**(4) (Aug 2017). https://doi.org/10.1145/3092566
8. Kouliaridis, V., Kambourakis, G.: A comprehensive survey on machine learning techniques for android malware detection. Information **12**(5), 185 (2021). https://doi.org/10.3390/info12050185
9. Krasner, H.: The cost of poor software quality in the us: a 2020 report. In: Proceedings of Consortium Information and Software QualityTM (CISQTM) (2021)
10. Mahindru, A., Singh, P.: Dynamic permissions based android malware detection using machine learning techniques. In: Proceedings of the 10th Innovations in Software Engineering Conference, pp. 202–210 (2017). https://doi.org/10.1145/3021460.3021485
11. McDermid, J.A., Jia, Y., Porter, Z., Habli, I.: Artificial intelligence explainability: the technical and ethical dimensions. Phil. Trans. R. Soc. A **379**(2207), 20200363 (2021)
12. Mitra, J., Ranganath, V.P.: Ghera: A repository of android app vulnerability benchmarks. In: Proceedings of the 13th International Conference on Predictive Models and Data Analytics in Software Engineering, pp. 43–52. PROMISE, Association for Computing Machinery, New York, NY, USA (2017). https://doi.org/10.1145/3127005.3127010
13. Nagaria, B., Hall, T.: How software developers mitigate their errors when developing code. IEEE Trans. Softw. Eng. **48**(6), 1853–1867 (2022). https://doi.org/10.1109/TSE.2020.3040554
14. Namrud, Z., Kpodjedo, S., Talhi, C.: Androvul: a repository for android security vulnerabilities. In: Proceedings of the 29th Annual International Conference on Computer Science and Software Engineering, pp. 64–71. IBM Corp., USA (2019). https://dl.acm.org/doi/abs/10.5555/3370272.3370279
15. NIST: National vulnerability database (2023). https://nvd.nist.gov/vuln. Accessed 21 Feb 2023
16. Rajapaksha, S., Senanayake, J., Kalutarage, H., Al-Kadri, M.O.: Ai-powered vulnerability detection for secure source code development. In: Bella, G., Doinea, M., Janicke, H. (eds.) SecITC 2022. LNCS, vol. 13809, pp. 275–288. Springer, Cham (2023). https://doi.org/10.1007/978-3-031-32636-3_16

17. Senanayake, J., Kalutarage, H., Al-Kadri, M.O.: Android mobile malware detection using machine learning: a systematic review. Electronics **10**(13), 1606 (2021). https://doi.org/10.3390/electronics10131606

18. Senanayake, J., Kalutarage, H., Al-Kadri, M.O., Petrovski, A., Piras, L.: Developing secured android applications by mitigating code vulnerabilities with machine learning. In: Proceedings of the 2022 ACM on Asia Conference on Computer and Communications Security. ASIA CCS '22, pp. 1255–1257. Association for Computing Machinery, New York, NY, USA (2022). https://doi.org/10.1145/3488932.3527290

19. Senanayake, J., Kalutarage, H., Al-Kadri, M.O., Petrovski, A., Piras, L.: Android source code vulnerability detection: a systematic literature review. ACM Comput. Surv. **55**(9) (2023). https://doi.org/10.1145/3556974

20. Senanayake, J., Kalutarage, H., Al-Kadri, M.O., Petrovski, A., Piras, L.: Labelled vulnerability dataset on android source code (lvdandro) to develop AI-based code vulnerability detection models. In: Proceedings of the 20th International Conference on Security and Cryptography - SECRYPT (2023, accepted)

21. Shezan, F.H., Afroze, S.F., Iqbal, A.: Vulnerability detection in recent android apps: an empirical study. In: 2017 International Conference on Networking, Systems and Security (NSysS), pp. 55–63. IEEE, Dhaka, Bangladesh (2017). https://doi.org/10.1109/NSysS.2017.7885802

22. Srivastava, G., et al.: XAI for cybersecurity: state of the art, challenges, open issues and future directions (2022). https://doi.org/10.48550/ARXIV.2206.03585

23. Statcounter: Mobile operating system market share worldwide (2023). https://gs.statcounter.com/os-market-share/mobile/worldwide/. Accessed 01 Apr 2023

24. Statista: Average number of new android app releases via google play per month from March 2019 to March 2023 (2023). https://www.statista.com/statistics/1020956/android-app-releases-worldwide/. Accessed 03 Apr 2022

25. Tang, J., Li, R., Wang, K., Gu, X., Xu, Z.: A novel hybrid method to analyze security vulnerabilities in android applications. Tsinghua Sci. Technol. **25**(5), 589–603 (2020). https://doi.org/10.26599/TST.2019.9010067

26. Thomas, G., Devi, A.: A study and overview of the mobile app development industry. Int. J. Appl. Eng. Manag. Lett. 115–130 (2021). https://doi.org/10.5281/zenodo.4966320

27. de Vicente Mohino, J., Bermejo Higuera, J., Bermejo Higuera, J.R., Sicilia Montalvo, J.A.: The application of a new secure software development life cycle (s-sdlc) with agile methodologies. Electronics **8**(11) (2019). https://doi.org/10.3390/electronics8111218

28. Zhuo, L., Zhimin, G., Cen, C.: Research on android intent security detection based on machine learning. In: 2017 4th International Conference on Information Science and Control Engineering (ICISCE), pp. 569–574. IEEE (2017). https://doi.org/10.1109/ICISCE.2017.124

A Dynamic Approach to Defuse Logic Bombs in Android Applications

Fausto Fasano[1,2] ⓘ, Michele Guerra[1,2,3](✉) ⓘ, Roberto Milanese[1],
and Rocco Oliveto[1,3] ⓘ

[1] University of Molise, DiBT, Pesche (IS), Campobasso, Italy
{fausto.fasano,michele.guerra,roberto.milanese,rocco.oliveto}@unimol.it
[2] MOSAIC Research Center, DiBT, Unimol, Campobasso, Italy
[3] Stake Lab, DiBT, Unimol, Campobasso, Italy

Abstract. Logic bombs are a critical security threat in Android applications that can be triggered by specific events or conditions, leading to serious consequences. In this work we focus on apps accessing mobile device resources for sensitive data leakage. Such malicious behaviour can exploit Android permission model by gaining access to sensitive related resources in a legitimate context and later using them in a dangerous one, once the logic bomb is triggered. We propose a dynamic approach by extending RPCDroid, a tool that monitors the behavior of an Android application whenever it accesses specific device resources. To defuse the logic bomb we force an explicit prompt to authorize access requests based on the usage context preventing accesses unbeknownst to the user. We assessed the effectiveness of our proposal using TriggerZoo, a publicly available dataset of apps injected with logic bombs. Our results show that a context aware permission model can effectively prevent uncontrolled access to privacy related data in case a logic bomb is triggered.

Keywords: Security and Privacy · Context Aware Permission Model · Dynamic Analysis · Android Permission Model

1 Introduction

Android is the most popular mobile operating system[1], with over 2.5 billion active users worldwide. The security of Android applications is a significant concern, as new threats are discovered regularly in the official Google Play app store [13]. One of the most significant threats to the security of Android applications is logic bombs, a malicious code that is triggered by specific events or conditions. When activated, a logic bomb can execute various harmful actions, such as stealing sensitive data or crashing the system. The AndroZoo [2] repository has collected over 22 millions of malicious app versions, among which over 19 millions were available on Google Play Store. Therefore, addressing the spread of malware in app markets is a prime concern for researchers and

---

[1] https://www.idc.com/promo/smartphone-market-share.

ⓒ IFIP International Federation for Information Processing 2023
Published by Springer Nature Switzerland AG 2023
V. Atluri and A. L. Ferrara (Eds.): DBSec 2023, LNCS 13942, pp. 358–365, 2023.
https://doi.org/10.1007/978-3-031-37586-6_21

practitioners. Unfortunately, automatically detecting logic bomb is still an open issue, due to several pitfalls, such as the high rate of false positives, thus requiring an analyst to verify the behavior [20]. In recent years, there has been growing interest in using dynamic analysis techniques for detecting logic bombs in Android applications. This is mainly due to the fact that static analysis can be deceived by different obfuscation schemes [12].

In this work, we propose to monitor the resources accessed by the app and regulate their access based on the usage context. It is worth noting that we do not aim at identifying the presence of the logic bomb, but we aim at preventing it from causing access to protected resources unbeknownst to the user. With the term protected resources we refer to all those features of the device that are associated with sensitive data and which Android protects by explicitly requiring access permission to the user. Examples of protected resources are: camera, microphone, contacts, SMS, and location. Although Android has improved the permission management system over the years, it still suffers from some limitations that allow a logic bomb to access protected resources without the user's awareness. For instance, an app can legitimately acquire access to a protected resource and later trigger the logic bomb so that the system would not warn the user. Even if Android allows the user to specify whether access to a resource should be limited to a single execution, it is very likely that if the legit functionality is frequent – sooner or later – the user will decide to grant the permission permanently. In such a circumstance the logic bomb would be triggered.

To mitigate this problem we propose an extension of the Android permissions model in which the authorization to access a protected resource is restricted to the execution context. By execution context we mean a combination of the functionality the app is involved in and the UI element the user interacted with. There are several ways to identify the execution context, such as using the list of active functions on the call stack [23], the calling context encoding [24], the execution index [25], as well as techniques to recording and reporting dynamic calling contexts [3]. By adopting the calling context as a new dimension of the permission model, the user continue using the functionality s/he has already granted permissions to without the need to confirm its choice, but any access to the same protected resource occurring in a different context will require a further authorization. Usually, the logic bomb does not trigger if the context has not been previously analyzed, but even if the logic bomb is designed to trigger independently of the context – e.g., because it is unaware of the modified permission model – access to protected resources would have to be explicitly granted by the user. This behavior would be an alarm bell for the user, who could identify it as malicious and mitigate the malicious behaviour.

In this paper, to identify the calling contexts and instrument the context-based permission model, we extend RPCDroid [10] – a tool for monitoring the resources accessed by Android applications – to enforce the permission model with context-aware access control policies. By analyzing the logs generated by RPCDroid, we can identify the context in which a logic bomb is triggered, providing a better understanding of its behavior and how it is activated. To assess the effectiveness of our proposal we used TriggerZoo [21], a publicly available dataset of apps injected with logic bombs. The achieved results confirm that our approach can prevent sensitive data from being leaked without the knowledge of the user even in case of a logic bomb.

The rest of the paper is organized as follows. Section 2 describes the context aware permission model implemented with RPCDroid. In Sect. 3 we provide a preliminary evaluation of the effectiveness of our proposal using TriggerZoo. Section 4 discussed related works, while Sect. 5 concludes the paper and gives indications for future work.

2   Context Aware Permission Model with RPCDroid

Our work is based on the premise that a logic bomb is triggered by a specific sequence of events, which can be identified by analyzing the runtime behavior of an application. To implement our approach, we extended the Android permission model by considering information to limit the access to protected resources to specific contexts. This offers several advantages over existing approaches. It allows us to identify context-specific behavior, reducing the risk of false positives and, obviously, the drawback of the approach is that we rely on the ability of the user to discern between legit and malicious behaviours.

We extended an existing dynamic analysis tool called RPCDroid designed to monitor the execution of mobile applications that access specific device resources. RPCDroid Analyzer is installed as an Xposed module on the Android device or emulator and collects information to identify resource usage contexts. Upon starting the application, RPCDroid Analyzer tracks any access to protected resources (e.g., camera, microphone, storage, or location) at the system level. We monitor any action performed on the user interface and any system call to the Android access control and validation mechanism. More details on the tool are available in [10].

RPCDroid has been modified to save each context in which the request for a protected resource has been analysed. To prevent some logic bombs from not trigger due to the denial of permissions, we automatically granted all the permissions declared in the Manifest file, in order to set the tool in the worst scenario. In fact, logic bombs are usually designed to trigger only if the user has previously granted access to the resource they want to exploit, so as not to betray their presence. By granting permissions outside of the trigger code, we simulated a situation where the logic bomb is free to trigger at any time. Currently, the system identifies a context based on actions on the UI (e.g., touching a button or changing activities) and permissions requested at runtime. It is worth noting that the approach can be enhanced to include more restrictive or exhaustive execution context identification approaches.

The proposed approach is depicted in Figure (Fig. 1). RPCDroid uses the Xposed framework to dynamically inject the services we developed. These services perform method hooking concerning the invocation of access permissions and use callbacks to inject code that dynamically displays the permission management prompt. Finally, we monitor the app's behavior in the application

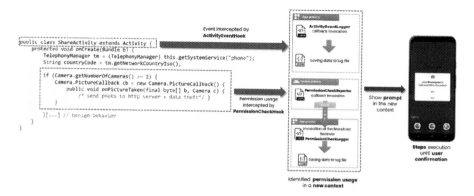

Fig. 1. The approach *dynamically identifies* individual permission usage contexts, showing the user the *decision prompt*.

process by intercepting the calls to access permissions associated to protected resources. We use this information to contextualize the permission requests and decide whether to display the appropriate prompt to the user. Note that the user's contextualized choice can be saved and used in case of further requests, thus avoiding the need to defuse the same bomb several times. Similarly, for each resource, impact on benign apps are limited by the number of different contexts exceeding the first one.

3   Preliminary Evaluation

To evaluate the effectiveness of our approach we conducted a preliminary evaluation on a dataset of Android apps called *TriggerZoo* [21], provided by Andro-Zoo [2]. This dataset contains 406 apps with **injected logic bombs** and includes descriptions of the logic bomb activation (e.g., the activity in which it is activated, permissions used, and return values). We executed our tool on an Android 11 (API 30) emulator. We randomly selected a subset including 70 apps and conducted an *in-depth analysis of their behavior* to understand the logic bomb triggering process and its relationship with permission misuse.

In Table 1 we report the results of our study. In particular, we were able to reproduce all the steps described in the dataset for 25 apps, while 45 of the selected apps could not be executed. More details on the selected apps details and the reasons why we could not execute them can be found in [7]. For 16 apps the tool displayed a prompt to request permission to access the protected resource exactly when the logic bomb trigger occurred. In 4 apps the bomb could not be triggered, in 3 apps the malicious behavior merely involved closing the application, and in 2 apps the malicious behavior did not involve using protected resources. In these cases, our tool did not warn the user since no protected resource was accessed. Despite the fact that this is a preliminary study, results are promising and confirm the overall effectiveness of our context aware fine grained permission model to defuse logic bombs or mitigate their impact on user privacy. In fact, even if the bomb is not actually removed, it cannot cause sensitive data access unless explicitly authorized.

Table 1. Summary of the execution results for the 70 apps

Category	Number of Apps
Non-executable apps	45
Incorrect permission declaration	10
Incompatible with Android version	6
RPCDroid related issues	9
Other errors	20
Executable apps	25
RPCDroid mitigation successful	16
Trigger condition not met	4
App closed by logic bomb	3
No access to protected resource	2

4   Related Works

Over the past decade, numerous approaches have been proposed to automate malware detection adopting static analysis techniques [8,11], dynamic execution [12], or a combination of both [4,26], as well as machine learning [16,19]. Although effective on benchmarks, these techniques may fail to detect new attacks that use sophisticated evasion techniques, code obfuscation [5] to bypass static analysis, or hide malicious code behind triggering conditions during dynamic analysis.

Logic bombs can be used for various malicious activities, such as adware [6], Trojan [17], and ransomware [27]. As the trigger and the malicious code are independent of the core application code, logic bombs can easily be added to legitimate apps and repackaged for distribution [14]. Therefore, detecting logic bombs is crucial, particularly in mobile devices containing critical personal information. Despite the challenges in detecting logic bombs, various approaches have been proposed in the literature exploring static-analysis-based heuristic or machine learning approaches [15] and dynamic-analysis-based approaches [28] to identify suspicious sensitive triggers. However, detecting logic bombs remains an open issue [1,18]. Static analyses may be limited by many conditional statements, making it challenging to identify suspicious sensitive triggers accurately. Moreover, high rate of false positives suggest that a manual analysis should be conducted to prevent a legitimate app from being erroneously considered to contain a logic bomb [20].

TriggerScope [9] uses symbolic execution to detect logic bombs but is limited to specific triggers and may not scale to large datasets. Dark Hazard [15] leverages a supervised learning approach with engineered features to identify sensitive triggers but flags up to 20% of apps, making it inefficient for isolating dangerous triggers. Unlike these approaches, we focus on identifying suspicious unexpected dangerous events and prevent protected resource access using dynamic analysis. Difuzer [22] proposed an approach that relies on unsupervised learning techniques and specific trigger/behavior features to identify suspicious hidden sensitive operations. In contrast, we focus on dynamic analysis and context-aware detection to prevent logic bombs triggered in dangerous contexts from being executed without the user approval, allowing for targeted mitigation strategies. Additionally, our approach does not block app execution in case of a false positive but informs the user of sensitive resource usage, allowing for continued app use. This capability is an improvement over existing techniques that rely solely on binary classification and often generate false positives, leading to unnecessary blocking of app execution.

5   Conclusion

In this work, we addressed logic bombs, a type of malicious code that is triggered by specific events or conditions. We proposed a dynamic approach to avoid privacy leakage in case the malicious code is activated. In particular, we aim at identifying execution contexts related to protected resources and prevent unauthorized access to privacy related data through logic bombs.

We assessed the effectiveness of our proposal with TriggerZoo [21], a publicly available dataset containing apps with injected logic bombs. The results are preliminary but promising since the approach allowed us to prevent the execution of malicious code behind a logic bomb trigger in all the situations in which the code actually tried to access a protected resource. We also collected logs generated by our enhanced version of RPCDroid to identify the exact conditions under which a logic bomb is triggered and permit a better understanding of its behavior. This gave us important insights on the behaviour of logical bombs while accessing privacy related resources that we plan to use to further improve the ability to automatically distinguish legitimate and malicious behaviors, reducing the effort required to the user for decisions regarding dangerous permissions.

The tool used to assess the proposed approach is a proof-of-concept. It requires root access to the mobile device and introduces a processing overhead making it unsuitable for a real context. However, it is desirable that in the future, a permission management aware of the execution context and the usage pattern of dangerous permissions will be integrated into the operating system. In this way, the approach could actually contribute to the overall security of the Android ecosystem and protect user privacy and sensitive data even in case of security threats like logic bombs, notoriously difficult to detect.

References

1. Agrawal, H., et al.: Detecting hidden logic bombs in critical infrastructure software (2012)
2. Allix, K., Bissyandé, T.F., Klein, J., Le Traon, Y.: AndroZoo: collecting millions of android apps for the research community. In: Proceedings of the 13th International Conference on Mining Software Repositories. MSR '16, pp. 468–471. ACM, New York, NY, USA (2016). https://doi.org/10.1145/2901739.2903508
3. Bond, M.D., Baker, G.Z., Guyer, S.Z.: Breadcrumbs: efficient context sensitivity for dynamic bug detection analyses. In: ACM-SIGPLAN Symposium on Programming Language Design and Implementation (2010)
4. Choudhary, M., Kishore, B.: HAAMD: hybrid analysis for android malware detection. In: 2018 International Conference on Computer Communication and Informatics (ICCCI), pp. 1–4 (2018). https://doi.org/10.1109/ICCCI.2018.8441295
5. Dong, S., et al.: Understanding android obfuscation techniques: a large-scale investigation in the wild. In: Beyah, R., Chang, B., Li, Y., Zhu, S. (eds.) SecureComm 2018. LNICST, vol. 254, pp. 172–192. Springer, Cham (2018). https://doi.org/10.1007/978-3-030-01701-9_10
6. Erturk, E.: A case study in open source software security and privacy: Android adware. In: World Congress on Internet Security, pp. 189–191 (2012)
7. Fasano, F., Guerra, M., Milanese, R., Oliveto, R.: A dynamic approach to defuse logic bombs in android applications: a technical report. Technical report, University of Molise, DiBT (2023). https://dibt.unimol.it/fasano/TR_DBSEC2023.pdf
8. Fereidooni, H., Conti, M., Yao, D., Sperduti, A.: Anastasia: android malware detection using static analysis of applications. In: 2016 8th IFIP International Conference on New Technologies, Mobility and Security (NTMS), pp. 1–5 (2016). https://doi.org/10.1109/NTMS.2016.7792435
9. Fratantonio, Y., Bianchi, A., Robertson, W., Kirda, E., Kruegel, C., Vigna, G.: TriggerScope: towards detecting logic bombs in android applications. In: 2016 IEEE Symposium on Security and Privacy (SP), pp. 377–396 (2016). https://doi.org/10.1109/SP.2016.30
10. Guerra., M., Milanese., R., Oliveto., R., Fasano., F.: RPCDroid: runtime identification of permission usage contexts in android applications. In: Proceedings of the 9th International Conference on Information Systems Security and Privacy - ICISSP, pp. 714–721. INSTICC, SciTePress (2023). https://doi.org/10.5220/0011797200003405
11. Kang, H., Jang, J.W., Mohaisen, D., Kim, H.K.: Detecting and classifying android malware using static analysis along with creator information. Int. J. Distrib. Sens. Netw. **2015**, 1–9 (2015). https://doi.org/10.1155/2015/479174
12. Khalid, S., Hussain, F.B.: Evaluating dynamic analysis features for android malware categorization. In: 2022 International Wireless Communications and Mobile Computing (IWCMC), pp. 401–406 (2022). https://doi.org/10.1109/IWCMC55113.2022.9824225
13. Kotzias, P., Caballero, J., Bilge, L.: How did that get in my phone? Unwanted app distribution on android devices. In: 2021 IEEE Symposium on Security and Privacy (SP), pp. 53–69 (2021). https://doi.org/10.1109/SP40001.2021.00041
14. Li, L., Bissyande, T.F., Klein, J.: Rebooting research on detecting repackaged android apps: literature review and benchmark. IEEE Trans. Softw. Eng. **47**(04), 676–693 (2021). https://doi.org/10.1109/TSE.2019.2901679

15. Pan, X., Wang, X., Duan, Y., Wang, X., Yin, H.: Dark hazard: learning-based, large-scale discovery of hidden sensitive operations in android apps (2017). https://doi.org/10.14722/ndss.2017.23265

16. Peiravian, N., Zhu, X.: Machine learning for android malware detection using permission and API calls. In: 2013 IEEE 25th International Conference on Tools with Artificial Intelligence, pp. 300–305 (2013). https://doi.org/10.1109/ICTAI.2013.53

17. Pieterse, H., Olivier, M.S.: Android botnets on the rise: Trends and characteristics. In: 2012 Information Security for South Africa, pp. 1–5 (2012). https://doi.org/10.1109/ISSA.2012.6320432

18. Rice, H.G.: Classes of recursively enumerable sets and their decision problems. Trans. Am. Math. Soc. **74**, 358–366 (1953)

19. Sahs, J., Khan, L.: A machine learning approach to android malware detection. In: 2012 European Intelligence and Security Informatics Conference, pp. 141–147 (2012). https://doi.org/10.1109/EISIC.2012.34

20. Samhi, J., Bartel, A.: On the (in)effectiveness of static logic bomb detection for android apps. IEEE Trans. Depend. Secure Comput. **19**(6), 3822–3836 (2022). https://doi.org/10.1109/TDSC.2021.3108057

21. Samhi, J., Bissyandé, T.F., Klein, J.: TriggerZoo: a dataset of android applications automatically infected with logic bombs. In: Proceedings of the 19th International Conference on Mining Software Repositories. MSR '22, pp. 459–463. Association for Computing Machinery, New York, NY, USA (2022). https://doi.org/10.1145/3524842.3528020

22. Samhi, J., Li, L., Bissyand'e, T.F., Klein, J.: Difuzer: uncovering suspicious hidden sensitive operations in android apps. In: 2022 IEEE/ACM 44th International Conference on Software Engineering (ICSE), pp. 723–735 (2021)

23. Sumner, W.N., Zhang, X.: Identifying execution points for dynamic analyses. In: 2013 28th IEEE/ACM International Conference on Automated Software Engineering (ASE), pp. 81–91 (2013). https://doi.org/10.1109/ASE.2013.6693069

24. Sumner, W.N., Zheng, Y., Weeratunge, D., Zhang, X.: Precise calling context encoding. IEEE Trans. Softw. Eng. **38**(5), 1160–1177 (2012). https://doi.org/10.1109/TSE.2011.70

25. Xin, B., Sumner, W.N., Zhang, X.: Efficient program execution indexing. In: Proceedings of the 29th ACM SIGPLAN Conference on Programming Language Design and Implementation. PLDI '08, pp. 238–248. Association for Computing Machinery, New York, NY, USA (2008). https://doi.org/10.1145/1375581.1375611

26. Xu, L., Zhang, D., Jayasena, N., Cavazos, J.: Hadm: hybrid analysis for detection of malware, pp. 702–724 (2018). https://doi.org/10.1007/978-3-319-56991-8_51

27. Yang, T., Yang, Y., Qian, K., Lo, D.C.T., Qian, Y., Tao, L.: Automated detection and analysis for android ransomware. In: 2015 IEEE 17th International Conference on High Performance Computing and Communications, 2015 IEEE 7th International Symposium on Cyberspace Safety and Security, and 2015 IEEE 12th International Conference on Embedded Software and Systems, pp. 1338–1343 (2015). https://doi.org/10.1109/HPCC-CSS-ICESS.2015.39

28. Zheng, C., et al.: SmartDroid: an automatic system for revealing UI-based trigger conditions in android applications. In: Proceedings of the Second ACM Workshop on Security and Privacy in Smartphones and Mobile Devices. SPSM '12, pp. 93–104. Association for Computing Machinery, New York, NY, USA (2012). https://doi.org/10.1145/2381934.2381950

Defense Mechanisms

AMOE: A Tool to Automatically Extract and Assess Organizational Evidence for Continuous Cloud Audit

Franz Deimling[1](✉) and Michela Fazzolari[2]

[1] Fabasoft R&D GmbH, 4020 Linz, Austria
franz.deimling@fabasoft.com
[2] IIT-CNR, 56122 Pisa, Italy
m.fazzolari@iit.cnr.it

Abstract. The recent spread of cloud services has enabled many companies to take advantage of them. Nevertheless, the main concern about the adoption of cloud services remains the lack of transparency perceived by customers regarding security and privacy. To overcome this issue, Cloud Service Certifications (CSCs) have emerged as an effective solution to increase the level of trust in cloud services, possibly based on continuous auditing to monitor and evaluate the security of cloud services on an ongoing basis. Continuous auditing can be easily implemented for technical aspects, while organizational aspects can be challenging due to their generic nature and varying policies between service providers.

In this paper, we propose an approach to facilitate the automatic assessment of organizational evidence, such as that extracted from security policy documents. The evidence extraction process is based on Natural Language Processing (NLP) techniques, in particular on Question Answering (QA). The implemented prototype provides promising results on an annotated dataset, since it is capable to retrieve the correct answer for more than half of the tested metrics. This prototype can be helpful for Cloud Service Providers (CSPs) to automate the auditing of textual policy documents and to help in reducing the time required by auditors to check policy documents.

Keywords: question answering · cloud security assessment · organisational measures · continuous audit · evidence extraction · MEDINA

1 Introduction

In recent years, cloud computing has emerged as a widespread solution for businesses seeking cost-effective and scalable IT infrastructure. The advantages

This work has received funding from the European Union's Horizon 2020 research and innovation programme under grant agreement No: 952633.
This work was partially supported by project SERICS (PE00000014) under the MUR National Recovery and Resilience Plan funded by the European Union - NextGenerationEU.

© IFIP International Federation for Information Processing 2023
Published by Springer Nature Switzerland AG 2023
V. Atluri and A. L. Ferrara (Eds.): DBSec 2023, LNCS 13942, pp. 369–385, 2023.
https://doi.org/10.1007/978-3-031-37586-6_22

brought by cloud services, such as flexibility, cost-efficiency and maintenance reduction, made them an attractive option for companies of all sizes.

Nevertheless, the adoption of cloud services also implies moving from direct control and governance of data and applications to an indirect form of control. Thus, several concerns have been raised about security, privacy, transparency and trustworthiness. To address these concerns, CSCs have become an effective solution to increase the level of trust in cloud services [15]. CSCs provide assurance that cloud services are compliant with industry standards and best practices, and that appropriate security controls are in place to protect sensitive data and applications. The goal is to obtain a certificate that proves compliance with one or more security schemes, allowing users and customers to trust the cloud service.

While traditional security certification approaches rely on periodic audits (annually or biannually), continuous auditing has emerged as a method to monitor and evaluate the security of cloud services on an ongoing basis [5,26]. Continuous auditing involves the collection, analysis, and evaluation of security-related data and events to provide real-time insights into the security posture of cloud services. Continuous auditing is particularly effective when applied to analyze technical/performance aspects, which can be represented with unambiguous and measurable objectives. On the contrary, when considering administrative/organisational aspects, they are generally not analysed, or their analysis is conducted manually. This is due to the fact that organisational aspects, by their nature, are generic, typically expressed by policies written in natural language and varying from one service provider to another. For these reasons, they are difficult to be transformed into objective quantities that can be measured and evaluated automatically. However, they play a critical role in establishing a strong security culture and ensuring compliance with security standards.

Given the challenge mentioned above, the novelty of this work resides in the proposal of a tool, namely Assessment and Management of Organisational Evidence (AMOE), to enable evidence extraction and assessment of policy documents containing organizational aspects. This tool has been developed within the context of the MEDINA project [18], which aims at providing a security framework for continuous audit-based certification in compliance with cloud security certification schemes, in particular with the European Cybersecurity Certification Scheme for Cloud Services (EUCS). These schemes, indeed, include both technical and organisational controls. The latter are not suitable to be automatically monitored like technical requirements, but they still need to be verified and checked in a way that enables the continuous and automatic issuing of security certificates.

The AMOE tool relies on a set of organisational metrics specifically defined for this purpose, which aim to measure concrete parts in the policy documents. The proposed approach is based on NLP techniques since policy documents contain organizational evidence expressed in Natural Language (NL). The audit information is then extracted from such texts, exploiting a QA system. Indeed, question answering has been successfully used in various information retrieval tasks, e.g. to build a search system for COVID-19-research documents [8].

To evaluate the suitability of our proposal, a set of retrieval pipelines has been tested utilizing QA to extract the relevant audit information. Then, the different evidence extraction pipelines have been tested by conducting a set of experiments, which show that the QA approach, combined with keyword-based paragraph filtering, leads to promising results.

The proposed tool can be useful for Cloud Service Provider (CSP) compliance managers or auditors to verify the compliance of a policy document with respect to a set of organisational metrics.

This paper is structured as follows: Sect. 2 discusses the related work in the domain of security transparency and audit in cloud computing. Section 3 provides some background information about techniques and methods used in this work. The data used for the experimentation are described in Sect. 4. Section 5 describes the methodology used in the approach proposed in this paper. The experimental results and a discussion are provided in Sect. 6. Finally, Sect. 7 concludes the paper and suggests some improvements that can be developed.

2   Related Work

Several contributions have been proposed in the last decade dealing with continuous auditing and dynamic certification of cloud services. In 2013, Cimato et al. [6] introduced the concept of cloud service certification and they drew an initial proposal containing a conceptual framework with the specification of certification models. Afterwards, Anisetti et al. [1, 2] proposed a test-based certification framework for automating the certification process and a cloud engineering methodology based on it.

The authors in [21] focus on Infrastructure-as-a-Service (IaaS) providers and propose an approach that aims to continuously detect ongoing changes in the services. To assess the impact of these changes on customer requirements, low-level metrics are used, which are derived from widely deployed IaaS components. Furthermore, the authors show how these low-level metrics can be used to construct complex metrics to support the validation of generic requirements. A further approach proposed in [22] focuses on security certification for Software-as-a-Service (SaaS) providers. In this work, the authors develop a method to support continuous certification of SaaS applications, using web application testing techniques. In particular, they exploit SQLMap, a tool for web application testing.

One of the first attempts to summarize contributions in this field can be found in the paper published by Lins et al. [16], where the authors conducted a systematic literature review to identify automated auditing methods that could be applied within the context of cloud computing. Then, they propose a conceptual architecture for continuous auditing of cloud services, identify the cloud services criteria that should be continuously audited, evaluate applicable methodologies, and highlight the components and processes required for successful implementation [15].

Work on the subject of continuous auditing has increased in recent years. In [12] the authors highlight the difficulties in the implementation of continuous auditing due to the lack of standardized approaches. In this regard, they propose a solution by defining a standardized way of establishing a continuous audit process and by providing a methodology to realize it, by leveraging an Audit API. The work in [13] discusses the challenges of integrating continuous certification checks in existing certification processes for cloud services. The authors analyze and generalize traditional certification processes and then propose a novel certification process model to address these challenges and support continuous certification techniques.

The work in [23] proposes a novel cloud security system, namely CSBAuditor, to continuously monitor and audit cloud infrastructure. CSBAuditor uses the reconciler pattern and state transition analysis to detect misconfigurations, malicious activities, and unauthorized changes. Furthermore, a new scoring system is proposed, i.e. Cloud Security Scoring System, which uses security metrics to compute severity scores for detected vulnerabilities. The authors also highlight the limitations of existing security management processes and the need for more customer-centric security mechanisms to protect cloud infrastructure.

While this is a broad topic and they do not provide technical implementation, research teams such as Banse et al. [4] focus on specific aspects such as static code analysis, which can be part of the evidence gathering needed for continuous audits. Some of the theoretical concepts are implemented in different technical evidence gathering tools (e.g. Clouditor[1]) and have been tested in audit use cases. However, we are interested in the technical feasibility of handling and integrating organisational evidence in the automated audit process.

3   Background

Audits of cloud computing services look for evidence that a cloud provider is using best practices, complies with appropriate standards and meets certain benchmarks in delivering its services. Thus, when performing a cloud audit, one of the first steps involves evidence collection, i.e. gathering, integrating and processing logs, policies and metadata coming from the cloud.

Security certification schemes such as the EUCS contain several objectives to define technical and organizational measures to ensure the security of the systems[2]. There are requirements that call for policies and procedures and provide guidelines for the content of the policies. Similarly, NIST classify some controls (similar to requirements in EUCS) to address administrative, technical and physical aspects[3]. The Continuous Audit Metrics Catalog[4] released by Cloud Security Alliance (CSA) lists metrics to deal with technical security measures. The authors make a distinction between the evaluation of technical measures and the evaluation of policy and procedural controls. They argue, that the technical ones can be managed by automated techniques to collect evidence to prove their

---

[1] https://github.com/clouditor/clouditor.
[2] https://www.enisa.europa.eu/publications/eucs-cloud-service-scheme.
[3] https://nvlpubs.nist.gov/nistpubs/SpecialPublications/NIST.SP.800-53r5.pdf.
[4] https://cloudsecurityalliance.org/artifacts/the-continuous-audit-metrics-catalog/.

effectiveness and that this idea can be extended partially to policy and procedural controls. Independent of the security scheme vendor, there is a distinction between technical and non-technical (administrative or organizational) measures that are specified by the security controls or requirements. However, the security control descriptions are too generic to classify them as organizational or technical. Most of them cover both technical and organizational aspects and call for automation if possible, especially for higher levels of assurance.

When considering the organizational part of a requirement, the evidence collected for the cloud audit is mostly available in textual form, thus a possible way to process it is to use Information Retrieval (IR) approaches, which has shown increasingly accurate results over the last years. In particular, NLP techniques can help retrieve accurate results from large amounts of text. In this section, we provide some background information regarding NLP that has been used in the creation of the AMOE tool.

3.1   Text Pre-processing

We exploited several text pre-processing techniques to clean the text analyzed by the AMOE tool.

Tokenization is the first step in any NLP pipeline and is the process of breaking a stream of textual data into words, terms, sentences, symbols, or some other meaningful elements called tokens [24]. A tokenizer breaks unstructured data and natural language text into chunks of information that can be considered as discrete elements.

Lemmatization, in contrast to stemming, does not remove the suffixes of words but tries to find the dictionary form of a word on the basis of vocabulary and morphological analysis of a word [3,20]. Furthermore, it could help to match synonyms such as "hot" and "warm" - or "car", "cars" and "automobile" [3].

Stop word removal involves removing common words that are irrelevant for a query, as they occur with the same likelihood over all documents. In fact, words such as "the", "if", "but", "and", etc. do not add additional content to the document. Removing such words can improve retrieval performance [25]. However, for some queries, not removing the stop words leads to more precise results [20].

3.2   Language Encoding Models

In the last decade IR research has brought us new ways to approach NLP tasks by developing Language Encoding Models, i.e. models designed to represent words or text with the goal of capturing their underlying meaning or semantic information.

An example of Language Encoding Model is the Bidirectional Encoder Representations from Transformers (BERT) model, which was introduced by Devlin et al. [7]. This model has been successfully applied over the last few years and additional research has been built upon it. A resulting refinement is A Robustly Optimized BERT Pretraining Approach (RoBERTa) [17], which manages to achieve very good performance on different datasets. We would like to mention one particular dataset in the following, e.g. Stanford Question Answering Dataset (SQuAD2) [19], as it has been used to fine-tune the QA model[5] applied in the evidence extraction pipelines described in Sect. 5.2. This dataset is based on a set of Wikipedia articles and annotated answers to 100,000+ questions. Further models based on FastText [10] for learning word vectors of languages have been presented by Grave et al. in [9]. These models are trained with data from Wikipedia and Common Crawl and evaluated on word analogy tasks. For a triplet of words $A : B :: C$, the goal is to guess D. For example, for the triplet $Paris : France :: Berlin$:?, the answer would be *Germany*. The resulting models can produce word vectors, which can be used for further applications, e.g. text classification or text similarity tasks.

3.3   Question Answering (QA)

Question Answering (QA) is a task of NLP which consists in retrieving one or more answers to a question, given an input text as *context*. Once trained, QA models do not require a complex setup to be used. Some QA models can work even without context. These systems are especially used in customer service chat-bots, evidence extraction or in semantic search engines [8]. The use of large numbers of documents increases the probability of including the correct answer, but the QA system's performance can be negatively affected. Therefore, Lee et al. [14] investigate paragraph ranking to improve answer recall in QA. To this aim, they introduce a Paragraph Ranker to increase answer recall and reduce noise. For a set of N documents containing K paragraphs on average, the system only selects the M top-ranked paragraphs. In this way, N is increased while the number of read paragraphs M is reduced, leading to higher answer recall. Lee et al. calculate the probability that a paragraph contains the answer to the question by using different similarity functions. This probability is then used in the loss function of the model.

We used an approach similar to the Paragraph Ranker described by Lee et al. [14] in the similarity-based evidence extraction method, as described in Sect. 5.3. The main difference is that instead of training a model to refine the ranking, the ranking of results for evidence extraction is done directly using the similarity score. The Paragraph Ranker approach is not applicable in our case because training a model given the two documents, it would likely over-fit.

To this aim, cosine similarity can be used to determine the similarity between documents and texts of different lengths. In fact, despite having different lengths, two documents might be similar. This happens because the relative term frequency could be similar, thus given similar term frequencies, it can be assumed that the content of the documents is similar as well. The denominator of the equation normalizes the length of the vectors [20]. The cosine similarity is defined as

---

[5] https://huggingface.co/deepset/roberta-base-squad2.

shown in Eq. 1, where A and B could be a document or word vector representations.

$$cos\ \theta\ =\ \frac{A \cdot B}{|A|\,|B|} \tag{1}$$

4   Dataset

The AMOE tool uses two different types of textual data. The first type of data is used for extracting evidence and it is represented by a set of organisational metrics. This set was specifically designed within the MEDINA project. Nevertheless, it includes metrics of general nature and can therefore easily be reused within other frameworks or extended by incorporating new metrics. The second type of data contains the policy documents of CSPs.

In the following, the two kinds of data will be described in detail.

4.1   Organisational Metrics

The organisational metrics are quantitative measures that can be associated with organisational requirements, with the aim of defining how compliance can be automatically assessed. In AMOE they represent the structured form of a query for the evidence to be assessed. Specifically, a metric consists of a set of attributes such as a name, a description, and some keywords found in the paragraph or section heading of the expected evidence to extract. The metric also includes values useful for the assessment, e.g. an operator, a target value and a data type. An example of metric and its attributes is reported in Table 1.

Table 1. Example of organisational metric.

Attribute	Value
name	PasswordPolicyQ2
description	What is the password's maximum age according to the password policy?
keywords	password, age, maximum
operator	$\leq$
target value	100
data type	Integer

Security certification schemes such EUCS aim at enhancing trust in cloud services by defining a set of security requirements. Within this context, metrics are linked to security requirements, thus to assess compliance with a requirement, we need to assess the corresponding metrics.

The description of each organisational metric is targeted to measure a specific part of a requirement. As the requirements are written in a generic way and allow some broader interpretation, multiple metrics are required to reflect the compliance status of a cloud service or policy to a requirement.

Therefore, the organisational metric description is formulated as a precise question targeted in consequence to measure and assess compliance. This way, the query is human-readable as well as usable by the evidence extraction pipeline. The keywords supplied in the metric can be used to reduce the search space for the evidence in the different approaches explained in Sect. 5.2.

4.2   Policy Documents

The policy documents are usually formatted as unstructured text in the form of Word documents or PDFs. In this case, the experiments are conducted using the documents supplied by two industry partners.

Since the documents contain text in natural language, they need to be pre-processed and prepared for evidence extraction. Moreover, they need to be annotated, in order to gain some insights into the performance of the whole system. For this, the INCEpTION software has been chosen [11], which is described as "A semantic annotation platform offering intelligent assistance and knowledge management". Thus, for a set of metrics, the expected evidence (i.e. the answer to the metric description question) is marked directly in the text. The annotations can be extracted as TSV (Tab-Separated Value) files and thus conveniently used for quality checks of AMOE.

The policy documents provided contain multiple policies, so they are addressing different requirements of the EUCS. Some documents contain more than 50 pages and this affects the processing duration as well as extraction accuracy. In fact, AMOE tool does not know apriori what policies are included in a document, thus every metric needs to be checked, even if it could not be answered since it is not covered by the document.

5   Methodology

In this section, we describe the methodology used within the AMOE tool to extract evidence based on metrics from certain documents linked to the organisational requirements and to process and prepare them for assessment.

5.1   Pre-processing

Both the policy documents and the metrics data need to be pre-processed to be used within the AMOE tool.

Policy Document Pre-processing. As already introduced, policy documents are provided in the form of PDF documents. To retain some of the structure given by e.g. section headings, these documents are transformed into HTML. Depending on the document's origin, some headings need further recognition,

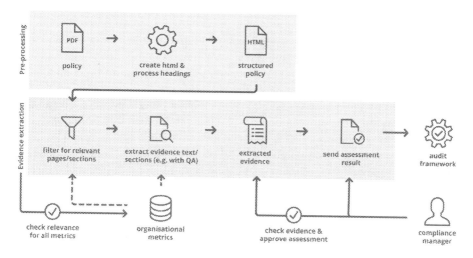

Fig. 1. Simplified overview of the AMOE evidence pipeline.

e.g. through rule-based approaches. This process is depicted in the upper part of Fig. 1.

The PDF document is transformed into an HTML with the help of the Poppler library[6], specifically by using the *pdftohtml* tool. While the document is processed, common errors for section headings are fixed. For example, it can occur that headings are not correctly detected by the initial conversion to HTML. Therefore, the heading tags are merged into a single tag, if the heading spans over multiple lines, or they are added if they have been missed. Short text spans are considered to be a heading if the text size is high (relative to the rest of the document) or if the font is bold.

The result of this process is a structured document containing headings and sections/paragraphs, that eases the information filtering task. In the last stage of the pre-processing, information such as the table of contents, or parts of the headings or footer are removed. The whole process depends heavily on the quality of the PDF, which is reflected in the final HTML document.

Transforming the document to HTML has at least three benefits: 1) it brings structure into an otherwise unstructured text (as seen by the program), 2) the obtained structure can be used to perform better analyses and to infer why something was found or could not be obtained and 3) the document in HTML format can be directly used to present the answers in a User Interface, without additional processing.

Metric Pre-processing. As for the policy documents, the metrics data need to be pre-processed as well. For example, the metric keywords can contain irrelevant words for queries and therefore they are removed. As a basis for the removal,

---

[6] https://poppler.freedesktop.org/.

common English stop words defined in the Natural Language Toolkit (NLTK) corpus have been used[7]. Furthermore, the remaining words are lemmatized and used in the different extraction processes.

5.2   Evidence Extraction

After pre-processing the document, the evidence can be extracted using different approaches. In the following, the basic approach is first explained, which consists in taking the entire policy document as input and feeding it to the QA model. However, as previously mentioned, processing very long documents may lead to a deterioration in performance. Therefore, alternative approaches to mitigate this problem are also described. In particular, in some approaches, the documents have been filtered in a preliminary step, in order to reduce the search space for the evidence.

The bottom part of Fig. 1 shows the pipeline steps for evidence extraction and connection to a hypothetical component that will use the assessment results somehow. For all the approaches, the extraction of evidence is based on a pre-trained QA model, specifically, the RoBERTa base model, fine-tuned using the SQuAD2 dataset (roberta-base-squad2[8]).

The evidence extracted by the QA model is then analyzed. If a target value has been set for a metric, the extracted evidence is translated into a similar datatype (if possible) and an assessment hint is computed by checking the output against the target value with the defined metric operator. Moreover, the QA model provides a score that could aid in determining whether the output is relevant since not all queries produce relevant outputs.

5.3   Baseline: Whole-Doc Approach

In the baseline approach, the text of the whole document is fed into the QA model to produce a single answer. In the following, we provide an example of how the extraction pipeline works for the metric shown in Table 1. In Fig. 2 an excerpt of a policy document is reported, which represents the context for the question. Table 2, instead, shows the question given as input to the QA model, which corresponds to the metric description, and the answer (marked in bold) as extracted from the evidence.

The assessment hint is generated by converting the answer from string to integer and by comparing this value with the metric target value, using the metric operator. Thus, for the example reported, the assessment hint will appear as follow:

$$60 \leq 100 \rightarrow True$$

An (internal) auditor or compliance manager can then approve the assessment result and initiate the workflow needed to obtain a certificate with the help of an audit framework.

---

[7] https://www.nltk.org/.

[8] https://huggingface.co/deepset/roberta-base-squad2.

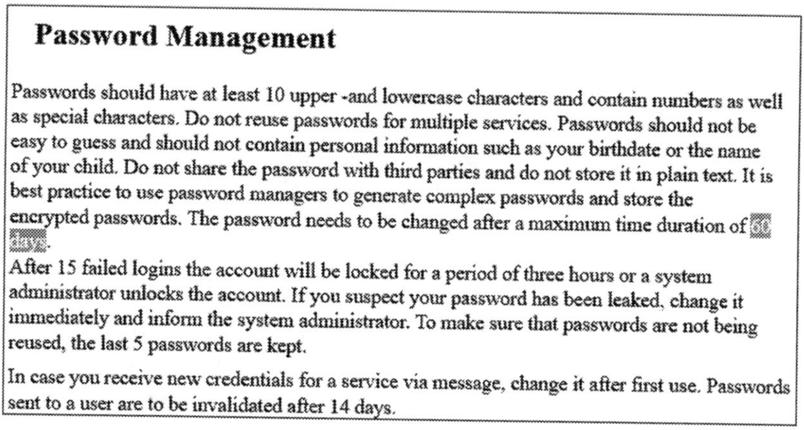

Password Management

Passwords should have at least 10 upper -and lowercase characters and contain numbers as well as special characters. Do not reuse passwords for multiple services. Passwords should not be easy to guess and should not contain personal information such as your birthdate or the name of your child. Do not share the password with third parties and do not store it in plain text. It is best practice to use password managers to generate complex passwords and store the encrypted passwords. The password needs to be changed after a maximum time duration of ▓▓ ▓▓▓.

After 15 failed logins the account will be locked for a period of three hours or a system administrator unlocks the account. If you suspect your password has been leaked, change it immediately and inform the system administrator. To make sure that passwords are not being reused, the last 5 passwords are kept.

In case you receive new credentials for a service via message, change it after first use. Passwords sent to a user are to be invalidated after 14 days.

Fig. 2. Excerpt of a policy document.

Table 2. Evidence extraction example.

Query
What is the password's maximum age according to the password policy?
Evidence/Answer
The password needs to be changed after a maximum time duration of **60 days**.

The approach described so far can retrieve relevant evidence from small documents containing only a few policies. However, for longer documents, the extraction quality suffers and the computation time is higher (as reported in Sect. 6). In the following, we describe alternative evidence extraction approaches developed to improve performances.

Keyword-Based Approach. The keyword-based approach tries to mitigate the negative effects of document length on performance. In fact, the documents can contain large amounts of text and multiple policies irrelevant to the metric, thus this information needs to be filtered out. The underlying idea consists in mimicking what a human auditor would do. First, search for the relevant section based on some keywords (derived from experience, similar policy documents, etc.), then read the section and decide whether the necessary information is included. Therefore, relevant sections are sought according to the metric keywords. If no sections can be found, the whole document is used. Stop words are removed from the metric keywords and the remaining words are lemmatized.

For this simple approach, a section is considered relevant if the lemmatized section heading words intersect with the metric keywords. Once the filtering is complete, the relevant sections are concatenated into a single input text. Lastly, the pre-trained QA model is fed with both the concatenated text as well as the metric question, and a single answer is retrieved. The process then continues as the baseline approach.

The main benefit of the keyword-based approach is that it is quite fast since the model is used only once per metric. However, some evidence could be missed, because sections are excluded based on the keywords. This error occurs if the evidence is in the document, just not in a section with a relevant heading. Therefore, in some cases, the results of this approach depend more on the keywords, than on the QA model's performance itself.

Score-Based Approach. To deal with the problem arising from the length of the text, one possibility is to consider individual sections instead of the entire document. Thus, in the score-based approach, multiple queries are presented to the pre-trained QA model, one for each section of the document. For each query, the context is the text of a section and the question is the metric description. With such an approach, the model provides not one, but as many answers as there are sections. As described in Sect. 5.2, the QA model also returns a score associated with each answer: the higher the probability that an answer correlates with a question, the higher the score.

Therefore, once all answers and scores are retrieved, the answer with the highest score is returned. This approach stems from the assumption that the section that produces the highest score would be the correct one. However, empirical results and also quantitative comparisons to the annotated samples showed that this is not always the case. This could be probably mitigated by fine-tuning the QA model with respect to the domain.

Similarity-Based Approach. The similarity-based approach was designed to make better use of the metric keywords. To this aim, the metric keywords are lemmatized and transformed into a feature vector by applying the FastText model ($qry\_features$), computed at sentence level instead than at word level. The same is done for each section in the document, and the feature vectors for sections are obtained ($section\_features$). At this point, the cosine similarity measure is computed between the $qry\_features$ and the $section\_features$ of each section. Finally, the pre-trained QA model is applied, considering each section as the context and the metric description as the question. Similar to the score-based approach, multiple answers are retrieved but this time the answer corresponding to the section with the highest cosine similarity is returned. This approach is highly dependent on the metric keywords.

Similarity + Score-Based Approach. This approach combines the similarity-based and score-based approaches and it works in the same way. This time, for each answer, both scores and cosine similarities are computed and added up. Finally, the answer with the highest sum is returned, with the idea of balancing out the flaws of the single approaches.

6   Experimental Results

To get an impression of how well the tool is working and to be able to research for better extraction methods, quality checks have been implemented. Two test cases have been constructed, in cooperation with the two industry partners, to determine the performance of the approach. Each test case is using a policy document and a set of organisational metrics for which the evidence has been annotated in the document. The two test cases differ mainly in the length of the policy document considered (14 vs 69 pages).

The annotations were edited using the INCEpTION tool, as explained in Sect. 4.2. A numerical analysis and a manual analysis were conducted for each approach. In the following, the two test cases are described and the results of the experiments are reported.

The first test case consists of a short document containing policies and 28 organisational metrics have been annotated for this document. The document belonging to the second test case is longer than the previous one and 50 organisational metrics have been annotated in it.

The annotations of the short document have been made by an expert person with in-depth knowledge of the context, while the longer document has been annotated by people in the field of cloud computing, but with only high-level knowledge of the context.

6.1   Computed Results

The various approaches presented in Sect. 5.2 have been evaluated and compared by computing a *quality* score that is defined as in Eq. 2.

$$score = \frac{\#correctly\ retrieved\ evidence}{\#total\ annotated\ evidence} \tag{2}$$

This value represents the ratio between the number of correctly retrieved answers and the total number of annotated answers. A piece of evidence is counted as correctly retrieved if the tokens of the retrieved answer intersect with the annotated tokens. Tokens are chunks of characters from a text and are separated by spaces or punctuation marks. The results for the test cases can be seen in Table 3.

The results show a clear deterioration when the long document is considered instead of the short one. This is because, for the short document, annotations are more specific and less ambiguous. Moreover, performance can suffer from the annotation bias introduced by non-expert annotators.

Further issues can derive from the particular choice of metric keywords included in each metric. Nevertheless, the keyword-based approach is the one that achieves the best performance for both test cases. On the other hand, the similarity-based and the similarity+score-based approaches seem not to benefit from the search space reduction based on keywords.

Table 3. Results obtained for each approach on the test policy documents

Approach	ShortDoc Score	LongDoc Score
Whole-doc	0.54	0.08
Keyword-based	0.68	0.26
Score-based	0.46	0.10
Similarity-based	0.25	0.12
Similarity + score-based	0.46	0.16

In general, the results obtained for the long document are limited and the division of the text into sections does not seem to lead to a particular improvement. This may also be due to inaccurate detection of sections or a poor structure of the document.

6.2 Empirical Results

As seen from the results obtained, the analysis of the long document is the most problematic. For this reason, an empirical analysis on the long document has been performed, by inspecting the answers retrieved. To this aim, a set of 118 metrics have been evaluated and assessed. Among these metrics, 82 entries were manually set to *compliant* and 36 were set to *not compliant*. In addition, a comment has been provided by the evaluator to describe why the result is compliant or not. According to the information found in the comment, the metrics have been then grouped into 4 categories:

- *Correct:* this category includes all the results assessed as compliant and no comment has been provided.
- *Partial matching:* it includes all results that have been marked as compliant but had additional comments indicating that the actual result would be in a different place. In any case, the systems' answer was correct.
- *False/other error:* it includes all results that have been set to not compliant and/or errors have been indicated within the comment.
- *Not in document:* there are all results that had a comment indicating that the metric target is not contained in the policy document.

Table 4 reports the results obtained by applying the manual assessment. In the first column, the 4 error categories are listed, while the second and the third ones report the number of results belonging to that category and the percentage with respect to the whole results, respectively.

As a consequence of the above, there are at least three reasons why a result can be not compliant:

1. The evidence is not in the document.
2. The wrong answer was retrieved.
3. The retrieved answer does not comply with the target value.

Table 4. Results from manual assessment. Each extracted evidence has been assessed and assigned an *error category*. The keyword-based approach was used for evidence extraction.

Error category	Count	Percentage
No error	68	57.63%
Partial matching	11	9.32%
False/other error	8	6.78%
Not in document	31	26.27%
Total	118	100%

The first type of situation (evidence not in the document) is the one occurring most often, but in reality, this should not be considered an error, since the metric sought is not really present in the text. This problem can be solved by applying a method that is able to automatically detect whether or not the answer is present in the text, or by defining a set of metrics that are definitely present in the text. For example, the set of metrics could be defined by the staff responsible for policy creation, as they know which requirements/metrics are covered by the document.

For a quality measurement of the actual evidence retrieval system, the metrics considered *not in document* have been excluded and the *partial matching* have been counted as false results. This leads to an accuracy of $68/87 = 78.16\%$ (67 correctly retrieved answers vs 19 that are either only partly correct or not at all).

7   Conclusion and Future Work

In this paper, we presented AMOE, a tool to process organisational evidence to enable computer-aided audits. Several approaches have been proposed, to facilitate the automatic assessment of organizational evidence, such as the one available in security policy documents of CSPs. This tool is also expected to reduce the time spent by auditors to check policy documents to filter and extract relevant information. The proposed approaches have been tested on an annotated dataset, providing promising results. The empirical results indicated that the correct answer could be retrieved for more than half of the tested metrics. In the future, these approaches need to be verified on larger sets of data and refined taking into account the context. Currently, the final decision on the assessment is still left to a human auditor, but once the system has been tested on a larger number of data and refined, the audit may be fully automated and only random samples need to be checked once in a while.

Furthermore, additional QA models could be used, and extractive text summarization techniques can be also applied. Generative text models could also be tested, e.g. those based on Generative Pre-trained Transformer-3 (GPT-3), but despite their powerfulness, they do not seem to be suitable for this task since

384 F. Deimling and M. Fazzolari

they suffer uncertainty and correctness issues. Moreover, incorporating context in generative models can increase the computational cost and time.

References

1. Anisetti, M., Ardagna, C., Gaudenzi, F., Damiani, E.: A certification framework for cloud-based services. In: Proceedings of the 31st Annual ACM Symposium on Applied Computing, pp. 440–447. Association for Computing Machinery, New York, NY, USA (04 2016). https://doi.org/10.1145/2851613.2851628
2. Anisetti, M., Ardagna, C.A., Damiani, E., Gaudenzi, F., Veca, R.: Toward security and performance certification of open stack. In: 2015 IEEE 8th International Conference on Cloud Computing, pp. 564–571 (2015). https://doi.org/10.1109/CLOUD.2015.81
3. Balakrishnan, V., Lloyd-Yemoh, E.: Stemming and lemmatization: a comparison of retrieval performances. Lect. Notes Softw. Eng. 2(3), 262–267 (2014)
4. Banse, C., Kunz, I., Schneider, A., Weiss, K.: Cloud property graph: connecting cloud security assessments with static code analysis. In: Ardagna, C.A., et al. (eds.) 14th IEEE International Conference on Cloud Computing, CLOUD 2021, Chicago, IL, USA, 5–10 September 2021, pp. 13–19. IEEE (2021). https://doi.org/10.1109/CLOUD53861.2021.00014
5. Çabuk, A., Aytaç, A.: The transformation of auditing from traditional to continuous auditing in the era of big data. In: Organizational Auditing and Assurance in the Digital Age, pp. 137–152. IGI Global (2019)
6. Cimato, S., Damiani, E., Zavatarelli, F., Menicocci, R.: Towards the certification of cloud services. In: 2013 IEEE Ninth World Congress on Services, pp. 92–97 (2013). https://doi.org/10.1109/SERVICES.2013.16
7. Devlin, J., Chang, M., Lee, K., Toutanova, K.: BERT: pre-training of deep bidirectional transformers for language understanding. CoRR abs/1810.04805 (2018). https://arxiv.org/abs/1810.04805
8. Esteva, A., et al.: Co-search: COVID-19 information retrieval with semantic search, question answering, and abstractive summarization. CoRR abs/2006.09595 (2020). https://arxiv.org/abs/2006.09595
9. Grave, E., Bojanowski, P., Gupta, P., Joulin, A., Mikolov, T.: Learning word vectors for 157 languages. CoRR abs/1802.06893 (2018). https://arxiv.org/abs/1802.06893
10. Joulin, A., Grave, E., Bojanowski, P., Douze, M., Jégou, H., Mikolov, T.: Fasttext.zip: compressing text classification models. CoRR abs/1612.03651 (2016). https://arxiv.org/abs/1612.03651
11. Klie, J.C., Bugert, M., Boullosa, B., de Castilho, R.E., Gurevych, I.: The inception platform: machine-assisted and knowledge-oriented interactive annotation. In: Proceedings of the 27th International Conference on Computational Linguistics: System Demonstrations, pp. 5–9. Association for Computational Linguistics, June 2018. https://tubiblio.ulb.tu-darmstadt.de/106270/, event Title: The 27th International Conference on Computational Linguistics (COLING 2018)
12. Knoblauch, D., Banse, C.: Reducing implementation efforts in continuous auditing certification via an audit API. In: 2019 IEEE 28th International Conference on Enabling Technologies: Infrastructure for Collaborative Enterprises (WETICE), pp. 88–92 (2019). https://doi.org/10.1109/WETICE.2019.00025

13. Kunz, I., Stephanow, P.: A process model to support continuous certification of cloud services. In: 2017 IEEE 31st International Conference on Advanced Information Networking and Applications (AINA), pp. 986–993 (2017). https://doi.org/10.1109/AINA.2017.106

14. Lee, J., Yun, S., Kim, H., Ko, M., Kang, J.: Ranking paragraphs for improving answer recall in open-domain question answering. CoRR abs/1810.00494 (2018). https://arxiv.org/abs/1810.00494

15. Lins, S., Schneider, S., Sunyaev, A.: Trust is good, control is better: creating secure clouds by continuous auditing. IEEE Trans. Cloud Comput. 6(3), 890–903 (2016). https://doi.org/10.1109/TCC.2016.2522411

16. Lins, S., Thiebes, S., Schneider, S., Sunyaev, A.: What is really going on at your cloud service provider? Creating trustworthy certifications by continuous auditing. In: 2015 48th Hawaii International Conference on System Sciences, pp. 5352–5361 (2015). https://doi.org/10.1109/HICSS.2015.629

17. Liu, Y., et al.: Roberta: a robustly optimized BERT pretraining approach. CoRR abs/1907.11692 (2019). https://arxiv.org/abs/1907.11692

18. Orue-Echevarria, L., Garcia, J.L., Banse, C., Alonso, J., et al.: Medina: improving cloud services trustworthiness through continuous audit-based certification. In: CEUR Workshop Proceedings. CEUR-WS (2021)

19. Rajpurkar, P., Zhang, J., Lopyrev, K., Liang, P.: Squad: 100, 000+ questions for machine comprehension of text. CoRR abs/1606.05250 (2016), https://arxiv.org/abs/1606.05250

20. Schütze, H., Manning, C.D., Raghavan, P.: Introduction to Information Retrieval, vol. 39. Cambridge University Press, Cambridge (2008)

21. Stephanow, P., Fallenbeck, N.: Towards continuous certification of infrastructure-as-a-service using low-level metrics. In: 2015 IEEE 12th International Conference on Ubiquitous Intelligence and Computing and 2015 IEEE 12th International Conference on Autonomic and Trusted Computing and 2015 IEEE 15th International Conference on Scalable Computing and Communications and Its Associated Workshops (UIC-ATC-ScalCom), pp. 1485–1492 (2015). https://doi.org/10.1109/UIC-ATC-ScalCom-CBDCom-IoP.2015.268

22. Stephanow, P., Khajehmoogahi, K.: Towards continuous security certification of software-as-a-service applications using web application testing techniques. In: 2017 IEEE 31st International Conference on Advanced Information Networking and Applications (AINA), pp. 931–938 (2017). https://doi.org/10.1109/AINA.2017.107

23. Torkura, K., Sukmana, M.I., Cheng, F., Meinel, C.: Continuous auditing and threat detection in multi-cloud infrastructure. Comput. Secur. 102, 102124 (2021). https://doi.org/10.1016/j.cose.2020.102124, https://www.sciencedirect.com/science/article/pii/S0167404820303977

24. Webster, J.J., Kit, C.: Tokenization as the initial phase in NLP. In: COLING 1992: The 14th International Conference on Computational Linguistics, vol. 4 (1992)

25. Wilbur, W.J., Sirotkin, K.: The automatic identification of stop words. J. Inf. Sci. 18(1), 45–55 (1992)

26. Windhorst, I., Sunyaev, A.: Dynamic certification of cloud services. In: 2013 International Conference on Availability, Reliability and Security, pp. 412–417 (2013). https://doi.org/10.1109/ARES.2013.55

VIET: A Tool for Extracting Essential Information from Vulnerability Descriptions for CVSS Evaluation

Siqi Zhang[1], Mengyuan Zhang[1], and Lianying Zhao[2]([✉])

[1] The Hong Kong Polytechnic University, Hong Kong, Hong Kong SAR, China
siqi0510.zhang@connect.polyu.hk, mengyuan.zhang@polyu.edu.hk
[2] Carleton University, Ottawa, Canada
lianying.zhao@carleton.ca

Abstract. Security vulnerabilities can be patched in order based on their severity as indicated by an assigned score, to minimize the chance and impact of potential exploits. However, it often takes several days for an analyst to assign a CVSS score, leaving a window of opportunity for attackers. Existing solutions heavily rely on the accuracy of current vulnerability scoring, which suffers from potential bias and errors introduced by human analysts. In this paper, we propose *VIET*, a tool that extracts essential information from vulnerability descriptions, which can be loosely mapped to CVSS metrics, and facilitates vulnerability evaluation. We trained a dedicated cybersecurity linguistic model based on 209,842 vulnerability descriptions and implemented a Bidirectional LSTM network trained on 800 labeled vulnerability descriptions. We evaluate the effectiveness of *VIET* through F1-scores and the efficiency of the models in terms of training time. The results show that *VIET* can extract essential entities to determining a vulnerability's severity level, reducing analysis time and addressing inconsistencies in the evaluation process.

Keywords: Cybersecurity · NER · Vulnerability Assessment

1 Introduction

Security vulnerabilities often lead to serious consequences for individuals, organizations, and society as a whole. Unpatched vulnerabilities can be exploited by cyber-criminals to launch attacks, such as ransomware, phishing, and denial-of-service. Due to such attacks, the number of compromised personal data has reached 300 million pieces in the beginning of the year 2023 [1]. The Common Vulnerabilities and Exposures (CVE) program [2] and the National Vulnerability Database (NVD) [3] are commonly used by organizations to discover and patch vulnerabilities before they are exploited by attackers. The CVE program assigns a unique CVE-ID to each of the vulnerabilities submitted by the public, which is then received by NVD for analysis and assigning a Common Vulnerability Scoring System (CVSS) [4] score. There are 199,786 vulnerabilities (March 2023) in

© IFIP International Federation for Information Processing 2023
Published by Springer Nature Switzerland AG 2023
V. Atluri and A. L. Ferrara (Eds.): DBSec 2023, LNCS 13942, pp. 386–403, 2023.
https://doi.org/10.1007/978-3-031-37586-6_23

the database, which are fetched by hundreds of security products [5] and used in security migration/network hardening solutions [6].

However, based on data collected for vulnerabilities published in 2022, the analysis of a vulnerability typically takes days (median processing time is 7 d). This may result in delays in identifying and thus patching high-severity vulnerabilities. Note that as vulnerability patching incurs costs [7] (e.g., service outage, risk of introducing new issues, manpower), it usually needs to be prioritized based on severity in enterprise environments. Furthermore, the process of assigning CVSS scores could be influenced by potential bias and limitations of individual analysts. To make things worse, erroneous or inconsistent evaluation may lead to a wrong decision in vulnerability prioritization systems that rely on CVSS scores for the severity level.

Existing solutions mainly focus on utilizing deep learning approaches to process vulnerability description text, e.g., one-layer shallow Convolutional Neural Network (CNN) [8], and multi-task learning approach [9], and predict a multi-class severity level of vulnerabilities. These methods heavily depend on the accuracy of *the current vulnerability scoring*, which is used as input for training. The aforementioned bias and inconsistency can be detrimental to the effectiveness and reliability, e.g., the same description text in different vulnerability entries may be assigned very different severity levels.

Instead of relying on existing scoring, this paper first reviews a large corpus of vulnerability descriptions and identifies the essential information needed for severity evaluation. Based on this, we propose a tool for extracting entities in vulnerability information, called *VIET*, which can facilitate the severity evaluation of vulnerabilities. It can reduce analysis time and help address inconsistencies in the evaluation process (see Sect. 2.2 and the example in Sect. 3). Specifically, we follow a novel data science pipeline to implement such a tool. First, we trained a dedicated cybersecurity linguistic model based on 9.7M words from 209,842 vulnerability descriptions (we include the rejected vulnerability descriptions to enlarge the possible corpus); Second, we implemented a Bidirectional long short-term memory (BiLSTM) network trained based on 40K labeled words from 800 vulnerability descriptions. Third, we conducted experiments to evaluate the effectiveness of our tool. Therefore, our main contributions are threefold:

- To the best of our knowledge, in the context of utilizing vulnerability descriptions, this is the first effort towards a novel entity extraction method for identifying vulnerability entities for assessing the severity level of vulnerabilities. The labeled data for training, to the best of our knowledge, is the largest dataset based on vulnerability descriptions.
- We train a specialized linguistic model for cybersecurity. This model is based on a large corpus of 9.7 million words from 209,842 vulnerability descriptions, which includes all the existing vulnerability descriptions. By training this model, this paper advances the state-of-the-art in cybersecurity NLP and creates a valuable resource for future research.
- We evaluate the effectiveness and efficiency of *VIET* based on different lengths of the vulnerability descriptions from different years. Our results demonstrate the effectiveness and efficiency of our solution.

Table 1. CVSS V3

	Base Score						
Attack Vector	Attack Comp.	Privileges Req.	User Interaction	Conf.	Inte.	Ava.	Scope
Network	Low	None	None	None	None	None	Unchanged
Adjacent							
Local	high	Low	Required	Low	Low	Low	Changed
Physical		High		High	High	High	

The remainder of the paper is organized as follows. Section 2 provides background information and a motivating example. Section 3 details the *VIET* methodology. Section 4 discusses the datasets and the technique used to process the datasets. Section 5 presents the experiment results. Section 6 reviews the related work and Sect. 7 concludes the paper with future directions.

2   Preliminaries

In this section, we first explain a few terms to facilitate subsequent discussions. Then, we present a motivating example and discuss the technical challenges of our work.

2.1   NVD and CVSS Metrics

NVD. The National Vulnerability Database (NVD)[1] is a government-maintained database of vulnerability information that follows industry standards. The NVD receives updates from MITRE's Common Vulnerability and Exposures (CVE) List, ensuring the database is up to date. Each CVE record in the CVE List is supplemented with additional information on the NVD website, such as severity scores, weakness enumeration, and security checklist references. The website also includes information on vulnerable product versions, components, attack vectors, and impact. Our paper primarily concentrates on vulnerability descriptions and CVSS vulnerability characteristics. As of march 2023, NVD contains 199,786 vulnerabilities.

CVSS. Each CVE record in NVD includes two severity scores, namely, CVSS Version 3 and CVSS Version 2, along with their respective characteristics. CVSS V2 has six basic vulnerability characteristics, namely, attack vector (AV), attack complexity (AC), authentication (AU), confidentiality (C), integrity (I), and availability (A), while CVSS V3 does not have AU but includes three new metrics: physical (P), privileges required (PR), and user interaction (UI) in vectors (See Table 1, highlighted cells are the newly introduced metrics). The new metrics in CVSS V3 aim to provide a more accurate and complete representation of the security risk of vulnerabilities. The scoring system ranges from 0 to 10, with higher scores indicating more severe vulnerabilities.

---

[1] https://nvd.nist.gov.

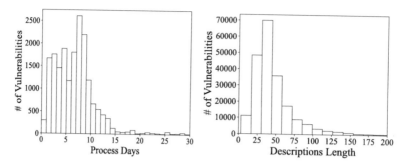

Fig. 1. Processing time (left), Length of the Descriptions (right)

Vulnerability Description. CVE Numbering Authorities (CNAs) are responsible for assigning unique CVE IDs to vulnerabilities. Before assigning a CVE ID, CNAs validate the submitted vulnerability to ensure it is not already assigned or fully patched. The vulnerability description [10], which includes information such as the affected product, version, component, vulnerability type, and conditions/requirements to exploit the vulnerability, is normally provided by the reporter or created using the CVE Assignment Team's template by CNAs. The MITRE CNA of Last Resort (CNA-LR) analyzes publicly available third-party reports on vulnerabilities, known as "references". It extracts the relevant information from each reference, resolves any conflicting information or inconsistent terminology usage, and then writes the vulnerability description. Although the National Vulnerability Database (NVD) is synchronized with the CVE List, the CVE description can only be submitted through the CVE List, and the NVD has no control over the CVE descriptions. An NVD analyst may manually search through the Internet to gather any other relevant publicly available materials and information during the analysis process. Due to the large number of vulnerabilities, it may take several days before the CVSS is attributed. Figure 1 (left) shows the process time for vulnerabilities, and Fig. 1 (right) shows that the most common length for a vulnerability description is around 25∼70 characters.

2.2 Motivating Example

Figure 2 depicts three vulnerabilities (CVE-2017-5807, CVE-2017-5808, CVE-2017-5809) having identical vulnerability description, and further assigned to three analysts to evaluate the severity level. The three analysts may make the following decisions based on their own judgement:

– The first analyst considers this vulnerability to be easily exploitable with only remote access, as indicated by the word `remote` in the description, and also believes `arbitrary code execution` will lead to a total compromise of confidentiality, integrity, and availability (see detailed CVSS metrics in Sect. 2). As a result, a severity score of 10/10 is assigned to this vulnerability, which means top priority to be patched.

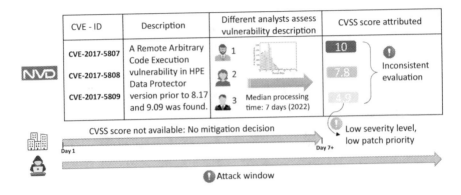

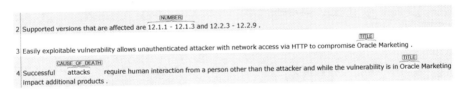

Fig. 2. The motivating example

- The second analyst also acknowledges `remote` access as with the first analyst. Nonetheless, different impact metrics are considered, i.e., only availability is undermined if this vulnerability is exploited. Hence, 7.8/10 is assigned.
- The third analyst mistakenly considers the required access to be `local` (which is inconsistent with *"a remote arbitrary code execution"*) and only leading to information disclosure (confidentiality) as the impact of this vulnerability. Thus, this vulnerability is scored 4.9/10.

Adding to the manual analysis time already leaving an attack window, improperly/wrongly assigned CVSS scores may further delay patching extending the attack window favoring the attacker. We thus propose to leverage NER techniques to extract vulnerability-specific entities from vulnerability descriptions for score derivation, which can serve as a new basis to complement the analysts.

Fig. 3. Name Entity Recognition with CoreNLP

Challenges. To extract entities, we first evaluated vulnerability descriptions using CoreNLP [11], which is currently the state-of-the-art name entity extraction implementation. However, we found that CoreNLP failed to process vulnerability descriptions, as it often misclassifies security-related terms, such as categorizing "attacks" under the concept of "cause of death" (see Fig. 3). This might be due to lacking vulnerability terminologies in the underlying linguistic model in CoreNLP. Therefore, a fine-tuned linguistic model is necessary to capture vulnerability-related entities. Previous research on attack entity extraction has focused on extracting entities related to creating attack graphs [12] and detecting inconsistencies in vulnerable versions [13]. A clear definition of the entities that are correlated with vulnerability evaluation is missing.

3   Design of *VIET*

This section first provides an overview of *VIET*, followed by the detailed methodologies for its major components.

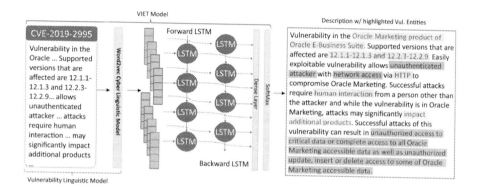

Fig. 4. The Architecture

3.1   Overview

Figure 4 depicts the two major components of *VIET*, vulnerability linguistic model and *VIET* model.

The vulnerability linguistic model is designed to train vulnerability-specific word embeddings using a dataset of 209,842 vulnerability descriptions (including rejected CVEs) from the NVD. Unlike existing works that rely on pre-trained models, our approach involves fine-tuning the linguistic model with vulnerability terminologies. Specifically, we fine-tune the linguistic model using the Word2Vec algorithm. We did not choose other language models like BERT [14] because, aside from training such complex and deep models being too expensive (while Word2Vec has only one hidden layer), specifically Binyamini et al. [12] showed that the pre-trained and fine-tuned BERT performed significantly worse than Word2Vec in such entity extraction tasks, and its visualization of the word embedding space is also poorly clustered. As a result, our approach can achieve good embedding representations with limited training data (9.7M corpus).

The *VIET* model utilizes the trained vulnerability linguistic model as input to its embedding layer. The embedding layer then feeds into a BiLSTM layer, which contains both forward and backward LSTM layers. The output from these layers is then passed through a dense layer and a Softmax layer to output the extracted vulnerability entities.

3.2   The Vulnerability Linguistic Model

In this section, we present the details of the vulnerability linguistic model with examples. We implemented both continuous bag-of-words (CBOW) and skip-gram (SG) variants of the Word2Vec algorithm. Both variants generate word embeddings that contain information about the surrounding words. In our case, we use vulnerability descriptions as inputs to fine-tune the word embeddings. In CBOW, we predict the center word from the context while in SG algorithm we try to predict the context words from the center word. In terms of training efficiency, CBOW is far better than SG, and it becomes more obvious as the corpus or window size increases, because CBOW only needs to do one representation (embedding) learning for each central word whereas SG needs (window size - 1) times. In dealing with low-frequency words, SG is more sensitive than CBOW, if there are many uncommon words in the text, SG will predict the usage environment of uncommon words to achieve a better prediction result.

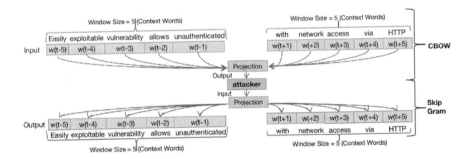

Fig. 5. CBOW and Skip Gram Algorithms

Example 1. Figure 5 illustrates the difference between the CBOW and SG algorithms when applied to the context "Easily exploitable vulnerability allows unauthenticated attacker with network access via HTTP". With window size 5, SG uses the word "attacker" as input to predict the surrounding 10 words "Easily, exploitable, vulnerability, allows, unauthenticated, with, network, access, via, HTTP", while CBOW takes the context set ⟨Easily, exploitable, vulnerability, allows, unauthenticated, with, network, access, via, HTTP⟩ as input and predicts the output word "attacker". In both algorithms, as a result of the training, the word "attacker" becomes closer to the set of context words ⟨Easily, exploitable, vulnerability, allows, unauthenticated, with, network, access, via, HTTP⟩ since they appear closely and frequently in the same part of the sentence. Hence, the word "attacker" will start to contain "vulnerability" meanings and be more effectively used in the vulnerability linguistic model for accurate entity extraction.

$$P(w_t \in C_t | w_c) = \frac{exp(w_c^T w_t)}{\sum_{wi \in C_t} exp(w_c^T w_i)} \qquad (1)$$

Equation 1 is the softmax function to predict a probability of 1 if the $w_t \in C_t$ or 0 otherwise, where C_t is the set of all context words based on a center word, and w_c, w_t, and w_i are the embeddings of the center word, target word, and any word in all available context words, respectively.

3.3 Vulnerability Entity Extraction

Named Entity Extraction (NER) is a technique used in many areas of Natural Language Processing (NLP). The main task of this technique is to extract named entities from text, which can include things like names of people, places, organizations, and dates, among others. NER is an important tool for many NLP applications, including sentiment analysis, document classification, and question answering, among others. By identifying and extracting named entities from text, NER can help improve the accuracy and effectiveness of these applications. To identify and define the entity categories, we conducted a thorough analysis of the language used in vulnerability descriptions. This involved studying a large corpus of vulnerability descriptions and identifying the various types of entities that were commonly mentioned.

Table 2. The List of Vulnerability Entities (S: Supplementary, E: Essential)

	Vul. Entity	Descriptions	Example	Dist.
S	Application	Vulnerable software	Openssl, Websphere	0.0636
	CVE ID	A CVE identifier	Cve-2015-1924	0.0101
	File	Vulnerable file	wp-admin/options.php	0.0038
	Update	Service pack installation	SP1	0.0026
	Vendor	The vendor names	Microsoft, Oracle	0.0125
	Version	The application versions	12.1.0.5	0.08
	Function	The vulnerable function	getdevices()	0.0027
	Network Protocol	The network protocol	HTTP, dns	0.0026
	OS	The operating system names	Android, windows	0.0112
E	Vul. Impact	The consequences of exploiting Vul.	Obtain sensitive information	0.0766
	Vul. Type	The Vul. types	Memory corruption vulnerability	0.0574
	Vul. Complexity	The technique that used to exploit the Vul.	via crafted encrypted data	0.0322
	Vul. Vector	The context that a vulnerability gets exploited	Remote attackers, physical access	0.0317
	Privileges	The privileges that required to exploit the Vul.	Remote authenticated users	0.0169
	O	Other words do not belong any of above	a, the	0.596

Our analysis revealed two main types of entities: supplementary entities and essential entities. Supplementary entities are those that cannot be directly mapped to CVSS metrics, but are still important for understanding the context of the vulnerability. Examples of supplementary entities include software names, version numbers, impacted components, and vendors, among others. On the other hand, essential entities are those that can be loosely mapped to CVSS metrics. These entities are critical for assessing the severity of a vulnerability and include things like vulnerability impact, vulnerability complexity, etc.

Table 2 shows the list of vulnerability entities with definition, examples, and the distribution of each entity in the labelled data.

By defining these two entity categories, we were able to develop a more effective approach for extracting and analyzing vulnerability-specific information from textual descriptions. This allowed us to build a tool that could automatically identify and extract essential entities, making it easier for security analysts to evaluate vulnerabilities and prioritize remediation efforts.

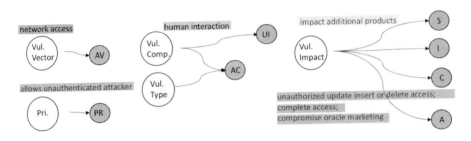

Fig. 6. A loose mapping between vulnerability entities and CVSS metrics

Example 2. Figure 6 illustrates the loose mapping between vulnerability entities and CVSS metrics. For example, with the extracted "allows unauthenticated attacker" entity from the description, the analyst can easily assign "None" to the privilege metric. Similarly, with the extracted "network access" entity, the analyst can assign "Network" to attack vector seamlessly.

4   Dataset

In this section, we first explain how to obtain our input dataset then we illustrate the techniques we used to process the dataset.

NVD Entries. The NVD data feed, which provides a JSON-formatted archive of security vulnerabilities from 1999 to March 2023, contains 209K vulnerability descriptions, including those labeled as **Rejected**, with a total of 9.7M words. In order to train a vulnerability linguistic model with a larger dataset related to the cybersecurity domain, we utilized all of the vulnerability descriptions, including those with rejected CVEs.

Tokenization. We take into account multiple factors when selecting and labeling inputs, e.g., time span, as dated vulnerability scoring issues may have been fixed or not reflect new insights/versions (e.g., CVSS v3.0), reasonable quantity, as manual annotation is very time-consuming. Considering in the work of Binyamini et al. [12] 650 vulnerability descriptions were labeled (and we can target slightly higher), we used a stratified sampling method to randomly select 800 vulnerability descriptions (40K words) from the past eight years (2015–2022), with 100 descriptions from each year. Due to the presence of specific words from the cybersecurity domain, it is not ideal to use common tokenization processes like NLTK tokenization for word segmentation. Such methods may split complete links or file names into meaningless pieces due to special symbols (e.g., `admin.php?m=admin&c=site&a=save`). To preserve the meaning of cybersecurity-specific words, we used the simple `split()` function to segment the descriptions by spaces between words. In cases where there were no spaces between punctuation marks and words (e.g., "(word," "word)."), we used Regex to remove stranded whitespace and punctuation for further processing of the segmented words.

Manual Labeling. To alleviate the time-consuming manual labeling process, we first employ an automatic labeling algorithm proposed by Bridge et al. [15] to label the entities such as, "application", "version", and "vendor" which reduced the proportion of "O" from 80% to 60%. However, as this autolabeling method labels vulnerability-specific entities only as relevant-terms, we have to further manually label those. Since Bridge et al. [15] used standard IOB-tagging for many multi-word names commonplace, they labeled the beginning word of an entity name with "B-X", any word in this entity name beside the beginning word is tagged with "I-X" and labeled unidentified words with "O" where X defined as a type of attack entity, we also applied this concept in the subsequent manual labeling after we generated the automatically labeled dataset through the automatic labeling process. For the subsequent manual labeling, we replaced the relevant term gazetteer that contains the words related to cybersecurity domain and 13 vulnerability categories [5] with Vulnerability type, Vulnerability impact, and Vulnerability vector which helped us to reduce the time of manual labeling. In this paper, we consider the following five essential vulnerability entities: Vulnerability vector, Vulnerability impact, Vulnerability type, Privilege, Vulnerability complexity as our mean Vulnerability vector, Vulnerability impact, Privilege, and Vulnerability complexity, 8 supplementary vulnerability entities: Vendor, Version, Application, CVE ID, Update, Function, and Network protocol, and other words not possessing any cybersecurity meaning labeled as "O". A short description and distribution of these entities are presented in Table 2.

Data Imbalanced. Despite the reduction of the proportion labeled with "O" from 80% to 60%, there still exist entities that are less common such as "Network protocol" and "Privileges". To better balance the data, we applied the weighted cross-entropy loss function [12] to cope with this issue.

5   Experiment

In this section, we first provide details about how the experiment was set up and then present the results for both models.

5.1   Experiment Setup

All the experiment steps are developed in Python 3.9 and executed on a Macbook Pro running macOS Monterey, with Apple M1 Pro chip and 16.0 GB of

RAM. For the vulnerability linguistic model, we leverage *Word2Vec* [16] with both algorithms, CBOW and Skip-gram, implementation from *Gensim* [17]. The embedding vector generated from the vulnerability linguistic model is fed into the embedding layer implemented based on *Keras* [18]. The deep learning model in *VIET*, e.g. BiLSTM, is implemented based on the *Keras.layers* library [18] to generate sentence embedding for the entire description and extract vulnerability entities. The evaluation metric, e.g., *loss* is implemented based on *scikit-learn* [19]. The data preprocessing and auto-labelling is based on *pandas* [20].

5.2   Evaluation of the Vulnerability Linguistic Model

To evaluate the proposed vulnerability linguistic models, we compared two fine-tuned models, CBOW and Skip-gram, with the default pretrained model. The pretrained vectors were trained on a subset of the Google News dataset, consisting of approximately 100 billion words. The model contains 300-dimensional vectors for 3 million words and phrases.[2] We chose not to use the Wikipedia pretrained model as it contains words from too many domains, and the performance of such a model is relatively slow.

The fine-tuned models take vulnerability descriptions as domain specific input and perform training based on the pretrained model. To evaluate the performance of the fine-tuned models, we examine the semantic similarities between a selected word and the top closest words. In this set of the experiment, we chose words "OS", "priviledges", "attackers", and "overflow".

Results. The word2vec model without fine-tuning as shown in Fig. 7(c) performs the worst in both separating the selected words and identifying meaningful neighbouring words. The word "attackers" cluster is very close the word "privilege" cluster. The words considered close to it are, "attacker" (the singular form of the chosen word), "assailant" (which only makes sense in natural languages), and other words that do not have a cybersecurity meaning. The word "priviledge" and "overflow" perform even worse as they only get different form or format of the original words such as, "priviledged" (the past tense), "priviledges" (the singular form), "Overflow" (the first word in upper case), "overflowing" (present participle), etc. The word "OS" cluster is surprisingly good. It contains different operating systems, e.g., "windows", "UNIX", and words related to "OS", e.g., "CPU". We assume that's because the pretrained model is based on Google news which might have security related articles that contribute to understanding a computer science related word. However, it is evident from this experiment that the pretrained model cannot fully capture vulnerability-specific terminologies.

The word2vec-CBOW model in Fig. 7(a) shows the best performance in clustering different selected words and their neighboring words. All the selected words are well separated in their respective clusters. In the "attackers" cluster, we observe the words that are used to describe attackers from vulnerability descriptions, such as, "remote", "allows", "arbitrary" (sample description from

---

[2] https://huggingface.co/fse/word2vec-google-news-300.

Table 3. Dataset summary and training time for the vulnerability linguistic models

Year	# of Vul. Des	# of Corpus	W2V-CBOW	W2V-SG
1999–2023	209K	9.7M	29.67 min	124.28 min

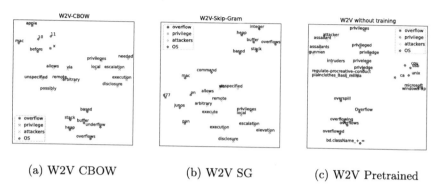

(a) W2V CBOW   (b) W2V SG   (c) W2V Pretrained

Fig. 7. A visualization based on e t-Distributed Stochastic Neighbor Embedding (t-SNE) of the word embedding space for selected words based on CBOW fine-tuned model(a), skip-gram fine-tuned model(b), and the pretrained model(c)

CVE-2015-0876: "allow remote attackers to inject arbitrary web script"), etc. The word cluster "priviledge" properly captured the words that are commonly close to it as well, e.g., "escalation" (CVE-2017-0313: "escalation of privileges"), "local" (CVE-2017-3740: "an attacker with local privileges"). This result demonstrates that with our input vulnerability description, we fine-tuned the model that captures cybersecurity-specific meanings. Similarly, the word2vec-SG model (Fig. 7(b)) could also capture cybersecurity-specific meanings after fine-tuning. However, as shown in Table 3, fine-tuning the word2vec-SG model may take four times more time than the word2vec-CBOW model. The performance of both models in vulnerability entity extraction will be studied in the second experiment thoroughly.

5.3   Evaluation of The *VIET* Model

In this set of the experiments, we evaluate the performance of the *VIET* model against four different metrics, i.e., accuracy, precision, F1-score, and recall. Then we study the efficiency and scalability of the model.

Performance of Vulnerability Entity Extraction. We train the model based on the 800 automatically and manually labeled vulnerability descriptions with different hyperparameters. The results, as shown in Table 4 and Table 5, follow the separation ratio 0.9:0.1 for the training and the testing dataset, i.e., 90% of the data goes for training and 10% for testing. We have experimented with other data separation; but the 0.9:0.1 separation yields the best performance. Although, we evaluated our model against four metrics, we choose F1-score as

Table 4. F1-scores of the different models in essential vulnerability entity extraction: CBOW vs. SG

Models	Vul. Vector	Vul. Impact	Vul. Type	Pri.	Vul. Comp.	Macro Ave.	Weighted Ave.
CBOW				w/o POS			
D100-L50	0.682	0.626	0.436	0.254	0.245	0.35	0.964
D100-L100	0.752	0.682	0.555	0.444	0.458	0.453	0.972
D100-L200	0.803	0.747	0.734	0.623	0.508	0.516	0.977
D300-L50	0.764	0.704	0.701	0.357	0.342	0.492	0.972
D300-L100	0.848	0.754	0.722	0.7	0.446	0.5	0.976
D300-L200	0.851	0.773	0.746	0.757	0.505	0.58	0.977
CBOW				w/ POS			
D100-L50	0.878	0.795	0.809	0.706	0.625	0.5961	0.9792
D100-L100	0.916	0.807	0.846	0.723	0.679	0.604	0.980
D100-L200	0.917	0.788	0.862	0.738	0.635	0.721	0.980
D300-L50	0.901	0.793	0.835	0.752	0.679	0.655	0.981
D300-L100	0.914	0.805	0.857	0.817	0.628	0.67	0.981
D300-L200	0.902	0.807	0.86	0.831	0.719	0.68	0.9839
SG-D300-L200	0.902	0.801	0.826	0.750	0.636	0.583	0.978

the main metric to compare between different models since our data is not balanced and F1-score offers the best comparison within such a dataset. We first trained the model without the part-of-speech (POS) module, then we added it back to demonstrate the improvement of such a module.

Table 5. F1-scores of the different models in supplementary vulnerability entity extraction: CBOW vs. SG

Models	Vendor	Version	Application	CVE ID	Update	Function	Network Protocol
CBOW				w/o POS			
D100-L50	0.522	0.637	0.367	0.35	0	0	0
D100-L100	0.641	0.716	0.565	0.836	0	0	0
D100-L200	0.675	0.746	0.617	0.852	0	0	0.286
D300-L50	0.718	0.691	0.572	0.324	0.667	0	0.4
D300-L100	0.694	0.734	0.604	0.735	0	0	0.154
D300-L200	0.675	0.7424	0.613	0.784	0.667	0	0.5
CBOW				w/ POS			
D100-L50	0.727	0.835	0.542	0.967	0	0.333	0.588
D100-L100	0.8	0.814	0.567	0.79	0.8	0.25	0.588
D100-L200	0.721	0.81	0.576	0.984	0.286	0.588	0.675
D300-L50	0.8	0.824	0.572	0.984	0.667	0.333	0.588
D300-L100	0.753	0.825	0.559	0.984	0.8	0.333	0.667
D300-L200	0.759	0.825	0.718	0.984	0.667	0.286	0.556
SG-D300-L200	0.741	0.452	0.636	0.984	0.000	0.333	0.588

Results. Table 4 presents the evaluation results for our model to extract essential vulnerability entities, including *vulnerability vector*, *vulnerability impact*, *vulnerability type*, *privilege*, and *vulnerability complexity*. We also provide the macro average and weighted average for each model. Our best F1-score was achieved when training the model without POS module, with 300 embedding dimensions and 200 LSTM units. The *vulnerability vector* entity achieved the highest F1-score of 0.851, followed by the *privilege* entity with an F1-score of 0.757. It is worth noting that in the closest related work [12], the F1-scores for different entities range from 0.4 to 0.94. Our results fall within this range, indicating that our approach is acceptable for this task.

To further improve the F1-score in our model, we perform training the same hyperparameter combinations with a POS module. In NLP, it's quite important to recognize parts of speech as it helps in sentence analysis and comprehension. The role a word plays in a sentence denotes its part of speech. In our design, we utilized "B-Entity" and "I-Entity" labels to identify the beginning and internal parts of entities. By integrating our labels with POS tagging, we can potentially improve the F1-score by accurately identifying entity boundaries. With 300 embedding dimensions and 200 LSTM units, our model with POS module achieves F1-score 0.902 and 0.831 for the *vulnerability vector* entity and the *privilege* entity, respectively. Despite taking four times longer to train the word2vec Skip-gram embedding model, it was only able to achieve relatively similar or slightly worse results when trained with POS tagging compared to the word2vec CBOW embedding model.

Table 5 shows the evaluation results for our model to extract supplementary vulnerability entities. Generally, the results are not as good as those for extracting essential vulnerability entities because supplementary entities are less commonly found in vulnerability descriptions. However, our results are still acceptable when we include the POS module in the training. For example, we achieve an F1-score of 0.825 for the version entity, while [12] achieves an F1-score of 0.77 for extracting versions.

Efficiency and Scalability. Figure 8 shows the training time of the *VIET* model in six different hyperparameter combinations. Figure 9 illustrates the

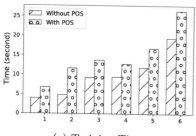

Type	CBOW	Training Time w/O POS	Training Time w POS
1	D = 100 L = 50	6.65 min	7.99 min
2	D = 100 L = 100	8.05 min	10.3 min
3	D = 100 L = 300	15.33 min	14.86 min
4	D = 300 L = 50	15.62 min	19.08 min
5	D = 300 L = 100	19.75 min	15.62 min
6	D = 300 L = 200	32.25 min	26.68 min

(a) Training Time   (b) Experiment D. vs. Total Training Time

Fig. 8. Training time of the Bi-LSTM model with and without POS tags vs. Different word embedding dimensions (D) and LSTM cells (L) (second per Epoch)(a), Total training time (min)(b)

accuracy and loss versus the number of training epoch. Finally, Fig. 10 demonstrates the prediction time based on different input lengths of the descriptions.

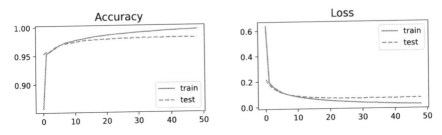

Fig. 9. Bi-LSTM model evaluation accuracy vs. epoch (left), loss vs. epoch (right)

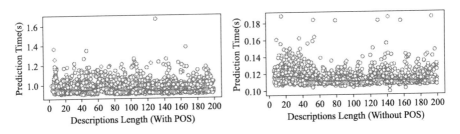

Fig. 10. Model prediction time vs. varying description lengths

Results. The training time results shown in Fig. 8 indicate that the POS module introduces an additional time cost to the model training. When comparing the best performance (Type 6) in Fig. 8b, the model with POS module required an extra 5 s per epoch for training. However, as early stopping was implemented in the model training, the training process stops when the validation *loss* increases while the training *loss* is still decreasing. The model with POS module only requires 26.68 min, while the one without POS needs 32.25 min to finish the training. This is because the model with POS module converges faster. The results in Fig. 9 suggest that, in general, the models can reach early stop after training for only 10–20 epochs. This indicates that training the models to a reasonable level of accuracy is relatively easy and does not require a large amount of computational resources. Additionally, Fig. 10 demonstrates that our solution is efficient, as the model with POS tagging takes an average of 0.96 s and only an average of 0.11 s is needed for the model trained without POS tagging to complete a prediction.

6   Related Work

In recent years, there has been a growing body of research on automating the prediction of severity scores, exploitability metrics, and impact metrics of vulnerabilities since vulnerability assessment is still primarily done manually. Researchers have focused on utilizing Natural Language Processing (NLP) to address various security problems, including vulnerability assessment.

One of the earliest works in the field of automated vulnerability assessment was conducted by Weerawardhana et al. [21]. They developed a tool that utilized Stanford Named Entity Recognition (NER) to automatically extract software names, versions, and impacts from vulnerability descriptions from the NVD.

To predict the CVSS exploitability metrics and impact metrics by extracting information from vulnerability descriptions, the majority of research has focused on three main learning approaches: single-task, multi-target, and multi-task. Yamamoto et al. [22] were the first to use descriptions of software vulnerabilities from the NVD with a supervised Latent Dirichlet Allocation topic model to predict these CVSS metrics. Gong et al. [9] utilized multi-task learning to predict CVSS characteristics based on the vulnerability descriptions. Each character had its own label and classifier that used a shared sentence representation based on a Bi-LSTM model with an attention mechanism for capturing implicit correlations among related vulnerability characteristics. There are also six well-known ML models that most researchers used to do vulnerability classification: Naïve Bayes (NB) [23], Logistic Regression (LR) [24], Support Vector Machine (SVM) [25], Random Forest (RF) [26], XGBoost - Extreme Gradient Boosting (XGB) [27] and Light Gradient Boosting Machine (LGBM) [28]. As shown in their results, these data-driven methods performed well with satisfactory accuracy in extracting information and predicting characteristics or severity scores from vulnerability descriptions. However, predicting scores for new vulnerabilities from description text, but based on existing past CVSS scores that were assigned by security analysts still suffers from the bias/inconsistency issues we pointed out earlier, such as the same vulnerability description being assigned different severity levels. Therefore, we choose to directly perform vulnerability entity extraction from description text without relying on existing scores, which can be subsequently mapped to exploitability and impact metrics in the CVSS score system to either derive a score, or provide a reference for security analysts, improving accuracy and reducing analysis time.

7   Conclusion

We have developed a novel, end-to-end tool for extracting vulnerability entities from the description text of a security vulnerability. This tool enables security analysts to easily identify the essential vulnerability entities that loosely map to the CVSS metrics. This does not rely on the existing CVSS scores avoiding potential bias or inaccuracy introduced by human analysts. In particular, we have trained a vulnerability linguistic model on a corpus of 9.7M words from over

200K vulnerability descriptions. This linguistic model can be applied to many other NLP tasks in the vulnerability domain. Furthermore, we have manually labeled 800 vulnerability descriptions containing 40K words, which is, to the best of our knowledge, the largest dataset for vulnerability descriptions. This dataset as well as the models can be utilized to further automate vulnerability evaluation and scoring, which we consider as future work.

References

1. TechTarget, "List of Data Breaches and Cyber Attacks in February 2023-29.5 Million Records Breached." https://www.techtarget.com/searchsecurity/feature/Publicly-disclosed-US-ransomware-attacks-in-2023
2. The MITRE Corporation, "CVE Website." https://cve.mitre.org/
3. The National Institute of Standards and Technology, "NVD Data Feeds." https://nvd.nist.gov/vuln
4. Mell, P., Scarfone, K., Romanosky, S.: Common vulnerability scoring system. IEEE Secur. Privacy **4**(6), 85–89 (2006)
5. CVEdetails, "List of Products." https://www.cvedetails.com/product-list.php
6. Wang, L., Islam, T., Long, T., Singhal, A., Jajodia, S.: An attack graph-based probabilistic security metric. In: Atluri, V. (ed.) DBSec 2008. LNCS, vol. 5094, pp. 283–296. Springer, Heidelberg (2008). https://doi.org/10.1007/978-3-540-70567-3_22
7. Anjum, M., Singhal, S., Kapur, P., Khatri, S.K., Panwar, S.: Analysis of vulnerability fixing process in the presence of incorrect patches. J. Syst. Softw. **195** (2023)
8. Zhuobing, H., Xiaohong, L., Zhenchang, X., Hongtao, L., Zhiyong, F.: Learning to predict severity of software vulnerability using only vulnerability description, pp. 125–136 (2017)
9. Gong, X., Xing, Z., Li, X., Feng, Z., Han, Z.: Joint prediction of multiple vulnerability characteristics through multi-task learning. In: International Conference on Engineering of Complex Computer Systems (ICECCS'19), pp. 31–40. IEEE (2019)
10. The MITRE Corporation, "How are the CVE Record DESCRIPTIONS created or compiled?." https://www.cve.org/ResourcesSupport/FAQs
11. Manning, C.D., Surdeanu, M., Bauer, J., Finkel, J.R., Bethard, S., McClosky, D.: The Stanford coreNLP natural language processing toolkit. In: Proceedings of the 52nd Annual Meeting of the Association for Computational Linguistics, ACL 2014, 22–27 June 2014, Baltimore, MD, USA, System Demonstrations, pp. 55–60 (2014)
12. Binyamini, H., Bitton, R., Inokuchi, M., Yagyu, T., Elovici, Y., Shabtai, A.: A framework for modeling cyber attack techniques from security vulnerability descriptions. In: Zhu, F., Ooi, B.C., Miao, C. (eds.) KDD '21: The 27th ACM SIGKDD Conference on Knowledge Discovery and Data Mining, Virtual Event, Singapore, 14–18 August 2021, pp. 2574–2583. ACM (2021)
13. Dong, Y., Guo, W., Chen, Y., Xing, X., Zhang, Y., Wang, G.: Towards the detection of inconsistencies in public security vulnerability reports. In: 28th USENIX Security Symposium (USENIX Security'19), pp. 869–885 (2019)
14. Devlin, J., Chang, M., Lee, K., Toutanova, K.: BERT: pre-training of deep bidirectional transformers for language understanding. In: Burstein, J., Doran, C., Solorio, T. (eds.) Proceedings of the 2019 Conference of the North American Chapter of the Association for Computational Linguistics: Human Language Technologies, NAACL-HLT 2019, Minneapolis, MN, USA, 2–7 June 2019, Volume 1 (Long and Short Papers), pp. 4171–4186. Association for Computational Linguistics (2019)

15. Bridges, R.A., Jones, C.L., Iannacone, M.D., Testa, K.M., Goodall, J.R.: Automatic labeling for entity extraction in cyber security (2014)
16. Mikolov, T., Chen, K., Corrado, G., Dean, J.: Efficient estimation of word representations in vector space. In: Bengio, Y., LeCun, Y. (eds.) 1st International Conference on Learning Representations, ICLR 2013, Scottsdale, Arizona, USA, 2–4 May 2013, Workshop Track Proceedings (2013)
17. Rehurek, R., Sojka, P.: Gensim-python framework for vector space modelling. NLP Centre, Faculty of Informatics, Masaryk University, Brno, Czech Republic, vol. 3, no. 2 (2011)
18. Chollet, F., et al.: Keras: Deep learning for humans (2015). https://github.com/fchollet/keras
19. Buitinck, L., et al.: API design for machine learning software: experiences from the scikit-learn project. In: ECML PKDD Workshop: Languages for Data Mining and Machine Learning, pp. 108–122 (2013)
20. McKinney, W., et al.: Data structures for statistical computing in python. In: Proceedings of the 9th Python in Science Conference, vol. 445, pp. 51–56, Austin, TX (2010)
21. Weerawardhana, S., Mukherjee, S., Ray, I., Howe, A.: Automated extraction of vulnerability information for home computer security. In: Cuppens, F., Garcia-Alfaro, J., Zincir Heywood, N., Fong, P.W.L. (eds.) FPS 2014. LNCS, vol. 8930, pp. 356–366. Springer, Cham (2015). https://doi.org/10.1007/978-3-319-17040-4_24
22. Yamamoto, Y., Miyamoto, D., Nakayama, M.: Text-mining approach for estimating vulnerability score. In: 2015 4th International Workshop on Building Analysis Datasets and Gathering Experience Returns for Security (BADGERS), pp. 67–73. IEEE (2015)
23. Russell, S.J.: Artificial Intelligence a Modern Approach. Pearson Education Inc (2010)
24. Walker, S.H., Duncan, D.B.: Estimation of the probability of an event as a function of several independent variables. Biometrika **54**(1–2), 167–179 (1967)
25. Cortes, C., Vapnik, V.: Support-vector networks, **20**, 273–297 (1995). Springer
26. Ho, T.K.: Random decision forests. In: Proceedings of 3rd International Conference on Document Analysis and Recognition, vol. 1, pp. 278–282. IEEE (1995)
27. Chen, T., Guestrin, C.: XGBoost: a scalable tree boosting system. In: Proceedings of the 22nd ACM SIGKDD International Conference on Knowledge Discovery and Data Mining, pp. 785–794 (2016)
28. Ke, G., et al.: LightGBM: a highly efficient gradient boosting decision tree. In: Advances in Neural Information Processing Systems, vol. 30 (2017)

An Analysis of Hybrid Consensus in Blockchain Protocols for Correctness and Progress

Sangita Roy[1]([⊠])[iD] and Rudrapatna K. Shyamasundar[2]

[1] Thapar Institute of Engineering and Technology, Patiala, Punjab, India
sangita.roy@thapar.edu
[2] Indian Institute of Technology Bombay, Mumbai, Maharashtra, India
rkss@cse.iitb.ac.in

Abstract. One of the key ideas for enhancing the scalability of block-chain lies in having consensus among a smaller set of nodes rather than the set of all nodes be it PoW (Proof of Work) or PoS (Proof of Stake). Such a transformation calls for analysis of trust in the transformed consensus, forking, progress, fairness, etc. Thus, one major requirement is to ensure the correct functioning of PoW or PoS under the BFT (Byzantine Fault Tolerance) of the network remains invariant in spite of the transformation. Note that the conditions for scalability of PoW and BFT are somewhat contradictory, in the sense that PoW is good for a large network with very low throughput and BFT is good for a small network with high throughput. For scalability, we need high node scalability as in permissionless blockchain, and high transaction throughput as in permissioned blockchain. In this paper, we analyse different consensus mechanisms used in blockchain platforms like Ripple, Algorand, Red Belly, etc, for the correctness and also conditions required for overcoming forking or avoiding not-making progress. Our analysis is based on the widely used *Rand Index* used similarity measurement of data clusters. Our results show that the scalability of blockchain platforms requires a subtle assessment of correctness, forking, not making progress, or unfairness issues and cannot be just based on the experimental evaluation.

Keywords: Hybrid consensus · Forking · PoS · PoW · Rand Index

1 Introduction

In the classic paper, Fischer et al. [1], show that it is impossible to reach a consensus in a fully asynchronous system with a single crash fault. A crash fault is a type of hardware or software fault in a network denoting that a node in a network has stopped responding. There is another type of fault known as, Byzantine fault wherein communication is possible but they can send erroneous

---

Supported by Center for Blockchain Research funded by Ripple Inc. USA.

© IFIP International Federation for Information Processing 2023
Published by Springer Nature Switzerland AG 2023
V. Atluri and A. L. Ferrara (Eds.): DBSec 2023, LNCS 13942, pp. 404–412, 2023.
https://doi.org/10.1007/978-3-031-37586-6_24

data to some other destination. [1] also establishes that it is impossible to achieve 'safety' and 'liveness' together at a time in a fully asynchronous environment. By 'safety', we mean the correct process will yield the correct output, and 'liveness' implies that the output will be produced within a finite amount of time. In classical distributed consensus, 'safety' is prioritized over 'liveness'. But the PoW has given more emphasis on 'liveness' than 'safety' which means participants may agree on a transaction that is not yet final in the chain [2]. Thus, two miners, can mine blocks simultaneously and realize avoiding double spending and forking, various strategies like a preference for the longest chain, etc. do exist.

There are several proposals in the literature to enhance the scalability in terms of the number of transactions/nodes in blockchain platforms. Vukolic [3] shows that the PoW-based consensus and the BFT-based consensus both lie in opposite directions. PoW is good for a large network with very low throughput and BFT is good for a small network with high throughput. However, there is no assessment of the PoW and its underlying BFT for the correctness of consensus. Note that for purposes of scalability of nodes, the preference is for the permissionless platform, and for high transaction throughput, the preference is for the permissioned platform. Researchers have been struggling to achieve decentralization, security, and scalability simultaneously in bitcoin-like platforms through *hybrid consensus* that has the idea to bootstrap fast permissionless consensus by combining an inefficient blockchain protocol with a permissioned consensus protocol; hybrid consensus uses the blockchain not to agree on transactions but to agree on rotating committees which in turn execute permissioned consensus protocols to agree on transactions [4]. All such systems have faced issues of fairness, or correctness of consensus.

In this paper, we shall analyze the various hybrid consensus mechanisms from the perspective of correctness and derive conditions that avoid forking, etc., and touch upon issues of fairness. We make use of the notion of *Rand Index* used in assessing clusters for our analysis for PoW/PoS variations as adopted in Ripple, Algorand, or Red Belly.

The rest of the paper is organized as follows: In Sect. 2, we provide an analysis of Ripple protocol for consensus and agreement in terms of *Rand Index* defined in Sect. 2.2. This is followed by a brief on Algorand in Sect. 3 and an analysis of Algorand in Sect. 3.1. Due to lack of space, we only touch upon on the analysis Red belly in Sect. 4. The paper concludes with Sect. 5.

2 Analysis of Ripple Consensus

2.1 A Brief on Existing Ripple Analysis

In Ripple [5], the entire network is divided into several UNLs (Unique Node Lists) under several servers. Servers play the role of proposer and for each server, there is a UNL. The other nodes in the UNL act as verifiers. The selection of UNL is not random rather nodes are cryptographically identifiable. The verification is achieved through two phases: correctness and agreement. In the first stage, the UNL checks if there are any fraudulent transactions or not. Once correctness is achieved, all UNLs collectively reach an agreement. According to [5], to reach consensus at least 80% nodes from every UNL must be honest and every UNL size must be greater than 20% of the size of the entire network size. Under this condition, correctness is achieved at the UNL level. The 80% of honest nodes is an upper bound and if 80% honest nodes check transactions and say 'yes' then we can say, strong correctness has been achieved. The lower bound of honest nodes is 20%. We can represent this scenario in another way: if there are f faulty nodes and N total nodes in the network, then the range of f must be as follows:

$$(N-1)/5 \leq f \leq (4N+1)/5 \tag{1}$$

Equation (1) depicts consensus; we often refer to this as correctness. As UNLs are different for each server, the agreement may not be guaranteed even after achieving correctness. For agreement, the size of UNLs must be greater than or equal to 20% of the total network size. Not only this, there must be an upper bound of intersection nodes of UNLs and this is given by:

$$|UNL_i \cap UNL_j| \geq 1/5 \, max(|UNL_i|, |UNL_j|) \; \forall i, j \tag{2}$$

Equation (2) depicts the agreement of the block to be added to the ledger. Thus, if the total number of the faulty nodes is less than the lower bound of f as in Eq. (1) and if the total number of intersection nodes is greater than the range given in Eq. (2), then we can say that correctness and agreement both are achieved.

Note that, Armknecht et al. [6] argue that overlap nodes must be at least 40% of the maximum size of UNLs and 20% overlap is not sufficient to stop forking.

Example 1: To make a connection between two UNLs, we need at least one edge which means at least one node from each UNL. Another way we can say, According to the base paper claim, the minimum number of nodes required to make a UNL must be greater than 10. In this situation, if the UNL size is less than or equal to 10, the rule mention in Eq. (1) must be violated. Now consider there are two ledgers L1 and L2 and 80% nodes from UNL$_i$ vote for L1 and 80% nodes from UNL$_j$ vote L2 and this scenario clearly can create the fork. Now if we make the 40% overlap, the minimum requirement of UNL nodes must be greater than 5. Towards the above claim of Armknecht et al. [6], the overlap percentage must be greater than 40%. Thus, fork will be impossible iff:

$$|UNL_i \cap UNL_j| > 2/5 \, max(|UNL_i|, |UNL_j|) \; \forall i, j \tag{3}$$

Note that [7] claims that the overlap size must be 41% of the average size of the UNLs.

Now consider a situation where $|UNL_i| < 5$. Any number of nodes in UNL below 5 will violet the Eq. (3) in the same manner discussed above. Consider just two nodes in UNL$_i$ and two nodes in UNL$_j$. In this scenario, the minimum overlap size must be 50% of their corresponding UNL size. Though we can consider the actual UNL size can be much higher but theoretically the overlap size must be

$$|UNL_i \cap UNL_j| > 1/2 \, max(|UNL_i|, |UNL_j|) \; \forall i, j \tag{4}$$

2.2 Ripple Analysis Using *Rand Index*

Before going to our analysis, we shall formally define below *Rand Index*.

Rand Index: A Brief Background - *Rand Index* is a similarity measurement of two data clusters [8]. By *Rand Index*, we can calculate the number of agreements and disagreements in terms of node pairs from the same or different clusters.

Consider the network with N number of nodes, and there are 2 different partitions or clusters of the network, say $C' = (C'_1, C'_2, \ldots, C'_r)$ and $C'' = (C''_1, C''_2, \ldots, C''_s)$. Here the meaning of partition/clusters is that of non-empty disjoint subsets of the network such that their union equals N. Observe that the set of all unordered pairs of the network having $\binom{N}{2}$ pairs is the disjoint union of the following defined sets:

$A = \{$pairs that are in the same clusters under C' and $C''\}$
$B = \{$pairs that are in different clusters under C' and $C''\}$
$C = \{$pairs that are in the same cluster under C' but different in cluster C'' $\}$
$D = \{$pairs that are in different cluster under C' but in the same cluster under $C''\}$

The *Rand Index* measure of similarity of clusters C' and C'' is given by

$$RI = \frac{|A| + |B|}{|A| + |B| + |C| + |D|} = \frac{|A| + |B|}{\binom{N}{2}} = \frac{2(|A| + |B|)}{N(N-1)} \quad (5)$$

Here $|A| + |B|$ can be considered as the number of agreements between C' and C'', and $|C| + |D|$ as the number of disagreements between C' and C''. Notice that as the denominator $|A| + |B| + |C| + |D|$ is the total number of unordered pairs of nodes, so it can be written as $\binom{N}{2}$.

Rand Index Adaptation for Ripple Analysis: UNLs in Ripple consensus can be treated as two different clusters. The agreement analysis of these two UNLs (UNL and cluster are used interchangeably) is similar to the 'similarity measurement' described in *Rand Index*. In Ripple, it is necessary for any two UNLs to actually overlap to achieve agreement. Consider the possibilities of the overlap of two UNLs and see its impact on the agreement of a block to be added and hence, shall 1 see the impact on the correctness of different configurations of UNLs. This is done by using the 'similarity measurement' between two UNLs by using *Rand Index*.

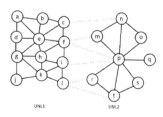

Fig. 1. Disjoint UNL1 and UNL2

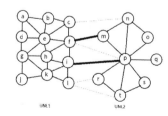

Fig. 2. Overlapped UNL1 and UNL2

Case 1: *UNL1 and UNL2 are disjoint* (Fig. 1). This means, there is no validator node common for two different proposers. In this case, it is possible to reach a correct consensus leading to confirmed (100%) forking. If two disjoint UNLs validate two disjoint transaction sets, obviously there will be correctness but there could be potential double spending and no agreement. As the two UNLs are disjoint, from Eq. 1 above, it follows that they can have all honest or 80% honest or all faulty nodes separately. In such cases, it follows that UNLs receive different sets of transactions. While the nodes come to a consensus, it does not guarantee agreement on the block of transactions. Figure 1 shows UNLs of two nodes 'e' and 'p' that are disjoint. For these two nodes, there are no common nodes as validators. For 'e', the UNL or the validator set is (a, b, c, d, e, f, g, h, i, j, k, l) and for 'p', this is (m, n, o, p, q, r, s, t).

Case 2: *UNL1 contains any number of honest nodes and UNL2 also contains any number of faulty nodes* (Fig. 2) It is not clear, whether the intersection nodes of two UNLs are honest or faulty. Figure 2 shows the overlapped UNL and the new UNLs are (a, b, c, d, e, g, h, i, j, k), (n, o, q, r, s, t), and (f, l, m, p). The analysis of the various scenarios is given below:

- *Scenario 1:* Cluster1, Cluster2 contains more than 80% honest nodes and Cluster3 which is the intersection of Cluster1 and Cluster2, also contains all honest nodes.

- *Scenario 2:* Cluster1, Cluster2 contains more than 80% honest nodes and Cluster3 contains all faulty nodes.

- *Scenario 3:* Cluster1 contains 80% honest nodes, Cluster2 contains all faulty nodes and Cluster3 also contains all faulty nodes.

- *Scenario 4:* Cluster1 contains all honest nodes and Cluster2 contains all faulty nodes and the Cluster3 contains more honest nodes and fewer faulty nodes.

- *Scenario 5:* Cluster1 contains all honest nodes and Cluster2 contains all faulty nodes and the intersection contains less honest nodes and more faulty nodes.

All the above scenarios, follow (1) and (2). In *Scenario 1*, the agreement/correctness is achieved as per the *Rand Index* iff Eqs. 1 and 2 are satisfied. In the example below, the correlation of the *Rand Index* with respect to (1) and (2) is illustrated. Suppose, the total number of nodes in the network N. Let N be divided into two UNLs. Let Cluster1 contain N_1 nodes and Cluster2 contain N_2 nodes and be disjoint, with $N_1 + N_2 = N$. When they are disjoint, there is 100% forking and even if consensus can be achieved for separate transaction sets, the agreement will never be achieved. I.e., both clusters will reach consensus separately with different sets of transactions. To achieve both consensus and agreement, consider the intersection of Cluster1 and Cluster2. Now we have three clusters: Cluster1$'$ contains N_1' nodes, Cluster2$'$ contains N_2' nodes and Cluster3 contains N_1'' nodes from Cluster1 and N_2'' nodes from Cluster2 which is actually the intersection of Cluster1 and Cluster2. *Rand Index* (RI) is calculated as per Eq. 5.

$$RI = \frac{X + Y}{Z} \tag{6}$$

If we compare Eq. 6 with Eq. 5 we will get

$$|A| = X = \binom{N_1'}{2} + \binom{N_1''}{2} + \binom{N_2''}{2} + \binom{N_2'}{2}, \quad |B| = Y = (N_1' * N_2') + (N_1'' * N_2'), \quad Z = \binom{N}{2}$$

If $N_1'' = N_2'' = 1$ the the value of X is $X = \binom{N_1'}{2} + \binom{N_2'}{2}$

Example 2 (Fig. 1): Cluster1 contains 12 nodes (a, b, c, d, e, f, g, h, i, j, k, l) and Cluster2 contains 8 nodes (m, n, o, p, q, r, s, t). Now we perform the overlap of 33.33% nodes of the maximum size of the cluster according to Fig. 2. After overlapping we get three clusters as follows: Cluster1' (a, b, c, d, e, g, h, j, k, l), Cluster2' (n, o, q, r, s, t), and Cluster3 (f, i, m, p). In this example, N = 20, $N_1 = 12$, $N_2 = 8$, $N_1' = 10$ and $N_2' = 6$, $N_1'' = 2$, $N_2'' = 2$

$$X = \binom{N_1'}{2} + \binom{N_1''}{2} + \binom{N_2''}{2} + \binom{N_2'}{2} = \binom{10}{2} + \binom{2}{2} + \binom{2}{2} + \binom{6}{2} = 45 + 1 + 1 + 15 = 62$$

$$Y = (N_1' * N_2') + (N_1'' * N_2') = (10*6) + (2*6) = 60 + 12 = 72$$

$$Z = \binom{N}{2} = \binom{20}{2} = 190$$

According to Eq. 5, *Rand Index* is

$$RI = \frac{X + Y}{Z} = \frac{62 + 72}{190} = \frac{134}{190} = 0.705 \approx 0.71$$

In this case, when $N = 20$, if Cluster3 contains only 2 nodes (one from Cluster1 and one from Cluster2), the *Rand Index* is ≈ 0.84. If Cluster3 contains 6 nodes and 8 nodes, the *Rand Index* is ≈ 0.59 and ≈ 0.49 respectively. It means, when we increase the number of overlap nodes, the *Rand Index* decreases. *Rand Index* implies here the forking. For two disjoint Clusters, the forking is 100% but once we perform an intersection between two Clusters, the forking percentage is reduced. from this calculation we can see, if the overlap is approx 67% nodes of the largest Cluster size then forking can be reduced to below 50% but if the overlap is approx 40% nodes of the largest Cluster size then forking is approx 71% as calculated above.

Now, if we consider *Scenario 2* and *Scenario 3*, at max, 40% overlapping nodes of the largest Cluster size can be all faulty. It is clearly a forking situation. For the rest of the *Scenarios* we need to explore more, how the system can perform on all these *Scenarios*. In the later section, i.e. in Sect. 3.1, we have shown the situation where these scenarios have appeared actually.

Discussion: In our analysis using *Rand Index*, we have tried to show how the increase of nodes in the overlapping sections of UNLs can influence agreement hence forking. The existing literature also does not focus on the type of members (honest or faulty) in the overlapping section. The *Rand Index* is clearly applicable when there are all honest nodes in the overlap part of two UNLs. This situation is similar to what we mentioned above in scenarios 4 and 5. According to Amores-Sesarsar et al. [9], one Byzantine node in the overlapping part may cause finality or liveness issues. The Byzantine node may follow the agreement statement separately with different values as per two different UNLs. Thus, there will be a possibility of forking.

3   Analysis of Algorand Consensus

In Algorand, the key idea is to achieve consensus through Byzantine Agreement Protocol. The major limitation of the Byzantine Agreement Protocol is the number of nodes that it supports [10]. The key assumption is, those who have more amount (stake) of Algorand with them, are more viable to become a part of the underlying consensus mechanism with the claim that the probability of a fork is very low. The architecture of Algorand depends on the selection of random users and random committees. First, a random user is selected to create and propagate the block through gossiping. Now the question is who will validate the block? A random committee is selected to run the Byzantine Agreement Protocol on the block created by the random user. If the committee validates the block, they will digitally sign the result and it propagated the digital signature to say the block is valid [11].

3.1   Our Analysis of Algorand Consensus

Let us consider the situation after the creation of a committee. Borrowing the results from Ripple, there must be 80% of honest validators in the committee. In every round of the random committee creation, there is a possibility to get Byzantine nodes in the committee. Assuming there are N nodes in the entire network. Consider various scenarios of the number of nodes that may qualify for being a validator for creating the committee through the following example below.

   Example 3: Let there be 20 nodes and assume that 90% nodes are qualified for being committee members - thus, there could be 18 nodes in the committee. Let there be 20% faulty nodes in the entire network. Thus, in a 20 nodes network, there will be at most 4 faulty nodes. Now, we may have the following partitions in the committee: (0-18), (1-17), (2-16), (3-15), and (4-14) which means 0, 1, 2, 3, 4 are the different numbers of Byzantine nodes with a different set of correct nodes of 18,17,16,15 and 14 respectively. More precisely, if the validator network or committee contains total of 18 nodes, then (0–18) means, there exist 0 Byzantine node and 18 honest nodes, and (1-17) means, there exist 1 Byzantine node and 17 honest nodes, and so on. If the system is 20% fault tolerant that means the committee may have at most 20% faulty nodes then the accepted partitions of the committee would be (0-18), (1-17), (2-16), (3-15). Partition (4-14) will be eliminated since 4 is more than 20% of the total number of committee members (18). Thus, probability of accepted committee partition (ACP) is:

$$P(\text{ACP}) \quad = \quad \frac{\text{No of accepted committee partition}}{\text{Total number of possible committee partition}} \quad = \quad \frac{4}{5}$$

If we generalize the above example for N number of total nodes in the network, consider the total number of the committee member is $C_p * N$ where C_p is the percentage of the committee members. $C_p * N$ is divided into two parts $(C_p * N)_{faulty}$ and $(C_p * N)_{honest}$, where $(C_p * N)_{faulty}$ is the number of faulty nodes in the committee and $(C_p * N)_{honest}$ is the number of honest nodes in the network. For any valid committee $(C_p * N)_{faulty} \leq 0.2 * (C_p * N)$ and $(C_p * N)_{honest} \geq 0.8 * (C_p * N)$. So the probability of accepted committee partition (ACP) is:

$$P(\text{ACP}) = \frac{(C_p * N)_{faulty}}{(f_p * N) + 1} \tag{7}$$

where, $(C_p * N)_{faulty} \leq (f_p * C_p * N)$ and f_p is the percentage of faulty nodes in the committee. The concept of committee partition is similar to the overlapping scenarios mentioned in Sect. 2.2. Now if we think that the committee members are not agreeing on the same set of transactions, the 'similarity measurement' or 'agreement' can be analyzed through *Rand Index* as mentioned in Sect. 2.2.

4   Analysis of Red Belly Consensus

In the Red Belly architecture, let there be P correct proposers and V correct verifiers. It uses leader free architecture [12]. Then, we have $P \cap V \geq f + 1$ where f is the number of faulty nodes. Unlike Ripple or Algorand, here the verification is done in two stages- primary_ and secondary_verification. As Red Belly is $N/3$ Byzantine Fault Tolerant [13], the fault handling follows on the lines of discussion Sects. 2.2–3.1.

5   Conclusion and Future Work

In this paper, we have described an analysis to show the impact of BFT on the consensus agreement in the scaled-up versions of PoS-based blockchains. Our analysis based on the *Rand Index* shows that various partitions of validator nodes, proposers, or UNLs in terms of crash/Byzantine/honest node, lead to inconsistencies in correctness. Our analysis based on *Rand Index* provides a concrete evaluation of the similarity measure that leads to affirmations about correctness and agreement. This work is just the beginning and further finer analysis with respect to each of the protocols needs to be done and have been working on fairness using distribution of stakes.

References

1. Fischer, M.J., Lynch, N.A., Paterson, M.: Impossibility of distributed consensus with one faulty process. J. ACM **32**(2), 374–382 (1985)
2. Nakamoto, S.: Bitcoin: a peer-to-peer electronic cash system. Consulted **1**(2012), 28 (2008)

3. Vukolić, M.: The quest for scalable blockchain fabric: proof-of-work vs. BFT replication. In: Camenisch, J., Kesdoğan, D. (eds.) iNetSec 2015. LNCS, vol. 9591, pp. 112–125. Springer, Cham (2016). https://doi.org/10.1007/978-3-319-39028-4_9

4. Pass, R., Shi, E.: Hybrid consensus: Efficient consensus in the permissionless model. Cryptology ePrint Archive (2016)

5. Schwartz, D., Youngs, N., Britto, A.: The Ripple protocol consensus algorithm. Ripple Labs Inc., available online. https://ripple.com/files/ripple_consensus_whitepaper.pdf (2014)

6. Armknecht, F., Karame, G.O., Mandal, A., Youssef, F., Zenner, E.: Ripple: overview and outlook. In: Conti, M., Schunter, M., Askoxylakis, I. (eds.) Trust 2015. LNCS, vol. 9229, pp. 163–180. Springer, Cham (2015). https://doi.org/10.1007/978-3-319-22846-4_10

7. Chase, B., MacBrough, E.: Analysis of the XRP Ledger Consensus Protocol (2018). arXiv preprint arXiv:1802.07242

8. Rand Index. https://en.wikipedia.org/wiki/Rand_index

9. Amores-Sesar, I., Cachin, C., Micic, J.: Security analysis of ripple consensus. In: Proceedings of 24th Int. Conf. Princ. Distrib. Syst. (OPODIS), pp. 10:1–10:16, November 2020

10. Lamport, L., Shostak, R., Pease, M.: The Byzantine generals problem. ACM Trans. Program. Lang. Syst. **4**(3), 382–401 (1982)

11. Gilad, Y., Hemo, R., Micali, S., Vlachos, G., Zeldovich, N.: Algorand: Scaling byzantine agreements for cryptocurrencies, In Proc. 26th SOSP, pp. 51–68. ACM, October 2017

12. Borran, F., Schiper, A.: A leader-free Byzantine consensus algorithm. In: ICDCN, pp. 67–78 (2010)

13. Crain, T., Natoli, C., Gramoli, V.: Red belly: a secure, fair and scalable open blockchain. In: 2021 IEEE S & P, San Francisco, CA, USA, pp. 466–483 (2021)

Author Index

© IFIP International Federation for Information Processing 2023
Published by Springer Nature Switzerland AG 2023
V. Atluri and A. L. Ferrara (Eds.): DBSec 2023, LNCS 13942, pp. 413–414, 2023.
https://doi.org/10.1007/978-3-031-37586-6

Printed in the United States
by Baker & Taylor Publisher Services